D0757965

ARISTIDES

I

458

ARISTIDES

IN FOUR VOLUMES

I

PANATHENAIC ORATION

AND

IN DEFENCE OF ORATORY

TEXT AND TRANSLATION BY

C. A. BEHR

CAMBRIDGE, MASSACHUSETTS

HARVARD UNIVERSITY PRESS

LONDON

WILLIAM HEINEMANN LTD

MCMLXXIII

American
ISBN 0-674-99505-8

British
ISBN 0 434 99458 8

Printed in Great Britain

CONTENTS OF VOLUME I

PAGE

INTRODUCTION vii

SELECTED BIBLIOGRAPHY . . . xxii

SIGLA xxvi

I. THE PANATHENAIC ORATION—

   Introduction 3
   Text and Translation 6

II. TO PLATO: IN DEFENCE OF ORATORY—

   Introduction 278
   Text and Translation:
     Book I 280
     Book II 464

INDEX 559

INTRODUCTION

LIFE [a]

PUBLIUS AELIUS ARISTIDES [b] was born at Hadriani in northern Mysia, on November 26, A.D. 117.[c] His father, Eudaemon, was a wealthy landholder in the region and a priest of the Temple of Zeus Olympius. The family were also citizens of Smyrna and in A.D. 123 were enfranchised by Hadrian with Roman citizenship. Aristides was given the finest education available. He first studied, probably at Smyrna, under the grammaticus Alexander of Cotiaeum, who later was called to Rome to be the tutor of Marcus Aurelius and Lucius Verus. Aristides' education was completed by attending the lectures of Antonius Polemo in Smyrna, Claudius Aristocles in Pergamum, and Claudius Herodes in Athens, the foremost sophists of their day. He also studied philosophy, per-

[a] See Behr, *Aelius Aristides and the Sacred Tales*, Amsterdam, 1968.

[b] He later added " Theodorus," gift of god. The full name is found in OGIS 709. A statue of Aristides is preserved in the Vatican Museum, a picture of which is reproduced in Bernoulli, *Griechische Ikonographie*, vol. 2, Tafel xxx ; see also Behr, *op. cit.*, p. 111, n. 64 ; A. Giuliano, Dialoghi di Arch. i (1967), pp. 72-81.

[c] See A.J.P. xc (1969), pp. 75-77, where I have corrected the birth date which I earlier proposed.

haps under the Platonists Caius at Pergamum and Lucius at Athens.

Aristides chose to become an orator and in A.D. 141 set out on a tour of Egypt, the traditional capstone of the education of that time. In the course of his trip, he stopped and declaimed at Cos, Cnidus, Rhodes, and Alexandria, with varying success. In Egypt, with Alexandria as the base of his operations, he travelled extensively, proceeding as far south as the first cataract, where he fell ill. Still unwell, he sailed home to Smyrna before April, A.D. 142. To alleviate his ill health, he turned to the healing god Sarapis, whom he invoked in or. xlv, his earliest preserved speech.

So far Aristides' career had been modest. He now extended his ambitions and, prompted no doubt by the presence of his former teachers, Alexander and Herodes, determined to lecture at Rome, the capital of the world, before the highly literate imperial court. A few days before setting out on his journey, in December A.D. 143, he contracted a heavy cold at his estate near Baris on the river Aesepus, but he declined to postpone his journey. It was a most unwise decision. The rigours of the trip exacerbated his condition, and he reached Rome after lengthy delays desperately ill and totally unable to fulfil his plans. He decided to return home and, after an unpleasant sea-journey, he arrived at Smyrna in November.

To improve his respiratory problems, his doctors sent him to the warm springs outside of Smyrna. But now neither medicine nor Sarapis helped. Aristides abandoned his hopes of a career and became more and more despondent when suddenly around

viii

INTRODUCTION

December a momentous change took place which was for ever after to govern his life. He received hi first revelation from Asclepius, the paramoun healing god of the ancient world. But although Aristides became increasingly devoted to Asclepius, he retained a real belief in many gods, Sarapis, Isis, Zeus, Apollo, Athena, Dionysus, and Heracles, beside numerous local divinities, an eclectic poly-theism typical of the time.

Still his health remained unimproved and in the summer of A.D. 145 the unhappy Aristides felt himself summoned by Asclepius to his temple in Pergamum, one of the chief healing sites of the ancient world. Here Aristides spent the next two years of his life as an incubant at the temple, a period which he called "the Cathedra," the time of inactivity. Incubation primarily consisted in sleeping in the temple precinct in the hopes of receiving a dream from the god, which contained a prescription to ease or to cure the patient's ailment. These dream prescriptions, given at Pergamum during this period and later wherever Aristides happened to be staying, have conferred a notorious cachet on Aristides' life. Yet many of these seemingly aberrant prescriptions, excessive bloodletting, enemas, and vomiting, were similar to others which are known and were consistent with contemporary medical praxis, although some of them, such as bathing in swollen rivers, were not. Aristides often insists on his preference for Asclepius over the human doctor, but it is significant that throughout his life he continued to consult, if not always follow, the advice of the latter. Furthermore of the greatest interest is the psychopathology of the 130 dreams which Aristides has preserved in the

INTRODUCTION

Sacred Tales, the account of his illness and the great hymn of thanksgiving to his god. The abundance of these dreams, over a span of twenty-five years, in combination with the rather full biographical and descriptive data which Aristides has provided, offers a unique opportunity to analyse to some degree the psychology of at least one individual of the ancient world.[a]

At the temple, Aristides joined a society of upper class Greeks and Romans, who formed a small, cultivated circle of neurasthenics similar to those found in European sanatoria in modern times. Among them were Salvius Julianus, the famous jurist,[b] Sedatius Theophilus, a praetorian, Tullius Maximus, a consular, Claudius Pardalas, a wealthy literary critic,

---

[a] In qualified hands, I mean those of a trained psychoanalyst, with an appreciation of cultural disparity and a good knowledge of antiquity, much can be done, as can be seen in another context in the excellent study, one of many, of George Devereux, *La Psychanalyse et l'histoire*, Annales (1965), pp. 18-44.

[b] I take this occasion to retract my earlier suggestion, Behr, *op. cit.*, p. 41, that in or. xlviii. 9 the name Sabinus should be read. At the time I was unaware of ILS 7776 which establishes a relationship between Salvius and Aristides through their common friend, the philosopher Euarestus or Euaretus (or. l. 23). It now seems to me that the best way to treat that perplexing passage is to emend the offending words τοῦ νῦν ὑπάτου to τοῦ τῶν ὑπάτων, "a man of consular rank." For the form of the expression *cf.* or. xlviii. 16 ἀνὴρ τῶν ἐστρατηγηκότων ; or. iv. 2 (47, p. 415 Ddf.) ἀνὴρ τῶν ἐκ τῆς γερουσίας τῆς Ῥωμαίων ; or. l. 61 σοφιστὴς τῶν—ἐπιφανῶν. The interesting suggestion of Bowersock, *Greek Sophists*, p. 80, that the jurist was cos. II in A.D. 175, does not seem to square with the history of the powerful Salvius Julianus (presumably cos. A.D. 175) who was slain by Commodus. I shall discuss this point more fully elsewhere.

INTRODUCTION

Cuspius Rufinus, a consular and great benefactor of the temple and of Pergamum, his native city, various descendants of Julius Quadratus, the foremost family in the city, many of them powerful figures in the Roman Empire,[a] and at a later time, Antoninus, son of the senator Antoninus Pythodorus, the munificent benefactor of Epidaurus.[b] Under the influence of his friends and his new religion, Aristides' ambition began to reassert itself, first in dreams, then in tentative efforts at public speaking before small, select audiences. When he finally left Pergamum in the latter part of A.D. 147, he was once again active as a writer and partly as a lecturer. An unfortunate result of this period of his life was the notion that his literary career was due to Asclepius' grace. To abandon his god (and his illness) now meant the abandonment of what he had salvaged of his career. And so his recovery was impeded. Furthermore this fusion of religion and rhetoric seems to have persuaded Aristides that his was a higher calling. Oratory became something sacred, his rivals profaners and debasers of a pure art.

---

[a] I was wrong to suggest, Behr, *op. cit.*, p. 30, that members of this family held the hereditary priesthood of Asclepius at Pergamum. They were merely θεραπευταί, a class of officials at the temple (*cf.* or. xxx. 15). Julius Apellas' " hereditary " office (or. xxx. 25) was that of agonothete at the Asclepieia, the games at the temple. The priesthood was vested in the descendants of Archias, now a family of the gens Flavia, who have left a number of inscriptions from around this period, *cf. Altertümer von Pergamon VIII*³, *Die Inschriften des Asklepieions*, 1969, pp. 97 ff.

[b] Mentioned in or. xlvii. 35, son of Sex. Julius Maior Antoninus Pythodorus (*cf.* IG IV², pp. xxxiii-xxxv). I should have added him to the personae whom I discussed in *Aelius Aristides*.

INTRODUCTION

While these literary feuds are very common, Aristides has tinged his controversies with religious overtones.

As Aristides' health improved, so did his activity. The next six years were consumed in travels, mostly between his estates in Mysia, the temple at Pergamum, and Smyrna, and in a series of legal battles to keep himself free from having to undertake civic offices in his two native cities. In December A.D. 147, his fellow citizens of Smyrna thought to honour him by nominating him as high-priest of Asia, the highest provincial office to which one could aspire. He was elected to the post,[a] fought his selection, and won the case in court. Five years later, in A.D. 151, he was elected a tax-collector in Smyrna, furiously appealed and at length had the election rescinded. His last battle came in the following year, when the well meaning Governor Julius Severus, on his own initiative, appointed him Eirenarch or chief police officer of the administrative district of Hadriani. After many pleas and intercessions from influential Romans and Greeks, he was finally granted immunity from further civil liturgies. The vehemence, which he displayed in his struggles for what he conceived to be his right to immunity, is of a piece with the rest of his life at this time. He was still too insecure to commit himself to any obligation, whether it was that of a paid lecturer and teacher, or of a functionary in the government.

[a] When I advanced my theory of the cyclical election of the highpriesthood of Asia, Behr, *op. cit.*, p. 64, I ought to have mentioned J. Deininger's alternative suggestion, *Die Provinziallandtage*, 1965, pp. 39-40, that uniquely in this province several highpriests served concurrently. I am not convinced.

INTRODUCTION

By A.D. 154 he felt well enough to resume his career on a full scale. He made lecture tours through Greece and at last successfully appeared at Rome. His neurasthenia faded into the background and so significantly did his interest in Asclepius. Now Aristides seems to have accepted students, which he had been unable to do up to A.D. 153. The most famous among them was the sophist Damianus. However, he eschewed taking fees for this service, so that even at this point he was bound by no contractual commitments.

But after this more normal interlude, in the summer of A.D. 165, Aristides succumbed to smallpox, which then began to ravage the Roman Empire. He survived it, but the after-effects and his neurotic predisposition marred the rest of his life. For the next ten years, he still made public appearances, but his physical complaints and his religious fixation resumed. In A.D. 176, when Marcus Aurelius visited Smyrna, he spoke before the imperial entourage, perhaps his last major public appearance. In A.D. 177, shortly after Aristides' departure from the city, Smyrna was destroyed by an earthquake. This disaster ended Aristides' active career. Although he wrote appeals to the emperor and speeches to the citizens and governor in celebration of the reconstruction of the city, he no longer left his estates in Mysia. Here he died, around the age of sixty-three.[a]

[a] Galen, in a passage preserved in an Arabic quotation from a lost work, claimed that Aristides died of consumption (CMG I, 1934, p. 33). But this diagnosis seems to be at second hand and Galen to have got this information from the diagnosis of an earlier ailment by his teacher Satyrus, who was personally acquainted with Aristides (*cf.* Behr, *op. cit.*, pp. 162-163, 165).

INTRODUCTION

THE WRITINGS OF ARISTIDES

Philostratus said that Aristides was weak in *ex-tempore* speaking, a charge which is not belied by Aristides' own comments. He was, however, justly famous for the precision of his style. His efforts to conform to the highest canons of Atticism [a] earned him the title "divine" among posterity [b] and commended him as a model to the theorists on composition, such as Hermogenes, to later orators such as Libanius and Himerius, and to the schools of Byzantine times. His early studies under Alexander, who lectured on Plato, made a great impression on his style, which contains many reminiscences in construction and disposition of that author. His ideal, whom he frequently approaches in intensity, was Demosthenes. He also occasionally imitates Isocrates, particularly in the evident attempts at the avoidance of hiatus in the major works. Also to be noted, in this brief survey, is his frequent epigrammatic sarcasm and the intentionally elliptical phrasing, which easily leads to obscurity. Reiske's judgement is worth repeating [c]: " Scriptorum graecorum quotquot legi, neque tamen perpaucos legi, qui quidem libero dicendi genere usi sunt, post oratorem Thucydidem unus Aristides, mea sententia, est omnium intellectu difficillimus, cum propter incredibilem argumentationum et crebritatem et subtilitatem, tum propter graecitatis exquisitam elegantiam." Nonetheless in moments

[a] See Boulanger, *Aelius Aristide*, pp. 395 ff., still the best study on this subject.
[b] Eunapius, p. 494 Boissonade.
[c] Reprinted in vol. III, p. 788, of Dindorf's edition.

of religious fervour or great excitement, Aristides found his Attic models insufficient [a] and turned instead to an extreme form of Asianism, the prose hymn, which with its short rhythmical cola and plangent tone could not be more unlike the stately periods of his epideictic compositions.[b]

Fifty-three works have been preserved in the corpus of Aristides' writings. Of these two (ors. xxv and xxxv) are certainly spurious. The extant works may be categorized as follows :

(1) treatises : ors. ii-iv, the writings against Plato, which make up nearly a third of Aristides' preserved work, and or. xxxvi on the Nile.

(2) panegyrics and symbouleutic speeches to cities and/or on public questions : ors. i, xvii-xxiv, xxvi, xxvii, xxix.

(3) speeches on rhetoric : ors. xxviii, xxxiii, xxxiv.

(4) speeches to individuals : ors. xxx-xxxii ; the latter two are funeral orations.

(5) religious speeches and writings : ors. xxxvii-liii.

(6) declamations : ors. v-xvi.

However, this classification needs much qualification. Firstly because many of these writings were not delivered speeches, but professedly treatises or letters : ors. ii-iv, xviii-xxi, xxiv, xxviii (?), xxxii xxxiii, xxxvi, xlvii-liii ; and secondly because there is much overlapping in the categories. So, for example, ors. ii-iv and xxix might be regarded as concerning rhetoric, or or. xxxvi as religious because

---

[a] *Cf.* or. xlv. 1-13 ; Behr. *op. cit.*, p. 21.
[b] Interestingly first used in or. xli, from the stressful time of Aristides' incubation at Pergamum.

of its peroration, and ors. xliv and xlvi have many
characteristics of the panegyric. The order of
Laurentianus LX, 8 (T), which Keil rightly made the
canon and which I shall briefly discuss below, has
much to recommend it.

An enormous amount of Aristides' work has been
lost. Of ors. lii and liii only the beginnings are
preserved. Aristides himself reports that he wrote
over 300,000 lines to Asclepius. He mentions an
oration *To Athena*, a *Defence of Running*, and an
unnamed work similar in tone to or. xxxiii, and
Menander refers to a speech to *Hygieia*, which have
perished. Gone too is his oration *Against the Dancers*,
many fragments of which are preserved in Libanius'
reply (or. lxiv). Philostratus cites seven declamations and Hermogenes one which have vanished.
And finally there is Aristides' poetry, scraps of
which are quoted in the *Sacred Tales*, but which
essentially—it was apparently quite extensive—
has also disappeared.

Three inscriptions of Aristides have been found in
Mysia (one of which survives only in a copy): an
elegiac couplet to Hera, a brief dedication to Dike
and Nemesis, and a second to Sarapis.[a] Another
dedication may exist in Epidaurus.[b]

[a] The first published in Athen. Mittheil., 1904, p. 208;
in the last line I would supplement ἐν δαπέδοις ['Απίοις].
The last two in L. Robert, *Études anatoliennes*, pp. 216, 218.

[b] IG IV² 1. 577; cf. Behr, *op. cit.*, p. 87, n. 90. For a very
doubtful attribution cf. also *op. cit.*, p. 7, n. 10 (*Die Inschriften von Pergamon*, Band 2, 616 B). For the reasons
cited in *op. cit.*, p. 52, n. 44, I still cannot believe that the long
elegiac inscription published and greatly emended by
Herzog, Sitzungsberichte der preussischen Akademie der
Wissenschaften, 1934, pp. 753-770 (*cf.* also *Die Inschriften
des Asklepieions*, p. 144) was written by Aristides.

INTRODUCTION

Text

A trace of the earliest edition of Aristides' works seems to be present in the subscriptions appended to several of his speeches, which contain highly valuable circumstantial information (ors. xvii, xxii, xxx, xxxiv, xxxvii, xl). The ultimate source of these must be Aristides' own notes, but the divergence in spelling the name Severus ($\Sigma\epsilon\nu\hat{\eta}\rho\sigma$ and $\Sigma\epsilon\beta\hat{\eta}\rho\sigma$) in the subscription to or. xxxvii and the text of the *Sacred Tales* may point to a different hand. In the fourth century A.D., Sopater of Apamea lectured on Aristides and was responsible for collecting and composing much of the extant scholia.[a] The earliest preserved remains of the writings themselves occur in two recently published papyrus fragments, one from or. i of the sixth or seventh century A.D. and the other from or. iii of the seventh century A.D. All of the mss. go back to an archetype (O), whose date cannot be fixed, except to say that if it did not emanate from Sopater's school, it long antedated the ninth century A.D. The oldest version of O should be found in the excerpts of the first four orations, which the Patriarch Photius included in his *Bibliotheca*, c. A.D. 850, but the source of Photius' text was very corrupt and represents a vulgar and inferior line of the tradition. His pupil Arethas, Archbishop of Caesarea, at the beginning of the tenth century A.D., caused a ms. of Aristides to be prepared for himself (A). It contains forty-two orations and is the only source for or. liii. The first nearly complete text of Aristides is presented in Laurentianus LX, 8 (T), which omits

[a] On the question of the authorship of the scholia, see F. W. Lenz's definitive study in *Aristeidesstudien*, pp. 1-99.

the fragmentary ors. lii and liii, although its exemplar certainly contained the former.

Keil knew of more than two hundred MSS. which contain at least some of Aristides' writings. Only a small portion of these has been examined, but all of the older MSS. and enough of the newer have been inspected, so that, I think, little or nothing will ever be added to our knowledge of O. The determination of the relationship of the MSS. to one another is complicated by the fact that there has been much borrowing between them of readings, emendations, and omissions of superfluous words. Furthermore most of these MSS. have a varying tradition, by which I mean that one MS., which agrees with another MS. in some orations, will not do so in all. Finally there exists among the MSS. a wide variation in the order of the orations, especially in ors. xvii-liii, as well as in the omission of speeches. The provisional attempt which Keil made at the classification of the MSS. does not fit the facts and must be rejected.

Because of lack of space, I shall limit myself to a few general remarks on this problem and shall detail only the factors upon which I have based the text of ors. i and ii. In the ensuing volumes, I shall supply the information pertinent to the writings contained therein. In determining the relationships of the MSS., I have found that their lacunae give the best criterium, for they were least subject to later manipulations, at least in every case in a speech. An examination of the lacunae of the major MSS. in ors. i and ii immediately establishes a pattern *for these two works*, which is not inconsistent with the *variae lectiones* (for the sigla, see opposite and on p. xxvi).

The lacunae in ϕ are far more serious than in ω.

INTRODUCTION

Furthermore the papyrus fragment of or. i, although this version differs from O for the worse in several respects, doubtless because of a normalizing tendency,[a] shows that in two places, where ω contains words absent in φ, these words are of ancient authority. ω seems to be consistently represented by T, which

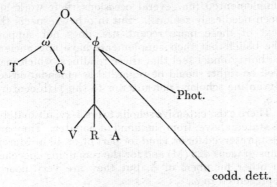

throughout the corpus forms, for better or worse, a polarity to the varying members of the other group. So I believe that the order of the speeches in T, which Keil chose to follow but thought a more recent innovation—one should not proceed from order to chaos—was the true order of O and that losses and subsequent additions in φ, as well as arbitrary rearrangement, led to the disorganization in members of that group. Indeed, R (Vaticanus graecus 1298), a consistent member of φ, in ors. i-iv follows T's order, whereas Photius and V use i ii iv iii and A uses i iii ii iv. I might add here that the

[a] Cf. Lenz, *Zu den neuen Aristeidespapyri*, published posthumously in *Philologus*, 113 (1969), pp. 301-306.

theory of the tomoi, first developed by Sieveking and carried further by Lenz,[a] seems specious to me, although it has some value if reapplied to the ruinous state of φ.

In a number of places all the ancient MSS. contain obvious lacunae, which more recent MSS. have supplemented (on several occasions their work has been needlessly zealous). But in other respects the text of these more recent MSS. does not support the belief that their supplements have any ancient authority and I feel that these readings, which may well be right, should be regarded as emendations of Byzantine scholars, not anterior to the 11th century A.D.

There exist extensive scholia to ors. i-xv, ultimately, as stated above, from the hand of Sopater. They are best preserved for or. i and for part of or. iii in Marcianus graecus 423 (M) and for the remaining speeches in other members of φ, but they are very poorly represented in ω.

Keil did not carry his magisterial edition of 1898 beyond ors. xvii-liii. His work was taken over by Lenz, who at the time of his own death in 1969 had prepared the text for ors. i and v-xvi. It is planned to complete this edition. Lenz most generously corresponded with me about doubtful points in the text of ors. i-iv, but for various reasons I decided to postpone the Loeb edition until his appeared in print. This is no longer possible. The text of ors. i and ii is my own, based upon the collation begun by Keil and continued by Lenz. In many places I have

***

[a] W. Sieveking, *De Aelii Aristidis oratione εἰς Ῥώμην*, Diss. Göttingen, 1919, pp. 7 ff.; Lenz, *Aristeidesstudien*, pp. 102 ff.

corrected or supplemented it by means of photostatic copies of the relevant MSS. All of this material, which belonged to Professor Lenz, including both Keil's and Lenz's own copies of Dindorf with marginalia, was kindly placed at my disposal by his wife.

For ors. i and ii, it seems sufficient to cite (and not completely for lack of space) the readings of only four major MSS., TQVA (with some references to Photius), though Q and A should be regarded as corrective subsidiaries to T and V respectively, which are the best representatives of their two classes. In the codices deteriores, I have included Vaticanus graecus 1298 (R), at times it could have been A, and a host of other MSS., among which are Parisinus graecus 2950 (E), Urbinas graecus 123 (U), Vaticanus graecus 75, and the canaille cited in Dindorf. They have no independent value.

SELECTED BIBLIOGRAPHY

I. ARISTIDES' LIFE AND TIMES

(Other literature can be found in the bibliographies of these works.)

Behr, C. A. : *Aelius Aristides and the Sacred Tales*, Amsterdam, 1968.

—— : *Aelius Aristides' Birth Date*, American Journal of Philology, xc (1969), pp. 75-77.

Bowersock, G. W. : *Greek Sophists in the Roman Empire*, Oxford, 1969.

Boulanger, André : *Aelius Aristide et la sophistique dans la province d'Asie au IIᵉ siècle de notre ère*, Paris, 1923, reprinted 1968.

Festugière, André-Jean : *Personal Religion Among the Greeks*, Berkeley, 1954, reprinted 1960.

v. Wilamowitz-Moellendorff, Ulrich : *Der Rhetor Aristeides*, Sitzungsberichte der preussischen Akademie der Wissenschaften, 1925, pp. 333-353.

II. GREEK EDITIONS OF ARISTIDES' WRITINGS

Aldus Manutius : *Isocratis Opera* (to which are appended ors. i and xxvi), Venice, 1513 ; a second edition in 1534.

Philippus Junta : *Orationes Aristidis* edited by Euphrosinus Boninus, Florence, 1517 (lacks ors. xvi and liii).

SELECTED BIBLIOGRAPHY

Henricus Stephanus : *Isocratis Orationes...et Aristidis quaedam*, Paris, 1593 (ors. i and xxvi).

Paulus Stephanus : *Aelii Aristidis...Orationum Tomi Tres*, Geneva, 1604 (lacks ors. xvi and liii).

Samuel Jebb : *Aelii Aristidis...Opera Omnia*, 2 vols., Oxford, 1722, 1730 (lacks or. liii).

Wilhelm Dindorf : *Aristides*, 3 vols., Leipzig, 1829 ; reprinted, 1964.

Bruno Keil : *Aelii Aristidis Smyrnaei Quae Supersunt Omnia*, vol. 2, Berlin, 1898 ; reprinted, 1958 (contains ors. xvii-liii).

James H. Oliver : *The Ruling Power*, Transactions of the American Philosophical Society, 43 (1953)(or. xxvi).

——: *The Civilizing Power*, Transactions of the American Philosophical Society, 58 (1968) (or. i).

Barns, J. W. B. and H. Zilliacus : *The Antinoopolis Papyri*, Part III, no. 182, London, 1967 (fragments of or. iii).

Browne, G. M. and A. Henrichs : *A Papyrus of Aristides, Panathenaikos*, Zeitschrift für Papyrologie und Epigraphik, 2 (1968), pp. 171-175 (fragments of or. i).

III. EDITIONS OF THE SCHOLIA

Frommel, Wilhelm : *Scholia in Aelii Aristidis... Orationes*, Frankfurt a/M., 1826.

Dindorf, Wilhelm : Volume III of his edition of 1829 (see Bibl. II).

Lenz, Friedrich Walter : *The Aristeides Prolegomena*, Mnemosyne Supplement V, 1959.

SELECTED BIBLIOGRAPHY

IV. STUDIES ON THE TEXT OF ORS. I AND II

Beecke, Eugen : *Die historischen Angaben in Aelius Aristides Panathenaikos auf ihre Quellen untersucht*, Diss. Strassburg, 1905.

Behr, C. A. : *Citations of Porphyry's Against Aristides...*, American Journal of Philology, lxxxix (1968), pp. 186-199.

Cobet, C. G. : *Variae Lectiones*, second edition, Leyden, 1873.

Haas, A. : *Quibus Fontibus Aelius Aristides in componenda declamatione, quae inscribitur πρὸς Πλάτωνα ὑπὲρ τῶν τεττάρων, usus sit*, Diss. Greifswald, 1884.

Haury, J. : *Quibus Fontibus Aristides usus sit in declamatione quae inscribitur Παναθηναικός*, Diss. Augsburg, 1888.

Holleck, Henricus : *Coniectanea Critica in Aelii Aristidis Panathenaicum*, Bratislava, 1874.

Lenz, Friedrich Walter : *Aristeidesstudien*, Berlin, 1964
―― : *Aristidea et Epigrammatica*, Wiener Studien, n.f. 2 (1968), pp. 28-45.
―― : *Scholien zu Aristeides Panathenaikos I 306, 3, Dindorf*, Philologus, 107 (1963), pp. 278-287.
―― : *Zwei Mishandlungen...*, Philologus, 112 (1968), pp. 276-281.
―― : *Zu den neuen Aristeidespapyri*, Philologus, 113 (1969), pp. 301-306.

Reiske, J. J. : *Animadversionum ad Graecos Auctores Volumen Tertium*, Leipzig, 1761 (reprinted in the notes of Dindorf's edition of 1829, see Bibl. II).

SELECTED BIBLIOGRAPHY

V. Translations of Ors. I and II

Canter, Willem : *Aelii Aristidis...tomi tres nunc primum Latine versi*, Basle, 1566 (contains all orations except ors. xvi and liii ; a brilliant work with many corrections of the text ; reprinted in its entirety in Stephanus' edition of 1604 and Jebb's of 1722, 1730).

Oliver, James H. : see Bibl. II, 1968.

SIGLA FOR ORS. I AND II

Pap. : P. Mich. inv. 6651 (6th or 7th century), see
    Bibl. II, under Browne & Henrichs 1968.

T : Laurentianus LX, 8 (11th century).

Q : Vaticanus graecus 1297 (12th century).

V : Marcianus App. VIII, 7 (11th century).

A : Parisinus graecus 2951 (10th century).

Phot. : Photius, *Bibliotheca*, codd. 246-248 (where
    cited Lenz's photostats of Marcianus gr. 450 and
    451 are used).

codd. dett. : any codex aside from those listed above.

Aldinae : see Bibl. II, under Aldus 1513, 1534.

Canter : see Bibl. V, under Canter 1566.

Cobet : see Bibl. IV, under Cobet 1873.

Ddf. : see Bibl. II, under Dindorf 1829.

Holleck : see Bibl. IV, under Holleck 1874.

Iunt. : see Bibl. II, under Junta 1517.

Keil : from the marginalia of his copy of Dindorf.

Lenz : see Bibl. IV, under Lenz, *Aristeidesstudien*,
    1964, and Philologus, 1968 ; and from the mar-
    ginalia of his copy of Dindorf.

Oliver : see Bibl. II, under Oliver 1968.

Reiske : see Bibl. IV, under Reiske 1761.

Stephanus : see Bibl. II, under Henricus Stephanus
    1593.

< > : supplement by Byzantine or modern scholars.

[ ] : words to be deleted in the major MSS.

I

THE
PANATHENAIC ORATION

ARISTIDES

INTRODUCTION

THE *Panathenaicus* was probably delivered at the
major Panathenaea in August, A.D. 155, in the course
of Aristides' second trip to Greece and Rome. The
speech, apart from its hugely disproportionate
account of the glories of Attic military history,
§§ 75-321, is typical of Aristides' other panegyric
orations on behalf of various cities and sites. So for
example, it commences with the standard portrait
of geographic features. It is the abstract of Athens'
military glory which doubtless earned the speech its
popularity in the schools of antiquity, but it should
be noted that, as Aristides himself comments, § 230,
we are not dealing with a jejune military chronicle.
Rather Aristides has chosen certain famous events
which he felt to be illustrative of the overriding
theme of the oration, Athens' generosity and self-
sacrifice ; and with little if any mention of the actual
circumstances of these actions, he has written eulo-
gies on the character which inspired them. It is
noteworthy in this respect how sparingly he has
employed proper names, as if he wished to submerge
the accomplishment of the individual into the lauda-
tion of the whole state. It was clearly Aristides'
intention to praise Athens for its contribution to the
arts. But the traditional course of the panegyric
thwarted this plan, although it does appear in the

3

highly incongruous transition from Athens' feats in war to the glories of her dialect and literature, §§ 322-330.

Though there exist several elaborate studies on the sources which Aristides allegedly used in composing this speech,[a] it seems most unlikely that the material contained in this work depends on much actual research as such. Aristides' thorough familiarity with the great historians, including Ephorus, as literary objects, and with the orators, poets, and Plato, would provide him with all the background which he required. At times his memory even led him into error. However, the curious argument concerning the three Olympiads in § 283, as well as the discussion based on the Athenian archon list in or. iii. 578 (p. 370 Ddf.) and iv. 51 (p. 435 Ddf.) may indicate that he used a handbook as an aid.[b]

OUTLINE OF THE CONTENTS OF THE ORATION

A. Proem : §§ 1-7.
B. Geography : §§ 8-23.
C. Indigenous Population : §§ 24-30.
D. The discovery of crops and their sharing : §§ 31-38.

[a] J. Haury, *Quibus Fontibus Aelius Aristides usus sit in declamatione quae inscribitur* Παναθηναικός, Diss. Augsburg, 1888 ; E. Beecke, *Die historischen Angaben in Aelius Aristides Panathenaikos auf ihre Quellen untersucht*, Diss. Strassburg, 1905 ; J. H. Oliver, *The Civilizing Power*, Transactions of the American Philosophical Society, n.s. 58, 1 (1968), with a translation, text, and apparatus, the last of which is unreliable.

[b] Perhaps Favorinus' *Miscellaneous History* or Apollodorus' *Chronica* ; *cf.* Behr, AJP, lxxxix, p. 195.

PANATHENAIC ORATION

E. The honour of the Gods toward Athens : §§ 39-48.
F. The city's generosity in the reception of exiles and the founding of colonies : §§ 49-74.
G. Deeds in war : §§ 75-321.
H. Attic tongue : §§ 322-330.
I. Honours shown to Athens : §§ 331-334.
J. Superiority of Athens : §§ 335-401.
K. Peroration : §§ 402-404.

I

ΠΑΝΑΘΗΝΑΙΚΟΣ

I 150 D.

1 Νόμος ἐστὶ τοῖς Ἕλλησιν παλαιός, οἶμαι δὲ καὶ τῶν βαρβάρων τοῖς πλείστοις, τροφεῦσιν χάριν ἐκτίνειν ἅπασαν, ὅση δυνατή. οὕστινας δ' ἂν τροφέας προτέρους ὑμῶν ἄγοι τις, ὦ ἄνδρες Ἀθηναῖοι, δοκῶν γε δή πως εἰς Ἕλληνας τελεῖν, οὐ ῥᾴδιον εὑρεῖν, ὥς γέ μοι φαίνεται. μάλιστα μὲν γὰρ καὶ τῆς νενομισμένης ταυτησὶ τροφῆς καὶ κοινῆς ὑμᾶς εὐθὺς ἂν εὕροι τις ἐπωνύμους καὶ ποριστὰς σκοπῶν ἐξ ἀρχῆς· ὥστε ἔξεστιν εἰπεῖν ἰδίᾳ μὲν ἄλλους ἄλλοις εἶναι τροφέας, οὓς ἂν ἡ τύχη καὶ ὁ συμπίπτων χρόνος ἑκάστοις παρασκευάσῃ, κοινοὺς δὲ ἁπάντων τροφέας ὑμᾶς εἶναι καὶ μόνους καὶ πρό γε αὐτῶν ἔτι τῶν τροφέων, ὥσπερ οὓς πατέρας πατέρων καλοῦσιν οἱ ποιηταί· δι' ἃ καὶ μόνα τὴν εὔνοιαν ἥρκει παρὰ πάντων ὑμῖν εἶναι κατὰ φύσιν.

2 οὐ μὴν ἀλλ' οἳ βλέπων τὸ δίκαιον ἐποιούμην καὶ περὶ ἧς εἶχον ἐν νῷ τροφῆς εἰπεῖν, τῆς ὡς ἀληθῶς καθαρᾶς καὶ διαφερόντως ἀνθρώπου, τῆς ἐν μαθήμασι καὶ λόγοις, τίς οὕτως ἔξω τούτων ἐστὶν ὥστ' ἀγνοεῖν παρ' ὑμῶν οὖσαν ἅπασι τὴν ἀρχήν; ὥστε

---

[a] Barbarians means non-Greeks, and in Aristides the Persians in particular.

[b] Source unknown ; cf. xxx. 10.

6

1

THE PANATHENAIC ORATION

THE Greeks, and, I think, also most of the bar-   1
barians,[a] have an old custom, to pay back, as far as
they can, every debt of gratitude to their foster-
fathers. But, it seems to me at least, it is not easy to
find persons whom anyone, who could somehow be
apparently classified as a Greek, would regard as
foster-fathers before you, O men of Athens. For
right at the start, in his initial considerations, one
would find that you were both named for and pro-
viders of this customary and general means of
fostering, so that others can be called foster-fathers
for people in a private sense, whomever chance and
coincidence made available to each, but you alone
can be called the common foster-fathers of all men
and even more, of the other foster-fathers themselves, just as those whom the poets call " fathers of
fathers." [b] This reason alone was a natural enough
cause for all men to show good will to you. However,   2
as to the purpose of the performance of my obligation
and in regard to the fostering of which I intended to
speak, that which is truly pure and particularly
proper to man, the fostering of studies and oratory,
to whom are these so foreign that he does not know
that all of them owe their origin to you ? Therefore

151 D. εἰκὸς καὶ τὸν περὶ τούτων λόγον δεῦρο κομίζειν καὶ
τιμᾶν τοῖς γιγνομένοις τὴν πόλιν. ὡς τὰς μὲν ἄλλας
χάριτας δικαίας μέν, οὐ μὴν τῶν πραγμάτων ἄντικρυς εἶναι συμβέβηκεν, μόνην δὲ ταύτην γνησίαν
τῆς εὐεργεσίας ἔξεστι προσειπεῖν. ἡ γὰρ ὑπὲρ λόγων λόγῳ γιγνομένη χάρις οὐ μόνον τὸ δίκαιον ἔχει
μεθ᾽ ἑαυτῆς, ἀλλὰ καὶ τὴν ἀπὸ τοῦ λόγου πρῶτον[1]
ἐπωνυμίαν βεβαιοῖ, μόνη γάρ ἐστιν ἀκριβῶς εὔλο-
3 γος. μηδεὶς δὲ ὑμῶν, ὦ νῦν τε παρόντες τοῖς
λόγοις καὶ χρόνῳ συνεσόμενοι, μηδεμίαν προπέτειαν
μηδὲ εὐήθειαν καταγνῷ τοῦ παντὸς ἐγχειρήματος,
εἰ μήτε προστησάμενοι σχῆμα φαυλότερον τοῦ λόγου μήτε ἃ πολλὰ καὶ ἐργώδη τῷ λόγῳ πρόσεστι
δείσαντες ὑπέστημεν ἐκ τοῦ φανεροῦ τοσοῦτον
ἀγῶνα. μάλιστα μὲν γάρ, εἰ καὶ τοῦτο ἄξιον αἰτίας,
οὐδὲ τὰ πρὸς τοὺς θεοὺς ἡμῖν γε παρεῖται τὸ μὴ
οὐ τετολμῆσθαι. ἔπειτ᾽ οὐδ᾽ ἐμὲ τοῦτο λέληθεν ὡς
ἐργώδης ὁ λόγος καὶ χαλεπὸς διενεγκεῖν καὶ τὰς
ἐκδρομὰς ὁπόσας ἔχει· ἃς καὶ συνιδεῖν ἁπάσας καὶ
διελέσθαι καθ᾽ ἑκάστην καὶ πληρῶσαι διὰ τέλους
ἀδύνατον μὴ οὐ σὺν μεγάλῃ καὶ λαμπρᾷ τῇ τύχῃ·
πρὸς δὲ τούτοις, ἐφ᾽ ὅσοις ἔθνεσιν τοῖς περὶ αὐτῶν
εἰρηκόσιν καὶ προκατειληφόσι τὰς ἀκοὰς ἐπερχό-
μεθα, μεῖζον ἔχοντες ἔργον ὅ τι φυλαξόμεθα ἢ ὅτῳ
χρησόμεθα εὑρεῖν. ἄλλων γὰρ ἄλλα κεκοσμηκό-
των καὶ διεξεληλυθότων τὰ πᾶσι παρειμένα πᾶσι
καὶ πεπλήρωται· καὶ συμβαίνει διπλοῦν τὸν ἀγῶνα
152 D. γίγνεσθαι τῷ μετὰ πάντας ἐγχειροῦντι, καὶ χωρὶς
4 πρὸς ἕκαστον καὶ κοινῇ πρὸς ἅπαντας. οὐ μὴν ἀλλ᾽

---

[1] πρώτην TQV.

it is reasonable to present here a speech on this subject and to honour the city in a fitting way. For it has chanced that other means of showing gratitude are just, yet not directly proper to the matter, but that this alone can be called a genuine means of expressing thanks for your kindness. For the expression of thanks for oratory delivered by means of oratory not only is right in itself but also first of all confirms the name given to this kind of speech. For it alone is, to be precise, "the use of fair speech." But you who are now present at my speech or will be acquainted with it later, let none of you condemn the whole attempt for rashness and simplicity if we undertook a contest so obviously great, neither having chosen a lesser subject for oratory nor having feared the many difficulties attendant on the speech. Indeed, even if this too is blameworthy, we at least have not been remiss in bold undertakings in respect to the Gods. Next, it has not escaped me that the oration is troublesome and difficult to accomplish, as well as offering many occasions for digression. To recognize, to classify, and to fulfil completely their requirements is impossible without a great deal of good luck. And in addition, we come forward after all the troops of writers who have spoken on this subject and preoccupied your ears, and we have a greater task in finding what we shall avoid than what we shall use. For although their subjects and laudations are different, that which has been neglected by each has been accomplished by all collectively. And it falls out that he who attempts to speak after all of them has a double contest, separately against each and commonly against all. Moreover this is the sole 4

9

(152 D.)

αὐτό γε τοῦτο ἐστὶν τὸ καὶ[1] μόνον πεποιηκός μοι
τὸν λόγον, ὅτι οὕτω πολλοῖς καὶ μεγάλοις τῆς
πόλεως ὑπερεχούσης, καὶ τόπον οὐδένα τοῖς βουλομένοις εὐφημεῖν ἀργὸν παρεικυίας, οὐδείς πω μέχρι
τῆσδε τῆς ἡμέρας εἰς ἅπαντα καθῆκεν ἑαυτὸν οὐδὲ
ἐθάρρησεν. ἀλλ' οἱ μὲν τοὺς ἄνω χρόνους ἐν τοῖς
ποιήμασιν ᾄδουσιν καὶ τὰ πρὸς τοὺς θεοὺς κοινὰ τῇ
πόλει, καὶ ταῦτα ἀπὸ τοῦ παρείκοντος,[2] οἱ δὲ τοὺς
ἐπὶ τῶν καιρῶν πολέμους πρὸς Ἕλληνας καὶ βαρβάρους αὐτῆς ἀφηγοῦνται μεμερισμένως· ἕτεροι δὲ
τὴν πολιτείαν καταλέγουσιν· οἱ δὲ ἐν τοῖς ἐπιταφίοις
λόγοις τῶν ἀποθανόντων ἐνίους προσειρήκασιν. εἰσὶν δὲ οἳ κἂν τούτοις οὐχ, ὡς νομίζεται, διὰ τῶν
πράξεων ἦλθον, ἀλλ' ἑτέραν ἐτράποντο, δείσαντες,
ἐμοὶ δοκεῖν, ἐλάττους γενέσθαι τῶν πραγμάτων, οὐκ
ἔξω μέν που συγγνώμης λαβόντες φόβον, ἀλλ' οὖν
οὕτω πολλοῦ τινος ἐδέησαν περὶ πάντων γε τῶν ὑπ-
5 αρχόντων τῇ πόλει διεξελθεῖν. καὶ μὴν οἱ μὲν τὴν
σοφίαν αὐτῆς ἐγκωμιάζουσιν, οἱ δὲ τὰς ἀποικίας
καταλέγουσιν, ἕτεροι δὲ αὖ τὴν κοινότητα καὶ φιλανθρωπίαν ὑμνοῦσιν, καὶ ταῦτα οἱ μὲν τοῖς συγ-
γράμμασί που τοῖς ἄλλοις ἐγκαταμιγνύντες, οἱ δ'
ἀπὸ στόματος οὑτωσὶ κατὰ τὸ συμβαῖνον τῆς μνήμης. ὡς δὲ ἁπλῶς εἰπεῖν, ἅπαντες ἢ τῷ βουλήματι
τῷ σφετέρῳ μεμετρήκασιν ἢ τῇ δυνάμει τὰ πρὸς
τὴν πόλιν, οὐ τῷ τῆς πόλεως μέτρῳ οὐδὲ τῷ τῶν
πραγμάτων, ἀλλὰ ὥσπερ πελάγους ἀπείρου καὶ τοῖς
ὀφθαλμοῖς οὐχ ὁρίζοντος ἕκαστος ὅσον καθορᾷ,
153 D. τοῦτο θαυμάζει· καὶ συμβέβηκεν ὥσπερ αἴνιγμα τῇ
πόλει· ᾗ γὰρ τοσοῦτον[3] εὐφημιῶν καὶ δόξης περίεστιν, ταύτῃ, κἂν ὡς ἐλάχιστον τούτων ὧν μέτεστιν
6 εἴπῃ τις, οὐ τοῦ παντὸς ἁμαρτήσεται. οὐ δὴ δίκαι-

10

reason which has caused me to speak, that, although
the city excels in many great attributes and has left
no topic untouched for those who wish to praise it,
no one up to the present day has set himself to the
whole subject, or had the courage to do so. But
some in their poems sing of former times and the
relations of the Gods with the city, as far as they
can ; others narrate its various occasional wars against
the Greeks and barbarians ; others describe the
constitution ; others have composed funeral orations
for some of the dead. And among these some did
not carry their narrative through the deeds of the
city as is customary, but went another way, in fear,
as it seems to me, of being inferior to their theme, a
terror not without compassion, but even so they
were far from recounting all of the city's attributes.
Indeed, some laud its wisdom, some list its colonies, 5
others again praise its generosity and liberality,
some including their praise in different writings, and
others just delivering it extemporaneously as they
chance to remember it. But to put it simply, all have
measured their praise of the city by their own wishes
or capacity, and not by the measure of the city or of
the facts, but as in a boundless sea which sets no
limits to the eye, each admires as much as he beholds.
And the city has become a riddle. For it has so
much fame and glory that even if someone mentions
its attributes in the most deficient way, he will not
be a complete failure. It is unjust that the imputa- 6

---

¹ codd. dett. : καὶ τὸ TQVA.
² παρήκοντος TQA p. corr.
³ τοσούτων VA.

(153 D.)

ον τὴν μόνην τοῦ τολμήματος αἰτίαν καὶ δι᾽ ἣν εἰκότως ἐδέησε τοῦ νυνὶ λόγου, ταύτην ἐκείνης ἀξιῶσαι
τῆς αἰτίας, ᾗ τὸ τῆς μέμψεώς ἐστιν ὄνομα. ἔπειτα
εἰ μὲν μὴ πολλῶν καὶ καλῶν καὶ μεγάλων ὄντων,
οὐ μὲν οὖν οὔτ᾽ ἀπαριθμῆσαι ῥᾳδίων οὔτε μετρῆσαι
δυνατῶν τῶν εἰς τοσοῦτον τὴν πόλιν ἠρκότων, ἔν τι
καὶ τοῦτο τὸ τῶν λόγων ἦν ἀγαθόν, οὐκ ἂν ἴσως
ἥρμοττε παρακινδυνεύειν, ἀλλ᾽ ἐὰν ὅπως ποτ᾽ εἶχε
τὰ τῆς δόξης αὐτῇ· νυνὶ δ᾽ ὥσπερ τῶν ἄλλων
ἁπάντων ἡγεμὼν τοῖς Ἕλλησιν, οἶμαι δὲ καὶ τοῖς
ἄλλοις ἀνθρώποις, γεγένηται, οὕτως ὅτι καὶ τῶν
154 D. λόγων πρώτη[1] γνώριμόν ἐστιν· ὥστε οὔτ᾽[2] ἀλλοτρίᾳ
τῇ πείρᾳ χρώμεθα, οὐδ᾽ ἑτέρωσε φέρουσαν ὁδὸν
προειλόμεθα, ἀλλ᾽ ἀκριβῶς ἐπὶ τὴν πόλιν καὶ τοὺς
Ἀθηναίους, οὔτε ἐλάττω τὰ τῆς πόλεως ποιοῦμεν,
ἀλλ᾽ ἔν τι τῶν τῆς πόλεως ἐκτίνομεν, εἰς ὅσον ἐγ-
7 χωρεῖ. εἰρημένον δὲ ὑπὸ πολλῶν πολλάκις ὡς ἄρα
οὐ ῥᾴδιον εὑρεῖν ὅθεν ἄρξεταί τις, ἐμόν, οὐκ ἄλλου
τοῦτον τὸν λόγον εἶναι νομίζω τῇ χρείᾳ. οὐ γὰρ
μόνον τῷ πρεσβυτάτην εἶναι τῶν ἐν μνήμῃ[3] τὴν
πόλιν συμβαίνει καὶ τὴν ἀρχὴν ἀνήκειν εἰς τὸ πλέον
τοῦ φανεροῦ καὶ προχείρου λαβεῖν, ἀλλ᾽ ὅτι καὶ πολλὰς ὥσπερ ἐν κύκλῳ τὰς ἀρχὰς ὁ λόγος προ-
δείκνυσιν, ἃς οὔτε ὁμοῦ ποιήσασθαι δήπου δυνατὸν
οὔθ᾽ ἥτις ἀρχὴ ταῖς ἄλλαις εἶναι νικήσει ῥᾴδιον
κρῖναι· ἄλλα γὰρ ἄλλων ἕνεκα ἁρμόττειν ὥς γ᾽ ἐκ
τοῦ προφαινομένου πρῶτα λεχθῆναι δόξαν παρί-
στησιν.

8 Ἣν δὲ ἁπασῶν ἐπικαιροτάτην ἀρχὴν ὑπολαμ-
βάνω καὶ πρὸς ἣν ἥκιστ᾽ ἂν ἁμαρτεῖν, ἅπαντα
καθιστάμενος τὸν λόγον, ταύτην καὶ δὴ ποιήσομαι·

tion of my audacity alone, which required the present defence, is felt deserving of that other imputation whose meaning is blame. If, next, this one virtue, that of oratory, were not among the many great and fair qualities of the city, which are neither easy to number nor possible to measure, and which have exalted it so greatly, perhaps it would be fitting not to run the risk, but to let the city's reputation stand as it is. But just as it has been the leader in all other things for the Greeks, and, I think, also for other men, so it is well known that it was also first in oratory. Therefore we do not employ an enterprise alien to it, nor did we choose a road which leads elsewhere than straight to the city and the Athenians, nor do we demean the attributes of the city, but we are showing our gratitude for one of them, as far as possible. Although many have often said that 7 it is not easy to find a starting point, I think that for all practical purposes this expression suits me and no one else : for not only does it happen, because it is the oldest city in memory, that its beginnings go back to a point which is no longer clear and easily comprehensible; but also because the argument reveals many beginnings almost everywhere, which cannot be used simultaneously, and because it is not easy to decide which beginning will take precedence over the others. But different points for different reasons suggest that they are clearly fit to be discussed first.

In the arrangement of my whole speech, I shall use 8 the beginning which I think is the most opportune of all and in which I should least err. But whether rightly

---

¹ πρῶτον VA.   ² οὐκ VA.   ³ τῇ μνήμῃ TQ.

(154 D.)

εἰ δ' ὀρθῶς, ἢ μή, πάρεστι κοινωνεῖν τῆς γνώμης.
οἶμαι δ', ἂν ὡς ὑπὲρ οἰκείας καὶ μετέχων τῶν
ἀγαθῶν ἔστιν οὗ φαίνωμαι τῷ λόγῳ χρώμενος, οὐδ'
ὑμῖν ἂν φέρειν αἰσχύνην. ἡ γὰρ τῆς χώρας ἡμῖν
φύσις τῇ φύσει τῶν ἀνδρῶν συμβαίνουσα φανήσεται
καὶ οὔτε ἡ γῆ πρέπουσα ἑτέρων εἶναι, οὔκουν οὐδὲ
ἐγένετο, οὔτε οἱ ἄνδρες ἄλλης ἀντὶ ταύτης ἄξιοι,
οὔκουν οὐδὲ ἠλλάξαντο, ἀλλ' ἔμειναν ἐφ' ἧς εἶχον·
ἄμφω δὲ ταῦτα ὄψει καὶ μνήμῃ κρίνεται. οἵ τε
155 D. γὰρ οἰκήσαντες ἀεὶ τὴν χώραν ἐναργῆ καὶ θαυμαστὰ
τῆς αὑτῶν ἐπιεικείας σημεῖα ἐξήνεγκαν ἐν παντὶ τῷ
παρασχόντι, τὰ μὲν ἦν οὑτωσί τις ἂν εἴποι φιλανθρωπίαν ἐπιδεικνύμενοι τῇ τῶν τρόπων πραότητι καὶ
ταῖς ὁμιλίαις, οὐδέσιν ἄλλοις ὁμοίως ἡμέροις εἶναι
δοκεῖν λιπόντες, τὰ δ' ἐν ταῖς χρείαις καὶ τοῖς κινδύνοις ἐν προβόλου μοίρᾳ τοῖς Ἕλλησι τεταγμένοι.
9 καὶ τὸ τῆς χώρας αὖ σχῆμα τοιοῦτον ἐκ γῆς καὶ
θαλάττης θεωροῦντι. πρόκειται γὰρ ἀντ' ἄλλου
φυλακτηρίου τῆς Ἑλλάδος τὴν γιγνομένην τάξιν
ἔχουσα πρώτη πρὸς ἥλιον ἀνίσχοντα, προμήκης εἰς
τὸ πέλαγος, καὶ μάλα ἐναργὴς συμβαλεῖν ὅτι τῆς
Ἑλλάδος ἐστὶν ἔρυμα ὑπὸ τῶν κρειττόνων πεποιη-
μένον καὶ μόνη ταύτῃ κατὰ φύσιν ἔστιν ἡγεῖσθαι
10 τοῦ γένους. εἶτα καὶ τῆς φιλανθρωπίας ὡσπερεὶ
σύμβολον ἐκφέρει· προβαίνει γὰρ μέχρι πλείστου,
τὴν θάλατταν ἡμεροῦσα, καὶ ταῖς νήσοις ἐγκατα-
μίγνυται, θεαμάτων ἥδιστον, ἤπειρος ἐν νήσοις, καὶ
τούτων ἐνίων νοτιωτέρα, πρώτη μὲν τοῖς ἐκ τοῦ
πελάγους ὡσπερεὶ χεῖρα προτείνουσα εἰς ὑποδοχήν,
παντοδαποὺς δὲ ὅρμους καὶ λιμένας παρεχομένη
κύκλῳ περὶ πᾶσαν ἑαυτήν, ἔτι δὲ ἀκτὰς ἄλλας κατ'

or not, it is time to share with you my resolve.
But I think that I should not shame you, if I appear
to speak as if on behalf of my own city and as a
participant in some of its virtues. For the nature of
our country will appear to agree with the nature of its
people. The land is not now, nor was it ever a
proper home for other people ; nor ought its people
to have inhabited another land instead of this, nor
did they ever change it, but they remained where
they were. Both these points are determined by
sight and tradition. For whoever dwelled in this
country showed at every possible opportunity
manifest and marvellous signs of his own goodness.
On the one hand they revealed through the gentleness of their manners and their accessibility that
which one would call generosity, in which they left
no room for others to seem equally mild, and on
the other hand in times of need and danger they were
arrayed like a bulwark for the Greeks. And again 9
the form of the country gives this appearance as seen
from both land and sea. For it is situated for Greece
like a means of protection in preference to any other,
in the proper position, the first land toward the east,
jutting into the sea, and making it very clearly comprehensible that it has been formed by the Gods as
the rampart of Greece, and alone possesses the natural leadership of the race. Again it displays a sort 10
of sign of its generous kindness, in that it projects far
into the sea, taming it. And it joins with the islands,
a most charming spectacle, a mainland among the
islands ; and more southerly than some of these,
it first as it were stretches forth its hand to receive
those from the sea, and provides various anchorages
and harbours all about itself, and also beaches at

15

(155 D.)

ἄλλα μέρη τῆς τε θαλάττης καὶ ἑαυτῆς, καὶ πορθμοὺς πρὸς τὰς ἐπικειμένας νήσους οὐ πλέον δια-
λείποντας[1] ἢ ὅσον αἱ νῆσοι πρὸς ἀλλήλας· ὥστε καὶ
παραπλεῖν καὶ περιπλεῖν καὶ πεζεύειν καὶ ἔτι πελα-
γίους εἶναι διὰ τῆς Ἀττικῆς ὥσπερ ἐν πομπῇ κατ᾽
11 ἐξουσίαν τὸ πρὸς ἡδονὴν αἱρουμένους. αἱ δὲ ἐπί-
κεινται πανταχόθεν πεποικιλμέναι Κυκλάδες καὶ
Σποράδες περὶ τὴν Ἀττικήν, ὥσπερ τῆς θαλάττης
156 D. ἐξεπίτηδες ἀνείσης ἀντὶ προαστείων τῇ πόλει, χοροῦ
σχῆμα σῴζουσαι, καὶ τὰ ἐκείνων κάλλη καὶ κόσμους
τῆς πόλεως κάλλη καὶ κόσμους εἶναι συμβέβηκεν.
δύνανται γὰρ ὅπερ τοῖς βασιλείοις τὰ προπύλαια, καὶ
σελήνην ἀστέρες ἐγκλείουσιν, ποιητὴς ἂν εἴποι τις,
μεῖζον φέρουσαι κέρδος ἢ ὅσον παρέχουσιν· λέγω δὴ
τοῦ προσοικεῖν. δι᾽ ἃ δὴ καὶ μόνῃ τῇ πόλει[2]
κυρίως ἄν τις φαίη τὴν ἀρχὴν αὐτῶν συμβῆναι καὶ
γνησίαν ἐπὶ τῶν Ἑλληνικῶν, τοὺς δ᾽ ἄλλους νόθους
εἰς τὴν θάλατταν ἐμβῆναι, ὥσπερ ὑποβολιμαίους, οὐ
πατρικαῖς ταῖς νήσοις ἐπιθεμένους, ἀλλ᾽ ἁρπάσαν-
τας τύχης ἀλογίᾳ, ὅπερ αὐτοὺς καὶ ταχέως πάλιν
12 ἐξήλασε. τοῦτο δὲ τὸ σχῆμα καὶ ταύτην τὴν θέσιν
τῆς χώρας ἐχούσης, τὸν μὲν ἀεὶ κατάπλουν τῶν
ἐμπόρων τε καὶ καθ᾽ ἱστορίαν ἢ χρείαν εἰσαφικνου-
μένων, μεθ᾽ ὅσης τῆς ῥαστώνης καὶ ψυχαγωγίας
γίγνεται καὶ τρυφῆς οὐ ῥάδιον εἰπεῖν, πλὴν εἰς
ὅσον αὐτούς τις ἐπιμαρτύραιτο· οὕτω γὰρ παντάπασιν ἡ ψυχὴ προκαθαίρεται καὶ μετέωρος καὶ
κούφη γίγνεται καὶ σφόδρα τῶν Ἀθηνῶν τῆς θέας
ἐν παρασκευῇ, ὥσπερ ἐν ἱεροῖς προτελουμένη.
ἐπίδηλον δὲ καὶ τοῖς ὀφθαλμοῖς πλέον τοῦ συνήθους

---

[1] διαλιπόντας VA.   [2] μόνης τῆς πόλεως VA.

different points on the sea and in its own territory, and crossings to the neighbouring islands at no greater distance than the islands are from one another, so that men sail by, sail around, and cross over on land and still are at sea in Attica, as if in a procession, choosing what pleases them according to their whims. There also lie nearby, on all sides of Attica, the vari- 11 ous Cyclades and Sporades, as if the sea puposely set them free to be like suburbs for the city, in the form of a chorus. And it has come to pass that their beauty and adornment have become the beauty and adorn- ment of the city. For they have the same meaning as gateways do for palaces, " and stars enclosing the moon," some poet would say,[a] receiving a greater advantage than they provide,—I mean by their nearness. Therefore one would say that in the time of the Greeks the proper and genuine rule of the islands belonged only to the city and that the others illegitimately entered upon the sea, like supposti- tious children, and did not attack the islands as being ancestral property, but stole them through the senseless behaviour of fortune, which circum- stance quickly expelled them again. Since this is 12 the form and situation of the land, it is not easy to describe with what delight, charm, and pleasure merchants or those who have come to learn or on business from time to time put into port, except in so far as one should call them as witnesses. For thus in every way the soul is first purified and exalted, indeed in preparation for the spectacle of Athens, as if receiving preliminary initiation in some sacred rites. But a clear and abnormally bright light strikes the

---

[a] Source unknown ; according to the scholiast, some held that Aristides was the author.

(156 D.)

τὸ φῶς ἐγγιγνόμενον, ἀφαιρούσης ἤδη τὴν πολλὴν
ἀχλὺν ὡς ἀληθῶς καὶ καθ' Ὅμηρον τῆς Ἀθηνᾶς
157 D. ἔτι τῇ χώρᾳ προσαγόντων. ὥστε ἔοικεν ὀνείρατος
εὐφροσύνῃ τὰ θεάματα καὶ χορείαν ἐξελίττειν, οὐ
πλοῦν ἀνύτειν δόξαις ἄν, οἷα τὴν ναῦν ἀεὶ κύκλῳ
περιΐσταται κάλλη παντοδαπὰ ἄγοντα μετ' εὐθυμίας
13 ἐπὶ τὴν Ἀττικήν. τοῖς δ' ὁρωμένοις συμβαίνει
καὶ τὰ λεγόμενα, οἷς οὐκ ἔνεστιν ἀπιστεῖν· πάντα
γὰρ ἑξῆς ὁμοίως ἔχει. Λητώ τε γάρ, εἰ καὶ μικρὸν
ὕστερον ἁρμόσει περὶ τῶν θείων διηγεῖσθαι, λυσα-
μένη τὴν ζώνην ἐν Ζωστῆρι τῆς Ἀττικῆς καὶ λι-
ποῦσα τὴν ἐπωνυμίαν τῷ τόπῳ, βαδίζουσα ἀεὶ[1] εἰς[2]
τὸ πρὸς ἕω τῆς Προνοίας Ἀθηνᾶς ἡγουμένης, ἀπ'
ἄκρας τῆς Ἀττικῆς ἐπιβᾶσα τῶν νήσων εἰς Δῆλον
καταίρει καὶ τίκτει δὴ τοὺς θεοὺς τήν τε Ἄρτεμιν
καὶ τὸν πατρῷον Ἀπόλλω τῇ πόλει, ἥ τ' ἀπὸ τῆς
158 D. Ἀσίας ἐπὶ τοὺς Ἕλληνας πρώτη διαβᾶσα δύναμις
διὰ τῶν νήσων προσέσχεν εἰς Μαραθῶνα, καλῶς
ὑπὸ τῆς φύσεως ἀχθεῖσα τοῦ τόπου πρὸς τὸ δοῦναι
14 δίκην ὧν ἐπεβούλευσε τοῖς Ἕλλησιν. οὕτω δὲ ἐν
ἀρχῇ τῆς Ἑλλάδος οὖσα ἡ χώρα ἐν μέσῳ τῆς πάσης
οὐχ ἧττόν ἐστιν. ὅποι γὰρ ἂν ἀπ' αὐτῆς κινηθείης,
τὰ γνωριμώτατα τῶν Ἑλλήνων ἐκδέχεται γένη, καὶ
ὥσπερ πόλιν ἡ οἰκεία χώρα προσοικεῖ, οὕτω καὶ
τὴν Ἀττικὴν ἅπασα ἡ Ἑλλὰς προσοικεῖ. διὸ δὴ
καὶ μόνη τὸ τῶν Ἑλλήνων πρόσχημα καθαρῶς
ἀνῄρηται καὶ τοῖς βαρβάροις ἐστὶν ἐπὶ πλεῖστον ἀλ-
λόφυλος· ὅσον γὰρ τῇ φύσει τοῦ τόπου κεχώρισται,
τοσοῦτον καὶ τοῖς ἤθεσι τῶν ἀνδρῶν ἀφέστηκεν.
οὔτε γὰρ ποταμοῦ μέσου κοινωνεῖ τινος οὔτε ἐστὶν

---

[1] ἀεὶ om. TQ.   [2] εἰς om. VA.

eye, since truly and to speak in Homeric terms [a]
Athena at once removes a great mist from those
still in the act of approaching the land. Therefore
the spectacle is like a joyful dream, and you would
believe that you were concluding the evolutions
of a dance, not finishing a voyage, when such various
kinds of beauty are always about the ship, joyfully
guiding it to Attica. And with the sights concur 13
those legends which cannot possibly be doubted.
All of them, everyone, are alike. For Leto, even
if a little later it is the place to tell of things divine,
loosed her girdle in Zoster in Attica and gave a
name to the place ; and walking ever to the east
under the guidance of the Athena of Providence,
from the tip of Attica to the islands, she stopped
at Delos and gave birth to Gods for the city, Artemis and Ancestral Apollo. And the first force, 490 B.C.
which crossed from Asia against the Greeks, passed
through the islands and put in at Marathon, rightly
drawn by the nature of the place to pay for their
plots against the Greeks. Thus although the land is 14
in the beginning of Greece proper, it is nonetheless
in the midst of all of Greece. For, in whatever
direction you would move from it, are at hand the
most famous races of the Greeks. And just as its
own territory is adjacent to a city, so the whole of
Greece is adjacent to Attica. For this reason it
alone has assumed the appearance of an unblemished
Greek people, and is to the greatest degree racially
distinct from the barbarians. For to the extent that
it is separated by the nature of its geography, it is
also removed from the barbarians in the customs of
its men. For it neither shares any common river,

---

[a] *Iliad* V. 127.

(158 D.)

αὐτῇ μεθόριον οὐδὲν τὸ αὐτὸ διαιροῦν καὶ μιγνύον
τὴν γῆν, ἀλλ' ὥσπερ πρὸς ἀσπίδος ἐπίσημον πάντα
πρὸς μέσον τοῦτο τὸ χωρίον ἐκ παντὸς ἄκρου τείνει
τὰ Ἑλληνικά, καὶ πανταχόθεν κύκλοι περιέχουσιν
τὴν χώραν Ἑλληνικοί, οἱ μὲν ἐκ θαλάττης, οἱ δ'
ἀπὸ τῆς ἠπείρου περικείμενοι, ὥσπερ εἰκὸς τῇ
15 κοινῇ τοῦ γένους ἑστίᾳ. τοσοῦτον δὲ πέφευγε τὴν
ἀλλοδαπὴν[1] καὶ βάρβαρον ὥστε καὶ ἐπὶ τῆς ἀντιπέρας ἠπείρου προὐβάλετο ἑτέραν Ἑλλάδα ἄποικον
ἑαυτῆς, ἢ νῦν ἤδη πλεῖστον βαρβάρων ἀφέστηκεν,
ὥσπερ φύσει ταχθεῖσα ἡ πόλις ἀντίπαλος τούτῳ
τῷ γένει καὶ πολεμία. ἐξ ὧν ἄδολον μὲν καὶ
καθαρὸν καὶ ἀδιάφθορον τὸ ἦθος ἀεὶ τοῖς ἐξ αὐτῆς
διαγέγονε παρεχομένη, εἰλικρινῆ δὲ καὶ καθαρὰν
159 D. καὶ ἄλυπον καὶ παράδειγμα πάσης τῆς Ἑλληνικῆς
16 ὁμιλίας φωνὴν εἰσηνέγκατο. ἡ δ' αὐτὴ θέσις τῆς
τε χώρας ἐν τῇ Ἑλλάδι καὶ τῆς πόλεως ἐν τῇ
χώρᾳ, μέση γὰρ ἐν μέσῃ κεῖται, τοσοῦτον πρὸς
θάλατταν ἐπικλίνουσα, ὅσον τοὺς λιμένας ἧς εἰσι
φαίνεσθαι. τρίτη δὲ ἀκόλουθος τούτων ἀνέχει,
περιφανὴς ἄνω διὰ μέσης τῆς πόλεως, ἡ πάλαι μὲν
πόλις, νῦν δὲ ἀκρόπολις, κορυφῇ παραπλησίως, οὐχ
ὡς ὕστατον εἶναι τῆς πόλεως, ἀλλ' ὡς περὶ αὐτὴν
πᾶν τὸ λοιπὸν σῶμα τῆς πόλεως, ἄκρου καὶ μέσου
ταὐτοῦ συμπεπτωκότος, τὸ διὰ πάντων ἤδη τοῦτο
κάλλος καὶ ὁ τελευταῖος ὅρος τῆς περὶ γῆν εὐκαιρίας.
ὥσπερ γὰρ ἐπ' ἀσπίδος κύκλων εἰς ἀλλήλους ἐμ-
βεβηκότων[2] πέμπτος εἰς ὀμφαλὸν πληροῖ διὰ πάντων ὁ κάλλιστος, εἴπερ ἡ μὲν Ἑλλὰς ἐν μέσῳ τῆς
πάσης γῆς, ἡ δὲ Ἀττικὴ τῆς Ἑλλάδος, τῆς δὲ χώ-
17 ρας ἡ πόλις, τῆς δ' αὖ πόλεως ἡ ὁμώνυμος. ἀλλ' ἐν-

---

[1] ἀλλοδαπῇ VA.   [2] συμβεβηκότων TQ.

nor does it have a boundary line, which can both separate and join a land. But as if to the bearing of a shield, all things Greek from every extreme are directed to this centrally located land, and on all sides Greeks encircle its territory, some from the sea, some nearby on the mainland, as is meet for the common hearth of the race. As if this city had 15 been naturally disposed as an opponent and enemy of the barbarian race, it has avoided foreign and barbarian land to such an extent that it even put forth as a bulwark another Greece, its colony, on the mainland opposite, which even now has kept far apart from the barbarians. From these causes it has always provided its people with pure and uncorrupted customs, and it also introduced, as a model for all Greek speech, a dialect which is clear, pure, and pleasant. The city occupies the same position in its 16 territory as the land does in Greece ; for it lies in the very centre of a central land, inclining only so far to the sea that the harbours show clearly whose they are. And as a third centrality, there rises clear aloft through the midst of the city, what was the old city and is now the present Acropolis, like a mountain peak, not to be the last part of the city, but so that all the remaining body of the city encloses it, where the high and central point coincide, a thoroughgoing adornment and the final boundary marker of the good position of the land. For as on a shield, where circular layers of hide have been put on in succession to one another, the Acropolis is the fifth at the boss, the fairest of all, which concludes the whole sequence : if Greece is in the centre of the whole earth, and Attica in the centre of Greece, and the city in the centre of its territory, and again its namesake in the

(159 D.)

ταῦθα μὲν ἡμᾶς ὁ λόγος παρήνεγκεν τῆς ἀεὶ παρα-
πιπτούσης ἀκολουθίας ἐχόμενος. ἐπιστρεπτέον δὲ
πάλιν πρὸς τὴν χώραν καὶ τὰ πρεσβεῖα φυλακτέον
αὐτῇ, ἧς τὴν μὲν πρὸς γῆς τε καὶ θαλάττης φύσιν
160 D. εἴπομεν δι᾽ ὅσων εἰκὸς ἦν, μῆκός τε φεύγοντες καὶ
18 τὸ παρελθεῖν ἃ μὴ χεῖρον εἰπεῖν. ἀλλὰ μὴν τόν
γε ὑπὲρ κεφαλῆς ἀέρα καὶ τὴν τῶν ὡρῶν κρᾶσιν οὕτω
σύμμετρον εἴληχεν ὥστε εἰ τῷ λόγῳ μετρίως εἰπεῖν
ἦν, εὐκτὸν ἂν ἦν. ἴσον γὰρ ἁπάντων ἀπέχει τῶν
δυσχερῶν καὶ μετέχουσα τῶν ἀγαθῶν τῆς δυνάμεως
ἑκάστης, ἃ λυπηρὰ πρόσεστιν ἑκάστῃ πέφευγεν. τεκ-
μαίρεσθαι δὲ ἔξεστιν οὐ μόνον τοῖς ὡραίοις νικῶσιν
καὶ παρὰ τὴν ἐπωνυμίαν καὶ τοσοῦτον τοῦ παντὸς
ἔτους κατέχουσι χρόνον, ἀλλὰ καὶ τῇ ἀποστάσει,
καθάπερ ἐν στάθμῃ, ὥσπερ ὅταν τι βουληθῶμεν
ἰδεῖν ἀκριβῶς.¹ ὅσον γὰρ ἄν τις ἀποστῇ τῆς
πόλεως δεῦρο ἢ ἐκεῖσε κινηθείς, ἢ τῇ θέρμῃ πλεῖον
τῆς χρείας ἢ τῷ ψύχει προστυγχάνει. ὥστε ἐν
τούτῳ μόνῳ νικᾶται ἐν ᾧ τὸ νικᾶν λυπεῖ καὶ οὗ τὸ
19 νικᾶσθαι λυσιτελέστερον. τοσαύτη δ᾽ ἐστὶν ἡ περιουσία τῆς εὐτυχίας ὥστε καὶ τῶν ἄλλων γενῶν αἱ
ταύτης ἄποικοι πόλεις αἱ τὴν νῦν Ἰωνίαν ἔχουσι
ἄριστα κεκρᾶσθαι δοκοῦσιν, ὥσπερ ἄλλο τι τῶν οἴκοθεν μετειληφυῖαι. ὥστε οὐ τὰ μὲν πρὸς ἄρκτον
ἂν εἴποι τις εἶναι τῆς χώρας, τὰ δὲ πρὸς μεσ-
161 D. ημβρίαν ὀνομάζων, οὐδ᾽ αὖ τὰ λοιπὰ δύο ὡσαύτως,
ἀλλ᾽ ἄνευ τῆς προσθήκης ἔξεστιν ὁρίσασθαι τὰ μὲν
ἔνθεν αὐτῆς ἄρκτον εἶναι, τὰ δὲ ἔνθεν μεσημβρίαν

¹ ὥσπερ—ἀκριβῶς secl. Oliver.

ᵃ Attica sent only part of the colonists of Ionia ; but they
included the founders of the important city Miletus. In

centre of the city. But here the argument, in 17
following whatever chances, has carried us from our
subject. Again we must turn back to the territory
and must carefully observe its superiorities. We
have discussed its nature in regard to land and sea
as fully as was reasonable, while avoiding both
tedium and unjust omissions. It has received so pro- 18
portioned a lot in its atmosphere overhead and the
blending of its seasons, that could it be said with
propriety, it would be a thing to be prayed for. For
it is free of everything unpleasant ; and equally while
it shares in every good faculty, it has escaped whatever disagreeable qualities attend each of these. It
is possible to judge this not only by its sea-
sonal fruits which abide beyond the seasons from
which they are named and remain for so long a part
of the whole year, but also by gaining perspective,
as in using a scale, as whenever we wish to make a
precise observation. For as far away as one stands
from the city, moving in this or that direction, he
finds either more heat or cold than necessary, so
that in this spot alone is there deficiency where
excess is painful and where deficiency is more advantageous. But such is the abundance of good fortune, 19
that the cities which hold Ionia and are colonies of *c.* 1100–
this city *a* seem to enjoy the best climate of all the 1000.
other races, as if they had shared in some other
natural attribute. Therefore one would not speak
of the northerly and southerly sectors by name, or
of the other two regions of the land. But without
qualification the region on the one side of it can be
defined as north, and on the other side as south,

legend Theseus participated in the refounding of Smyrna,
Aristides' native city.

(161 D.)

ἤδη, ἀνατολάς τε καὶ δύσεις ὅσον τὸ ἄνω καὶ κάτω,
αὐτὴν δ' εἶναι πάντων ὡσπερεὶ μεθόριον, κοινόν τινα
χῶρον, οὗ πάντα τὰ τμήματα συγκεράννυται, ὑπ'
αὐτήν, ὡς εἰπεῖν, τὴν ἀκρόπολιν τοῦ οὐρανοῦ καὶ
τὴν τοῦ Διὸς ἀρχὴν ὡς ἀληθῶς γιγνομένην λῆξιν τῆς
Ἀθηνᾶς καὶ τῶν ταύτης ἔργων τε καὶ θρεμμάτων
τόπον οἰκεῖον. οὐ γὰρ ἔστιν ὅστις τῶν περὶ γῆν ἀέ-
ρων τοσοῦτον ἀφέστηκεν γῆς τῇ φύσει οὐδ' αἰθέρι
20 μᾶλλον εἴκασται. γῆς μὲν δὴ καὶ θαλάττης καὶ ἀέ-
ρων εἰς τοῦτ' ἔθεσαν τὴν Ἀττικὴν οἷς ταῦτα ἔπρεπεν δημιουργοῖς. ἃ δὲ τούτοις τοιούτοις οὖσιν ἕπεται πολλὴ ῥᾳστώνη δεικνύναι, πεδίων τε κάλλη καὶ
χάριτας τῶν μὲν πρὸ τῆς πόλεως εὐθὺς ἀπὸ τοῦ τείχους, μᾶλλον δὲ ἀπὸ τῆς ἀκροπόλεως κεχυμένων καὶ
ἐγκαταμιγνυμένων τῇ πόλει, τῶν δὲ ἐφ' ἑκάστῃ τῇ[1]
θαλάττῃ τοῖς αἰγιαλοῖς ἐφορμούντων,[2] τῶν δ' ἐν τῇ
μεσογείᾳ τοῖς ὄρεσι τοῖς περιέχουσιν ὥσπερ ἄλλοις
ὁρίοις διειλημμένων ἐν κόλπων θαλαττίων τινῶν
21 σχήματι. καὶ μὴν τήν γε τῶν ὀρῶν φαιδρότητα καὶ
χάριν τίς οὐκ ἂν ἀγασθείη; οἷς γε τοσοῦτον κόσμου
περίεστιν ὥστε καὶ τὰς πόλεις αὐτὰ δὴ κοσμεῖ· ὃ γὰρ
εἰκὸς ἔχειν τὴν χώραν, ἔργον θεῶν οὖσαν, σπέρμα
162 D. τῆς χάριτος τῆς πρὸς τοὺς θεούς, τοῦτο δείκνυσιν ἐν
τοῖς πρώτοις, καὶ προξενεῖ διὰ τῆς φύσεως τὴν
χάριν. ἔστι δὲ ἐπιτηδειοτάτη πρὸς κάλλη νεῶν καὶ
ἀγαλμάτων, ὥστε δὶς ἡγεμὼν τούτων ἂν εἴη. καὶ
γὰρ ἐνθένδε ταῦτα πάντα ἤρξατο τῷ νόμῳ καὶ τὴν
22 χορηγίαν οἴκοθεν ἡ πόλις ἔσχηκεν εἰς αὐτά. ἀλλὰ
γὰρ οὐκ ἔχω τί χρήσωμαι, ἐπέρχεται γάρ μοι
καὶ κατὰ μέρη τὴν ἐπιτηδειότητα ἀποφαίνειν τῆς

---

[1] τῇ om. TQ.   [2] ἐφορμώντων VA.

and east and west whatever is upland and lowland, and it can be said that the territory itself is as it were at the crossway of all points, a kind of common ground, where all the sectors are blended, beneath, one might say, the very Acropolis of heaven and the empire of Zeus, and which in fact is the lot of Athena and a place proper to her deeds and nurslings. For no climate of the earth is so unlike the earth in nature, nor closer to the thinness of the upper air. Indeed, the creators, to whom belonged the task, set 20 Attica at this point of earth, sea, and air. But what is consequent upon such circumstances is very easy to show, the beauty of the fields, and the charm of the suburbs beginning at the walls, moreover starting at the Acropolis and poured over and intermingled with the city, the charm of the regions fronting each sea, at anchor by the strands, the charm of the interior cut off by the surrounding mountains, which are like other boundaries in the form of a kind of marine gulf. Indeed, who would not marvel at the 21 grace and charm of the mountains? They so abound in adornment that they even adorn other cities.[a] The city reveals in the first place a seed of gratitude toward the Gods, which the land ought to possess, that is a work of the Gods, and it presents its gratitude through the help of nature. The city is most well endowed to care for the beauty of her temples and images, so that in two ways she would be a guide in these matters. For this whole custom began here and the city has provided from its own resources the material for it. But I am in a quandary. Just now it 22 has occurred to me to depict the individual endow-

---

[a] Because of the marble-quarries; *cf.* § 364; the same conceit is found in xxvii. 14-15.

(162 D.)

χώρας, οἷον εὐθὺς τὸ μήτε ὑπτίαν εἶναι διὰ πάσης
μήτε ὄρειον παντελῶς, ἀλλ' ἐσχηματίσθαι πρὸς
τὴν ἑκατέρου χρείαν ἐν μέρει καὶ πεποικίλθαι, ὥστε[1]
πῶς οὐκ ἂν ὀρθῶς εἴποι τις εἶναι ⟨ταῦτα χώρας[2]⟩
τελέας καὶ πάσης τῆς οἰκουμένης οἱονεὶ μίμημα
23 σῳζούσης; ἔτι δὲ ἡ τῆς θαλάττης τε καὶ γῆς διὰ
τῶν λιμένων συζυγία καὶ συμφωνία, τῶν δ' αὖ
πεδίων καὶ τῶν ὀρῶν ἡ σὺν ὥρᾳ μίξις καὶ χάρις οὐ
τῶν ὅπου τις ἂν εἴποι συμβεβηκότων οἶμαι. ἔξεστι
δὲ ὁρᾶν καὶ τὰς φλέβας τὰς ἀργυρίτιδας ὥσπερ
νοτίδας διὰ πάσης τῆς ὀρείου διηκούσας, ὅπως ἄρα
μηδὲν ἀργὸν εἴη τῆς Ἀττικῆς μηδ' εἴη ταῖς προσ-
όδοις δυσχωρία μηδαμῇ, ἀλλὰ τὴν ἑτέρων εὔγεων
ἢ τῇδε ἄσπορος νικᾷη. ἔπρεπεν δ' ἄρα καὶ τοῦτο
ἐλευθερίας ἐφόδιον καὶ μεγαλοψυχίας παρεσκευάσθαι
τῇ πόλει. ἔτι τοίνυν ἀενάων ποταμῶν ῥεύματα
ἄλυπα καὶ πηγὰς ἀφθόνους καὶ καρπῶν ἁπάντων
φοράν, ὧν ὁ πάντων ἡμερώτατος ἐνταῦθα[3] τῶν
πανταχοῦ κάλλιστος περιφανῶς.

24   Ἀλλὰ ταῦτα μέν ἐστιν ὥσπερ ἀπὸ τῶν τρα-
γημάτων τὴν εὐωχίαν σεμνύνειν· τὸν δὲ οἰκειότατον
καὶ μέγιστον τῆς χώρας καρπόν τε καὶ κόσμον καὶ
163 D. ὃς ἅπασαν ἔχει τὴν ἐπιτηδειότητα συλλαβὼν αὐτῆς
25 ἤδη δίειμι. ἀρχὴ δέ μοι τοῦ λόγου κατελήλυθεν εἰς
ἀρχήν τινα ἑτέραν. ἄλλας μὲν γὰρ χώρας ἐλέφαν-
τες καὶ λέοντες κοσμοῦσιν, τὰς δὲ ἵπποι καὶ κύνες,
τὰς δὲ ἃ τοὺς παῖδας ἀκούοντας ἐκπλήττει· τὴν δὲ
ὑμετέραν[4] χώραν κοσμεῖ τῶν ἐπὶ γῆς τὸ κάλλιστον,
οὐ κατὰ τοὺς ἐν Ἰνδοῖς μύρμηκας ὑποπτέρους

---

[1] ὥστε om. TQA.
[2] add. Reiske.
[3] ⟨ὁ⟩ ἐνταῦθα ci. Reiske ; ἐνταῦθ' ὁ ci. Oliver.
[4] Aldinae : ἡμετέραν TQVA.

26

ments of the land, for example to begin with, that it is
neither entirely flat nor completely mountainous,
but has been formed and varied for each use in turn.
Therefore how would one not rightly say that this is
the character of a land which is complete and as it
were preserves an imitation of the whole world?
There is also the union and harmony of the sea and 23
the land through its harbours, and again the charming mixture and grace of fields and mountains, which
is not to be found, I think, anywhere you might
mention. And the veins of silver can be seen like
drops passing through the whole mountain district,
so that no part of Attica may lie idle, and no region
be too inhospitable for revenue, but that barren land
here may be superior to the fertile land of other
parts. So it was right that there was provided in
this too a means of freedom and nobility for the city.[a]
Also there can be seen the pleasant streams of ever-
flowing rivers, unstinting springs, crops of every
kind, and the most cultivated of all of them here is
clearly the fairest of all everywhere.

But this is like beginning to praise a feast from the 24
dessert. Now I shall tell of the most native and
greatest fruit and adornment of the land, that which
comprises and contains all of its endowments.
And the beginning of my speech has become another 25
beginning. For some lands elephants and lions
adorn, and others horses and dogs, and some things
the tales of which frighten children. But your land
the fairest thing on earth adorns, which should not
be merely spoken of like the winged ants in India.

[a] An allusion to Themistocles' use in 482 B.C. of the
revenues from the mines at Laureium to make Athens a naval
power; cf. Herodotus VII. 144.

(163 D.)

ἄξιον εἰπεῖν. πρώτη γὰρ ἤνεγκεν ἄνθρωπον καὶ
πρώτη πατρίς ἐστιν ἀνθρώπου, καὶ ὅπερ τοῖς πᾶσι
ζῴοις τοῖς ἐγγείοις ἐστὶν ἡ πᾶσα γῆ, τοῦτο ἤδε νενίκηκεν εἶναι τῷ τῶν ἀνθρώπων γένει, μήτηρ καὶ τρο-
φὸς κοινὴ καὶ τῆς φύσεως ἀφορμή, χῶρός τις ἀνθρώπων ἴδιος ἐκ πάσης γῆς ἐξῃρημένος, ὥσπερ οἱ τῶν
τεμενῶν ὅροι. διὸ δὴ καὶ πάντα κρατίστους καὶ
τῆς γιγνομένης ἀρετῆς ἐπὶ πλεῖστον ἥκοντας ἤνεγκεν, ἅτε οἰκείας αὐτῇ τῆς φορᾶς οὔσης, οὐκ ἐπεισ-
άκτου. οὐ γὰρ πλάνην καταλύσαντες οὐδὲ ὥσπερ
ἐπὶ σκότους πατρίδα ζητοῦντες διὰ πάσης γῆς καὶ
θαλάττης, οὐδὲ δυοῖν δυστυχίαιν ἡγησαμέναιν,
κατέσχον τὴν χώραν, βιασάμενοι τὴν ἐπωνυμίαν,
εἴξαντες μὲν τοῖς κρείττοσιν, ἐκβαλόντες δὲ τοὺς
ἥττους, ἀλλ' ὥσπερ τὸ ἐκ τῶν πηγῶν ὕδωρ ἐκ τῶν
κόλπων τῆς γῆς ἀνῆλθεν τὸ γένος, αὐτὸ ἐξ αὐτοῦ
26 λαβὸν τὴν ἀρχήν. καὶ ξένοι καὶ πολῖται μόνῃ[1] τῇ γῇ
ταύτῃ πρέπουσι διῃρῆσθαι. οἱ μὲν γὰρ ἄλλοι καθάπερ
164 D. θέαν καταλαβόντες οὕτω ταῦτα κρίνουσιν, οὐ τῷ
μᾶλλον ἑαυτοῖς προσήκειν τῶν χωρίων τοὺς ἄλλους
ἀφορίζοντες, ἀλλὰ τῷ φθῆναι κατασχόντες, καὶ
ξένους ὀνομάζουσι τοὺς δευτέρους ἐλθόντας, ἀγνοοῦντες ὅτι πάντες ὁμοίως εἰσὶ ξένοι, μᾶλλον δὲ
αὐτοὶ ξένοι πρῶτοι, καὶ τοσοῦτον τῶν δημοποιήτων,
οὓς αὐτοὶ ποιοῦνται, διαφέρουσιν, ὅσον οὐ κριθέντες
ἄξιοι τῆς πολιτείας, ἀλλ' εἰσβιασάμενοι προὐ-
βάλοντο τὴν πατρίδα, ὥσπερ ὅπλων ἀπορίᾳ τῷ
φανέντι χρησάμενοι· μόνοις δ' ὑμῖν ὑπάρχει καθαρὰν

---

[1] μόνοι VA.

[a] For another interpretation cf. J. H. Oliver, Greek,

28

For it first bore man, and it is the first country of man, and what the earth is to all terrestrial animals, this land has in fact become for the human race, mother and common nurse, and beginning of all nature, a certain place chosen from the whole earth as private to man, like the sacred enclosures.[a] For this reason it bore men who were best in every way and who advanced the farthest in proper virtue, since its crop was native and not imported. For they did not seize the land and at the end of their wanderings impose their name by force nor, as if in the dark, in search of a country through every land and sea, nor as the consequence of two misfortunes, yielding to the stronger and expelling the weaker. But like spring-water, the race arose from the bosom of the earth, taking its beginning from itself. And the distinction between foreigners and citizens ought only to be made by this land. For other people, as if they occupied a seat in the theatre, make these distinctions, not keeping apart other men because the land is any more theirs, but because they were the first to seize it. And they call those who have come afterwards foreigners, not realizing that all of them are equally foreigners, moreover that they themselves were the first foreigners, and that they differ from the citizens whom they themselves create only to the extent that they were not judged worthy of citizenship, but forced their way in and employed " their country " merely as a means of defence, as if through want of weapons they used whatever was available. But you alone can boast

Roman, and Byzantine Studies ii, pp. 141-143. For the alleged gold-digging winged " ants " in India *cf.* Herodotus III. 102.

(164 D.)

27 εὐγένειάν τε καὶ πολιτείαν αὐχῆσαι. καὶ δυοῖν
ὄντοιν ὀνομάτοιν ἑκάτερον κύριόν ἐστι τῇ χώρᾳ διὰ
τὸ ἕτερον· εἰκότως. οἵ τε γὰρ ξένοι διὰ τοὺς ἄλλους
πολίτας γνησίους ὄντας ἐνέχονται τῷ προσρήματι οἵ
τε πολῖται βεβαιοῦσι τὴν ἐπωνυμίαν τῷ καθαροὶ
28 ξένων εἶναι τὸ ἐξ ἀρχῆς. οὔκουν ἐξούλης γε μόνοις
ὑμῖν, εἰ οἷόν τ᾽ ἐστὶν εἰπεῖν, οὐδ᾽ ἂν εἷς λάχοι τῆς
29 γῆς, οὐ μᾶλλόν γε ἢ τῆς μητρός τινι. καὶ τοίνυν μόνοις τοῖς τῇδε γενομένοις[1] δημοποιήτοις οὐκ ἔπεστι
γέλως· ὄντες γὰρ ἅπαντες φύσει πολῖται τῆς χώρας
νόμῳ τοῖς ἄλλοις τὴν τιμὴν ἀπενείματε· τῶν δ᾽ ἄλ-
165 D. λων οἱ πλεῖστοι κινδυνεύουσι νόθοι νόθους εἰσποιεῖ-
σθαι, χρόνῳ τὴν ἀρχαίαν φύσιν διαφθείραντες, ὥσπερ
ἐν συνοικίᾳ τῇ πάσῃ γῇ ζῶντες, ἐκ περιόδων
καλοῦντες οἰκείαν οἱ τελευταῖοι τῶν ἄλλων οἰκησά-
30 μενοι. καί μοι δοκεῖ τις ἂν εἰπεῖν παραιτησάμενος
τὸν φθόνον ὅτι οἱ μὲν ἄλλοι τὰς πόλεις οἰκοῦσιν,
ὥσπερ στρατόπεδα, οἷς[2] κατέλαβον ἐμμείναντες,
μόνοις δὲ τοῖς ταύτης ἐγγόνοις τῆς χώρας ἡ πόλις
ἐστὶ κυρία καὶ μόνη πόλεων, ἢ κομιδῇ γε ἐν ὀλίγαις
ἑστίαν ἀκίνητον πρυτανείου δικαίως νέμει.

31 Πολλῶν δὲ ἐπιρρεόντων καὶ πάντων αὐτὸ ἕκαστον
εἰπεῖν ἐπειγόντων αἱροῦμαι τὸ τῇ φύσει δεύτερον
καὶ τὸ πρὸ αὐτοῦ βεβαιοῦν ἐφεξῆς ἀποδοῦναι.
ἐπειδὴ γὰρ ἀνῆκεν ἡ χώρα τοὺς ἄνδρας, ἐκόσμει
καὶ κατεσκεύαζε τὸν βίον αὐτοῖς, ἃ μητρὸς ἦν ἔργα
ποιοῦσα, καὶ οὐ περιεῖδεν ὥσπερ ἀλλοτρίας τῆς
τροφοῦ δεηθέντας, ἀλλ᾽ ἐκ τῶν αὐτῶν κόλπων

---

[1] codd. dett. : γινομένοις vel γιγνομένοις TQVA.
[2] Reiske : ὡς TQVA.

of a pure race and citizenship. And each of these 27
two names is proper to this land through the other.
With good reason. For foreigners are subject to
the term because the others are genuine citizens and
the citizens confirm their title by the fact that
they were free of foreign contagion from the start.
Then against you alone, if the expression can be used, 28
no one could file a suit for illegal possession of the
the land, no more than against someone for illegal
possession of his mother. And only those who 29
have been made citizens here are not ridiculous.
For you who are natural citizens of the land have
given this honour to others by law. But most
other people are in danger of adopting bastards
while being bastards themselves, having at length
corrupted their original nature, living everywhere
on earth as if this was all one transient hotel, the
last of them to live there in turn calling it their
native land. And it seems to me that one would say, 30
after excusing the invidious comparison, that other
people inhabit their cities like camps, remaining in
those which they seized, but that this city, alone of
cities, is the rightful possession only of the offspring
of this land, and that among very few cities it has
the right to administer " an unmoved hearth " in
the town hall.

Although many things occur to me and all of 31
them have a claim to a detailed discussion, I choose
to present next what naturally comes second and
proves that which preceded it. For when the land
put forth men, it arranged and prepared for them a
means of life, performing the task of a mother, and it
did not leave them in need as it were of an alien
nurse, but from the same bosom gave them its

31

(165 D.)

ἐδωρεῖτο τὰ δεύτερα. καὶ γίγνεται δὴ πανήγυρις
ὡς ἀληθῶς ἱερὰ καὶ ὑπὲρ γῆς πάσης τῆς οἰκουμένης ἐνταυθοῖ καὶ ὥσπερ ἐν θεωρίᾳ πάντα εἰς ἅμιλλαν
32 κατέστη. ἔρρωτο μὲν ἡ γῆ πρὸς ἁπάσας γονάς,
θεοὶ δὲ συμφέροντες παρεῖχον οἱ μὲν φυτά, οἱ δὲ
σπέρματα, οἱ δὲ βοσκήματα, ὧν ἔμελλεν ἡ φορὰ τὸ
τοῦ ἀνθρώπου σῶμα κοσμήσειν οὐχ ἧττον ἢ τὸ
οἰκεῖον καὶ παρέξειν τὴν σκέπην κοινὴν τοῖς μὲν
τὴν ἐπέτειον καὶ πρώτην ἀεί, τοῖς δὲ εἰς ὅσον
166 D. ἐξικνεῖτο[1]· τέχνας δὲ ἐπὶ τούτοις ἔφαινον τὰς μὲν
πυρὶ συγκεραννύντες, τὰς δὲ καὶ πυρὸς χωρίς.
33 καίτοι ταῦτα οὐ μόνον τοῦ πλήθους ἔνεκα τῶν
ἐνταῦθα καὶ φύντων καὶ φανέντων φιλοτιμίαν ἔχει
τῇ πόλει καὶ χάριν, ἀλλὰ καὶ τεκμήρια παμμεγέθη
τοῦ πρώτου λόγου, καὶ παντός ἐστιν ἐναργέστερα,
ὅτι πρῶτον ἄνθρωπος ἐπὶ τῆσδε τῆς γῆς ἔστη, καὶ
ταὐτὰ[2] συμβαίνει πλήθει τε ὑπερφέρειν καὶ σημεῖα
τῆς ἀληθείας ἀλλήλοις ἑξῆς εἶναι. πρώτους μὲν[3]
γὰρ φύντας ἔδει πρώτους καὶ δεηθῆναι, δεηθέντας
δέ που καὶ τυχεῖν· καὶ μὴν τοῦτό γε ἀμήχανον μὴ
θεοφιλεῖς ὄντας, θεοφιλεῖς δ' αὖ τιθέναι τοὺς
πρώτους ἀξιωθέντας φῦναι πῶς οὐκ εὔλογον; πάλιν
34 γὰρ εἰς ταὐτὸν ἐπανέρχεται. καὶ μὴν τούς γε θεοὺς
ἀμφοτέρων χάριν εἰκὸς τῇ γῇ τὴν φορὰν πληρῶσαι, τοῦτο μὲν τῆς χρείας, ὅτι πρώτους, ὥσπερ
ἔφην, τοὺς ἐν ταύτῃ κατελάμβανεν, τοῦτο δὲ τῆς
τιμῆς, ἢ τοῖς ἀρίστοις ὠφείλετο. λαβόντες δὲ οὕτω
τὰς παρὰ τῶν θεῶν δωρεὰς οὕτως εὖ τοὺς δόντας
ἐμιμήσαντο ὥστε αὐτοὶ τοῖς ἄλλοις ἀνθρώποις ἀντὶ

[1] ἐξικνοῖτο VA.

second gift. And here took shape a national assembly, truly sacred and for the sake of every land in the world, and just as in a festival there was every kind of rivalry. The earth grew strong for all sorts of 32 produce ; and the Gods made their contributions, some gave plants, some seed, some livestock, whose harvest would adorn the body of man no less than their own and provide a common covering, for the former of a year's duration and always new, for the latter for as long as it lasted. And after this, they revealed the arts, combining some with fire, and others without. Yet these things bring not only 33 glory and favour to the city because of the abundance of what grew and appeared here, but also great proofs of my first argument, and they are clearer evidence than anything that man stood first upon this land. And it turns out that the same proofs are exceedingly numerous and are in turn evidence for one another of their truth. For those who were first born must also have the first needs, and having the first needs must also somewhere have satisfied them. And this is impossible if they were not dear to the Gods. And again how is it not good sense to regard as dear to the Gods those who were first given the privilege of birth ? For once more the conclusion is the same. Indeed, it is likely that the 34 Gods compassed the fertility of the land for two reasons : first for need, because, as I said, the first men were found to be in need ; and second for the honour which is owed to the best men. Thus having received gifts from the Gods, so well did they imitate the givers that they themselves became like Gods

---

² Reiske : ταῦτα TQVA.　　³ Reiske : τε TQVA.

(166 D.)

τῶν θεῶν κατέστησαν, καὶ πεῖραν ταύτην πρώτην
ἔδοσαν τοῦ κατ᾽ ἀξίαν τυχεῖν, τὸ χρήσασθαι τοῖς
167 D. ὑπάρχουσιν ὡς προσῆκεν. οὐ γὰρ ἠξίωσαν αὐτὸ δὴ
τοῦτο γῇ κρύψαντες ἐξαρκεῖν, ἀλλὰ τοσοῦτον ἀπέσχον τοῦ φοβηθῆναι μὴ ἄρα τοὺς ἄλλους ἐξ ἴσου
σφίσιν ποιήσωσιν, ὥστ᾽ οὐκ εἶναι κάλλιον ᾠήθησαν
ὅσῳ τῶν ἄλλων προέχουσιν ἐνδείξασθαι ἢ εἰ πάντας
35 εὖ ποιοῦντες ὀφθήσονται. δοκεῖ δέ μοι καὶ
Ἡρακλῆς ὕστερον παράδειγμα τοῦ βίου τήνδε τὴν
πόλιν ποιησάμενος τὴν διάνοιαν ἐκείνην ὑπὲρ
ἁπάντων ἀνθρώπων λαβεῖν, ἢ μετὰ τῶν θεῶν αὐτὸν
καταστήσασα ἔχει. καὶ τὸ σημεῖον ἐναργὲς ἡ πρὸς
Θησέα φιλία οὐ μόνον τῶν ἐκείνοις πρὸς τοὺς
ἄλλους, ἀλλὰ καὶ τῶν οἰστισινοῦν πρὸς ἀλλήλους
καθ᾽ ἑταιρείαν[1] γενομένων παμπληθὲς ὑπερέχουσα.
ἀνθ᾽ ὧν αὖ καὶ πρώτη πόλεων ἥδε ἐτίμησεν ἐκεῖνον
ταῖς τῶν θεῶν τιμαῖς καὶ τοὺς παῖδας διετήρησεν
μόνη. ἀλλ᾽ ὁ λόγος γὰρ ὥσπερ ῥεῦμα φέρων
ὑπήνεγκεν βίᾳ· ἀναχωρεῖν οὖν ὅθεν ἐξέβην καιρός.
36 Πέμπουσι δὴ θείᾳ πομπῇ γῆν ἐπὶ πᾶσαν ἀφορμὰς
τοῦ βίου, καθάπερ θεωρικοῦ τινος διάδοσιν ἐπι-
στήσαντες τῶν Δήμητρος, ὡς λέγεται, τροφίμων ἕνα,
καὶ τὸ ἅρμα πτερωτὸν εἶναι φήμη κατέσχεν, ὅτι
θᾶττον ἐλπίδος ᾔει πανταχοῦ, καὶ πρόσαντες οὐδ᾽
ἄβατον οὐδὲν[2] ἦν αὐτῷ, ἀλλ᾽ ὥσπερ διὰ ψιλοῦ τοῦ
37 ἀέρος, οὕτως ἐκομίζετο. δοκοῦσι δέ μοι κἀκεῖνον
τὸν λόγον ἔργῳ πρῶτοι βεβαιῶσαι, καὶ καταδεῖξαι
τὰς χάριτας ταχείας εἶναι τὴν φύσιν· εὖ γὰρ ποιοῦντες ἔφθανον τὴν ἐπιθυμίαν τῶν εὖ παθεῖν δεομένων. μνημεῖον δὲ καὶ σύμβολον τῆς θείας ἐκείνης
πομπῆς καὶ τῆς εἰς ἅπαντας εὐεργεσίας αἱ παρὰ

---

[1] ἑταιρίαν VA.   [2] οὐδὲν om. VA.

for other men and gave this first proof of the merited achievement of their needs, the proper employment of what they had. For they did not think that it was enough if they buried their gift beneath the earth, but they were so far from fearing to make others their equals that they thought that they could not make a fairer demonstration of how superior they were to others than if they should be seen benefiting all men. It seems to me that later it was 35 with this city as a model for his life that Heracles [Legend.] formed that resolve on behalf of all mankind, which in the end placed him among the Gods. And a clear proof is his friendship with Theseus, which not only [C. 1250.] far surpassed the comradeship of those two men with others, but of any men at all with one another. For which reason again this was the first city to give that man divine honours, and it alone guarded his children. But the argument like a rushing river has somewhat carried me away by its force. It is time to return to where I digressed.

They sent, in a divine mission, the first means of 36 life to every land, just like a festival-distribution, having put in charge, as is said, one of the foster-children[a] of Demeter ; and tradition told that his chariot was winged because he went everywhere faster than anticipated, and he found nothing steep and impassable, but was carried as it were through the clear air. And first of all men they seem 37 to me to have proven true the old adage and to have shown that " kindness is naturally swift." For in their generosity they outstripped the desires of those who needed it. But the memorial and proof of that divine mission and benefaction to all men are

[a] Triptolemus.

35

168 D. τῶν Ἑλλήνων ἀπαρχαὶ δεῦρ' ἀφικνούμεναι καθ'
ἕκαστον ἔτος τῶν σπερμάτων ἐπὶ τῶν πρότερον[1]
χρόνων. ἔτι δὲ αἱ τοῦ θεοῦ μαντεῖαι, δι' ὧν μητρόπολιν τῶν καρπῶν ὀνομάζει τὴν πόλιν, ἄμφω
μαρτυρῶν, καὶ πρώτην ἔχειν καὶ τοῖς ἄλλοις παρ'
38 αὐτῆς γενέσθαι. τίθησι δὲ καὶ ἀγῶνας πρώτη
πόλεων ἁπασῶν καὶ τὸ ἆθλον ἐκ τῶν εὐεργεσιῶν,
καλῶς τὰ δοθέντα πιστουμένη. καίτοι πῶς οὐκ
ἀληθῶς ἐκεῖνοι θεῶν μὲν παῖδες, θεῶν δὲ καὶ
τρόφιμοι, πρόγονοι δὲ τοῦ κοινοῦ βίου πᾶσιν ἀνθρώποις; οἱ μετὰ τοιαύτην τιμὴν παρὰ τῶν θεῶν
αὐτοῖς ὑπάρξασαν ἄλλα καλλίω τοῖς ἐξ ἑαυτῶν
εἰς φιλοτιμίαν κατέλιπον, τοιοῦτοι μὲν πρὸς τοὺς
δόντας θεοὺς γενόμενοι, οὕτω δ' αὖ καὶ τοῖς ἄλλοις
39 ὁμιλήσαντες ἀνθρώποις. καὶ τοῦτο μὲν ἐνταυθοῖ
λῆξαν τελέως ἡμῖν διήνυσται, τὰ δ' ἐντεῦθεν ὥσπερ
ὁδοῦ διττὰ φέρει καὶ πλείω τμήματα τοῖς μὲν
εἰρημένοις ἕκαστον ἐφεξῆς, ἐν μέρει δὲ εἰπεῖν, εἰ
σῴζοντα ἐν ἀλλήλοις τὴν διαδοχήν, οὔπω δῆλον.

40 Κράτιστον δ' ἴσως περὶ τῶν θείων πρῶτον διεξελθεῖν, εἶθ' οὕτως καὶ περὶ τῆς ἄλλης ἐκείνων ἀρετῆς
διαλέγεσθαι· ἔτι δὲ ὧν καθ' αὑτούς τε καὶ ἐν κοι-
νωνίαις εἰργάσαντο οἱ καθ' ἑκάστους ἀεὶ τοὺς
169 D. χρόνους. μικρὸν δὲ ἀναλήψομαι· οὐ γὰρ μόνον οἷς
εἶπον ἐτίμησαν οἱ θεοὶ τὴν γῆν ὑμῖν,[2] ἀλλὰ καὶ
πολλοῖς ἄλλοις μεγάλοις, μεγίστῳ δέ, ὃ καὶ μόνον
εἰπεῖν ἴσως ἐξήρκει. περὶ γὰρ μόνης ταύτης τῶν

---

[1] προτέρων V.   [2] edd. : ἡμῖν TQVA.

[a] Repeated in § 399 ; cf. also xxxiv, vol. 1, p. 667 Ddf.
Perhaps from the time of a plague (so the scholiast).

the yearly offerings of the first fruits of the seed, which came here in former times from the Greeks. And there are also the oracles from the God in which he names the city " the mother city of the crops," [a] and attests two things : that it first had crops and that the others received them from it. It also was 38 the first of all cities to establish games and, in its generosity, a prize,[b] in a fair way confirming what had been given to it. Yet how were those men not truly the sons of the Gods, and also the foster-children of the Gods, and the ancestors of the common way of life of all men, who after they had received such honour from the Gods, left other fairer reasons for pride to their descendants, behaving in such fashion toward their benefactors the Gods and so comporting themselves among other men ? And we 39 have fully expressed the argument here concluded. From this point the themes lead as it were on a road in two or more ways, each of which follows what has already been said ; but if we discuss them in turn, it is not at all clear whether the narrative will preserve its consistency.

Perhaps it is best to speak about divine matters 40 first, and next to discuss the other virtues [c] of those men ; and finally their deeds alone and in common with other Greeks in each successive age. I shall go back a little. For the Gods did not give only the honours which I mentioned to your land, but also many other great ones, and the greatest of all, which perhaps it was enough to have mentioned alone. For the highest of the Gods struggled for this [Legend.]

[b] An ear of wheat.
[c] [Or " discuss the virtues also." But their virtue of generosity has been mentioned (§ 38).—*E.H.W.*]

(169 D.)

ὑφ' ἡλίῳ πόλεων ἤρισαν καὶ καταλαμβάνουσι τὴν
ἀκρόπολιν ὥσπερ ἐπὶ μοναρχίᾳ σχεδὸν ὡς εἰπεῖν οἱ
41 πρῶτοι τῶν θεῶν. ταύτης δὲ τῆς τιμῆς οὐχ ἥττω
τὴν δευτέραν ἐπεδείξαντο, ἐπιτρέψαντες δικασταῖς
καὶ κριταῖς αὐτοῖς τοῖς τότε τὴν χώραν ἔχουσι,
νομίσαντες χάριεν καὶ κοῦφον ἐπ' ἀμφότερα ἐν
τοῖς παιδικοῖς κριθῆναι. φανέντων δὲ τῶν συμβό-
λων ἑκατέρωθεν, τοῦ τε ῥοθίου καὶ τοῦ θαλλοῦ, νικᾷ
μὲν Ἀθηνᾶ καὶ καταδείκνυσι τὸν θαλλὸν νίκης εἶναι
σύμβολον, Ποσειδῶν δὲ ὑπεχώρησεν μέν, οὐ μὴν
42 κατέλυσε τὸν ἔρωτα. τῆς δὲ παρ' ἀμφοτέρων σπουδῆς τε καὶ τιμῆς οὐκ ἐλάττω σημεῖα τὰ δεύτερα·
ἡ μὲν γὰρ σοφίᾳ νικᾶν ἔδωκε τῇ πόλει, ὁ δὲ ταῖς
ναυμαχίαις οὐ μόνον τοὺς ἀνταγωνιστὰς νικᾶν,
ἀλλὰ καὶ τοὺς τῶν αὐτῶν μετασχόντας, οἶμαι δὲ
καὶ οἷς ὅλως ἀγῶνες καὶ νῖκαι ναυτικαὶ γεγόνασιν.
ἀλλ' ὁ μὲν περὶ τούτων ἐκδέχεται λόγος αὐτίκα.
43 λαβοῦσα δὲ τὰς ψήφους ἡ θεὸς τὴν ἐπωνυμίαν τῇ
πόλει δίδωσιν ὡς ἑαυτῆς οὔσῃ καὶ κατεσκευάσατο
ὡς κτῆμα ἑαυτῆς, διαρκῆ πρὸς εἰρήνην τε καὶ
πόλεμον, πρῶτον μὲν λόγους τε καὶ νόμων τάξιν
καταδείξασα καὶ πολιτείαν δυναστείας ἀπηλλαγ-
170 D. μένην. ἀφ' ὧν μαθήματα πάντα εὑρέθη καὶ βίων
παραδείγματα[1] εἰσῆλθεν. αὖθις δὲ ὅπλων τε χρῆσιν
διδάξασα καὶ κοσμήσασα πρώτους ᾧ νῦν ἡμεῖς
ἐκείνην σχήματι, ἔτι δ' ἵππων ἁμιλλητηρίων καὶ
πολεμιστηρίων ἔφηνεν ὀχήματα· καὶ ζεύγνυσιν ἐν
τῇδε τῇ γῇ πρῶτος ἀνθρώπων ὁ τῆσδε τῆς θεοῦ
πάρεδρος ἅρμα τέλειον σὺν τῇ θεῷ καὶ φαίνει πᾶσι
44 τὴν τελείαν ἱππικήν. ἐπὶ δὲ τούτοις χορεῖαι καὶ
τελεταὶ καὶ πανηγύρεις ἐπεκράτησαν ἄλλαι δι' ἄλ-

---

[1] παραδείγματα πάντα TQ.

city alone of those under the sun and seized the Acropolis almost one might say for a monarchy. But they showed a second honour no less than this 41 one, by turning the case over to those who then held the land to judge and decide, both parties believing that it was a charming and pleasant thing to be judged before one's favourite. But when their tokens had been presented on each side, the waves and the bough, Athena won her case and made the bough a sign of victory. And Poseidon withdrew ; however his love did not end. What en- 42 sued is no less proof of the zeal and honour of both Gods. For she granted the city to surpass in wisdom, and he not only to surpass its opponents in naval warfare, but also those who were trained in this same discipline, and even, I think, those who in every way had contended and triumphed at sea. But the tale about these matters soon follows. Having won the 43 contest by vote, the Goddess gave her name to the city as if it were hers, and prepared it, as her own possession, to be sufficient in peace and war, and first of all she revealed oratory and the order of the laws and a form of government free from the rule of one man. And all the sciences were invented thereby and various ways of life entered the scene. Again she instructed them in the use of weapons and dressed them first in the form in which we now dress her. And she also revealed racing chariots and war-horses ; and in this land first of all men, the assessor of this Goddess [a] yoked a fully equipped chariot with the aid of the Goddess and revealed to all the complete art of horsemanship. And after this, 44 dancing, ceremonies, and national assemblies came

[a] Erichthonius.

(170 D.)

λων θεῶν ἐπιδημίας. ταῖς γὰρ τιμαῖς τῶν θεῶν
ἠκολούθει τὰ δῶρα διδόντων καὶ λαμβανόντων ἐκ
45 τῶν αὐτῶν τὰ ἐπιβάλλοντα ἑκατέροις. οὐ μόνον δὲ
ὑπὲρ τῆς πόλεως θεοὶ πρὸς ἀλλήλους ἤρισαν, ἀλλὰ
καὶ ὧν ἤρισαν πρὸς ἀλλήλους ἐν τῇδε τῇ πόλει τὰς
κρίσεις ἐποιήσαντο, πανταχόθεν πάντας ἀνθρώπους
ἐπιστρέφοντες πρὸς τὴν πόλιν καὶ πάντων ἀρχὰς
καὶ δείγματα βουλόμενοι καταθέσθαι παρ' αὐτῇ,
καθάπερ οἱ τοὺς παῖδας προδιδάσκοντες, ἵν' ὥσπερ
πανταχοῦ τῶν ἄκρων προδιδαξάντων καλῶς ἔχει
τοῖς ζηλοῦσιν, οὕτω κἀκεῖνοι τέλειοι τὴν γιγνομένην
ἀρετὴν ἀποβαῖεν, οἷς χρῆν ἑπόμενοι, καὶ μὴ μόνον[1]
τῶν πυρῶν καὶ κριθῶν εἴη τὰ σπέρματα αὐτοῖς,[2]
ἀλλὰ καὶ δικαιοσύνης καὶ τῆς ἄλλης ἁπάσης διαίτης
τε καὶ πολιτείας ἐκ θεῶν αὐτοῖς εἴη τὰ σπέρματα.
46 καὶ λαγχάνει Ποσειδῶν Ἄρει τὴν ὑπὲρ τοῦ παιδὸς
καὶ νικᾷ ἐν ἅπασι τοῖς θεοῖς καὶ τὴν ἐπωνυμίαν ὁ
τόπος λαμβάνει τὴν αὐτὴν τοῦ τε συμβάντος
171 D. σύμβολον[3] καὶ δικαιοσύνης ὥσπερ ἄλλο τι μαρτύριον
καὶ πίστιν εἰς ἀνθρώπους. οὐ γὰρ ἔστιν ὑπὲρ τὸν
Ἄρειον πάγον οὐδὲν εὑρεῖν, εἴ τις ὑπερβολὴν ζητοίη.
ἀλλ' ὥσπερ τὰ ὕδατα ὅσα μαντικὰ καὶ πνεύματα
αὐτόθεν ⟨ἐν τοῖς θεοφορουμένοις⟩[4] ἰσχύει, οὕτως καὶ
οὗτος ὁ χῶρος ὥσπερ ἀνιέναι δοκεῖ τὴν τοῦ δικαίου
γνῶσιν ἐναργῆ καὶ τῆς παρὰ τοῖς θεοῖς ὡς δυνατὸν
47 ἐγγυτάτω. καὶ τοσούτῳ τετίμηται παρὰ πάντων
τῷ συγκεχωρηκότι, ὥσθ' οἱ μὲν ἡττώμενοι στέρ-

---

[1] μόνων VA.   [2] τὰ—αὐτοῖς om. TQ.
[3] συμβόλου VA.
[4] add. Behr, cf. scholium vol. III, p. 65, 29 Ddf., cuius

into force, through the visits of different Gods. For there followed upon the honours from the Gods gifts given and received, which were appropriate to each party. But not only did the Gods contend with one 45 another because of the city, but also they decided in this city the matters over which they contended with one another, turning the attention of all men everywhere to the city and wishing to deposit in its keeping the first principles and patterns of all things, just as those who give preliminary instruction to children, so that as it always makes for good imitation when the best have given the preliminary instruction, those men also might turn out perfect in a fitting virtue by following the proper teachers, and that they not only have the seeds of wheat and barley, but that they also have from the Gods the seeds of justice and every other means of life and government. And Poseidon obtained a suit against Ares 46 concerning his son and won it before all the Gods, and the site of the trial took its name from this,[a] being both a token of the event and another evidence and proof of justice in the eyes of mankind. For nothing can be found beyond the Areopagus, if one should seek the ultimate of justice. But just as all mantic waters and exhalations have a direct effect on divine inspiration, so this place seems, as it were, to emit the clear understanding of justice and one as close as possible to that which the Gods possess. And 47 the Areopagus has been honoured with such great deference by all, that those who lose their cases are

---

[a] The Areopagus.

---

verba manifeste corrupta correxerim in πνεύματα δὲ ἐνέπνει τοῖς θεοφορουμένοις κτλ. ; ἀνίσχει ci. Canter ; ἰσχυροῖ Lenz.

(171 D.)

γουσιν ὁμοίως τοῖς κεκρατηκόσιν, ἀρχαὶ δὲ πᾶσαι
καὶ συνέδρια τά τε ἄλλα καὶ τὸ μέγιστον ὁ δῆμος
πάντες ἰδιῶται πρὸς τὰς ἐν τούτῳ τῷ τόπῳ δίκας
172 D. εἰσὶν εἴκοντες.[1] καὶ μεταβολὴ τοῦ χωρίου τούτου
μόνου ἤδη σχεδὸν οὐχ ἥψατο, οἷα δὴ τὰ ἀνθρώπινα,
ἀλλ᾽ ὥσπερ ἀγωνιστήριον τοῖς θεοῖς ἀνεῖται καὶ οἷς
ἐξ ἐκείνου καθήκει καὶ πάντες παράδειγμα δικαιοσύνης νομίζοντες οὕτω τιμῶσιν αἰδοῖ τῶν θεῶν.
48 ἑτέρα δὴ[2] γίγνεται κρίσις ὕστερον μικτὴ τοῖς
ἀγωνισταῖς, θεία δὲ καὶ αὕτη τοῖς δικασταῖς, ἣν
ἀγωνίζεται τῶν Πελοπιδῶν ἀνὴρ δυστυχῶν πρὸς
τὰς νῦν προσοίκους τῷ τόπῳ θεὰς σεμνάς, κατα-
φυγὼν καὶ δοὺς ὥσπερ ἔφεσιν εἰς τὴν πόλιν, ὡς
ἐνταῦθα εἴπερ που τὴν δικαίαν φιλανθρωπίαν οὖσαν,
καὶ τυχὼν τῆς θεοῦ τῶν μανιῶν ἀπαλλάττεται.
49 Περὶ μὲν δὴ γένους καὶ τροφῆς καὶ τῆς ἐκ θεῶν
τιμῆς καὶ τῶν δωρεῶν, ἃς αὐτοί τε εὕροντο καὶ
τοῖς ἄλλοις ἔνειμαν, εἴρηται, τῶν μὲν πραγμάτων
ἴσως ἧττον, οὐχ ἧττον δὲ ἢ τοῖς πρὸ ἡμῶν. νῦν δὲ
παντοδαπῶν ἐπιόντων ἀκόλουθον ἴσως ἐστὶ λέγειν
173 D. ὧν μέρος ἐγγέγραπται τοῖς εἰρημένοις, ὅσῃ τινὶ καὶ
οἴᾳ[3] τῇ περιουσίᾳ τῆς φιλανθρωπίας εἰς ἅπαντας
ἐχρήσαντο καὶ ὅπως εἰς τὸ κοινὸν ἐπολιτεύσαντο.
50 ἄνειμι δὲ κἀνταῦθα μικρόν. ὥσπερ γὰρ τοῖς θεοῖς
οὐκ ἀπέχρησε δι᾽ ἑνός τινος τρόπου τὴν εὔνοιαν
ἀναδείξασθαι[4] τῇ πόλει, οὕτως οὐδ᾽ ἐκεῖνοι τοῦ

---

[1] ἤκοντες TQ ; ἑκόντες ci. Reiske.
[2] δὲ VA.
[3] τινὶ—οἴᾳ TQ : om. VA.
[4] ἐνδείξασθαι codd. dett.

---

[a] The reference is to the trial of Orestes, who in mythology
was arraigned for matricide by avenging Furies, tried before
a court of human councillors set up at Athens by the Goddess

42

as content as those who have won, and every office, and the assemblies, and the greatest among them, the people are all private citizens, submissive to the justice of this place. And change almost uniquely, such is the nature of human affairs, has not touched this spot ; but it is left open to be as it were a place of contest for the Gods and for those whom it befitted thereafter, and all men, thinking it a model of justice, so honour it with the reverence due to the Gods. There was another trial later on,[a] where the 48 contestants were mixed but the jurors were Gods, in which an unfortunate man, one of the Pelopidae, contended against the present neighbours of the place, the Reverend Goddesses, when he fled to the city for refuge and made as it were his appeal to the city, since here if anywhere there was justice and generosity, and having won the support of the Goddess was freed from his madness.

I have now discussed their birth, food, honour 49 from the Gods, and the gifts which they obtained and gave to others, perhaps in a way inferior to the facts, but not inferior to the discussions of those before us. At the present, although all sorts of things occur to me, perhaps it is consistent to speak next on a subject part of which has been included in my previous remarks, the greatness and the nature of the abundant generosity which they displayed toward all men and how they directed their policy to the common welfare of the Greeks. Here, too, I 50 shall go back a little. For just as the Gods were not satisfied to have shown their good will toward the city in a single way, so those men too did not judge

Athena, defended by the God Apollo, and acquitted by Athena's casting vote.

(173 D.)

σίτου τὴν κοινωνίαν τοῖς ἀνθρώποις ἔκριναν ἐξαρκεῖν, ἀλλ᾽ ὁδῷ προῄεσαν αὔξοντες τὴν φιλοτιμίαν, ὥσπερ οἱ[1] τὰ σπέρματα. μεγίστη δὲ καὶ
κοινοτάτη τῶν εὐεργεσιῶν ἡ τῶν πανταχόθεν
δυστυχούντων ὑποδοχὴ καὶ παραμυθία. οὐ γάρ
ἐστι γένος οὐδὲν τῆς Ἑλλάδος, ὡς ἔπος εἰπεῖν, ὃ
τῆσδε τῆς πόλεως ἀπείρατόν ἐστιν, οὐδ᾽ ἄοικον ἐπὶ
καιρῶν, ἀλλὰ καὶ πόλεις καὶ ἔθνη μετελήλυθεν εἰς
αὐτὴν καὶ καταπέφευγεν, καὶ κατ᾽ ἄνδρα σχεδὸν
οἱ γνωριμώτατοι, ὧν ἁπάντων μὲν ἀμήχανον καὶ
μνημονεῦσαι πρῶτον καὶ τῆς μνήμης τοὺς λόγους
συμμέτρους ἀποδοῦναι, μὴ ὅτι τῶν ἰδίᾳ λέγω
μεταστάντων κατὰ συμφοράς, ἀλλ᾽ οὐδὲ τῶν κοινῇ·
ἃ δ᾽ ἐστὶν τῶν παλαιῶν ἐντιμότατα καὶ ὥσπερ ἀρχὴ

174 D. τοῖς πολλοῖς διηγεῖσθαι, Ἡρακλέους ἀπελθόντος ἐξ
ἀνθρώπων ἡ μὲν πόλις καὶ νεὼς καὶ βωμοὺς ἱδρύεται
πρώτη, καθάπερ καὶ πρόσθεν τοῖς μυστηρίοις ἐτί-
51 μησεν πρῶτον ξένων. καὶ διατελεῖ δὴ θεὸς ὢν καὶ
δοκῶν ἐξ ἐκείνου. οὐ γὰρ μόνον[2] τοὺς πρεσβυτά-
τους ἄρα τῶν θεῶν ἦρξε τιμᾶν, καὶ ταῦτα διαφερόντως καὶ ὑπὲρ πάντας τοὺς ἀκολουθήσαντας, ἀλλὰ
καὶ τοὺς ἐπήλυδας αὕτη μετὰ τῶν ἄλλων θεῶν[3] ἐν-

175 D. έκρινεν, ὥσπερ συμπολιτευομένη τοῖς θεοῖς· ἅμα δὲ[4]
ἐκεῖνοί τε ἐδέχοντο καὶ ταύτην οὐκ ἐλελήθει, ἀλλ᾽
ἐξηγεῖτο τοῖς ἄλλοις ἀνθρώποις καὶ ἀνεκήρυττεν,
ὥστε ἀπέφηνεν τούς τε Θηβαίους ὀλίγον τῇ φύσει
προσήκοντας αὐτῷ, κατὰ ταὐτὰ δὲ καὶ τοὺς ἄλλους
οἷς τι μέτεστιν ὡς οἰκείοις ἐκείνου μνήμης. μόνη γὰρ
52 οἶδεν[5] τίνων ἦν ἄξιος. αὐτῷ μὲν οὖν[6] ταύτην ἀποδε-
δώκει τὴν χάριν, δι᾽ ἣν καὶ ὅσων παρὰ τῶν ἄλλων

---

[1] καὶ ci. dubitanter Lenz. [2] μόνους TQ.
[3] θεῶν om. VA. [4] γὰρ codd. dett.
[5] εἶδεν VA. [6] δὴ VA.

the sharing of their wheat with mankind to be sufficient, but they continued enlarging on their glory, just as the sowers of seed do not end their labour here. The greatest and most universal of their benefactions was the reception and consolation of unfortunates from every place. For there is no race in Greece, one might say, which is unfamiliar with this city, and on occasion did not dwell here. But cities and races came and found refuge in it ; and of individuals almost all the most famous men. To name all of them and to present an account consistent with their memory is first of all impossible, I mean not only those who moved here privately, through some misfortune, but also those who came in groups. But here is the most honoured of all ancient tales, and as it were the first one for most writers to relate. When Heracles departed from mankind, the city was the first to establish for him temples and altars, just as even before it honoured him first of foreigners with initiation into the mysteries. And 51 from that time he has always been and has seemed to be a God. For not only was the city the first to honour the eldest of the Gods, and especially so, and beyond all who followed its lead, but it also admitted strangers into the company of the other Gods, as if it shared the Gods' authority. But the Gods immediately received him in their company, and it did not escape the city's notice, but it announced and heralded the event to other men, so that it showed that the Thebans had little kinship with him, and on the same grounds the others, who had some share in his memory as relatives. For it alone knew what he deserved. Therefore it showed such grati- 52 tude to him, through which one would justly say

(175 D.)

ἔτυχεν Ἡρακλῆς ἁπάσας τῆς πόλεως χάριτας δικαίως ἄν τις λέγοι· ταύτην γὰρ ἅπαντες μιμησάμενοι
τὰ δίκαια συνωμολόγησαν. Εὐρυσθέως δ' ἐλάσαντος
μὲν ἐκ Πελοποννήσου τοὺς παῖδας αὐτοῦ, προσθέν-
τος δὲ ἑτέραν ἀγνωμοσύνην ἔτι μείζω καὶ δεινοτέραν,
τὸ μηδὲ τῶν ἄλλων πόλεων μηδεμίαν δέχεσθαι
προκηρύξαι, καὶ[1] τὰ ἔσχατα ἀπειλήσαντος, οἱ μὲν
ἄλλοι πάντες ἐσχετλίαζον, βοηθεῖν δὲ οὐκ εἶχον· ἡ
πόλις δὲ ὑπεδέξατο μόνη τῶν πάντων, μισήσασα
μᾶλλον τὰς ἀπειλὰς ἢ φοβηθεῖσα, καὶ τὴν προστασίαν, ἣν ἁπάντων ἀνθρώπων Ἡρακλῆς ἔσχεν, ταύτην
αὐτὴ τοῖς ἐκείνου παισὶν ὥσπερ τινὰ ἔρανον φορὰν
διεσώσατο· εἰκότως. καὶ γὰρ ἐκείνῳ τῶν πλείστων
176 D. διὰ Θησέως συνεπείληπτο, καὶ πάλαι κοινωνὸν
53 ἦγεν, ἀφ' οὗ ταὐτὰ ἑώρα γιγνώσκοντα ἑαυτῇ. καὶ ἃ
μὲν κατειργάσατο μετ' αὐτῶν καὶ ὑπὲρ αὐτῶν[2] ἐν
ἑτέρᾳ τῶν λόγων καθήκει δηλῶσαι μερίδι· τὴν δ'
οὖν ἐπιτροπὴν οὕτω λαμπρὰν αὐτῶν ἐποιήσατο ὥστ'
αὐτοῖς τὴν συμφορὰν λυσιτελῆσαι. οὐ γὰρ μόνον[3]
τὴν ὀρφανίαν ἄδηλον κατέστησεν, ἀντὶ τοῦ πατρὸς
αὐτοῖς[4] γενομένη, ἀλλὰ καὶ ὡς πατρόθεν εὐεργέτας
τῶν ἀνθρώπων οὕτως ἐτίμησεν, τέτταρας μὲν δοῦσα
νέμεσθαι πόλεις[5] τῶν τότε οἰκουμένων ἐν τῇ χώρᾳ,
πρώτους δὲ θρέψασα δημοσίᾳ, πατρὸς εὐεργέτου
παῖδας, ὥσπερ[6] οὓς ὕστερον τῶν ἐν τῷ πολέμῳ
54 τελευτησάντων τρέφειν ἐνόμισεν. καὶ μέντοι καὶ τὰ
τροφεῖα πρέποντα ἐκομίσατο ἑαυτῇ· τῶν γὰρ ὑπ-
ηργμένων ἀξίους εὗρεν· ἡ δ' ἐκείνων ὁδὸς τὸ δεῦρο
κοινῇ[7] πάντων ὕστερον τῶν ἐκπιπτόντων ἐγένετο,

[1] καὶ om. VA.
[2] καὶ—αὐτῶν Pap. TQ: om. VA.
[3] Pap. : ὀρφανίαν μόνην TQVA.
[4] αὐτῇ Pap.

that all of the gratitude which Heracles received from other men came from the city. For all men, in imitation of her, agreed upon what was just. But when Eurystheus drove Heracles' children from the Peloponnesus, and added a second act of cruelty, still greater and more terrible, the prohibition of any city from receiving them, and made the most extreme threats, all other men were angry, yet could not help; but the city, alone of all, received them, hating rather than fearing the threats. And it preserved the protection, which Heracles maintained for all men, for his sons, as its own private contribution. With good reason. For he had been aided in most of his enterprises by Theseus, and of old the city held him as a comrade, from the time that it saw him holding the same views as it did. And in another part of the speech must be revealed 53 what it accomplished with them and in their behalf. But its guardianship of them was so glorious that they profited by their misfortune. For not only did it obscure their orphaned state, by being like a father to them, but also it honoured them as benefactors of mankind because of their father, giving them four of the cities then settled in the land to hold, and raising them first at public expense, as the children of a father who was a public benefactor, just as it was its custom later on to raise the sons of those who died in war. And, moreover, it acquired for itself a 54 proper payment for its nurture. For it found them deserving of what they had received. The journey of those men here was shared by all men who were

---

[5] πόλεις νέμεσθαι Pap.
[6] ὥσπερ Pap. TQ : om. VA.
[7] κοινὴ δὲ VA a. corr.

(176 D.)

μᾶλλον δὲ ἐπὶ πολλοῖς τοῖς πρότερον[1] κἀκεῖνοι
κατέφυγον. ἅπασι γὰρ ἡ πόλις ἑαυτὴν παρέσχεν
τοῖς ἐν χρείᾳ κοινὴν εὐθὺς ἐξ ἀρχῆς, καὶ πάντες ἐπὶ
δυοῖν ὁρμεῖν ἔδοξαν οἱ Ἕλληνες ἀληθῆ νομίσαντες,
ἰδίᾳ μὲν ἕκαστοι τὴν ἀρχαίαν, κοινὴν δ' ἅπαντες
ταύτην προσονομάζοντες πατρίδα, καὶ τὴν μὲν προτέραν δευτέραν, τὴν δὲ ὑστέραν προτέραν ἄγοντες
τῇ δυνάμει. τοσούτῳ γὰρ βεβαιοτέραν ταύτην
αὐτοῖς εἶναι καὶ λυσιτελεστέραν, ὅσῳ μᾶλλον ἀν-

177 D. άλωτον καὶ ὡς ἀληθῶς ἱερὰν καὶ μετὰ τῆς πείρας
ἔγνωσαν, ὀρθῶς βουλευόμενοι, τοῦτο μὲν οἱ περὶ
Θήβας ἀτυχήσαντες καὶ πάσης τῆς Βοιωτίας συνεκ-
πεσόντες, τοῦτο δὲ Θετταλῶν οἱ ταύτῃ τραπόμενοι
καὶ Ταναγραίων οἱ μεταστάντες, Δωριέων Πελοποννήσου κρατησάντων, ὑπὸ τῶν εἰξάντων ἀναστάν-

55 τες· οὗτοι δ' ἦσαν Ἰωνία πάντες. τὸ δ' αὐτὸ πρὸς
⟨τοὺς ἀπ'⟩[2] ἀμφοτέρων τῶν αἰγιαλῶν ἐποίησεν, τοῦ
θ' ἑσπερίου καὶ τοῦ ἑῴου. καὶ γὰρ καὶ τούτους
κἀκείνους ἐν ταῖς ἀνάγκαις ὑπεδέξατο. ἔστι δὲ ἃ[3]
καὶ παντάπασιν ἐκκεχωρηκότα νῦν γένη τῶν
Ἑλλήνων καταφεύγοντα εἰς αὐτὴν ἀνέλαβεν, ὥσπερ
Δρύοπας καὶ Πελασγούς· ὧν ἔτι καὶ νῦν σημεῖα τῆς
σωτηρίας λείπεται. αἱ γὰρ ἀπ' αὐτῶν ἐπωνυμίαι

178 D. σύμβολον οὖσαι τῆς οἰκήσεως αὐτῶν ἅμα καὶ τῆς[4]
56 σωτηρίας [αὐτῶν][5] εἰσίν. οὕτω δ' ἐκ παλαιοῦ
πᾶσιν ἑαυτὴν δοῦσα διετήρησεν ὥσπερ νόμον εἰς
τέλος τὴν γνώμην, καὶ διεξῆλθεν διὰ πάντων τῶν
Ἑλληνικῶν καιρῶν, ἅπασι τὰς πύλας ὑπανοίγουσα
τοῖς ἐκ τῶν πολέμων, ἢ καὶ κατὰ στάσιν, ἢ καὶ κατ'

---

[1] προτέροις TQ.   [2] add. codd. dett.
[3] ἃ om. VA.   [4] τῆς om. TQ.

later exiled ; moreover the sons of Heracles took [1104.]
refuge here after many came before them. For the
city right from the start gave herself for all in need to
share. And all the Greeks thought that they were
secured by two anchors, a true belief : each privately
called his original land his country, but all named
this their common home, and ranked the former
second, and the latter first. For they thought that
this was so much more secure and advantageous to
them, to the degree that they recognized by experience and good sense that it was unassailable and
truly sacred. There were those who suffered misfortune at Thebes and were expelled from all
Boeotia,[a] and those of the Thessalians who turned
here and those of Tanagra who left their homes when
they were uprooted by others who fled before the
Dorian conquest of the Peloponnesus. But all of *c.* 1050.
these formed Ionia. Its conduct was the same to 55
those on both shores, western and eastern. For it
admitted both in times of necessity. And it received
Greek races in search of refuge, who have now
entirely disappeared, like the Dryopians and the
Pelasgians, and signs still now remain of their
preservation. For the names which they left exist
both as a proof of their dwelling here and their
preservation. Thus of old it gave itself to all men 56
and preserved its resolve to the end like a law.
And it passed through all of Greek history with its
gates open to all men, to those in exile from war or

---

[a] The Seven against Thebes traditionally dated in 1213
B.C. For those of Tanagra in Boeotia *cf.* Herodotus V. 57
and 61.

---

[5] αὐτῶν om. codd. dett.

49

(178 D.)

ἄλλην τινὰ φεύγουσι τύχην πόρρωθεν προκηρύτ-
τουσα θαρρεῖν, ὡς οὐδεὶς ἔσται τῶν Ἑλλήνων
ἄπολις, ἕως ἂν ἡ τῶν Ἀθηναίων ᾖ πόλις, ἀλλ' ἢ πα-
57 τρίδα μεταλλάξουσιν οἷς συμβαίνει. μιᾶς μέν γε τῶν
τριῶν ἐν Πελοποννήσῳ μοιρῶν διαφθαρείσης τῆς
Μεσσηνίων μόνη διετήρησεν τοὺς λοιποὺς αὐτῶν,
δεξαμένη τε καὶ σκεψαμένη τόπους ἐν οἷς ἔμελλον
ἱδρύσεσθαι.[1] καὶ νῦν εἰσὶ Μεσσήνιοι διὰ τὴν πόλιν.
179 D. αὖθις δὲ τοῦ περὶ Βοιωτίαν πάθους συμβάντος καὶ
τῆς παρασχούσης ποθ' αὐτὴν[2] ἐνευτυχῆσαι τοῖς
Ἕλλησι πόλεως ἀπροσδοκήτως καὶ παρ' ἀξίαν ἀναι-
ρεθείσης, οὐδένες εἰς τὴν χρείαν ἀπεμνημόνευσαν
οὐδ' ἐπεκούφισαν, ἀλλὰ τὸ μὲν τῶν ἄλλων μέρος
ἐξήκει τὸ Πλαταιέων γένος, ἡ δὲ πόλις μετὰ καλοῦ
τοῦ σχήματος τὴν δυστυχίαν ἐπηνώρθωσεν αὐτοῖς,
Ἀθηναίους ἀντὶ Πλαταιέων ἀποφήνασα καὶ φυλάξασα τῷ τόπῳ τὸ μνημεῖον, ὥσπερ εἰκὸς ἦν τὴν
κοινῇ[3] τότε πάντων προστᾶσαν· τοὺς δὲ πταίσαντας
58 τῶν ἐκεῖ φανερῶν ἀνώρθωσε.[4] πάλιν τοίνυν
Θηβαίων κακῶς ὑπὸ τῆς φρουρᾶς τῆς Λακωνικῆς
διακειμένων ἐδέξατο τὸν δῆμον καὶ διέτριβον οἱ
φεύγοντες ὡς Ἀθηναῖοι τὸν χρόνον τοῦτον, ἕως
180 D. ἔμελλον διὰ τῆς πόλεως αὖθις κομιεῖσθαι τὴν ἑαυ-
59 τῶν. αὖθις αὖ Πλαταιέας δεύτερον ἐξοικισθέντας
καὶ Θεσπιέας ἅμα ἐκείνοις δέχεται[5] πανοικησίᾳ.
καὶ πάλιν Θηβαίους ἐπὶ τοῖς ἐσχάτοις ἀτυχήμασιν
καὶ πρὸ τούτων τοὺς ἐπὶ Θρᾴκης κακῶς πράξαντας

---

[1] ἱδρύσασθαι VA.
[2] edd. : ποτε αὐτὴν TQVA.
[3] κοινὴν VA.   [4] ἀνορθῶσαι VA.
[5] δέχεσθαι VA.

---

[a] The reference is to the Heraclidae.

faction or through some other chance, and it promulgated abroad a word of encouragement, that no Greek will be without a city, so long as there is a city of the Athenians, but to whomever this befalls, they will find a new country. When one of the 57 three parts of the Peloponnesus was destroyed,[a] that of the Messenians, it alone preserved those who were left, receiving them and looking for places where they would settle. And even now Messenians exist because of the city. Again when misfortune befell in Boeotia and the city which had offered itself to the Greeks as the scene of their success unexpectedly and undeservingly was destroyed, no peoples repaid it in a time of need or alleviated its suffering, but as far as the others were concerned, the race of the Plataeans had vanished.[b] But the city in a fair way compensated for their misfortune, by making them Athenians instead of Plataeans and by preserving a memorial for this place, a consistent act for the city who then championed all men in common. It set right the leading men there who had stumbled. Then again when the 58 Thebans were in troubled circumstances because of the Lacedaemonian garrison, it received their people and the exiles passed the time as Athenians until they should get back their own land with the help of the city. Again it received *en masse* the 59 Plataeans who had been driven from their homes a second time and with them the Thespians. And again it received the Thebans after the most extreme misfortunes and before them those in Thrace who

Legendary [1104].

429-428.

382-379.

372.

335.

[b] For the Plataeans *cf.* Thucydides III. 55, and for their later sufferings, alluded to just below, Xenophon, *Hellenica* VI. 3.

(180 D.)

δύο καὶ τριάκοντα πόλεων ὅσον λοιπόν, τοὺς[1] ἐκ Κορίνθου καὶ Θάσου καὶ Βυζαντίου καὶ πανταχόθεν
60 τίς ἂν ἐξαριθμήσειεν; οἶμαι μὲν οὐδὲ τοὺς ἐκ τῶν
νήσων μόνον εἶναι ῥᾴδιον. μόνη γὰρ ὡς εἰπεῖν
διαγέγονεν πρὸς τὴν ἁπάντων τύχην ἁμιλλωμένη
καὶ πειρωμένη πᾶσιν περιτρέπειν τὰς συμφορὰς
ἐπὶ θάτερα. καὶ τὴν παροιμίαν ἐνήλλαξεν· οὐ γὰρ
ἐκποδὼν εἶναι κατέδειξε φίλου κακῶς πράξαντος,
ἀλλὰ πολλοὺς καὶ τῶν πρόσθεν διαφόρων ἐπὶ τοῖς
ἀτυχήμασιν φίλους πεποίηται. οὐδ' εὖ μὲν πράτ-
τουσι κέχρηται, κακῶς δ' ἀπαλλάξαντας ἠτίμακεν,
τῇ τύχῃ μετροῦσα τὴν φιλανθρωπίαν, ἀλλὰ τοὺς τοῦ
δυστυχεῖν καιροὺς τοῦ πράττειν εὖ πεποίηκεν,[2] τοῖς
πολλοῖς τὰ παρ' αὑτῆς[3] ἀγαθὰ προσθεῖσα καὶ ποι-
ησαμένη κοινωνούς, ὧν ὅτε κάλλιστα ἔπραττον οὐδ'
181 D. ἐλπὶς ἦν αὐτοῖς. καὶ γάρ τοι πάντες ἐν ἅπασι τοῖς
τῆς χρείας καιροῖς μίαν ταύτην ὁδὸν εἶδον τὴν δεῦρο
61 φέρουσαν. καὶ πρεσβυτάτη τῶν Ἑλληνίδων οὖσα
τῷ δέχεσθαι τοὺς πανταχόθεν μᾶλλον ἢ τῷ προει-
ληφέναι τῷ χρόνῳ τοῦ γένους ὡσπερεὶ πατρίς ἐστι
καὶ ἑστία κοινή. καὶ τὴν ἐπιτηδειότητα τὴν πρὸς
ἅπαντας οὐ μόνον οἷς αὐτὴ παρ' αὑτῆς ἀπέστειλεν
ἐδήλωσεν, ἀλλὰ καὶ τῷ τοὔδαφος παρέχειν τοῖς
ἔξωθεν καταφεύγουσιν εἰς αὐτὴν καὶ προσίεσθαι
πάντας ὡς μέρος αὑτῆς.

62 Ἓν μὲν οὖν[4] τοῦτο τοιοῦτον καὶ τοσοῦτον εἶδος
εὐεργεσίας τοῖς προϋπηργμένοις ἀκόλουθον· ἕτερον
δ', ὃ καὶ τοῖς πράγμασίν ἐστιν ἐφεξῆς καὶ μεγέθους
χάριν οὐ λείπεται, προσλαβοῦσα γὰρ τὸν κοινὸν

---

[1] codd. dett. : ταῖς TQVA. [2] πεποιήκει VA.
[3] αὑτῆς TQA. [4] οὖν om. TQ.

52

had fared badly, all that was left of thirty-two cities. Who would number those from Corinth, Thasus, Byzantium, and all the world ? [a] I think that it is not 60 even easy to count only those from the islands. For the city alone passed its time, one might say, in vying against the fortune of every man and in attempting to reverse their ill-luck. And it changed the old adage [b] : For it showed that it did not stand aside when a friend was in trouble, but it even made many of its former enemies friends after their misfortunes. Nor did it deal with the successful, but treat with dishonour the unfortunate, measuring its generosity according to a man's luck. But it turned the occasions of misfortune into success, giving to many its own possessions and making them its partners, of which they had not even a hope when they were most successful. For all men in every time of need saw one road which led here. And 61 although it is the oldest of Greek cities, it is as it were the country and common hearth of the race by its admission of those from everywhere rather than by its precedence in time. And it showed its usefulness for all men not only by what it sent them of its own, but also by the offer of its soil to those who sought refuge in it from without and its acceptance of all men as a part of itself.

Then this one kind of benefit, of such quality and 62 greatness, is consistent with its former deeds. But there is a second one contingent on these acts and which because of its greatness is no less important.

[a] The scholiast refers to Alexander's destruction of Thebes in 335 B.C. For the two other victories of Philip *cf.* § 319 and Demosthenes IX. 26 ; XX. 52, 59-60.
[b] *Cf.* xx. 18 and Nauck, *FTG*² 667 (Sophocles).

(181 D.)

τῶν Ἑλλήνων ἐξηγητήν, ἑαυτῇ δὲ πατρῷον, τὸν
Ἀπόλλω τὸν Πύθιον, ἐξήγαγε πανταχῇ[1] γῆς τὸ
Ἑλληνικόν, τὴν αὐτὴν φυλακὴν ἅμα καὶ προσθήκην
63 τῷ γένει ποιουμένη. καὶ πρῶτον μὲν τὴν ἐπικει-
μένην ἐκάθηρε θάλατταν, ἔοικα δὲ οὐ τὸ πρῶτον
λέγειν τῶν ἔργων, καὶ τῆς Ἑλλάδος ὥσπερ λήμην
ἀφεῖλεν, τοὺς ἐπὶ τῶν προθύρων ὀχληροὺς ἀνα-
στήσασα, λέγω τὸ ληστικὸν ἅπαν καὶ βαρβαρικόν,
καὶ καταναγκάσασα ὡς πορρωτάτω τῆς Ἑλληνικῆς
182 D. παραλίας καὶ τῶν[2] εἴσπλων ἀποχωρῆσαι. ἐξ ὧν ὁ
τῶν νήσων κύκλος ᾠκίσθη βεβαίως καὶ διὰ τῶν
ἡμερωτάτων τὸν Αἰγαῖον ὑπῆρξε πλεῖν σύνδυο καὶ
σύντρεις πόλεις, ὥσπερ ἐν ἠπείρῳ νήσου μιᾶς ἀμεί-
βοντας ἔστιν οὗ· οὕτως εὖ κατεσκεύασε τὴν
64 θάλατταν. πρὸς δὲ τούτοις τὰς ἐπικειμένας τῇ
Πελοποννήσῳ νήσους ᾤκισε, τοὺς ἑσπερίους τόπους
οἰκειουμένη καὶ πανταχόθεν τοὺς βαρβάρους ὥσπερ
προβόλοις ἀνείργουσα· ὡς δ᾽ αὐτῇ διχόθεν κατεσκεύ-
αστο ἡ τῆς Ἑλλάδος φρουρὰ καὶ συνεκέκλειστο
ὥσπερ λιμέσι κλειστοῖς, οὕτως ἤδη καὶ μέχρι τῆς
ὑπερορίας ᾔει διὰ τῆς θαλάττης, καὶ διεβίβαζεν εἰς
τὴν Ἀσίαν τὰς πολλὰς καὶ μεγάλας ἀποικίας,
συνάπτουσα τὴν γῆν ὡς μίαν οὖσαν τῇ φύσει, καὶ
τὰ πέραν τῆς Ἑλλάδος οὐ κεχωρισμένα, ἕως κατεσκεύασε τὸ ἐπὶ τῆς Ἀσίας ἀντίπρωρον, εἰ οἷόν τ᾽
εἰπεῖν, Ἑλλάδι[3] τῇ παλαιᾷ, μεγάλη μὲν αὔξουσα
μοίρᾳ τὰ ὑπάρχοντα τοῖς Ἕλλησι, μέγα δ᾽ εἰς
ἀσφάλειαν προϊδοῦσα τὴν κοινήν, ὡς ἔδειξεν ὁ
μέλλων χρόνος. κάλλιστον δὲ κόσμον ἀμφοτέρῳ
τῷ γένει περιθεῖσα οὐ μόνον τῷ πλήθει καὶ ἅμα

---

[1] πανταχοῖ VA.   [2] τῶν om. VA.   [3] Ἑλλάδα VA.

For in company with the common interpreter of the Greeks, and its own ancestor, Pythian Apollo, it led forth the Greek people all over the world, creating at the same time both a protection and an addition to the race. And first of all, it cleansed the neighbouring 63 sea—but I think that I do not speak of the first of its acts—, and it removed as it were rheum from the eye of Greece, by uprooting the trouble-makers at its gateways, I mean every barbarian and pirate band, and by compelling them to withdraw as far as possible from the Greek sea-coast and harbour entrances.[a] Thus the surrounding islands were firmly settled, and it was possible to sail the Aegean by way of the most cultivated regions, in some places, on one island, passing two or three cities at a time, as if on the mainland. So well did it dispose of the sea. Besides, it settled the islands near the Pelo- 64 ponnesus, taking over the regions in the west and fending off the barbarians on all sides as if with bulwarks. But when it had prepared a double means of protecting Greece and it had been enclosed as it were with fortified harbours, now it crossed the sea up to the regions abroad, and carried to Asia *c.* 1100- many great colonies, joining the earth as if it were 1000. naturally one and as if the regions beyond Greece were not distinct, until it brought Asia, if the expression can be used, face to face with old Greece, increasing the Greeks' existing strength by a great degree, and with much foresight for their common safety, as the future proved ; and it gave the fairest adornment to each race not only through increased

---

[a] [Aristides in §§ 63 and 64 is recording not what the Athenians did from 478 B.C. onwards but what they are supposed to have done long before that.—*E.H.W.*]

(182 D.)

καιρίῳ τῆς χώρας, ἀλλὰ καὶ τῷ δεῖξαι τὴν ὁμόνοιαν
65 ὅσων καὶ οἵων ἀγαθῶν αἰτία γίγνεται. ταύτης δὲ
τοιαύτης ὥσπερ κρηπῖδος ἢ ῥίζης ὑποκειμένης
ἐξεφοίτησαν καὶ διὰ πάσης ἤδη γῆς αἱ τῶν Ἑλλήνων
ἀποικίαι. τοῖς γὰρ πεμφθεῖσι καὶ κρατήσασιν
ἔρως ἐμπίπτει μιμήσασθαι τὴν μητρόπολιν. καὶ
183 D. διαλαβόντες ᾤκιζον τὴν γῆν, ἐκτείνοντες ὥσπερ[1]
ἄλλο τι μέτρον τὸ τῆς Ἑλλάδος, ἕως ἐξεπλήρωσαν
66 ἅπαν τὸ δεχόμενον. καὶ νῦν ἐπ᾽ ἀμφοτέροις τοῖς
πέρασι τῆς γῆς ὑμετέρων[2] παίδων παῖδες οἰκοῦσιν,
οἱ μὲν ἄχρι Γαδείρων ἀπὸ Μασσαλίας παρήκοντες,
οἱ δ᾽ ἐπὶ τῷ Τανάιδι καὶ τῇ λίμνῃ μεμερισμένοι.
ὥστ᾽ ἐμοὶ μὲν γέλως ἐπέρχεται ἀκούοντι τῶν νῦν
πόλεων τοῖς σφετέροις κόσμοις φιλοτιμουμένων καὶ
φρονουσῶν ὡς ἐπὶ λαμπροῖς, ὅταν εὑρίσκω θεωρῶν
ὑπὸ τῆς ὑμετέρας πόλεως γῆν καὶ θάλατταν κεκο-
σμημένην ἄνευ τῶν ἄλλων πολλῶν καὶ πολλῷ
μειζόνων.

67 Τοῦτο δὴ βούλομαι διὰ βραχέων ἐπανελθὼν ἐξε-
τάσαι καὶ δεῖξαι τὴν συνέχειαν τῆς πολιτείας, ᾗ
κέχρηται πρὸς τὸ Ἑλληνικὸν ἡ πόλις, καὶ ὅτι οὐκ
ἔστι πρόσρημα βέλτιον ἐπενεγκεῖν οὗ νῦν ἐφθεγ-
ξάμην. ὅτε μὲν γὰρ τοῖς Ἡρακλέους παισὶν ἔδει
βοηθείας, παρέσχεν μόνη καὶ μετέδωκεν ἁπάντων,
παρελθοῦσα τὴν χρείαν τῇ μεγαλοψυχίᾳ. ἐπεὶ δὲ
ἔδει τὴν Πελοπόννησον Δωριέων γενέσθαι, συγ-
68 κατήγαγεν πάλιν αὐτοὺς μετὰ τοῦ θεοῦ. γενομένης
δὲ τῆς Ἡρακλειδῶν καθόδου καὶ νεωτέρων συμβάντων ἐν τῇ Πελοποννήσῳ, πάλιν τὸ κινηθὲν ἐδέξατο.

---

[1] ὡς ἐπ᾽ ci. Oliver.   [2] ἡμετέρων VA Phot.

population and the advantageous positions gained, but also by showing the number and nature of the blessings for which concord is responsible. But once 65 there came into existence as it were such a foundation or root, the colonies of the Greeks went forth through every land. For those who had been sent out and won their land desired to imitate their mother city. And they divided up and settled the earth, extending as it were the measure of Greece until they filled the capacity of every place. And 66 now at both ends of the earth the sons of your sons dwell, some having gone from Massalia as far as Gadira, others scattered at the Tanais and the Lake.[a] Therefore I smile when I hear that the cities of to-day are proud and haughty over their adornments as if they were glorious, when in my observations, aside from many other and much greater achievements, I discover that earth and sea have been adorned by your city.

Now in a brief résumé I wish to examine all this 67 and demonstrate " the continuity of the policy " which the city employed in respect to the Greek race and that there is no better term to apply than what I now used. For when the children of Heracles were in need of help, it alone provided it and gave them a share of everything, surpassing their need by its generosity. But when it was fated that the *c.* 1050– Dorians possess the Peloponnesus, together with the 1000. God,[b] again it assisted in their restoration. Again, 68 when the Heraclidae returned and there was unrest in the Peloponnesus, it received the displaced races.

[a] Marseilles, Cadiz, the River Don and the Sea of Azov. Such were literary bounds of the Greco-Roman world ; *cf.* § 324 and xxxvi. 87.   [b] Apollo.

184 D. ἐν ᾧ τὰ μὲν τῶν προτέρων ἱκετῶν ἀσφαλῶς εἶχεν,
69 ἕτεροι δὲ αὖ τὸ ἐκείνων σχῆμα μετειλήφεσαν. δεξαμένη δὲ ἤδη πάντας ἀνθρώπους καὶ μεταδοῦσα χώρας καὶ νόμων καὶ πολιτείας ἐπενόησεν ὑπὲρ τῆς
Ἑλλάδος χρῆσθαι τῷ πλεονεκτήματι καὶ τὰς παρ᾽
αὐτῇ[1] πόλεις πολλὰς συμπεφευγυίας ἀφορμὴν τῶν
ἔξω πόλεων πολλῶν καὶ μεγάλων ποιήσασθαι.
70 καίτοι πῶς ἂν φιλανθρωπότερον ἡ πόλις ἢ πῶς
λαμπρότερον περὶ τῶν ἑαυτοὺς δόντων ἐβουλεύσατο;
ἢ πρῶτον μὲν[2] τῆς ἑαυτῆς χώρας καὶ πολιτείας
μετέδωκεν, ἔπειθ᾽ ἑτέραν ὅπως κτήσονται[3] συμπαρ-
εσκεύασεν, ὁμοίως τῇ τε οἰκείᾳ καὶ τῇ ἀλλοδαπῇ
δέχεσθαι τοὺς δεομένους ἀξιοῦσα, καὶ τὰ πρέποντα
ἑκατέροις τοῖς καιροῖς ἐτήρησεν. ὅτε μὲν γὰρ
ἀσθενεῖς ἦσαν, τὸν φόβον περιεῖλεν αὐτῶν καὶ τὰς
ἀπορίας ἐπηνώρθωσεν· ὡς δὲ ἄμεινον ἢ κατὰ
συμφορὰν ἐπεπράγεσαν, οὕτως ἤδη διεκόσμει καὶ
προέπεμπεν,[4] ἡγεμόνας τε ἑκάστοις ἐφιστᾶσα, ὥσπερ
αὐτὴ συμπάντων ἡγεμὼν καὶ φύλαξ ἐγεγόνει κοινή,
71 καὶ λεὼν οἴκοθεν παραζευγνῦσα. ταῦτα δ᾽ οὐ
μόνον ταῖς πράξεσιν εὕροι τις ἂν συνεχῆ, ἀλλὰ καὶ
τῷ βουλήματι. ὥσπερ γὰρ τοὺς προτέρους δεξαμένη κατήγαγεν, τοὺς Ἡρακλείδας εἶπον, οὕτω καὶ
τοὺς μετ᾽ ἐκείνους δεξαμένη πρῶτον, εἶτ᾽ ἐπεξήγαγε,
διπλῆν ἀνθ᾽ ἁπλῆς τὴν εὐεργεσίαν ἐπ᾽ ἀμφοτέρων
τιθεμένη. καὶ προϊοῦσα ἀπὸ τοῦ πρώτου πρὸς τὸ
τελευταῖον ἀεὶ οὕτως, ὅπερ εἶπον, πολιτείᾳ προσέοι-
κεν ἡ τῆς πόλεως ὑπὲρ τῶν Ἑλλήνων πρόνοια καὶ
185 D. διὰ πολλῆς καὶ συνεχοῦς τῆς ἀκολουθίας σῴζεται.
72 καὶ μὴν τὸ μὲν τοὺς φεύγοντας δέχεσθαι, εἰ καὶ
μηδὲ[5] τοῦτ᾽ ἐκφεύγει κοινῆς εἶναι δεῖγμα φιλ-

---

[1] edd. : αὐτῇ TQVA.　　　　[2] ἢ πρῶτον μὲν εἰ VA.

When the former suppliants were secure, others again took over their part. But when it had re- 69 ceived all men and let them share in lands, laws, and citizenship, it conceived of the idea of using its surplus population in behalf of Greece and of making the many cities which had sought refuge with it the source of many great cities abroad. Yet how could 70 the city form a more generous or glorious resolve concerning those who entrusted themselves to it ? It first of all let them share in its land and citizenship. Next it arranged for their possession of another land, thinking that it should receive those in need into a foreign land as well as its own land. And it carefully followed the requirements of each circumstance. For when they were weak, it removed their fear and corrected their distress. But when their success exceeded their misfortune, it equipped them accordingly and then sent them forth, setting leaders over each group, just as if it had become the common leader and guardian of all, and it added its own people from home. One would find a continuity 71 not only in action, but also in purpose. For just as it received and restored the former group, the Heraclidae whom I mentioned, so it received those who came after them and next sent them forth, in both cases conferring a double instead of a single benefit. And always proceeding in this fashion from beginning to end, as I said,[a] the city's concern on behalf of the Greeks is like a policy and is maintained with great and lasting consistency. Indeed, even if the 72 acceptance of exiles must be considered an example

[a] § 67.

(185 D.)

ἀνθρωπίας, ἀλλ' οὖν εἴποι γ' ἄν τις ὡς ἐκείνους ἦν
εὖ ποιούσης μόνους, ὅσοι ταύτης τῆς τύχης ἐπειράθησαν. αἱ δὲ τῶν ἀποικιῶν κατασκευαὶ κοινὸν
τῶν Ἑλλήνων κέρδος εἰσίν, οὐ μόνον τῶν ἀπελθόν-
των. καὶ γὰρ πόλεις καὶ χώρας καὶ δυνάμεις
πολλὰς καὶ μεγάλας εἰς τὸ κοινὸν προσέλαβον, ἐξ
73 ὧν οὐκ ὀλίγῳ μείζους ἐγένοντο. οὕτως ἐγώ φημι
τῆς πόλεως οὐχ ἧττον τὸ ἐκπέμψαι παρ' αὐτῆς ἢ
τὸ εἰσφρέσθαι[1] τοὺς δεηθέντας πρὸς τὴν παρὰ τῶν
Ἑλλήνων εἶναι χάριν. καὶ γάρ τοι συμβέβηκεν μόνοις τοῖς ταύτῃ καὶ διὰ τῶν ἐναντίων εὐδοκιμεῖν. οἱ
γὰρ αὐτοὶ πρεσβύτατοι τῶν ἄλλων Ἑλλήνων εἰσὶν
καὶ εἰς νέους Ἕλληνας τελοῦσιν πολλαχῇ,[2] καθάπερ τὸν Διόνυσον γράφουσιν. ἐπελθόντες δὲ οὐδα-
μόθεν, ἀλλ' αὐτόθεν φύντες τοὺς πανταχόθεν πόλεως δεηθέντας ἐδέξαντο. καὶ μὴν δεξάμενοι τοὺς
ἀπανταχόθεν, πανταχῇ[3] καὶ πεπόμφασιν, σώζοντες
κἂν τούτοις τὸ προσῆκον ἑξῆς. καὶ γὰρ τῶν πρε-
σβυτάτων πλείστους εἶναι τοὺς ἀπογόνους εἰκός,[4]
καὶ μᾶλλον ἢ τινῶν ἄλλων καὶ τὸ δέχεσθαι τοὺς δεο-
74 μένους τῶν κρειττόνων ἐστίν. καὶ μὴν τῷ γε τὸν
σῖτον ἐν ἀρχῇ διανεῖμαι πῶς οὐκ εἰς ταὐτὸν ἥκει τὸ
186 D. καὶ τὰ τῶν ἀποικιῶν σμήνη διαπέμψαι καὶ κατοι-
κίσαι τὴν γῆν; ἄλλως τε καὶ ἐξουσίας ἤδη πᾶσιν
οὔσης ἐργάζεσθαι καὶ τὰ τοῦ βίου τίθεσθαι ῥᾶον
ἀφορμῆς ἕνεκα.
75 Ἐκδέχεται δ' ἡ πάλαι τοῦ λόγου προσδοκωμένη
μοῖρα, ὡς ἐμοὶ δοκεῖ, καὶ ὑπὸ πολλῶν, αἱ μετὰ τῶν
κινδύνων πράξεις, ἃς ἐγὼ δέδοικα μὴ τῷ λέγοντι

---

[1] Cobet : εἰσφέρεσθαι TQVA.
[2] πανταχῇ TQ.   [3] πανταχοῖ VA.

of public generosity, still one might say that it
benefited only those who experienced this kind of
fortune. But the establishment of the colonies was a
gain shared by all the Greeks, and not only by the
colonists. For they acquired to their common
advantage cities, lands and many great means of
power, from which they became not a little greater.
So I say that the city is owed no less thanks by the 73
Greeks for sending people from it than for taking in
those in need. And it has chanced that those here
alone are famous for quite opposite reasons. For
they are both the oldest of the Greek people and in
many places they can be classified as young Greeks,
like the portraits of Dionysus.[a] They arrived from
nowhere, but grew up on the spot, and they received
those from everywhere who were in need of a city.
And after they received those from everywhere, they
sent colonies everywhere, even in this act behaving
consistently. For it is likely that the eldest have
the greatest number of offspring ; and the reception
of those in need is the act of a people of superior
power rather than of anyone else. Indeed, the dis- 74
patch of swarms of colonies and the settling of the
land has the same significance as the original distribution of wheat, especially when all can work the
land, and it is easier as far as means are concerned
to provide for the requirements of life.

Now follows the part of the speech long expected, 75
I think, and by many too ; the deeds of daring,
which I fear may be more dangerous for the speaker

[a] Who was represented as a young or mature person ; *cf.*
xli. 5, 13.

---

4 distinxit Oliver.

(186 D.)

κίνδυνον ἔχωσιν εἰπεῖν μᾶλλον ἢ τῇ πόλει τῶν ἔργων ὅτε ἐπραγματεύετο. οὐ μὴν ἀλλ' ἀναγκαῖον ἅψασθαι καὶ τούτων ἤδη δυοῖν ἕνεκα, ἑνὸς μὲν ὅτι τῶν ἀπὸ τῆς εἰρήνης ἀγαθῶν καὶ οἷς κατεσκεύασεν τὸν βίον ἡμῖν ἀποχρώντως μνημονεύσαντας εἰκὸς ἦν δήπου καὶ τὰς ἐπὶ τῶν ἑτέρων καιρῶν πράξεις μὴ παρελθεῖν, ἄλλως τε καὶ πλείους μὲν ἢ τὰς τῶν ἄλλων συμπάντων, μείζους δὲ ἁπασῶν οὔσας ὧν παρειλήφαμεν· ἑτέρου δ' ὅτι συμπίπτει τῇ πάσῃ φιλανθρωπίᾳ τῆς πόλεως, ἣν ἄρτι διεξιόντες ἐπαυσάμεθα, ὁ τῶν ἔργων τῶν ἐν τοῖς πολέμοις ἐξετασμός, ὥσθ' ἡμῖν πάλιν ἀρχὴν ἐκ τελευτῆς ἐπανήκειν.

76 σχεδὸν μὲν οὖν οὐδὲ τὰς ἀποικίας εὕροι τις ἂν τοῦτο τὸ μέρος τῶν λόγων διαπεφευγυίας. οὐ γὰρ ἄνευ μεγάλων ἀγώνων οὐδὲ τοῦ πανταχοῦ κρατεῖν οὐδ' αὗται δήπου συνέβησαν.

77 Ἐπάνειμι δ' ὅθεν ἐπαυσάμην. οὐ τοίνυν μόνον ταῖς ἄλλαις δωρεαῖς οὐδὲ τῇ τῶν καταφευγόντων δήπου θεραπείᾳ καὶ προστασίᾳ, οὐδ' οἷς, ὡς εἴπομεν, ηὔξησε τὸ Ἑλληνικὸν τῆς εἰς πάντας ἀρετῆς καὶ μεγαλοψυχίας ἐναργῆ δείγματα ἐξήνεγκεν ἡ πόλις ἡμῖν, ἀλλ' οὐδείς ἐστιν ἀγὼν ὅτου δεῆσαν ὤκνησεν,

187 D. ἀλλ' ἀμείνων περὶ τοὺς δεηθέντας ἢ 'κεῖνοι συνεβούλοντο ἐγένετο.

78 ἀφ' ὧν δ' ἠρξάμεθ' ἀρτίως τὴν ὅλην φιλανθρωπίαν ἐξετάζειν, ταῦθ' ἡμῖν καὶ νῦν τῆς ἐπὶ τῶν ἀγώνων ἀρχέτω, τοὺς σὺν Εὐρυσθεῖ Πελοποννησίους μεθ' ὅσου τοῦ κρείττονος ἠμύνατο ὑπὲρ τῶν Ἡρακλειδῶν καὶ τὸ πρᾶγμα ὡς μετέθηκεν. ὃν γὰρ οὐ πόλις, οὐκ ἀνήρ, οὐ γένος οὐδὲν τῶν ἐν τοῖς Ἕλλησιν ὑφίστατο, καὶ ᾧ τοσοῦτον περιῆν ὥστ' ἀπειλεῖν ἀπειλὰς κοινὰς τοῖς τε Ἡρακλέους παισὶ καὶ ταῖς πόλεσι, τοῖς μέν, εἰ φανήσονται, ταῖς

than for the city when the acts were performed. However, it is necessary to touch on these also for two reasons : first because after we covered the goods of peace and the means by which the city sufficiently provided for our way of life, we ought not to omit the deeds committed in the other circumstances, especially since they are more numerous than those of all other peoples put together, and greater than all the deeds of which we have reports; second, because when its acts in war are examined, they are found in agreement with all the generosity of the city which we just now recounted, so that after concluding this subject we have returned to our starting point. Nor would one in general find the 76 colonies excluded from this part of the argument. For surely even these were not established without great contests and victory everywhere.

But I shall return to the point where I left off. 77 The city not only has presented clear proofs to us of its virtue and generosity to all by its other gifts, and by its care and protection of those who sought refuge with it, and by the acts in which, as we said, it increased the Greek race, but there was no necessary contest which it shirked, but it behaved better toward those in need than they requested. But let us 78 now start at the point where we began to examine its generosity as a whole, that war-time act, its great superiority against Eurystheus and the Pelopon- [Legend.] nesians in defence of the Heraclidae and its disposition of the affair. For here was a man whom no city, no man, none of the Greek peoples resisted, and who was so strong that he made threats against both the children of Heracles and the cities, against the one if they should be seen again and against the

(187 D.)

δέ, εἰ δέξονται,[1] τοῦτον εἰς τοῦτ' ἤγαγεν ὥστ' αὐτὸν
οἴκοι ταφῆς μὴ τυχεῖν, καὶ τῆς ἐξουσίας, ἧς παρ'
ἀξίαν ἀπέλαυσεν Εὐρυσθεύς, τὴν τελευτὴν ἡ πόλις
79 εὗρεν κατ' ἀξίαν. καὶ τοῦτ' ἄρ' ἐκεῖνος ἐν καιρῷ
μόνον ὕβρισεν· τοῖς γὰρ ὑπάρχουσι θαρρήσας ἔδωκε
δίκην. καὶ τοῦτο μὲν ἐν τῇ Ἀττικῇ τὸ ἔργον
ἐκρίθη, καὶ διὰ τῆς τῶν ἱκετευσάντων σωτηρίας
ἅπασαν τὴν Πελοπόννησον ἠλευθέρωσεν, τοσούτῳ
χεῖρον ἐκείνων διακειμένην ὅσῳ τοῖς μὲν μὴ καταφεύγειν ἀπορρηθέν, τοῖς δὲ μὴ δέχεσθαι, οἱ μὲν διὰ
τῆς πόλεως ἄδειαν εὕροντο, οἱ δ' οὐκ εἶχον ὅπως
μὴ ποιήσωσι τὸ κελευόμενον.

80 Ἕτερον δὲ πρὸ τούτων ἐν μέσῃ τῇ Βοιωτίᾳ τῆς
πόλεως ἔργον γίγνεται, καὶ μάλα[2] μέντοι τῆς
188 D. πόλεως, ὃ τῷ μὲν ἀκοῦσαι καὶ τῇ χρείᾳ τῶν ἱκετῶν
ὑπὲρ Ἀργείων οἱ τότε ἔπραξαν, τῇ δ' ἀληθείᾳ καὶ
τῷ σχήματι τῆς εὐεργεσίας ὑπὲρ τῆς φύσεως ἁπάσης
τῆς ἀνθρωπείας κατεπράχθη. ὡς γὰρ ἤκουσαν
τοὺς ὑπὸ τῇ Καδμείᾳ δυστυχήσαντας ἀτάφους ἐρ-
ρίφθαι, οὐ φοβηθέντες τὴν ὕβριν τῶν ταῦτα τετολμη-
κότων οὐδ' οἷα βουλευομένοις[3] περὶ ὧν ἂν κρα-
τήσωσιν ἐπίασιν, ἀλλὰ τὴν μὲν τοῦ νικήσειν ἐλπίδα
τῷ συνειδότι τοῦ κρείττονος δόντες, τὴν δ' ὀργὴν
ὥσπερ ἂν αὐτοὶ πεπονθότες, οὕτω λαβόντες ὑπὲρ
τοῦ κοινοῦ νόμου πρέπουσαν τοῖς μὲν τὴν τιμήν,
τοῖς δὲ τὴν τιμωρίαν ἀπέδοσαν.

81 Καὶ μὴν αὐτὸ τοῦτο πρῶτον τὸ πάντας τοὺς ἐν

---

[1] distinxit Holleck.
[2] Reiske: τἆλλα TQVA ; ⟨κατὰ⟩ τἆλλα ci. Oliver.
[3] βουλομένοις TQA.

others if they should receive them. And the city brought Eurystheus so low that he did not obtain burial at home, and it found a proper means of ending the power which he improperly enjoyed. Thus that man committed this one crime oppor- 79 tunely. Though confident in his resources, he was punished. And this deed was judged in Attica, and through the preservation of the suppliants, it liberated the whole Peloponnesus, which was in a much worse condition than those men to the degree that, when the one was forbidden to seek refuge and the others to receive them, the former found freedom through the city, but the latter had no way of not obeying their orders.

There was another act of the city before this, in the 80 middle of Boeotia, indeed characteristic of the city, which the men of those days performed on behalf of the Argives, as far as tradition and the need of the suppliants was concerned ; but it was done in truth and in the nature of benefit on behalf of the whole human race. For when they heard that those who Legendary. had suffered misfortune beneath the Cadmea [a] were cast out unburied, they attacked, not fearing the criminal behaviour of the men who dared this act, or their plans for those whom they defeated. But leaving the expectation of victory to the conscience of what was right, and being enraged in defence of universal law, as if they themselves had been the victims, to the Argives they paid a proper honour, and to the others a proper punishment.

First then, the very fact that all men in need of 81

[a] [Not in the historical event of 382 B.C. but in the legendary story of the Seven against Thebes ; cf. Euripides' *Suppliant Women.—E.H.W.*]

(188 D.)

χρείᾳ βοηθείας καταφεύγειν ἐπὶ τὴν πόλιν ὥσπερ ἐκ
δυοῖν ποδοῖν ὡς ἀληθῶς καὶ μηδεμίαν τῶν ἄλλων
πόλεων ὁρᾶν μέγα καὶ φανερὸν σύμβολόν ἐστιν καὶ
στήλης ἄμεινον τοῦ προέχειν εὐθὺς ἐξ ἀρχῆς, οὐχ[1]
ὅσον λανθάνειν, καὶ μαρτύριόν γε δυοῖν τοῖν καλ-
λίστοιν ἀνδρείας καὶ φιλανθρωπίας, εἰ δὲ βούλει,
λέγω δικαιοσύνης ἀντὶ τῆς φιλανθρωπίας. ὥσπερ
γὰρ κήρυκες ἅπαντες οὗτοι περὶ αὐτῆς γεγόνασιν
καὶ τὴν ἀνάρρησιν ἀπ᾽ αὐτῶν τῶν ἔργων πεποίηνται,
μήτε μέλειν τισὶ τοῦ δικαίου μᾶλλον τῶν Ἀθηναίων
μήτε ἀμείνους εἶναι κωλύειν ὅσα ἂν ἔξω τοῦ καλοῦ
γίγνηται, ἀλλ᾽ εἶναι τὰς μὲν ἄλλας πόλεις τῆς

189 D. Ἀθηναίων δεομένας αὐτὰς ἐφ᾽ αὑτῶν ἀριθμὸν πλη-
ρούσας τῇ Ἑλλάδι, τὴν δ᾽ ὡς ἀληθῶς ὥσπερ πόλιν
ἐν χωρίοις ἀνέχουσαν ὁμοίαν τῇ κατασκευῇ καὶ τοῖς
λογισμοῖς, τῶν μὲν τὰ δίκαια τιμώντων ὀχυρωτέραν,
τῶν δὲ τὰς δυνάμεις ἐχόντων ἐπιεικεστέραν, μᾶλλον
δὲ τῶν μὲν τὰ δίκαια τιμώντων ἀκριβεστέραν εἰς
αὐτὸν τὸν τοῦ δικαίου λόγον, τῶν δὲ[2] ἐπὶ τοῦ βιάζεσθαι δυνατωτέραν εἰς τέλος· ὥστ᾽ ἄμφω τὼ γένη
δι᾽ ἀμφοῖν νικᾶν.

82 Ταυτὶ μὲν οὖν κοινὰ δείγματα, ὅπερ εἶπον, ἀνδρείας τε καὶ φιλανθρωπίας ὑπαρχέτω τῶν ἀρχαίων
ἐξειλεγμένα. ἀλλὰ μὴν ἅ γε ὑπὲρ τῆς οἰκείας ἐπεδείξαντο πρὸς τοὺς ἑκάστοτε ἐπιόντας ἀνήκοος μὲν
οὐδεὶς οἶμαι, λεκτέον δὲ καὶ τούτων μικρὰ προ-
83 χειρισαμένους. Ἀμαζόσι μὲν γάρ, αἳ παρῆλθον τοῖς
ἔργοις τὴν φύσιν, ἱππομαχίαν συνάψαντες παν-
ωλεθρίᾳ διέφθειραν, οὐδενὸς ἀνταίροντος τῶν μέχρι
τῆς Ἀττικῆς, ἀλλ᾽ ἐξισώκεσαν[3] ἤδη τὰς ἠπείρους,

190 D. ὥσπερ ἀπὸ σημείου τοῦ Θερμώδοντος ὁρμώμεναι,

---

[1] οὐδ᾽ ci. Holleck.   [2] δὲ ⟨τὰς δυνάμεις ἐχόντων⟩ ci. Holleck.

help took refuge with the city, truly " as fast as they could," and that they looked to no other city, is a great and certain proof, better than any monument, that the city was preeminent, and quite clearly so, right from the start. And it is evidence of the two fairest qualities, courage and generosity, or if you wish, I will substitute justice instead of generosity. For all these men have been like heralds in respect to it and have declared from the deeds themselves that no one cares for justice more than the Athenians or is better able to prevent any impropriety, but that the other cities are in need of Athens, in themselves mere ciphers for Greece, but that this is truly like a city towering over the countryside, consistent in conduct and plan, more secure than those who honour justice, more decent than those who possess power, moreover more exact even in its definition of justice than those who honour justice, and in its accomplishment more powerful than those who can use force, so that it surpasses both groups in both ways.

Let these be proofs, chosen from ancient examples, 82 as I said, both of courage and of generosity. But no one, I think, has not heard of their conduct in behalf of their own land against whoever attacked them. Yet we must also select and discuss a small part of these stories. They fought a cavalry engagement 83 against the Amazons who surpassed their nature by [Legend.] their deeds, and they annihilated them, although no one up to Attica opposed them. Now they had extended their lines equally through both continents, beginning from Thermodon, as it were the centre

---

³ ἐξισώκεσαν μὲν TQ.

(190 D.)

τὴν μὲν ᾿Ασίαν μέχρι Λυκίας καὶ Καρίας καὶ
Παμφυλίας παρατείνουσαι, ὥσπερ ἐν¹ στρατοπέδῳ,
τὴν δ᾿ Εὐρώπην ἄχρι τοῦ στρατοπέδου τοῦ πρὸς
84 τὴν πόλιν. ἐντεῦθεν δὲ ἤδη πάντα ὥσπερ κάλω²
ῥαγέντος ἐχώρησεν ὀπίσω, καὶ διελέλυτο ᾿Αμαζόσιν
ἥ τε ἀρχὴ καὶ ὁ δρόμος, καὶ ἡ πόλις κἀνταῦθα
ἐβοήθησεν τῇ κοινῇ φύσει, καὶ νῦν εἰς ἄπιστον
περιέστηκεν εἴ ποτε ἐγένοντο.

85   Οἶμαι δ᾿ οὐδὲ Θρᾷκας αὐτοῖς³ μέμψασθαι τῆς
191 D. συμφορᾶς, οἳ δεῦρ᾿ ἔτι πρόσθεν ἐλθόντες σὺν
Εὐμόλπῳ καὶ Ἑλλήνων τοῖς τἀκείνων ἑλομένοις
ἔγνωσαν παραπλήσια βουλεύσαντες ὥσπερ ἂν εἰ τὴν
θάλατταν ἐνεχείρουν περαιοῦσθαι πεζῇ.

86   ῎Αξιον τοίνυν κἀκεῖνο προσθεῖναι, ὃ τοῖς πολλοῖς
τῶν εἰωθότων λέγειν ἐπὶ τῷ τάφῳ τῷ δημοσίῳ
παρεῖται, ὅτι οὐ μόνον ἡ κοινὴ τῆς πόλεως προθυμία
τε καὶ ῥώμη τοσαύτη περὶ πάντα ἃ δεῖ γεγένηται,
ἀλλὰ καὶ ἰδίᾳ πεφήνασιν ἐνταῦθα βουλόμενοί τινες
χρήσασθαι συμφοραῖς ὑπὲρ τοῦ κοινοῦ, καὶ μάλα
εὐλόγως. ᾧ γὰρ ἑώρων τρόπῳ τὴν πατρίδα τοῖς
῞Ελλησιν ὁμιλοῦσαν, τοῦτον⁴ ᾤοντο δεῖν αὐτοὶ προσ-
φέρεσθαι τῇ πατρίδι, ἡνίκα⁵ ὁ καιρὸς καλοίη· ὥστε
καὶ ἐκ τῶν κοινῶν καὶ ἐκ τῶν ἰδίων διπλῆν εἶναι τῇ
πόλει τὴν ὅλην φιλοτιμίαν. ὃ δέ γε ἔτι τούτου
μεῖζόν ἐστιν, ὅτι καὶ τῶν ξένων τινὲς οὕτω πρὸς
87 αὐτὴν διετέθησαν. λέγεται γὰρ ᾿Ερεχθεὺς μὲν ἐν
τῷ πρὸς Εὔμολπον τούτῳ πολέμῳ τὴν θυγατέρα
ὑπὲρ τῆς πόλεως ἐπιδοῦναι, τοῦ θεοῦ χρήσαντος,

---

¹ ἐνὶ ci. Reiske, ἓν στρατόπεδον ci. Keil.
² codd. dett.: κάλου TQVA.
³ Aldinae Q p. corr. (αὐ-): αὐταῖς TVA.
⁴ τούτῳ TQ.
⁵ Ddf.: ἡνίκ᾿ ἂν TQVA.

of a circle, and passing through Asia up to Lycia, Caria, and Pamphylia, as if part of their encampment, and through Europe up to their encampment at the city. But now from this point, as if a rope had 84 broken, all snapped back, and the Amazons' march of empire was undone. And here too the city aided the whole race, and now it is doubtful if the Amazons ever existed.

I think that not even the Thracians blame them- 85 selves for their misfortune. Still earlier they came here with Eumolpus [a] and those Greeks who took their part, and their plan was similar to attempting to walk across the sea.

The following point also should be added, one 86 which has been omitted in many of the traditional public funeral orations, that not only was the general enthusiasm and strength of the city far beyond all need, but that also privately some men there were seen willing to suffer misfortune on behalf of the common good, and this was quite reasonable. For they thought that they should comport themselves in the same way toward their country, whenever the occasion called, as they saw their country behave toward the Greeks. Therefore both publicly and privately the city has in sum a double reason for pride. Still more marvellous than this is the fact that certain foreigners were also so disposed toward the city. Erechtheus is said in this war against 87 Eumolpus to have given his daughter in behalf of [Legend.] the city because of the God's oracle ; and her mother

---

[a] Legendary leader of the Thracians, who were summoned by the Eleusinians in their war against Athens. He was slain by Erechtheus.

(191 D.)

προσαγαγεῖν δ' αὐτὴν κοσμήσασα ἡ μήτηρ ὥσπερ
192 D. εἰς θεωρίαν πέμπουσα· Λεὼς δὲ ὅμοια τούτῳ βου-
λεύσας, ἐκστῆναι τῶν θυγατέρων καὶ οὗτος ἐν τῷ
λοιμῷ· Κόδρος δὲ ἐν τῷ πρὸς Δωριέας πολέμῳ καὶ
Πελοποννησίους αὐτὸς ἐθελοντὴς ὑπὲρ τῆς χώρας
ἀποθανεῖν. ὥστε καὶ οἷς τοιαῦτα ὑπάρχει τῶν
σφετέρων διηγήσασθαι, καὶ τούτοις μηδὲν εἶναι
πλέον εἰπεῖν τῶν παρ' ὑμῖν,[1] ἀλλὰ καὶ τῶν τοιούτων
ἔργων ἄρχειν τὴν πόλιν διὰ τοσούτων καὶ ἔτι
πλειόνων τῶν παραδειγμάτων, καὶ μηδεμίαν λείπεσθαι μήτε κοινὴν ὑπερβολὴν μήτ' ἰδίαν.

88   Οὐ τοίνυν τῶν μὲν ἄλλων οὐδὲ καθ' ἓν ἡττᾶσθαι
τῇ πόλει συμβέβηκεν, οὐδὲ τῶν πολεμίων ὅσων[2] εἶπον κεκρατηκέναι, τῶν δὲ παρ' αὐτῇ ταῦτα γνόντων
ὑπὲρ αὐτῆς ἀπολειφθῆναι περὶ τὴν χάριν, ἀλλὰ καὶ
193 D. τούτους ταῖς εὐεργεσίαις νενικηκυῖα φανήσεται,
Κόδρῳ μὲν δοῦσα τὴν ἀρχὴν εἰς τοὺς παῖδας καὶ
κοσμήσασα καὶ παρ' αὐτῇ κἂν τῇ ὑπερορίᾳ τὸ γένος,
τῶν δὲ κορῶν ἱερὰ ἱδρυσαμένη καὶ θείας μοίρας ἀντὶ
θνητῆς ἀξιώσασα ταῖς τιμαῖς, Ἐρεχθέα δὲ τοῖς ἐν
ἀκροπόλει θεοῖς πάρεδρον ἀποδείξασα.

89   Καὶ ταῦτα μὲν ἡμῖν εἰς τοσοῦτον ἀνήχθω τοῦ λόγου, δείγματα τῆς τε πρὸς τοὺς ἔξωθεν φιλανθρωπίας
τῶν προγόνων καὶ τῆς ὑπὲρ αὐτῶν εὐψυχίας ἐν τοῖς
ἐπείγουσιν, καὶ αὖ τῶν[3] ἐπιφανῶν τε καὶ πολλῶν
194 D. ὡς ἀλλήλοις[4] ὡμίλουν. χρὴ δὲ καὶ τῶν λοιπῶν ἴσως
καθ' ὅσον ἐγχωρεῖ μνησθῆναι, ἐπισκοποῦντας τά θ'

[1] codd. dett. : ἡμῖν TQVA.
[2] codd. dett. : ὅσον VA, οἷς TQ.
[3] codd. dett. : αὐτῶν TQVA.
[4] ἀλλήλους VA.

---

[a] Codrus was traditionally the last king at Athens.

is said to have led her forth after adorning her as if for a festival. And Leos is said to have reached the same resolve, in a time of plague : to abandon his daughters. And Codrus [a] is said in the war against [C. 1100.] the Dorians and Peloponnesians voluntarily to have died on behalf of his land. Therefore even those people who can tell of such acts of their fellow citizens can say nothing more than what you have done, but the city initiated such acts through its great and still more numerous examples, and was wanting neither publicly nor privately in extremes of patriotism.

Then it has befallen to the city not to be inferior 88 to other peoples even in a single respect, nor when it defeated all the enemies whom I named, to have been deficient in gratitude to those who on its side made these resolves on its behalf. But it will also appear to have surpassed its benefactors in its benefits : in respect to Codrus by having given office [b] to his sons and by having honoured his race at home and abroad ; and for the daughters, by having established a temple for them, and by having thought them worthy of the honour of a divine instead of a mortal portion ; and by having given Erechtheus a share in the ceremonies of the Gods on the Acropolis.

And let us carry this argument so far, as an 89 example of the generosity of your ancestors toward foreigners and their courage in their behalf in times of need, and again of the relations between the nobility and the people. But perhaps we should also mention the rest, as far as possible, and review both

[b] One of his sons, Medon, became Archon at Athens, another, Neleus, led a colony to Miletus.

(194 D.)

ὑπὲρ τῶν ἄλλων καταπραχθέντα καὶ ὅσα ὑπὲρ τῆς
οἰκείας ὑπέστησαν, ὅπως ἂν συμπίπτῃ τῷ λόγῳ
τοῦ μὴ πολὺ τὰς πράξεις τῷ χρόνῳ παρενεγκεῖν.
ἔξεστι δ' ἀκούοντας ἐπ' αὐτῶν τῶν ἔργων διαιρεῖν
90 τά τε κοινὰ καὶ τὰ ἴδια. εἰ μὲν οὖν περὶ ἄλλης
τινὸς ἦν πόλεως ὁ λόγος, οὐκ ἂν ἦν παρελθεῖν ἃς
νῦν δεήσει πράξεις, ἀλλὰ μόνας ἂν ταύτας ἀπέχρησεν
εἰπεῖν· εἰσὶ γὰρ οἵας ἄν τις ἐζήτησεν, καὶ πολλοὶ
πολλῶν ἂν χρημάτων, εἰ δύναιντο, πρίαιντο αὐτοῖς
εἶναι. νῦν δ' ἐξ ἴσου καθεστῶτος τοῦ θ' εὑρεῖν ἃ
χρὴ παραλιπεῖν καὶ τοῦ πρὸς ἀξίαν εἰπεῖν τὰ νικήσαντα, καὶ οὐδενὸς μὲν οὐδ' ἐν ἁπλῇ διηγήσει πάντα
πω διεξελθόντος, πλεῖστα δ' ὑπὲρ μιᾶς πόλεως
ταύτης ἁπάντων εἰρηκότων, μᾶλλον δ' ὑπὲρ μόνης
πλείω σχεδὸν ἢ τῶν ἄλλων ἁπασῶν, οὐκ ἐνδέχεται
διεξιέναι καθ' ἕκαστον ἀκριβῶς, ἀλλ' ἀνάγκη τὰ
πλεῖστα παραλιπεῖν, ἵνα τοῖς μεγίστοις χρησώμεθα.

91 Ἐπεὶ τίς οὐκ ἂν ἀσμένως[1] καὶ ταῦτα εἰς μέσον
ἤνεγκεν ἃ ἑτέροις γ' ἂν ἧρκει καὶ μόνα; τριῶν γὰρ
195 D. ἐθνῶν τῶν μεγίστων ἐν τοῖς Ἕλλησιν ἐπιθεμένων
τῇ πόλει, τὸ μὲν αὐτῷ φυγῆς τιμήσαν ἀπῆλθεν, τὸ
Δωρικόν, Βοιωτοὶ δὲ χερσὶν ἡττῶντο, καὶ τῆς αὐτῆς
ἡμέρας Εὐβοεῖς ἐν Εὐβοίᾳ· τοσοῦτον περιῆν τῇ
πόλει.

92 Ἀλλ' ἵνα μὴ πολλὰ τοιαῦτα λέγων πόρρω τοῦ
καιροῦ γένωμαι, παρεὶς ἅπαν τὸ μέσον καὶ προσχρησάμενος καὶ πρὸς αὐτό γε τοῦτο τῇ τῆς πόλεως
μεγαλοψυχίᾳ καὶ δὴ πρὸς αὐτὰ τὰ κύρια τοῦ λόγου
τρέψομαι. ὅτε γὰρ τοῖς Ἕλλησιν καὶ βαρβάροις[2]

---

[1] ἄσμενος TQV Phot.
[2] τοῖς βαρβάροις TQ.

[a] Cf. Herodotus V. 74-78.

what was done on behalf of others and all that they
endured on behalf of their own country, but in such
a way that in my speech the accounts of their deeds
do not take an excessive time. In the discussion of
these actions the audience can define between
those which were for the whole race and those for the
city. Then if the speech were about some other city, 90
it would not be possible to omit the deeds which will
have to be omitted, but it would have been enough
to mention these alone. For they are the sort for
which one would have searched ; and many, if it
were possible, would pay much to buy them as their
own. But now since it is equally difficult to choose
what must be omitted and to discuss properly the
best material, and since no one even in a simple
narrative has ever recounted everything, but all
speakers have had very much to say on behalf of
this single city, moreover nearly more on behalf of
it alone than on behalf of all the others together, a
detailed account of each individual act is impossible,
but it is necessary to omit most things, so that we
may employ what is the greatest.

Who would not gladly proclaim these deeds, 91
which alone would be enough for another people ?
For when the three greatest tribes in Greece attacked 506.
the city,[a] one of them, the Dorian, departed self-
condemned to flee, and the Boeotians were defeated
in combat, as well as the Euboeans on the same day
in Euboea. By so much did the city excel them.

But so as not to overrun my time by mentioning 92
many such actions, I shall omit all that intervenes,
acting in this respect with the openhandedness of the
city, and turn to the primary portion of the speech.
For when the trial between the Greeks and bar- 490–479.

(195 D.)

τὰ πράγματα ἐκρίνετο καὶ μικρὸν πρὸς πολὺ τῆς
γῆς μέρος ἠγωνίζετο, ὁ δ' ἀγὼν ἦν ὑπὲρ τῆς
σωτηρίας ἅμα καὶ ἀρετῆς, τότ' ἐνίκησεν ἡ πόλις
ἄμφω τὼ γένη κάλλιον εὐχῆς, ὡς τὸ μὲν προσθήκην

196 D. μικρὰν αὐτῆς ἀποφανθῆναι, τὸ δὲ πλέον χεῖρον ἢ
93 ὅσῳ πλεῖον ἐδόκει. ἔξεστι μὲν οὖν καὶ θεῶν τινα
αἰτιάσασθαι τοῦ παντὸς ἔργου βουλόμενον ὥσπερ
κρίσιν τινὰ ποιήσασθαι τῶν ὑφ' αὑτῶν ἀνθρώπων
καὶ τὸν ἀγῶνα τοῦτον διαθεῖναι, καθάπερ τοὺς
εἰωθότας ἡμεῖς, οὐ μὴν ἀλλ' οὐκ ἐλάχιστον μέρος ἡ
τῆς πόλεως ἀρετὴ συνεβάλετο,[1] καὶ μάλ' εἰκότως
καὶ μετ' ἀξίου τοῦ λόγου τῆς μελλούσης τύχης.
ὥσπερ γὰρ ἐπὶ τούτῳ κινοῦσα τοὺς βαρβάρους, ἵν'
αὐτήν[2] τε καὶ πᾶν τὸ Ἑλληνικὸν ἐκφήνειε[3] καὶ
δείξειε[4] τίς οὖσα τίνων προέστηκεν, οὕτως ἐφειλ-
κύσατο αὐτούς, οὐκ ἄδικον τὴν ἀρχὴν παρασχομένη
οὐδ', ὥσπερ οἱ ὕστερον διαβάντες εἰς τὴν Ἀσίαν,
ἔρωτι τοῦ πλείονος, ἀλλ' ἤδη τότε ἀμυνομένη καὶ
δίκην ἀξιοῦσα λαβεῖν τῶν ἐν τῇ ἠπείρῳ ⟨τῇ⟩[5] τῶν
Ἰώνων δεδουλωμένων Ἑλλήνων, οὓς μόνη μὲν ἐδέξατο φθειρομένους κατὰ πᾶσαν τὴν Ἑλλάδα, μόνη

94 δὲ εἰς τὸ δέον κατέστησε. καὶ πρῶτοι δὴ τῶν εἰς
ἐκεῖνον τὸν χρόνον Ἑλλήνων ἀναβάντες εἰς Σάρδεις
στρατιᾷ κοινῇ πορθήσαντες ᾤχοντο· τέως δὲ ἐν
Βαβυλῶνος τάξει καὶ τῶν ἐν Ἰνδοῖς Ἕλληνες Σάρδεις ἐθαύμαζον.

95

197 D. Λαβὼν δὲ ταύτην πρόφασιν Δαρεῖος ἡσυχίαν ἄγειν
οὐκ ἠδύνατο, ἀλλ' ἐξήταζεν τὴν ἀρχὴν καὶ τὰς
δυνάμεις συνεκρότει, καὶ πᾶν μικρὸν ἦν αὐτῷ. καὶ

---

[1] συνεβάλετο VA.   [2] αὐτήν T a. corr. VA.
[3] ἐκφήνῃ TQ.   [4] ἀποδείξῃ TQ.   [5] τῇ add. Reiske.

---

[a] [In Asia Minor, conquered by Cyrus the Persian. In

74

barians occurred and a small part of the world contended against much of it, and the contest was a matter of both self-preservation and virtue, then the city was superior to both races in a way fairer than could be hoped for, so that the Greek race appeared as a small appendage to it, and the larger race of the barbarians appeared worse to the degree that it seemed larger. Some God can also be named 93 as responsible for the whole deed, who wished to hold a kind of trial over the men beneath him and to arrange this contest, just as we arrange our customary contests. However, the virtue of the city was not the least contributor to the war, and indeed this was reasonable and worthy of coming fortune. For as if it were goading the barbarians to this, so that it might reveal itself and all the Greek race and show who it was and whom it championed, in this way it attracted them, not unjustly starting the affair, nor *c.* 479. because of greed like those who later crossed over to 400. Asia, but in its own defence and in the belief that it should avenge those Greeks [a] who had been enslaved 546–545. in Ionia, whom the city alone received when they were perishing throughout Greece and whom it alone restored to their rightful state. And first of the *C.* 497. Greeks till then, they went up to Sardis, and left, 94 having sacked it with their common force. Before, the Greeks marvelled at Sardis as if it were to be ranked with Babylon and the wonders of India.

But Darius, with this excuse, could not keep still, 95 but he searched through his empire and marshalled 490. his forces, and all was easy for him. His pretext

c. 497 some Athenians, helping the Ionians in Asia Minor to revolt, penetrated to Sardis. If " because of greed " alludes to the Spartans' act in 400 B.C., it is very unfair.—*E.H.W.*]

(197 D.)

τὸ μὲν πρόσχημα τοῦτο ἦν ἀμύνασθαι Ἀθηναίους
καὶ Ἐρετριέας· παρενθήκην γὰρ τοὺς Ἐρετριέας
ἐποιήσατο, ἵνα δὴ πιστὸν ᾖ. δύο δ' ὡς ἀληθῶς ἦν
τὰ κινοῦντα, ἓν μὲν δὴ[1] φόβος καὶ ὑποψία τῆς
πόλεως μὴ ἄρα οὐδὲν ἀποχρῆν ἀξιώσῃ· ἕτερον δ'
ἐπιθυμία καὶ πόθος αὐξῆσαι τὴν ἀρχὴν ἐνδόξῳ
προσθήκῃ τῇ τοῦ Ἑλληνικοῦ καὶ τῆς γῆς μὴ διηρ-
96 ημένως ἄρχειν, ἀλλὰ καὶ πάσης. τοῦτο δ' οὐ παντάπασιν ἀνέλπιστον ἦν αὐτῷ, διὰ πλῆθος τῶν ἤδη
δεδουλωμένων ἐθνῶν, ἃ καὶ ὀνομαστὶ[2] γνωρίσαι
φιλοτιμίαν εἶχεν καὶ ψιλῇ πορείᾳ διελθεῖν ἐλπίδος
κρεῖττον ἦν. πάντα γὰρ τότε Πέρσαις εἵπετο, ὥσπερ ἄλλως ζῆν οὐ δυνάμενα. ἔχων δ', ὡς εἶπον,
μέσην τινὰ τοῦ τε φόβου καὶ τῆς ἐπιθυμίας ἦλθεν.
αὐτὸς μὲν γὰρ ἀπέγνω μὴ διαβαίνειν, τὰ δ' ἔθνη
97 πέμπειν ἐπενόει. καὶ πρῶτον μὲν ἡ τῶν κηρύκων
περίοδος ἡ γιγνομένη κατὰ τὴν Ἑλλάδα ὑπ' ἐκείνου τε καὶ τοῦ μετ' ἐκεῖνον βασιλέως περὶ τῆς γῆς
καὶ τοῦ ὕδατος ἀπὸ ταύτης τῆς πόλεως ἤρχετο,
καὶ πάντα πρὸς ταύτην διελέγοντο· ἔν τε ταῖς
ἐπιστολαῖς ταῖς Ἑλληνικαῖς καὶ ὅσαι πυκναὶ
τοῖς ὑπάρχοις[3] ᾖσαν οὐδὲν ἦν ὅτι μὴ Ἀθῆναι, ὡς
ταὐτὸν ὂν εἰπεῖν τὴν Ἀθηναίων πόλιν καὶ τὴν
Ἑλλάδα, καὶ οὐκ εἰπεῖν μόνον, ἀλλὰ καὶ ἔργῳ
συμβαῖνον πάσας ἔχειν τὰς πόλεις, εἴ τις κατάσχοι
98 ταύτην. καὶ μὴν ὅσα γε αὖ τούτοις ἔδει χρήσασθαι
καὶ προβουλεῦσαι περὶ τῶν ὅλων, ἅπαντα ἡ πόλις
198 D. ἐξήταζεν, ἀπ' ἀρχῆς προτάξασα τῶν Ἑλλήνων
ἑαυτήν. καὶ διχόθεν ἤδη ἀπὸ Περσῶν καὶ Ἀθηναίων συνεκροτεῖτο ὁ πόλεμος, τοῦ μὲν ἀπειλοῦντος

---

[1] δὴ TQ : φόβος ἤδη VA.
[2] Reiske : ὀνόματι TQVA.
[3] ἐπάρχοις TQ.

was that he was defending himself against the Athenians and Eretrians.[a] For he added the Eretrians, to make the excuse plausible. But two things really moved him : first, a fear and suspicion of the city, that it might never be satisfied ; and second, a desire and a longing to increase his empire by the glorious addition of the Greek race and to rule over not a part of the earth, but the whole of it. This was not at all a hopeless venture for him because 96 of the many races already enslaved, to know whose names was a source of pride, and to traverse their countries in a simple journey beyond hope. For then all followed the Persians, as if life were otherwise impossible. But he took, as I said, a middle course between fear and desire. For he himself despaired of making the crossing, but he contrived to send the barbarian nations. And first of all, 97 heralds were sent throughout Greece by him and the king who succeeded him for earth and water,[b] and they began with this city, and all their words were in regard to it : both in their letters to the Greeks and all those to the kings' lieutenants there was nothing except Athens, as if the city of the Athenians and Greece meant the same, and not only meant the same, but that one would in fact come to hold all Greek cities, if he should possess this city. The city 98 also considered all matters, what means they must employ and devise for the whole situation, and at the start placed itself at the head of the Greeks. And now both sides prepared for war, the Persians and the Athenians, the one with threats and attempts,

[a] Eretria (in Euboea island) as well Athens had helped in the Ionian revolt.
[b] Traditional symbols of surrender.

(198 D.)

καὶ πειρωμένου, τῆς δ᾽ ἀνθεστηκυίας καὶ νικώσης
εὐθὺς ταῖς ἀποκρίσεσιν. καὶ παρ᾽ ἀμφοτέρων τούτων ἐμαρτυρεῖτο ὅτι ᾿Αθηναίων καὶ Περσῶν ἐστιν
ὁ πόλεμος περὶ τῆς ῾Ελλάδος, τῶν μὲν λαβεῖν πει-
99 ρωμένων, τῶν δὲ κωλῦσαι. ἐν ἐκείνοις μέντοι τοῖς
καιροῖς ἔργα λόγων ἡττήθη—λέγω δὲ τὰ τῶν ἄλλων
ἔργα λόγων τῶν παρ᾽ ὑμῖν[1]—καὶ ψήφισμα τροπαίου
κρεῖττον εἰς μνήμην ἐνίκησεν ἅμα λόγῳ καὶ ἔργῳ
νικῆσαν. εὐθὺς γὰρ ἐν χεροῖν κύριον ἦν οὐ τῇ
χειροτονίᾳ μόνον, ὡς νόμος, ἀλλὰ καὶ τῷ διαφθεῖραι
τοὺς ἀγγέλους. τῷ δ᾽ ἑρμηνεύσαντι τὰ γράμματα
διαχειροτονίαν μὲν ἀπέδοσαν, ἵν᾽, ἐπειδήπερ ῞Ελλην
ἦν, ἔχοι[2] πλέον τὴν τῆς κρίσεως εἰκόνα, ἀπέκτειναν
δὲ καὶ τοῦτον, ὡς οὐδ᾽ ἄχρι φωνῆς διακονῆσαι
προσῆκον τοῖς βαρβάροις. καὶ τὸ ἰσχυρὸν περιῆλθεν
αὐτῷ. τὸν γὰρ τῆς πόλεως ἄποικον οὐκ ἠξίουν
κατὰ τῆς πόλεως καὶ τῶν ῾Ελλήνων ἑρμηνέα τῷ
φύσει πολεμίῳ γίγνεσθαι. καὶ οὕτω δὴ ῥίπτουσιν
199 D. εἰς τὸ βάραθρον, ὥστ᾽ ἄλλους ἀναγγεῖλαι τῷ βασιλεῖ
τὰς ἀποκρίσεις καὶ παρὰ τῶν πεμφθέντων μὴ ἐκγε-
100 νέσθαι μαθεῖν. ὁ δὲ δὴ καὶ δὴ λαμπρῶς ἐκινεῖτο,
καὶ τοῦτο μὲν τοῖς ὑπάρχοις ἐκέλευεν ἑτοιμάζειν
αὐτόθεν τὰς πέδας ὑπερβαλὼν ἢ καθ᾽ ὅσους ᾤετο
τοὺς ᾿Αθηναίους εἶναι, ἵνα δὴ μηδεὶς ἄδετος αὐτῶν
διαφύγοι, καὶ τῆς ὀργῆς ἀπολαύων ἕως ἐξῆν, τοῦτο

---

[1] ἡμῖν TQ Phot.   [2] ἔχῃ TQ.

[a] For the messengers cf. Herodotus VII. 133; for the
interpreter, Plutarch, *Themistocles* 6. 2. The latter event is
confused with an incident (481 B.C.) in the early stages of
Xerxes' attack; cf. § 125 and iii. 229 (p. 247 Ddf.) and A.
Haas, *Quibus Fontibus Aelius Aristides in componenda
declamatione quae inscribitur* πρὸς Πλάτωνα ὑπὲρ τῶν

the other with resistance and with a victory straight away in its replies. Both parties attest that the war between the Athenians and Persians was for Greece, the one side attempting to seize it, the other to prevent them. Moreover, in those times 99 deeds were less than words, I mean the deeds of the others were less than your words—and, greater than a trophy, a decree achieved the status of a memorial, supreme both in word and deed. For at the start the city acted with authority, not only constitutionally by its vote, but also by its execution of the messengers.[a] But they gave to the interpreter of the letters the right of having a vote taken, so that, since he was a Greek, he might have more of the appearance of a trial ; yet they slew him too, since serving the barbarians was wrong, even if only in the use of one's voice. And his reason for confidence betrayed him. For they did not think that a colonist from the city should become an interpreter for their natural enemy against the interests of the city and the Greeks. And therefore they flung them into the pit, so that others reported their replies to the king, and it was impossible to learn of them from those who were sent. But he was notice- 100 ably moved, and ordered his lieutenants to prepare fetters on the spot, increasing their number beyond what he thought the population of Athens to be, so that none of them might escape unchained, and he enjoyed his anger while he could. And he gave

τεττάρων, *usus sit*, Diss. Greifswald, 1884, pp. 21-22. The " decree " apparently is not the famous one proposed at Athens by Miltiades—that the Athenians should march to Marathon and fight the Persians who had landed near that place.

(199 D.)

101 δὲ τοῖς πλήθεσιν ἄλλα[1] ἄλλοις ἐπέταττεν. ἐκ δὲ
τούτου κήρυκες μὲν οὐκέτι ἐφοίτων εἰς τὴν Ἑλλάδα,
αὐτάγγελον δὲ ἤδη κατέπεμπε τὸν στόλον, προστή-
σας ἄρχοντας Περσῶν τοὺς ἀρίστους, καὶ δίδωσι
πλῆθος στρατιᾶς, οὗ τὸ διαλλάττον παρ' ἑκάστους
τοὺς ἀφηγουμένους τοσοῦτόν ἐστιν ὥστ' εἶναι τὸν
μέγιστον ὅρον στόλου, βουλόμενος μηδεμίαν πρόφασιν λιπεῖν μήτ' ἐκείνοις μήτ' αὐτὸς αὑτῷ τὸ μὴ οὐ
πρᾶξαι περὶ ὧν ἐνετέλλετο. ταῦτα δ' ἦν τὴν μὲν
πόλιν καταποντίσαι, τὸ δὲ φῦλον κομίζειν ἅπαν ὡς

102 αὑτὸν[2] ᾧ δὴ προειρήκειν[3] τῷ σχήματι. θυμοῦ μὲν δὴ
καὶ παρασκευῆς οὕτως εἶχεν τὰ τοῦ βασιλέως, οἱ
δ' ἐφέροντο ὑπερηχοῦντες μὲν τὸν Αἰγαῖον, ἀποστε-
ροῦντες δὲ τὴν ὄψιν τοὺς ἐντυγχάνοντας, φυγῆς δ'
ἐμπιμπλάντες τὴν θάλατταν· ὥστ' οὐδεὶς ἦν ὅστις
νῆσον τότ' ἂν οἰκεῖν ἐβούλετο.[4] ἔτι δ' αὐτοῖς οὖσιν
ἐν πλῷ καὶ μικρὸν πρὸ τῆς καταγωγῆς ἔδοξεν

200 D. ἀπάρξασθαι τοῖς τοῦ βασιλέως ἐπιτάγμασιν καὶ
ὥσπερ τι προοίμιον ᾆσαι τοῦ πολέμου· καὶ δόξαν
οὕτως Ἐρετριέας ἐπιβάντες ᾤχοντο φέροντες,

103 σαγήνην τινὰ μιμησάμενοι ναυτικήν. καὶ τὸ μὲν
Ἐρετριέων γένος οὕτως ἀνήρπαστο, οἱ δ' ἐπὶ τὸν
δεύτερον ᾖσαν, ὡς ἀνασπάσοντες αὐτοὺς ἤδη τοὺς
Ἀθηναίους καὶ τὴν Ἑλλάδα ἀναρπασόμενοι, ὥσπερ
οἱ παρ' ἄλλου τινὸς τῶν κρειττόνων [ἀναρπασθέν],[5]
κακῶς εἰδότες οἵαν θήραν μετέρχονται καὶ ὅτι οὐκ
ἐνέχονται τῷ λόγῳ ὡς ἄρα οὐ τὰ φεύγοντα διώκου-

104 σιν, ἀλλὰ μᾶλλον τὰ τῷ[6] διώκειν συνήθη. οὕτω
δὲ τούτων κεχωρηκότων καὶ φερομένων αὐτῶν πρὸς
τὴν ἤπειρον ὥσπερ ἄλλου τινὸς ἐκ τοῦ πελάγους

---

[1] codd. dett. : ἄλλη TQVA. [2] edd. : αὐτὸν TQVA.
[3] προειρήκει VA. [4] ἠβούλετο VA.

various orders to the other multitudes. After this 101
heralds no longer came to Greece, but he now sent
unannounced his expedition, having put in command
the best of the Persians, and he gave them an enormous army, whose number varies according to each
reporter so greatly, that this fact is the greatest
definition of the size of the expedition, since he
wished to leave neither them nor himself any excuse
for not fulfilling his commands. And these were to
sink the city, and bring the whole race to him in the
dress which I mentioned before. Such was the 102
temper and the preparation of the king. But they
were carried along, outroaring the Aegean, dazzling
those who met them, and filling the sea with flight,
so that no one then would have wished to live on an
island. And while they were still at sea and a little
before landing, they decided to make a beginning
with the king's commands and to sing a kind of
prologue to the war. And when this was decided,
they attacked the Eretrians and went off with them, 490.
having imitated a fisherman's net with their fleet.
Thus the Eretrian race had been carried off. But 103
they went against their second opponent, now to
drag away the Athenians themselves and to carry
off Greece, like emissaries from a God, badly understanding the kind of hunt in which they were engaged
and the irrelevance of their action to the old adage,
since they were not " in pursuit of what was elusive,"
but rather of what was accustomed to pursue. When 104
these events had taken place, and the Persians were
being brought to the mainland, like some evil from

---

⁵ transposuit et scripsit Behr : post οὕτως ἀνήρπαστο erant
ὡσπερεὶ παρ' ἄλλου—ἀναρπασθέν.

⁶ τῷ om. TQ.

(200 D.)

κακοῦ, οἱ μὲν ἄλλοι πάντες Ἕλληνες καὶ πάλαι προ-
ϊδόντες τὴν διάβασιν καὶ τότε ὁρῶντες ἤδη καθῆντο
ἐκπεπληγμένοι, τὸ μέλλον ἀποσκοποῦντες, ὀνειρο-
πολοῦντες ἕκαστοι τὰς Ἐρετριέων συμφοράς, καὶ
τοσοῦτον τῶν δεινῶν ἀπέχειν νομίζοντες ὅσον τὸν
στρατὸν αὐτῶν. ἡ δὲ πόλις πομπὴν ἄγουσῃ προσ-
εῴκει μᾶλλον ἢ πρὸς ἀγῶνα κοσμουμένη. ἱερά τε
γὰρ πάντα ἀνέῳγεν καὶ τὰ τῶν ἱερέων γένη[1] συνῆγεν καὶ διεπρεσβεύετο πρὸς τοὺς θεοὺς τὸν ἀρχαῖον

201 D. τρόπον, συμμάχους τε καλοῦσα καὶ ἡγεμόνας ποιου-
105 μένη. ὡς δ' αὐτῇ τὸ θεῖον ἤσκητο, οὐδὲν ἦν ἀργὸν
ἔτι, ἀλλ' οἱ μὲν φύλακες τῶν ἱερῶν οἱ γέροντες καὶ
τῆς πόλεως ὑπελείποντο, ἡ δὲ νεότης ἐχώρει. καὶ
πρῶτον μὲν τοὺς ἐν τοῖς στεφανίταις δρόμους ἀπέκρυψαν, ὅσῳ περὶ καλλιόνων τῶν ἄθλων ἠγωνίζοντο, τοσούτῳ θαυμαστοτέραν τὴν προθυμίαν παρα-
σχόμενοι· ἔπειτα κρείττους ἦσαν τὰ τελευταῖα ἢ τὰ
106 ἀπὸ τῶν πυλῶν. καίτοι μεσοῦντας μὲν[2] ἔτι τῆς πορείας προσέβαλεν[3] ὥσπερ πνεῦμα ἀπὸ θαλάττης βοὴ
συμμιγὴς ἵππων καὶ ἀνδρῶν καὶ τῶν ἄλλων ἐφολ-
κίων τῷ στρατοπέδῳ, τῶν μὲν χρείας ἕνεκα, τῶν δὲ
καὶ ψυχαγωγίας βαρβαρικῆς κεκομισμένων. ὑπερ-
βαλόντες[4] δ' οὐκ εἶχον ὅ τι ἴδωσι, πλὴν τῶν πολεμίων καὶ τῶν ἀτόπων ἐκείνων φασμάτων. [χαλκὸς
δὲ καὶ σίδηρος πόρρωθεν εἶργεν μὴ προσιέναι.][5]
τοσαύτη δ' ἦν ὑπερηφανία τῆς παρασκευῆς καὶ
τῶν ποιουμένων ὥστ' ἐξαρκεῖν ἐδόκει τοῖς βαρβάροις ὀφθῆναι μόνον. ᾤοντο γὰρ ὥσπερ ἐν ἄθλοις

---

[1] ἱερῶν πάντα TQ.   [2] μὲν οὖν VA.
[3] προσέβαλλεν VA.   [4] ὑπερβάλλοντες TQ.
[5] secl. Behr.

[a] i.e. to Marathon.

the sea, all the other Greeks, who had long ago
foreseen the crossing, and who then saw it, now sat
dumbstruck, watching for what would come, each
with his fantasies of the misfortune of the Eretrians,
and believing that they were only as far from danger
as the army was from them. But the city seemed to
be celebrating a holiday rather than to be preparing
itself for combat. For it was opening all the temples,
and it was assembling the various priests, and
performing supplications to the Gods in the ancient
fashion, calling on them as allies and making them
their leaders. And when it had performed the divine 105
rites, still everyone was active. The old men were
left behind to guard the temples and the city, and
the youth went off.[a] And first they outshone the
races in the great games,[b] displaying a much more
wonderful enthusiasm, to the degree that they
were contending for fairer prizes. Next they were
stronger at the finish than when they started at the
gates. Yet while they were still in the middle of 106
their journey, there struck them, like a breeze from
the sea, the mingled din of horses, men and the other
appendages of the camp, some of which were brought
to use and others for barbarian pleasure. But when
they had crested the hills, they could see nothing
except the enemy and those strange apparitions.
[But bronze and iron kept them from approaching].[c]
And so great was the barbarians' contempt based on
their preparations and actions, that they decided
that merely to be seen was enough. For they
thought that as if in a contest for a prize everyone

---

[b] The Greek means games wherein the prizes were crowns
or wreaths.

[c] [Parts of two lines of poetry?—*E.H.W.*]

(201 D.)

ἅπαντας εὐθὺς ἀπογνώσεσθαι καὶ δώσειν ἑαυτοὺς
107 ἀκονιτί. αὕτη πρώτη δημοτελὴς κρίσις ἐν τῷ μέσῳ
κατὰ ἀνθρώπους[1] ἐγένετο ἀρετῆς πρὸς πλοῦτον καὶ
φρονήματος Ἑλληνικοῦ πρὸς βαρβάρων πλῆθος
καὶ παρασκευήν, οὐ λόγων εὐφημίᾳ κριθεῖσα, ἀλλ'
ἔργων ἀποδείξει καὶ τῷ καλοῦντι τοῦ καιροῦ. οὐ
202 D. γὰρ εἰς φόβον τὴν θέαν ἔτρεψαν, ἀλλ' εἰς προθυμίαν
κατεχρήσαντο, οὐδ' ἐξεπλάγησαν τῶν ὁρωμένων
τὴν ἀήθειαν,[2] ἀλλ' ἤσθησαν ὁρῶντες ὅσων κρείττους γενήσονται, καὶ νομίσαντες ὥσπερ ἀφορμὴν εἰ-
ληφέναι παρὰ τῆς τύχης ὑπερβαλέσθαι πάντας
ἀνθρώπους ἀνδραγαθίᾳ καὶ τοῦτ' εἶναι πλέον τῆς
τοσαύτης στρατιᾶς ἔχειν ὥσπερ χρήμασιν ἀφθό-
νως χρήσασθαι, καὶ διανοηθέντες ὅτι νῦν ὥσπερ
ἑστιάσονται λαμπρῶς ὑπὸ τῶν βαρβάρων καὶ τῆς
ἀρετῆς ἀξίως τῆς ἑαυτῶν. καὶ γὰρ ἵπποι καὶ
βέλη καὶ νῆες καὶ ψέλια καὶ στρεπτοὶ καὶ κύνες καὶ
πάντα χρήματα δῶρα τῆς τύχης ἐστὶν προκείμενα
τοῖς κρείττοσι, καὶ πάντα ταῦτα ἡ νίκη παραδίδωσι.
108 ταῦτα καὶ στρατηγοὶ πρὸς ἑαυτοὺς εἰπόντες καὶ
πρὸς ἀλλήλους[3] ἕκαστοι διαλεχθέντες, ἐκ θεῶν ἀρ-
ξάμενοι καὶ τοῦ φίλου παιῶνος,[4] ἐχώρουν δρόμῳ,
καθάπερ διὰ ψιλοῦ τοῦ πεδίου θέοντες, καὶ τοῖς
βαρβάροις οὐκ ἔδωκαν ἰδεῖν ὅ τι ἐστὶ τὰ γιγνόμενα,
ἀλλ' ἅμα τε[5] τάξεις ἐρρώγεσαν καὶ ἄνδρες ἐκτείνοντο
καὶ ἵπποι συνελαμβάνοντο καὶ νῆες εἵλκοντο καὶ
χρήματα ἤγετο καὶ χορεία Πανὸς ἦν τὰ ποιούμενα.
ἤδη δέ τις καὶ τελευτήσας εἱστήκει περιτοξευθεὶς
203 D. ὑπὸ τῶν βαρβάρων, φοβῶν τοὺς λοιπούς, ὥσπερ
109 ἀθάνατος ὤν. ἀπολλύμενοι δὲ οἱ τὰ μεγάλα τολ-

---

[1] τοὺς ἀνθρώπους TQ.   [2] ἀλήθειαν TQA.
[3] αὑτοὺς Phot., αὐτοὺς VA.

would immediately despair and surrender without a
struggle. This was the first public and open trial, 107
among mankind, of virtue against wealth and of
Greek pride against barbarian numbers and preparations, and it was not decided by fair eloquence,
but by the proof of deeds and by the call of that
critical moment. For they were not turned by the
spectacle to fear, but they used it to whet their
enthusiasm ; nor were they frightened by the
strangeness of what they saw, but they delighted to
see all that they would win, in the belief that they
had been given by fortune, as it were, a means of
surpassing all men in valour, and that the advantage
of so great an army was the power, as it were, to use
its riches unstintingly, and it occurred to them that
they would, as it were, feast gloriously and worthily
of their virtue because of the barbarians. For the
horses, weapons, ships, bracelets, necklaces, dogs,
and all the money were exposed to the winners as
gifts of fortune, and victory bestowed all these
prizes. When the generals had spoken of this 108
privately and all had discussed it together, beginning
with an invocation of the Gods and the friendly
paean, they went at a run, as if they were dashing
through an empty plain, and they did not give the
barbarians time to see what was happening. But
in an instant their lines were broken, the men slain,
the horses captured, the ships dragged off, the money
carried away, and what was done was " a Panic
dance." Even a corpse, shot through with arrows by
the barbarians, stood erect, frightening the survivors,
as if he were immortal. But as the Persians per- 109

---

⁴ παιᾶνος TQ.   ⁵ τε om. VA Phot.

(203 D.)

μήσαντες καὶ τρόπαια φέροντες ἐν ταῖς ναυσὶ πλείους αὑτοῖς ἐφάνησαν ἢ πρότερον. οὔτε γὰρ τὸ ἕλος οὔτε ἡ θάλαττα ἀρκούντως αὐτοὺς ἐδέχετο, οὐδ' ἦν εὐρυχωρία τοῖς κακοῖς οὐδὲ διέξοδος, ἀλλὰ τότε ὡς ἀληθῶς ὄχλος ὄντες ᾐσθάνοντο καὶ μέγιστον ἐναντίωμα ἑαυτοῖς, καὶ τοῖς πλείοσιν ἥττους ἐγένοντο ἢ ὅσοις ἄν τις ἐξ ἀρχῆς ἐθάρρησεν ἀντιστῆναι. ὥστε οἱ τοῦ αἵματος ῥύακες ἤρκουν ἐν νοτίῳ ταῖς ναυσὶν εἶναι.

110   Τοσαύτη δὲ ἡ λαμπρότης τῶν ἀνδρῶν ἐκείνων ἐγένετο καὶ τοσοῦτον τῆς νίκης τὸ ἀξίωμα, ὥστε καὶ τὸ χωρίον ὥσπερ τι σύμβολον ἀρετῆς κατέστησαν. οὔκουν ἔστι γε οὐδεὶς ὅστις ἀκούσας τὸ τοῦ Μαραθῶνος ὄνομα οὐκ ἀνίσταται τῇ ψυχῇ οὐδ' ὥσπερ ἄλλο τι τὴν ἐπωνυμίαν ἀσπάζεται καὶ σέβεται σὺν χαρᾷ. καὶ συνέβη δὴ[1] τῇ πόλει πρώτῃ μὲν κινδυνεῦσαι τῶν κατὰ τὴν ἤπειρον Ἑλλήνων, μόνῃ δὲ ἀρκέσαι νικῆσαι, τῶν δὲ ἰδίων κινδύνων κοινὰ τὰ ἆθλα ἅπασι καταστῆσαι καὶ τροφὸν οὖσαν τῆς Ἑλλάδος τοὐναντίον τοῦ νενομισμένου ποιῆσαι. τοὺς μὲν γὰρ ἄλλους τὰ τροφεῖα κομίζεσθαι παρὰ τῶν ἐκτραφέντων ὁ νόμος λέγει, ἡ δὲ πόλις πρὸς ταῖς τροφαῖς καὶ οἷς ἔδωκεν ἐξ ἀρχῆς καὶ τὴν ἐλευθερίαν μετὰ τῆς σωτηρίας ἐν τοῖς αὑτῆς κιν-

204 D. δύνοις ἀπέδωκεν τῇ Ἑλλάδι, ὥσπερ τοῦτο ὀφείλουσα τοῖς Ἕλλησιν, ποιεῖν διὰ παντὸς αὐτοὺς εὖ καὶ τοῦτο ὡμολογηκυῖα τοῖς πρὸ τοῦ πᾶσιν. ὥστ' εἰκότως εἰπεῖν εἶναι τὴν μὲν πόλιν τὸν ἐλευθέριον Δία τιμᾶν ἐπὶ τοῖς πραχθεῖσιν προσήκειν, τοῖς δὲ ἄλλοις Ἕλλησι τὴν πόλιν, καὶ νομίζειν τὸν Ἀθηναίων δῆμον ὥσπερ ἐλευθέριον τοῖς Ἕλλησιν εἶναι.

86

ished, those who had attempted great deeds of daring, and carried trophies in their ships, seemed to themselves more numerous than before. For neither the swamp nor the sea sufficed to contain them, nor was there space or exit for their evils. Then truly they perceived that they were a disorganized mob and the greatest obstacle to themselves, and they lost more men than at the start one would have had the courage to resist, so that the flow of blood was enough to carry the draught of the ships.

But so great was the glory of those men of yours 110 and so great the distinction of the victory, that they even made the place, as it were, a symbol of virtue. Nor is there anyone who, hearing the name Marathon, does not feel his heart rise, and who does not welcome the word as a gift and revere it with joy. And it befell that it was the first Greek city on the mainland to face danger, and that it was able to achieve victory unaided, and that it shared the prizes of its own dangers with all men, and that being the nurse of Greece, it acted contrary to custom. For the law declares that other men receive payment for their nurture from those whom they raised, but the city in addition to nurture and all that it gave in the beginning, also paid to Greece with its own danger freedom and preservation, as if it owed to the Greeks continual benefits and had conceded this in all its previous acts. Therefore it can be said with good reason that it was proper for the city to honour Zeus Giver of Freedom after what was done, and for the other Greeks to honour the city, and to believe in the people of Athens as a Giver of Freedom for the

---

¹ δὲ V.

(204 D.)

111 δοκεῖ δέ μοι συγκληρωθῆναι τῇ τύχῃ τῆς πόλεως ἡ
μάχη καὶ μηδένων ἄλλων εἶναι κατὰ γένος ἢ τῶν
Ἀθηναίων. ἐκείνη γάρ, εἰ καὶ νεανικώτερον εἰπεῖν,
ὥσπερ μητρόπολις καὶ ἀφορμὴ τῶν ὕστερον πάντων
ἐγένετο τοῖς Ἕλλησιν, οὐ μόνον τῶν ἐν τοῖς πολέμοις ἀγώνων ἀντὶ κρηπῖδος ἢ παραδείγματος προτε-
λεσθεῖσα,[1] ἀλλὰ καὶ πάντων ἐπιτηδευμάτων καὶ βίου καὶ προαιρέσεως καί, τὸ σύμπαν εἰπεῖν, τοῦ τῶν
Ἑλλήνων σπέρματος. καὶ[2] εἰ μὴ τότε ἡ πόλις οὕτω
διήνεγκεν, ἅπαντ' ἂν ἔρρει καὶ σώματα καὶ πρά-
112 ξεις καὶ λόγοι καὶ τὰ κοινὰ τῆς φύσεως. οἱ μὲν οὖν
πολλοὶ θαυμάζουσιν ὅσας μυριάδας τῶν βαρβάρων
205 D. ἐνίκων, ἐμοὶ δὲ δοκοῦσιν ἅπαντας ἀνθρώπους, οὐ
μόνον πρὸς οὓς ἠγωνίσαντο, ἐκεῖνοι νενικηκέναι, εἰ
δεῖ παραιτησάμενον τὸν φθόνον εἰπεῖν, οὐ μόνον
τῷ πᾶσι τοιούτων ἀγαθῶν αἴτιοι καταστῆναι, ἀλλὰ
καὶ τῷ μηδένας ἐγγὺς εἶναι τοῖς ὑπάρχουσιν. ὥστ'
εἰ τὸ μὴ ἔχειν ἐξ ἴσου γενέσθαι τῶν ἡττόνων ἐστίν,
113 ἅπαντας νενικήκασιν. οἶμαι μὲν οὖν εἰ καὶ μόνα
ταῦτα ἐκλέξας ἐπεπαύμην, ἔχειν ἂν πέρας ἀρκοῦν
τὸν λόγον καὶ μηδὲν ἂν προσδεῖν τῇ πόλει φιλοτιμίας μηδ' ἀρετῆς εἰς τὸ ὁμόφυλον. τὴν γὰρ πρώτην
μὲν ἀνεῖσαν ἀνθρώπους, πρώτην δὲ βίου χρῆσιν
εὑροῦσαν, θρέψασαν δ' οὐ μόνον τοὺς ἐξ αὑτῆς, ἀλλὰ
καὶ πάντας, δεξαμένην δὲ τοὺς ἐκπίπτοντας πρώτην
τε καὶ πλείστους, ἑκάστους τε καὶ σύμπαντας,
πλείστους δὲ αὖθις ἀποστείλασαν πανταχοῖ,[3] πάλιν
δ' ἐν τοῖς ὑπὲρ σωτηρίας ἀγῶσιν ἀμφοτέρων προ-
στᾶσαν, τῶν τ' ἐν τῇ ὑπερορίᾳ καὶ τῶν ἐπὶ τῆς

---

[1] προτεθεῖσα TQ. [2] edd. : ἦν TQVA.
[3] πανταχῇ TQ.

Greeks. The battle seems to me to have been part 111
of the allotted fortune of the city and to have been
suited to the nature of no one other than the Athenians. For that battle, even if it is a rather bold
expression, was like a mother city and starting
point for all later deeds for the Greeks, not only in
warfare, being an initiation, like a foundation or
model for future contests, but also for all the practices of life, for the choice of ways, and to sum up,
for the seed of the Greeks. And if the city had not
then concluded the battle in this way, everything
would have been ruined, bodies, deeds, words, the
common ties of nature. Then most men marvel 112
at the many tens of thousands of barbarians whom
they conquered, but they seem to me to have
conquered all men, not only those against whom they
fought—if I must say so with apologies for the invidious remark—not only because they were responsible
for such good things for all men, but also because
no one approaches their accomplishments, so that if
the inability to be equal is a characteristic of the
inferior, they have surpassed all men. Then, I 113
think that if I had stopped after only having selected
these deeds, the speech would still have had a
satisfactory conclusion, and the city would not be
lacking in honour or virtue in respect to its fellow
Greeks. For when it was the first to produce mankind, the first to discover the means of life, and
nourished not only its own sons, but also all men,
and was first to receive exiles and the largest number
of them besides, individually and in groups, and
again sent out the largest number of colonists to
every part of the earth, and besides in the struggle
for survival championed both those abroad and

(205 D.)

ἀρχαίας Ἑλλάδος, πῶς οὐ διὰ παντὸς ἂν εἴποι τις
ἀφῖχθαι καὶ καθάπερ τοὺς δρομέας τὸ γιγνόμενον πεπληρωκέναι; ὥστε μηδεμίαν πρὸ ταύτης ἐγ-
χωρεῖν ἐν τοῖς Ἕλλησιν κηρύττεσθαι. πρὶν γὰρ
ἄρχεσθαι τῶν ὁμοίων ἑτέρους, τοσοῦτον ἡ πόλις
προελήλυθει.[1]

114   Οὐ μὴν ἐῶσίν γε ἀπελθεῖν[2] αἱ πράξεις, ἀλλὰ καλοῦσιν καὶ προσάγουσιν εἰς τὸ πρόσω τοῦ λόγου,
καὶ τοσούτῳ μᾶλλον ὅσῳ ταῦτα ἀκριβέστερον ἐξήτα-
σται. τοσαύτην γὰρ ὑπερβολὴν τοῖς ἐφεξῆς ἐποιήσατο ἡ πόλις ὥσθ' ὑπερῆρεν αὐτὴν τοσοῦτον
206 D. ὅσονπερ πρὸ τοῦ τοὺς ἄλλους. καὶ πρὶν τὰ πρῶτα
ἀξίως τινὰ θαυμάσαι, ἐπέθηκε τὰ δεύτερα, ὥσπερ
αὐτὴ πρὸς αὐτὴν ἁμιλλωμένη. γενομένου γὰρ τοῦ
Μαραθῶνι τολμήματος καὶ τῶν βαρβάρων ἐλαθέν-
των ἐκ τῆς Ἑλλάδος ὥσπερ κονιορτοῦ, Δαρεῖος μὲν
οὐκ εἶχεν ὅ τι χρήσηται,[3] ἀλλ' ὥσπερ ἐκ θεοῦ
πληγεὶς ὑποπεπτώκει τῇ πόλει καὶ τοὺς αἰτίους τῆς
διαβάσεως κατεμέμφετο, ὡς κακῶς προξενήσαντας
αὐτῷ τοὺς Ἀθηναίους, καὶ τελευτᾷ δή, πρίν τι
115 δεύτερον κακὸν αὐτὸν ἐξεργάσασθαι. ὁ δὲ πάντας
βασιλέας παρενεγκὼν ταῖς ἐπινοίαις καὶ μηδὲν καταλιπὼν ἄτοπον νομίσαι, Ξέρξης ὁ Δαρείου, κατα-
γνοὺς μὲν τοῦ πατρὸς ὡς ἐνδεῶς ἐπιχειρήσαντος,
ὑπεριδὼν δὲ τῆς πόλεως καὶ τῶν Ἑλλήνων ὡς οὐδαμοῦ φανησομένων, ἀγῶνα διπλοῦν ἀγωνίζεται,
τὸν μὲν ὑπερβαλέσθαι, τὴν δὲ τιμωρήσασθαι, μετὰ
πολλοῦ τοῦ κρείττονος. καὶ τοσοῦτον ὕβρισε τῇ
ὑπερβολῇ ὥστ' ἔγνω τὸν πρότερον στόλον ὡσπερεὶ
116 παιδιὰν ἀποφῆναι. δοκεῖ δέ μοι καὶ πρὸς τὰς διο-

---

[1] παρεληλύθει TQ.

those in ancient Greece, how would one deny that
it had done everythinga nd, like runners, completed
its proper course ? Therefore no city can be proclaimed victor among the Greeks before this one.
For the city had taken a very long lead before the
others began to do deeds which were like theirs.

Indeed, the account of these actions does not 114
permit us to depart, but summons and leads us on
in our speech, and so much the more strongly to the
degree that these matters have been more carefully
investigated. For in its following deeds the city
reached such a peak of superiority that it surpassed
itself as much as it formerly surpassed others.
And before one had properly admired its first acts,
it added the second ones, as if it were vying against
itself. For when the daring at Marathon had taken 490.
place and the barbarians were driven from Greece
like a dust-storm, Darius did not know what to do,
but as if smitten by God he collapsed before the city,
and blamed those responsible for the crossing, as if
they had wrongly recommended the Athenians to
him, and at length he died before he did himself a
second injury. But Xerxes, the son of Darius, who 115
surpassed all kings in his conceptions and was 485.
wanting in no bizarre idea, condemned his father
for his deficient attempt, scorned the city and the
Greeks as sure to put in an appearance nowhere
at all, and fought a double contest, to surpass his 480, 479.
father and to punish the city, with a much stronger
force. And his behaviour reached such a peak of
criminality that he resolved to make the former
expedition appear like a child's game. But it seems 116

---

² παρελθεῖν TQ.   ³ χρήσαιτο TQV.

ARISTIDES

σημίας τότε Ξέρξης οὐ μόνον πρὸς τὸν πατέρα ἀμιλ-
λήσασθαι καὶ πρὸς ἅπασαν ὄψιν τε καὶ ἀκοὴν ἀνθρώποις ἀνέλπιστον ὥσπερ ἐνδείξασθαι βουλόμενος
ὅτι αὐτοῦ[1] βεβαίως ἐστὶν ἡ γῆ. ποίαν γὰρ κυμά-
των ἐπιρροήν, ἢ τίνας σκηπτούς, ἢ τίνας σεισμούς, ἢ
ποίαν νεφῶν ἢ χαλάζης ἐμβολήν, ἢ ποίους ἀήθεις
ἀστέρας οὐκ ἐλαφροτέρους ἐκεῖνός γε ἀπέδειξεν; ἢ
ποίους φόβους ἐγγείους ἢ θαλαττίους οὐχὶ συνέστειλε
117 τοῖς παρ' αὐτοῦ ; οὗ τὰς ἀπειλὰς πρῶτον οὐκ ἦν
ἑστῶσι τοῖς ὠσὶν ἀκοῦσαι, ἀλλ' ἀπῆγον εἰς ἔσχατα
207 D. [γῆς],[2] καὶ προὔλεγον ἃ μηδενὸς ἦν εὑρεῖν πλὴν ἐκείνου μόνου.[3] αἰτεῖν μὲν γὰρ ἔφασκεν οὐδὲν τῶν
ἀλλοτρίων, ἀλλ' ἀπαρχὰς γῆς καὶ ὕδατος· πάντων
δ' εἶναι τούτων κύριος. τῆς δ' ἀγνωμοσύνης τῆς
Μαραθῶνι λύσιν μίαν εἶναι καὶ παραίτησιν, εἰ ταῦτα
συγχωρήσαιεν καὶ μετὰ τῶν ἄλλων ἀνθρώπων γένοιντο καὶ τὸν κοινὸν δεσπότην γνοῖεν· εἰ δὲ μή, δι-
δάξειν αὐτοὺς καλῶς μετὰ τῶν προπατόρων θεῶν·
οὕτω γὰρ θεοῖς τε καὶ Ξέρξῃ δοκεῖν ὑπὲρ τῶν Ξέρ-
ξου πραγμάτων· ἥξειν γὰρ ἄγων ἅπαντα, ναῦς μὲν
ὅσας ἡ Ἑλληνικὴ θάλαττα οὐχ ὑποδέξεται, ἵππῳ δὲ
καὶ πεζοῖς ἀποκρύψειν τὴν Ἀττικήν, καὶ τὴν πόλιν
ἱππόκροτον καταστήσειν, ἱερά τε[4] συμφλέξειν καὶ
118 θήκας ἀναρρήξειν καὶ μετασκευάσειν ἅπαντα. ἔτι δὲ
Ἀτλαντικοῦ πελάγους κληρουχίας ἀτίμους ἠπείλει
καὶ γῆς ποίησιν ἔξω τῆς οἰκουμένης, ἣν ἀναγκάσειν

[1] Stephanus : αὐτοῦ TQVA.   [2] secl. Behr.
[3] μόνου om. VA Phot.   [4] δὲ VA.

[a] " Cleruchiae," " allotment-holdings," were settlements

92

to me that Xerxes then also vied with the elements, not only with his father, and with every sight and sound unanticipated by man, as if he wished to show that the earth was under his control. For what onflow of waves, or what thunder-bolts, or what earthquakes, or what onset of clouds or hail, or what strange stars did he not make less significant? Or what terrestrial or marine terrors did he not diminish with those of his own causing? At first it 117 was impossible to hear his threats with a stout heart, but they reduced men to extremities of fear, and proclaimed what no one would think of except him alone. For he said that he did not ask for anything which belonged to another, but for the first fruits of the land and water, and that he was lord of all these; and that there was one expiation and plea for the folly at Marathon, if they would make these concessions, and join with other men and recognize him as their common master; and that if they would not, he in company with the Gods, his ancestors, would teach them a good lesson. For thus the Gods and Xerxes had decided concerning the affairs of Xerxes. He said that he would come in full force, with more ships than the Greek sea would hold, and that he would cover Attica with his cavalry and infantry, and make the city resound to his horses, and that he would burn the temples, break open the tombs, and transform everything. Further he threatened to assign them miserable 118 allotments[a] in the Atlantic Ocean, and with the task of reclaiming land outside the inhabited world, in which he would compel them, after they had been

of Athenians, on Greek soil, of which the male members remained citizens of Athens.

(207 D.)

208 D.
119

ἠκρωτηριασμένους προχοῦν εἰς τὸ πέλαγος, ὕδωρ
μὲν ἀντλοῦντας, πέτρας δὲ ὀρύττοντας, τοσαῦτ'
ἔχοντας τοῦ σώματος, ὅσα τοῖς ἔργοις ἀρκέσει. καὶ
οὐκ ἠπείλει μὲν οὕτως ἀήθη καὶ ὑπερόρια καὶ φο-
βου μείζω, ἐτελεύτησεν δ' ἐνταῦθα, ἀλλ' ἀπέκρυψεν
τοῖς ἔργοις τὰς ἀπειλάς, ἄνευ γε τοῦ τι δυνηθῆναι,
λέγω δὴ χρήσασθαι τῇ πόλει. τίνα γὰρ μεσόγειαν
ἢ ποίαν Ἀτλαντικὴν ῥαχίαν οὐκ ἔσεισεν; ἢ ποῖον
κόλπον ὧν ἴσασιν ἄνθρωποι, λέγω τῶν εἰσεχόντων
ἀπὸ τῆς ἔξω θαλάττης, παρῆκεν ἀσύμβολον ; οὐ
τὸν εἰς Φᾶσιν, οὐ τὸν ἄνω τὸν Περσικόν, οὐκ ἐρυ-
θρὰν θάλατταν, οὐχ Ὑρκανίαν, οὐ πάντας συνήγα-
γεν; οὐ διηρευνήσατο πάντας τῆς γῆς τοὺς μυχοὺς[1]
ἀκριβέστερον ἢ Δᾶτις τὴν Ἐρετρικήν; οὐκ ἐσχα-
τιαῖς γῆς καὶ θαλάττης τὸν στόλον ὡρίσατο, ὥσπερ
σαγηνεύων τὴν ἀρχὴν τὴν αὐτὸς αὑτοῦ; ποῖον δὲ
τότε φάσμα οὐκ ἐκινήθη; ἢ τί τῶν ὄντων οὐχ
ὑπερώφθη; ἢ τί τῶν οὐκ ὄντων οὐκ ἐγένετο; οὐχ
οἱ πορθμοὶ τοσοῦτον αὐτῷ τῶν ποταμῶν διαφέρειν
ἐδόκουν ὅσον οὐ παρέχειν πιεῖν ἐξ αὐτῶν; οἱ δ' ἀε-
ναοι ποταμοὶ τῶν χειμάρρων οὐδὲν ἀλλοιότερον διε-

209 D.
120

_____

[1] τοὺς μυχοὺς τῆς γῆς TQ.

_____

[a] [In this passage the outside sea is the Ocean (outside
the Mediterranean) rightly conjectured as surrounding the
whole one partly known land-mass Europe *plus* Asia *plus*
Africa. From this Ocean there spread into the land-mass
several sea-" gulfs ": the present-day Mediterranean (literally
" mid-land "), which in classical times had no overall name
except as " Our Sea " ; the Red Sea ; and the Persian Gulf ;
for many people (not the better-informed Herodotus, 5th
century B.C. and Claudius Ptolemy, 2nd century A.D.) the
inland sea—the Caspian (called by Aristides Hyrcanian)—was
another such gulf supposed to belong to a not far distant

94

mutilated, to heap up earth into the sea, dredging
up the water, digging up the rocks, with as much
of their body left as would suffice for the work.
And he did not stop with such strange and extra- 119
ordinary threats, which were beyond terror. But he
outdid his threats by his deeds, without any effect,
I mean upon the city. For what inland region or
what sort of Atlantic beach did he not cause to
tremble ? Or what gulf of those known to man, I
mean those that flow in from the outside sea, did he
bypass without exacting a contribution ? Did he not
bring together the gulf leading to the river Phasis,
the Persian gulf above, the Red Sea, the Hyrcanian,
all of them ?[a] Did he not search through all the
corners of the earth more thoroughly than Datis
searched through Eretria ? Did he not define the
complement of his expedition by the farthest reaches
of the land and sea, as if netting his own empire ?
What strange apparition was not then set in motion ?
Or what naturally existing means was not scorned ?
Or what non-existent one did not come into being ?
Did not the straits seem to him to differ from the 120
rivers only in so far as they did not provide drinking-
water from themselves ? The ever flowing rivers
were affected in a way no different from torrents ;

northern or north-eastern part of the Ocean outside Europe
and Asia. The " gulf " leading to the river Phasis (Rion) is
the Black Sea, here carelessly included among the " gulfs."
The word μεσόγειαν, " mid-land," here translated " inland
region," may really go with ῥαχίαν, " inland beach " as
opposed to " Atlantic " or " Oceanic " beach. In either case
the word has no association with the application of the name
" Mediterranean " to a sea. Aristides speaks of the Persian
gulf as " above." This apparently means " to the north " of
the Red Sea.—E.H.W.]

(209 D.)

τέθησαν, μᾶλλον δὲ τοῖς χειμάρροις εἰς τοὐναντίον
περιέστησαν· ὥσπερ γὰρ τὰ ἐκείνων ῥεύματα ἐκ
Διὸς αὔξεται, οὕτως ὑπὸ Ξέρξῃ πάντα ἐπέλιπεν.

121 ἐδέχετο δ᾽ αὐτὸν οὔτε γῆ οὔτε θάλαττα ἱκανῶς, καὶ
ταῦτα εἶκεν πρὸς τὴν ἐκείνου χρείαν καὶ μετέβαλ-
λεν εἰς ἄλληλα. γῆ τε γὰρ ἡ μὲν ἐγίγνετο, ἡ δ᾽ ἀπ-
ώλλυτο, καὶ θάλαττα ὑπεχώρει καὶ πάλιν συνῄει τῷ
βασιλεῖ—καὶ νῦν ἐστι τῆς νέας θαλάττης ὅσος τῆς

210 D. ἐκείνου διαβάσεως χρόνος καὶ ὁ Ἄθως ἀντὶ στήλης
τῷ ἔργῳ λέλειπται—ὡς δ᾽ εἰπεῖν πάντα κινου-
μένοις ἐῴκει καὶ μεθισταμένοις ὡς ἐκείνῳ δοκοίη.

122 κάμηλοι δὲ χρυσοῦ καὶ ἀργύρου κατέλαμπον, ὅσον
μήκιστόν ἐστιν ἀνύσαι, τοσοῦτον ἐπέχουσαι.[1] εἰ δ᾽
ἐπιθυμήσειε σκιᾶς, δένδρον ἦν αὐτῷ χρυσοῦν ἡ
σκιά. ὥστε νύκτωρ μὲν ἤστραπτεν ἀργύρῳ καὶ
χρυσῷ, μεθ᾽ ἡμέραν δὲ νύκτα ἐπῆγεν ὁσαχοῦ τοξεῦ-
σαι κελεύσειεν. πολλοῖς δ᾽ ἦν ἀφανὴς ὢν ἦγεν οὗ
γῆς εἴη τὰ νῦν. οὐδὲν δ᾽ ἦν ἔθνος τῶν κατὰ τὴν
πορείαν μεῖζον ἢ κρύπτεσθαι. φιλονικήσας δὲ
μαθεῖν ὁ πάντα ἄτοπος βασιλεὺς ὁπόσους ἄγει,
χρῆν[2] γὰρ καὶ τοῦτο ἐκείνῳ γενέσθαι δυνατόν, ἠναγ-
κάσθη μετρῆσαι τρόπον δή τινα μᾶλλον ἢ ἀριθ-
μῆσαι τὴν στρατιάν, καὶ κατασκευασάμενος τεῖχος

123 μυρίανδρον πρὸς μέτρον ἠρίθμει. καὶ ὁ μὲν οὕτω
πάντα κινῶν ᾔει, τοσαῦτα προσλαμβάνων ὁπόσοις
ἐντύχοι, καὶ κατεπτήχει καὶ ἔθνη καὶ πόλεις καὶ
πάντα γένη καὶ Εὐρωπαῖα καὶ τὰ ἐπὶ τῆς Ἀσίας
πάντα, καὶ πρὸς τὴν κίνησιν εἶκεν ὥσπερ τὰ κοῦφα

124 σὺν πολλῷ τῷ φόβῳ. ἡ πόλις δ᾽ ἕτερα ἀντεπεδεί-

---

[1] ὑπέχουσαι VA.   [2] χρὴ VA.

---

[a] When Dieneces, a Lacedaemonian soldier killed at the
Battle of Thermopylae in 480 B.C., heard that the Persian

moreover their fate was quite the opposite. For just
as the flow of those rises from the rain of Zeus, so all
of these dried up under Xerxes. Neither land nor 121
sea had sufficient capacity to receive him, and they
yielded to his need, and changed into one another.
For land came into being, and land was destroyed,
and sea gave way and again was united for the
king. And now the duration of the new sea is
reckoned as the time of his passage, and Athos has 483.
been left as a monument of the deed. But, one
might say, everything seemed to be in motion and
to be changing its place, just as he might decide.
The camels shone with gold and silver, occupying 122
ground enough for the greatest possible journey.
If he desired shade, his shade was a golden tree,
so that at night he gleamed with silver and gold, but
in the day, he brought on night, whenever he ordered
a volley of arrows.[a] It was unclear to many in his
column in what land he was now. No race of people
in his line of march was too great to be obscured.
When that king, strange in all his acts, obstinately
desired to know how many men he led—for even this
must be possible for him—he was compelled in a
way to measure rather than count his army ; and
having prepared a walled-in pen with a capacity of
ten thousand men, he counted them by volume. 123
And so he went stirring up everything, adding to his
ranks all that he came upon ; and the tribes, cities, 481–480.
and all the races of Europe and all those of Asia
with great fear cowered before him, and yielded
to his course, like weightless objects. But the city 124

forces were so vast that their launched arrows hid the sun, he
cheerfully indicated a good result—the Greeks would be
fighting in the shade. Herodotus VII. 226.

(210 D.)

211 D.
125

126

κνυτο, οὐδ' ἦν Ξέρξην μᾶλλον θαυμάσαι τῆς ὑπερηφανίας ἢ τὴν πόλιν τοῦ μηδὲν τῶν ἐκείνου θαυμάσαι· ἢ θορύβου τοσούτου διὰ γῆς ἁπάσης καταρραγέντος καὶ τῶν ἠπείρων ἀμφοτέρων κρινομένων ἐπὶ τῆς Ἑλλάδος ἀντέσχεν, ὥσπερ ἔρυμα καὶ πρόβολος, ἀπ' ἀρχῆς ἀρξαμένη καὶ αὐτὴ τὰ αὑτῆς ἐπιδεικνύναι. πρῶτον μὲν τοῖς περὶ τὰς ἐπιστολὰς ἀκροβολισμοῖς καὶ πείραις τοσοῦτον ὑπερέσχεν φρονήματι καὶ τοσοῦτον ἀπέσχεν τοῦ πτοηθῆναι πρὸς τὰς τῶν ἀτόπων ⟨ἐκείνων⟩[1] φόβων ἐπαγωγάς, ὥστε οὐκ ἐδεήθη ψηφίσματος πρὸς ταῦτα ἔτι, ἀλλ' ὥσπερ ἑνὸς κοινοῦ νενικηκότος τοῦ κατὰ Δαρεῖον, μηδένα ἀκούειν βαρβάρων, πρὶν ἐκκλησίαν ἀποδοῦναι, ἀφανίζει τοὺς ἀγγέλους αὐτῇ σκευῇ καὶ ποικίλμασι, καὶ τοῖς εὖ φρονοῦσι τῶν Ἑλλήνων ἡγεμὼν τῆς ἀποκρίσεως ἐγένετο. ἔπειτα πάντων ἀγγελλόντων τὰ δεινὰ δὴ ταῦτα, ὅτι πάντα χρήματα μίγνυται καὶ τῶν Ἑλλήνων κερδανοῦσιν οἱ τελευταῖοι, πάντες δὲ ὥσπερ ὑπὸ κύματος τοῦ πολέμου καλυφθήσονται, καὶ τοσαύτης κατεχούσης ἐκπλήξεως τοῦ βαρβάρου[2] ὥστ' εἰκάζειν θεῶν τινος εἶναι πορείαν μετὰ τῶν λοιπῶν ἀνθρώπων ἐπὶ τὴν Ἑλλάδα ἐλαύνοντος, οὐδὲν μᾶλλον ὑφεῖτο οὐδὲ μετέγνω περὶ ὧν ἐβουλεύσατο, οὐδὲ ἐμέμψατο αὐτῇ[3] τῆς ἀποκρίσεως, ἀλλὰ τούς τε Ἕλληνας συνεκάλει πρὸς τὸν ἀγῶνα τὸν κοινόν, αἰσχυνομένη μοι δοκεῖν μόνη φανῆναι τῷ βαρβάρῳ, καθάπερ πρότερον Μαραθῶνι. οὐ γὰρ αὐτή γε ἐν ἄλλοις εἶχεν τὰς ἐλπίδας τῆς σωτηρίας, ἀλλὰ πάντες εἶχον ἐν αὐτῇ τὰς ὑπὲρ αὑτῶν, οἵ γε ὁμοίως[4] τε σωτηρίας δεό-

---

[1] add. A codd. dett. [2] τοὺς βαρβάρους TQV.

gave a counter display in turn, nor was there more wonder at Xerxes' scorn than at the city's not wondering at any of his acts. For when this great disturbance burst through every land and both continents came to trial in Greece, like a bulwark and a shield, it continued right from the start to display its qualities. First of all in the skirmishing 125 and attempts in the matter of the letters,[a] it was so proud and was so far from cowering at the introduction of those strange terrors, that there was no longer a need for a decree for these things, but as if that decree in respect to Darius, that nobody should listen to the barbarians, had become one common decree for all, before granting them an assembly, it removed the messengers with their trappings and adornments, and was leader for those Greeks who had the good sense to give this answer. Next when 126 everyone was reporting these terrors, that everything was in utter chaos and the last of the Greeks to be reached would profit thereby, and all would be covered over by the war as by a tidal wave, and when such great fear of the barbarian was current, so that it was conjectured that one of the Gods was marching with the rest of mankind against Greece, the city did not any more slacken its purpose nor repent its decision, nor blame itself for its answer, but it summoned the Greeks to the common contest, embarrassed, I think, to appear alone against the barbarian, as formerly at Marathon. For the city did not have its hopes of safety in the others, but all had their own hopes in it, since they were equally

---

[a] Herodotus VII. 133; for the reference to Darius cf. § 99.

---

[3] αὐτῇ T a. corr. VA edd.   [4] ὁμοίας TQV.

(211 D.)

μενοι καὶ ἐλευθερίας, καὶ τὸ παράδειγμα ὑπῆρχεν
ἀμφοῖν ἐγγύθεν ἡ προτέρα κρίσις, ἐσκόπει τε ὅ τι
212 D. βουλευσαμένη πρῶτον ἀντεκπλήξει τὸν βάρβαρον.
127 καὶ παρῆλθέ γε αὐτὸν τοῖς θαύμασι. μετοικίζεται
γὰρ ἐξαναστᾶσα, καὶ τὸ μέγιστον ἁπάντων, γῆς μὲν
οὐδαμοῦ, πᾶσα γὰρ εἴχετο, ἡ δὲ εἰς τὴν θάλατταν
ἀπεχώρει,¹ καὶ τῆς περὶ τὸν Ἄθω² διωρυχῆς καὶ
τοῦ πορθμοῦ τῆς γεφύρας οὔτε εἰς ἀκοὴν ἀηδέστερον οὔτε γνώμῃ φαυλότερον τοῦτο τὸ³ τόλμημα
ἀντεπεδείξατο ἐπὶ τῆς θαλάττης φανεῖσα, καὶ
Ξέρξῃ καταλιποῦσα τὸ ἴχνος μόνον προσιδεῖν· ὥστε
ἐλθὼν οὐχ εὗρεν τὴν πόλιν οὐδὲ εἶχεν λαβεῖν ἔχων
128 ὡς ᾤετο. οὕτως εἰς ἄπορον καὶ ὑπερφυὲς αἴνιγμα
συνηλάθη. ἀλλ᾿ ὥσπερ τῶν ποιητῶν φασί τινες τὸν
Ἀλέξανδρον τῆς Ἑλένης τὸ εἴδωλον λαβεῖν, αὐτὴν
δὲ οὐ δυνηθῆναι, οὕτω καὶ Ξέρξης τῆς πόλεως
τοὔδαφος εἶχεν, αὐτὴν δὲ οὐχ εὗρεν, πλήν γε δὴ
καλῶς εὗρεν ἐπ᾿ Ἀρτεμισίῳ καὶ Σαλαμῖνι, καὶ τὴν
θέαν οὐκ ἤνεγκεν, ὥσπερ τινὸς ἐν μύθῳ Γοργόνος,
ἀλλ᾿ ἐκπλαγεὶς ἔδεισεν οὐ μόνον περὶ τῶν λοιπῶν,
213 D. ἀλλὰ καὶ περὶ τοῦ σώματος, πάντα τὸν ἔμπροσθεν
χρόνον ἀήθης ὢν τούτου καὶ τῷ φοβεῖν συνεζηκώς.
129 ὅπερ δὲ καὶ πρὶν ἅπτεσθαι τῶν λόγων τούτων
προειρήκειν, ὅτι ἄμφω τὼ γένη τῆς πόλεως ἡττᾶτο
λαμπρῶς, τό τε Ἑλληνικὸν καὶ τὸ βαρβαρικόν, τὸ
μὲν ἁπάντων ἀποτυχόν, τὸ δὲ οὐδ᾿⁴ ἐγγὺς γενόμενον, καὶ πάλιν ὃ μικρῷ γε πρόσθεν ἔφην, ὅτι μᾶλλον αἰσχυνομένη συνῆγεν τοὺς Ἕλληνας ἢ δεο-

---

¹ ἀπεχώρησεν VA.   ² codd. dett. : Ἄθων TQVA.
³ τὸ om. VA.   ⁴ οὐκ VA.

ᵃ The Athenians left their city, sending their women and
children to safer places, and entrusting the future to their
ships.

in dire need of safety and freedom, and the city's former decision was an example ready at hand for both these needs. And it considered by what plan it would first of all frighten the barbarian in turn. And it surpassed him in its extraordinariness. 127 For the city rose up and moved away, and what was the greatest of all, nowhere on the earth—for this was all occupied, but it withdrew to the sea.[a] And it displayed this act of daring in return, its appearance on the sea and its leaving Xerxes the sight of its tracks alone ; which was no less pleasant to hear, nor less important to conceive than the canal at Athos and the bridge over the strait, so that when he came he did not find the city, and although he held it, he could not take it, as he thought. Thus he 128 was forced into a difficult and extraordinary kind of riddle. But just as some of the poets say that Alexandros[b] took a shadow of Helen, but could not take _her_, so Xerxes also held the ground, but did not find the city, except that he found it well at Artemisium and Salamis, and did not endure the 480. sight, as it were of some mythical Gorgon, but he was terrified and feared not only for the future, but also for his very life, although during all the previous time he was unaccustomed to this and had passed his life in causing fear. But this should be said and 129 can be learned from the facts—what I had formerly stated before undertaking these arguments[c]—that both races, Greek and barbarian, were clearly inferior to the city, the one having failed in everything and the other not even coming near it, and again what I said a little before,[d] that the city gathered the Greeks together more through a sense of embarrassment

[b] Also called Paris.   [c] § 92.   [d] § 126.

(213 D.)

μένη, νῦν τοῦτο ἄξιον εἰπεῖν καὶ πάρεστι διὰ τῶν πραγμάτων καταμαθεῖν. φανεῖται γὰρ πανταχῇ σκοπουμένῳ τοσοῦτον ὑπερβαλλομένη ὥστε μὴ πρώτη τῶν Ἑλληνίδων μηδὲ μάλιστα αἰτία τῆς ἐλευθερίας μᾶλλον ἢ μόνη δικαίως ἂν ἀκοῦσαι πάντα κατειργασμένη. πρῶτον μὲν γὰρ ἐκεῖνο πάντες ἂν συμφαῖεν ὅτι τοῖς τοσοῦτον λειπομένοις καὶ ναυσὶν καὶ ὅπλοις καὶ σώμασιν καὶ χρήμασιν καὶ πάσῃ τῇ τοῦ πολέμου παρασκευῇ ἓν μόνον ἀντίρροπον κατελείπετο καὶ ὡς ἀληθῶς Ἑλληνικόν, τὸ βουλεύεσθαι καλῶς, ἢ χρῆναι ἀτίμως συμπατηθῆναι, καθάπερ τὰ μικρὸν τῆς γῆς ὑπερέχοντα. μὴ γὰρ ὅτι εἰς ἀντιπάλων μέρος ἐξήρκουν, ἀλλ' ἐν προσθήκῃ τῷ βασιλεῖ
130 γενομένων οὐκ ἂν ἦν τὸ ἐπίδηλον. τούτου δ' οὕτω κειμένου καὶ πάντων ἂν ταύτῃ [κατὰ ταὐτὸ ψηφιζομένων ἢ]¹ θεμένων καὶ σοφῶν καὶ πολλῶν οὐκ ἔστιν ἀντειπεῖν ὡς οὐχ ἥδ' ἐστὶν ἡ παρασχομένη τὸν βουλευσάμενον καὶ περὶ αὑτῶν καὶ περὶ τῶν
131 ἄλλων ἃ σώσειν ἔμελλεν.² ὃ δὲ τούτου τ' ἐξήρτηται
214 D. καὶ καθ' αὑτὸ διαρκῆ τὴν ἐπίδειξιν ἔχει πάλιν σκεψώμεθα. οὐδεὶς γὰρ οὕτω σκαιός ἐστιν οὐδὲ τἀναντία τοῖς φανεροῖς φρονῶν ὅστις οὐ συμφήσει ὡς οὐκ εἰς τὰς ναῦς ἧκεν τότε τοῖς Ἕλλησι τὰ πράγματα, οὐδὲ ὡς τοῦτο ἄριστον ἦν τῆς γνώμης· οἱ μὲν γὰρ εἰς Πύλας ἐξελθόντες καὶ τάξαντες ἑαυτοὺς ἐπὶ τὰς παρόδους οἱ μὲν ὥσπερ νεφέλην προσιοῦσαν οὐκ ἤνεγκαν, ἀλλ' αἰσχρῶς τὴν ἐπίνοιαν διέφθειραν, δραπετεύειν ἀναγκασθέντες καὶ σῴζειν

---

¹ secl. Ddf. ² codd. dett. : ἔμελλον TQVA.

ᵃ Themistocles.
ᵇ Thermopylae (" Hot Gates " because of warm sulphurous springs of water), the pass where in 480 B.C. the Persians

than actual need. For upon every consideration,
it will obviously be so superior that in justice, since
it accomplished everything itself, it should not be
called the first of the Greek cities or the one especially responsible for freedom, but rather the only one.
For first of all, everyone would agree that though
they were very deficient in ships, weapons, men,
money, and every means of war, one thing alone was
left to even the balance, and that a truly Greek
quality, sound advice ; otherwise they must have
been trampled down in dishonour, like little uneven-
nesses on the ground. For to say nothing of their
being sufficient for the role of opponents, if they had
joined the king, there would have been nothing
notable in their addition. When this was the situa- 130
tion, and all men, both the wise and the masses,
would have agreed with this interpretation, it is
indisputable that it was this city which provided
the man *a* who gave the advice on this and other 493-472.
matters which was going to save them. Again let 131
us consider what results from this consideration
and in itself is sufficient proof of my contention.
For no one is so stupid or in his beliefs so opposed to
the obvious truth as not to agree that the Greeks'
position then depended on the fleet, and that this
was the best decision. For of those who went out 480.
to the Gates *b* and took their stand at the entrance
ways, some did not endure as it were the approaching
cloud, but shamefully ruined the plan of campaign,
each of them being forced to run away and save

destroyed King Leonidas and his three hundred fellow
Lacedaemonians, and also some Thebans and Thespians,
after soldiers of other Greek states had retired. Whether
there was any cowardice is doubtful.

(214 D.)

ἑαυτοὺς χωρὶς ἕκαστοι μελλόντων ἔτι τῶν δεινῶν·
οὕτως ἀνομοίως τὴν Μαραθῶνι μάχην ἐμιμήσαντο·
οἱ δὲ ὑπολειφθέντες οὐκ ἠδυνήθησαν ταὐτὸν τοῖς
Μαραθῶνι διαπράξασθαι, ἀλλ᾽ εὐθύς τε ἔμειναν ὡς
πεισόμενοι μᾶλλον ἢ δράσοντες καὶ καταχωσθέντες
ἀπώλοντο, ἑνὶ τούτῳ κοσμήσαντες τὴν Ἑλλάδα, τῷ
καλῶς ἀποθανεῖν, καὶ τοσοῦτον ἐπιδειξάμενοι μόνον·
οἱ δ᾽ ὥσπερ χειμάρρους ἐχώρουν διὰ πάντων ἤδη

215 D.
132   δεχομένων. καίτοι τοῦτο δυοῖν ἐστι σημεῖον, τοῦ
μήτ᾽ ἐν τῇ γῇ φανῆναί τινας τῶν Ἑλλήνων ὁμοίους
τῇ πόλει καὶ οἷς ἐκεῖνοι πρότερον κατέπραξαν,
μᾶλλον δὲ τοῦ μηδὲ σύμπαντας ὁμοίους καὶ τοῦ τὰ
ἐν τῇ θαλάττῃ μόνα τότε τοῖς Ἕλλησιν λειφθῆναι·
οὕτω δ᾽ αὖ τούτου σαφοῦς ὄντος καὶ διπλῆν γενέσθαι τὴν γνώμην οὐδενὶ λείποντος τοσοῦτον διήνεγκεν ἡ πόλις ἐν τούτοις ὥστε κἂν αἰσχυνθῆναί τινα

133   ὑπὲρ τῆς λοιπῆς Ἑλλάδος. πρῶτον μέν γε τῷ
πλήθει τῶν τριήρων οὕτω λαμπρῶς ὑπερῆρεν ὥστε,
εἴ τις χωρὶς ἀφέλοι τὸ τῆς πόλεως ἀξίωμα καὶ τὴν
δύναμιν πρός γε τὸν συλλεχθέντα τοῦ ναυτικοῦ
ἀριθμόν, ἐξεῖναι τὰς μὲν τῆς πόλεως ναῦς νομίσαι
τὰς ἀπάντων εἶναι, τὰς δὲ κοινὰς ἁπάντων μιᾶς
τινος τῶν ἐν τοῖς Ἕλλησιν πόλεως. ὥστ᾽ εἴ τις
θεῶν ἤρετο τοὺς Ἕλληνας τότε εἰ μὴ δέοι πάσας
ἀγωνίσασθαι μηδὲ ἐξείη, πότερον τὰς ἁπάντων τῶν
ἄλλων παρούσας δέξαιντο ἂν μᾶλλον ἢ τὰς Ἀθήνηθεν μόνας, οὐχ αἵρεσιν εἶναι πάντες ἂν εἶπον, ἀλλ᾽
Ἀθηναίους ὑπὲρ σφῶν ἀγωνίζεσθαι λείπεσθαι. κἂν
εἰ πάλιν αὐτὸς ὁ θεὸς αὐτοὺς ἐπανήρετο, οὐκοῦν
ὁμολογεῖτ᾽ Ἀθηναίοις γε θαρρεῖν ὑπὲρ αὑτῶν

themselves separately, while the danger was still in the future. In such a dissimilar fashion did they imitate the battle at Marathon. But those who were left behind were unable to achieve the same accomplishment as those at Marathon, but from the start they remained at their post to suffer rather than to act, and they were overwhelmed and perished, having honoured Greece by this single action, their noble death, and offering no more. But the barbarians passed like a torrent through all and now were unopposed. Yet this is a proof of two things : that 132 on land none of the Greeks appeared equal to the city and to its former accomplishments, moreover that not even all of them together were equal ; and that at this time only action on the sea was left to the Greeks. And again when this fact was so clear and allowed no one to hold two opinions on the matter, the city was so distinguished in this regard that one would even feel shame for the rest of Greece. First of 133 all it so clearly had the largest number of triremes that if someone should compare the proud force of the city against the whole number of the fleet, it could be thought that the ships of the city were those of all the rest, and that the ships of all the rest together were those of one Greek city. Therefore if one of the Gods then asked the Greeks whether if it were not fated or impossible for all the ships to engage in the contest, they would prefer the presence of those of the others to those from Athens alone, all would say that there was no choice, but that the Athenians should be left to contend on their behalf. And if again the God asked them, " do you then confess that you are more confident in the Athenians for your defence than in yourselves ? ",

(215 D.)

μᾶλλον ἢ ὑμῖν αὐτοῖς, ἄρνησις οὐκ ἦν δήπουθεν.
οὐ γὰρ μέρος εἰς τὸ κοινὸν εἰσήνεγκαν, ἀλλ' ἡ παρὰ
πάντων συντέλεια μέρος τῶν ἰδίων τῆς πόλεως ἐγένετο, ἀλλὰ μὴν τήν γε εὐψυχίαν καὶ τόλμαν τοσαύτην συνεισήνεγκαν ὥστε μικρὸν εἶναι τὸ ταῖς ναυσὶ
τοσοῦτον ὑπερέχειν. μόνοι μὲν γὰρ ἁπάντων ἀνθρώ-

216 D. πων ὑπέμειναν τὴν ἑαυτῶν ἐκλιπεῖν ὑπὲρ τοῦ μὴ
τὴν τῶν ἄλλων ἁπάντων ἀνάστατον γενομένην ἐπ-
ιδεῖν, μόνοι δὲ οὐχ ὑπὸ πολεμίων τοῦτο παθόντες,
ὑπὸ σφῶν αὐτῶν ἐξῳκίσθησαν ὑπὲρ νίκης, οὐ κατὰ
συμφορὰν ὑφ' ἑτέρων, ἀλλ' ἃ τοῖς ἄλλοις πέρας
εἶναι δοκεῖ τῶν ἐν τοῖς πολέμοις ἀτυχημάτων, ταῦτ'
εἰς ἀρετὴν ἔτρεψαν καὶ παρείλοντο Ξέρξην τὰς
ἐλπίδας τὸ καθ' αὐτούς, ἐνδειξάμενοι τοῦθ', ὅτι κἂν
μυριάκις κατάσχῃ τὴν χώραν, κἂν τὰς ἑστίας διερευ-
νήσηται, κἂν ἐκ βάθρων ἅπαντα ἀνασπάσῃ, οὐδὲν
μᾶλλον τὸ τῶν Ἀθηναίων ἀξίωμα καθαιρήσει οὐδὲ
ἀφαιρήσεται σφᾶς τό γε Ἀθηναίους εἶναι, ἀλλ'
ἀπέραντα πονεῖ καὶ τοῖς ἐν Ἅιδου καταδίκοις προσ-

134 όμοια. καίτοι τίς προθυμία λαμπροτέρα, τίς εὐψυ-
χία φανερωτέρα τίνων Ἑλλήνων ἢ καθάπαξ εἰπεῖν
ἀνθρώπων ἐξετάζοντι φανήσεται; οἳ τῆς γῆς ἐξέστησαν ὑπὲρ τοῦ μήτε ἐν γῇ μήτε ἐν θαλάττῃ
δουλεῦσαι, τὸ μὲν τηρεῖν τὰ ὑπάρχοντα δουλείας
ἀρχὴν νομίσαντες εἶναι, τὴν δὲ τῶν ὄντων στέρησιν
ἀφορμὴν τῶν μελλόντων ἀγαθῶν ποιησάμενοι, καὶ
τοὺς ἔχοντας τὰ ἑαυτῶν ἔσῳζον ἀφ' ὧν αὐτοὶ

135 προεῖντο[1] τὴν αὑτῶν. ἡ μὲν δὴ πρὸ τῶν κινδύνων
τε καὶ πρὸς τοὺς κινδύνους προθυμία τοσαύτη καὶ
οὕτως ἄλογος ὡς εἰπεῖν, ἢ τό γε ἀληθέστερον[2]
εἰπεῖν, οὕτως εὔλογος· ἡ δὲ παρ' αὐτὸν τὸν ἀγῶνα

---

[1] προοῖντο TVA Phot. [2] codd. dett. : ἀληθὲς TQVA.

they certainly would not deny it. For they did not
contribute a part to a joint force, but everyone's
contribution was a fraction of the personal contingent of the city. Indeed, they contributed so
much courage and daring, that their great superiority
in ships was a small thing. For alone of all men they
endured to leave their country, so that they might not
see all the others uprooted from theirs, and alone,
without suffering this at the hands of the enemy,
they were driven from their homes by themselves
for the sake of victory, not through defeat at the
hands of the enemy. But they made a virtue out of
what to others seems to be the extremity of misfortune in war time, and by themselves they deprived
Xerxes of his hope, by making this clear, that even if
he captures their territory over and over again,
or plunders their homes, or pulls everything down
to the foundations, he will still not destroy the
honour of the Athenians, nor will he deprive them
of being Athenians, but he will labour endlessly and
like the condemned in Hades. Yet upon examination, 134
where will be found an enthusiasm more glorious,
where a courage more manifest among the Greeks,
or to say it once and for all, among mankind ? They
left their land so that they might not be slaves either
on land or sea, in the belief that the preservation of
their property was the beginning of slavery, but they
made the loss of their possessions the start of their
future good. And they saved those who kept their
possessions by the act of abandoning their land.
Their enthusiasm before the time of danger and 135
in face of danger was so great and so contrary to
reason, one might say, or to speak more truly, of such
glorious reason, and during the contest and danger

(216 D.)

καὶ κίνδυνον οὕτω περιφανὴς ὥστε μόνους ἔξεστιν
εἰπεῖν ἐπὶ σφῶν αὐτῶν νικῆσαι· πρῶτοι γὰρ ἐποίη-
136 σαν τὴν τροπήν. βούλομαι δὲ ἐπαναχωρήσας ἔτι μικρὰ πρὸ τῆς ναυμαχίας προειπεῖν. οἱ μὲν γὰρ ἄλλοι
πάντες τὸ τῶν νεῶν πλῆθος καὶ τὴν προθυμίαν τῆς
πόλεως καὶ τὰς πράξεις ἐγκωμιάζουσιν, ἐγὼ δέ, εἰ
καὶ παράδοξον εἰπεῖν, ἔν τι φημὶ πάντας αὐτοὺς
παραλιπεῖν, οὐδενὸς ἧττον τούτων ἄξιον ἰδεῖν καὶ
217 D. θαυμάσαι, ὃ νῦν αὐτὸς εἰς μέσον θήσω, τἀληθὲς
οὐκ αἰσχυνθείς· ὡς ὅστις αἰσχύνῃ τοῦτο παρέρχεται
καὶ δι' εὔνοιαν τὴν πρὸς τὴν πόλιν, παραπλήσιον
ποιεῖ ὥσπερ ἂν εἰ τὴν ναυμαχίαν παρέρχοιτο δι'
εὔνοιαν τὴν πρὸς τὴν πόλιν. ἀμφοτέρας γὰρ τὰς
νίκας ἀνείλοντο σαφέστατα ἀνθρώπων οἱ τότε,
πάλαι τε δὴ τὰς Ἀθήνας οἰκοῦντες καὶ ἔτι κάλλιον κομισάμενοι· τοὺς μὲν γὰρ ἐχθροὺς τοῖς ὅπ-
137 λοις, τῇ δ' ἐπιεικείᾳ τοὺς φίλους ἐνίκησαν. τὸ γὰρ
τοσαύτην μὲν προθυμίαν παρεχομένους ὑπὲρ τῆς
ἁπάντων σωτηρίας, τοσαύτην δὲ εἰσφορὰν εἰσεν-
εγκόντας τῇ κοινῇ χρείᾳ, πάντα δὲ αὐτοὺς ὄντας,
καὶ τῶν μὲν πραγμάτων εἰς τὴν θάλατταν καὶ τὰς
ναῦς, τῶν δ' ἐν ταῖς ναυσὶν εἰς τὴν πόλιν ἀνακειμέ-
νων, τῶν δ' ἄλλων, ὥσπερ χειμῶνος ὥρα, κατα-
πεφευγότων πρὸς τὴν ἐκείνων δύναμιν καὶ ἐπὶ τῆς
ἐκείνων ἀρετῆς τε καὶ τύχης ὁρμούντων, καὶ μηδ'
ἂν αὐτῶν, ὅπερ εἶπον, ἐξάρνων γιγνομένων ὡς οὐχ
οὕτως ταῦτ' ἔχει, τοσοῦτον πραότητος καὶ μεγαλοψυχίας προσθεῖναι ὥστε ἑτέροις ἡγεῖσθαι συγχωρῆσαι τὴν ἐπὶ σχήματος ἡγεμονίαν, καὶ μὴ φιλονικῆσαι,

---

ᵃ At Salamis.

was so manifest, that it can be said that they conquered alone by themselves. For they were the first to turn the enemy. But going back, I wish to 136 preface a few remarks to the naval battle.[a] For all 480. other writers praise the multitude of ships, and the enthusiasm and the deeds of the city. But I, even if it is a strange thing to say, declare that they all have overlooked one point, no less deserving to be considered and marvelled at, which now I shall reveal, since I am not ashamed of the truth. For whoever omits this out of shame and because of his good will toward the city, does the same as if he should omit the naval battle because of his good will toward the city. For those then, who of old dwelt in Athens and recovered it in a still fairer way, won a double victory most clearly of all men : they conquered the enemy in armed prowess and their friends in goodness. For when they had shown such 137 great enthusiasm for the safety of all men, and made such a great contribution to the common need, and were all-important, and when the situation depended on the sea and the fleet, and the fleet depended on the city, and when the others, as in a time of storm, took refuge in the Athenians' power and were securely anchored in their virtue and fortune, and when none of them would deny, as I said,[b] that such was the case,—for the Athenians then to add such gentleness and nobility, so that they conceded to 481. others a formal leadership, and did not argue the

[b] [§ 132. Though the Athenians could claim the right to command at sea, they yielded, because of other cities' jealousy, the sea-command to the Lacedaemonian Eurybiadas, while the Lacedaemonian Leonidas led the Greek armies. See also note to § 148.—*E.H.W.*]

(217 D.)

μηδὲ ἃ κἂν[1] οἱ νωθρότατοι τὴν φύσιν εἶπον, κἂν
ὑπὲρ αὐτῶν ἕτεροι μηδὲν[2] μήτε φθέγξασθαι μήτε
μελλῆσαι μήθ' ὅλως φωνὴν ἔχουσιν ἐοικότας ὀφθῆ-
218 D. ναι τούτων ἕνεκα, πῶς οὐ πᾶσαν ἤδη σοφίαν παρ'
ἐκείνοις οὖσαν ὡς ἀληθῶς ἀποφαίνει καὶ πάντων
ἄνδρας ἀρίστους ἐκείνους καὶ κατὰ ἔθνη καὶ καθ'
ἕνα καὶ ὁπωσοῦν ἐξετάζοντι; εἰ γὰρ τότε ἐκεῖνοι
δυσχεράναντες τὴν τοιαύτην ἀγνωμοσύνην ἐκποδὼν
ἔστησαν, ἢ πρὸς φιλονικίαν ἐχώρησαν, τίς μηχανὴ
σωτηρίας, ἢ ποῖον ὄναρ χρηστὸν κατελείπετο τοῖς
ἄλλοις, ἢ τίς τῶν εἴτε πλεόνων εἴτε ἐλαττόνων νεῶν
138 ὑπῆρξεν ἂν εἰς τὸ δέον τοῖς Ἕλλησιν ἔτι; φέρε
γὰρ πρὸς θεῶν, ἵνα μικρὸν προσδιατρίψωμεν τῷ
λόγῳ καὶ τὸ ἦθος αὐτῶν καὶ πᾶν ὃ λέγω σαφέστερον κατίδῃ τις, εἰ τὴν ἡγεμονίαν αὐτοὶ τότε τοὺς
Ἕλληνας ᾔτησαν, λέγοντες ὡς, ἂν μὲν κρατηθῶσι
τῇ ναυμαχίᾳ, οὐκ ἔσονται κύριοι σφίσιν αἱρεῖσθαι
τοὺς ἡγεμόνας οὐδὲ ὑπὲρ τῶν ἐν ἑαυτοῖς ἡγησομέ-
νων ὁ βάρβαρος αὐτοῖς εἶναι ποιήσει τὸν λόγον, ἀλλ'
ἀκολουθεῖν αἰσχρῶς ἐκείνῳ δεήσει καὶ δούλους καὶ
ἀνασπάστους[3] γενέσθαι, ἴσως δὲ οὐδ' ἀκολουθεῖν,
ἀλλ' ἀφανισθέντας τρόπον ὅντινα ἐκείνῳ δόξειεν
ἀπελθεῖν ἐξ ἀνθρώπων αὐτοῖς ἱεροῖς καὶ ὅπλοις καὶ
νόμοις· λέγοντες δ' ὅτι ταῦθ' ἡμεῖς προορώμενοι
τὴν πόλιν εἰς τὰς τριήρεις πᾶσαν μετεσκευάσαμεν,
καὶ εἴτε δεῖ τὰ μέγιστα τετολμηκέναι, ἐκλέλειπται
τὰ κοινὰ τῆς ἀνθρωπείας φύσεως ἡμῖν ὑπὲρ ὑμῶν,
εἴτε παρασκευῆς ⟨οὕτως⟩[4] ἔχενι, ὡς ἀβίωτον ὂν
ἡττηθεῖσιν, ἡμεῖς τοῦτο διανενοήμεθα· καὶ μόνοις

---

[1] ἡνίκα ci. Oliver.
[2] codd. dett. : μηδενὶ TQVA (prob. Oliver).

matter, and neither said nor intended to say,
what even those of the most slothful nature would
have said or others on their behalf, nor as far as
this matter was concerned seemed to be able to
speak at all : how does not such conduct truly prove
upon investigation that they already possessed
every kind of wisdom and were the best of all men
both race by race, and man by man, or however it
may be ? For if then in anger at such folly they had
stood aside, or became argumentative, what means of
preservation or what fair dream was left to the others,
or which of the larger or smaller fleets would have
any longer satisfied the Greeks' need ? Come, 138
by the Gods—to devote a little time to this argument
so that their nature and all that I am discussing
may be more clearly seen—, if they then had themselves asked the Greeks for the command, saying
that if the Greeks were defeated in the naval battle,
they would have no authority to choose their commanders, nor would the barbarian regard their
feelings as to who would be their leaders, but they
would have to follow him shamefully, and be enslaved and uprooted, and perhaps not even follow,
but be removed in whatever way he might decide
and be erased from mankind with their temples,
weapons, and laws, and saying that we have foreseen
these things and changed the structure of our whole
city into triremes, and if the greatest daring is
needed, we have abandoned those things common to
human nature for your sake, and if we must be so
prepared, as if life would not be livable should we be
defeated, we have taken thought for this and for us

---

¹ἀναστάτους QT p. corr.   ⁴ add. codd. dett.

(218 D.)

ἡμῖν ἀναγκαῖόν ἐστιν τὸ νικᾶν· ὥστ' εἴτε τι νίκης

219 D. δεῖσθε,[1] τοσοῦτον ἡμῖν προκέκοπται, εἴτε καὶ τὴν
συντέλειαν δεῖ σκοπεῖν, δύο τοῦ παντὸς μέρη μόνοι

139 πληροῦμεν, οὗτοι δὲ εἰκοστὸν τοῦ παρ' ἡμῶν· εἰ
ταῦτα ἔλεγον καὶ κεφάλαια προσετίθεσαν, ὅτι εἰ
μὲν δέχεσθε ἐπὶ τούτοις· εἰ δὲ μή, σκοπεῖτε μὴ οὐχ
ἡμᾶς μειζόνων ἢ ὑμᾶς αὐτοὺς ἀποστερήσετε· εἰ δὲ
δὴ καὶ προσέθηκαν, ἐῶ γὰρ τὸν ἡγούμενον, ὃς
τοσοῦτον ἁπάντων ὑπερεῖχεν ὥσθ' εἷς ἀντὶ πάντων
ἦν, ὃς μόνος καὶ τόπους καὶ καιροὺς καὶ τὰ τῶν
βαρβάρων ἀπόρρητα καὶ τὰ μέλλοντα ὥσπερ μάντις
ἐξηγεῖτο· ἀλλ' εἰ προσέθηκαν ἐκεῖνο μόνον τῇ
προκλήσει, ὅτι, εἰ δ' ἄρα ἄλλως ἐγνώκατε ὑμεῖς,
ἡμῖν δ' ἕτερος δώσει τὴν ὑμετέραν ἡγεμονίαν
ἄσμενος καὶ προσθήσει χρήματα Μηδικὰ καὶ
δωρεάς, πρὸς ταῦτα αἱρεῖσθε ὁπότερα βούλεσθε, ἆρ'
ἢ τῷ δικαίῳ λόγους οὐχὶ συμβαίνοντας, ἢ ταῖς
παρούσαις ἀνάγκαις οἵους ἐγχωρεῖ παριδεῖν, εἶ-

140 πον ἄν, εἰ τούτοις ἐχρῶντο; μὴ γὰρ ὅτι λειπο-
μένης μὲν τῆς θαλάττης μόνης, τοσαύτας δὲ ναῦς
αὐτοὺς ἰδίᾳ παρεχομένους, τῶν δ' ἐλπίδων ὄντας τὸ
κεφάλαιον, ἐφεστηκότας δὲ τῇ ῥοπῇ τῆς σωτηρίας,

220 D. μόνους δὲ ἀγωνιστὰς ὄντας τοῦ πράγματος ἀξιόχρεως, πάντων δὲ προβεβληκότας αὑτούς, οὐχ ἡγεμόνων τάξιν μόνον, ἀλλὰ καὶ πατέρων, ἔχοντας δ'
ὡς εἰπεῖν παρ' αὐτῶν ὧν ἐποίουν τὴν ἡγεμονίαν·
ἀλλ' εἰ κοινὰ μὲν πάντα ἦν, μηδεὶς δὲ ὑπερεῖχεν
μηδενός, πάντες δ' ἐξ ἴσου συνετέλουν, οἱ δὲ ναύ-
αρχοι παραπλησίως εἶχον τὰς φύσεις ἀλλήλοις,

[1] δεῖσθαι ΤΩΛ.

alone is victory necessary; therefore if you have
any need of victory, we have already made great
progress in that direction, and if our contribution
must be considered, we alone make up two thirds of
the whole, but these people a twentieth part of our
force [a] ; if they said these things and added as their 139
main point, that if you accept us, accept us on these
terms, but if not, consider that you will not deprive
us of more than you will deprive yourselves ; and
if they also added,—for I omit their commander [b]
who was so superior to all men, that one man alone
he was worth all of them, and who alone like a seer
expounded the places and times of battle, the secret
plans of the barbarians, and the future—, but if they
added to their appeal only the following, that if
you have decided otherwise, and another will
gladly give us command of you and will add Persian
money and gifts besides, so choose which ever you
wish : then would not their arguments have been
consistent with right and the present necessities,
and such as cannot be overlooked, if they used them ?
For, to say nothing about the sea being the only 140
means left, and that they themselves contributed so
many ships, and were the sum of their hopes, and
could tilt the balance of safety, and were the only
suitable contestants for the affair, and had gone
forth in defence of all, not only in the position of
commanders, but also as fathers, and, one might say,
held the command as a result of their actions—but
if everything was shared, and no one outranked another, and all contributed equally, and the admirals'
natures were similar to one another, and it was a

[a] *Cf.* Herodotus VIII. 1, 61.
[b] Themistocles.

(220 D.)

ἔρανος δ' ἦν, ἔδει δ' ἐκ τῶν ὑπαρχόντων σκεψα-
μένους τοὺς ἡγησομένους καταστῆσαι, πῶς οὐκ
ἐκεῖνοι διὰ πάντων ἐξέλαμπον ὥσπερ ἀστέρες; ἢ
πῶς οὐχ ὑπὲρ σύμπαντας ἦσαν ⟨πάσαις⟩¹ ταῖς
141 ψήφοις, οὐ μόνον κατὰ τὴν ἐπιστήμην; καίτοι
τοῦτο ἔσχατον εἶναι δοκεῖ τῶν δικαίων ἐν τοῖς
τοιούτοις· οὐ² γὰρ δήπου κατὰ μίαν μὲν ἂν τῶν
τριήρων αὐτοῖς οὕτως ἦρχον οἱ κυβερνῆται τέχνῃ
προκριθέντες, πασῶν δὲ λαβεῖν τὴν ἡγεμονίαν οὐ
τοῖς ταῦτα κρατίστοις ὠφείλετο, ἀλλὰ καὶ τοῦτο
μικρὸν ἐκείνοις τὸ δίκαιον. ἀλλ' ἐκεῖνό γε δὴ καὶ
πρόδηλον καὶ μόνον ἀρκοῦν, τῶν συνειλεγμένων
δέον τινὰς ἡγεῖσθαι τοῦ πρὸς τὸν βάρβαρον πολέμου,
οὐ τοὺς πρὸς τὸν πρότερον στόλον τῶν αὐτῶν
τούτων βαρβάρων μόνους κινδυνεύσαντας ὑπὲρ
πάντων, τούτους ἡγεῖσθαι ἔδει;³ οἷς γὰρ τὰ παρόντα
κοινὰ πρὸς τοὺς μετέχοντας ἦν, οὗτοι τοῖς ἰδίοις
ἐνίκων ἅπαντας· καὶ τοσούτῳ γε ἐλάττω τὴν χάριν
ἐκομίζοντ' ἄν, ὅσῳ πάντας μὲν ἠλευθέρωσαν, τῶν
221 D.
142 παρόντων δὲ ἔμελλον ἡγήσεσθαι. καὶ μὴν εἰ μὲν
οὐδεὶς ἀντεῖπεν αὐτοῖς πρὸς ταῦτα, ἀλλὰ πάντες
ἀμφοῖν χεροῖν ἀπέστησαν, πῶς οὐκ ἄξιον τῆς μεγαλοψυχίας ἀγασθῆναι; οἳ πανταχῇ παρεῖδον τὰ καθ'
ἑαυτούς, καὶ τοσοῦτον μὲν τὸν πρόσθεν ἀράμενοι,
πάλιν δὲ ἐν τῷ τότε ὑπὲρ τὴν φύσιν φιλοτιμούμενοι
143 πλέον οὐδὲν ἐζήτησαν. εἰ δὲ μὴ προσέξειν ἔμελλον
αὐτοῖς οἱ Ἕλληνες, οἱ δὲ πρὸς ὀργὴν ἐγκατέλιπον, τί
ἦν ἐν μέσῳ ⟨τοῦ τότ' οὐ μόνον ἀφαιρεθῆναι⟩⁴ τῆς
οὐδ' ἐν τοῖς βαρβάροις ἀπεστερημένης Ἑλλάδος τὸ

---

¹ add. Behr.   ² εἰ ci. Holleck.
³ codd. dett. : δεῖ TQVA.   ⁴ add. Oliver, p. 122.

joint effort, and it was necessary to appoint a city to command in consideration of its existing qualities, how did they not shine out in every way like stars ? Or how were they not superior to all of them together on every count, not only in their technical skill ? Yet in such circumstances this seems to be the 141 most important claim. For it cannot be said that, if their helmsmen, having been selected by their skill, commanded the individual triremes, the command of all the ships was not owed to the people who were best in this respect. But even this claim is a modest one to make on their behalf. The following one is both clear and sufficient by itself : since it was necessary that some one of those assembled take command of the war against the barbarian, should not those hold the command, who against the former expedition of these same barbarians alone faced danger on behalf of all ? For they who now shared in the present circumstances with the other participants, surpassed all in their private action. And their recompense would be so much the less, to the degree that they then liberated all, but would now command only those who were present. Indeed, if no one argued 142 with them on those points, but all yielded entirely, how should we still not marvel at their generosity ? For in every way they neglected their own affairs, and although they had formerly undertaken so great a contest, and again in the present struggle were zealous beyond what was natural, they still sought nothing more than the command. But if the 143 Greeks did not intend to pay attention to them, and they had left then in anger, what would prevent Greece, which had not lost its reputation among the barbarians, then not only to be deprived of it,

(221 D.)

144 θαυμάζεσθαι ἀλλ' οὐδ' ὄνομα νῦν λείπεσθαι; ἀλλὰ
μὴν τριῶν γε ἕν τι κατηνάγκαστο, ἢ πάντων εἰξάντων ἔχειν¹ τὴν ἡγεμονίαν, οὗ μεῖζον οὐδὲν ἂν εἴποι
τις δεῖγμα τῆς ἐκείνων ἀρετῆς καὶ τοῦ προῖκα τοὺς
Ἕλληνας ἐλευθεροῦν, ἢ μηδενὸς ταῦτα συγχωροῦντος

222 D. ἅπαντας οἴχεσθαι καταλειφθέντας, ἢ δίχα τὰς ψήφους ἐλθεῖν, ἐν ᾧ στασιάζειν καὶ πολεμεῖν πρὸς ἀλλήλους ἦν, οὐκ ἔχοντας ὅπως χρὴ² τοῖς βαρβάροις· ὃ τῇ
μὲν τοῦ πράγματος φύσει συμβάν, τῇ δὲ ἐκείνων

145 προνοίᾳ κωλυθὲν φαίνεται. καὶ μὴν εἰ μὲν ἐκίνει
ταῦτα αὐτοὺς ἃ νῦν διεξῆλθον, εἶτα κατεῖχον σιγῇ
τοὺς λογισμούς, ἐσχάτης³ βάσανον καρτερίας παρεῖχον. εἰ δ' οὐδὲν ᾤοντο ἐλαττοῦσθαι, τίνας εἰς
ταὐτὸν ἄξιον ἐκείνοις θεῖναι, οἳ μόνοις ᾔδεσαν τοῖς
βαρβάροις ὀργίζεσθαι; ἀλλ' οἶμαι πρὸς ἓν τοῦτο
ἅπαντα συνετάξαντο, ὅπως καὶ τοὺς παρόντας καὶ
τοὺς ἀπόντας τοὺς μὲν ἑκόντας, τοὺς δ' ἄκοντας
ἐξαιρήσονται καὶ τοῦτο δίκαιον ἑώρων μόνον, ἐπεὶ
πάντα γε εἰ καθαρῶς ἐξήταζον, οὐδεὶς ἂν Ἑλλήνων
τότ' ἦν ἐν Σαλαμῖνι. προσθήσω γὰρ εὐφημίας ἕνεκα

146 τὴν Σαλαμῖνα. νῦν δὲ τοῦτο σφίσιν ἔκριναν ἐξαρκεῖν, καταστῆναι τοῖς Ἕλλησι τὰ πράγματα. καὶ
διὰ τοῦτο οὐ μόνον τῆς ἡγεμονίας, ἀλλὰ καὶ τῆς

223 D. πόλεως αὐτῆς ἀπέστησαν, ἁπάσης ἰδίας ἀσφαλείας καὶ πλεονεξίας τὰ κοινῇ συμφέροντα προκρί-
ναντες, καὶ νομίζοντες ταύτην ὡς ἀληθῶς καὶ μεγάλην ἡγεμονίαν κατεργάσεσθαι,⁴ ἐὰν ἡγήσωνται
τοῖς Ἕλλησιν πρὸς τὴν ἐλευθερίαν καὶ τὸ σωθῆναι.

---

¹ ⟨αὐτοὺς⟩ ἔχειν ci. Holleck.
² χρὴ ⟨προσιέναι⟩ Iunt.; χρήσονται codd. dett.
³ Canter : ἐσχάτην TQVA.
⁴ Ddf. : κατεργάσασθαι TQVA.

116

but not even to be left its name? Indeed, one of 144 three things must have necessarily happened: either, when all of them yielded, the Athenians would have held the command, in which case one would say that there was no greater proof of the Athenians' virtue and that they liberated Greece without charge; or when no one conceded their demands, they would all have been left to be annihilated; or the votes would have been split, which meant faction and warring with one another, not knowing how to war with the barbarians, which was obviously likely in the nature of the situation, but obviously has been prevented by their foresight. Indeed, if they were moved by the considerations 145 which I have now recounted, and next kept their reasons silent, they gave proof of the most extreme self-control. And if they thought that they were in no way worse off, to whom should they be compared, when they knew how to be angry at the barbarians alone? But, I think, they arranged everything for this single end, that they might liberate both those present and absent, and those willing and unwilling, and this was their only consideration, since if they had weighed every point, no Greek then would have been left alive at Salamis. For I shall add "at Salamis" to soften this invidious remark. But now they decided that it was enough 146 for them, to set to rights the affairs of the Greeks. And for this reason, they not only gave up the command, but also their city, since they preferred what was expedient for all in common to every private means of safety and advantage, in the belief that they would make this also a truly great command, if they led the Greeks to freedom and safety.

147 Λακεδαιμονίους δέ, ὥσπερ οἱ τοὺς παῖδας προδιδάσκοντες, ἐβουλήθησαν προθυμοτέρους ποιῆσαι.
καὶ διὰ τοῦτ' ἤγαγον εἰς τὸ πρόσθεν παρακλήσεως
ἕνεκα καὶ τοῦ τὰ πραττόμενα ὑπὸ σφῶν μιμεῖσθαι.

148 ταῦτα δὲ ἐποίουν καὶ τοῖς ψηφίσμασιν. οὐ μὴν
ὥσπερ τῷ ῥήματι καὶ τῷ κέρᾳ τῆς παρατάξεως,
οὕτω κἂν ταῖς πράξεσιν τὴν ἡγεμονίαν ἑτέροις παρεῖσαν, πόθεν; ἀλλ' οἱ μὲν ὄνομα ἡγεμόνων, οἱ δ'
ἔργα παρείχοντο, καὶ τοσούτῳ κάλλιον αὐτοῖς τὸ
σχῆμα καθίστατο ὅσῳ τῶν ἡγεμόνων αὐτῶν εἶχον
τὴν ἡγεμονίαν. ὅ τι γὰρ μὴ δόξειεν Ἀθηναίων ἑνί,
πάντ' ἦν ἄκυρα, ὥσθ' ὁ μὲν Λακεδαιμονίων ναύ-
αρχος τῶν ἀφ' ἑκάστων ἀρχόντων ἦρχεν, ὁ δὲ τῶν

149 Ἀθηναίων ἄρχοντος ἀρχόντων· ἅπερ οὖν καὶ οἱ
Ἕλληνες συνιδόντες τὰ ἀριστεῖα τῶν ναυμαχιῶν

224 D. ἀπέδοσαν τῇ πόλει, καὶ μαρτυρίαν παρόντων ὡς
ἀληθῶς καὶ ἑωρακότων παρέσχοντο τίνες ἦσαν
οἱ πρὸς τὴν σωτηρίαν αὐτοῖς ἡγησάμενοι. καὶ συνέβη τῇ πόλει διχόθεν τὰ πρωτεῖα ἀνελέσθαι. τὰς
μὲν γὰρ πόλεις ὑπερεῖχον Ἀθῆναι, τοὺς δὲ ἄνδρας
ἀνὴρ Ἀθηναίων εἷς. οὕτως ὃ μὲν ἦν τρόπου
πραότητος ἐν τῷ συγχωρῆσαι παρέσχοντο, ὃ δὲ
ἀληθινῆς ἡγεμονίας ἦν παρὰ πάντων ἐκείνοις ἀν-

150 ετέθη. καὶ μὴν καὶ πρὸς τὰ λοιπὰ τοῦ πολέμου
τὴν πόλιν ἤδη καθαρῶς προεστήσαντο οἱ Ἕλληνες·
πάντες γὰρ οἱ σύλλογοι καὶ αἱ σύνοδοι πρὸς Ἀθηναίους καὶ παρ' Ἀθηναίων ἐκ τούτων ἐγίγνοντο,
καὶ κατέστη κοινὸν βουλευτήριον ἡ πόλις τοῦ πρὸς

ᵃ The Lacedaemonian Eurybiadas was theoretically in

As for the Lacedaemonians, they wished to arouse 147
their enthusiasm, like teachers of children. And for
this reason, they brought them out in front of everybody to encourage them and so that they might
imitate their teachers' actions. And they did this
also in their decrees. However, in their actions they 148
did not also give up their leadership to others, as in
the matter of a title and the wing of a battle line.
How was it possible ? But the former people had
the name of commanders, and the latter the respon-
sibilities, and their position became so much the
fairer, to the degree that they held command over
the commanders themselves. For everything of
which one man of the Athenians did not approve,
was without authority, so that the admiral of the
Lacedaemonians commanded the commanders of
each city, but the admiral of the Athenians commanded the commander of the commanders.[a] So 149
the Greeks, conscious of this fact, gave the prize of
valour for the sea-battles to the city, and provided
the evidence of actual participants and observers of
the event as to who led them to safety. And it
befell to the city to win first prize in two ways.
For Athens excelled the other cities, and one of the
Athenians the other men. Thus in their concession
they showed a gentle nature, but all attributed to
them the real command. Indeed, for the rest 150
of the war, the Greeks now gave the city full charge.
For all the meetings and assemblies thereafter took
place in the presence of the Athenians and because
of the Athenians, and the city became a common
council chamber for the war against the barbarians.

command at sea, but the Athenian Themistocles was the
guiding spirit.

(224 D.)

151 τὸν βάρβαρον πολέμου. ἀλλὰ γὰρ ἡ περὶ τὰς
ἀποδείξεις σπουδὴ καὶ λόγος λόγῳ παραδιδοὺς ἡμᾶς
παρήνεγκεν περαιτέρω. εἶμι δὲ ἐπ' αὐτὰς πάλιν τὰς
πράξεις, ἐπειδὴ περὶ ὧν ἐβουλόμην ἐν τῷ μέσῳ
διέλαβον. μηδεὶς δὲ ἡμᾶς ἡγείσθω πέρα τοῦ δέοντος διατρίβειν μηδ' ἐπ' ἐξειργασμένοις ἀναλαμ-
βάνειν, ἀλλὰ σκοπείσθω τὴν χρείαν ὅση¹ καὶ τὴν
ἑκάστου τοῦ λόγου πρόφασιν καὶ ποῖ φέρει. κἂν
οὕτω σκοπῇ, πολλὰ μὲν εἶναι δόξει τὰ λεγόμενα,
ἕκαστον δ' εἰσάπαξ εἰρῆσθαι, καὶ τῇ μὲν ἀνάγκῃ
ἐφάμιλλα πάντα, ὥστε μηδὲν εἶναι παραλιπεῖν
ἀτιμάσαντα, τῇ τάξει δὲ ἑτέρως οὐκ ἐγχωροῦντα
συμβῆναι, τὸ δὲ ἀεὶ παρενεγκὸν τῆς συνεχείας ὂν
καὶ τῆς ἀκολουθίας εἴσεται, ἀναλαμβάνων τῷ νῷ
225 D. ταῦτα παρ' αὑτῷ καὶ σκοπῶν εἴ πως ἑτέρως μᾶλλον
152 ἥρμοττεν. ἔτι δὲ εἰ μὲν περὶ μηδενὸς ἀξίων πραγμάτων ἢ περὶ ὧν ἐκ γειτόνων ἐστὶ τὰ παραδείγματα
τὴν ἐξέτασιν ταύτην καὶ σπουδὴν ἐποιούμεθα,
εἰκότως ἄν τις ἡμᾶς ἔφη μικρολογεῖσθαι· νῦν δὲ
ὑπὲρ ὧν πάντες μὲν ποιηταὶ λέγοντες ἐλάττους
γεγόνασιν, πᾶσα δὲ ἡ περὶ τοὺς λόγους δύναμις
ἥττηται, πάντες δὲ ὥσπερ ὑπ' ἐκπλήξεως θαυμά-
ζουσι μᾶλλον ἢ οἱ² δι' ἀκριβείας ἕκαστα ἑωρακότες,
περὶ τούτων ἀγωνιζόμεθα οὐδὲν ἐλάττω κατὰ τοὺς
λόγους ἀγῶνα μικροῦ δεῖν ἢ κατὰ τὰς πράξεις
153 ἐκεῖνοι τότε. οὐδὲν οὖν ἀργὸν οὐδ' ἀνεξέταστον
εἰκὸς παραλιπεῖν, ὡς ὁμοίως ἥ τ' ἐπὶ τοῖς μικροῖς
σπουδὴ φέρει μέμψιν καὶ τὸ τοῖς τηλικούτοις μὴ
τὴν ἀξίαν διὰ πάντων φυλάξαι. καὶ γὰρ τοῦτο

---

¹ ὅση om. VA. ² οἱ om. VA.

But my enthusiasm for demonstration and the suc- 151
cession of arguments has carried us rather far off
course. I shall return to the account of the action
itself since I interrupted in the middle that about
which I wished to speak. Let no one think that we
dwell on these matters unnecessarily and take them
up after they have been thoroughly treated, but
let the critic consider their importance, and the
reason and aim of each argument. And if he so
considers, it will appear that much has been said,
but that each point has been stated once and for all,
and that it so happens that all these matters necessarily compete with one another so that nothing
can be omitted unhonoured, and that no other
arrangement is possible. And he will recognize
that there is a quality which always detracts from
continuity and sequence, if he ponders these matters
by himself and considers whether there was some
other more harmonious arrangement. Also if we 152
conducted this investigation and displayed this
enthusiasm over matters of no importance or for
which there are immediate parallels, one would
reasonably say that we were being trivial. But in
fact these are acts in the discussion of which all
poets have been inferior, all the power of oratory
has been worsted, and at which all men, as if in
astonishment, marvel more than those who carefully
observed each detail, and concerning these we
undergo almost no less a contest in oratory than
those men then did in battle. So it is reasonable to 153
leave nothing untouched or unexamined, since
enthusiasm over little things incurs blame equally
with not maintaining throughout the dignity of
great events. For one would say that this too was

(225 D.)

ἕτερον τρόπον ἄν τις εἶναι[1] φαίη μικρολογουμένου.
154 ἀλλ᾽ ἐπάνειμι δή. συμβάντος γὰρ τοῦ περὶ τὰς
Πύλας πάθους καὶ τῆς Ἑλλάδος λαμπρῶς καὶ
σφαλερῶς ἀνοιχθείσης οἱ μὲν ὥσπερ πύλας τείχους
ῥήξαντες εἰσεχέοντο, δυοῖν μερίδοιν οὐδετέρας στε-
ρόμενοι. οἱ μὲν γὰρ ἑκόντες, οἱ δ᾽ ἀνάγκῃ προσ-
εχώρουν, περιρρέοντος τοῦ πολέμου καὶ πάντων
ἐφεξῆς ὥσπερ πῦρ ἐπιὸν ὑποφευγόντων, οἱ δὲ τῆς
Ἀθηνᾶς ἐν πολλοῖς ἤδη πολλάκις δείξαντες ὡς
ὀρθῶς εἰσιν ἐπώνυμοι καὶ μάλα ἵλεῳ τῇ τῆς θεοῦ
χρῶνται διανοίᾳ, καὶ συνειδότες ἔξωθεν οὖσαν τῇ
226 D. πόλει τὴν φυλακὴν ψήφισμα ποιοῦνται τὴν μὲν
πόλιν ἐπιτρέψαι τῇ πολιούχῳ θεῷ, παῖδας δὲ καὶ
γυναῖκας εἰς Τροιζῆνα παρακαταθέσθαι, αὐτοὶ δὲ
γυμνωθέντες τῶν περιττῶν προβαλέσθαι τὴν θάλατταν, καὶ πάντων ὅσα[2] τις εἴποι μέγιστα κατ᾽ ἀνθρώπους ἐν ἡμέρᾳ μιᾷ παρασχόμενοι σύμβολα
εὐσεβείας, καρτερίας, φρονήσεως, φιλανθρωπίας,
155 μεγαλοψυχίας· εὐσεβείας μὲν διὰ τὴν πίστιν ἣν ἐν
τοῖς θεοῖς εἶχον· καρτερίας δὲ παίδων καὶ γυναικῶν
καὶ τῆς τῶν οἰκειοτάτων συνηθείας ἀπεζευγμένοι
φέροντι τῷ θυμῷ· φιλανθρωπίας δὲ ὅτι ταῦτα ὑπὲρ
156 τῆς τῶν ἄλλων σωτηρίας ὑπέμενον. καὶ μὴν καὶ
μεγαλοψυχίᾳ γε τίς ἀνθρώπων ἐκείνοις ὅμοιος, οἳ
τῶν ὄντων ὑπὲρ τῆς ἐλευθερίας ἀπέστησαν; ἀλλὰ
μὴν τό γε γνῶναι τὸ μόνον μέλλον διασῴζειν ἅπαντα
τὰ πράγματα, τὴν σοφίαν λέγω, δι᾽ ἣν καὶ τῆς ὑπὸ

---

[1] εἶναι om. TQ. [2] ὅσ᾽ ἄν ci. Oliver.

---

[a] Rather they were overrun by the Persians.
[b] Cf. or. iii. 247 (p. 256 Ddf.). This " invented " version of
the decree agrees in some of its context and phraseology

122

another way of being trivial. But I shall return to
the subject. Well, when the misfortune at the 154
Gates took place and Greece was quite dangerously 480.
laid open, as if they had broken down the gates
of a wall the enemy poured in, and they did not lack
assistance from either side. For some joined them
willingly and others out of necessity, when the war
streamed about them, and all, one after another
fled [a] as it were an advancing fire. But the people of
Athena, who had already often and in many ways
showed that they were rightly named after her and
that they found the Goddess' intentions most kindly
disposed towards them, and who had recognized
that the city's protection lay without, passed a
decree,[b] to entrust the city to the Goddess City-
Holder, and to deposit their wives and children at
Troezen, and themselves stripped of excess encum-
brance, to use the sea as their shield, in one day
giving proof of all the qualities which are called the
greatest among mankind, piety, moral strength,
intelligence, generosity, and nobility. Piety, through 155
the faith which they had in the Gods. Moral
strength, by having separated themselves with a
staunch heart from their children, wives, and the
company of all who were most dear. Generosity,
because they endured these things for the safety of
others. Indeed, who among mankind was their 156
equal in nobility, when they abandoned their possessions for the sake of freedom ? And I call " wisdom "
the recognition of that policy which alone is going
to secure everything,—wisdom through which in their

with Plutarch, *Themistocles* X. 2 and with the inscription
published in Hesperia, XXXI (1962), pp. 310-315. On the
whole subject *cf.* Habicht, Hermes, 89 (1961), pp. 10-11.

123

(226 D.)

πάντων ἐν τοῖς λόγοις τιμωμένης τοῖς ἄρχουσιν
157 εὐπειθείας τοὺς πώποτ' ἐνίκησαν τῷ δόγματι. καὶ
οἱ μὲν οὕτως ἀπεσκευασμένοι πρὸς τῇ Σαλαμῖνι
κατεῖχον τοὺς Ἕλληνας, ὁ δὲ ἀμφοτέρᾳ τῇ χειρὶ
παρῆν, ἄγων τοὺς μέχρι τῆς Ἀττικῆς Ἕλληνας
227 D. ὁμοῦ καὶ βαρβάρους, καὶ πέμπει δὴ πάλιν εἰς τὴν
Σαλαμῖνα, κελεύων ἃ πρὸ τοῦ, γῆν καὶ ὕδωρ λαβεῖν,
νομίζων, εἰ παρόντων καὶ ὁρωμένων τῶν δεινῶν
γίγνοιντο οἱ λόγοι, μᾶλλόν τι καμφθήσεσθαι καὶ
158 παραδώσειν τὰ ὦτα αὐτούς. ἐνταῦθα δὴ καὶ πλεῖστον
ἐλπίδος ἐσφάλη. οὕτω γὰρ πόρρω δέους ἢ τοῦ
μεταθέσθαι περὶ τῶν ἐξ ἀρχῆς ἐγνωσμένων ἐγένοντο
ὥστ' ἐπειδή τις ἐτόλμησεν εἰπεῖν ὡς χρὴ συγχωρεῖν,
αὐτοὶ μὲν αὐτόν, αἱ δὲ γυναῖκες τὴν γυναῖκα ἐπελ-
θοῦσαι διέφθειραν ἐκ χειρός. καὶ παράκλησις αὕτη
πρώτη[1] πρὸς τὴν ναυμαχίαν τοῖς Ἕλλησιν ἐγένετο
159 κοινὴ τῶν τε ἀνδρῶν καὶ τῶν[2] γυναικῶν. οὐ μὴν
κατῄσχυναν ταύτην τοῖς ἔργοις ἐφεξῆς, ἀλλὰ πρῶτον
μὲν ἀνάξια τῶν Ἑλλήνων βουλευομένων τῆς ἐπ'
Ἀρτεμισίῳ τόλμης καὶ τῆς Ἀθηναίων παρουσίας
καὶ νικῶντος ἤδη τοῦ δρασμοῦ, διεκώλυσαν αὐτοὶ
καὶ κατηνάγκασαν ὥσπερ παῖδας ἄκοντας ὑποστῆναι[3] τῇ θεραπείᾳ πάντα πραγματευσάμενοι, τὸ μὲν
πρῶτον ἐνδεχομένους μόλις φωνὴν πείθοντες, ἔπειτα,
ὡς ἀπέραντον ἦν, ἀπροσδοκήτως περιθέντες τὰς
ἀνάγκας καὶ συσκευάσαντες τὴν ναυμαχίαν, ὥστε
160 πρὸς βίαν θαρρῆσαι. ἔπειτα γιγνομένης τῆς συν-
όδου καὶ[4] τῶν βαρβάρων περικαλυψάντων ταῖς ναυ-

---

[1] πρώτη om. VA.   [2] τῶν om. VA.
[3] ὑποσχῆναι TQ.   [4] καὶ τῆς συμβολῆς TQ.

decree they also surpassed all men who ever lived, although all give lipservice to obedience to one's rulers. And when they were thus unencumbered, 157 they induced the Greeks to hold fast to Salamis. But the barbarian was present with both his forces, leading both those who inhabited Greece up to the borders of Attica and the barbarians. And he sent again to Salamis, with the same demands as before, the bestowal of earth and water, in the belief that they would be somewhat less unbending and would pay heed if the discussion should take place when the danger was present and visible. Here 158 indeed he was much deceived in his expectations. For they were so far from being afraid and from changing their original resolve that when someone [a] dared to say that they should yield, they immediately attacked and slew him, and their wives his wife. This act was the first exhortation, by both men and women, made to the Greeks for the naval battle. Indeed, 159 they did not shame this by their subsequent actions ; but first when the Greeks were making plans which were unworthy of the daring action at Artemisium and the presence of the Athenians, and flight now prevailed, they restrained them and compelled them, like unwilling children, to submit to the cure, and they used every contrivance, first of all trying to persuade those who scarcely listened to their voice, and next when this was proving endless, unexpectedly forcing them to act and contriving the naval battle, so that they were compelled to be courageous. Next when they met and the bar- 160 barians blanketed the outlying region with their

[a] Cyrsilus; *cf.* Demosthenes XVIII. 204; Habicht, *op. cit.*, p. 21.

228 D. σὺν ἅπαντα τὸν ἔξω τόπον, τότε ἤδη καὶ γῆς καὶ
θαλάττης παρὰ τοσοῦτον ἐξειργόμενοι, παρ' ὅσον
αἱ τριήρεις ἐπεῖχον, καὶ ὡς ἀληθῶς ὥσπερ ⟨ἐν⟩[1]
θαλάττῃ καὶ κύμασι πανταχῇ ταὐτὸν ὁρῶντες ὅποι
βλέψειαν, πολεμίους, οὐδὲν παρεῖσαν ἑτέροις, ἀλλὰ
πρῶτοι μὲν αὐτοὶ κατῆρξαν τῆς ναυμαχίας, ὥσπερ
ἐν Εὐβοίᾳ πάντων ἀποκνούντων, μόνοι δὲ τὸ πᾶν
ἐξειργάσαντο, ὅσα μὲν στρατηγοῦ προνοίᾳ κακῶσαι
τὸν βασιλέα[2] ἔδει πρότερον παρασκευάσαντες, ὥστε
ἐν τοῖς πολεμίοις φιλίων καὶ τῶν συνευξομένων
εὐπορῆσαι—λέγω δὲ τὴν περὶ τοὺς Ἴωνας πρᾶξιν—
ἃ δὲ χειρῶν νόμῳ καὶ μετὰ κοινῆς ⟨τῆς⟩[3] εὐψυχίας
ἔδει πραχθῆναι, κάλλιστα δὴ τῶν ὑφ' ἡλίῳ μάρτυρι
καὶ τολμήσαντες καὶ τελεσάμενοι, τάξαντες μὲν
αὐτοὺς ἐναντία ἐκείνοις, οἵπερ ἦσαν κεφάλαιον τοῦ
ναυτικοῦ τῶν πολεμίων, τρεψάμενοι δὲ πρῶτοι καὶ
διαφθείραντες ἄλλας ἀλλαχοῦ τῶν νεῶν ἐν παντοδα-
ποῖς τῶν ἔργων εἴδεσιν, παρασχόντες δὲ τοῖς λοι-
ποῖς διώκειν ἀντὶ τοῦ ναυμαχεῖν. ὥστ' ἐμοὶ μὲν
παραπλησίως οἱ Ἕλληνες δοκοῦσιν νικῆσαι τὴν
ναυμαχίαν ἐκείνην ὥσπερ ἂν εἰ καὶ Μαραθῶνι παρόντες μετέσχον τῆς νίκης. ἐκεῖ τε γὰρ ἤρκεσεν ἡ
πόλις αὐτῇ καὶ ἐν Σαλαμῖνι τῶν γιγνομένων ἀπέλαυ-
σαν οἱ λοιποί. καὶ τότε μὲν ἡμέρᾳ μιᾷ τῆς μάχης

229 D. ὑστέρησαν Λακεδαιμόνιοι, ἐκείνῃ δὲ τῇ ἡμέρᾳ αὐτῆς
161 ὑστέρησαν τῆς τροπῆς οἱ συντελεῖς. καὶ τοσοῦτον
διενήνοχεν ὥστ' εἰκότως ἄν τινα φῆσαι μὴ μόνον
τῆς ἐλευθερίας μηδὲ τῶν ἄθλων τῶν ἐκ τῆς ναυμαχίας χάριν ἂν τῇ πόλει τοὺς Ἕλληνας ἔχειν δικαίως,

[1] add. Reiske.
[2] codd. dett. : τῶν βασιλέως TQVA.
[3] add. codd. dett.

[a] At the Battle of Artemisium.

ships, and they were already cut off from land and sea except for as much as their triremes held, and in fact as on the sea and the deep, everywhere they looked, they saw the same, the enemy, they left nothing to the others' discretion, but they began the naval battle themselves when all were hesitating, just as at Euboea.[a] And by themselves they accomplished everything, having prepared through the foresight of their general all which would injure the king, so that among the enemy they were rich in friends and men ready to support them. I refer to their action concerning the Ionians.[b] But as to what had to be accomplished by the law of arms and with common courage, they displayed and brought to pass the fairest deeds of daring of those beneath the witness of the sun, having placed themselves opposite those who were the mainstay of the enemy's fleet, and having been the first to turn and destroy ships everywhere in various kinds of action, and having enabled the others to pursue the enemy instead of engaging him in sea-battle. Therefore the Greeks seem to me to have won that naval battle in the same way as if they had been present at Marathon 490. and shared in the victory. For there the city was self-sufficient, and at Salamis the other Greeks enjoyed the fruits. And on the former occasion [c] the Lacedaemonians were one day too late for the battle, but on that day even as participants in the battle they were too late for the turning of the enemy line. And the city was so superior that one would have 161 reasonably said that the Greeks would justly give thanks to it not only for their freedom and the

[b] *Cf.* Herodotus VIII. 19-22.
[c] At the Battle of Marathon, 490 B.C.

ἀλλὰ καὶ τῆς νίκης αὐτῆς. καὶ γὰρ ταύτην ὥσπερ
ἄλλο τι κέρδος προσλαβόντες φαίνονται καὶ τῆς φι-
162 λοτιμίας κοινῇ μετασχόντες. ἐνταῦθα δὴ πᾶσα μὲν
ἀκτὴ ναυαγίων ἐπέπληστο, πάντες δὲ οἱ πορθμοὶ
συνεκέχυντο, ἔφερεν δὲ ὁ πόρος πρὸς τὴν ἤπειρον
ἔξω τῷ βασιλεῖ δεινὰ θεάματα καὶ μάλα ἀπᾴδοντα
163 τῆς ἐκείνου περινοίας καὶ τρυφῆς. ἄξιον δὲ καὶ τῆς
ἐπιθήκης τῶν κακῶν ⟨τῶν γενομένων⟩¹ τοῖς βαρβάροις μνησθῆναι. τὸ γὰρ δὴ πάρεργον τῶν ἔργων
164 οὐκ ἀτιμότερον προσεξείργασται. τί οὖν ἦν τοῦτο;
τρεῖς τόπους οἱ βάρβαροι κατέλαβον τὸ κατ' ἀρχάς,
τὴν ἤπειρον, τὴν θάλατταν, τὴν πρὸ τῆς Σαλαμῖνος
νῆσον, ὅπως ἀκριβέστερον ἢ δικτύῳ συγκλείοιντο
οἱ Ἕλληνες. δοκεῖ γὰρ εἶναι μεγάλη συμφορὰ καὶ
παρὰ τὸν νόμον τὸν Μηδικόν, εἴ τις τῶν ἀνταίρειν τῷ
165 βασιλεῖ τολμησάντων διαφεύξεται. κατὰ οὖν τοὺς
ἐκπίπτοντας ἐκ τῆς ναυμαχίας ἐτάχθη τὰ κύρια
τῆς στρατιᾶς, ἄνδρες Περσῶν οἱ πρῶτοι, καὶ κατέσχον τὴν νῆσον ἐφεστηκότες ὡς ἐφ' ἑτοίμοις. ὡς δὲ
τῶν πρώτων ἀπέτυχον καὶ μετὰ τῶν Ἑλλήνων ἦν
ἡ τύχη καὶ περιέστραπτο ἡ πεῖρα, ἀνὴρ Ἀθηναίων
εἷς ἐθελοντὴς τὸν κίνδυνον ὑφίστατο καὶ λαβὼν τοὺς
230 D. ὄντας αὐτῶν ἐν Σαλαμῖνι τοὺς πρεσβύτας ἀποβιβά-
σας εἰς τὴν νῆσον κτείνει πᾶν τοῦτο τὸ Περσικόν.
166 Ξέρξης δὲ καθῆστο μὲν ἐπὶ τῆς ἠπείρου κεκοσμημ-
ένος, ὥσπερ ἄλλον τινὰ ἀγῶνα ποιῶν, ἤ τις τῶν
ἐξ οὐρανοῦ κριτὴς τῶν γιγνομένων, οἰόμενος τοῖς
ἑαυτοῦ τὸν παρ' αὐτοῦ φόβον ἀρκέσειν. καὶ τοσοῦτον ἦν ἄρα τὸ ἔργον αὐτῷ ὅσον τοῖς μὲν ὀργισθῆναι,

---

¹ add. codd. dett.

prizes of battle, but also for the victory itself. For
they obviously got this victory like a gift and shared 480.
in the Athenians' glory. Here every beach was filled 162
with wrecks, all the straits were choked, and the
current bore onto the mainland, to the king, dread-
ful sights, much out of tune with his arrogance
and luxury. Mention too should be made of a further 163
evil which befell the barbarians. For this side-
action was an added accomplishment having no
less honour than those deeds. What was it? At 164
the start, the barbarians seized three places, the
mainland, the sea, and the island [a] before Salamis,
so that the Greeks might be enclosed more closely
than in a net. For it is held to be a great misfortune
and contrary to the law of the Medes, if any of those
who dared to oppose the king are going to escape.
Then against those who fled from the naval battle 165
there was stationed the pick of the army, the leading
men of the Persians, and they held the island,
ready as if for what was sure to come. But when
their first efforts failed, and fortune was with the
Greeks, and their attempt had turned against them,
a man of the Athenians,[b] a volunteer, faced the
danger, took their old men who were in Salamis,
disembarked them on the island, and slew this
whole Persian force. But Xerxes sat on the main- 166
land, in regal splendour as if he were holding a
contest, or were a heavenly judge of these events,
thinking that the terror which he inspired was
sufficient for his people. And his only action was to
show anger toward some of his soldiers, and to

[a] Psyttalea.
[b] Aristides, son of Lysimachus. On the question of " the
old men " cf. Oliver, p. 124.

(230 D.)

τοὺς δὲ τιμῆσαι τῶν στρατιωτῶν. ὡς δ' ἑώρα τὴν
θάλατταν αἵματι καὶ ῥοθίῳ ζέουσαν καὶ πάντα
νεκρῶν καὶ ναυαγίων μεστὰ καὶ κυριωτέρους ἑτέρους
φοβεῖν καὶ τοὺς ἐκείνου καὶ αὐτόν, ἐκπλαγεὶς καὶ
νομίσας θαυματοποιὸν εἶναι τὴν πόλιν παλινῳδίαν
ᾖδεν, καὶ μεταστρέψας ᾔει τὴν αὐτήν, οὐ μετὰ τοῦ
αὐτοῦ σχήματος, ἐν ἤδη τοῦτ' ἀγώνισμα ποιούμενος
167 τὴν σχεδίαν καταλαβεῖν. οὕτω διὰ πάντων ἡ πόλις
πᾶν ἔσωσε τὸ Ἑλληνικόν, καὶ τοῖς πᾶσιν ἐδείχθη
μόνον φυλακτήριον οὖσα τοῖς Ἕλλησιν, οἶμαι δὲ καὶ
τῷ λοιπῷ μέρει τῆς οἰκουμένης. τίσιν δὴ¹ λέγω
τοῖς πᾶσιν; οἷς ἐνίκα πρότερον μόνη Μαραθῶνι,
οἷς ὕστερον τοσοῦτον παρῆλθεν τοὺς συστάντας, οἷς
αὐτὴ κεφάλαιον τοῦ πολέμου τοῖς στόλοις ἀμφοτέροις ἦν, τοῖς ἐν Πύλαις ἀτυχοῦσιν ἄνευ τῆς πόλεως,
τοῖς ἐπ' Ἀρτεμισίῳ νικῶσιν διὰ τῆς πόλεως, ταῖς
231 D. τοῦ θεοῦ μαντείαις, ὧν αἱ μὲν τῆς Ἀθηνᾶς εἶναι τὴν
δωρεάν, αἱ δὲ ἀπολέσθαι τοὺς Ἕλληνας ἔφραζον, εἰ
συσταῖεν Ἀθηναῖοι μετὰ τῶν βαρβάρων. ὥστε καὶ
ἐξ ὧν οὐκ ἔπαθον οἱ Ἕλληνες καὶ ἐξ ὧν ἔμελλον
πείσεσθαι καὶ οἷς ἐποίησεν ἡ πόλις καὶ οἷς οὐκ ἐποί-
168 ησεν μόνη φέρεται τὴν τοῦ παντὸς κρίσιν· ἔτι πρὸς
τούτοις τῇ τοῦ στρατηγοῦ συντελείᾳ, τῷ πλήθει τῶν
τριήρων, τῷ κατάρξαι τῶν ναυμαχιῶν, τῷ τοὺς
τόπους εὑρεῖν, τῷ τοὺς Ἕλληνας κατασχεῖν, τῷ πρώτην νικῆσαι καὶ τὴν μεγίστην τοῦ ναυτικοῦ μοῖραν,
τῷ πλεῖστον διαφθεῖραι, τοῖς ἀπ' Ἐλευσῖνος φάσμα-

¹ δὲ V.

ᵃ Over the Hellespont.
ᵇ The campaigns of Darius and Xerxes.
ᶜ Cf. Herodotus VII. 141.

honour others. But when he saw that the sea was
boiling with blood and foam, and that everything
was full of corpses and wrecked ships, and that the
other side were better able to inspire terror both
in his own people and in himself, terrified and believing that the city had the power to work magic,
" he sang a recantation " and turned and left by the
same route, but not with the same pomp, now with a
single aim, to secure his bridge of rafts.[a] So in every 167
way, the city saved the whole Greek race, and it was
proved in full that not only was it a means of protection for the Greeks, but also, I think, for the rest of
the world. What do I mean by " in full " ? By the
fact that formerly it triumphed alone at Marathon, 490;
by the fact that later it so greatly excelled its allies, 480–479.
by the fact that it was the mainstay of the war in
both campaigns,[b] again by those who failed at the
Gates without the city's help and by those who
conquered at Artemisium through the city, by the
oracles of the God, one of which spoke of the gift of
Athena,[c] and the other, which said that the Greeks
would perish if the Athenians should join with the
barbarians. Therefore the city alone wins the decision on every count, because of what the Greeks
did not suffer, because of what they were going to
suffer, by what it did, and by what it did not do.
Besides, by the contribution of its general, by the 168
number of its triremes, by its starting the naval
battles, by its discovery of the best battle sites, by its
restraining the Greeks from flight, by its being the
first to be victorious and at that over the largest
part of the enemy fleet, by its causing the most
destruction, by the apparitions from Eleusis,[d] by the

[d] *Cf.* xxii. 6 ; Herodotus VIII. 65.

(231 D.)

σιν, τοῖς ἐν Ψυτταλίᾳ περιττοῖς, τῇ ⟨τε παρὰ τῶν
συμμάχων μαρτυρίᾳ καὶ τῇ⟩[1] παρὰ τῶν ἐχθρῶν· οἱ
μὲν γὰρ τὰ ἀριστεῖα ἔδοσαν τῇ πόλει, καὶ ταῦτα
ἡγεῖσθαι ἐφ᾽ ὧν ἦν, ὁ δὲ ἐκείνων βασιλεὺς φεύγων
ᾤχετο· ὥστε καὶ παρὰ θεῶν καὶ παρὰ ἀνθρώπων
καὶ φίλων καὶ πολεμίων τῇ πόλει δεδόσθαι τὰς ψή-
169 φους. καὶ ταύτῃ αὖ διχόθεν ταῦτα συμβαίνει, τὰ μὲν
232 D. ἐξ ὧν κοινῇ προὐκρίθη καὶ κατέπραξεν, τὰ δ᾽ ἐξ
170 ὧν διὰ τοῦ στρατηγοῦ. καὶ τὰ μὲν αὖ τοῦ βασιλέως
οὕτως εἶχεν· Μαρδόνιος δὲ ὑπελείπετο μὲν θανατῶν,
συνειδὼς ἑαυτῷ μέρος τι τῆς στρατείας αἴτιος γεγονώς, τῆς δ᾽ αὐτῆς μονῆς καὶ τύχης ἔγνω ⟨ἄξιόν⟩[2]
τι καὶ τολμήσας καὶ λαβὼν παρὰ τοῦ βασιλέως τὰ
171 κράτιστα τοῦ πεζοῦ προσεκάθητο. οὐ μὴν οὐδὲ πρὸς
ταῦτα ἑτέρων ἐδέησεν τοῖς Ἕλλησιν, ἀλλ᾽ ὥσπερ
ἄλλο τι λοιπὸν καὶ τοῦτο προσεξειργάσατο ἡ πόλις
καὶ διεξῆλθεν μέχρι τῆς τελευτῆς, ὥσπερ οἱ τοὺς
172 στεφάνους συνείροντες. οἱ μὲν οὖν ἄλλοι τῇ μετου-
σίᾳ τῆς μάχης σεμνύνονται, ὅσοι δὴ καὶ παρεγένοντο,
καὶ ταῦτα οὐδένες αὐτῶν ἐγγὺς τῆς πόλεως οὔτε
πλήθει στρατοπέδου οὔτε προθυμίᾳ γενόμενοι, ἡ δὲ
ὑμετέρα[3] πόλις πολλῷ πρότερον τῆς μάχης ἐνίκησεν
αὖθις καὶ Μαρδόνιον καὶ βασιλέα ὡς ἀληθῶς ἰδίαν[4]
νίκην ἑαυτῆς καὶ μόνοις τοῖς Ἀθηναίοις προσήκου-
σαν. ὡς γὰρ πρὸς αὐτὴν ἑώρα πᾶν τὸ Ἑλληνικὸν
καὶ παρ᾽ ἀμφοτέρων ἔγνωστο καλῶς οὗ τῶν πραγμά-
233 D. των ἐστὶν τὰ κύρια, καὶ παρὰ τῶν Ἑλλήνων λέγω

---

[1] τῇ ⟨τε παρὰ τῶν φίλων μαρτυρίᾳ καὶ τῇ⟩ add. Beecke :
συμμάχων pro φίλων Behr.
[2] add. Behr ; μεμνῆσθαι pro μονῆς καὶ ci. Oliver.

additional action in Psyttalea, and by the testimony of the allies and of the enemy. For the allies conceded that the first prize belonged to the city, that it indeed commanded wherever it was ; and the enemies' king went off in flight. Therefore the city won the votes of the Gods, and of mankind, both friend and foe. And in two ways the city took 169 first prize, because of the popular preference shown to it and its accomplishments, and because of its general's actions. The king's position, then, was 170 such as I said. But Mardonius was left behind, eager to die because he was conscious that in some part he had been responsible for the campaign. And his plan was worthy of the king's constancy and fortune and having got the best part of the infantry from the king, he boldly began his siege. Even for 171 this the Greeks had no need for any other resources, but just as some leftover detail, the city accomplished this too and saw it through to the end, like people stringing together crowns of victory. All the others, 172 who were present, were proud of participating in the 479. battle,[a] although none of them came near the city either in the number of their army or in their zeal. But your city long before the battle won another victory over Mardonius and the king, which was truly its own and proper only to the Athenians. For when the whole Greek race was looking to it and both sides, I mean the Greeks and the barbarians,

---

[a] [The Battle of Plataea, the chief credit for which should go to the Lacedaemonians and the Lacedaemonian commander-in-chief Pausanias, much credit also to the soldiers from Tegea, not much to the Athenians.—E.H.W.]

³ edd. : ἡμετέρα TQVA.
⁴ codd. dett. : διὰ VA, δὴ TQ.

(233 D.)

καὶ παρὰ τῶν βαρβάρων, ἐνθύμιον βασιλεῖ καὶ
Μαρδονίῳ γίγνεται· ὃ καὶ φρόνιμον καὶ εὔηθες
ἔξεστι προσειπεῖν. ἦν μέν γε τὸ πάντων κράτιστον
περιφανῶς, εἰ προὐχώρησεν. τοῦτο δὲ ἦν παντὸς
173 μᾶλλον ἀδύνατον. τί δὴ τοῦτο ἦν; ἐσκέψαντο
μεταστῆσαι πρὸς αὐτοὺς[1] τὴν πόλιν καὶ ψιλῶσαι τὸ
Ἑλληνικὸν αὐτῆς, οὐ μόνον τὰ παρελθόντα συνειδότες, ἀλλὰ καὶ τὰ παρόντα ὁρῶντες ὡς δι' ἐκείνων
ἤγετο· πρὸς δὲ τούτοις καὶ τῶν ἐκ Δελφῶν λογίων,
ὡς λέγεται, διαρρήδην μαρτυρούντων, εἰ γένοιντο
Ἀθηναῖοι μετὰ τούτων, οἰχήσεσθαι τοῖς Ἕλλησι
174 τὰ πράγματα. ἐδόκει δὴ τῷ βασιλεῖ καὶ τὸν φόβον
ὠνουμένῳ καὶ τὸ κέρδος ἐνθυμουμένῳ πειρᾶσθαι τῆς
πόλεως· καὶ πέμπει δὴ κήρυκας τἀναντία τοῖς
πρόσθεν λέγοντας. ἀντὶ γὰρ ὧν ᾔτει πρότερον γῆς
καὶ ὕδατος, ταῦτα ἐδίδου τότε, οὐκ ἀπὸ ἴσου τοῦ
μέτρου, ἀλλὰ τοῦτο μὲν τὴν πόλιν καὶ τὴν χώραν
αὐτοῖς ἀπεδίδου πᾶσαν, τοῦτο δὲ τὴν λοιπὴν Ἑλλάδα δωρεὰν προσετίθει. χωρὶς δὲ τούτων ἐπῆν
χρήματα ὑπὲρ πάνθ' ὅσα ἐν Ἕλλησι καὶ φίλους καὶ
συμμάχους εἶναι βεβαίως· ἐξ ὧν ὅτι καὶ μόνους
ἐδεδίει καὶ μόνοις ἐθάρρει μᾶλλον ἢ πᾶσιν οἷς εἶχεν,
175 εἰ πείσειεν, ἐμαρτύρει. καὶ τὸ μὲν κεφάλαιον τῆς
πρεσβείας τοιοῦτον ἦν. ἐκηρύκευεν δὲ Ἀλέξανδρος
βασιλεὺς Μακεδονίας. οἱ δὲ τοσοῦτον ἀπέσχον τοῦ
θαυμάσαι τὰς ἐπαγγελίας, ἢ καὶ σύμπαντα ἃ κέκτηται διδόντα ἄξια σφῶν εἶναι νομίσαι, ὥστε ἔσωσεν
τὸν πρεσβευτὴν τὸ σχῆμα τῆς προξενίας. οὐ μὴν
234 D. οὐδὲ οὕτως ἀδεᾶ καθάπαξ ἀπέστειλαν, ἀλλ' εἰ μὴ
πρὸ ἡλίου δύνοντος ἐκτὸς ὅρων εἴη, καὶ τοῦ λοιποῦ

---

[1] codd. dett. : αὐτὸν TQVA.

had fairly judged where the power lay, the king and
Mardonius had an idea, which can be called both
wise and silly. It was clearly the best idea of all if it
succeeded, but it was more impossible than anything.
What was it? They considered how to bring the city 173
over to their side and to denude the Greek race of her,
since they were not only conscious of what had passed,
but they also saw that the Athenians guided the present circumstances, and besides even the oracles from
Delphi, as it is said, expressly testified that if the
Athenians should join them, the Greek cause would
perish. The king, buying off his fear and considering 174
the advantages of this project, decided to make trial
of the city. And he sent heralds whose speech was
opposite to the one before. For instead of the earth
and water which he formerly demanded, on this
occasion he offered these, but not in equal measure.
He offered to restore to them their city and all its 479.
territory, and he added the rest of Greece as a gift.
And apart from this, he offered more money than
there was in all of Greece, and a firm friendship and
alliance. And thereby he bore witness that he
feared them alone and had more confidence in them
alone, if he should persuade them, than in all his
possessions. Such was the purport of the embassy. 175
Alexander,[a] the king of Macedonia, acted as the
herald. Yet they were so far from being awestruck
by these promises, or from believing that even if he
gave all that he possessed, it was worthy of them,
that only the forms of diplomatic courtesy saved the
ambassador. However, not even so did they simply
dismiss him with impunity, but, if he should not be
outside their borders before sunset—, prefacing that

[a] Alexander the First.

(234 D.)

προειπόντες ἄλλο τι τοῖς Ἀθηναίοις μᾶλλον
προξενεῖν, ὡς οὐκ ἄνευ θανάτου τοιαῦτα πρεσβεύ-
σοντα· καὶ ἅμα ἀγωγοὶ διὰ τῆς χώρας αὐτὸν ἦγον,
176 ὅπως μήτε τις ἅψηται μήτε τῳ διαλέξηται. ταύτην
ἐγὼ τὴν ἀπόκρισιν τῆς ἐν Σαλαμῖνι ναυμαχίας καὶ
τῶν τροπαίων οὐχ ἧττον ἀξίαν ἡγοῦμαι θαυμάσαι
οὐδὲ ἐλάττω φιλοτιμίαν παρέχειν οὔτε τοῖς δοῦσιν
οὔτε τῷ πείσαντι. εἰς μὲν γὰρ ἐκεῖνα ὅπλοις καὶ τρι-
ήρεσι καὶ ὀργάνοις ἔδει προσχρήσασθαι, ἐνταῦθα δὲ
τοῖς σφετέροις αὐτῶν καθαρῶς ἐχρήσαντο, γνώμῃ
177 καὶ λόγῳ. τίνες οὖν ἀρετῆς ἀγωνισταὶ καλλίους, ἢ
τίνες τῶν πώποτε διαρκέστερον τὴν ἐπίδειξιν αὐτῆς
ἐποιήσαντο; οἳ καὶ χρυσῷ καὶ ἀργύρῳ καὶ σιδήρῳ
καὶ τοῖς πᾶσιν ἀήττητοι διεγένοντο καὶ πάντα ἀπέφηναν ὁμοίως ἄχρηστα τῷ βασιλεῖ ὥσπερ ἂν εἰ
ἐκρύπτετο ὑπὸ γῆς ἔτι, πενίαν μὲν ἀντὶ πλούτου τι-
μήσαντες, κινδύνους δ' ἀντ' ἀσφαλείας ἑλόμενοι, δικαιοσύνην δ' ἀντὶ τῆς βασιλέως τοσαύτης φιλανθρω-
178 πίας. καὶ οὐ πρὸς μὲν τὰς βαρβαρικὰς ὑποσχέσεις
οὕτως ἐχθρῶς καὶ παρατεταγμένως εἶχον, πρὸς δὲ τὰς
Ἑλληνικάς, εἰ προσείη σχῆμα χρείας, ὑποπεπτωκό-
235 D. τως, ἢ ὡς ἐπὶ πλεῖον ἀκοῦσαι λόγου. ἀλλὰ ἐλθόντων
Λακεδαιμονίων περιφόβων καὶ δεομένων ἐναντία τῇ
τοῦ βασιλέως πρεσβείᾳ καὶ τοὺς παῖδας καὶ πρεσβύτας καὶ γυναῖκας αὐτοῖς θρέψειν ὑπισχνουμένων,
ἕως ἂν ὁ πόλεμος ᾖ, συνέγνωσαν μᾶλλον ἢ ἀπεδέ-
ξαντο, τῷ μὲν φόβῳ χρηστοὺς νομίζοντες, οἷς δ'
179 ἐπηγγέλλοντο ἀπείρους ἔτι τῶν Ἀθηναίων. καὶ τὴν

in the future he had better make other recommendations to the Athenians, since he would not again bear such messages and remain alive. And at the same time guides conducted him through their territory so that no one might touch him and that he might not speak to any one. I think that this answer 176 is no less worthy of admiration than the battle at Salamis and its trophies and that it gave no less honour to those who made it or to the man who persuaded them. For those actions really required the use of weapons, triremes, and engines of war ; but on this occasion they employed only their own faculties, their resolve and power of reason. Were 177 there ever fairer contestants in the struggle for virtue, or did men ever give a more satisfactory demonstration of it ? For they remained undefeated by gold, silver, iron, and everything, and they made it all equally useless to the king, as if it were still buried beneath the earth, since they honoured poverty before wealth, preferred danger to safety, and justice to such great generosity on the part of the king. And they were not so inimically and obstin- 178 ately disposed to the promises of the barbarians, and at the same time submissive toward those of the Greeks, even if apparently practical, or disposed to listen to them longer than they took to tell. But when the Lacedaemonians came in fear and desired the opposite of the embassy of the king, and promised that they would care for their children, old people, and wives, so long as the war lasted, they pardoned rather than accepted their offer, in the belief that fear inspired their generosity, but that they were still unfamiliar with the Athenians as their promises showed. And they displayed no less 179

(235 D.)

μεγαλοψυχίαν οὐχ ἧττον ἔδειξαν τῷ τὴν ὀργὴν κατασχεῖν ἢ τῷ τὰς ἐπαγγελίας διώσασθαι· εὖ γὰρ
ποιεῖν, οὐκ εὖ πάσχειν πεφυκότες ᾔδεσαν καὶ μισθὸν
ὀφείλειν αὐτοὺς[1] τοῖς εὖ ποιοῦσι τὸ Ἑλληνικόν, ἀλλ'
οὐχ αὐτοὺς[2] δεῖν παρ' ἑτέρων μισθὸν τῆς ἀρετῆς
λαμβάνειν, οὐδ' ἐπὶ κέρδει φιλεῖν τοὺς δόντας
αὐτούς, οὐδέν γε μᾶλλον ἢ τοὺς παῖδας καὶ γονέας
ἐπὶ κέρδει φιλεῖν, ἀλλὰ καὶ μετὰ τῶν ἀναλωμάτων
σῴζειν, ὥσπερ εἰκὸς τοὺς ὡς ὑπὲρ οἰκείων ταῖς
180 γνώμαις διακειμένους. καὶ τοῦτο μὲν τοσοῦτον καὶ
τηλικοῦτον ἔργον εἰς ἀρετῆς λόγον ἐν τοῖς τοῦ
πολέμου καιροῖς ἐξέλαμψεν, μέσον τῆς ἐν Σαλαμῖνι
236 D. ναυμαχίας καὶ τῆς Πλαταιᾶσι μάχης. ἔδειξαν δ'
αὖ κἀκ[3] τούτων χωρὶς ὧν καὶ πρόσθεν διεξῄειν καὶ
βασιλεὺς καὶ οἱ Ἕλληνες ἐξ ἁπάντων τοῖς Ἀθηναίοις
τιθέμενοι ὁ μὲν διὰ Μαρδονίου καλῶν ἐπὶ τούτοις,
οἱ δὲ μὴ ποιεῖν ταῦτα διὰ Λακεδαιμονίων δεόμενοι·
τὸ γὰρ ἀνθέλκειν καὶ καλεῖν ὡς αὐτοὺς ἑκατέρους
ψῆφος ἦν[4] φανερὰ καὶ πίστις ἐναργὴς παρ' ἀμφοῖν
ὅτι καὶ σφῶν αὐτῶν καὶ τῶν ἐναντίων συνίσασιν
181 κρείττους ὄντας οὐ μικρῷ τινι. οὕτω δ' ἐλπίσαντες
ἐξ ἀρχῆς ἔτι μᾶλλον θαυμάσαντες ἀπῆλθον· τῶν μὲν
γὰρ οὐκ ἠνέσχοντο, τοὺς δὲ ἀπὸ πολλοῦ τοῦ κρείττονος προσεδέξαντο. ὥστε καὶ τὸ εἰκὸς προσγε-
νέσθαι, τὸ καὶ αὐτοὺς ὑπὲρ σφῶν αὐτῶν τὴν ἀξίαν
προσθέσθαι ψῆφον καὶ τρεῖς εἶναι τοὺς μάρτυρας
ἑξῆς, τοὺς πολεμίους, τοὺς συμμάχους, αὐτοὺς ἑαυ-
182 τοῖς ἔργῳ διὰ πάντων ὁμοίους γεγενημένους. συν-
αγαγόντες δὲ τοὺς Ἕλληνας ἤδη μᾶλλον αὐτοῖς ἀκο-

[1] αὐτοὶ ci. Reiske. [2] edd. : οὐκ αὐτοὺς TQVA.
[3] Ddf. : καὶ TQVA. [4] ἦν om. TQ.

138

nobility in containing their anger than in rejecting the promises. For they knew that it was their nature to bestow benefits, not to receive them, and that while they owed payment to the benefactors of the Greek race, still they should not take payment from others for their virtue, nor form self-advantageous friendships with those who sought their help, any more than show love for their parents and children in order to gain advantage from them, but they should preserve them even at their own expense, as those so resolved as if on behalf of their own kin should do. And this act of such greatness and magnitude in 180 regard to virtue shone forth in time of war, between the battle at Salamis and that at Plataea. And afterwards, apart from what I formerly recounted, the king and the Greeks showed that in every way they preferred the Athenians, the former through Mardonius proposing an alliance on these terms, and the latter through the Lacedaemonians begging them not to accept. For when each side drew them in a different direction and solicited their alliance, they cast a clear vote and manifestly showed that they recognized that the Athenians were superior in no small degree both to themselves and their enemies. But although they had such expectations 181 at the start, they departed still more awestruck. For the barbarians they did not endure, and the Greeks they accepted as allies although they were in a far superior position. Therefore it is not unexpected that they added their own vote worthily in their own behalf and that there are three successive witnesses, the enemy, their allies, and themselves ever consistent in their activity. When they had 182 assembled the Greeks, who were now better able to

(236 D.)

λουθεῖν δυναμένους Πλαταιᾶσιν γίγνονται. καὶ τὸ
μὲν ἀξίωμα τῶν στρατοπέδων, ἢ τὴν παράταξιν τῶν
βαρβάρων, ὡς ἐτάχθη διὰ τῆς Βοιωτίας, ἢ τὰ πρὸ
τῆς μάχης διηγεῖσθαι διατριβή ἐστι τῆς σπουδῆς
237 D. οὐκ ἐφικνουμένη. μαρτυρία δ' αὖθις γίγνεται τῇ
πόλει θαυμαστὴ παρ' ἀμφοτέρων ἐπὶ τῆς μάχης.
Λακεδαιμόνιοι μὲν γὰρ Ἀθηναίοις ἐξέστησαν τῆς
ἐπὶ Πέρσας τάξεως, ὥσπερ ἀνάγκῃ τινὶ καὶ φύσει
συγκεκληρωμένον Πέρσας Ἀθηναίων ἡττᾶσθαι.
αὖθις δὲ ἀνθυπῆγε Μαρδόνιος τοὺς Λακεδαιμονίους
ἀνθαιρούμενος, ἡγούμενος λυσιτελεῖν αὐτῷ[1] Λακεδαιμονίους καλῶς ἀποθνήσκοντας μᾶλλον ἢ[2] Ἀθηναίους καλῶς νικῶντας. ταῦτα γὰρ ἐκ τῶν πρὸς
183 αὐτοὺς παραδειγμάτων εὕρισκεν.[3] ὥσπερ οὖν οἱ
πύκται περὶ τῆς στάσεως πρῶτον ἠγωνίσαντο, οἱ δὲ
ἐδέχοντο μὲν Πέρσας, ἐδέχοντο δὲ πάντας ἀνθρώπους, ὑπῆρχον δὲ εἰς ἅπαντα νικῶντες, τοὺς μὲν
βαρβάρους ἀρετῇ, τοὺς δ' Ἕλληνας ἀρετῇ τε καὶ
πλήθει. καὶ τήν τε μάχην κρίνουσιν διὰ πάντων
ἐξελθόντες καὶ τοὺς ἡγουμένους τῆς ἵππου διαφθείραντες. καὶ δεῆσαν τειχομαχίας, ὅσον αἰσχυνθείη
τις ἂν εἰπεῖν οἱ ἄλλοι πρὸς αὐτοὺς ἦσαν, ἕως τῶν
βαρβάρων οἱ μὲν οὐχ ὁμοίως καὶ πρόσθεν κατεῖχον
τὴν Βοιωτίαν κείμενοι, οἱ δ' ὥσπερ ἐκ ναυαγίας
ἄοπλοι καὶ ἀσύντακτοι νύκτα ἡμέρας τιμιωτέραν

---

[1] edd. : αὐτῷ TQVA.
[2] Reiske : ἢ μᾶλλον TQVA.   [3] ηὕρισκεν VA.

---

[a] [The great Greek army was organized, and led out of the
Peloponnese to Plataea, not by Athens but by the Lace-

140

follow them, they came to Plataea.[a] The account of 479.
the glory of the armies, or how the battle line of the
barbarians was marshalled through Boeotia, or the
events before the battle, requires a delay not
appropriate to my haste. Again both sides, at the
time of battle, bore remarkable testimony to the
city. For the Lacedaemonians yielded their position
against the Persians to the Athenians, as if the
Persians were fated by some natural law to be
defeated by the Athenians. And Mardonius withdrew in turn, preferring the Lacedaemonians, in the
belief that Lacedaemonians who die nobly were
more advantageous to him than Athenians who
conquer nobly. For he discovered this from his
previous actions against them. So, like boxers, they 183
first struggled for position, and the Athenians took
on the Persians, and then all mankind, and they were
victorious in every way, over the barbarians in
virtue, and the Greeks in virtue and number. And
they decided the battle by doing everything and by
destroying the commanders of the cavalry.[b] And
when siege tactics were required, it would be shameful to say how much the others depended on them,
until some of the barbarians did not hold Boeotia
in the same way as before but lay dead in it, and
others like those from a shipwreck, unarmed and in
disorder, viewing the night as more helpful than the

daemonian Pausanias, whose force of Peloponnesians and
others was joined at Eleusis by Athenians under Aristides.—
E.H.W.]

   [b] [Unscrupulously pro-Athenian though Aristides' account
is, the Athenians did have a hand in the destruction of
Masistius and his cavalry. But the decisive factor came later
in Lacedaemonian prowess and the death of Mardonius
during the battle.—E.H.W.]

(237 D.)

ἄγοντες, ἐκ πολλῶν ὀλίγοι καὶ πολλοὶ κατ' ὀλίγους
ἐξεχώρησαν, πολλὰ τῆς ὑπερηφάνου στρατιᾶς καὶ
184 τῶν Ἀθηναίων μεμνημένοι. τούτων δ' οὕτω καταστάντων οἱ μὲν ἄλλοι πάντες Ἕλληνες ἀσμένως
ἀναπεπνεύκεσαν, οὐχ ὅσον ἂν καὶ προσεδόκησαν
διαπεφευγότες χειμῶνα, καὶ τὴν πόλιν ἐστεφάνουν,
ἐθαύμαζον, πᾶν ὅ τι εἴποιεν αὐτὴν μικρὸν ἡγοῦντο.
οὕτω πολλοῦ τινος αὐτοῖς ἔδει ποιῆσαι ὅ τί γε δο-
238 D. κεῖν ἔχειν ἄξιον αὐτῆς· ἡ δὲ ἐνταῦθα δὴ καὶ μάλιστα τὴν περιουσίαν τῆς ἀρετῆς ἐπεδείξατο. τοσοῦτον
γὰρ ἐπεξῆλθεν[1] ἐν τοῖς πράγμασιν ὥστ' ἔτι μᾶλλον ἔξω δεῖξαι τοῖς βαρβάροις τίνες ἦσαν οἱ καὶ τὰ
ἐν τῇ Ἑλλάδι ταῦτα δράσαντες αὐτοὺς καὶ τίνας
φεύγειν κρίναντες ἀγαπητὸν ἀπῆλθον.
185 Ὁρῶ μὲν οὖν καὶ τὸν λόγον ἐκτεινόμενον καὶ ἐπὶ
τοιούτοις τοῖς προειρημένοις οὐ ῥᾴδιον ὂν πρὸς
ἡδονὴν οὔτε αὐτὸν ἔτι εἰπεῖν οὔτε τυχεῖν ἀκουόν-
των, ὥσπερ μετ' ἀγωνιστὴν εὐδοκιμηκότα εἰσιόντα
ἕτερον. οὐ μὴν ψυχαγωγίας χάριν μᾶλλον ὑπέστην
τοὺς λόγους ἢ τοῦ δεῖξαι μετὰ ἀληθείας τὴν τῆς
πόλεως ἀξίαν· ὥστε ἀδικήσω καθυφεὶς μᾶλλον ἢ
186 διοχλήσω λέγων. ἔπειτα ἐνθυμητέον καὶ ἀπ' αὐτοῦ
τοῦ συμβόλου τῶν λόγων ὅτι οὐδὲ τὴν τῶν Πανα-
239 D. θηναίων αὐτῶν ἑορτὴν ἡμῖν ἡμέρας μιᾶς[2] ἀνάγκη
μετρεῖν, ἀλλ', εἴ γε καὶ τοῦτο δεῖ προσθεῖναι, καὶ
τὸ πλῆθος τῶν ἡμερῶν κόσμου χάριν καὶ σεμνότητος
ἀνεῖται· ὥστε οὐδὲ τὸ τῶν λόγων πλῆθος ἄκαιρον

---

[1] ἐπεξῆλθον VA. [2] ἡμέρᾳ μιᾷ ci. Reiske.

---

[a] The reference is to the Panathenaea, called πεντετηρίς,
"quinquennial," celebrated every four years, in August.
It was the view of the scholiast and the author of the

day, withdrew, a few out of many, yet many left, a
few at a time, recalling again and again their proud
expedition and the Athenians. When matters had 184
been settled in this way, all the other Greeks gladly
took a respite, since they had escaped a tempest
even greater than they would have expected, and
they crowned the city, marvelled at it, and believed
that whatever they might say of it was too little.
So far were they from thinking that anything which
they could do was worthy of it. Here also it displayed the fullness of its virtue. For its subsequent
actions were so great that outside Greece it gave still
greater proof to the barbarians of who were the
people who had done these things to them inside
Greece and from whom the barbarians were glad to
escape when they had decided to retreat.

I see indeed that my speech is becoming long and 185
that it is not easy after what has been already said
still to speak to please or to win my audience, just
like a second contestant who enters after the first
has distinguished himself. However, I did not
undertake these arguments to entertain, but to show
truthfully the worth of the city, so that I shall do
more wrong by slackening than I shall cause annoy-
ance by speaking. Next it must be borne in mind 186
even from the title of this speech that there is no
necessity for us to measure the festival of the
Panathenaea within a single day,[a] but if this point
must also be made, the number of days has been
extended as a means of conferring adornment and
dignity, so that a number of arguments at the time

---

[a] *Prolegomena* to Aristides' works, probably Sopater, *c.* A.D.
300, that the speech was given over a four-day period. *Cf.*
Behr, *Aelius Aristides*, p. 87. See also n. *b*, p. 258.

(239 D.)

187 ἐν τοιούτῳ τῶν ἔργων καιρῷ. σύνισμεν δὲ δήπου
καὶ τὸν ἀγῶνα τὸν γυμνικὸν καὶ ἔτι μᾶλλον τὸν τῆς
μουσικῆς οὐκ εἰσάπαξ ὁριζόμενον, ἀλλ' ἐφ' ἑκάστῃ
τελευτῶντα ὡς εἰπεῖν τῇ ἡμέρᾳ καὶ πάλιν ἐξ ἀρχῆς
καθιστάμενον, καὶ οὐδὲ τοῖς εἴδεσι τῶν θεαμάτων
ἐκπληρούμενον αὐθημερόν. ὥσθ' ὅσα καὶ τὸν νῦν
καιρὸν ἐκφεύγει τὸν ὅλον γε δήπου τῆς πανηγύρεως
οὐ παρελήλυθεν. ἢ κομιδῇ γ' ἂν εἴη τῶν ἀτόπων,
εἰ οἱ μὲν νομοθέται τούτου χάριν ἐξέτειναν τὰς
συνόδους, καὶ νὴ Δία γε αὐτὸ τοὔνομα τῆς ἱερομηνίας
παρέβησαν, πλείω τὸν χρόνον προσθέντες, ὅπως ἐπὶ
πλεῖστον ἀλλήλοις ὁμιλοῖμεν, ἡμεῖς δ' ἀντὶ τοῦ
188 χρήσασθαι τούτῳ μεμφοίμεθα.[1] ὥσπερ οὖν τοῖς
τῶν ἄθλων γυμνασίοις οὐκ ἀχθόμεθα ἐντυγχάνοντες
ἐφ' ἡμέρᾳ,[2] ἀλλ' ἐν κέρδους μέρει τῆς ἀεὶ παρούσης
θέας ἀπολαύομεν, οὕτω καὶ περὶ τῶν λόγων ἔχειν
εἰκός, καὶ ταῦτά γε τῶν τῇ πανηγύρει συγκεκλη-
ρωμένων, πάντως οὐχ ἑώλοις[3] ἀεὶ τοῖς ὑπολειφθεῖ-
σιν ἐντεύξεσθε, οὐδ' ἀτιμοτέροις ἐκείνων συνεῖναι.

189 Ἀλλ' ἵνα μὴ πλείω τῶν ἀναγκαίων παραιτούμενος
αὐτῷ τούτῳ μηκύνω, πρὸς τοὺς ἐφεξῆς τῶν λόγων
καὶ συνεχεῖς καὶ δὴ τρέψομαι. ἐπειδὴ γὰρ ἡ Ἑλλὰς
240 D. ἑαυτῆς ἐγένετο καὶ πάντα ἐξεκεχωρήκει, νῆες, ἵπποι,
τὸ πεζόν, ὕπαρχοι, βασιλεύς, πρῶτον μὲν πανηγύρεις καὶ πρόσοδοι τοῖς θεοῖς ἦσαν οἵας οὔτε πρότερον οὔθ' ὕστερον οὐδεὶς μέμνηται γεγονυίας ἐν
ἐλευθέρᾳ τῇ Ἑλλάδι. οὐ γὰρ νόμος ἦν ὁ συνάγων
οὐδὲ χρόνου τακτὴ περίοδος, ἀλλ' ἐκ τῶν πραγμάτων ἦν καὶ κατὰ ἄνδρα καὶ πόλεις εὐθυμεῖσθαι καὶ
στεφανηφορεῖν καὶ τοὺς θεοὺς μαρτύρεσθαι τῆς

---

[1] Reiske : μεμφόμεθα TQVA.
[2] ἡμέρᾳ ⟨ἡμέραν⟩ ci. Oliver.   [3] Ddf. : οὐκ ἑώλοις TQVA.

of such activity is also not inopportune. We know, I 187
suppose, that gymnastic contests and, still more, musical contests have no set limits, but, one may say, conclude each day and again begin anew, and do not
even finish on the same day with particular kinds of
spectacles, so that all which escapes the present
moment has not exceeded the whole time of the
festival. Or it would be a very strange thing if the
lawgivers increased the length of the assemblies for
this purpose, and by Zeus, transgressed the very
name of the Sacred Month *a* by extending its time
so that we might converse with one another for the
longest period, but that we should criticize this
practice instead of employing it. Then just as we are 188
not annoyed if we daily attend gymnastic contests,
but enjoy each present spectacle as our gain, it is
reasonable to be so disposed about speeches, and
indeed those which have been allotted to this festival.
You will not find the rest to be completely stale, nor
to be less worthy to hear than what has preceded.

But so that I may not lengthen my speech by 189
this very process of making a longer apology than
necessary, I shall indeed turn to the arguments
which are next in order. For when Greece got
control of herself, and all had departed, ships, horses,
infantry, lieutenants, king, first of all there were
festivals and processions to the Gods, such as no one
remembers to have taken place either before or
afterwards in a free Greece. For it was not custom
which now gathered them together nor a fixed
periodical celebration ; but these actions were the
reason why every man and every city rejoiced,
wore crowns, and called on the Gods to witness their

a The "Sacred Month " was the name of a single day.

145

(240 D.)

190 παρούσης εὐδαιμονίας. καὶ τοῦτο μὲν βωμὸς ἐλευ-
θερίου Διός, αὐτῷ τε τῷ θεῷ χαριστήριον καὶ τοῖς
κατορθώσασιν μνημεῖον ἐπ᾽ αὐτοῦ τοῦ τόπου τῶν
ἔργων ἐστάθη, κοινὴν ἔχον¹ παράκλησιν τοῖς Ἕλλησιν εἴς τε ὁμόνοιαν καὶ τὸ τῶν βαρβάρων κατα-
φρονεῖν· τοῦτο δὲ τὸ κοινὸν τῶν Ἑλλήνων ἱερὸν τὸ
ἐν Δελφοῖς ἐξεκοσμήθη σὺν καλοῖς καὶ πρέπουσι
τοῖς ἐπιγράμμασιν, αἵ τε πόλεις οὐ τὸν ἐξ ἀρετῆς

241 D. μόνον, ἀλλὰ καὶ τὸν ἐκ τῆς κατασκευῆς κόσμον
προσέλαβον, καὶ ὁ τῶν βαρβάρων πλοῦτος εἰς τοὺς

191 κρείττους ἐμερίσθη. καὶ μέντοι κἂν τούτοις αὖ πάλιν ἡ πόλις τοσοῦτον ὅσονπερ ἐν αὐταῖς ταῖς πρά-
ξεσι διενεγκοῦσα φανήσεται· [καὶ]² τοῦτο μὲν γὰρ
τὴν ἀκρόπολιν κατεκόσμησε τοῖς τῶν ἔργων ὑπο-
μνήμασιν, καὶ τῷ τῆς φύσεως κάλλει τὸ παρὰ τοῦ
πλούτου καὶ τῆς τέχνης ἐφάμιλλον προσέθηκεν, ὥστ᾽
εἶναι πᾶσαν ἀντ᾽ ἀναθήματος, μᾶλλον δὲ ἀντ᾽ ἀγάλ-
ματος· τοῦτο δὲ τὰς ἄλλας τιμὰς τοῖς θεοῖς ἀνῆψεν,
κρεῖττον ἁπάσης Ἑλληνικῆς δυνάμεως, τὰ μὲν
οἴκοι, τὰ δ᾽ ἐν τῇ ὑπερορίᾳ· αὐτή τε παρῆλθε τοὺς
ἀρχαίους ὅρους πανταχῇ κατ᾽ ἀξίαν τῶν ἔργων
καὶ τὴν τοῦ κύκλου προσθήκην ποιουμένη· ὡς δ᾽
εἰπεῖν συνελόντι, μόνη μὲν δι᾽ ἀρετὴν ἀοίκητος ἐγέ-

242 D. νετο, μόνη δ᾽ ἐξ ἀρετῆς³ ᾠκίσθη τε αὖθις καὶ τῶν
πρόσθεν ἀοικήτων ἐπέλαβεν ἅμα τοῖς ἔργοις καὶ τῇ
δόξῃ καὶ τῷ κόσμῳ καλλίων τε καὶ μείζων γενομένη.

192 Ἀλλὰ γὰρ ἐνταῦθα μὲν ὥσπερ ἄκων ἐνέπεσον
καὶ καθ᾽ ὁδὸν τοῦ λόγου μᾶλλον ἢ προειδόμενος· οὐ
γὰρ εἰς ταῦτα ὁρῶν ἠπειγόμην, ἀλλ᾽ ἐκεῖνο ἐπιδεῖ-

---

¹ ἔχων TVA.   ² add. TQVA : om. codd. dett.
³ ἀρετῆς καὶ TQ.

ᵃ [One of these has survived. The Greeks sent to Delphi a

146

present felicity. For one thing, an altar of Zeus the 190
Liberator was erected on the very site of the action
as both a thank-offering to the God himself and a
monument to their success, embodying a general
appeal to the Greeks to be concordant and to despise
the barbarians. For another the common temple
of the Greeks in Delphi was adorned with fair and
fitting inscriptions.[a] And the cities acquired not only
the adornment of virtue, but also one of a material
kind, and the wealth of the barbarians was divided
among better men. Moreover, even in these matters 191
the city obviously will have excelled as much as in
the action itself. For one thing, it adorned the 450-430.
Acropolis with monuments of its deeds, and added
to its natural beauty the rival beauty of wealth and
art, so that the whole Acropolis was like a dedication,
or rather like a statue. And again, it conferred
other honours on the Gods in a way beyond the
power of all of Greece, some at home and some
abroad. And it itself extended its old boundaries,
everywhere adding to the circuit of its walls, in
keeping with the dignity of its deeds. To sum up,
one might say that it alone because of its virtue was
left uninhabited, and it alone as a result of its virtue
was refounded and occupied lands formerly uninhabited, at the same time becoming fairer and greater
through its deeds, glory, and adornment.

But I stumbled into this argument, as it were 192
unintentionally in the course of my speech rather
than because I planned it so. For I did not press on
with an eye to it, but from the desire to show that

golden tripod on a pillar of three bronze snakes having a base
on which they inscribed the names of Greek peoples who fought
with Pausanias. The pillar can be seen in Istambul.—*E.H.W.*]

(242 D.)

ξαι βουλόμενος, ὅτι εἰ κάλλιστον ἀνθρώποις καὶ τὸ
αὐτὸ λυσιτελέστατόν τε καὶ νικῶν ἡδονῇ, θεῶν πρόσοδοι καὶ ὁμιλίαι, καὶ τοῦτ᾽ εἰς τοσοῦτον τότ᾽ ἐπ-
ανθῆσαν τοῖς Ἕλλησιν μιᾷ δὴ πόλει ταύτῃ μάλιστ᾽
ἄν τις προσθείη δικαίως, πρῶτον μὲν κατ᾽ αὐτὴν ὡς
ἀληθῶς τὴν τῶν θεῶν τιμήν· τούς τε γὰρ θεοὺς ὡς
αἰτίους δήπου τῶν ἀγαθῶν ἅπαντες ἀμειβόμεθα, ἥ
τε πόλις τό γ᾽ εἰς ἀνθρώπους ἐλθὸν τότ᾽ ἐπὶ πλεῖστον αἰτία τῶν ἀποβάντων φαίνεται· ἔπειτα τῷ καὶ
τοῖς ἀναθήμασιν αὐτοῖς καὶ τοῖς χαριστηρίοις τοσοῦτον ὑπερσχεῖν. τὰ γὰρ σύμβολα τῆς εὐσεβείας
αὐτῆς ταῦτα τοῦ κάλλους καὶ μεγέθους ἐστὶ τεκμήρια.

193   Οὐ μὴν ἐξαρκεῖν τοῦτ᾽ ἐνόμισε, χάριν τοῖς θεοῖς
ἔχειν τῶν γεγενημένων καὶ μηδὲν πλέον ζητεῖν οὐδ᾽
ἐπὶ τοῖς τροπαίοις καθῆσθαι, ὥσπερ ἀπιστοῦσαν
ἑαυτῇ, ἀλλ᾽ ὥσπερ ἐπίβασιν τῶν μελλόντων τὰ
ὑπάρχοντα κρίνασα αὐτὴ πρὸς ἑαυτὴν ἡμιλλήσατο,
καλῶς καὶ τῷ καιρῷ προσήκοντα βουλευσαμένη· ἐν
243 D. γὰρ τοῖς δευτέροις χρόνοις τὰ δεύτερα πράττειν
ἠξίου. ταῦτα δ᾽ ἦν ἀντεπεξελθεῖν τοῖς προτέροις ἐπι-
στρατεύσασιν καὶ τοὺς φόβους καὶ τοὺς κινδύνους
194 εἰς τὴν ἐκείνων μεταστῆσαι. ὃ καὶ μάλιστ᾽ ἄξιον
τῶν ἐν τοῖς ἔργοις ἐκείνοις ἀγασθῆναι τὸ σχῆμα
τοῦ πολέμου καὶ τὴν σύστασιν. δυοῖν γὰρ ὄντοιν
ἑτέροιν πολέμοιν, τοῦ μέν, ἂν ἄρχῃ τις ἐξ ἀρχῆς,
τοῦ δέ, ἂν ἀμύνηται, τῷ μὲν οὐχ ἕπεται τὸ δίκαιον,
τοῦ δὲ ἀφαιρεῖ τὴν φιλοτιμίαν¹ ἡ τῆς ἀνάγκης
προσθήκη, διὰ τὸ φύσει γνώμην ἀνάγκης κεχωρί-
σθαι. ἀλλ᾽ ἀμείνων μὲν ὁ ποιῶν οἶμαι τὰ δίκαια ἀναγκαίως τοῦ παραβαίνοντος ἑκόντος, οὐ μὴν αὐτοῦ
γε τὸ πᾶν ὡς εἰπεῖν γίγνεται. καὶ δὴ καὶ τότε τοῦ

if what is most profitable and most pleasant is the fairest thing for mankind, that is processions for the Gods and associations with the Gods, justly would this quality, which then so flourished among the Greeks, be attributed to this city alone, first of all in actually paying honour to the Gods—for we all requite the Gods since they are responsible for what is good, and the city appears then to have been most humanly responsible for what resulted—, and next because it so excelled in the erection of dedications and thank-offerings. For this testament to its beauty and greatness is the mark of its piety.

However, it did not think that it was enough to be 193 thankful to the Gods for what had taken place and to do no more, to rest on its laurels, as if it had no confidence in itself; but it judged the present as a stepping-stone to the future, and it entered into competition with itself, with a plan which was fair and suited to the moment. For it thought that in the ensuing times it should perform the ensuing tasks : a counterattack against the aggressors, and 479-468; the transfer of fear and danger to their territory. 459- And in that action the form and character of the 194 war was particularly admirable. For there are two varieties of war : aggression and self-defence. The former is unjust, and the latter, by being subject to compulsion also, inglorious, because determination is by nature distinct from compulsion. But, I think, he who acts justly under compulsion is better than a willing transgressor. However, one might say that he is not master of the situation. And then the

---

¹ Canter : τῆς φιλοτιμίας TQVA.

(243 D.)

προτέρου πολέμου τὸ μὲν αἰσχρὸν εἰς τοὺς βαρβάρους ἦλθεν, τὸ δ᾽ ὀφειλόμενον παρὰ τῶν Ἑλλήνων
ἀπήντησεν· ὥστ᾽ ἐνενικήκεσαν μέν, τὸ δ᾽ ἐκ περι-
195 ουσίας οὐ προσῆν. ὃ δὴ τρίτον ἄν τις φαίη τοῦ
πολέμου σχῆμα, τὸ τοῖς προτέροις ἐπιβουλεύσασιν
ἀντεπελθεῖν αὐτούς, ἐλευθερίᾳ μὲν τῇ τῶν ἀρχόντων,
δικαιοσύνῃ δὲ τῇ τῶν ἀμυνομένων χρωμένους, τοῦτ᾽
οὖν ἡ πόλις ἐσκέψατο καὶ ὑπὲρ αὑτῆς καὶ ὑπὲρ τῶν
ἄλλων Ἑλλήνων ἐπιδεῖξαι τοῖς βαρβάροις, ὅτι οὐκ
ἐπ᾽ ἐκείνοις ἐστίν, ὅταν ἥκωσι,[1] ποιεῖν ἀγαθοὺς
244 D. τοὺς Ἕλληνας, οὐδ᾽ ἀνάγκης τύχῃ ταῦτα πέπρακται
σφίσιν, ἀλλὰ τῷ προτέρους ἄρχειν μὴ καλῶς ἔχειν
ἡγεῖσθαι· νῦν δ᾽ ὅτε ἡ ἀρχὴ περιέστηκεν εἰς δικαίου
τάξιν, εὖ καὶ καλῶς εἴσεσθε τίνας κεκινήκατε.
196 οὕτως ἐγώ φημι καὶ πρὸς δικαιοσύνης καὶ πρὸς
ἀνδρείας ἐπίδειξιν ἀληθινῆς τὰ δεύτερα, ἵνα μηδὲν
ἐπαχθὲς εἴπω, τῶν πρότερον οὐχ ἧττον ἐναργῆ
197 πεπρᾶχθαι τῇ πόλει. πρὸς δὲ τούτοις καὶ τῶν
Ἑλλήνων ἀσφάλειαν εἶναι καὶ σωτηρίαν ὑπελάμβα-
νεν οὐκ εἰ καθείρξασα αὐτοὺς ἐπὶ τῆς ἑστίας τηροίη,
οὐδ᾽ εἰ μηδὲν μήτ᾽ αὐτὴ πρὸς αὐτῶν ⟨αἰτοίη⟩[2]
μήτ᾽ αὐτοὶ πράττοιεν ὑπὲρ σφῶν αὐτῶν, ἀλλ᾽ εἰ
τοὺς βαρβάρους ὡς ἐπὶ πλεῖστον ὤσαιντο ἀπὸ τῆς
Ἑλλάδος, οὕτως ᾤετο ἀρίστην καὶ καθαρὰν ἡσυχίαν
ἅπασιν ἔσεσθαι, ὀρθῶς λογιζομένη καὶ τὰ πράγματα
ὡς πέφυκεν ὁρῶσα. μόνοι γὰρ σχεδὸν οὗτοι καθαρῶς ἡσυχάζουσιν οἵτινες ἂν δείξωσιν μὴ πάντως
ἡσυχίαν ἄγειν δεόμενοι.
198 Ὁ μὲν λογισμὸς οὗτος ὁ τῆς πόλεως, ἅπαντα
ἔχων ὅσα ἄν τις εἴποι κάλλιστα ἐν ἀνθρώπου φύσει.
διανοηθέντες δὲ οὕτω τί χρὴ πρῶτον, ἢ τί τελευταῖον

---

[1] εἴκωσι VA.

barbarians experienced the shameful side of the
former war, and they got their due from the Greeks.
For the Greeks had conquered, but not thoroughly.
Then what could be called a third kind of war, a 195
counter-attack against those who first plotted
hostilities, with the freedom of action of the aggressor
and the just cause of the defender, was the means by
which the city planned on behalf of itself and the
other Greeks to show to the barbarians that it did not
rest with them on any invasion of theirs, to make the
Greeks good men, nor had they acted so from for-
tuitous compulsion, but because they did not believe
that it was right to be aggressors. But now when
aggression has been classed as just, you will know
well whom you have provoked. So I say that the 196
city accomplished the ensuing actions no less clearly
than the earlier ones for the demonstration of
justice and true courage, not that I denigrate the
former deeds. Besides, it realized that the Greeks 197
had no safety and security if it should shut them up
and keep them at home, or if it should ask nothing of
them, or they should do nothing in their own behalf.
But if they should drive the barbarians as far as
possible from Greece, in this way it thought that all
would have the best and fullest peace, and it judged
well and with a regard for how matters stood.
For it is generally true that they alone are most fully
at peace who show that they do not desire to remain
entirely at peace.

This was the city's judgement, embodying all of 198
the finest things which one would say are in human
nature. But with this resolve—what should first

---

² add. Behr dubitanter : δι' αὐτῶν codd. dett., edd.

245 D. εἰπεῖν,[1] ἐνίκων μὲν τὴν ἐν Μυκάλῃ μάχην οὐκ ἐν
ὀλίγῳ τῷ μέσῳ, διηρευνήσαντο δὲ τῆς Εὐρώπης
τὰς ἀκτάς, εἴ πού τις ἔτι κρύπτοιτο τῶν ἐπελθόντων,
καὶ τοὺς μὲν ἀπὸ Στρυμόνος ἤλασαν, τοὺς δὲ ἀπὸ
199 Σηστοῦ, τοὺς δ' ἀπὸ Βυζαντίου. πάντα δὲ ὥσπερ
ἄγος καθαίροντες ἐπῆλθον, οὐκ ἐλάττω δὲ τῶν κατ'
ἐμπορίαν πλεόντων ἐπ' ἀγκυρῶν ὡρμίσαντο.[2] τὴν
δὲ Τριπτολέμου διὰ τοῦ ἀέρος λεχθεῖσαν πορείαν, ἐν
ᾧ παρῆκεν ἐκεῖνος, ἐμιμήσαντο. ὁ μὲν γὰρ εὖ ποιῶν
εἰς τὸ κοινὸν ἅπαντας, οἱ δὲ παρ' ὧν δίκην ἔδει
λαβεῖν κολάζοντες ἐπῄεσαν, ἡγούμενοι καὶ τοῦτο
τῷ κοινῷ γένει τῶν ἀνθρώπων λυσιτελεῖν, τοὺς
246 D. ὑβριστὰς καὶ μεῖζον τῆς φύσεως φρονοῦντας ταῖς
200 πρεπούσαις ὑπάγειν ζημίαις. γνόντες δὲ οὕτως
ἅμα μὲν περιέπλεον τὴν Ἀσίαν, ἅμα δὲ ἀνέπλεον
διὰ τῶν δεχομένων ποταμῶν, ἅμα δ' ἠκούοντο, ἅμα
δ' ἑωρῶντο· θαυμαστὴν δ' ἐπεδείξαντο καὶ ὡς
ἀληθῶς ἐνόπλιόν τινα καὶ πολέμου χορείαν. οὕτω
δὲ πυκνὸν καὶ σύντονον ἐξήλαντο ἐν τοῖς πράγμασιν
ὥστε καὶ Λακεδαιμόνιοι τοῖς μὲν πρώτοις τῶν
ἔργων παρεγένοντο, ἔπειτ' ἀπῆραν, ὥσπερ πτηνοῖς
201 ἀκολουθεῖν οὐ[3] δυνάμενοι. τὸ δ' αὐτὸ τοῦτο καὶ
τῶν ἄλλων Ἑλλήνων οἱ καὶ τὰ πρῶτα συνεκπλεύ-
σαντες ἰλιγγιάσαντες ἀπῆραν, οἱ δὲ τοὺς ἀπὸ τῆς
Ἀσίας ἔχοντες, οὓς βασιλεὺς πρότερον ἐπ' ἐκείνους
καὶ τὴν Ἑλλάδα ἧκεν ἄγων, τούτοις ἐχρῶντο ἀπο-
χρῶσιν. καὶ ἦν αὐτοῖς ἀφορμὴ κατὰ τοῦ βασιλέως
τὰ τοῦ βασιλέως πράγματα. καὶ γὰρ ὅρμοι καὶ
τείχη καὶ χαρακώματα καὶ πάντα ἐκείνους ἐδέχετο,
καὶ ὅπλα καὶ νῆες ἐκείνων ἐγίγνοντο.
202   Παρεῖσαν δ' οὐδὲν ἀπείρατον τῆς ἑαυτῶν ἀρετῆς,

---

[1] ποιεῖν ci. Holleck.

be told, or what last ?—, they won the battle at
Mycale by no small measure, and they searched 479.
the shores of Europe, in case any of the invaders
should still be lurking somewhere ; and some they
drove from the Strymon, some from Sestus, and 478-475.
others from Byzantium. They went everywhere, 199
as if they were cleansing a pollution, and they rode at
anchor no less often than merchantmen. And they
imitated the journey, already mentioned, of Triptolemus through the heavens,[a] in a way which he overlooked. For his arrival benefited all men in common,
but theirs chastised those who deserved it, since they
believed that it was advantageous to the whole
human race to subject criminals and the unnaturally
arrogant to appropriate punishments. With this 200
resolve, they sailed about Asia, and sailed up the
navigable rivers, and were rumoured and seen at the
same instant. They displayed a wonderful and real
armed rhythm and war dance. So often and force-
fully did they leap in their performance that the
Lacedaemonians, who were present at their first
actions, departed, as if they could not follow winged 479.
men. So too, among the rest of the Greeks, those, 201
who first sailed out with them, became dizzy and
departed. But they had those from Asia whom the
king formerly led against them and Greece, and
found them satisfactory. And they used the king's
own works as a starting point against him. For
anchorages, walls, pallisades, all received them, and
they took over their weapons and ships.

They left nothing untouched by their virtue, 202

---

[a] Cf. § 36.

² ὡρμήσαντο TQA.   ³ μὴ TQ.

(246 D.)

ὁμοῦ μὲν Φοίνιξι καὶ Κίλιξι καὶ Κυπρίοις ναυμα
χοῦντες ἐν μέσῳ τῷ Αἰγυπτίων πελάγει καὶ ναυ
τικὰ ἀθρόα λαμβάνοντες, ὁμοῦ δὲ πρὸς πᾶσαν τὴν
Περσῶν ἀρχὴν διακινδυνεύοντες ἐν τῇ γῇ ἀντ' ἀριθ
μοῦ σωμάτων ἐθνῶν ἀριθμοὺς διαφθείροντές τε καὶ
λαμβάνοντες. ἤδη δὲ καὶ δύο τρόπαια εἰς μίαν
247 D. ἡμέραν ἦλθεν καὶ ναυμαχία πεζομαχίᾳ παρισώθη.
τοσοῦτον δὲ τῷ βασιλεῖ περιεγένετο ὥστε ἐνδοξο
τέραν αὐτοῦ τὴν ἀρχὴν καὶ τοὺς τόπους ταῖς νίκαις
203 ἐποίησαν. ὁ δ' οὖν Εὐρυμέδων οὐχ ἥκιστα δὴ διὰ
τούτους ᾄδεται. ἔδειξαν δ' ὅτι οὐ λινοδέσμῳ σχεδίᾳ
τοὺς πορθμοὺς ζευγνύντα δεῖ διαβαίνειν οὐδὲ τοῖς
ὑψηλοτάτοις τῶν ὀρῶν προσπαλαίειν, ὥσπερ τι κάλ
λιον, ἀλλ' ἀνδρείᾳ καὶ γνώμῃ προέχοντας[1] κρατεῖν
πανταχοῦ καλλίστοις ἁπάντων ἐφοδίοις οἶμαι καὶ
καθαρῶς οἴκοθεν· μόνα γὰρ τῶν ἐχόντων διὰ τέλους
ἐστίν, τὰ δ' ἄλλα κοινὰ πρόκειται πᾶσιν ὡς εἰπεῖν
τύχης δῶρα, εἰ δὲ βούλει, ἀρετῆς. ὑπάρχει μὲν γὰρ
καὶ τοῖς χείροσιν ἐξ ἀρχῆς, σῴζεται δὲ ἐπιεικῶς
τοῖς κρείττοσιν.

204   Οὕτω δ' ἅπασαν τὴν ἀρχὴν ἐξήλεγξαν, καὶ διέ
σεισαν καὶ πρὸς τοσοῦτον ἀφίκοντο οἱ μὲν εἰς τὸ
Περσικὸν τελοῦντες τοῦ καταφρονηθῆναι, ἡ πόλις
δὲ τοῦ πάντας αὐτῇ θαρρεῖν, ὥστ' ἐκινήθησαν μὲν
οἱ πρὸς Φάρῳ Λίβυες, συναπέστησαν δὲ Αἰγύπτιοι,
248 D. βασιλεὺς δὲ καίτοι τὰ ἄλλα κατὰ νοῦν περὶ αὐτοὺς

---

[1] Reiske : προσέχοντας TQVA.

---

[a] [In 468 B.C. at the Battle of the river Eurymedon in
Pamphylia in Asia Minor, the forces of Athens' new Confederacy (" of Delos ") under the Athenian general Cimon
won a great victory over the Persians and Phoenicians by
land and sea, and freed the Greeks from all real danger. The

154

simultaneously fighting a sea battle with the Phoenicians, Cilicians, and Cyprians in the middle of the 450–449. Egyptian sea and capturing whole fleets, and on land too facing danger against the whole of the Persian Empire, killing or capturing instead of a number of men, great numbers of races. Even two trophies were raised in a single day, and naval battle was like land battle. But the king profited only to the extent that they made his empire and these places more glorious by their victories. The river Eury- 203 medon is famous especially because of these men.[a] They showed that there was no need to cross the 468. straits by bridging them with " flax-bound pontoons," [b] nor to wrestle with the highest mountains, as if that were a fairer achievement, but by excelling in courage and resolve, the fairest, I think, and most native resources of all, to be everywhere victorious. For these qualities alone always remain with their possessors, but other things are promiscuously available to all, gifts of fortune, one might say, or if you wish, of virtue. For even inferior men possess them at the start, but they are mostly kept by the superior.

Thus they exposed and jarred the whole empire, 204 and the members of the Persian race became so despised and all men had such confidence in the city, that the Libyans near Pharus revolted, and the Egyptians joined the defection. Although in other 459. respects the king apparently had his way with them,

same general in 450–449 B.C. died while freeing Cyprus from Persian and Phoenician domination ; and his fleet then won a victory by sea and land over Phoenicians and Cilicians. Peace with Persia followed in 448 B.C.—*E.H.W.*]

[b] Aeschylus, *Persians* 69.

(248 D.)

πρᾶξαι δοκῶν ἀπόλλυσιν Αἰγύπτου μοῖραν οὐκ
ὀλίγην τὸ ἕλος. πρότερον δ' ἡρήκει πᾶσαν δὶς ἤδη.
205 ἦν δὲ τὸ τῶν Ἀθήνηθεν τριήρων οἷόν τι τῶν ἐξ
οὐρανοῦ βελῶν. μόνοι γὰρ ἀνθρώπων τῶν εἰς κοινὸν
πολιτευσαμένων τὴν μὲν οἰκείαν ὥσπερ ἀλλοτρίαν
ἐνόμισαν, τὴν δὲ ἀλλοτρίαν οὐχ αὑτῶν ἀλλοτρίαν,
ἀλλὰ τῶν σὺν κακίᾳ νεμομένων. φυλάκων δ'
ἐβίωσαν βίον, οὐδὲ τούτων ἱδρυμένων, οὐδέ γε ἑνὸς
τόπου τινὸς περιπόλων, ἀλλὰ τοῦ διὰ πάσης γῆς
206 Ἑλληνικοῦ περιπόλους ἐκείνους χρὴ καλεῖν. πολεμίους δὲ οὐ τοὺς ἀσθενεστάτους εἵλοντο, ἀλλὰ τοὺς
πλεῖστα ἀνασχέσθαι δυνατωτάτους, δυοῖν ἐναγόν-
τοιν, ἑνὸς μὲν τοῦ μηδὲν τῶν ἐσχάτων, ὅσον εἰς
γνώμην καὶ παρασκευὴν ἧκεν τῶν βαρβάρων, ἐλλε-
λεῖφθαι τοῖς Ἕλλησι τὸ μὴ οὐ πεπονθότας εἶναι,
ἀνθ' ὧν δεῖν ἀμύνεσθαι καὶ μηδαμῶς μικρῶς, ἑτέρου δὲ τοῦ πρὸς τὸν λοιπὸν χρόνον ἀσφαλοῦς τῇ
Ἑλλάδι, ἕως ἔγνω βασιλεὺς παραπλήσιον ποιῶν
ἀνταίρων τῇ πόλει ὥσπερ ἂν εἰ πρὸς φλόγα πολλὴν
ἐπιοῦσαν ὕλην ἐπηρμένος ἠγωνίζετο. οὐδὲν γὰρ ἦν
ὅ τι οὐκ ἔπασχεν, ἀλλ' ἀνηλίσκετο αὐτὸς ἐξ αὑτοῦ
καὶ τὴν χώραν ἐπιτείχισμα τῆς ἑαυτοῦ σωτηρίας
ἔχων ᾔσθετο.
207   Καὶ προῆλθεν ὁδῷ τὸ τρίτον κάλλιον τοῦ πρώτου
νομίσας, μᾶλλον δὲ ἀναγκαιότερον. ἐπεθύμησεν
⟨μὲν γὰρ⟩¹ τὸ ἐξ ἀρχῆς τὴν Ἑλλάδα προσλαβεῖν καὶ
τῆς Εὐρώπης τὸ λοιπόν, ᾔσθετο ⟨δὲ⟩² οὐ δυνατῶν
ἐρῶν. δεύτερον ἦν αὐτῷ τὴν ὑπάρχουσαν ἀρχὴν

¹ add. codd. dett.
² add. codd. dett.

ᵃ [Egypt had been conquered by the Persians in 525 B.C.
In 459 B.C. Athens and her confederates answered a call from
a rebel Libyan chief Inarōs, went up the Nile and besieged

he lost no small part of Egypt, the Marsh. But before this he had captured all of it twice already.[a] The Athenian triremes had a character somewhat 205 like that of shafts from heaven. For they alone of those concerned with all people's welfare thought of their own land as if foreign, but foreign land as not foreign to them but to those who inhabit it badly. They lived the life of guards, not the kind who are in garrisons or the patrols of some single region, but they should be called the patrols of the Greek race throughout the earth. They did not choose the 206 weakest men as their enemies, but those who had the most endurance, for two reasons : first because for all that the barbarians had planned and prepared, the Greeks would have been spared no extremity of suffering, in return for which they must also defend themselves, and in no small way ; and second for the future security of Greece, until the king realized that in opposing the city he acted just as if he fought the advance of a great forest fire by heaping fuel on it. For there was nothing which he did not suffer, but he financed his own destruction, and he found that his territory was a military threat to his own safety.

And he was more successful after he realized that 207 his third plan was better, or rather more necessary, than his first one. For initially he desired to add Greece and the rest of Europe to his empire, but he perceived that he hoped for the impossible. His second plan was to preserve his existing empire ;

some Persians in Memphis. But in 456 B.C. Megabyzus was sent against the besiegers, whose efforts collapsed in 454 B.C. An Athenian relief-force was destroyed by Phoenicians in the Mendesian mouth of the Nile ; and Persian rule was restored in Egypt.—E.H.W.]

249 D.

208 διασώσασθαι, οὐδὲ τοῦθ' ἡ πόλις ἠνέσχετο. τὴν σωτηρίαν καὶ δὴ πλείονος ἀξίαν ἐποιήσατο, καὶ ὑποχωρεῖ τῇ πόλει τοσοῦτον ἐκ γῆς καὶ θαλάττης, οὐχ ὅσον, φασίν, πρύμναν κρούσασθαι οὐδ' ὡς ἐπὶ πόδα ἀναχωρῆσαι, ἀλλ' ἀφῆκε πάντα μὲν τὸν κάτω τόπον, μυριάδας σταδίων τῆς Ἀσίας οὐκ ἔλαττον ἢ μεγάλης ἀρχῆς εἶναι τὸ σύμπαν· ὥστε μὴ μόνον τὰς νήσους καὶ τοὺς ἐν ταύταις παντοδαποὺς Ἕλληνας ἐλευθέρους εἶναι, ἀλλὰ καὶ τοὺς τὴν ἐκείνου χώραν κατοικοῦντας πλέον τῆς ἐκείνου δυναστείας καὶ ἀρχῆς ἀπέχειν ἢ πρότερον τοὺς τὴν ἀρχαίαν Ἑλλάδα. εἶχεν μέν γε πρὸ τοῦ τὸν μέχρι Πηνειοῦ τόπον·

209 καίτοι τὸ θαυμαστὸν ἀφεῖλον, ὡς δή τι θαυμαστὸν λέγων· εἶχέ γε¹ πάντα τὸν μέχρι τῆς Ἀττικῆς, ἕως ἐνέτυχε τοῖς ἐκ τῆς Ἀττικῆς ἐν τῇ θαλάττῃ· τοσοῦτον παρελήλυθεν τὸν ὀμφαλὸν τῆς γῆς τε καὶ τῆς Ἑλλάδος, τοὺς Δελφούς. ἐκ δὲ τῶν τῆς πόλεως ἀγώνων καὶ ἀποστόλων εἰς τοῦτο κατῆλθεν ὥσθ' ὡμολόγησεν δυοῖν μὲν ὅροιν εἴσω μηκέτι πλευσεῖσθαι, πρὸς μεσημβρίαν μὲν Χελιδονέας, πρὸς

250 D. δὲ ἄρκτον Κυανέας θέμενος, θαλάττης δὲ ἀφέξειν ἴσον πανταχῇ σταδίους πεντακοσίους· ὥστ' εἶναι τὸν κύκλον τοῦτον ἀντ' ἄλλου τινὸς στεφάνου τοῖς Ἕλλησιν ὑπὲρ κεφαλῆς καὶ τὴν φρουρὰν ἐξ αὐτῆς τῆς χώρας τοῦ βασιλέως.

210 Τοιοῦτον μὲν τὸν πόλεμον τὸν πρὸς τοὺς βαρβάρους ἡ πόλις, τόν τ' ἐπὶ τῆς οἰκείας καὶ τὸν ἐν τῇ ἐκείνων, τοιαύτην δ' αὖ καὶ τὴν εἰρήνην ἐποιήσατο, ἐξ ἀμφοτέρων δείξασα ὅτι οὐ πλοῦτον διώκουσα οὐδ' ἡδονῇ κέρδους ἐπεξῆλθεν, ἀλλ' ἐν τοῦτο θηρωμένη, βεβαίαν τοῖς Ἕλλησιν ἐλευθερίαν ἀπὸ τῶν

and even this the city did not allow. He valued his 208
safety more, and he retreated before the city on land
and sea not the distance, as the saying goes, of a
ship's backwater, nor of a step backwards, but he 448.
gave up all his land down by the sea, tens of thousands of stades in Asia, in all no less than the area
of a great empire,[a] so that not only the islands and the
various Greeks in them were liberated, but even
the inhabitants of his territory were farther from his
control and rule than those of ancient Greece were
formerly. Once he held everything up to the
Peneus.[b] Yet as if I had said something remarkable, 209
I omitted what is remarkable. For he held every- 492.
thing up to Attica, until he met those from Attica 480.
on the sea. So far had he travelled beyond Delphi,
the centre of the earth and Greece. But after the
struggles and expeditions of the city, he sank so low
that he agreed that he would no longer sail within
two boundaries, the Chelidonean Isles to the south, 448.
and the Cyanean to the north, and that he would
everywhere keep five hundred stades away from the
sea, so that this very circle was like a crown upon
the head of the Greeks, and the king was under sur-
veillance from his very territory.

Such was the war that the city waged against the 210
barbarians, both in its own territory and in theirs,
and such was the peace it made, having shown in
both instances that it did not counterattack in
pursuit of wealth or for the pleasure of gain, but in
the hunt for this single quarry, a secure freedom for

---

[a] The reference is to the Peace (of Callias, so called) with
Persia. For the terms see §§ 209 and 274.   [b] In Thessaly.

---

[1] τε aut δὲ codd. dett.

(250 D.)

211 βαρβάρων. καίτοι τί κάλλιον ἂν εἴποι τις εἰρήνης
ἢ πολέμου κεφάλαιον ἢ πρὸς Ἕλληνας ἢ πρὸς βαρβάρους, ᾧ κατέκλεισεν τότε τὰς πράξεις ἡ πόλις;

212 Καὶ ταῦτα μέντοι τὰ τοσαῦτα καὶ τοιαῦτα διῆλθε
σὺν πολλοῖς ὅμως ἐναντιώμασιν τῶν Ἑλλήνων καὶ
πάντων ὥσπερ ἀνθελκόντων, ἀφεστηκότων μὲν τῇ

251 D. γνώμῃ Λακεδαιμονίων, Βοιωτῶν δ' ἐναντία πολεμούντων, Αἰγινητῶν δ' ἐναντία ναυμαχούντων, οὓς
εἶναι τὰ ναυτικὰ πρώτους ἐν ἐκώλυσεν, ἡ πόλις
πολὺ νικῶσα· πρὸς δὲ τούτοις Κορινθίων διὰ Με-
γαρέας παρωξυμμένων καὶ πολεμούντων καὶ κατὰ
γῆν καὶ κατὰ θάλατταν, Ἐπιδαυρίων δὲ καὶ Σικυωνίων σὺν Κορινθίοις ἐξεταζομένων, Ναξίων δὲ καὶ
Θασίων καὶ Καρυστίων κακῶς περὶ τῆς συμμαχίας
βουλευομένων, καλούντων δὲ Φωκέων, καλούντων
δ' αὖθις Λακεδαιμονίων, θαυμαστοῦ δὲ κύκλου
πραγμάτων ὄντος κατὰ τὴν Ἑλλάδα· ὥστ', εἰ καὶ
μόνοις τούτοις ἐξήρκεσεν[1] καὶ μόνας τὰς Ἑλληνικὰς
πράξεις εἴχομεν αὐτῆς εἰπεῖν ἐν τῷ τότε συμβάσας,
Μηδικαὶ δὲ μηδαμοῦ προσῆσαν λαμπρότητες, ἐξ-

213 αρκεῖν ἂν τοῖς χρόνοις εἰς ἀφήγησιν. ᾗ καὶ διαφερόντως ἄξιον συνησθῆναι τῇ πόλει οὐ μόνον τῆς
ῥώμης χάριν, ἀλλὰ καὶ τῆς μεγαλοψυχίας· τὸ γὰρ
ἐν πολέμῳ καὶ φιλονικίᾳ τῶν Ἑλλήνων πρὸς αὐτὴν
καθεστηκότων τῆς ὑπὲρ τῶν Ἑλλήνων προνοίας
μηδὲν μᾶλλον ἀφεῖσθαι, ἀλλ' ὑπὲρ τῶν κοινῇ συμ-
φερόντων βασιλεῖ πολεμεῖν διὰ γῆς ἁπάσης καὶ
θαλάττης πόσῃ τινὶ χρὴ τῇ μεγαλοψυχίᾳ προσθεῖναι,

---

[1] Reiske: ἐξήρκεσαν TQVA.

---

[a] [Athens' Confederacy of Delos is meant, 478 B.C.; and
the suppression of these states (Naxos c. 469 B.C.; Thasos
in 463; Carystos in 472–471; Aegina, after much hostility

the Greeks from the barbarians. Yet what fairer 211
consummation of peace or war against Greeks or
barbarians could be mentioned than that by which
the city concluded its acts ?

Moreover it accomplished these great and noble 212
deeds despite frequent opposition from the Greeks,
all of whom as it were pulled against it ; the Lacedaemonians stood aloof in their counsel, the Boeotians
waged open war, and the Aeginetans, who were
prevented by the great superiority of the city alone *C.* 595;
from being the first naval power, fought with them $\begin{smallmatrix}C.498-491\\488-481\\;\end{smallmatrix}$
at sea ; and in addition to this the Corinthians were $458-456.$
enraged because of the Megarians and waged war 459-458.
on land and sea, and the Epidaurians and Sicyonians
were counted with the Corinthians, and the Naxians, $\begin{smallmatrix}472-471,\\469,465-\end{smallmatrix}$
Thasians, and Carystians were treacherous toward 463; 478;
the alliance,*a* and the Phocians and again the Lace- 457.
daemonians summoned their help, and there was an 464.
extraordinary succession of troubles throughout
Greece. Therefore even if the city had sufficed only
for these affairs and we could only speak of its
actions then in regard to the Greeks, and there
were no Persian glories, there would be enough
to tell for years. For this reason, the city should be 213
particularly congratulated not only because of its
strength, but also because of its generosity. For to
how noble a concept of generosity should be attributed the fact that the city did not any the more
abandon its concern for the Greeks, although they
warred and fought with it, but that for the sake of
what was expedient for all it waged war with the
king throughout every land and sea, apart from the

over the years, in 456), as a result of disagreements, marked
progress of Athens towards empire.—*E.H.W.*]

252 D. χωρὶς τοῦ τοσαῦτα μερισθῆναι καὶ πάντων ὡς μόνων
ἑκάστων ἐφικέσθαι, τῆς μὲν γνώμης τὴν ἀνδρείαν,
τῆς δὲ παρασκευῆς τὴν ὑπερβολὴν παρέχειν θαυμάσαι; τά τε γὰρ πρὸς τοὺς βαρβάρους ὡς πᾶσαν
ἄγουσα ἀπὸ πάντων σχολὴν οὕτω διῳκήσατο, καὶ
τοῖς ἐνοχλοῦσι τῶν Ἑλλήνων οὐδὲν μᾶλλον ὑπῆρ-
χεν¹ χρήσασθαι τῷ καιρῷ, ἀλλὰ καὶ τούτοις οὕτως
ἀπήντησεν ὥστε σύμπεντε καὶ συμπλείω ταῦτ' ἔχειν
ἀπαριθμεῖν ὥσπερ ἄλλ' ἄττα συλλήβδην ἀριθμού-
μενα.

214
253 D.   Ἐνίκων μέν γε ναυμαχίᾳ Πελοποννησίους ἐπὶ
Κεκρυφαλίᾳ, ἐνίκων δ' Αἰγινήτας πρὸς Αἰγίνῃ, καὶ
Πελοποννησίους αὖθις. Μεγαρεῦσιν δ' ἔστησαν
τείχη μέχρι θαλάττης, καὶ τὴν ἐλευθερίαν ἅμα καὶ
χώραν διεφύλαξαν· ἐνίκων δὲ Κορινθίους πρὸ Με-
γαρέων, καὶ πρὶν δώδεκα ἐξήκειν ἡμέρας ἐνίκων
αὖθις ἑτέραν, οὐ καλῶς τὸ τρόπαιον ὑφαρπάζοντας.
215 καὶ οὔπω ταῦτα μεγάλα· ἀλλ' εἰρήσεται γάρ, κἂν
ἐπείγωμαι· ἡ γὰρ προσθήκη δείξει τὸ πᾶν. ἀπῆσαν
μὲν γὰρ αἱ δυνάμεις τῇ πόλει, ἡ μὲν κατὰ τὴν
⟨τῶν⟩² Αἰγυπτίων χρείαν, νῆες πλείους ἢ τότε ἦσαν
ἐν τοῖς Ἕλλησιν αἱ σύμπασαι σχεδόν· ἡ δ' Αἴγινα
προσεκάθητο, ὅπερ καὶ τοὺς ἐναντίους μᾶλλον ἐπῆρεν ὁρμῆσαι πρὸς τὰ Μέγαρα. ᾤοντο γὰρ εἶναι
σχολὴν Ἀθηναίων εἰς τὸ ἔργον ἑαυτοῖς. εἰ δ' ἄρα
καὶ τὰ δεύτερα νικῷη, ἀλλ' ἑτέραν λύσειν πολιορκίαν,
τὴν Αἰγίνης³· οὐ γὰρ ἄλλοθέν γε λοιπὸν ἥξειν αὐτούς.
216 οἱ δὲ τοσοῦτον κατεγέλασαν τοῦ σοφίσματος ὥστ'
254 D. οὐδὲν μᾶλλον οἱ πρὸς Αἰγίνῃ τότ' ἐκινήθησαν τῶν

---

¹ ὑπῆρχεν om. A.   ² add. codd. dett.
³ τῆς Αἰγίνης Phot.

ᵃ Cf. Thucydides I. 105.

enormous division of its activities, and its complete success in all of them as if each were the only one, so that it gave occasion to admire the courage of its resolve and the surpassing greatness of its preparations ? For it acted toward the barbarians, as if it were utterly and completely at leisure ; and the Greeks who were troubling the city were still unable to take advantage of this opportunity, but the city so encountered them that it could number these actions at five or more together, just as other trivial things which are numbered in lots.

They defeated the Peloponnesians in a naval 214 engagement at Cecryphalea,[a] and they defeated the 458. Aeginetans at Aegina, and again the Peloponnesians. For the Megarians they built walls up to 459. the sea, and they protected their freedom and territory. They defeated the Corinthians in defence of the Megarians, and before twelve days had passed, they defeated them again in another battle when they basely stole the Athenian trophy. And these 215 deeds are not great, but they will be mentioned 458. even if I am pressed for time. For this added point will prove the whole argument. The forces of the city were away, one in the service of the Egyptians, almost more ships than the total number then of the other Greeks ; another was besieging Aegina, which 458-456. circumstance still more impelled the enemy to attack Megara. For they thought that the absence of the Athenians aided their enterprise. But even if the city should win the second action, they still thought that they would end the other siege, that of Aegina. For no other place remained from which they would come. But the Athenians so ridiculed 216 the clever trick that their men at Aegina were no

(254 D.)

ἐν Αἰγύπτῳ καὶ μηδὲν πεπυσμένων, ἀλλὰ τὸ λοιπὸν
τῆς ἡλικίας οἱ πρεσβύτατοι καὶ νεώτατοι βοηθοῦσιν
εἰς τὰ Μέγαρα, καὶ δυοῖν μάχαιν ἑξῆς κρείττους
τῆς ⟨τῶν⟩¹ Κορινθίων καὶ Πελοποννησίων ἀκμῆς
ἐφάνησαν· ὥστ' ἐκείνους ἀκριβῶς ἤδη συγχωρῆσαι
καὶ μηδὲν ἔχειν εἰπεῖν ἔτι, μηδ' ὡς οὐ δικαίως τά γε
217 δὴ νῦν ταῦτα προσανιμήκεσαν. καί μοι δοκεῖ θεῶν
τινος εὐνοίᾳ καὶ σπουδῇ πρὸς τὴν πόλιν συσκευα-
σθῆναι τοῦτο τὸ δεύτερον, ὥσπερ ἐν δράματι. εἰ
μὲν γὰρ ὡς ἅπαξ ἐπλήγησαν, ἀπῆλθον, τάχ' ἄν τις
ἦν αὐτοῖς ὕστερον ἀντιλαβή, τὸ δ' ὀνειδίζεσθαι μὲν
ὑπὸ τῶν οἰκείων, ὀνειδιζομένους δὲ αὖθις ἐξελθεῖν,
ἀνθιστάντας δὲ τρόπαιον μεῖζω τῶν πρότερον προσ-
παθεῖν, αὐτοὺς ἐποίησεν ἐπισφραγίζεσθαι τὴν νί-
255 D. κην, ὡς μὴ δοκεῖν τύχῃ μᾶλλον ἢ τῷ τοῦ κρείττονος λόγῳ τὸ ἔργον κριθῆναι καὶ νῦν καὶ πρότερον.
οὔκουν τοῦ τρίτου γε ἐπειράθησαν, καίτοι τοὺς
ἀγωνιστὰς αὐτοὶ προσαναγκάζοντες ἐν Ἰσθμῷ.
218   Ἆρ' οὖν ταῦτα καὶ μόνα τῶν ἀνδρῶν ἐκείνων
ἔχομεν λέγειν; πολλῶν μεντἂν καὶ μεγάλων ἀπο-
στεροίημεν αὐτούς· οἳ περιέπλευσαν μὲν τὴν Πελοπόννησον, οὐχ ὡς ἁπλῶς εἰπεῖν περίπλοις ναυτικοῖς,
ἀλλ' ὥστε κρατεῖν μὲν τῶν ἐπικαίρων τῆς χώρας,
νικᾶν δὲ τοὺς ἀντιστάντας ἐν φαύλῳ, στρατηγὸς
ἐπὶ στρατηγῷ. διέβησαν δὲ εἰς τὴν ἀντιπέρας ἤπειρον, παντὸς τοῦ προστυχόντος εἴκοντος.
219   Αὖθις δ' ἐπὶ Φωκέας Λακεδαιμονίων παρελθόντων
256 D. ἐκέκλειστο μὲν ὁ Κρισαῖος κόλπος, ἀπήντων δ' ἐπὶ

¹ τῶν om. TQV ; τῆς solum A p. corr.

ᵃ Cf. Thucydides I. 108.   ᵇ Cf. Thucydides I. 107.

more disturbed than those in Egypt who had heard nothing of the matter, but what remained of their age groups, the oldest and the youngest, went to help Megara. And in two successive battles they appeared superior to the pick of the Corinthians and Peloponnesians, so that these now completely gave way and no longer could make any claims, not even how at the present they had not justly drawn up this additional bucket of woe. And it seems to me, 217 as if in a play, that this second act was arranged by the goodwill and eagerness of some God toward the city. For if the enemy had gone off after the first 458. blow, perhaps later they would have had a point to argue. But the fact that they were reviled by their own people, and having been reviled, marched forth a second time, and having erected as a countermove their own trophy, suffered much worse than before, all of this caused them to confirm the victory, so that both the present and previous action seem to have been decided not by chance but rather on the grounds of superiority. Therefore they did not make a third attempt, although at the Isthmus they do indeed force the contestants to do this.

Then can we only speak of these deeds of those 218 men ? But we should deprive them of many great achievements. They circumnavigated the Pelopon- C. 455-453? nesus,[a] not, to put it simply, in a naval circumnaviga- tion, but so that general after general got control of the strategic points of the land and easily defeated those who opposed them. And they crossed over to C. 453. the mainland opposite, and all that met them gave way. 219

Again when the Lacedaemonians marched against 457. the Phocians,[b] the Athenians blocked the Crisean

165

(256 D.)

τοὺς ὅρους. χωρὶς δὲ ὑπὲρ Μεγάρων ἦσαν ἐν
Γερανείᾳ· ὥστε μὴ ἔχειν Λακεδαιμονίους ὅ τι
χρήσονται, ἀλλ' ἀπορεῖν ἑστῶτας ἐν Βοιωτοῖς ὅποι
σωθήσονται· οὕτω περιέπτυξεν αὐτοὺς ἡ πόλις.
220 τέλος δὲ συμβάλλουσιν ἐν Τανάγρᾳ τῆς Βοιωτίας,
καὶ γενομένων ἀμφοτέρων ἀνδρῶν τοῦ τολμήματος
ἀξίων ἔδοξαν καθ' ἓν τοῦτο Λακεδαιμόνιοι πλέον
ἐσχηκέναι, πῶς ἂν εἴποιμι εὐπρεπῶς; ὀκνῶ γὰρ
εἰπεῖν ὅτι οὐκ ἀπώλοντο. καὶ γὰρ ἦν ὅρος οὗτος
Ἀθηναίοις μὲν κλεῖσαι τὴν πάροδον, Λακεδαιμονίοις
δὲ σωθῆναι οἴκαδε. καὶ κινδυνεύει μόνον τοῦτο τὸ
ἔργον τὴν φυγὴν σύμβολον τῆς νίκης ἐσχηκέναι,
ἐπεὶ τούς γε καὶ παρὰ τὴν μάχην κρείττους καὶ
[παρὰ]¹ τοῖς ὅλοις ἄνευ πολλῶν τῶν καὶ πρότερον
κρινάντων τὰ ἐφεξῆς εὐθὺς ἔδειξεν. τρεῖς γάρ εἰσιν
οἱ μαρτυρήσαντες παραχρῆμα Ἀθηναίων εἶναι τὴν
221 νίκην, Ἀθηναῖοι, Λακεδαιμόνιοι, Βοιωτοί. Λακεδαιμόνιοι μὲν γὰρ ἠγάπησαν ἀποχωρήσαντες, Ἀθηναῖοι δὲ προῆλθον κατὰ πόδας τῆς μάχης, Βοιωτοὶ
δὲ οὐκ ἀντέσχον, ἀλλ' ἡττηθέντες ἐν Οἰνοφύτοις
ὑπέκυψαν, καὶ μετ' αὐτῶν Φωκεῖς καὶ Λοκροὶ νίκῃ
μιᾷ. καὶ παρὰ μὲν τούτων ταύτην ἔλαβεν ⟨τὴν⟩²
δίκην ἡ πόλις ἀνθ' ὧν τῷ βαρβάρῳ συνέστησαν ἐν
τοῖς κοινοῖς τῆς Ἑλλάδος κινδύνοις.
222 Ἕτερον δ' ἔργον αὐτῆς ἄξιον εἰπεῖν καὶ σφόδρα
μέντοι καὶ τοῦτο βοῶν καὶ δηλοῦν ἔτι πόρρωθεν
257 D. ὅτων εἴη· γενομένου γὰρ τοῦ περὶ τὴν Λακωνικὴν
σεισμοῦ καὶ Λακεδαιμονίους τῶν περιοίκων περι-

---

¹ παρὰ secl. Reiske.   ² add. codd. dett.

ᵃ Cf. Thucydides I. 102 ; the Perioeci, " dwellers round

166

Gulf, and went to meet them along their own borders, and also were in Gerania in defence of Megara. Therefore the Lacedaemonians did not know what to do, but because of their position in Boeotia despaired at how they would be saved. So the city encompassed them. But finally they clashed at Tanagra in Boeotia ; and although the men of both sides were worthy of their daring, in this one respect the Lacedaemonians seemed to have had the advantage. How should I put it properly ? For I hesitate to say, because they were not destroyed. For it was the goal of the Athenians to block their passage and for the Lacedaemonians to get back home safely. And this action alone is in danger of having flight as a sign of victory, since apart from many earlier decisive points the following events immediately proved that the Athenians were in every way superior during the battle. For right on the spot there were three witnesses who attested that the victory belonged to the Athenians : the Athenians, the Lacedaemonians, and the Boeotians. For the Lacedaemonians were satisfied to have got away, but the Athenians advanced on the heels of the battle ; and the Boeotians did not withstand them, but yielded in defeat at Oenophyta, and with them the Phocians and Locrians in a single victory. And the city punished these for joining with the barbarian during the common dangers of Greece.

Another of its deeds should be mentioned, very much so, which shouts out and makes clear even from afar whose it was. When the earthquake had taken place in Laconia,[a] and the Perioeci surrounded the

220
457.

221
457.

222
464.

about," were Lacedaemonian communities which managed their own affairs, but had no political rights in Sparta.

(257 D.)

στάντων καὶ πάντων ὡς ἀληθῶς ὥσπερ ἐν σεισμῷ
ταραχθέντων τῶν ἐν Πελοποννήσῳ πραγμάτων, οὐκ
ἔφθησαν Λακεδαιμόνιοι καλέσαντες, καὶ παρῆν ὁ
δῆμος ἐν τοῖς ὅπλοις, τῇ μὲν ἀνδρείᾳ θαρρῶν, ὑπὲρ
δὲ ἐκείνων ὡς ὑπὲρ τῆς αὐτοῦ σωτηρίας περιδεής· ὃ
καὶ τοὺς παρόντας ἔλυσεν φόβους τῇ Λακεδαιμονίᾳ
καὶ δίκην λαβεῖν εἰσαῦθις παρεσκεύασεν αὐτῶν.

223 οὕτως ἄρα οὐδαμοῦ τὰς πράξεις οὐδὲ τὰ τολμήματα
τῆς πόλεως ἀσπάσασθαι μᾶλλον ἔστιν ἢ τὸ τῶν
ἔργων ἦθος, ἀκριβέστερον τροπαίου σημαῖνον τοὺς
εἰργασμένους.

224 Τὸν δ' ὑπὲρ Μιλησίων ἔκπλουν καὶ τὰς ἐν Σάμῳ
ναυμαχίας καὶ τὴν Εὐβοέων σωφρονισθεῖσαν ἀπό-
στασιν καὶ πολλὰ ἕτερα ἔξεστι δὴ[1] καὶ παραλιπεῖν.

225 Τέλος δὲ κρατήσασα πάντας εἰρήνην ποιεῖται, ἧς
ἄξιον μνησθῆναι. οὐ γὰρ τὸν αὐτὸν τρόπον ὅνπερ
πρὸς τοὺς βαρβάρους καὶ πρὸς τοὺς Ἕλληνας ἐ-
σπείσατο, ἀλλ' ἐνήλλαξεν. ἐκείνων μὲν γὰρ ἀφεῖλε
πᾶσαν τὴν κάτω χώραν καὶ τὴν ἐντὸς ὦν εἶπον
θάλατταν, τοῖς δὲ Ἕλλησιν ὦν ἐπὶ τοῦ πολέμου
κατέστη κυρία, ταῦτ' ἀπέδωκεν, Μέγαρα, Τροιζῆνα,
Πηγάς, πᾶν τὸ Ἀχαϊκόν. ᾧ καὶ δῆλον ὡς κρατοῦσα
τὴν εἰρήνην συνέθετο· οὐ γὰρ ἦν ὅ τι ἀνταπέλαβεν,
ἀλλὰ δυοῖν ἓν τὸ αὐτὸ σύμβολον ἐξήνεγκεν, καὶ τοῦ
περιεῖναι τῷ πολέμῳ καὶ τῆς ἐμφύτου χρηστότητος,

258 D. ἡγουμένη πρὸς μὲν τοὺς βαρβάρους δεῖν πολεμεῖν
ἄχρι παντὸς τοῦ δυνατοῦ, πρὸς δὲ τοὺς Ἕλληνας

226 ἁπλῶς μέχρι τοῦ κρείττονος. οὕτω μὲν τὸν πρὸς

---

[1] Iunt.: δὲ TQVA.

[a] Cf. Thucydides I. 114-117.   [b] § 208.

Lacedaemonians, and everything in the Peloponnesus was truly in turmoil as in an earthquake, the Athenian people was present under arms, confident in its courage and fearful for the Lacedaemonians as if for its own safety, before the Lacedaemonians even summoned its aid. This action put an end to the current fears of Lacedaemonia, and enabled the Lacedaemonians later to punish the Perioeci. Thus 223 in no case can we more approve the actions and the daring of the city than the character behind the deeds, which more clearly than a trophy reveals who performed them.

But the naval expedition in defence of the Mile- 224 sians, and the naval engagements at Samos and the 440. chastisement of the Euboeans' revolt, and many 447–446. other deeds can be omitted.[a]

Finally when it had conquered everyone, it made 225 a peace which should be mentioned. For it did not 446–445. make the same terms with the Greeks as it had with the barbarians, but completely changed them. For it deprived the latter of all their territory by the sea and the sea within the boundaries I mentioned.[b] But it gave back to the Greeks whatever it got control of during the war : Megara, Troezen, Pegae, all of Achaia [c] : which proves that it made peace from a position of strength. For there was nothing for it to take back in return. But it presented one piece of evidence as an equal proof of both its superiority in war and in native goodness, its belief that it must wage total war against the barbarians, but against the Greeks must fight simply to the point of attaining superiority. In this way having 226

[c] *Cf.* Thucydides I. 115 and IV. 21, who says nothing of Megara ; also in § 278 and or. iii. 120 (p. 199 Ddf.).

(258 D.)

τοὺς βαρβάρους ἀγῶνα, οὕτω δ' αὖ τὸν πρὸς τοὺς
Ἕλληνας διενεγκοῦσα, τοιαύτην[1] μὲν τὴν πρὸς
ἐκείνους, τοιαύτην δὲ καὶ τὴν πρὸς τούτους εἰρήνην
ἐποιήσατο, ἀμφοτέρων ὁμοῦ καὶ χωρὶς κρείττων
227 γενομένη. ἀλλὰ μὴν μόνη μὲν ἁπασῶν πόλεων ἰδίοις κινδύνοις κοινὴν ἅπαντι τῷ γένει τὴν ὠφέλειαν
ἐπορίσατο, μόνη δ' ἐκ τῶν κοινῶν εὐεργεσιῶν τὴν
ἡγεμονίαν ἐκτήσατο καὶ μετέθηκε τὸν θεσμόν· οὐ
γὰρ ἐξ ὧν κατεδουλώσατο τὰς πόλεις ἔσχε τὴν ἀρχήν, ἀλλ' ἐξ ὧν ἐποίησεν ἐλευθέρας· ὥστε συμβῆναι τοὺς αὐτοὺς χρόνους τοῖς μὲν Ἕλλησιν τὸ τῆς
ἐλευθερίας, τῇ δὲ πόλει τὸ τῆς ἀρχῆς κέρδος ἐν-
εγκεῖν· μόνοι γὰρ ἑκόντων ἦρξαν, καὶ μόνος οὗτος
δήμων ὥσπερ εἷς ἄρχων αἱρετὸς ἐξ ἁπάντων ἐνίκησεν, τοὺς μὲν βαρβάρους τοῖς ὅπλοις βιασάμενος,
τοὺς δ' ὁμοφύλους οὐ πείσας, ἀλλ' ὑπ' αὐτῶν
ἄρχειν πεισθείς, σύμβολον δικαιοσύνης ἔχων τὴν
ἀρχήν, οὐκ ἀδικίας. εἰ δὲ δεῖ διελόντα εἰπεῖν, μόνη
πόλεων τῶν μὲν βαρβάρων ἀκόντων, τῶν δὲ Ἑλλήνων δεηθέντων ἔσχεν τὴν ἀρχήν.

228 Οὕτω δὲ τούτων προκεχωρηκότων μέχρι μέν τινος ἦν ἡσυχία καὶ τῆς ὑπαρχούσης εὐδαιμονίας αἱ
πόλεις ἀπέλαυον,[2] τῆς δὲ κοινῆς τύχης ἀνθρώπων,
ἣ πάντα κινεῖ, μετέσχον ἄρα καὶ οἱ Ἕλληνες καὶ ἡ
πόλις· οἱ μὲν γὰρ οὐχ ὧν εὖ ἔπαθον χάριν ἔσχον διὰ
τέλους, ἀλλ' ἐφθόνησαν τῶν ἔργων ταῖς ὑπερβολαῖς,
ἡ δ' ὑπὲρ ὧν ἅπαντα ὑπέστη, τούτοις συνέρραξεν,
δυοῖν δείξασα ὡς ἄκουσα, τῷ τε κατ' ἀρχὰς ἔτι κι-
259 D. νουμένους κατασχεῖν καὶ δεῖσθαι λόγῳ κρίνεσθαι
περὶ τῶν διαφόρων καὶ τῷ πολεμεῖν ἀναγκασθεῖσα,

---

[1] τοσαύτην VA.
[2] codd. dett. : ἀπήλαυον TQVA.

concluded its contest against the barbarians, and in that way against the Greeks, it made terms of peace with the former and with the latter accordingly, being superior to both, together and separately. Indeed, alone of all cities at its personal risk it 227 brought help to the whole race. And alone because of its benefits to all, it acquired its leadership and 478. changed the law of nature. For it did not hold its empire from its enslavement of the cities, but from its liberation of them, so that it befell that the same period brought the Greeks the advantage of freedom and the city that of empire. For they alone ruled willing subjects, and this people alone, as if it were the sole elected ruler, won its office on every count : it crushed the barbarians by force of arms, yet it did not need to persuade its fellow Greeks but ruled at their persuasion, with its empire as a proof of its justice, not injustice. But if the distinction must be made, alone of cities it held its empire to the despite of the barbarians and at the wishes of the Greeks.

When these affairs had been successfully settled, 228 for some time there was peace and the cities enjoyed their good fortune, but then the Greeks and the city shared in the common fate of mankind, which disrupts everything. For the Greeks were not always grateful for their benefits, but they were jealous of these extraordinary actions ; and the city came into conflict with those on whose behalf it had endured everything, proving in two ways that it did so unwillingly : by still restraining their unrest at the start and desiring that their differences be decided by reason ; and by its seeking no advantage, when, having been compelled to wage war, it was

(259 D.)

ὅτε ἐνίκησε, μηδὲν πλέον ζητῆσαι, ἀλλ᾽ ἀφεῖναι
τοὺς ἐρίσαντας αὐτῇ περὶ τῆς ἡγεμονίας καὶ μηδὲν
ἀηδέστερον ἐξαγαγεῖν ἐκ τοῦ δεσμωτηρίου ἢ κρατή-
229 σασαν τὸ ἐξ ἀρχῆς ἐμβαλεῖν. τουτοισὶ δὲ ἤδη τί
τις ἂν χρήσαιτο; αἰσχύνομαι μὲν γὰρ καὶ τὰς ἐν
Ναυπάκτῳ ναυμαχίας παραλείπων,[1] ἃς οὔτε παρὰ
μικρὸν ἐνίκων οὔτε ὀλίγῳ πλείονας, ἀλλ᾽ ὡς ἐφ᾽
ἕρμαιον πλεύσαντες,[2] καὶ νίκας ἑτέρας ἐπὶ Θρᾴκης
καὶ ὡς Κέρκυραν ἐξείλοντο καὶ τὰ κατ᾽ Ἀμπρακίαν
ἔργα μέγιστα τῶν κατ᾽ ἐκεῖνον τὸν χρόνον Ἑλληνικῶν, καὶ ταῦτα ἀρετῇ πραχθέντα, οὐ χρείᾳ, καὶ
τὰ κατ᾽ αὐτὴν δὴ τὴν Πύλον, ναυμαχίας τε ἀπὸ
260 D. γῆς καὶ μάχας πεζὰς ὕστερον ἐν τῇ νήσῳ γενομένας, καὶ πρὶν ταῦτ᾽ ἐξήκειν, ἑτέρους Λακεδαιμονίους
ἐκ Κυθήρων ἀγομένους καὶ τρόπαια Κορινθίων καὶ
230 πολλὰ ἕτερα ἐφάμιλλα καὶ εἰπεῖν καὶ θαυμάσαι. ὁ
δὲ καιρὸς οὐ φέρει, ἀλλὰ μείζονος εὐτυχίας εἶναί μοι
δοκεῖ κατασχεῖν αὐτόν. ἔτι δέ, ὥσπερ εἴπομεν, οὐ
συγγραφῆς ἔργον ψιλῆς προειλόμεθα ἀφηγεῖσθαι τὰ
πεπραγμένα τῇ πόλει, καὶ γὰρ ἂν εἰς τὴν ἐπιοῦσαν
πεντετηρίδα ἐκτείνοιτο ὁ λόγος, ἀλλὰ τῶν μὲν κατὰ
τοὺς πολέμους πράξεων τὰς γνωριμωτάτας εἰπεῖν,
τῶν δ᾽ ὑπαρχόντων ἀγαθῶν τῇ πόλει καθ᾽ ὅσον
δυνατὸν μηδὲν παραλιπεῖν. ταῦτα δ᾽ ἐστὶν οὐκ ἂν
διὰ πάντων ἕκαστα λέγωμεν, ἀλλ᾽ ἂν μηδὲν εἶδος
εὐφημίας παραλείπωμεν.
231 Ὡς δὲ ἐδόκει τῷ δαίμονι μήπω ταῦτα ἀποχρῆν τῇ

---

[1] Aldinae : παραλιπὼν TQVA.
[2] codd. dett. : πλεύσαντας TQVA.

---

[a] The prisoners from Cleon's victory at Sphacteria, *cf.*
Thucydides IV. 3-23.

[b] Naupactus, Thucydides II. 83-92 ; Thrace, I. 61-65,

victorious, but by freeing those who struggled with it
for the leadership of the Greeks and releasing them 421.
from prison with no less pleasure than with which it 425.
had initially confined them after their defeat.[a] How 229
should the following deeds be treated ? For I am
ashamed to omit the naval engagements at Naupac- 429.
tus,[b] which they won by no small degree and in no
little number, but as if in their sailing they had
come upon a pot of gold ; and the other victories in
Thrace and how they liberated Corcyra, and their 436. 433
actions in Ambracia, the greatest Greek achievement 430-429.
of that time, and accomplished by virtue, not necessity ; and those at Pylus itself, and the naval engagements on land and the infantry battles which later 425.
took place on the island ; and before this was done,
the other Lacedaemonians brought as prisoners from 424.
Cythera ; and the victories over the Corinthians, 433 and
and many other things which vie for praise and earlier.
admiration. Yet time does not allow, but it seems to 230
me too much to hope for to prevent it from passing.
Further, as we have said,[c] we did not choose the task
of writing a jejune history, of narrating the deeds of
the city, for even that speech would extend into the
following penteterid.[d] But we chose to mention its
most famous actions in war, and as far as possible to
omit none of the city's good qualities. This cannot
be, if we discuss each point fully, but only if we omit
no category of praise.

When the evil spirit decided that not even these 231

II. 70 ; Corcyra, I. 48-55 ; Ambracia, III. 105-114 ; Pylus,
IV. 3-23 (the island is Sphacteria) ; Cythera, IV. 53-54 ;
Corinthians, IV. 42-45.

   [c] § 90.
   [d] To the next Panathenaic festival, *cf.* note to § 186.

(260 D.)

Ἑλλάδι, ἀλλ' ἔτι καὶ κατὰ γῆν καὶ κατὰ θάλατταν
κλυσθῆναι τὰς πόλεις, καὶ τοὺς μὲν ἐκ τῆς ὑπερορίας ἐπελθεῖν πολεμίους, τοὺς δ' εἰς τὴν ὑπερορίαν

261 D. ἐκπλεῦσαι κατὰ συμφοράς, τίς Ἑλλήνων ἢ τίς βαρβάρων ἐστὶν ὅστις τὸ ἐξ ἴσου τοῖς ἀπὸ τῆσδε τῆς

232 πόλεως ἑτέρους ἂν ἔχοι λέγειν; οἷς ἐπῄει μὲν πλεῖν
ὑπὲρ τῆς Λεοντίνων ἐλευθερίας, ἐδόκει δὲ κινδυνεύειν ὑπὲρ τῆς Ἐγεσταίων,[1] διενοοῦντο δὲ διαβαίνειν
ἐπὶ Καρχηδονίους ἀνθ' ὧν ἐκεῖνοι πρότερον[2] ἐπὶ τοὺς
Ἕλληνας τοὺς ἐν Σικελίᾳ, τριήρεις δὲ ἐπλήρουν καὶ
ὁλκάδας, ὥσπερ ἀπὸ πάσης τῆς Ἑλλάδος ἐκπέμ-

233 ποντες. καὶ τὰς μὲν[3] πεζομαχίας καὶ ἱππομαχίας
ἧττον ἴσως ἄξιον ἐκπλαγῆναι διὰ τὴν ἀεὶ τοῦ νικᾶν
συνήθειαν καὶ τὸ δεδόσθαι τῇ πόλει καθάπερ γέρας
τὴν τῶν κρειττόνων μοῖραν ἐν τοῖς πλείστοις· τὸ δὲ
μηδ' ὡς ἀντέπεσεν τὰ πράγματα μηδὲν μᾶλλον ἀπο-

262 D. στῆναι, ἀλλ' ἀπόντων μὲν ὁπλιτῶν, ἀπόντων δὲ
ἱππέων, οἷς οὔτε πλῆθος οὔτε ἀρετὴν ἴσους εὑρεῖν
ἦν· ἔτι δὲ νεῶν τοσούτων καὶ βελῶν καὶ σκευῶν καὶ
τεχνῶν καὶ συμμάχων καὶ πάσης ὡς ἔπος εἰπεῖν
τῆς κατασκευῆς μεθεστηκυίας, ὥσπερ ἄρτι τῆς
πάσης Σικελίας οἰκιζομένης, κεκενωμένης μὲν τῆς
ἀκροπόλεως ταλάντων ὀλίγου δεῖν μυρίων, Λακεδαιμονίων δὲ καὶ Βοιωτῶν καὶ τῶν ἄλλων οὐκέτ'
ἐκ Πελοποννήσου τὰς εἰσβολὰς ποιουμένων, ἀλλ' ἐκ
μέσης τῆς Ἀττικῆς, ἐκ Δεκελείας, μεθεστηκότων

---

[1] Ddf. : Αἰγεσταίων TQVA.
[2] πρότερον ἐπετέθησαν TQ.
[3] μὲν ⟨ναυμαχίας νικᾶν καὶ⟩ ci. Oliver.

---

[a] Cf. Plato, Menexenus 243 A ; Thucydides VI. 6-19.
[b] The final defeat before Syracuse.

things were enough for Greece, but that the cities
should be further overwhelmed on land and sea,
and that some people should come from abroad as
enemies, and that others sail abroad to their own
destruction, what Greek or what barbarian could
speak of the others in the same terms as those from
this city ? It occurred to them to embark an expedi- 232
tion in defence of the freedom of Leontini,[a] they 433.
decided to risk danger in defence of the freedom of 458, 416.
the Egestaeans, they planned to cross over from
Sicily against the Carthaginians in return for their
former crossing against the Greeks in Sicily, and they 481–480.
manned triremes and merchant vessels as if they were
sending them from the whole of Greece. And 233
perhaps we should be less astonished at the infantry
and cavalry battles because they were always
accustomed to win and the fate of being victorious
in most things had been given to the city like a
prize. But with what kind of human spirit can the
following conduct be compared, what good fortune
is not less admirable ? When circumstances were
reversed,[b] it still did not desist, but in the absence of 413.
its hoplites, in the absence of its cavalry, who were
incomparable in number and courage, and further
after the transfer of so many ships, weapons, material,
crafts, allies, and every means of preparation, one 415.
might say, as if now all of Sicily were being settled, 407–406.
and after the Acropolis was stripped of nearly ten
thousand talents and the Lacedaemonians, Boeotians,
and the others no longer made their incursions from 431–425.
the Peloponnesus, but from the middle of Attica,
from Decelea,[c] and no fewer slaves defected than 413.

---

[c] In northernmost Attica and fortified permanently for the
war against Athens.

175

(262 D.)

δὲ καὶ τῶν οἰκετῶν οὐκ ἔλαττον ἢ πλήρωμα ἔθνους
εἶναι δοκεῖν, ἀδείας δ᾽ ὑπαρχούσης αὐτομολεῖν τοῖς
βουλομένοις, τοσούτου δὲ ὄντος πολέμου περὶ τὴν
πόλιν, τοσαύτην περιουσίαν καρτερίας ἅμα καὶ
ῥώμης καὶ φιλοτιμίας ἐπιδείξασθαι ὥσθ᾽ ἕτερον
στόλον πέμπειν ἀντίρροπον τῷ προτέρῳ καὶ στρα-
τηγοὺς ἐφαμίλλους, καὶ Λακεδαιμονίους ἀξιοῦν ἐκεῖ
πολιορκεῖν μετὰ τῆς συμμαχίας, ποίᾳ ταῦτ᾽ ἔνεστι
ψυχῇ παραβαλεῖν ἀνθρωπίνῃ, καὶ τίνος οὐκ εὐτυχίας
μᾶλλον θαυμάσαι;

234 Γενομένου δὲ τοῦ μεγάλου πάθους—οὐ γὰρ οὖν
σιωπήσομαι, ἀλλὰ καὶ τοῦτο ἔτι μείζω μοι δοκεῖ δεικνύναι τὴν πόλιν—οὕτω γὰρ τοῖς ὑπολοίποις προσ-
ηνέχθη πράγμασιν ὥσπερ ἂν εἰ πᾶσαν εἰλήφει τὴν
Σικελίαν. οὐ γὰρ ἐστερημένη δυνάμεως ἐῴκει, ἀλλ᾽
ἄρτι προσκεκτημένη. καὶ τὴν μὲν τῶν τρόπων εὐ-
263 D. κολίαν καὶ σωφροσύνην καὶ τάξιν διαίτης, ἣν ὑπὲρ
τοῦ μηδὲν αἰσχρὸν συγχωρῆσαι προείλοντο, οὐδ᾽ ἂν
235 εἷς ἀξίως εἴποι. περιστάντων δὲ αὐτοὺς τῶν Ἑλλήνων ἁπάντων, καὶ τῶν μὲν ὑπαρχόντων πολεμίων
τότε πρῶτον λαβόντων ἐλπίδας καὶ παροξυνθέντων
ὑπὸ τῆς τύχης, ἐπελθόντων δὲ τῶν ἐκ Σικελίας,
μεταστάσης δὲ τῆς συμμαχίας ὀλίγου δεῖν ἁπάσης,
καὶ νήσων καὶ ἠπείρου καὶ πάντων ὡς εἰπεῖν πολεμίων καταστάντων καὶ πανταχόθεν κεκυκλωμένων,[1]
ἔτι δ᾽ ἀγνωμοσύνης ἀπροσδοκήτου συμβάσης ὥστε
καὶ βασιλέα κληθῆναι κατὰ τῆς πόλεως ὑπὸ τῶν ἀπ᾽
ἐκείνου σωθέντων ταῖς ἀπὸ τῆς πόλεως πράξεσιν,
προσγενομένου δὲ κἀκείνου μάλα ἀσμένως, καὶ
συμπολεμοῦντος καὶ σώμασιν καὶ ναυσὶ καὶ χρυσῷ

---

[1] κεκυκλωμένοι VA.

seemed to be the population of a whole nation, and those who wished were free to desert, and so great a war surrounded the city, then it displayed at the same time so much self-control, strength, and pride that it sent out a second expedition [a] equal to the 413. former one and rivalling generals, and decided to besiege the Lacedaemonians and their allies over there.

But when that great misfortune took place— 234 for I shall not keep silent, but even this, I think, 413. proves the city to be greater still—it behaved in its future conduct as if it had taken all of Sicily. For it was not like a city deprived of its power, but one which now had acquired more. And the calmness of their behaviour, their moderation, and the disciplined life which they chose so as not to make any shameful concessions could not be convincingly described. When all the Greeks surrounded them, 235 and those already their enemies then first took hope and were spurred on by their good luck, and when those in Sicily joined the attack, and nearly all their 412. allies changed sides, and the islands, mainland, and everything, one might say, became their enemy and encircled them, and further when an unexpected piece of folly occurred, so that even the king was 412. called in to fight against the city by those who were saved from him by the actions of the city, and when he very gladly joined them and waged war with men,

---

[a] [Led by Demosthenes (not the orator) and Eurymedon, who were colleagues not rivals (ἐφαμίλλους, "matching"?), though Nicias the commander-in-chief at Syracuse did (disastrously) oppose Demosthenes' advice that the Athenians should leave Syracuse. In § 387 ἐφαμίλλους ἐν σφίσιν αὐτοῖς certainly means "equal among themselves." So perhaps here also.—E.H.W.]

(263 D.)

καὶ τίνα γῆς ἢ θαλάττης τόπον οὐ παρέχοντος
ἀφορμὴν τῷ πολέμῳ; ἦν μὲν οὐδεὶς ὅστις οὐκ ἂν
ἤλπισεν, ἔξωθεν οὑτωσὶ σκοπῶν, ἀναρπασθήσεσθαι
νῦν ἤδη τὴν πόλιν, οὕτω κοινῷ πολέμῳ βαρβάρων τε
καὶ Ἑλλήνων συνεχομένην· οἱ δ' οὕτω μετέστησαν
τὰ πράγματα ὥσπερ ἁπάντων τούτων ὑπὲρ αὐτῶν,
ἀλλ' οὐ κατ' αὐτῶν γιγνομένων, ἢ στρατηγούντων
σφίσι τῶν πολεμίων.

236
264 D.
Τὸ δὲ πάντων μέγιστον ὅτι καὶ τῆς πολιτείας
κινηθείσης καί τινων ἀλλοτριωθέντων σφίσι τῶν
οἴκοι, τόπον οὐδένα ἔχοντες οὗ χρὴ στῆναι πλὴν
Σάμου, καθάπερ ἐν τῷ Μηδικῷ κινδύνῳ τῆς Σαλαμῖνος, ἀλλ' ἕτερον δή τινα καὶ οὗτοι τρόπον εἰς
ταὐτὸν ἐλθόντες τοῖς τότε, καὶ τὴν πόλιν ἐκλιπόντες
μέρει τῷ πλείστῳ, κατεστήσαντο μὲν τὰ οἴκοι,
ἐκράτησαν δὲ τοὺς ἔξω, διέλαβον δὲ τροπαίοις τὸν
Ἑλλήσποντον, ἄλλους ἄλλοσε καταδιώκοντες, ὥσπερ μελέτας μᾶλλον ἐν σφίσιν αὐτοῖς ἢ ναυμαχίας
πρὸς τοὺς ἐντυγχάνοντας ἀεὶ ποιούμενοι. [εἴρηταί
τε καὶ ἐνεθυμήθην ὡς ἑτέρῳ προείρηται.][1]

237
265 D.
Τέλος δ' ἐπὶ Κυζίκῳ συμπεσόντες ὁμοῦ Λακεδαιμονίοις καὶ τοῖς ἀπὸ τῆς Ἑλλάδος καὶ τοῖς ἀπὸ
τῆς Ἀσίας βαρβάροις καὶ Φαρναβάζῳ λαμβάνουσι
τὰς ναῦς παρὰ τοσοῦτον οὐ πάσας παρ' ὅσας δι-
έφθειραν· καὶ Φαρναβάζου κακῶς τὸ συμβὰν ἰωμέ-

---

[1] secl. Behr.

---

[a] The oligarchic revolution of the Four hundred.
[b] Particularly at Cynossema in 411 B.C.
[c] This phrase, which I have hesitantly bracketed, may
have been a marginal note by Aristides himself. The
reference seems to be to Thucydides I. 18. 5, not to Plato, as

ships, and gold, and spared no part of the earth or
sea as a means for war, anyone, viewing the matter
superficially, would have expected that the city
would now be annihilated, since it was involved in a
common war with the barbarians and the Greeks.
But they reversed the situation, as if all these things
were in their favour, and not against them, or as if
the enemy commanded its army to suit them.

But finest of all is that even when the constitution 236
was overthrown and some of those at home were 411.
estranged from them,[a] and when they had no place
where they might stay except Samos, like Salamis
in the time of danger from the Medes, but when these
men were in the same situation as those of that time
in a somewhat different way, having abandoned the
city in company with the majority of the citizens,
then they settled affairs at home, defeated those 411-410.
abroad, and split the Hellespont with their victories,[b]
pursuing their enemies in different directions, as if
they were only practising by themselves, rather than
fighting naval engagements against whomever they
encountered. [The remark has been already made
and I realized that it has been formerly said for
another purpose].[c]

Finally at Cyzicus,[d] having come upon the Lace- 237
daemonians, and those from Greece, and the bar- 410.
barians from Asia, and Pharnabazus, they captured
almost all their ships other than those which they
destroyed. And when Pharnabazus badly tried to

the scholiast thought; though *cf. Politicus* 286 **A** : there is a
similar idea in xvii. 4.
[a] *Cf.* Xenophon, *Hellenica* I. 6. 1-27 ; Diodorus XIII.
49-53. Pharnabazus was Persian satrap of Hellespontine
Phrygia ; he supported the Lacedaemonians against Athens.

(265 D.)

νου καὶ τὴν ἵππον ἐπεισάγοντος ⟨οἱ μὲν⟩[1] ἐκ ποδὸς
ἱππομαχήσαντες, οἱ δ' ἀπὸ τῶν νεῶν πάντα ὁμοῦ
χειροῦνται, ναυτικόν, ἱππικόν, τοξότας τοὺς ἀπὸ
Σικελίας, τοὺς ἐκ Πελοποννήσου, τὴν βασιλέως
χορηγίαν, τὰς Λακεδαιμονίων ἐλπίδας, καὶ κενὸς
ἤδη τοῖς ἐναντίοις ὁ πόλεμος ἦν καὶ πάντα φροῦδα
ὥσπερ ἐκ ναυαγίας τινὸς ⟨ὡς⟩[2] ἀληθῶς. ὥσθ' ἡ
μὲν τοσοῦτον ὑπερβληθεῖσα ὑπὸ τῆς στάσεως[3] πόλις
οὐδ' ὄνομα εἰρήνης ἐπ' ἐκείνων τῶν χρόνων ἐνενόη-
σεν, οἱ δ' ἀπὸ τοσούτων καὶ τηλικούτων πλεονεκτη-
μάτων ὁρμώμενοι πληγέντες κατέφυγον εὐθὺς ἐπὶ
τὴν εἰρήνην.

238 Ἀεὶ μὲν οὖν ἔγωγ' ἐμεμψάμην τοῖς ἐπιτιμῶσι τῇ
τῶν Λακεδαιμονίων πόλει καὶ τοῦθ' ὑπὲρ τῆς ὑμετέρας ἀξιοῦσιν ποιεῖν· ἐκείνοις μὲν γὰρ ἀπεχθά-
νονται, ὑμᾶς δ' οὐ κοσμοῦσιν, ὡς οἴονται. ἀλλ'
266 D. εἴ γέ τι δεῖ καὶ παράδοξον εἰπεῖν, τοὐναντίον μοι δοκοῦσι δρᾶν ἢ βούλονται· μᾶλλον γὰρ ἐκείνους αἴρου-
σιν ἢ τὴν πόλιν ἐγκωμιάζουσιν καὶ πλείω χάριν ἂν
παρ' ἐκείνων αὐτοῖς οἶμαι τῆς βλασφημίας ἢ τῶν
εὐφημιῶν εἶναι παρ' ὑμῶν. οἱ μὲν γὰρ οὐχ ὅτι δεύ-
τεροι τῆς πόλεως ἀκούουσι, τοῦτο ζημιοῦνται, ἀλλ'
ὅτι πρὸς τὴν πόλιν κρίνονται, τοῦτο κερδαίνουσιν·
ὑμᾶς δ' οὐχ ὅτι κρείττους ἀποφαίνουσι σεμνύνου-
σιν, ἀλλ' αὐτῷ τῷ παρεξετάζειν ἐοίκασιν οὐ γι-
γνώσκειν· ὥστ' οὐδὲν ἀπεικὸς ὑμᾶς ἀηδέστερον ἢ
Λακεδαιμονίους ἔχειν, ὁπόταν ταῦτα ἀγωνίζωνται.

239 οὐ μὴν ἀλλ' ἐπειδήπερ ἐν τούτῳ τῷ μέρει τοῦ λόγου
γεγένημαι, ἐν ᾧ τὰ πρὸς ἄλληλά ἐστι ταῖς πόλεσιν,

---

[1] add. codd. dett.   [2] add. Reiske.
[3] Aldinae : συστάσεως TQVA.

remedy what had happened and introduced his cavalry, with some of them fighting the cavalry on foot, and others on board ship, they conquered all, naval force, cavalry, archers from Sicily, those from the Peloponnesus, the war-equipment furnished by the king, and the expectations of the Lacedaemonians. And now the war was purposeless for the enemy, and everything was gone as if truly in some shipwreck. When the city was overwhelmed by faction, in those days it did not even think of the word peace ; but when they, who began with great and huge advantages, were struck down, they immediately took 425–421. refuge in peace.

I have always been critical of those who find fault 238 with the city of the Lacedaemonians [a] and who think that they should do this on behalf of your city. For they are hateful to the former, but they do not honour you, as they think. But if I must make a paradoxical remark, they seem to me to do the opposite of what they wish. For they exalt the Lacedaemonians rather than praise the city ; and I think that they would have more thanks from them for the defamation than from you for the praise. For the Lacedaemonians are not injured because they are called second to the city, but it is to their advantage that they are compared with the city. Yet they do not praise you because they show that you are superior, but by the very act of comparison they seem not to understand you, so that it is not unlikely that you are less pleased than the Lacedaemonians whenever they debate these points. However, since I have reached the part of my speech which involves the relationship between these ci- 239

---

[a] Cf. Isocrates, *Panathenaicus* 41 ff.

(266 D.)

ἀνάγκη καὶ τοῦτο ἴσως ὑπομεῖναι, ἵνα μὴ μόνον ἐν
τοῖς ἀγῶσιν ὅσῳ κρείττων ἡ πόλις ἀποφαίνωμεν,
240 ἀλλὰ καὶ τοῖς ὅλοις. φανήσονται γὰρ Λακεδαιμόνιοι
μὲν τριακοσίων ἀνδρῶν στερηθέντες οὐκ ἐνεγκόντες,
ἀλλ' εὐθὺς ἐγκλίναντες· ὃ μείζω φιλοτιμίαν ἔχει τῇ
πόλει τοῦ νικῆσαι τῇ μάχῃ· ἐν ἐκείνῃ μὲν γὰρ τῶν
ἀντιστάντων κρείττων ἐγένετο, ἐν οἷς δ' ἀπηγό-
267 D. ρευσαν οἱ λοιποὶ σχεδὸν πάντων, ὥσπερ ἐν ἄθλοις,
ὅταν πᾶς τις εἴκῃ. αὕτη δὲ τοσαύτῃ χρησαμένη
συμφορᾷ μετὰ ταῦτ' ἐν Σικελίᾳ οὐ μόνον οὐ κατα-
πτήξασα οὐδ' ἐπὶ τὴν εἰρήνην ἀσμένως καταφυγοῦσα,
ἀλλ' οὕτω διαθεῖσα τοὺς πολεμίους ὥστ' ἀσμένους
ἂν ἐκείνους ἰδεῖν, εἴ τις εἰρήνην ἄγειν δυνηθείη πεῖσαι
241 τὴν πόλιν. καὶ μὴν οἱ μὲν ὡς ἤκουσαν τὴν Κόνωνος
ἐν Μυτιλήνῃ πολιορκίαν, οὐκ ἐξεπλάγησαν, ἀλλὰ
πλεύσαντες ἐπ' Ἀργινούσαις ὅσαις οὐδ' ἂν εἷς εἰκά-
σειεν ναυσίν, ἐλάττοσιν δὲ ὅμως ἔτι τῶν ἀντιπάλων,
ἀντετάξαντο παντὶ τῷ ναυτικῷ τῶν πολεμίων, ὥσπερ
ἄλλου μέν τινος ἀεὶ παρέχοντος σφίσι τὰς τριήρεις,
ἐν δὲ τῷ Καρὶ καὶ οὐκ ἐν τοῖς αὑτῶν σώμασιν τὰς
242 πείρας ποιούμενοι· καὶ οὔτε πλήθους τῶν ἀντιτεταγ-
μένων ἐφρόντισαν οὔτε τῆς Καλλικρατίδου δόξης,
οὔτε νήσων ἐχομένων οὔτε ἡλλοτριωμένης ὡς εἰπεῖν
ἤδη τῆς τύχης· οὐ χειμῶνος ἡττήθησαν, οὐχ ὅσον
τοῦ πολέμου τὸ λοιπὸν ἐνεθυμήθησαν, ἀλλ' ὥσπερ
ἐξαρκοῦν εἰς τὴν θάλατταν ἰδεῖν, τρέπονται μὲν

---

^a Cf. § 238.
^b In fact on Sphacteria the Athenians captured 292 men,
of whom about 120 were full Spartan citizens. Thucydides
IV. 38. ^c Cf. Xenophon, *Hellenica* I. 6. 24-34.
^d An expression which refers to the cheapness of Carian
slaves, somewhat like our " cannon-fodder."
^e Lacedaemonian admiral, defeated and killed by the
Athenians at the Arginusae islands in 406 B.C.

ties, perhaps we ourselves must undergo the same objection,[a] so that we may not only show how superior the city is in times of struggle, but also at all times. For the Lacedaemonians will clearly 240 appear not to have endured the loss of three hundred 425. men,[b] but to have yielded immediately, which circumstance confers greater distinction upon the city than victory in battle. For in that battle it was superior to its opponents, but where all the rest despair, it was superior to nearly everyone, just as in the games, when all give way to the champion. Now this city, although it had experienced such great 413. misfortunes afterwards in Sicily, will clearly appear not only not to have cowered, or gratefully to have taken refuge in peace, but so to have treated its enemies that they would have been glad to discover if anyone could have persuaded the city to make peace. Indeed, when the Athenians heard that 241 Conon was besieged in Mytilene,[c] they were not 406. frightened, but sailed to Arginusae with so many ships that one could not even guess at their number, though still fewer than their opponents, and they arrayed themselves against the whole fleet of the enemy, as if someone else were always providing them with triremes, and they were running risks " with Carian " and not their own bodies.[d] And they 242 were concerned neither about the number of their antagonists nor about the reputation of Callicratidas,[e] 407–406. nor about the islands held by the enemy nor about their luck which had now, one might say, changed against them. They were not overcome by the storm, they did not even consider the future length of the war. But as if it were enough to look to the sea, they routed the Lacedaemonians, and defeated 406.

(267 D.)

Λακεδαιμονίους, κρατοῦσι δὲ σύμπαντας Πελοποννησίους, τριήρεις δὲ τὰς μὲν αἱροῦσιν, τὰς δὲ κατα-
δύουσιν ὁμοῦ τῷ σκηπτῷ καὶ τοῖς πολεμίοις
μαχόμενοι. τοσοῦτον ἐποίησαν τῆς πολιορκίας τὸ
243
διάφορον. τὸ δὲ πάντων μέγιστον, ὅτι ἄνδρα ῥύονται
268 D.
ὃς μόνος ἤρκεσεν τὴν Λακεδαιμονίων ὕστερον δυ-
ναστείαν καταλῦσαι. οἱ δ᾽ ὥσπερ ἅπαντες κατα-
ναυμαχηθέντες εἰρήνης αὖθις ἐδέοντο, οὕτως οὐ
μόνον τοὺς ἐν τοῖς ἀγῶσιν παρόντας εἴθιστο τότε
νικᾶν ἡ πόλις, ἀλλὰ καὶ τοὺς ἄλλους ἐξέπληττεν
καὶ διὰ πάντων ἐνίκα.

244 Ἀλλὰ μὴν φανήσεται νίκας τε μεγίστας τῶν
πώποτε ἀνῃρημένη καὶ συμφορὰς οὕτως ἐνεγκοῦσα
ὡς μᾶλλον ἄν τινα τῆς πόλεως ἄγασθαι τὴν ἐν τοῖς
δεινοῖς εὐψυχίαν ἢ τὰ ἔργα τῶν κεκρατηκότων,
ὥστ᾽ ἔμοιγ᾽ ἐπέρχεται καὶ τοῦτ᾽ εἰπεῖν, ὅτι νικῶσα
ταῖς εὐπραξίαις οὐχ ἧττον ἐν οἷς ἠτύχησεν διενήνοχεν, εἴπερ μηδεὶς ὁμοίως ἐνήνοχε ⟨τὰς⟩[1] συμφο-
245 ράς. τοῦ μὲν οὖν οἷς κατώρθωσεν νικᾶν ἄνευ τῶν
πρὸς αὐτοὺς πεπραγμένων τοὺς ἀντιπολιτευσαμένους
ἄλυτα ὑπάρχει διττὰ σημεῖα· ἅ τε γὰρ καθ᾽ αὑτὴν
ἔπραξεν τῶν ἰδίᾳ τισὶ πραχθέντων ὑπεραίρει οὐχ
ὅσον ἀγνοῆσαι, ἅ τ᾽ ἐν ταὐτῷ γενομένων ὁμοῦ
246 πάντες ἐλάττους ἀντιθεῖναι. καὶ μὴν ἔν γε τοῖς
δυσκόλοις κρείττων γέγονε τῶν νενικηκότων· οἱ
μὲν γὰρ εἴκοντες, ἡ δ᾽ ἀντέχουσα δέδεικται τῇ τύ-
247 χῃ. οὐκοῦν ἀμφοτέρας τὰς νίκας οὐ παρὰ μικρὸν
φέρεται καὶ νικᾷ τὰς πόλεις ὁμοίως οἷς τε κατ-
248 ώρθωσεν καὶ ἐν οἷς ἀπέτυχεν. καὶ μὴν αὐτὴ[2] μὲν

184

all the Peloponnesians, and took some of the triremes, and sank others, fighting against the thunder-bolts and with the enemy. They effected an outcome far 407-406. different from the Lacedaemonians' siege. Most 243 important of all was that they saved a man [a] who later 394. alone sufficed to destroy the empire of the Lacedaemonians. The enemy, as if they had all been defeated at sea, again sued for peace. In those days the city not only customarily defeated its actual opponents, but also frightened the others into submission and won a total victory.

Indeed, it will clearly appear to have won the 244 greatest victories which ever were and to have borne its misfortunes in such a way that one would more admire the courage of the city in adversity than the acts of its conquerors. Therefore it occurs to me to say also that although it was victorious in success, it was not less triumphant in misfortune, if no one endured their reverses in like manner. There are two irrefutable proofs that in its success it 245 was superior to those who opposed its policy, apart from its actions against them. For its independent actions were unmistakably superior to those of anyone else ; and as to joint ventures, all are inferior in comparison. Indeed, in its difficulties, it was 246 superior to its victors. For they have been shown to have yielded to fortune, but the city to have held out against it. Then it wins on each count by no 247 small margin and is superior to the other cities both in success and in misfortune. At the same time, 248

---

[a] Conon, who at the Battle of Cnidus in 394 B.C. destroyed the Lacedaemonian maritime power.

---

[1] add. codd. dett.   [2] Reiske : αὕτη TQVA.

(268 D.)

έθνῶν ἅμα καὶ πόλεων κεκράτηκεν, αὐτῆς δ᾽ οὐδεὶς
269 D. ὅστις οὐ μετὰ πολλῶν συμμάχων. ἔτι δ᾽ αὐτὴ[1] μὲν
πρὸς ἅπαντας ὁμοῦ πολεμεῖν ἠνάγκαστο τοὺς ἐπιόντας, ἢ κινοῦντας, τῶν δ᾽ ἐναντίων οἱ πλεῖστοι πρὸς
μέρος αὐτῆς ἀντήρκασιν, ἀθρόας δὲ τῆς δυνάμεως
ἢ τὶς ἢ οὐδεὶς ἐπειράθη. ὥσθ᾽ ἡ τῶν Ἀθηναίων
πόλις νενίκηκεν μὲν πολλὰ δὴ πολλάκις, αὐτὴ δ᾽
249 ἴσα καὶ ἀήττητος ἐστίν. τὸ δὲ πάντων μέγιστον ὅτι
αὐτῆς μὲν οὐδεὶς ἐκράτησεν—οὐδεὶς γὰρ αὐτῆς τὴν
γνώμην παρεστήσατο, ἀλλὰ στρατιᾶς γέγονεν πάντα τὰ τοιαῦτα ἀτυχήματα—αὐτὴ[2] δὲ τὰς γνώμας
τῶν ἐναντίων ἅμα τοῖς ἔργοις δεδούλωται, Ξέρξη[3]
μὲν φεύγειν ἀπὸ τῶν πραγμάτων ποιήσασα ἐν εὐχῆς μέρει, Λακεδαιμονίους δὲ ἀνακλίνασα οὐχ ἧττον
τοὺς ἀκούοντας ἢ τοὺς ἐν ταῖς μάχαις παρόντας καὶ
250 πταίσαντας αὐτῶν. γνοίη δ᾽ ἄν τις ὡς οὐκ ἴσον
οὐδ᾽ ὅμοιον τὸ τῶν πόλεων τούτων οὔτε τῷ μεγέθει
τῶν ἔργων οὔτε τοῖς τολμήμασιν οὔθ᾽ ὅλως οὐδενὶ
τῶν ὑπαρχόντων. Λακεδαιμόνιοι μὲν γὰρ ἐν
270. Λεύκτροις ἀτυχήσαντες οὐκ ἀνήνεγκαν, ἀλλ᾽ ὥσπερ
ἀνδρὸς τελευτὴ κἀκείνοις συνέβη.[a] εἰρήνην μὲν γὰρ
ἀπηξίωσαν ποιήσασθαι πρὸς Θηβαίους, μόνῃ τῇ
τῶν Ἀθηναίων πόλει νομίζοντες εἴκειν εὐπρεπῆ
συμφορὰν εἶναι, ἀναμιχθέντες δὲ τοῖς ἄλλοις Πελοποννησίοις οὐ μᾶλλον σῴζειν ἑτέρους εἶχον ἢ τῶν
251 ἄλλων ἐδέοντο σῴζειν σφᾶς. καίτοι τὸ μέγιστόν γε
αὐτοῖς ἡ πόλις ἤρκεσεν, τὸ μὴ ὥσπερ καταιγίδος ἢ
στροβίλου τινὸς ἐμβολῇ καθάπαξ ἀναρπασθῆναι.
252 Ἡ δὲ πόλις κλαπεῖσα τῇ ναυμαχίᾳ τῇ καθ᾽ Ἑλ-

---

[1] Reiske : αὕτη TQVA.   [2] Stephanus : αὕτη TQVA.
[3] codd. dett. : Ξέρξην TQVA.

---

[a] At the hands of Epaminondas. Aristides himself wrote

186

it conquered foreign nations and the Greek cities, but no one conquered it except with many allies. Further, it was compelled to wage war simultaneously against all men, invaders or trouble-makers ; but most of its enemies held out against only a fraction of it, and few or none experienced its collective power. Therefore the city of the Athenians has conquered often and in many ways, but itself is as it were unconquered. Most important of all, 249 no one prevailed over it—for no one deflected its resolve, but all its defeats belonged to the military sphere—yet it itself along with its tangible accomplishments enslaved the resolves of its opponents, by its actions causing Xerxes to regard flight from his circumstances as desirable, and humbling the Lacedaemonians who heard of its deeds no less than those of them who participated in the fighting and lost. It is obvious that the accomplishments of 250 these other cities were not equal or similar in magnitude, daring, or in any quality at all. For when the Lacedaemonians suffered misfortune at Leuctra,[a] 371. they did not recover, but their empire ended like a human life. For they disdained to make peace with the Thebans, in the belief that yielding to the city of Athens alone was an honourable defeat. But jumbled together with the other Peloponnesians, they still could not save their allies, rather they needed the others to save themselves. Most impor- 251 tantly, the city helped them, so that they were not once and for all swept away as if by the onset of a hurricane or tornado.

But after the city had been tricked by the Lace- 252

five declamations on the results of this famous battle, orations xi-xv, not included in this series.

(270 D.)

λήσποντον, καὶ στερηθεῖσα τῶν[1] νεῶν καὶ τῶν
τειχῶν, καὶ μετὰ τοῦτο ἐν αὑτῇ στάσει χρησαμένη,
καὶ Λακεδαιμονίων οὐδὲν μέτριον ποιούντων, ἐκείνους μὲν δι' ἑνὸς ἀνδρὸς ἀφείλετο τῆς θαλάττης τὴν
271 D. ἀρχήν, αὐτὴ[2] δ' ἐπέστη τοῖς Ἑλληνικοῖς ὥσπερ
253 ἄρτι παριοῦσα ἀπὸ τῶν Μηδικῶν. οὐ τοίνυν μόνον
τὰ τῶν πολέμων ἐλαττώματα κάλλιον ἤνεγκεν ἢ
τὰς εὐπραξίας ἕτεροι, ἀλλὰ καὶ τὰς οἴκοι δυσκολίας
οὕτω διέθετο ὥσθ' ὅρον εἶναι σωφροσύνης πᾶσιν ἀνθρώποις καὶ μηδένα μηδ' ὕστερον ἐξευρεῖν ἔχειν βέλτιον τῶν ὑπ' ἐκείνων γενομένων[3] μηδέν. ἔδειξε δὲ
τῇ τ' ἐπὶ τῶν τετρακοσίων μεταστάσει τῆς πολιτείας, ἣν ἀψοφητὶ κατέλυσε, καὶ τῷ πρὸς τοὺς τριάκοντα πολέμῳ, μηδέν τι πρὸς πλείους μετ' ἐκεί-
254 νους γενομένῳ. ἀλλὰ μὴν ἅμα σωφροσύνης τε
καὶ τόλμης οὐδένες ἀνθρώπων σαφέστερα δείγματ'
ἐξήνεγκαν, οἵ γε ὀλίγῳ μὲν πλείους ὄντες ἢ πεν-
τήκοντα οἱ πρῶτοι ταῦτα βουλεύσαντες ὁμοῦ πρός
τε τὴν Λακεδαιμονίων ἀρχὴν γῆς καὶ θαλάττης
οὖσαν καὶ πρὸς τοὺς ἐν αὐτῇ τῇ πόλει κινδυνεύειν
ὑπέστησαν, οἰόμενοι δεῖν ἢ ζῆν ἐν ἐλευθερίᾳ, ἢ μὴ
προσορᾶν τὸν ἥλιον, κακίας μάρτυρα ἑαυτοῖς γενό-
255 μενον. ἐπεὶ δ' ἠγωνίσαντο μὲν πρὸς τοὺς ἀπὸ τοῦ
ἄστεος, ἀντετάξαντο δὲ Λακεδαιμονίοις, ἔσχον δὲ
τὸν Πειραιᾶ, παράδειγμα δὲ ἀνθρώποις τῶν ἐν τοῖς
272 D. δεινοῖς ἐλπίδων ἐγένοντο, ὁ δῆμος ἤδη συνειλεγ-
μένοι ἅμα τ' εἰς χεῖρας παρῆσαν καὶ σχεδὸν εἰς
λόγους, ὥσπερ ὑπὲρ ἀλλήλων, οὐχ ὑπὲρ αὑτῶν

---

[1] καὶ τῶν VA.
[2] Ddf. : αὕτη TQVA.
[3] A : γεγενημένων TQV.

daemonians' naval victory at the Hellespont [a] and 405–403.
was deprived of its ships and walls, and later suffered
faction at home, and when the Lacedaemonians
did not act with restraint, through one man it took
from them their sea-empire,[b] and turned its attention 394.
to Greek affairs as if it had just now come from the
wars with the Medes. It not only bore more grace- 253
fully its defeats in war than others their successes,
but it also settled its troubles at home in such a
way that all mankind had a definition of moderation
and no one later could discover a better arrangement
than theirs.[c] And it proved this both in the change 403.
in the constitution under the Four Hundred to which 411.
it quietly put an end, and in the war against the
Thirty, and against no more, which took place after 404–403.
the Four Hundred. Indeed, no men produced 254
clearer proof both of moderation and of daring than
those who first formed this plot, and numbering
little more than fifty,[d] at the same time endured to
face the danger of the Lacedaemonians' land and
sea-empire and of those in the city itself, in the belief
that they must either live in freedom or not gaze
upon a sun which had become a witness of their
cowardice. When they had struggled against those 255
in the city, and had opposed the Lacedaemonians,
and held the Piraeus, and had become for mankind
an example of good hope in adversity, the assembled
populace at once came ready for battle and almost
at the same time to make terms, as if each side were

---

[a] Aegospotami.   [b] Conon.
[c] The "Amnesty" after the fall of the Thirty; *cf.* Plato,
Menexenus 243 E.
[d] The number is usually given as seventy; *cf.* Xenophon,
Hellenica II. 4. 2 and Pseudo-Aristides xxv. 65.

(272 D.)

πολεμήσοντες[1] ἑκάτεροι· ὥστε μὴ εἶναι διελέσθαι
πότερον τῶν ἐναντίων ἦν καταρᾶσθαι τὴν στάσιν, ἢ
τῶν εὔνων συνεύξασθαι τῇ πόλει, τοῦτόν γε λυθεῖ-
σαν τὸν τρόπον. ἐνόσησεν μὲν γὰρ τῇ τῶν πάντων ἀνθρώπων φύσει, ἰάθη δὲ τῇ ἑαυτῆς· ὥστε καὶ
τοῦτο ζῆλον αὐτῇ μᾶλλον ἐνήνοχεν ἢ συμφοράν.

256 βούλομαι δὲ τοσοῦτον ἔτι ὑπὲρ τῶν ἀνδρῶν ἐκείνων
εἰπεῖν, ὅτι τῇ μὲν τόλμῃ παρῆλθον οὐ μόνον Λακεδαιμονίους, ἀλλὰ καὶ τοὺς Μαραθῶνι σχεδὸν τῶν
προγόνων. οἱ μὲν γάρ, εἰ καὶ πολὺ τῶν ἐναντίων
ἥττους, ἀλλ' οὖν ἐν πλήθει συντάγματος ὄντες
ἐθάρρησαν, οἱ δ' ὀλίγῳ πλείους ὄντες οἱ σύμπαντες
ἢ πρὸς ὅσους τοὺς τυράννους ἠγωνίζοντο Φυλὴν
κατέλαβον. καὶ οἱ μὲν εὐθενούσης[2] τῆς πόλεως
ξένους καὶ βαρβάρους, οἱ δ' ἑτέρως πεπραγυίας Λακεδαιμονίους τῶν Ἑλλήνων ἄρχοντας καὶ τοὺς
257 ἐκ τοῦ ἄστεος ἑαυτῶν ἐκράτησαν. κρατήσαντες
δὲ εὐψυχίᾳ τοὺς ἐχθρούς, ἐπιεικείᾳ τοὺς οἰκείους
ἐνίκησαν. χρησάμενοι δ' ἀμφοτέροις, καὶ τῇ παρὰ
τοὺς ἀγῶνας ἀνδρείᾳ καὶ τῷ μετὰ τὰς πράξεις ἃ δεῖ
βουλεύσασθαι, οὕτως ἀνεκτήσαντο τὴν πόλιν ὥστ'
εἴ τις βούλοιτο μὴ πάντα διηγεῖσθαι, ἐνεῖναι κλέψαι
273 D. τὴν συμβᾶσαν ἐπὶ τοῦ πολέμου συμφοράν· οὕτως
ἀκολούθους ταῖς ἄνω πράξεσιν τὰς ἐφεξῆς καὶ προ-
258 είλοντο καὶ κατώρθωσαν. καίτοι ἧς,[3] ὅτε πάντων
ἀπεστέρητο, τοσοῦτον ἡττῶντο Λακεδαιμόνιοι, πόσῃ
τινὶ τῇ περιουσίᾳ χρὴ νομίζειν ταύτην ὑπεραίρειν;

---

[1] πολεμήσαντες TQVA a. corr. Phot.
[2] codd. dett. : εὐθηνούσης TQVA.
[3] εἰ TQ.

going to wage war on behalf of one another, and not themselves alone, so that it is impossible to decide whether it was an act of an enemy to curse the city with such faction or of men of good will to pray for it, since it was concluded in this manner. For in the nature of mankind the city was diseased, but it was cured by its own nature, so that this circumstance brought it admiration rather than misfortune. But I also wish to say on behalf of those men, that 256 they not only surpassed the Lacedaemonians in daring, but also almost the men of Marathon among their ancestors. For even if the men of Marathon were far fewer than their opponents, still they were confident in having the numbers of a corps ; but these later heroes, though their total number was little more than that of the tyrants against whom they struggled, seized Phyle. And the former conquered foreigners and barbarians, when the city flourished, but the latter the Lacedaemonians who were the rulers of the Greeks as well as those in their own town, when the city fared ill. But having 257 surpassed their enemies by courage, they conquered their own people by decency. And by the application of both courage during the struggle and the proper decisions after the time of action, they recovered their city in such a way that if someone preferred not to tell the whole tale, it would be possible to conceal the misfortune which befell them during the war. So consistent with their former deeds was the subsequent course of action which they chose and successfully implemented. Yet how superior to the 258 Lacedaemonians should this city be believed, if the Lacedaemonians were so inferior to it when it had been stripped of everything ?

(273 D.)

259 Ὁ δ' οὐδενὸς ἧττον τῶν ὑπ' ἐκείνων πραχθέντων
ἄξιον εἰπεῖν τε καὶ τιμῆσαι, Λακεδαιμονίων γὰρ ἃ
τοῖς τριάκοντα ἐδάνεισαν ἐπὶ τὸν δῆμον ἀπαιτούν-
των, ἐπειδὴ συνέβησαν, συνεξέτισεν ὁ δῆμος, ἵν'
260 ἔργῳ τὰς συνθήκας βεβαιώσηται. καὶ μὴν Λακεδαιμόνιοι μὲν ὅπως ὡμίλουν ἀλλήλοις οὐκ ἂν ἔχοιμεν
εἰπεῖν· ἔκρυπτον γάρ· ἡ δὲ πόλις πρὸς τῷ τὰ σφέτερα
αὐτῆς οὕτω θέσθαι μετὰ πολλῶν μαρτύρων καὶ τοῖς
261 ἄλλοις παράδειγμα κατέστη. τὸ γοῦν Ἀργείων
πλῆθος νοσοῦν ὕστερον ἰάσατο καὶ ἔργῳ καὶ λόγῳ·
πέμψασα γὰρ ὡς αὐτοὺς καὶ ὑπομνήσασα τῶν
262 ἑαυτῆς διήλλαξεν. φαίνονται τοίνυν ὁμοίως τά τε
οἰκεῖα καὶ τὰ κοινὰ τῶν Ἑλλήνων πολιτευσάμενοι
μόνοι τῶν ἄλλων. τούς τε γὰρ Ἕλληνας οὐ μόνον
ἐκ τῶν πολεμίων ᾤοντο δεῖν ῥύεσθαι, ἀλλὰ καὶ νο-
σοῦντας ἐν αὑτοῖς[1] ἀπαλλάττειν, αὐτοί τε καὶ πρὸς
τοὺς ἔξω πολέμους καὶ πρὸς τὰς οἴκοι δυσκολίας
263 παρεσκευασμένοι κρεῖττον ἐλπίδος ἑωρῶντο. οὐ
δὴ ⟨τὸ⟩[2] τοὺς ἄλλοθεν ἥκοντας καὶ πολλῷ νεωτέ-
ρους πρὸς αὐτόχθονας καὶ πρεσβυτέρους [οὐδὲ τὸ][3]
⟨διατελεῖν μηδένα δεχομένους⟩,[4] τῆς πόλεως ἑτέροις
274 D. καταδειξάσης, οὐδὲ τὸ μηδενὸς ἄλλου πλὴν τῶν εἰς
τὸν πόλεμον προνοουμένους, τῆς πόλεως πλέον τοῖς
ἄλλοις ἢ ταύτῃ νικώσης, οὐ ταῦτα μόνον δείκνυσιν
τὸ οὐκ ἴσον, ἀλλὰ καὶ τὸ ἐν αὐτοῖς τοῖς τοῦ πολέμου
πράγμασιν καὶ καιροῖς τοσοῦτον φαίνεσθαι κρατοῦ-
σαν τὴν πόλιν, εὖ τε καὶ ὡς ἑτέρως χωροῦσιν, ὡς τά
τε εἰρημένα δηλοῖ καὶ δι' ὧν προσθήσομεν ἔξεστιν

---

[1] codd. dett. : αὐτοῖς TQVA.
[2] add. Iunt.; οὐ δὴ τὸ (ex Iunt.) ⟨κρύβδην μελετᾶν τὴν τῶν
ὅπλων ἄσκησιν⟩ ci. Oliver.

And the following act is no less worthy of mention 259
and praise than any of their deeds. When the
Lacedaemonians demanded the money which they
had lent to the Thirty against the people, after the
settlement was made, the people paid it, so that by
their action they might confirm the compact.
Indeed, we could not discuss the internal affairs of the 260
Lacedaemonians. For they kept these concealed.
But the city, beside arranging its own affairs in this
way in the presence of many witnesses, also became a
model for other people. Later it cured by its 261
actions and counsel the masses of the Argives when
they were sick with faction. For it reconciled them
by sending to them and reminding them of its own
history. Clearly the Athenians alone among all 262
equally have administered the private and the public affairs of the Greeks. For they not only thought
that they must save the Greeks from their enemies,
but also that they must reconcile them when they
were sick with faction at home. And they appeared
unexpectedly prepared for foreign wars and do-
mestic troubles. Indeed, the fact that the Lace- 263
daemonians, who were émigrés and a much younger
people, compared to a native born and older people,
never admitted anyone into their country, while
the city taught others to do this, and that they were
never concerned for anything except war, while
the city was superior in other things more than in
this, does not alone prove their inequality, but also
the fact that in the very acts and times of war, favour-
able and otherwise, the city obviously was so much
better, as the previous discussion shows and as can

(274 D.)

264 θεωρεῖν. πάσχω δ' ἔγωγε πρὸς τὰς τῆς πόλεως
πράξεις ὅπερ οἱ πρὸς τοὺς ἐν ὥρᾳ· ἀεὶ γάρ μοι τὸ
προφαινόμενον τῶν ἔργων κάλλιστον φαίνεται καὶ
265 τίθεμαι τούτῳ κατὰ τὸν λόγον. ταῦτα μὲν οὖν θεῶν
τις ἂν κρίνειεν καλῶς, ἐγὼ δέ, ὥσπερ ὑπεσχόμην,
δίειμι τῶν λοιπῶν τὰ γνωριμώτατα, ἐξ ὧν ἅμα τήν
τε γνώμην καὶ τὴν δύναμιν τῆς πόλεως ἔξεστι λογίζεσθαι.

266 Ἕνα μὲν τοίνυν καὶ πρῶτον ἄτοπον πόλεμον
καὶ θαυμαστὸν ἤρατο ὑπὲρ Θηβαίων. ἐπειδὴ γὰρ
ὡς ἀπειρηκότων ὑμῶν[1] Λακεδαιμόνιοι παιδιὰν τὰ
λοιπὰ κρίναντες ἤρχοντο τῆς δυναστείας ἀπὸ τῶν
ἑαυτῶν συμμάχων καὶ φρουρὰν ἐπὶ Θηβαίους ἔφαινον, ἀμφότερα ἐξέπληξεν τοὺς Ἕλληνας· οὔτε γὰρ
ἡ πόλις ἐχθροῖς πικροτέροις οὔτ'[2] αὖ Λακεδαιμόνιοι
συμμάχοις προθυμοτέροις ἅμα καὶ δυνατωτέροις
ἐπ' αὐτὴν ἐκείνην ἐκέχρηντο, οὐ μόνον ἀρχομένου
τοῦ πολέμου καὶ μεσοῦντος, ἀλλὰ καὶ τὰ τελευταῖα
267 πεπαυμένου. ἀλλ' ὅμως ὁ δῆμος οὐκ ἐφήσθη τοῖς
275 D. γιγνομένοις, οὐδ' αὖ τὴν ἀκαιρίαν κατεμέμψατο τῷ
μήτε ναῦς μήτε τεῖχος ἔχειν πω τότε, ἀλλ' ὥσπερ
οὗ Λακεδαιμόνιοι κινοῦνται, ἐνταῦθα σφᾶς δέον
εἶναι τοὺς ἀπαντῶντας, παραβάλλοντες μέσην τοῖς
τοῦ πολέμου κινδύνοις τὴν πόλιν, παρ' αὐτὰ τὰ
τῶν συμφορῶν ὑπομνήματα, ἐξελθόντες εἰς Ἁλίαρ-
τον ἐναντία Λυσάνδρῳ καὶ Παυσανίᾳ τὴν Βοιωτίαν
268 ἐξείλοντο. καὶ τότε δὴ Λύσανδρος ἀκριβῶς ᾔσθετο
ὅτι οὐχ, ὡς ᾤετο, ἐνενικήκει τὴν τῶν Ἀθηναίων πόλιν, ἀλλ' ὥσπερ ὠνειροπόλησεν τοῖς παισὶ παρα-

------

[1] codd. dett. : ἡμῶν TQVA.

be observed in what we shall add. But my feelings in 264
regard to the actions of the city are like those of men
toward handsome youths. For whatever I gaze upon
seems to me to be the finest deed and I favour it
while I speak. One of the Gods would best judge 265
the matter ; but as I promised,[a] I shall recount the
most important acts which are left, from which the
resolve and power of the city can both be estimated.

On behalf of the Thebans it undertook a unique 266
and very strange and remarkable war.[b] When, as if 395.
you had given up, the Lacedaemonians judged all
the rest as child's play and began their tyranny with
their allies and ordered a garrison to be stationed in 383-382.
Thebes, the Greeks were astounded for two reasons.
For the city had had no more bitter enemies than
the Thebans, nor had the Lacedaemonians more
hostile and more potent allies against the city, not
only at the beginning and middle of the war, but also
when it finally had stopped. Still the people were not 267
pleased at what was taking place. Nor again did it
blame its want of opportunity, because then it had
neither fleet nor wall. But as if they must always be
the opponents of the Lacedaemonians wherever they
are engaged, they cast the city right into the dangers
of war, marched out even past the reminders of their
misfortune, to Haliartus, against Lysander and 395.
Pausanias, and rescued Boeotia. And then Lysander 268
clearly perceived that he had not conquered the city
of the Athenians, as he thought, but had something
very like a childish dream. For the city had made a

---

[a] §§ 90, 230.
[b] *Cf.* Demosthenes XVIII. 96.

---

[2] codd. dett. : οὐδ' TQVA.

(275 D.)

πλησίως· ἡ μὲν γὰρ εὐθὺς ἀνειλήφει τὰς συμφοράς,
ὁ δ' οὐ τὰ τῶν Ἑλλήνων διώκει, ἀλλ' ὁμοῦ τοῖς
ἄλλοις ἔκειτο.

269 Οὐ πολλῷ δ' ὕστερον καὶ Κορινθίους Ἑλληνικὴ
καὶ τῇ πόλει πρέπουσα μετῆλθεν δίκη, καὶ καταφεύγουσι καὶ οὗτοι πρὸς τὴν πόλιν· ἣν ὁτιοῦν δρῶσαν
κακὸν αὐτοὺς οὐκ ἄν ποτε τὴν ἱκανὴν δίκην ἔχειν
νομίσαι πᾶς τις ἂν εἴκασεν ἐκ τῶν ὑπαρχόντων, οἱ
δ' ἅπερ περὶ Θηβαίων, ταῦτα καὶ περὶ τούτων
γνόντες βοηθοῦσιν εἰς Κόρινθον, ὡς ἄν τις ὑπὲρ τῆς
270 οἰκείας. καὶ γενομένου τοῦ πολέμου πολλοῦ καὶ
συνεχοῦς ἐν Κορίνθῳ, μάχας τε πολλὰς προκιν-
δυνεύσαντες, καὶ τειχίσαντες αὐτοὺς καὶ τὴν πόλιν
διὰ πάντων φυλάξαντες, κάλλιστον ἐκεῖνο ἐπέθη-
καν· ἔχοντες γὰρ τὸν Ἀκροκόρινθον καὶ παρὸν αὐτοῖς κατασχεῖν τὴν πόλιν, ἡνίκ' ἐβούλοντο, οὐκ
ἐξεδέξαντο οὐδ' ἐβουλεύσαντο, ἔργῳ δείξαντες ὅτι
τὸν[1] τῶν προστατῶν πολεμοῦσιν, οὐχ αὐτοῖς[2] ἰδίᾳ
τι πράττοντες.

271
276 D. Καὶ τέλος εἰς τοῦτ' ἀπορίας κατέστησαν Λακεδαιμονίους ὥστ' ἐπὶ τὸν[3] Περσῶν βασιλέα πάλιν
καταφεύγουσιν καὶ δι' ἐκείνου ποιοῦνται τὴν θρυ-
λουμένην εἰρήνην, τοὺς τὴν Ἀσίαν οἰκοῦντας Ἕλληνας προέμενοι, περὶ ὧν οὐδὲν ἔγωγε κατηγορῶ·
ἀλλ' εἴ τις ἔροιτο αὐτοὺς πότερον ἑκόντες ταῦτα
συνεχώρησαν, ἢ βιασθέντες, εἰ μὲν ἑκόντες φήσουσιν, ἀνάγκη προδεδωκέναι φάσκειν, ὃ τίς ἂν πιστεύσειεν; εἰ δ' ἄκοντες καὶ δι' ἀνάγκην, ὁμολογοῦσιν

___

[1] om. TQ ; τὸ codd. dett.
[2] Reiske : οὐκ αὐτοῖς TQVA.   [3] τῶν VA.

___

[a] During the Corinthian war, 395–390 B.C.

swift recovery from its misfortune ; whereas he no longer administered Greek affairs, but lay dead with the others.

Not much later a truly Greek retribution, appropri- 269 ate to the city, befell the Corinthians,[a] and they 394. also took refuge with the city. Even if it had in some way mistreated the Corinthians, everyone would have thought from their past conduct that it would never have felt itself sufficiently revenged. Yet the Athenians also decided the same about them as they did about the Thebans, and went to the aid of Corinth, as one would in defence of his own country. And when a great and uninterrupted war had taken 270 place in Corinth, and they had faced the danger of many battles, and had built them a wall and protected the Corinthians' city in every way, their last act was the finest of all. For although they held Acrocorinth, and they could hold the city whenever they wished, they did not take advantage of this or plan for it, having proven in fact that they waged war in the role of protectors, and not for any personal benefit for themselves.

And finally they reduced the Lacedaemonians to 271 such desperation, that they again took refuge with the king of the Persians and through his agency made that notorious peace,[b] abandoning the Greeks who 387–386. lived in Asia. I make no accusations concerning this act. But if someone should ask them whether they made these concessions willingly or under compulsion, if they will say that they did it willingly, it must be agreed that they were traitors, and who would believe this ? But if they will say that they did it unwillingly and out of necessity, they admit

[b] " The King's Peace."

197

(276 D.)

ἡττῆσθαι δήπου πρὸς τὴν πόλιν τοῖς ὅλοις· οὐ γὰρ
ἄν, εἴ γ' εἶχον ὅ τι χρήσονται τοῖς πράγμασιν, εἶτ'
ἐξεπίτηδες τοιαύτην αἰσχύνην ὑπέστησαν. ὥστε τῷ
μόνῳ λειπομένῳ τῶν λόγων αὐτοὶ[1] μαρτυροῦσιν
προέχειν τῷ πολέμῳ τότε τὴν πόλιν, καὶ ταῦτ' οὐχὶ μικρόν.

272 Ἐπεὶ δὲ τῆς εἰρήνης ἐμνήσθην, πάλιν ἐνταῦθα ἐπ-
ανελθεῖν βούλομαι βραχύ τι. δυοῖν γὰρ ὄντοιν ἐξ ὧν
κρίνονται πόλεις, πολέμου καὶ εἰρήνης, καὶ τούτων
ἀμφοτέρων τοῖς Ἕλλησι πρὸς τοὺς βαρβάρους γενομένων, ἐπὶ μὲν τοῦ πολέμου τοσοῦτον διήνεγκεν
ἡ πόλις ὥσθ' ἃ μόνη κατειργάσατο, μέγιστα τῶν
ἔργων ἐστίν· ἢ τοῖς ὕστερον εἴ τις τιθοῖτο, τοσοῦτον
τῶν μετασχόντων ὑπερῆρεν, ὅσονπερ ἂν εἰ καθ'
273 αὑτὴν ἠγωνίζετο. χωρὶς δὲ τούτων τοῖς τρισὶ καιροῖς μαρτυρεῖται· τὰ μὲν γὰρ πρῶτα τοῦ πολέμου
μόνη κατέπραξεν, ἐν δὲ τοῖς δευτέροις καὶ πρὸς τὸν
βασιλέα προκινδυνεύσασα τὰ ἀριστεῖα ἠνέγκατο· τὰ
δ' αὖ τελευταῖα αὐτῆς ἐστιν ἴδια, αἱ περὶ Κύπρον
καὶ Παμφυλίαν ναυμαχίαι καὶ πεζομαχίαι καὶ ὁ
277 D. πολὺς δρόμος· ὥστε καὶ μόνη τοὺς βαρβάρους καὶ
πρώτη νενίκηκεν, καὶ σὺν ἄλλοις γενομένη οὐκ
ἔλαττον τοὺς συμπαρόντας ἢ τοὺς ἀντιπάλους ἐνίκα·
274 καὶ παρέμεινεν μόνη. ἀλλὰ μὴν τῆς γε εἰρήνης ὅσον
τὸ διάφορον· ἡ μέν γε τῆς πόλεως ἐπιτάττει τῷ
βασιλεῖ κἀκεῖνόν φησι δεῖν τὸ κελευόμενον ποιεῖν·
οὐ γὰρ ἐᾷ πλεῖν εἴσω Χελιδονέων καὶ Κυανέων, εἰ δ'
ἐπὶ τῇ ἵππῳ μέγα φρονεῖς, οὐδὲν μᾶλλον ἐλᾷς ἄχρι

---

[1] Reiske : αὐτοῖς TQVA.

---

[a] Especially at Marathon.
[b] Cimon's land and sea victory at the Eurymedon in Pamphylia and his destruction of the Phoenician ships off Cyprus.

that they are inferior to the city in every way. For if they knew what to do, they would not intentionally have undertaken such a shameful act, so that by the only argument left they themselves bear witness that the city then was superior in war, and not a little at that.

But since I mentioned the Peace, here again I 272 wish to return to a point for a moment. For when there are two criteria by which cities are judged, war and peace, and both of these involved the Greeks against the barbarians, in war the city was so superior that the greatest deeds were accomplished by it alone.[a] Or if its later deeds are preferred, it surpassed those who participated with it, as much as if it had fought by itself. But apart from this, 273 its superiority is attested by three different periods. The first part of the war it accomplished alone ; 490. and in the second part, it also faced the danger of 480–479. the king and won the prize of valour ; and again the final action was its alone, the naval and infantry battles at Cyprus and Pamphylia, and the long- 468. distance race between them.[b] Therefore it was the first to conquer the barbarians and it conquered them alone ; and when it allied itself with other Greeks, it conquered its allies no less than its opponents ; and it alone kept up the war. But in the 274 matter of the Peace what a great difference there is ! 448. For the city's peace gave orders to the king and said that he must do what he was commanded. For it did not allow him to sail within the Chelidonian and Cyanean Islands.[c] And if you are proud of your cavalry, no longer will you ride up to the sea, but, it

[c] The so-called Peace of Callias between Athens and Persia ; cf. xxvi. 10 ; Demosthenes XIX. 273.

(277 D.)

θαλάττης, ἀλλ' αὐτῆς, φησί, τῆς ἵππου δρόμον
ἡμέρας τῆς θαλάττης ἀποσχήσεις, καὶ ἀκούσῃ
περὶ τῶν Ἑλλήνων ὁμοίως τῶν τε ἐν τῇ Ἑλλάδι καὶ
275 τῶν ἐν τῇ σεαυτοῦ. ταῦτα μὲν ἡ τῆς πόλεως εἰρήνη
λέγει, ἡ δ' ἑτέρα τοὺς τὴν Ἀσίαν οἰκοῦντας Ἕλληνας ἀκούειν τοῦ βασιλέως κἀκεῖνον ποιεῖν ὅ τι ἂν
278 D. βούληται περὶ αὐτῶν καὶ τοῖς ἄλλοις τὰ δίκαια
276 ὁρίζειν προστέθεικεν. ἆρ' ἴσον τὸ κεφάλαιον, ἢ
μικρὸν τὸ διάφορον, ἀλλ' οὐ πᾶν τοὐναντίον;

277 Πάλιν δὴ τὰ πρὸς τοὺς Ἕλληνας καὶ τὰς τῶν ἐν
αὐτοῖς πολέμων καταλύσεις. ἡ μὲν τοίνυν πόλις οὓς
εἷλεν Λακεδαιμονίων οὐδὲν κακὸν ποιήσασα ἀπ-
έπεμψε μετ' εἰρήνης, ὥσπερ ἀρκοῦν ἀρετῇ νενικη-
κέναι· οἱ δ' ἐν Ἑλλησπόντῳ Λακεδαιμονίων, οὕτω
γὰρ εὐπρεπὲς εἰπεῖν, οὓς ἔλαβον τῇ ναυμαχίᾳ
κλαπέντας Ἀθηναίων ἀπέσφαξαν παραχρῆμα, καὶ
πλέον οὐδὲν προστίθημι, καὶ ταῦτα ὑπάρχοντος τοῦ
παραδείγματος αὐτοῖς οἴκοθεν, οἷα περὶ τοὺς
δυστυχήσαντας ἡ πόλις ἐστίν· ἀλλ' ὅμως οὐδ'
οὕτως ἐμιμήσαντο, τοσοῦτον[1] ἀπέσχον τοῦ πρῶτοί
278 γ' ἂν αὐτοὶ δυνηθῆναι καταδεῖξαι. ἔτι δ' οἱ μὲν οὐδὲν ἀποχρῶν ἡγήσαντο, ἀλλ' ἄχρι τῆς τῶν τειχῶν
ἦλθον καθαιρέσεως, ἡ πόλις δ' ἅπαντας Πελοποννησίους κατὰ τοὺς ἄνω χρόνους νενικηκυῖα, ὡς ἐκομίσατο τὴν Εὔβοιαν, οὐ προῆλθεν περαιτέρω, ἀλλὰ
καὶ ἃ τῷ πολέμῳ προειλήφει, καὶ ταῦτ' ἀπέδωκεν
ἑκοῦσα, Μέγαρα, Νίσαιαν,[2] Τροιζῆνα, Ἀχαῖαν,
279 Πηγάς. δοκεῖ δ' ἔμοιγε καὶ τὸ τῶν αἰχμαλώτων καὶ
πᾶν ὅλως τὸ τοιοῦτον διπλῆς ἀρετῆς εἶναι τῇ πόλει σημεῖον, οὐχ, ὡς ἄν τις φήσαι, μόνον οὑτωσὶ

---

[1] τοσοῦτ' TQV.
[2] codd. dett. : Νήσαιαν TQVA.

says, you will stay away from the sea the distance of a day's ride of that very cavalry, and you will hear as much about the Greeks who live in Greece as about the Greeks who live in your own land. Such were the terms of the city's peace. But the terms of the other peace were that the Greeks living in Asia obey the king, and it added that he act however he wished concerning them and be the arbiter of justice for the others. Then was the purport the same or the difference slight ? Was it not entirely the opposite ? 275 387–386. 276

Again consider the conduct of both toward the Greeks and how they concluded the wars in Greece. The city made peace and sent back the Lacedaemonians, whom it had captured, without harming them, as if it were enough to have conquered in virtue. But those of the Lacedaemonians who were in the Hellespont—for this is a seemly way to express it—slaughtered on the spot the Athenians whom they had captured by the ruse of the naval battle, and I say no more, although they had an example from home of the city's behaviour toward unfortunates. Still, they did not even imitate it in this ; they were so far from being the first to be able to teach this. Further they were satisfied with nothing, but they went as far as to tear down the walls. Yet earlier when the city had conquered all the Peloponnesians, after it had got back Euboea, it went no farther ; but it even voluntarily returned what it had formerly taken in the war : Megara, Nisaea, Troezen, Achaia, and Pegae.[a] But it seems to me that the affair of the prisoners and indeed every event of this nature is a proof of two virtues of the city, and not as one would say, of generosity alone. 277 421. 405. 278 404. 446–445. 279

[a] *Cf.* Note on § 225.

279 D. φιλανθρωπίας. ὅσοις μὲν γὰρ οἶμαι παρ' ἐλπίδας
ἢ δύναμιν τὰ τοιαῦτα κατορθοῦται, τῆς παρούσης
ἔχονται τύχης, ὥσπερ οἱ θηρᾶν ἀδύνατοι τὸ ληφθὲν
ἀπροσδοκήτως οὐ μεθιᾶσιν, οὐδ' ἂν ἀποδόσθαι τις
ἀξιώσῃ, τῆς ἀξίας τιμήσαιντ'[1] ἄν, ἀλλὰ τὴν αὑτῶν
ἀδυναμίαν προστιθέντες πλεονάζουσιν. ἡ δ' οἶμαι
συνειδυῖα ἑαυτῇ κρείττων οὖσα τοῖς ὅλοις οὐδε-
πώποτ' ἐμικρολογήσατο, ἐξ ἴσου τοῖς παροῦσι τὰ
ἀπόντα ἐλπίζουσα· διὸ πάντα ῥᾷον τοῖς πολεμίοις
ἀπέδωκεν ἢ 'κεῖνοι τὰ σφέτερα αὐτῶν ἀπήτησαν.

280 καὶ μὴν ὅστις μὲν εἷς Λακεδαιμονίων τῆς πόλεως
ἐκράτησεν οὐδ' ἂν εἷς εἰπεῖν ἔχοι, ὅπου γε μηδ' ἀπὸ
κοινοῦ μόνοι· Ἀθηναίων δ' ἀνὴρ εἷς τῆς θαλάττης
Λακεδαιμονίους ἀφείλετο τὴν ἀρχήν, μόνος ἀνθρώπων ἅμα τῷ βασιλεῖ στρατηγήσας καὶ τῇ πόλει, μᾶλλον δὲ τοῖς Ἕλλησιν. οὐδ' ὁτιοῦν γὰρ τὸν
πιστεύσαντα ἀδικήσας ἐτείχισε τὴν πόλιν καὶ τοὺς
Ἕλληνας ἠλευθέρωσεν, Λακεδαιμονίους κατὰ νῆσον

281 καὶ πόλιν νικῶν. αὐτὴν τοίνυν τὴν τῆς θαλάττης
ἀρχὴν ἡ μὲν πόλις ἐξ ὧν τοὺς βαρβάρους τοὺς
φύσει πολεμίους ἐνίκησεν ἐκτήσατο, οἱ δ' ἐξ ὧν ἡ

282 πόλις ἠτύχησεν. κτησάμενοι τοίνυν τὴν ἀρχὴν οἱ
μὲν οὕτως ἕκαστα διεῖλον ὥστε τὸν διοικήσαντα

280 D. παρ' αὐτοῖς τοῖς Ἕλλησιν δίκαιον κληθῆναι μόνον
Ἑλλήνων ἀπὸ τούτου καὶ μηδὲν δεῖν περιττότερον
σύμβολον εἰπεῖν τῆς ἐπωνυμίας, ἣν δι' ἐκείνου τότε
ἡ πόλις ἐκτήσατο, οἱ δ' οὕτω τοὺς παραδόντας
αὑτοὺς διέθηκαν ὥστε κάλλιστ' ἀνθρώπων ἀπε-

---

[1] τιμήσαιτ' VA.

---

[a] Conon.
[b] Aristides, the son of Lysimachus, assessed the principles

For, I think, all who in such enterprises are successful beyond their expectation or real strength, cling fast to their present good fortune, just as bad hunters do not let go of an unexpected catch, nor if someone desires to sell it, would they set a fair price, but they add their own weakness into consideration and exaggerate its value. So the city, I think, conscious of its total superiority, was never petty-minded, since it had the same expectations about what it did not have as about what it did. For that reason it returned to its enemies all their territory faster than they asked for it. Indeed, no one could name a 280 Lacedaemonian who by himself conquered the city, since they did not even do this as a group acting alone. But a single man of the Athenians[a] deprived 394. the Lacedaemonians of their sea-empire, the only man who simultaneously served as a general of the king and the city, and moreover of the Greeks. For without violating the king's trust, he fortified 393. the city and liberated the Greeks, conquering the Lacedaemonians, island by island and city by city. The city acquired its sea-empire because it con- 281 quered the barbarians, its natural enemy ; but the 478-453. Lacedaemonians acquired theirs, because the city 404. suffered misfortune. After acquiring their empire, 282 the Athenians so arranged its particulars that the man who administered the tribute,[b] alone of the 478. Greeks, among the Greeks themselves, henceforth was called " just " and no further superfluous argument need be made than this title which the city then acquired through him. But the Lacedae-monians so treated those who entrusted themselves

on which the allies of the new Athenian confederacy of Delos should contribute to its fund.

(280 D.)

λογήσαντο ὑπὲρ τῶν κατὰ καιρούς τινας αἰτιῶν
γενομένων παρ' ἐνίων τῇ πόλει· αἴτιον δ' οὐκ
ὠμότης οὐδ' ἅ τις ἂν φαίη τῶν ῥᾳδίως εἰωθότων
ἐπιτιμᾶν, ἀλλὰ τὸ μὴ ἐξικνεῖσθαι τὰς φύσεις ἄχρι
283 τοῦ ἴσου. καὶ μὴν οἱ μὲν πλέον ἢ ἑβδομήκοντα
ἔτη κατέσχον, οἱ δὲ οὐδ' εἰς τρεῖς 'Ολυμπιάδας διε-
φύλαξαν τὴν ἀρχήν· οὔκουν ὡς ἀληθῶς ἄλλως γε
ἂν εἴη, εἰ μὴ τὸ πρῶτον 'Ολυμπίων προσαγόντων
παρέλαβον.

284 Ταῦτ' ἐστὶν ἀγὼ τοῖς παρεξετάζειν βουλομένοις
ἄχθομαι. ἴσως μὲν οὖν κἀγώ τισιν ποιεῖν ἄτοπον
δοκῶ, μεμφόμενος μέν, αὐτὸς δ' εἰς τοὺς ὁμοίους
λόγους προεληλυθώς, καὶ δι' αὐτά γε ταῦτ' εἰρηκὼς
285 αὐτοὺς δι' ἅ φημι δεῖν μὴ λέγειν. οὐ μὴν ἀλλ' ἐξ
αὐτῶν τούτων καὶ μάλιστ' ἄν τις κατίδοι ὡς οὔτε ἡ
χάρις θαυμαστή, ἣν οἴονται τῇ πόλει κατατίθεσθαι,
οὔτε ἐξεπίτηδες τά γε τοιαῦτα ἀγωνιστέον. ὥστ'
281 D. εἴ τις ἀξιοῖ καὶ ἡμῖν ἄρρητα ταῦτ' εἶναι, σχεδὸν
286 τούτου χάριν εἴρηται. χωρὶς δὲ τούτων ἄνευ βλασφημίας οἱ λόγοι γεγόνασιν καὶ τῆς παραπεσούσης
χρείας ἕνεκα. οὐ γὰρ ἦν ἄλλως ὃ προειλόμην ἀπο-
δεῖξαι,[1] ὥστ' ἐξ ὧν ἔφευγον, ἐκ τούτων προήχθην
εἰπεῖν. δοκοῦσιν γάρ μοι Λακεδαιμόνιοι τὸ τοῦ
παρ' 'Ομήρῳ Τεύκρου πρὸς τὸν Αἴαντα πεπονθέναι
πρὸς τὴν πόλιν. καὶ γὰρ ἐκεῖνος τῶν ἄλλων προ-

---

[1] ἐπιδεῖξαι TQV.

ᵃ The years 404–394 B.C. are meant, and the distinction is
drawn between the four years of the Olympic period and the
Olympic festival itself. The Lacedaemonians' hegemony
survived three of the latter only because Athens fell in 404 B.C.
several months before the celebration of the 92nd Olympic
Games. Their power was shattered at Cnidus and Coronea in
394 B.C. after less than eleven years.

to them that they of all men offered the finest
defence for the charges made by some at certain
times against the city. The cause for this was not
cruelty nor whatever fault-finders would readily say,
but the fact that the natures of the two did not
develop equally. Indeed, the Athenians held their 283
empire for more than seventy years, but the Lace- 478-404.
daemonians did not even preserve theirs for three
whole Olympiads. Actually, it would not have been 404-394.
even three Olympiads, if they had not first succeeded
to power when the Olympic festival was approaching.[a]

These are the very things which annoy me in 284
those who wish to compare the two cities.[b] Perhaps
I seem to some to act strangely when I blame these
critics and yet have proceeded to similar arguments,
and have made them for the very reasons, for which I
claim they should not be made. However, from 285
these arguments, it would certainly be clear that the
gratitude which they think they are storing up with
the city is not large, nor should these points be
intentionally brought into the debate. Therefore if
someone thinks that they also should have been left
unsaid by us, I reply that they have been said almost
for this very purpose. Besides, the arguments have 286
been made without defamation and because of a
chance need. For it was not otherwise possible to
prove my point, so that I was carried away into
discussing these matters because I was avoiding
them. The Lacedaemonians seem to me to have
had the same experience in respect to the city as
Teucer in Homer did in respect to Ajax.[c] For although he faced danger on behalf of the others, he

[b] Cf. § 238. [c] Iliad VIII. 271.

205

(281 D.)

κινδυνεύων ὡς τὸν Αἴαντα ἀναχωρεῖ καὶ δι' ἐκείνου
φαίνεται, ὡς δ' αὔτως καὶ κρύπτεται, καὶ Λακεδαιμόνιοι οἱ τῶν Ἑλλήνων προέχοντες καὶ προ-
κινδυνεύοντες ἐν ταῖς χρείαις παῖδες τῇ πόλει
287 παραβαλεῖν εἰσίν. τεκμήριον δέ. τῶν γοῦν ὑπαρχόντων καὶ πεπραγμένων αὐτοῖς μέγιστα ταῦτ'
ἐστὶν ὧν κεκοινωνήκασι τῇ πόλει· καὶ τούτων ἃ μὲν
διείλοντο ἀπέτυχον, ἃ δὲ σὺν τοῖς ἀπὸ τῆς πόλεως
ἔπραξαν, ἐνδοξότατα ἀνθρώπων κατώρθωσαν. οὕτω
διὰ τῆς πόλεως καὶ φαίνονται καὶ κρύπτονται πάλιν.
288 οὐ μὴν ἀλλ' ἔγωγε οὕτω παρὰ γνώμην εἰς τούτους
ἐξήχθην τοὺς λόγους, ὥστ' ἐβουλόμην ἂν καὶ τὰ
τρόπαια ἃ μέλλω λέγειν ἀπ' ἄλλων ὑπάρχειν ἀνακεί-
μενα τῇ πόλει καὶ μὴ ἀναγκαῖον εἶναι προστιθέναι
289 τοῖς πολλοῖς ὅτι ἀπὸ Λακεδαιμονίων. νῦν δ' αὐτὰ
τὰ πράγματα ταύτην ἄγει, ὥστ' οὐ τοῦ παρεξετάσαι
χάριν εἰρήσεται, ἀλλὰ τοῦ μὴ παντάπασιν τὰς πράξεις παρελθεῖν· καὶ γὰρ εἰσὶν ἃς παρεξέλιπον· δεῖ
δέ, ὡς ἔοικεν, οὐ τοῦ τυχόντος δρόμου.

290 Ἐνίκησαν μὲν τοίνυν ἐν Λεχαίῳ καὶ διέφθειραν
282 D. μικροῦ πᾶν τὸ στρατόπεδον, εἷλον δὲ τὰ ἐν τῇ
Κορίνθῳ φρούρια καὶ τοὺς ἐγκαθεστῶτας Λακεδαι-
291 μονίων ἐξήλασαν καὶ τὰ τείχη κατέσκαψαν· ἦλθον
δὲ εἰς Ἀρκαδίαν καὶ μέχρι τῆς Λακωνικῆς, κατέ-
κλεισαν δὲ τοὺς ἐν Φλιοῦντι, καὶ τῶν ἐπεξελθόν-
των τρόπαιον ἔστησαν, καὶ Μαντινέων πάλιν καὶ
Σικυωνίων αὖθις ἐν τῷ πεδίῳ καὶ τῶν συμμάχων·
292 παρέπλευσαν δ' ἄχρι Βυζαντίου, καὶ πάντα τὸν περὶ

withdrew to Ajax, and he became famous and again was overshadowed on account of him. And the Lacedaemonians, who stood before the Greeks and faced danger in their behalf in times of need, are children in comparison with the city. There is 287 proof of this. For their greatest accomplishments and deeds are those which they shared with the city. And they failed in those which they took for themselves alone, but enjoyed the most glorious success of mankind in those which they performed with the Athenians. So they became famous and again were overshadowed on account of the city. How-288 ever, I stumbled into these arguments so contrary to my intention, that I would wish that the trophies which I am going to discuss were dedicated by the city for the defeat of other people and that it was not necessary to append to this large number that they were for the defeat of the Lacedaemonians. But now the circumstances lead me this way, so that 289 they will be discussed, not for the sake of comparison, but so as not to omit the events entirely; for some I have left out. But, it seems, a haphazard course must not be pursued.

Well then, they were victorious at Lechaeum and 290 destroyed almost the whole camp.[a] They captured the forts in Corinth and expelled the Lacedaemo- 392-390. nians stationed in them, and tore down the walls. They went to Arcadia and as far as Laconia, and 291 they blockaded those in Phlius; and when these marched out, they defeated them, and later the Mantineans, and still later the Sicyonians and their allies in the plain. They sailed as far as Byzantium, 292

---

[a] The events at Lechaeum, Corinth, Phlius, and Mantinea and in Arcadia were the exploits of the Athenian Iphicrates.

(282 D.)

Θράκην τόπον δι' αὐτῶν¹ ἐποιήσαντο, ἐνίκησαν δὲ
τοὺς ἐπιλοίπους τῶν ἁρμοστῶν καὶ τὰς φρουρὰς ἐν
Μηθύμνῃ καὶ πρὸς Ἀβύδῳ. τοσοῦτον ⟨δ'⟩² αὐτοῖς
περιῆν ὥστε καὶ τοὺς Θρακῶν βασιλέας διήλλαξαν.

293 Γενομένου δὲ τοῦ περὶ τὴν Καδμείαν ἀπροσδοκήτου κακοῦ μόνοι τῶν Ἑλλήνων καὶ τὸ τῆς αἰσχρᾶς
εἰρήνης δίκαιον καὶ τὰ τῶν Ἑλλήνων καλὰ καὶ ὡς
ἀληθῶς δίκαια ἐτήρησαν Λακεδαιμονίοις ἐπεξελθόν-
τες· ὧν ἀμφοτέρων τί χρὴ μεῖζον εἰπεῖν περὶ τῆς
πόλεως; τήν τε γὰρ εἰρήνην ἔσχατοι τῶν Ἑλλήνων
συνεχώρησαν καὶ οὐ πρότερον πρὶν ἔγνωσαν ὅτι οὐ
μόνον Λακεδαιμονίοις ἅμα καὶ βασιλεῖ καὶ Σεύθῃ
καὶ Διονυσίῳ καὶ Πελοποννησίοις ἀνάγκη πολεμεῖν, ἐπεὶ πρὸς τοῦτό γε ὑπῆρχον παρεσκευα-
283 D. σμένοι, ἀλλὰ καὶ τοῖς συμμάχοις τοῖς σφετέροις
αὐτῶν· οὕτω προὐδόθησαν καὶ οὐδ' οὕτως ἁπάσαις
ταῖς ψήφοις ὑπέμειναν, ἀλλὰ τῶν γε πεισάντων
κατέγνωσαν, ἡγούμενοι παρὰ τὴν αὑτῶν³ εἶναι
φύσιν καὶ οὐ θεμιτὸν πρὸ τῶν τροπαίων ὁντινοῦν
τῶν Ἑλλήνων βασιλέως ἀκροᾶσθαι συγχωρῆσαι.

294 ἐπειδὴ δὲ καὶ παρὰ ταύτην τὴν εἰρήνην παρῆλθον
εἰς Θήβας ὧν ἐγὼ φεύγω λέγειν τοὔνομα ἐπὶ τοιούτοις, οὐ μόνον πρῶτοι τῶν Ἑλλήνων, ἀλλὰ καὶ
μόνοι τῶν πραγμάτων ἀνθήψαντο, ὥσπερ ἑρμαίου
λαβόμενοι, καὶ οὐχ ἓν εἶδος εὐεργεσίας ἐπεδείξαντο, ἀλλ' οὐδὲν εἶδος εὐεργεσίας ἀπέλιπον, δεξάμενοι μὲν τὴν φυγὴν καὶ τὴν πρᾶξιν αὐτοῖς συνθέντες

---

¹ Ddf. : αὐτῶν TQVA.
² add. codd. dett. ³ Ddf. : αὐτῶν TQVA.

ᵃ Byzantium and Methymne were the scenes of victories
by Thrasybulus in 390 B.C. ; Abydus by Iphicrates in 389 B.C.
ᵇ The citadel of Thebes, seized by the Lacedaemonians in
382 B.C.

and got control of the whole region of Thrace,[a] and 390.
they conquered the remaining Harmosts, and the
garrisons in Methymne and at Abydus. So great 389.
was their superiority that they even reconciled the
Thracian kings.

When that unexpected evil took place at the 293
Cadmea,[b] they were the only Greeks to observe 383-382.
both the requirements of that shameful peace and
the real rights and just claims of the Greeks by
counter-attacking the Lacedaemonians. And what
more could be said about the city than these two
points ? For they were the last of the Greeks to 387-386.
concede the peace [c] and not before they realized
that they would not only have to wage a simultaneous
war with the Lacedaemonians, the king, Seuthes,
Dionysius,[d] and the Peloponnesians, since they were
prepared for this, but also with their own allies.
Thus they were betrayed. And not even so did they
submit wholeheartedly, but they condemned those
who persuaded them, in the belief that it was contrary
to their nature and improper in view of their
trophies to concede that any Greek be obedient to the
king. But when even contrary to the terms of this 294
peace, Thebes was invaded by a people whose name
I will not mention in such circumstances, the Athenians were not only the first of the Greeks to seize
upon the matter, as if they had found some treasure,
but also the only ones. And they displayed not only
one kind of benefit, but they omitted no kind of
benefit, receiving the fugitives, preparing a course of

[c] " The King's Peace."
[d] King Artaxerxes II of Persia ; Seuthes a ruler in Thrace ;
and Dionysius I, " tyrant " (that is, unconstitutional despot)
of Syracuse from 405 to 367 B.C.

καὶ προδείξαντες ὥσπερ δρᾶμα παρ᾽ αὐτοῖς, ἀτέλειαν
δὲ καὶ πολιτείαν καὶ πάντων μετουσίαν δόντες,
ὥσπερ τοῖς ἐκ Κορίνθου καὶ Θάσου καὶ Βυζαντίου μεταστᾶσιν. ἔπειθ᾽ ὡς καὶ τῆς διὰ τῶν ὅπλων
ἐδέησεν βοηθείας, ἐξελθόντες μικροῦ δεῖν ἅπαντες
ὥσπερ πομπῆς ἀλλ᾽ οὐ κινδύνων μεθέξειν μέλλοντες,
τὴν προτέραν αὐτῶν ἔξοδον μιμησάμενοι, τῇ δὲ
γνώμῃ καὶ ὑπερβαλόμενοι. τότε μὲν γὰρ οὐκ οὔσης
αὐτοῖς συμμαχίας πρὸς Θηβαίους ἐξῆλθον, ἐν δὲ τοῖς
χρόνοις τούτοις καὶ τῶν στηλῶν τῶν περὶ τῆς συμμαχίας ὑπὸ Θηβαίων καθῃρημένων, ἀλλ᾽ ὅμως οὐχ
ὑπελογίσαντο τὴν ἄνοιαν αὐτῶν τῇ χρείᾳ, οὐδὲ μᾶλλον τοῖς δικαίως κινδυνεύουσιν ὠργίσθησαν ἢ τοῖς
295 ἀδίκως ἐπελθοῦσιν. οὕτω δὲ λαμπροῖς τοῖς λογισμοῖς χρησάμενοι πρέπουσαν τὴν τελευτὴν ἐπέθη-
284 D. καν. οὐ γὰρ παρὰ μικρὸν ἐνίκησαν οὐδ᾽ ὡς φοβῆσαι
[μᾶλλον]¹ μόνον Λακεδαιμονίους, ἀλλ᾽ ἐκβαλόντες
τὴν φρουρὰν καὶ τοὺς ἁρμοστὰς ὑποσπόνδους ἀνήγαγον εἰς τὴν ἐξ ἀρχῆς τάξιν τὴν πόλιν.

296   Καὶ τοῦτον μὲν ὑπὲρ τῆς ἐλευθερίας τὸν ἀγῶνα
τῆς Θηβαίων, τὸν δ᾽ ἐφεξῆς ὑπὲρ αὐτῆς ἤραντο τῆς
σωτηρίας αὐτῶν. παροξυνθέντων γὰρ Λακεδαιμονίων πρὸς τὸ συμβὰν καὶ μετὰ πάσης συμμαχίας
ἐπελθόντων ἀντετάξαντο πρὸ τῆς πόλεως τῆς
Θηβαίων, στρατηγούς τε φοβερωτέρους ἐκείνοις
ἀντεπιστήσαντες ἢ 'κεῖνοι τοὺς σὺν Ἀγησιλάῳ
παρείχοντο, καὶ διὰ πάντων σωτῆρες τῇ πόλει
γενόμενοι.

---

¹ om. codd. dett. ; secl. Reiske.

ᵃ The battle at Haliartus in 395 B.C. Aristides seems to
confuse the Athenians' victory at Coronea (394 B.C.) with the
Thebans' expulsion of the Spartans from the Cadmea in
378 B.C.

action with them, coaching them as it were about the drama taking place among them, and offering them freedom from taxation, citizenship, and a share in everything, just as they did for those who were banished from Corinth, Thasus, and Byzantium ; and next when armed assistance was needed, nearly all of them marching out, as if they were going to participate in a procession and not danger, in imitation of their former expedition, but with even a nobler resolve.[a] For then they marched out when they had no alliance with the Thebans, but then even after the pillars containing the alliance had been torn down by the Thebans. Nonetheless they did not consider the Thebans' folly in view of their need, nor were they more angry at those who risked danger in a just cause than at those who were unjust aggressors. Thus they reasoned in a noble way and fittingly concluded the matter. For they were victorious by no small margin, nor so as only to frighten the Lacedaemonians. But they expelled the garrison and the Harmosts under a truce, and restored Thebes to its original state.

And they undertook this struggle on behalf of the Thebans' liberty, but the following one on behalf of their very existence. For when the Lacedaemonians were enraged at what happened and attacked with all their allies, they drew up their battle line before Thebes, putting more terrifying generals [b] in command against the Lacedaemonians than the latter presented in the person of Agesilaus and his fellows, and being in every way the saviours of the city.

^b margin note: 395, 394 ? 378 ?

margin note: 296 377.

[b] Chabrias was the Athenian general, *cf.* Xenophon, *Hellenica* V. 4. 47 ff.

(284 D.)

297   Περίσταται δέ με παντοδαπὰ ὥσπερ ἐν συγ-
γραφῇ τῶν αὐτῶν χρόνων, ἃ μὴ ὅτι πάντα διεξελθεῖν
εὔπορον, ἀλλ᾽ οὐδὲ ἑνὸς στρατηγοῦ πάντα ἑξῆς.
ὧν τί παρεὶς τίνος μνησθῶ; πότερον τῆς ἐν Νάξῳ
ναυμαχίας, ἔργου τοσούτου; ἢ τῶν περὶ Κέρκυραν
ἀγωνισμάτων; ἢ τῶν ἐπὶ Θρᾴκης ὑπὲρ τῆς ἐκεῖ
πραχθέντων Ἑλλάδος; ἢ τῶν ἐν Ἀκαρνανίᾳ; ἢ
τῶν πανταχοῦ;

298   Ἡ πάντα τὰ ἄλλα ἀφεὶς ὃ μέγιστον ἔχω καὶ θαυ-
μαστότατον καὶ μόνον ὡς ἀληθῶς τῶν Ἀθηναίων
ἄξιον πρᾶξαι, τοῦτο εἴπω, τὸ ἐπειδὴ Θηβαῖοι
285 D. Λακεδαιμονίους ἐν Λεύκτροις κρατήσαντες ἐξελεῖν
ἐπενόουν καὶ κατελέλειπτο τὰ πράγματα ἐν τούτῳ
Λακεδαιμονίοις ὥστε δεῖν ἢ θεῶν τινα χεῖρα ὑπερέχειν, ἢ τὴν πόλιν κληρονομῆσαι τῶν ἐκείνοις
299 ὄντων κινδύνων ἐθελοντάς. καίτοι ἀφῖκτο μὲν κατ᾽
ἀρχὰς εὐθὺς κῆρυξ παρὰ τῶν Θηβαίων, ὡς ἐπ᾽ εὐ-
αγγελίοις ἐστεφανωμένος, ἧκεν δ᾽ ἡ Πελοπόννησος
ἅπασα διδοῦσα ἑαυτήν, κελεύουσα ἐπ᾽ ἀναιρέσει
τῆς Σπάρτης ἡγεῖσθαι· εἰ δὲ μή, Θηβαίοις ἠπείλουν
300 προσθήσεσθαι. οἱ δ᾽ ἐπὶ μὲν τοῖς παρὰ τοῦ κήρυκος
οὕτως ἐδάκρυσαν ὥσπερ οἰκείαν τινὰ συμφορὰν
ἀκούσαντες καὶ ἀπέπεμψαν ὥσπερ ἐκ τῶν βαρβάρων ἥκοντα, πλεῖστον δὴ δόξης ψευσθέντα· τὴν
δὲ Λακεδαιμονίων ἐρημίαν ἀντὶ τῆς Πελοποννησίων ἑκουσίου συμμαχίας καὶ τῆς φιλίας τῶν
κεκρατηκότων εἵλοντο, οὐχ ὧν ἐπεπόνθεσαν αὐτοὶ
μνημονεύσαντες, ἀλλ᾽ ἃ πείσονται Λακεδαιμόνιοι
301 περιοφθέντες αὐτῶν[1] εἶναι λῦσαι νομίσαντες. ὃ δὲ[2]

[1] codd. dett.: αὐτῶν TQVA.   [2] post δὲ add. καὶ Q, T ssc.

[a] Naxos was the scene of Chabrias' victory in 376 B.C.;
Corcyra, Iphicrates' in 373 B.C.

212

But various events of the same time occur to me, 297
as it were in a chronicle, and not only is it impossible
to narrate all of them, but not even all of the successive actions of one general. Which of these should I
omit and which should I mention? The naval battle 376.
at Naxus,ᵃ which was so great a deed? Or the
struggles at Corcyra? Or the deeds done in Thrace 373.
on behalf of what was Greek there? Or those in
Acarnania? Or those anywhere?

Or, omitting all these things, should I speak of an 298
act which I regard as the greatest, most remarkable,
and truly alone worthy of the Athenians to accomplish?—when the Thebans had defeated the Lace- 371.
daemonians at Leuctra and planned to destroy
them, and for the Lacedaemonians matters had been
left at this point, that either some God must hold
up his hand to protect them, or the city voluntarily
accept the perils which confronted them.ᵇ Yet right 299
at the start a herald had come from the Thebans,
wearing a crown as a bearer of good tidings. And all
the Peloponnesus came offering itself, and asking the
Athenians to lead them in the destruction of Sparta.
If not, they threatened that they would join the
Thebans. But they wept over the report of the 300
herald as if they had heard some personal misfortune
and they dismissed him, most thoroughly deceived
in his expectation, as if he had come from the
barbarians. They preferred the lonely condition
of the Lacedaemonians to the voluntary alliance of
the Peloponnesians and the friendship of the victors,
not remembering what they had suffered, but thinking that it was their duty to put an end to what the
Lacedaemonians would suffer if they were aban-

ᵇ *Cf.* Xenophon, *Hellenica* VI. 4. 19-20.

(285 D.)

δὴ μάλιστα ἄξιον τῆς ἐκείνων φύσεως ἀγασθῆναι
καὶ κρεῖττον ἢ κατ᾽ ἄνθρωπον ἡγήσασθαι, ἐξὸν γὰρ
ἑαυτοῖς ἀκολουθοῦντας ἔχειν Λακεδαιμονίους καὶ
286 D. κατὰ γῆν καὶ κατὰ θάλατταν, ἢ περιιδεῖν ἐπὶ κεφαλὴν ὠσθέντας, συμμάχων, περιοίκων, οἰκετῶν,
ἁπάντων ἐπανεστηκότων, ἐπὶ τοῖς ἴσοις ἐδέξαντο,
καὶ πορευομένης ὥσπερ φλογὸς τῆς Θηβαίων δυνάμεως ἐπὶ τὴν πόλιν τῶν Λακεδαιμονίων καὶ τὰ
λοιπὰ τῆς Πελοποννήσου μόνοι καὶ Ἑλλήνων καὶ
βαρβάρων προστάντες ἐκώλυσαν. ἐξ ὧν οὕτως ὑπὸ
πάντων ἑωρῶντο ὥστε καταστῆναι τὴν πόλιν συνέδριον τῆς συμμαχίας ἁπάσης.

302   Θαυμάζω τοίνυν τῶν τὰ Μηλίων καὶ Σκιωναίων
τολμώντων προφέρειν τῇ πόλει ποῦ γῆς ἢ θαλάττης
ὄντες ταῦτα κατηγοροῦσιν, πότερον ταῦτα μόνα
ἀκούσαντες τῶν πεπραγμένων τῇ κατὰ ἦθος πόλει,
ἢ ταῖς ἑαυτῶν πατρίσιν οὐκ ἂν συμβουληθέντες καὶ
ταῦτα καὶ τἆλλα ὑπάρχειν ὅσα τῇ πόλει; εἰ μὲν
γὰρ οὐ συμβούλεσθαι φήσουσιν, ἀντεπιδειξάντων
οἷς ἀγάλλονται· εἰ δ᾽ οὐκ ἂν φύγοιεν τὴν αἵρεσιν,
εἴ τις αὐτοῖς διδοίη θεῶν, παυσάσθωσαν[1] μείζοσιν
303   ἢ καθ᾽ αὑτοὺς λόγοις ἐγχειροῦντες. ἔτι τοίνυν πότε-
287 D. ρον τῆς πόλεως ἢ τῶν συμβάντων κατηγοροῦσιν· εἰ

---

[1] παυσάσθων edd.

* Cf. Xenophon, *Hellenica* VII. 1. 14.
[b] Cf. Thucydides V. 116. 4 and V. 32. Scione, won over
from Athens' empire to the Spartan side in the Peloponnesian
War in 423 B.C., was recaptured in 421. All the males were
put to death by the Athenians. In 416 B.C., when Melos

214

doned. The following conduct should be especially 301
admired in their nature and should be regarded as
better than human behaviour. For although it was
possible for them to have the Lacedaemonians as
their subordinates on land and sea, or to stand idly by
while they were overthrown headlong, since their
allies, the Perioeci, their slaves, everyone had risen
up against them, they accepted them as allies on
terms of equality *a* ; and although the power of the
Thebans, like a conflagration, was making its way
toward the city of the Lacedaemonians and the rest
of the Peloponnesus, they alone among the Greeks
and barbarians acted as their protectors and prevented it. Therefore they were so regarded by all
that the city became the headquarters of the whole
alliance.

I am amazed at those who dare to cast in the 302
city's face the affair of the Melians and the Scioni- 416, 421.
ans.*b* What part of land or sea do they inhabit,
that they make these charges ? Have they only
heard of these of all the deeds performed by the city
acting in its proper character ? Or would they not
have wished for their own countries to have accomplished these and all the other works of the city ?
For if they shall claim that they do not wish this,
then let them show in turn what they admire.
But if they could not avoid the choice, should some
God give it to them, let them stop engaging in
arguments beyond their capacity. Furthermore, 303
are they accusing the city or blaming what took
place ? For if they are accusing the city, they have

refused to join the Athenians, the island-city was attacked
and conquered by them ; they put to death all the males of
military age and enslaved the rest of the people.

(287 D.)

μὲν γὰρ τῆς πόλεως, οὐδέν, ὡς ἔοικε, τῶν μεγίστων
ἐπίστανται, ἀλλ' ἐκπέφευγεν αὐτοὺς ἀφ' ὧν ἡ πόλις γνωρίζεται· εἰ δὲ τὰ συμβάντα μέμφονται, οὐχ
ὅμοια τοῖς ἄλλοις, ὡς ἔοικεν, οἷς προείλετο ἡ πόλις
νομίζοντες οὕτω μέμφονται ὥστ' ἐξ ὧν τὸ πρᾶγμα
κακίζουσι τὴν πόλιν ἐγκωμιάζουσιν. τότε γὰρ κα-
κία καὶ πόλεως καὶ ἰδιώτου δείκνυται, ὅταν ἢ μόνα
τῳ προσῇ τὰ ὑπαίτια, ἢ πλείω τὰ φαῦλα τῶν ἐπι-
304 εικῶν ἐλέγχῃ τις ἢ μείζω· προσκείσθω γάρ. ὅταν
δὲ ἐξετάζων διὰ πάντων ἑνὸς καὶ δυοῖν λαμβάνῃ,
λέληθας ἐπαινῶν οἷς ἀφίῃς, ἄλλως τε εἰ μηδ'
ἰδιώτου ποιῇ τὴν κρίσιν, ἀλλὰ πόλεως καὶ ταύτης
πρεσβυτάτης τῶν Ἑλληνίδων καὶ ᾗ πλεῖστα ὑπάρχει
305 τὰ δέοντα συμβάντα. εἰ δὲ δεῖ καὶ περὶ τούτων
ἀποκρίνασθαι, οὐκ ἐρῶ πῶς οἱ μετὰ ταῦτα δυνηθέν-
τες προσηνέχθησαν τοῖς αὐτοῖς τούτοις πράγμασιν·
οὔτε γὰρ λυπεῖν ἔγωγε οὐδένα τῶν Ἑλλήνων
προῄρημαι, ἀλλ' ἀνεῖται τῷ γένει τῶν Ἑλλήνων ὁ
λόγος φιλοτιμία κοινή,[1] οὔτ' ἂν ἑτέρους ἐπιδείξω
δήπου μείζω καὶ δεινότερα εἰργασμένους, ἀπολογία
τοῦτ' ἐστὶν ὑπὲρ τῆς πόλεως, ἀλλ' ὁμολογία μᾶλ-
306 λον εἰς συγγνώμην καταφεύγουσα. οὐδὲν οὖν δέομαι τοιαύτης ἀπολογίας. ἀλλά μοι δοκοῦσιν ὅλως
ἠγνοηκέναι τὴν τῶν πραγμάτων φύσιν καὶ ὥσπερ
ἐξοικεῖν[2] τῆς οἰκουμένης οἱ τοὺς τοιούτους παρα-
φέροντες λόγους. πῶς γὰρ ἂν καὶ λογίζεσθαι φαίη
τις αὐτοὺς περὶ τῶν ὄντων μετρίως, ἢ πῶς ὑπὲρ
288 D. ἀρχῆς χρῆναι διαλέγεσθαι, εἰ τοῦτο πρῶτον ἠγνοή-
κασι, τὴν φύσιν αὐτῆς; ἅπασα γὰρ δήπουθεν ἀρχὴ

---

[1] κοινή TA.
[2] cf. xvii. 13 ; ἔξω οἰκεῖν ci. Aldinae.

not learned, it seems, of any of its very great accomplishments, but the reason for the city's fame has eluded them. But if they are censuring what took place, they do so because of their belief that these acts were not, as it seems, like the others, which the city chose to commit, so that they praise the city for the very reasons for which they condemn its action. For the wickedness of both city and private citizen is proved when only blameworthy actions are connected with them, or when it is shown that the evil outnumbers or is greater than the good. For this qualification should be added. But when after a 304 complete examination, you seize on one or two incidents, you have unwittingly praised it in all those matters in which you acquit it, especially if you are not judging a private citizen, but a city and the oldest Greek city at that, and one which has to its credit the largest number of proper actions. But if 305 these accusations must be answered, I shall not say how those who afterwards came into power behaved in similar circumstances. For I have chosen not to cause pain to any Greek, but my speech has been offered to the Greek race for the glory of all. Nor if I prove that others have committed greater and more terrible acts, is this a defence of the city, but rather a confession which seeks refuge in compassion. I need no such defence. But those who bring for- 306 ward such arguments seem to me to have misunderstood entirely the nature of the matter and, as it were, to live outside the civilized world. For how could it be said that they show a balanced consideration for the realities of life or that they ought to discuss empire if they have misunderstood this point to begin with, its nature ? For every empire obvi-

(288 D.)

τῶν κρειττόνων ἐστὶν καὶ παρ' αὐτὸν τὸν τῆς ἰσό-
τητος νόμον· εἰ δὲ μή, πῶς ἴσον ἢ ποῦ δίκαιον ἢ
φόρους ἐκλέγειν ἀπὸ τῆς ἀλλοτρίας, ἢ νόμους τιθέναι
τοῖς οὐδὲν δεομένοις, ἢ κρίνειν τἀκείνων, ἢ προστάττειν, ἢ πολεμεῖν, ἢ κτᾶσθαι τὰ μὴ προσήκοντα;
ὅλως γὰρ οὐδὲν τούτων ἀπὸ τοῦ ἴσου γίγνεται. ὥστ'
εἴ τις ἀκριβολογεῖται περὶ τῶν δικαίων καὶ σοφιστὴς εἶναι μᾶλλον βούλεται ἢ τῇ τῶν πραγμάτων
φύσει συγχωρεῖν, οὐκ ἂν φθάνοι διαγράφων πάσας
ἀρχάς τε καὶ δυνάμεις ἁπλῶς· ὡς ἅπαντά γε ταῦτά
307 ἐστιν ἐν τῷ θεσμῷ τοῦ κρείττονος. εἶθ' ὑπὸ σοφίας
ἄνεισι μέχρι τῶν θεῶν, ἐλέγχων, καὶ λέγων ὡς οὐδὲ
οὗτοι τοῖς ἀνθρώποις ἐξ ἴσου προσομιλοῦσιν, ἀλλ'
ᾕρηνται κρείττους εἶναι. ἀλλ' οἶμαι ταῦτ' ἐστὶν
γωνίας ἀξίων ἀνθρώπων καὶ τὸν ἥλιον οὐχ ἑωρακότων, ὃς ἀφαιρεῖται τοὺς ἄλλους ἀστέρας τὸ φαίνε-
308 σθαι. εἰ δὲ ἀναγκαῖον τὸ ἁπάσῃ δυναστείᾳ καὶ πάσῃ
περιουσίᾳ τὰ τοιαῦτα προσεῖναι, καὶ οὗτός ἐστιν
ἀρχῆς θεσμός, μὴ ἀπὸ τοῦ ἴσου πρὸς τοὺς ὑπηκόους
κρίνεσθαι, τότε νικῶν ἀπίτω τις, ὅταν δείξῃ τῶν
ἄλλων εἴτε Ἑλληνικῶν δυνάμεων εἴτε καὶ βαρβα-
ρικῶν βασιλειῶν ἡντινοῦν ἐλάττονι τῷ τῆς πλεονεξίας γιγνομένῳ χρησαμένην ἢ τὸν τῶν Ἀθηναίων
ἔστι δῆμον εὑρεῖν. φανήσεται γὰρ ἃ μὲν διαφερόντως ἐβουλεύσατο ἑνὸς ἀνδρὸς ἤθει κεχρημένος τοῦ
βελτίστου, ἃ δ' ἐγκαλοῦσίν τινες, οὐ τῇ κοινῇ φύσει
τῶν ἀνθρώπων ἐξαμαρτών, ἀλλὰ τῇ τῆς ἀρχῆς
ἀκολουθήσας ἀνάγκῃ, καὶ δυνάμει μὲν ἄρχων κατα-
289 D. στὰς τὸ ἐξ ἀρχῆς, φιλανθρωπίᾳ δὲ τὸ τῆς ἀρχῆς
218

ously belongs to the stronger and is contrary to the very law of equality. But if this is not so, how is it fair or in what way is it just to collect tribute from a foreign land, or to legislate for those who do not desire it, or to judge their affairs, or to give them orders, or to wage war, or to possess what is not properly one's own? In general, none of these circumstances is equitable. Therefore if someone is uncompromising about equal rights and prefers to be a sophist rather than to admit the nature of the matter, he would lose no time in erasing every empire and power without distinction, since they all rest on the law of the stronger. Next he will cleverly 307 proceed to the Gods, proving and arguing that not even these have an equitable association with mankind, but have chosen to be superior. But, I think, these are the arguments of men who deserve their obscure nooks and who have never beheld the sun which deprives the other stars of being seen. If it is 308 necessary for every rule and every kind of superiority to have such attributes and this is the law of empire, not to be judged on a level of equality against one's subjects, then let someone go off having won his case when he shows any of the other Greek powers or even barbarian kingdoms which made less use of the prerogatives of their advantage than the people of Athens can be found to have done. For it will be obvious that the Athenians in their remarkable decisions have behaved like a very good man, and in the matters for which some blame them, have not erred through the ordinary nature of mankind, but have followed the imperatives of empire; and in respect to power have been a ruler from the start, but in generosity, have voluntarily dispensed with

219

(289 D.)

δεδοικὼς¹ ἑκὼν μεθεὶς καὶ σχεδὸν ⟨αὐτὸς⟩² αὑτῷ
τῶν ἐγκλημάτων αἴτιος γεγονώς. πλείστῳ γὰρ τῷ
κοινῷ καὶ μετρίῳ πρὸς ἅπαντας χρησάμενος καὶ
τρόπον τινὰ τῆς πολιτείας μᾶλλον κοινωνοὺς ποιησάμενος ἢ δυναστείας νόμῳ κατέχων, ταὐτὸν τοῖς
χρηστοῖς ἔπαθεν τῶν δεσποτῶν· οὐ γὰρ διὰ τὴν
ἄλλην ἐπιείκειαν χάριτος παρ' ἐνίων ἔτυχεν, ἀλλ'
εἴ τι προσηνάγκασεν, ἐπιφανῶς ἔδοξεν βιάζεσθαι.

309 καὶ μὴν εἰ μὲν ἔχοντας τὸ τῶν ὑπηκόων σχῆμα
ταῦτ' εἰργασμένος φαίνεται, δῶμεν τοῖς ἐθέλουσιν
βλασφημεῖν· εἰ δὲ τοὺς μὲν ἀποστάντας καὶ παρ'
ἀξίαν ὑβρίσαντας εἰς αὐτόν, τοὺς δὲ ἐκ τοῦ φανεροῦ
πολεμίους ὄντας, ποτέροις ἄξιον ἐγκαλεῖν; οἶμαί
γε τοῖς τὴν ἀνάγκην παρασχοῦσιν· ἐπεὶ κἀκεῖνοί
μοι δοκοῦσιν ὥσπερ ἐνέχυρον αὐτὸ τοῦτ' ἔχοντες ἐπ-
αρθῆναι καὶ τούτῳ μάλιστα πιστεύσαντες ἁμαρτεῖν,
οὐ τῷ διὰ τέλους κρατήσειν τῆς πόλεως, ἀλλὰ τῷ
μηδ' ἂν ληφθῶσιν μηδὲν δεινὸν πείσεσθαι, ὡς Ἀθη-
310 ναίους γε πεφυκότας σῴζειν. δῆλον δέ· ἃ γὰρ περὶ
290 D. Μυτιληναίων³ μετέγνωσαν τίς ἔχει νικῆσαι πόλις οἷς
ἐξ ἀρχῆς ἐβουλεύσατο; ἐκεῖνοι γὰρ ἃ μὲν τῇ προτε-
ραίᾳ διέγνωσαν τῆς κρίσεως ἦν καὶ ὧν ἠδίκηντο, ἃ
δὲ τῇ ὑστεραίᾳ μετέγνωσαν τῆς πόλεως ἦν μόνης
311 καὶ ἡ τριήρης τὴν τριήρη κατειλήφει. θαυμάζω δὲ
εἰ τῶν μὲν ἰδιωτῶν τὴν ἔργῳ πάντες ἀπολογίαν τι-

---

¹ Phot. codd. dett. : δεδωκὸς V, δεδωκὼς TQA.
² add. Reiske.
³ schol. ad A : Μιτυληναίων mss.

ᵃ Cf. Thucydides III. 2-50. In 428 Mytilene on Lesbos
island revolted from the Athenian empire. The Athenians
subdued it in 427 B.C. and sentenced all the adult males to
death and the rest of the people to slavery. The Athenians

the terror of empire and have almost themselves been responsible for the complaints. For when they behaved most democratically and moderately toward all and in a way made everyone partners in their government rather than restraining them under the law of empire, they had the same experience as good masters. For they received no gratitude from some because of their other goodness ; but if they used any compulsion, their application of force appeared particularly noticeable. Indeed, if they 309 clearly have treated in this way those who had the guise of subjects, let us grant to whoever wishes the right to slander them. But if those who were in revolt and undeservedly committed crimes against them, and those who were open enemies, which side is culpable ? I think, the one which made this necessary ; since they seem to me to have been encouraged by possessing, as it were, this very guarantee against retaliation, and to have erred particularly through their confidence in this : not in the thought that they would permanently master the city, but that even if they were captured, they would suffer nothing terrible, since the Athenians were born to be saviours. This is clear. For what 310 original decree of any city can surpass their repentance in the matter of the Mytilenaeans ? Their decision on the day before came from an act of judgement and the crime which was committed against them. But their repentance on the following 427.¹ day came from the city alone and one trireme overtook the other.ᵃ I am amazed if everyone respects 311 the defence of private citizens when they appeal to

repented and sent a counter-order by trireme next day just in time. Only a small number of the rebels were executed.

221

μῶσιν, τῆς πόλεως δὲ οὐχ ὁρῶσιν οἱ σεμνοὶ τὰ ἔργα
δι' οἵων καὶ ὅσων ἀπολελόγηται περὶ τούτων. καὶ
ἡλίου μὲν καὶ σελήνης οὐχ ὅσα βλάπτουσιν κατη-
γοροῦμεν, ἀλλ' ὅσων ἀγαθῶν αἴτιοι γίγνονται θαυ-
μάζομεν, τὴν πόλιν δ' ἐξ ὧν ἐνίοις προσέκρουσεν,
ἀλλ' οὐκ ἐξ ὧν ἅπασιν ὡμίλησεν, οὐδ' ἐκ τῆς ὅλης
φύσεως κρινοῦμεν; οὐκ οἶμαί γε. ὥσπερ ἂν εἴ
τις[1] καὶ τῶν θεῶν κατηγοροίη τοὺς σκηπτοὺς καὶ
τὰς βροντάς, κἂν εἴ τι σεισθῇ, τὰς ὅλας καὶ κοινὰς
312 εὐεργεσίας αὐτῶν ἀμελήσας σκοπεῖν. ἡ τοίνυν
πόλις Σκιωναίους μὲν ἀνέστησεν, τοὺς δ' Ἕλληνας
ἅπαντας καὶ κοινῇ καὶ καθ' ἑκάστους ἔσωσεν, καὶ
ταῦτα μυριάκις. ἡδέως δ' ἂν πυθοίμην τῶν ῥᾳδίως
ἀξιούντων αὐτοὺς τὰ τηλικαῦτα κατηγορεῖν τίνας
τοιούτους αὐτὴν ἀναστάτους ποιῆσαί φασιν οἵους
291 D. ἀναστάτους ἐκώλυσεν γενέσθαι Θηβαίους, ἢ τίνων
τείχη καθελεῖν οἷα Κορινθίοις ἀνέστησεν, ἢ τίνας
τοιούτους ἀνελεῖν οἵους διετήρησεν Λακεδαιμονίους
καὶ τὰς μετ' ἐκείνων πόλεις, ἄλλοις τε πολλοῖς παλαιοῖς καὶ καλοῖς ἔργοις, καὶ τὰ τελευταῖα τῇ περὶ
Μαντίνειαν ἀρίστη τῶν Ἑλληνικῶν, οἶμαι δὲ καὶ
τῶν μνημονευομένων, ἱππομαχία.

313   Ὁ δ' ὡσπερεὶ κεφάλαιον τῶν χρόνων ἐκείνων
ἐστὶν καὶ ὃ πάσας τῇ πόλει καὶ τὰς ἄνω καὶ τὰς τότε
πράξεις ἐπεσφραγίσατο, Διονυσίου γὰρ τοῦ Σικελίας
μὲν τυράννου, πολλῶν δὲ καὶ τῶν ἐν Ἰταλίᾳ πόλεων ἐπάρχοντος εἰς νοῦν ἐμβαλομένου[2] ἐπιθέσθαι τῇ

---

[1] εἴ τις post θεῶν TQ.
[2] ἐμβαλλομένου codd. dett. edd.

[a] [Cf. Xenophon, Hellenica VII. 5. 16–17. This cavalry
skirmish was followed by the second great victory (that at
Leuctra in 371 B.C. was the first) won by the Theban Epaminondas over the Lacaedemonians, with whom the Athenians

some past act, but in the case of the city if these haughty men do not see the nature and number of the actions by which it has exonerated itself in this regard. And we do not accuse the sun and moon for all the harm which they do, but we are amazed at all the good which they cause. But shall we judge the city from those matters in which it offended a few people, but not from those where it maintained a friendly association with everyone, nor from its complete nature ? I think not. As if someone would blame the Gods for thunderbolts and lightning, and if an earthquake occurs, while having neglected to consider all their benefits at large. The city uprooted 312 the Scionians, but it saved all of the Greeks as a 421. group and individually, and at that countless times. I should be pleased to ask of those, who lightly undertake such great accusations, what people do they say the city uprooted comparable to the Thebans whom it prevented from being uprooted, or whose 378. walls it tore down comparable to those which it erected for the Corinthians, or what people did it 394. destroy comparable to the Lacedaemonians whom it preserved as well as the cities allied with them, in 464 etc. many other actions, ancient and fair, and finally in the cavalry battle at Mantinea,[a] which was the 362. finest of such Greek engagements, and I think, also of those anywhere recorded ?

The following event was as it were the embodi- 313 ment of those years and set a seal of approval on all of the acts of the city before and then. When Diony- sius, the tyrant of Sicily and ruler also of many cities 405–367. in Italy, took up the idea of attacking Greece which

were now allied. Epaminondas was killed in the battle, and Thebes' greatness died with him.—*E.H.W.*]

(291 D.)

Ἑλλάδι, τῷ μήκει τῶν πολέμων κεκακωμένῃ, καὶ
τοῦτο μὲν τοὺς προσοίκους τοῖς Ἕλλησι βαρβάρους
τεθεραπευκότος ἐκ πολλοῦ, τοῦτο δὲ τὸν¹ Περσῶν
βασιλέα καλοῦντος, καὶ τοῦ πράγματος ἤδη ζέοντος,
ἔσχον τὴν πεῖραν Ἀθηναίων στρατηγοὶ δύο, ὁ μὲν
τὰς ἀπὸ Σικελίας ναῦς προσπλεούσας ἁπάσας λαβὼν
αὐτοῖς ἀνδράσιν, ὁ δὲ καταναυμαχήσας Λακεδαιμονίους ἐπὶ Λευκάδι καὶ τὴν θάλατταν δι’ αὑτοῦ² ποιησάμενος. μόνη γὰρ πόλεων οὐ τύραννον ἐπηγάγετο,
οὐ πλοῦτον ἐθαύμασεν, οὐκ ἀσφάλειαν, οὐχ ἡδονὰς
ἀντὶ τῶν δικαίων ἠλλάξατο, ἀλλ’ ὥσπερ ἅπασι
πεφυκυῖα ζῆν οὕτως ἑαυτὴν ἤγαγεν. καὶ γάρ τοι
πάντες, ὅσοι τῆς τῶν³ Ἑλλήνων ἀρχῆς ἐπεθύμησαν
τῇ πόλει πολεμοῦντες διεγένοντο.

314   Καὶ Φίλιππος τοὺς μὲν ὑπερεῖδεν τῶν ἄλλων Ἑλλήνων, τοὺς δ’ ἐλπίσι καὶ δωρεαῖς αὑτῷ⁴ συμπράτ-
292 D. τειν ἔπεισεν· πρὸς δὲ τὴν πόλιν πολεμῶν ἐξ ἀρχῆς
διετέλεσεν, ὥσπερ ὅρον τινὰ ἀναγκαῖον ἐκπληρῶν.
315 ἡ δὲ ἕως μὲν ἐξήρκει, τοὺς μὲν ἐξῃρεῖτο, τοῖς δ’ ἐν
πατρίδος μοίρᾳ κατέστη, πάντων δὲ ὥσπερ μήτηρ
ὑπὲρ παίδων προὔκαμεν, μόνη δὲ τὸ σύμβολον τῆς
Ἑλλάδος διετήρησεν καὶ συνεσκίασεν τὰς κατεχού-
316 σας τότε συμφοράς. ἐπεὶ δ’ ἔκλινεν⁵ τὰ πράγματα,
οὐδὲν ἦν ἐμποδὼν Φιλίππῳ, ἀλλ’ ἐδείχθη σαφῶς ὅτι
καὶ αἱ νῖκαι τῆς πόλεως τῶν Ἑλλήνων εἰσὶ νῖκαι καὶ
τὰ τῆς πόλεως ἐναντιώματα τῶν Ἑλλήνων ἁπάν-

---

¹ τῶν VA.   ² αὑτοῦ TQA.   ³ τῶν om. A.
⁴ Ddf. : αὐτῷ TQVA.
⁵ codd. dett. : ἔκλιναν TQVA.

ᵃ Iphicrates captured all but one of the ships sent in 373 or
372 B.C. by Dionysius I, tyrant of Syracuse, to help the
Lacedaemonians against Corcyra. Timotheus had achieved
something against the Lacedaemonians in 375 B.C.

had been injured by the length of its wars, and when he had long cultivated the friendship of the barbarian neighbours of the Greeks and was appealing to the king of the Persians for help, and now the matter was at a boil, then two generals of the Athenians stopped the attempt,[a] one of them having captured all the ships, which sailed from Sicily, together with their crews, and the other having defeated the Lacedaemonians in a naval engagement at Leucas and having got control of the sea. For this was the only city which did not support tyrants, was not awestruck by wealth, or security, did not trade justice for pleasure. But it behaved as if it were born to live on behalf of all men. For everyone who desired empire over the Greeks was an enemy of the city. 373 or 372.

375.

And Philip scorned some of the other Greeks, and some he persuaded through hopes and bribes to ally themselves with him. But he was in a state of war with the city from the start, as if fulfilling an unalterable law.[b] So long as the city sufficed, it freed some of the Greeks, and for the others it became like a new country, and it toiled on behalf of all, like a mother for her children, and alone preserved what was the hallmark of Greece, and obscured the misfortunes which then prevailed. But when its power of action declined, there was nothing to impede Philip, but it was clearly shown that the city's victories were the victories of the Greeks and the city's reverses were those of all the Greeks. 314

c. 355–338.

315

316

[b] Philip II of Macedon began to spread his power in Greece c. 355 B.C., and crowned his achievements by winning hegemony over all Greece through the Battle of Chaeronea in 338 B.C.

(292 D.)

των ἐστίν. οὐ γὰρ πρότερον τῆς ἡγεμονίας ἀπέστησαν Φιλίππῳ πρὶν ἢ πόλις τὴν εἰρήνην παρεδέξατο.

317 Ἔχων δὲ πολλὰ καὶ τῶν ὕστερον εἰπεῖν καὶ μάχας
ἀτόπους καὶ τολμήματα θαυμαστὰ καὶ καρτερίας
ὑπερφυεῖς, οὐκέθ᾽ ὁρῶ τὸν καιρὸν ἀρκοῦντα. τοσοῦτον δ᾽ ἔτι προσθεὶς τοῖς περὶ τούτων λόγοις ἀπαλ-

318 λάττομαι· τέτταρας ὡς διελέσθαι γένει πολέμους ἡ
πόλις πεποίηται, τοὺς μὲν αὑτῆς[1] ἰδίους, τοὺς δὲ ὑπὲρ
τοῦ κοινοῦ τῆς Ἑλλάδος, τοὺς δ᾽ ὑπὲρ τῶν ἐν μέρει
δεηθέντων, κἂν τούτοις αὐτοῖς τοῖς δεηθεῖσιν ἔν-
εισιν ὑφ᾽ ὧν ἠδίκητο καὶ οἷς ἐγκαλεῖν εἶχεν ἐκ τῶν

319 πρόσθεν. φημὶ τοίνυν ἐγὼ τουτὶ μόνον τὸ σχῆμα
τοῦ πολέμου πάσας ὁμοῦ τὰς Ἑλληνικὰς πράξεις
ἐλέγχειν ὑστέρας οὔσας. πλείους γάρ εἰσιν οὓς ἡ
πόλις ἀγνωμονήσαντας εἰς αὐτὴν[2] ἔσωσεν ἢ ὅσοις

293 D. μᾶλλον χάριν εὖ ποιήσασιν ἀπεμνημόνευσεν, λέγω
δὴ[3] Θηβαίους ἀπὸ Λακεδαιμονίων, Κορινθίους ἀπὸ
Λακεδαιμονίων, Λακεδαιμονίους ἀπὸ Θηβαίων,
Εὐβοέας ἀπὸ Θηβαίων,[4] ὅτε διττῆς ἀρετῆς δείγματα
ἐξήνεγκεν, τοῖς μὲν τὰς πόλεις φυλάξασα καὶ τὴν
χώραν ὑφ᾽ ὧν ἀπεστέρητο τὴν[5] αὑτῆς, τοὺς δ᾽ ὡς
ἐκράτησεν ὑποσπόνδους ἀφεῖσα, αὖθις Εὐβοέας ἀπὸ
Φιλίππου, Βυζαντίους, Περινθίους, Χερρονησίτας,
Χαλκιδέας τὸ καθ᾽ αὑτήν,[6] ἑτέρους μυρίους. ἀνθ᾽ ὧν
εἰ χρῆν ὥσπερ ἰδιώτου πόλεως εἰκόνα ποιήσασθαι,

---

[1] αὑτῆς VAT ante corr.
[2] Ddf. : αὐτὴν TQVA.   [3] codd. dett. : δὲ TQVA.
[4] Εὐβ. ἀπὸ Θηβ. om. V, in mg. add. T.
[5] τῶν TQV.   [6] ἑαυτὴν TQ.

---

[a] It protected the Thebans at the battles of Haliartus
(395 B.C.) and Coronea (394 B.C.) ; the Corinthians at the
battle of Corinth (394 B.C.) ; the Lacedaemonians between

For they did not cede the command to Philip until the city accepted his peace.

Although I could speak of many later events, 317 strange battles, remarkable deeds of daring, and extraordinary acts of endurance, I see that there is no longer enough time. After adding this further point to the discussion of my subject, I am done. The city has waged four kinds of war, to define them 318 generically : its own personal wars ; wars on behalf of the general welfare of Greece ; wars on behalf of those who in particular desired aid ; and among those who desired aid are people by whom the city had been wronged and against whose former conduct it could complain. I say that this last kind of war 319 by itself proves all the actions of the Greeks combined to be inferior. For there are more people whom the city has saved after they behaved senselessly against it than all of its benefactors who were amply repaid. I mean, it saved the Thebans from 395–394. the Lacedaemonians, the Corinthians from the Lacedaemonians, the Lacedaemonians from the 369–366. Thebans, the Euboeans from the Thebans,[a] at which 357. time it gave evidence of two kinds of virtuous conduct, by preserving the cities and territory of a people by whom it had been deprived of its own, and by letting the others leave under truce when it conquered them— ; and again it saved, from Philip, the Euboeans, Byzantines, Perinthians, 343–342, Chersonesans, Chalcideans, as far as it could, and 340. countless others. In return for this, if it were fitting to erect a statue to a city as it is to a private citizen, it was proper to erect one to Athens alone

369 and 366 B.C. ; and the Euboeans in 357 B.C. For the last cf. especially Aeschines, Ctesiph. 85.

(293 D.)

τῆς Ἀθηναίων προσῆκε μόνης καὶ τιμᾶν ὥσπερ ἄ-
γαλμα κοινὸν τῆς Ἑλλάδος. ὅπερ γὰρ τῇ πόλει τὸ
πρυτανεῖον, τοῦτο ἡ πόλις πᾶσι κοινῇ γέγονεν τοῖς
Ἕλλησιν ἐν ταῖς χρείαις, τῶν τροπαίων καὶ τῶν
ἐπιγραμμάτων καλλίους ἀεὶ παρασχομένη τὰς ὑπο-
θέσεις.

320 Ὁ τοίνυν ἔξω μὲν κινδύνων πέπρακται, οὐδενὸς δ'
ἧττον ἐμφανίζει τί ποτ' ἦν τὸ τῶν Ἀθηναίων
πρᾶγμα, ἐν μὲν τοῖς ἄνω λόγοις ἡμᾶς διέφυγεν, νῦν
δ' ἴσως οὐ χεῖρον ἀποδοῦναι. γενομένων γὰρ
αὐτοῖς συνθηκῶν πρὸς Λακεδαιμονίους, ἐὰν κρατήσωσι τῶν βαρβάρων, ἀνελεῖν τοὺς μηδίσαντας,
ἐπειδὴ παρῆλθον οἱ κίνδυνοι, τῆς ἔχθρας ἐπελά-
θοντο. καὶ Λακεδαιμονίους ὡρμημένους ποιεῖν τὰ
δεδογμένα διεκώλυσαν, ὁρῶντες τῶν πόλεων τὸ
πλῆθος, αἷς ἔμελλεν ἡ Ἑλλὰς ἐλάττων γενήσεσθαι.

321 οὕτως οὐ μόνον τῷ κοινῷ γένει τῶν Ἑλλήνων, ἀλλὰ
καὶ τοῖς ἐξ ἀρχῆς ἁμαρτοῦσι καὶ εἰς αὐτὴν[1] καὶ εἰς
τοὺς Ἕλληνας ἐλυσιτέλησεν ἀεὶ δή ποτε ἡ πόλις,
καὶ ὅσα ἐνίκησεν ἀκριβῶς ὑπὲρ ἁπάντων ἐνίκησεν.

294 D.
322
Καὶ περὶ μὲν τούτων ἱκανά. ὧν δ' οὐδεὶς τὸ μέχρι
τοῦδε, ὅσα γ' ἡμεῖς σύνισμεν, ἐν ταῖς κοιναῖς
εὐφημίαις ἐμνήσθη, ταῦτα οὐ πρὶν εἰπεῖν παύσομαι.
καὶ γὰρ ὥσπερ οὐ θεμιτόν μοι φαίνεται λόγοις τὰς
πράξεις κοσμοῦντα τοῦ κατ' αὐτοὺς τοὺς λόγους
μέρους παρελθεῖν τὴν μνείαν. μόνοι γὰρ ἁπάντων
ἀνθρώπων, τὸ λεγόμενον δὴ τοῦτο, ἀναίμακτον
τρόπαιον ἐστήσατε, οὐκ ἀπὸ Βοιωτῶν οὐδ' ἀπὸ Λακεδαιμονίων οὐδὲ Κορινθίων, ἀλλ' ἀπὸ τῶν ὁμοφύλων ἁπάντων,—λέγω δὲ οὐχ ὡς ἄν τις Ἕλληνας

and to honour it as if the image belonged to Greece in common. For what the Town Hall is to the city, the city has become to all of the Greeks in common at times of need, always providing subjects of praise which are fairer than its trophies and inscriptions.

A deed of no danger, but no less revealing of the 320 conduct of the Athenians, was overlooked by us in the above discussion, and now perhaps should be presented. For although they had made an agree- 481. ment with the Lacedaemonians, that if they conquered the barbarians, they would destroy those who favoured the Persians,[a] when the danger passed, they forgot their enmity. And when the Lacedaemonians were eager to accomplish what they had agreed upon, they prevented them, since they realized the number of cities which Greece would lose. Thus the city was always of help not only to 321 the whole Greek race, but also to those who at first erred against it and the other Greeks ; and in all in which it prevailed, it prevailed without exception on behalf of all men.

And enough about these matters. But I shall not 322 stop before I discuss a subject which, as far as we know, no one has mentioned up to this time in these public recitals of praise. For it seems to me as it were improper to praise actions with speech and then to omit mentioning the topic of speech itself. You alone of mankind have erected " a bloodless trophy," as the expression goes, not by defeating the Boeotians, or Lacedaemonians, or Corinthians, but all kindred races—I do not mean in the way one would

---

[a] *Cf.* Herodotus VII. 132.

---

[1] Ddf. : αὐτὴν TQVA.

(294 D.)

προσείποι πρὸς βαρβάρους ἀντιδιαιρούμενος, ἀλλ'
ἀπὸ τοῦ κοινοῦ γένους τῶν ἀνθρώπων—καὶ νίκην
ἀνείλεσθε ἔντιμον καὶ μεγάλην κατὰ παντὸς τοῦ
χρόνου, οὐ κατὰ τὴν ἐν Τανάγρᾳ μάχην τὴν ἀμφισ-
βητήσιμον οὐδὲ μὰ Δία κατὰ τὴν ἐν Μαραθῶνι τὴν
τοσοῦτον νικῶσαν, ἀλλ' ὡς ἀληθῶς τὴν πρέπουσαν
ἀνθρώπῳ καὶ διηνεκῆ καὶ ἣν Διὸς παῖδα προσειπεῖν
εὐσεβές. ἅπασαι γὰρ αἱ πόλεις καὶ πάντα τὰ τῶν
ἀνθρώπων γένη πρὸς ὑμᾶς καὶ τὴν ὑμετέραν δίαιταν
323 καὶ φωνὴν ἀπέκλινεν. καὶ οὐ φρουραῖς ἐγκαθεστηκυί-
αις ἡ δύναμις τῆς πόλεως συνέχεται, ἀλλ' ἁπάντων
ἐξεπίτηδες τὰ ὑμέτερα[1] ᾑρημένων καὶ εἰσποιούντων
ἑαυτούς, ὡς δυνατόν, τῇ πόλει, συνευχομένων καὶ
παισὶ καὶ ἑαυτοῖς τοῦ παρ' ὑμῖν καλοῦ μεταλαβεῖν.
324 καὶ οὔτε Ἡρακλέους στῆλαι κωλύουσιν οὔτε Λιβύης
κολωνοῖς ταῦτα ὁρίζεται, οὐδ' αὖ Βοσπόρῳ καὶ[2]
ὁποτέρῳ βούλει, οὐδὲ στενοῖς Συρίας καὶ Κιλι-
κίας, ἀλλὰ πᾶσαν τὴν γῆν τύχῃ τινὶ θείᾳ ζῆλος ἐπέρχεται τῆς ὑμετέρας σοφίας καὶ συνηθείας, καὶ
ταύτην μίαν φωνὴν κοινὴν ἅπαντες τοῦ γένους ἐνό-
325 μισαν. καὶ δι' ὑμῶν ὁμόφωνος μὲν πᾶσα γέγονεν
ἡ οἰκουμένη, ἴδοις δ' ἂν καὶ τοὺς Ἡνιόχους[3] καὶ τοὺς
295 D. νομέας καὶ τοὺς ἀπὸ τῆς θαλάττης ζῶντας καὶ
πάντα ὅσα ἔθνη καὶ κατὰ πόλεις καὶ κατὰ χώρας
τῆς παρ' ὑμῶν φωνῆς ἐχομένους καὶ πειρωμένους
τῆς γῆς[4] ἀνθάπτεσθαι, καθάπερ τοὺς νεῖν ἀδυνάτους.
326 ταύτην ἐγώ φημι τὴν μαρτυρίαν, ὦ Λακεδαιμόνιοι

---

[1] codd. dett. : ἡμέτερα TQVA.   [2] καὶ om. VA.
[3] Oliver : ἡνιόχους TQVA.
[4] τῆς γῆς om. VA.

---

[a] Athena Nike was the child of Zeus.
[b] The strait at Byzantium and that leading from Lake

describe Greeks in distinction to barbarians, but the whole human race—, and you have won an honoured and great victory for all time, not like the disputed battle at Tanagra, nor by Zeus, like that at Marathon, 457. which was an outstanding success, but a victory 490. truly suited to mankind, continuous, and one which 't is an act of piety to call a child of Zeus.[a] For all the cities and all the races of mankind turned to you and your form of life, and dialect. And the power of the 323 city is not contained in the establishment of garrisons, but in the fact that all men of their own accord have chosen your ways and enrolled themselves as far as possible into the city, praying that their sons and they themselves may have a share in the beauty which is yours. And the Pillars of Heracles are no 324 barrier, nor are these ambitions limited by the hills of Africa, nor again by the Bosporus, whichever Bosporus you wish,[b] nor by the passes of Syria and Cilicia. But emulation of your wisdom and way of life has spread over every land by some divine fortune, and all men have come to believe that this is the speech of the human race. And through 325 you the whole of the inhabited world has come to speak the same tongue. One might see the Heniochi, both the herdsmen, and those who get their living from the sea,[c] and all peoples, city by city and land by land, clinging to your dialect and trying to get to your land, like those unable to swim. O Lacedae- 326 monians and all other Greeks,[d] I say that every day

Maeotis to the Pontus Euxinus were both called the Bosporus; *cf.* § 66.

[c] Such is J. H. Oliver's interpretation, *The Civilizing Power*, pp. 140-141, for the otherwise meaningless "charioteers." The Heniochi were a fierce tribe of barbarians living near the Black Sea.   [d] Perhaps attending at the Panathenaea.

(295 D.)

καὶ πάντες Ἕλληνες, καὶ παρ' ὑμῶν αὐτῶν καὶ τῶν
παρ' ὑμῖν πρώτων διαφερόντως εἰσέτι νῦν ἐφ' ἑκάστῃ ἡμέρᾳ τελεῖσθαι τῇ πόλει τῆς νίκης· οἳ τὰς μὲν
πατρίους φωνὰς ἐκλελοίπασιν καὶ καταισχυνθεῖεν ἂν
καὶ ἐν σφίσιν αὐτοῖς διαλεχθῆναι τὰ ἀρχαῖα παρόντων
μαρτύρων, πάντες δὲ ἐπὶ τήνδε ἐληλύθασιν ὥσπερ
327 ὅρον τινὰ παιδείας νομίζοντες. ταύτην ἐγὼ τὴν
μεγάλην ἀρχὴν καλῶ τὴν Ἀθηναίων, οὐ τριήρεις
διακοσίας, ἢ πλείους, οὐδ' Ἰωνίαν, οὐδ' Ἑλλήσποντον, οὐδὲ τὰ ἐπὶ Θρᾴκης, ἃ μυρίους μεταβέβληκεν
ἄρχοντας. τοσοῦτον γὰρ τὸ διάφορον τῶνδε τῶν
λόγων πρὸς ἅπαντας τοὺς ἄλλους ἐξ ἀρχῆς τε ἦν καὶ
ἔτι μᾶλλον ἐξεφάνη τῷ χρόνῳ, ὥστ' οὐ μόνον ἐκλε-
λοιπότων σχεδὸν ἤδη τῶν ἄλλων οἵδε τοσοῦτον
ἀνθοῦσιν, ἀλλὰ καὶ φήσειεν ἄν τις ἁπάσας τὰς τῶν
ἄλλων φωνὰς καὶ μὴ ὅτι βαρβάρων, ἀλλ' αὐτῶν τῶν
Ἑλλήνων τοῖς τῶν ψελλιζομένων παίδων ῥήμασιν
προσεοικέναι ὡς τῇ παρ' ὑμῶν παραβαλεῖν.[1] μέχρι
μὲν γὰρ δυοῖν καὶ τριῶν ῥημάτων κἂν ἀκούοι τις
κἂν τέρποιτο ὥσπερ ἐν παιδιᾷ, τὸ δὲ λοιπὸν κόρος
ἤδη καὶ πάντα ἐλέγχεται· μόνη δὲ ἥδε πάσαις μὲν
πανηγύρεσι, πᾶσι δὲ συλλόγοις καὶ βουλευτηρίοις
σύμμετρος, ἔτι δὲ ἅπασιν καὶ καιροῖς καὶ τόποις
ἀρκεῖ καὶ δι' ἴσου πρέπει· δύο γὰρ τὰ πρῶτα
σχεδὸν ὡς εἰπεῖν κέκτηται μόνη, σεμνότητα λέγω
328 καὶ χάριν. ἀλλὰ μὴν τοῦ γε διὰ πάντων ἀγῶνος καὶ
296 D. τόνου καὶ δρόμου καὶ κράτους τίς ἂν οἷός τ' εἴη
πλησίον ἐλθεῖν, ἑτέραν κομίζων γλῶτταν, καὶ οὐχ
ὡς ἀληθῶς παῖς ἀνδρὸς ἡττηθεὶς ἄπεισιν, ἵν' εὐπρεπῶς εἴπω; καὶ γάρ τοι πᾶσα μὲν ποίησις ἡ παρ'

this proof of the city's victory is still confirmed by you yourselves and especially by the first men among you ; they have abandoned their native dialects and would be ashamed to speak in the old way even among themselves with witnesses present. And all men have come to accept this dialect, in the belief that it is as it were a mark of education. This I call 327 the great empire of the Athenians, not two hundred triremes, or more, and not Ionia, or the Hellespont, or the regions in Thrace, which have changed their rulers countless times. For at the start so great was the difference between this form of speech and all the others—and still greater did it appear in time— that not only is this dialect flourishing while all the others have almost vanished, but also it could be said that all other dialects—to say nothing about the barbarians, but I mean of the Greeks themselves— were like the words of lisping children in comparison with yours. One would listen to the extent of two or three words and would enjoy it as it were in a game. But more brings satiety, and it is all rejected. This dialect alone is suitable for all national festivals, all assemblies and council chambers, and it also suffices and is equally appropriate for all times and places. For it was, one might say, almost the only dialect to have possessed the two first essentials of language, I mean dignity and charm. Indeed, who would be 328 able to come near the requirements of the full scale oratorical contest, its pitch, rapidity, and power, if he introduced another dialect ? And will he not go off truly a child defeated by a man, to put it mildly ? All your poetry is excellent and fully perfected,

---

¹ παραβάλλειν VA.

296 D.)

ὑμῶν ἀρίστη καὶ τελεωτάτη, καὶ ὅση σεμνότητος
καὶ ὅση χαρίτων προέστηκεν. εἰ δὲ δεῖ καὶ τῆς
Ὁμήρου μνησθῆναι, μετέχει καὶ ταύτης τῆς φιλοτιμίας ἡ πόλις, οὐ μόνον διὰ τῆς ἀποίκου πόλεως,
329 ἀλλ' ὅτι καὶ ἡ φωνὴ σαφῶς ἐνθένδε. ἅπαντες γὰρ[1]
οἱ λόγοι διὰ πάντων τῶν εἰδῶν οἱ παρ' ὑμῖν ἄριστοι
καὶ οὓς οἱ παρ' ὑμῶν ἐποίησαν, καὶ σχεδὸν οἱ διὰ
πάντων ἐν Ἕλλησι νικήσαντες ἅπαντες τῇ τῶν
Ἀθηναίων δυνάμει νενικήκασιν. εἰ δὲ δή τι καὶ τὸ
καθ' ἡμᾶς—τοῦτο νῦν ἐστι θεῶν ἵλεων ὄντων—καὶ
τοῦτ' εἰς ὑμᾶς ἀναφέρει, οὔκουν ξενίαν γε ἔστιν τῶν
λόγων καταγνῶναι· ὥσπερ γὰρ προειδυῖα ἐξ ἀρχῆς
ἡ φύσις περὶ τῆς πόλεως ὅσον τοῖς ἔργοις προέξει
τῶν ἄλλων, κατεσκευάσατο αὐτῇ πρὸς ἀξίαν τοὺς
λόγους, ἵνα αὐτή τε κοσμοῖτο ὑπὸ τῶν ἑαυτῆς
ἀγαθῶν κἄν τισι τῶν ἄλλων δέῃ, καὶ τοῦτ' ἔχοι[2]
330 μετὰ τῶν ἄλλων χαρίζεσθαι. πρότερον μὲν οὖν
τοὺς καταφεύγοντας ἐφ' ὑμᾶς τῶν Ἑλλήνων διε-
σῴζετε, νυνὶ δ' ἀτεχνῶς πάντας ἀνθρώπους καὶ
πάντα γένη τῇ καλλίστῃ τῶν εὐεργεσιῶν ἀνέχετε,
ἡγεμόνες παιδείας καὶ σοφίας ἁπάσης γιγνόμενοι
καὶ πάντας ἁπανταχοῦ καθαίροντες. τῇ μὲν γὰρ
τῶν Ἐλευσινίων τελετῇ τοῖς εἰσαφικνουμένοις ἐξηγηταὶ τῶν ἱερῶν καὶ μυσταγωγοὶ κέκλησθε, διὰ

297 D. παντὸς δὲ τοῦ χρόνου πᾶσιν ἀνθρώποις τῶν εἰς τὸ
μέσον εἰσφορῶν ἱερῶν ἐξηγηταὶ καὶ διδάσκαλοι
καθεστήκατε· ἀνθ' ὧν ἅπαντας ταῖς πρεπούσαις

---

[1] δὲ VA.   [2] Q p. corr. : ἔχει TA, ἔχῃ V.

---

[a] Tragedy and comedy.
[b] Like many others, Aristides regarded Homer as a fellow Smyrnaean, cf., e.g., xvii. 15.
[c] So I interpret τὸ καθ' ἡμᾶς, cf. xx. 23 τι καὶ τοὐμόν :

234

both that which is the patron of dignity and that which is the patron of charm.[a] If Homer's poetry must also be mentioned, the city shares in this honour not only because his city was a colony but also because his dialect clearly came from here.[b] For all of your oratory in all of its forms and that which others have written in your tradition is excellent, and almost all orators, who have been fully successful among the Greeks, have been successful through the faculty of the Athenians. If our part is also something—it is now such because the Gods are gracious—it goes back to you.[c] It is certainly not possible to condemn our oratory for falsely claiming citizen's rights. For as if nature had foreseen from the start how far in its actions the city would excel all the others, it created for it an oratory of commensurate value, so that it might be praised by means of its own advantages, and if anyone else needed this, it could bestow it along with its other gifts. Formerly you saved those Greeks who sought refuge with you. But now you sustain all mankind and every race with the fairest of benefits, becoming the leaders of all education and learning and purifying all men everywhere. For in the ceremonies of the Eleusinian mysteries you have been called the interpreters and guides of the sacred ritual for those who attend. But for all men you have always been interpreters and teachers of this sacred and public offering. Therefore you attract all men with appropriate incantations,

---

Canter also rendered it " Quodsi et nos aliquo loco habendi sumus . . . ." But Oliver translates : " And even as to this engagement of ours, if in any respect—now is a time for gods who are propitious—if in any respect this also traces its ancestry back to you, . . ."

(297 D.)

ἐπῳδαῖς ἐφέλκεσθε, οὐκ ἴυγγι ὑποκινοῦντες, ἀλλὰ
τῷ καλλίστῳ τῶν φαρμάκων, τῷ λόγῳ, ὅπερ οἱ
θεοὶ πάντων ἀντάξιον ἀνθρώπῳ μόνῳ τῶν ἄλλων
ἐδωρήσαντο. ὥστε τὰς μὲν ἄλλας πόλεις, ἃς ἕκαστοι τιμῶσι, μετὰ τὴν ἑαυτῶν φαῖεν ἂν οἶμαι
πατρίδα, ἐπὶ δὲ τῆς Ἀθηναίων ἀντέστραπται,[1] καὶ
πάντες οὐ τὴν ὑμετέραν εἴποιεν ἂν τιμᾶν μετὰ τὴν
ἑαυτῶν, ἀλλὰ τὴν ἑαυτῶν μετὰ τὴν ὑμετέραν, ὡς
ταύτην οὖσαν τὴν ὡς ἀληθῶς οἰκείαν καὶ προτέραν,
καὶ οὐδ᾽ ἂν εἷς νεμεσήσαι. ὥσπερ γὰρ τοὺς θεοὺς
καὶ πρὸ τῶν γονέων τιμᾶν νενόμισται, ὡς κοινοὺς
ὄντας ἁπάντων γονέας τε καὶ εὐεργέτας, οὕτω τὴν
κοινὴν πατρίδα τοῦ γένους πρὸ τῆς ἰδίας εὐσεβὲς
τιμᾶν.

331 Ἄξιον τοίνυν καὶ τὸ τῆς αἰδοῦς εἰπεῖν ὅσον παρὰ
πάντων ἐστί τε καὶ γέγονεν τῇδε τῇ πόλει καὶ κατὰ
πάντας ἀεὶ τοὺς χρόνους. οὐ γὰρ μόνον εὐθενούσης[2]
τῆς Ἑλλάδος ἠξιοῦτο τῶν πρωτείων, ἀλλὰ κἂν ταῖς
μεταβολαῖς οὐδεμία ἐστὶν ἥτις ἐξ ἴσου ταύτῃ γεγένηται. Φίλιππός τε γὰρ εὐτυχήσας τῇ περὶ Χαιρώ-
νειαν μάχῃ τὴν μὲν Θηβαίων πόλιν εὐθὺς φρουρᾷ
298 D. κατέλαβεν, τὴν δὲ τῶν Ἀθηναίων [εὐθὺς][3] οὐδ᾽ ἰδεῖν
ὑπέμεινεν, ἀλλ᾽ ἔστη κατὰ χώραν αἰδοῖ τοῦ κρείττονος. καὶ σιωπῶ τὸν Ἀλέξανδρον, ὡς ἀεὶ πρὸς
332 αὐτὴν ἔσχεν θεραπευτικῶς. ἥ τε νῦν ἀρχὴ[4] γῆς τε
καὶ θαλάττης, εἴη δὲ ἀθάνατος, οὐκ ἀναίνεται τὰς
Ἀθήνας μὴ οὐκ ἐν διδασκάλων καὶ τροφέων μέρει

---

[1] ἀνέστραπται VA.
[2] codd. dett.: εὐθηνούσης TQVA.
[3] secl. Reiske.
[4] ἄρχει T p. corr. QA p. corr.

---

[a] Cf. Theocritus II. The bird, attached to a revolving
wheel, served as a charm to win back errant lovers.

not moving them slightly with the charm of the wryneck,[a] but with speech, the fairest drug of all,[b] which the Gods gave to man alone of all the animals as a gift equal in value to all the rest. So each man would say, I suppose, that he honours after his own country the other cities which he respects; but the situation has been reversed in the case of Athens, and all would deny that they honour your city after their own, but rather their own after yours, since it is truly their own and takes precedence, and no one would resent this. For just as it is our custom to honour the Gods even before our parents, since they are the common parents and benefactors of all, so it is an act of piety to honour the common country of the human race before one's own.

We should also speak of how much reverence 331 everyone shows and has shown continuously at all times to this city. Not only when Greece flourished was it thought worthy of the first prize, but even in the times of change no city has been equal to this one. For after Philip had been successful in the battle at Chaeronea, he immediately occupied the city of 338. Thebes with a garrison; yet he did not even endure to visit the city of Athens, but stayed where he was out of reverence for something which was greater than ordinary. And I omit the fact that Alexander 336- was always solicitously disposed toward it. The 332 present empire of both land and sea [c]—and may it be immortal—is not unwilling to adorn Athens as a teacher and foster-father, but so great are its

---

[b] *Cf.* ii. 412 (p. 140 Ddf.), possibly from Plato, *Critias* 106 B; see also what I have noted on that similar passage of Aristides.

[c] The Roman empire is meant.

(298 D.)

κοσμεῖν, ἀλλὰ τοσαύτη τῶν τιμῶν ἐστιν ἡ περιουσία
ὥστε τοσοῦτον ἑτέρως ἡ πόλις πράττει τὰ νῦν ὅσον
οὐ πραγματεύεται. τὰ δὲ τῆς ἄλλης εὐδαιμονίας
μικροῦ δεῖν παραπλήσιά ἐστιν αὐτῇ τοῖς ἐπ᾽ ἐκείνων τῶν χρόνων, ὅτ᾽ εἶχεν τῆς Ἑλλάδος τὴν ἀρχήν,
καὶ προσόδων ἕνεκα καὶ προεδρίας καὶ τοῦ παρὰ
333 πάντων συγκεχωρηκότος. ὃ δὲ πάντων θεοφιλέστα-
τον, ὅτε μὲν γὰρ ἤνθει τὰ τῶν Ἑλλήνων, διετέλει
καὶ Ἕλληνας καὶ βαρβάρους νικῶσα, ὧν δὲ μόνων[1]
ἔδοξεν ἔλαττον ἔχειν ἐν τοῖς ὕστερον, τούτων
τοσούτῳ κάλλιον ἀπήλλαξε καὶ εὐτυχέστερον εἰς
τέλος, ὥστε τῶν μὲν αἱ πόλεις ἀπολώλασιν, ὅσαι δὲ
καὶ λοιπαί, τῷ τῆς ἀρχῆς ἄγονται νόμῳ καὶ φόροις
καὶ τοῖς ἄλλοις ἀναγκαίοις ὑποκείμεναι ὑποτελεῖς·
ἡ δ᾽ οὐ τοσοῦτον ἠλαττώθη τότ᾽ οὐδ᾽ εἰς τοσοῦτον
τοῦ χρόνου ἐξ ὅσου καὶ ὅσῳ μέχρι τοῦδε οὐ μόνον
πρὸ ἐκείνων, ἀλλὰ καὶ πρὸ τῶν ἄλλων τετίμηται.
334 δῆλον δέ· Πέλλῃ μὲν γὰρ οὐδεὶς ἂν φιλοτιμοῖτο
πατρίδι οὐδὲ Αἰγαῖς, Ἀθηναῖος δὲ οὐδείς ἐστι
299 D. Ἑλλήνων ὅστις οὐκ ἂν εὔξαιτο μᾶλλον ἢ τῆς
ὑπαρχούσης πόλεως πολίτης γεγονέναι. οὐ μόνον
δὲ τὰ τῶν ἰδιωτῶν οὕτω πρεσβεύουσι τὰς Ἀθήνας,
ἀλλὰ καὶ πόλεις αἱ μὲν ὡς ἀληθῶς ἐνθένδε καὶ παρ᾽
ὑμῶν οἰκισθεῖσαι ἥδιον ἂν ὡς ἀφ᾽ ὑμῶν[2] εἰσιν
εἴποιεν ἢ τὴν ἴσην ὑμῖν κτήσαιντο δύναμιν, αἱ δὲ
κύκλῳ περιέρχονται ζητοῦσαι τρόπον τινὰ εἰς ὑμᾶς
ἀνενεγκεῖν.
335 Ἀλλὰ μὴν πέντε μέν ἐστιν μνήμη βασιλειῶν, μὴ

---

[1] μόνον TQV.   [2] ἡμῶν TQ.

[a] The Macedonians.

honours that now the only difference in the city's condition is that it does not engage in serious affairs. But for the rest, it is almost as fortunate as in those times, when it held the empire of Greece, in respect to revenues, precedence, and the privileges conceded by all. The following is the greatest sign of all 333 of divine favour. When the power of the Greeks flourished, it was always triumphant over the Greeks and the barbarians ; and as for those to whom alone it seemed inferior in later times,[a] its end was so much fairer and more fortunate than theirs, that some of their cities have perished, and all which are left are bound by imperial law, being subject both to tribute and to other requirements ; but then its subordination was less severe and briefer than the magnitude and duration of the honours which it has received to this day, not only above them, but also above other people. And this is clear. For no one 334 would be proud to have Pella or Aegae [b] as his country ; but there is no Greek who would not wish to have been born an Athenian rather than a citizen of his own city. Not only do private citizens prefer Athens in this way, but also in the case of cities, those which have been actually founded from here and by you would rather boast that they descend from you than possess power equal to yours ; and the others go about seeking somehow to trace themselves back to you.

There is a tradition of five empires [c]—and may 335

[b] Both in Macedonia. Pella was the birth place of Alexander the Great (*cf.* or l. 49 and Behr, *op. cit.*, p. 50, n. 35) ; Aegae, also called Edessa, lay nearby, and Aristides is known to have stopped there (or. xlix. 62).

[c] The five empires : Assyria, Media, Persia, Macedonia, Rome ; *cf.* xxvi. 91.

(299 D.)

γένοιτο δὲ πλειόνων· τούτων δὲ ἐπὶ μὲν τῆς Ἀσσυ-
ρίων τῆς πρεσβυτάτης αἱ πρῶται τῆς πόλεώς εἰσιν
πράξεις, καὶ ὅσα τῶν θείων, εἰς τοῦτον ἐμπίπτει
τὸν χρόνον· ἐπὶ δὲ τῆς δευτέρας ἤρετο ἡ πόλις· τὴν
δὲ τρίτην διὰ τέλους ἐνίκησεν· ἐν δὲ τῇ τετάρτῃ
μόνη μὲν ἀντέσχεν, ἄριστα δὲ ἀπήλλαξε τῶν ἄλλων.
ἐπὶ δὲ τῆς πάντα ἀρίστης καὶ μεγίστης τῆς νυνὶ
καθεστηκυίας τὰ πρεσβεῖα παντὸς ἔχει τοῦ Ἑλ-
300 D. ληνικοῦ, καὶ πέπραγεν οὕτως ὥστε μὴ ῥᾳδίως ἄν
τινα αὐτῇ τἀρχαῖα ἀντὶ τῶν παρόντων συνεύξασθαι.

336   Γνοίη δ᾽ ἄν τις ὅσον τῇ πόλει περίεστιν ἐκ τοῦ
παντὸς αἰῶνος, εἰ τὰ ὑπάρχοντα αὐτῇ, πάντα μὲν
οὐκ ἴσως δυνατόν, μᾶλλον δὲ σαφῶς ἀδύνατον, ἀλλ᾽
ὅσα γε ἐγχωρεῖ μερίσας ἄλλο[1] ἄλλῃ πόλει καὶ χώρᾳ
προσθείς, εἶτα ἀγῶνα τῷ λόγῳ ποιήσειεν, καθάπερ
ποιητῶν ἢ χορῶν· οὐ[2] γάρ μοι δοκεῖ τὴν νικῶσαν
εὑρεῖν ἂν ῥᾳδίως· οἷον εἰ φιλοτιμοῖτο ἡ μὲν ὡς
πρώτη τεκοῦσα τὸ τῶν ἀνθρώπων γένος, ἡ δὲ ὡς
πρώτη δείξασα τοὺς καρπούς, ἡ δὲ ὡς πλείστοις
μεταδοῦσα, ἡ δέ τις ὡς νόμους καταδείξασα, ἡ δὲ
⟨ὡς⟩[3] πανηγύρεις, ἡ δ᾽ ὡς ἐν καλλίστοις κεῖται γῆς
ἅμα καὶ θαλάττης, ἡ δὲ τοῖς τῆς σοφίας ἀγαθοῖς
ἀγάλλοιτο, ἡ δὲ τὰς ἐν τοῖς πολέμοις πράξεις κατα-
λέγοι, ἄλλη δὲ ὅσους ὑπεδέξατο τῶν Ἑλλήνων, ἡ δὲ
τὰς ἀποικίας ἃς ἀπέστειλεν, ἡ δ᾽ ὅ τι καὶ δοίη τις
αὐτῇ τῶν ὑπαρχόντων τῇ πόλει, φήμ᾽ ἔγωγε μάλιστ᾽
ἂν οὕτω γενέσθαι καταφανὲς ὁπόσοις τισὶ τοῖς κρείτ-

---

[1] Phot. codd. dett. : ἄλλος TQVA.
[2] οὕτω ci. Reiske.   [3] add. codd. dett.

there be no more. Of these, the first acts of the city took place under the oldest, that of the Assyrians, and all that pertains to the Gods falls into this period. Under the second, the city grew great. It completely conquered the third. In the time of the fourth, it was the only city to resist, and its end was the best of all peoples'; and under the one at present existing, which is in every way the best and greatest, it has precedence over all the Greek race, and has fared in such a way that no one would readily wish for its old state instead of its present one.

The city's superiority in every age would be clear, 336 if its accomplishments were taken—perhaps it is not possible with all of them, moreover it is clearly impossible, but as far as can be done—and divided up and a different accomplishment was assigned to a different city and land, and an imaginary competition was held, as of poets or choruses. For it seems to me that it would not be easy to find the victorious city. For example, if one city should be proud because it first produced the human race, and another because it first taught the practice of agriculture, and another because it let most people share in it, and another one because it taught the use of laws, and another because of the national assemblies, and another because it was situated in the fairest part of both the earth and sea, and if another should glory in the advantages of its wisdom, and if another should enumerate its deeds in war, and another all of the Greeks it received in protection, and another the colonies which it sent out, and another whatever of the city's accomplishments would be attributed to it, then I say that it would be especially clear how many and how superior were the ways in which

(300 D.)

τοσιν ἡ πόλις ὑμῖν[1] τὰς ἄλλας παρελήλυθεν. ἃ γὰρ
301 D. ἐξαρκεῖ νειμαμένη τῇ Ἑλλάδι, ταῦτα μόνα συλλήβ-
337 δην ἔχει. καὶ τοίνυν ὥσπερ τοῖς ἅπασι τοσοῦτον
περίεστιν, οὕτω καὶ καθ' ἕκαστον αὖ πολλοῖς τοῖς
εἰς ταὐτὸν φέρουσιν ἀγάλλεται.

338   Οἷον τῶν μὲν θείων εὐθέως δύο μὲν τὰ πρῶτα καὶ
μέγιστα, ἥ τε ἐκ τῶν θεῶν τιμὴ καὶ ἡ περὶ τοὺς
θεοὺς σπουδή. τούτων δ' αὖ τῆς μὲν παρὰ τῶν
θεῶν τιμῆς πότερον τὰς ἐπιδημίας εἴποι[2] τις, αἷς τὸ
κοινὸν ἐτίμησαν, ἢ τὰς τροφὰς αἷς ἔθρεψαν τοὺς ἐν
τέλει καθάπερ παῖδας ἑαυτῶν; ἢ τὰς δίκας ἃς
ἐποιήσαντο; καὶ τῶν γε δικῶν αὖ πότερον[3] ἃς
πρὸς ἀλλήλους περὶ τῆς πόλεως ἐποιήσαντο, ἢ τὰς
ἐν τῇ πόλει πρὸς ἀλλήλους ὑπὲρ τῶν διαφόρων,[4]
ἢ τὰς ἀναμὶξ ἥρωσι καὶ θεοῖς ἐν θεοῖς δικασταῖς
339 ἐνταυθοῖ γενομένας; καὶ μὴν τῶν γε δωρεῶν ὡσαύτως οὐ ῥᾴδιον τὴν μεγίστην εὑρεῖν. ἁμιλλάσθω
δὲ καὶ περὶ τούτων ἄλλη πρὸς ἄλλην πόλις, ἡ μὲν
τοὺς Δήμητρος καρποὺς κομίζουσα, ἡ δὲ τοὺς τοῦ
Διονύσου, καὶ τούτους οὐ μόνον τοὺς ἀπὸ τῆς ἀμπέ-
λου, ἀλλὰ καὶ τῶν ἄλλων ἡμέρων· ἡ δὲ τρίτη λε-
340 γέτω τὴν τῆς Ἀθηνᾶς δωρεάν, καὶ ταύτην διπλῆν.
302 D. ἆρ' οὐ πολλαῖς πόλεσιν μεριζόμενα ἐξαρκεῖ τὰ ἐκ
τῶν θεῶν ἑκάστῃ φιλοτιμεῖσθαι ὡς ἐχούσῃ τὸ κάλλιστον;

341   Αὖθις τοίνυν τὰ πρὸς τοὺς θεούς, τοῦτο μὲν οἱ
νεῴ, τοῦτο δὲ αἱ δι' ἔτους θυσίαι καὶ πρόσοδοι· ὧν
τὰ μὲν παρ' ὑμῖν πρώτοις γεγένηται, τὰ δ' εἰς
ὑπερβολὴν ἔτι καὶ νῦν γίγνεται· τὰς δ' ἀρρήτους

---

[1] Ddf. : ἡμῖν TQVA.
[2] εἴπῃ TVA.
[3] codd. dett. : πότερα TQVA.
[4] Reiske : διαφορῶν TQVA.

242

your city has surpassed the others. For it alone has combined what is enough for all Greece if divided. And just as it is so superior in its collective accom- 337 plishments, so also in particular matters it takes pride in many things which pertain to the same end.

For example, in matters concerning the Gods, 338 two immediately take precedence and are most important, honour shown by the Gods and care for the Gods. And again of these two, in respect to the honour shown by the Gods, should their visits be discussed, by which they honoured the whole state, or the nurture by which they raised those in authority like their own children ? Or the law-suits which they instituted ? And again in respect to the law-suits, those which they instituted against one another concerning the city, or those in the city against one another because of private differences, or those which took place here with a combination of heroes and Gods before the Gods as judges ? In the same way, it is not 339 easy to find which is the greatest of their gifts. Let one city also compete against another concerning these: one bringing in the fruits of Demeter; another those of Dionysus, and not only those from the vine, but also from other cultivated plants ; and let the third city speak of the gift of Athena, and that too a two-fold one.[a] Are not these gifts from the Gods, even 340 when divided among many cities, sufficient for each city to feel proud as if it held the fairest one ?

Again in respect to their care for the Gods, 341 there are the temples, and the annual sacrifices and processions, some of which took place first among you, and others still take place in the most elaborate way. And who would deny that the secret cere-

---

[a] Obscure. Apparently olive oil, as food and ointment, *cf.* § 362.

(302 D.)

τελετάς, ὧν τοῖς μετασχοῦσιν καὶ μετὰ τὴν τοῦ
βίου τελευτὴν βελτίω τὰ πράγματα γίγνεσθαι δοκεῖ,
τίς οὐκ ἂν ἐξαρκεῖν φαίη πᾶσιν ἐν ἀντιθεῖναι;

342 Ἀλλὰ μὴν ἥ γε πρὸς τοὺς ἀνθρώπους ὁμιλία τίν'
ἐκπέφευγεν τρόπον εὐεργεσίας; πρῶτον μέν γε ἡ
τῶν καρπῶν μετάδοσις, ἔπειθ' ἡ τῶν τελετῶν ἑτέρα,
τρίτον ἡ κατὰ τοὺς πολέμους προστασία, τέταρτον
ἡ διὰ τῆς σοφίας ἀεὶ πᾶσι γιγνομένη καὶ εἰς τοὺς
ἰδίους οἴκους καὶ εἰς τὰ κοινὰ τῶν πόλεων ἐπικουρία.

343 τῆς τοίνυν σοφίας αὐτῆς πότερον τοὺς νόμους εἴ-
πωμεν, οἷς ἔτι νῦν οἱ πολλοὶ χρῶνται τοῖς ὑμετέροις,
ἢ τοὺς λόγους; καὶ τῶν λόγων πότερον τοὺς περὶ
τὴν ῥητορείαν, ἢ τοὺς διαλεκτικούς, ἢ τὴν ποίησιν,

303 D. ἢ τὴν ἄλλην συγγραφήν, εἰ δὲ βούλει, τί τῆς ποιή-
σεως εἶδος; ὅ τι γὰρ πρῶτον ἢ τελευταῖον εἴποις
τῆς πρώτης ἐστὶ τῇ πόλει.

344 Σκόπει δὴ καὶ τὰ τῶν πολέμων, τοῦτο μὲν τοὺς
ἰδίους ἀγῶνας, τοῦτο δὲ τοὺς ὑπὲρ τῶν ἄλλων,
αὖθις αὖ τὰ ἐν τῇ οἰκείᾳ κατορθώματα, καὶ πάλιν
γε τὰ ἐν τῇ ὑπερορίᾳ ὁμοίως Ἑλλάδι καὶ βαρβάρῳ·

345 καὶ πότερον τὴν ἀνδρείαν, ἢ τὴν φιλανθρωπίαν ἐρεῖς
τὴν ἐν αὐτοῖς τοῖς πολέμοις ἐνοῦσαν; ὥσπερ γὰρ
ἐν μιᾷ πηγῇ πάνθ' ὅσα ἂν μερίσῃς πάλιν εἰς ἄλληλα
συρρεῖ καὶ μίγνυται, εἰς μὲν τὰς εὐεργεσίας οἵ τε
πόλεμοι τῇ χρείᾳ τῶν δεηθέντων καὶ τὰ ἀπὸ τῆς
σοφίας ἀγαθά, εἰς δ' αὖ τοὺς πολέμους τά τε οἰκεῖα

346 καὶ τὰ ὑπὲρ τῶν δεηθέντων. πάλιν τοίνυν τῶν ἢ
ὑπὲρ αὐτῶν ἢ ὑπὲρ τῶν ἄλλων πολέμων πότερον τὰς
ναυμαχίας χρὴ λέγειν, ἢ τὰς πεζομαχίας, ἢ τὰς
ἱππομαχίας, ἢ τὰς τειχομαχίας; πάντα γὰρ ταῦτα

monies, whose followers believe in a better life after
death, are sufficient by themselves to weigh against
everything ?

Well now, what sort of benefit has it neglected in 342
its relation with mankind ? First of all there is the
sharing of the crops, and next another sharing, that
of the ceremonies ; third, its protection in times of
war ; fourth, its continual assistance both to private
houses and to the corporate bodies of the cities,
given to all through knowledge. Then in the 343
matter of knowledge itself, are we to speak of your
laws, which many men still use, or of your literature ?
And in the matter of literature, are we to speak of
oratory, or philosophy, or poetry, or some other form
of composition ? And if you wish, what kind of
poetry ? For whatever you would mention first, or
last, belongs in the highest degree to the city.

Consider also matters of warfare, the city's 344
personal struggles, and those in defence of others ;
and again the successes at home and further those
abroad, both in Greek and barbarian territory.
And will you speak of the courage or the generosity 345
which is inherent in the wars themselves ? For just as
all the segments of a single spring, no matter how
many the parts into which you divide it, flow back to
one another and are combined, so the wars fought
through the need of those who asked for help and
the advantages deriving from knowledge combine
with the city's benefactions, and the city's activity
on behalf of itself as well as those who asked for
help combine with the wars. Again in the matter 346
of wars either in defence of themselves or others,
should we speak of the naval battles, or land battles,
or cavalry battles, or sieges ? For the city was

(303 D.)

κρατίστη ἡ πόλις. εἰ δ' αὖ βούλει, τί τῶν ἐν τῇ
θαλάττῃ μέγιστον αὐτῆς, ἢ τί τῶν κατ' ἤπειρον;
347 τρεῖς δ' οὖν ὅροι ταύτῃ κείσθων, οἷς εἰ[1] μὴ ἑαυτήν, ἀλλὰ τούς γε ἄλλους ἀναμφισβητήτως ὑπερ-
βέβληκεν· πεζομαχία μὲν ἡ Μαραθῶνι, ναυμαχία
δὲ ἡ ἐν Σαλαμῖνι, ἱππομαχία δέ, ἀπορῶ μὲν ἥντινα
κρινῶ, ἔστω δὲ ἡ ἐν Μαντινείᾳ· τειχομαχίας μὲν
348 γὰρ οὐδ' ἠμφισβήτησεν οὐδεὶς πώποτε. καὶ τοίνυν
πότερον τῷ πλήθει τῶν τροπαίων, ἢ τῷ μεγέθει τῶν
304 D. ἔργων θησόμεθα; ἢ πῶς τὴν ἀξίαν ἀποδώσομεν;
οὕτω καὶ διὰ πάντων καὶ δι' ἑκάστου πολλαχῶς νικᾷ.
καὶ γὰρ ἀγῶνας πλείστους καὶ μεγίστους καὶ ὑπὲρ
καλλίστων ἐποιήσατο, καὶ τρόπαια πλεῖστα καὶ
κάλλιστα ἐκ τῶν Ἀθηνῶν, καὶ λόγοι πλεῖστοι καὶ
κάλλιστοι καὶ διὰ πάντων ὑπερέχοντες οἱ τῆσδε
τῆς πόλεως· προσθήσω δὲ καὶ παρὰ τῆσδε καὶ
στρατηγοὶ σοφώτατοι καὶ ὀξύτατοι καὶ ἀσφαλέ-
στατοι καὶ δικαιότατοι καὶ πλείους ἢ σύμπαντες
οἱ τῶν Ἑλλήνων.

349 Ἵνα δὲ εἴπω κεφάλαιον, τρισὶ τούτοις ὁ τῶν
ἀνθρώπων βίος πληροῦται, τῇ τῶν ἀναγκαίων εὐπο-
ρίᾳ, τοῖς τῆς παιδείας καλοῖς, τῇ τῶν πρὸς τὸν
πόλεμον κατασκευῇ· δυοῖν γὰρ ὄντοιν καιροῖν,[2]
εἰρήνης καὶ πολέμου, τὸ μὲν ἀμφοῖν κοινόν ἐστι, τὸ
δὲ τῷ τῆς εἰρήνης ἀνεῖται καιρῷ, τὸ δὲ ἀμύνεσθαι
350 δυνατοὺς εἶναι ποιεῖ περὶ τῶν ὑπαρχόντων. τούτων
τοίνυν ἔστω μὲν ὅ τί τις βούλεται μέγιστον· τριῶν
δ' εἶναι πόλεων δεδόσθω πάντα,[3] ἑκάστῃ ἕκαστον·
φημὶ τοίνυν ἐγὼ καθ' ἣν ἄν τις αὐτῶν κρίνῃ, τῆς

---

[1] εἰ om. TQA.   [2] codd. dett. : καιρῶν TQVA.
[3] ταῦτα codd. dett. (prob. Ddf.).

best in all these respects. Again if you wish, what
was its greatest action at sea or what on land?
Let three landmarks be established in this matter, 347
in which if the city has not surpassed itself, still it has
indisputably surpassed all other people : as land
battle, that at Marathon ; as naval battle, that at 490.
Salamis ; and as cavalry battle—I do not know 480.
which to select—, but let it be that at Mantinea. 362
For in the matter of sieges, no one ever disputed its
preeminence. And then shall we prefer the multi- 348
tude of its trophies or the magnitude of its accomplishments ? Or how shall we give it its due ? Thus
both in general and particular it is superior in many
ways. It undertook the largest number and the
greatest struggles for the sake of the fairest purposes ; and the largest number and the fairest
trophies came from Athens ; and the largest number,
the fairest and in every way most excellent exhortations [a] were made by this city ; and I shall add, the
wisest, cleverest, soundest, and most just generals
also are from this city, and there are more of them
than all those of the other Greeks put together.

To sum up, the life of man is fulfilled by these three 349
activities : possession of the necessities ; culture ;
and the acquirement of the means for war. In the
two diverse occasions of peace and war, the first
activity has a part in both ; the second has been left
to the time of peace ; and the third makes men
able to defend their possessions. Then let any one of 350
these three be the most important and let it be
assumed that all these activities are found in three
cities, one in each. I say that whichever city one

---

[a] This interpretation of λόγοι seems confirmed by its use in
§ 394. Oliver renders " traditions."

(304 D.)

πόλεως εἶναι τὸ νικᾶν. πάντα γὰρ αὕτη δείξασα
καὶ πάντων ἐπὶ πλεῖστον προελθοῦσα φανήσεται·
οὕτω πᾶσι τοῖς κριταῖς νικᾷ καὶ πρός γε ἔτι ταῖς
χώραις ἁπάσαις· ὥστ' οὐκ ἄν τις ὀκνήσειεν εἰπεῖν
ὅτι χρὴ καὶ πρώτην καὶ δευτέραν καὶ τρίτην αὐτὴν
ἐν τοῖς Ἕλλησι κηρύττειν, ὥσπερ ἐν ἅρμασιν, εἰ
δὴ καὶ ἅρμα γε ἀπὸ τῶν Ἀθηνῶν τὸ ἀρχαῖον, οὐκ
305 Ð. ἀπὸ τῆς Σικελίας. εἶεν. ἀλλὰ ταῦτα μὲν τοιαῦτα.
351 Τὰ δ' αὖ τοῦ μεγέθους καὶ τῆς ἄλλης κατασκευῆς
τίς οὐκ ἂν[1] ἄξια τῆς ὅλης τύχης εἴποι καὶ τοῦ
μεγάλου τῶν Ἀθηναίων ὀνόματος; τοῦτο μὲν
αὐτὸν τὸν κύκλον τοῦ ἄστεος, μέγιστον μὲν τῶν
Ἑλληνικῶν, κάλλιστον δὲ τῶν πανταχοῦ. καὶ
σιωπῶ τείχη καθήκοντά ποτε ἐπὶ θάλατταν, ἡμε-
ρησίας ὁδοῦ μῆκος τὰ σύμπαντα, καὶ πρὸς τῇ
θαλάττῃ κύκλους ἑτέρους ἀντιστρόφους τῶν περὶ
τὴν πόλιν. ἀλλὰ τοὺς δήμους πάρεστιν δήπου
θεωρεῖν, ὧν ἔνιοι λαμπρότερον τῶν ἀλλαχοῦ πόλεων
εἰσιν κατεσκευασμένοι, καὶ πάντα δὴ τὸν κόσμον
καὶ τὸν παρὰ τῆς φύσεως καὶ τὸν παρὰ τῆς τέχνης
352 ἐφάμιλλον κἂν τῇ πόλει κἂν τῇ χώρᾳ. τῶν μὲν
αὐτοφυῶν, ἀήρ τε οὗτος ἐξαίρετος τοῦ πολλοῦ καὶ
λιμένες τοσοῦτοι, ὧν εἷς ἕκαστος ἀντάξιος πολλῶν.
ἔτι δ' αὐτῆς τῆς ἀκροπόλεως ἡ θέσις καὶ τὸ ὥσπερ
353 αὔρας εὔχαρι προσβάλλον πανταχοῦ. ὃ δὲ καὶ ἐν
αὐτοῖς τούτοις ἄξιον ἐπισημήνασθαι, ταῖς μὲν γὰρ
ἄλλαις πόλεσιν, ὅπως ἂν ἔχωσι τοῦ οὐρανοῦ, τῆς γε
αὐτῶν[2] χώρας ἐπιεικῶς ἡττᾶσθαι συμβέβηκεν, τοῦ

---

[1] ἂν οὐκ TQV Phot.   [2] edd. : αὐτῶν TQVA.

---

[a] [Athens had walls as follows : (i) a wall right round the
city itself ; (ii) a wall right round its harbour-town Piraeus
(3 miles to the S.W.) ; (iii) two straight parallel walls, joining

prefers, your city emerges the victor. For this city clearly will have taught all these activities and have made the farthest progress in all of them. Thus it wins by the votes of all the judges, and in addition it takes all three places, so that there would be no hesitation in saying that it should be heralded before the Greeks, as first, second, and third, just as in the chariot races—since the chariot originated in Athens, not Sicily. However, so much for this.

Again as to the city's magnitude and other adorn- 351 ment, who would not say that they were worthy of the general fortune and great name of the Athenian people? So the very circuit of the city is the greatest in Greece and the fairest anywhere. And I will not mention the walls which once descended to the sea, the length of a day's journey all told, and at the sea another set of walls in a circle to answer those about the city.[a] We can consider the country hamlets, some of which have been adorned more gloriously than cities elsewhere, and all the beauty, both natural and artificial beauty, vying with each other in the city and the country-side. In respect to 352 natural phenomena, the climate here is exceptional, and the harbours so great that each one of them has the capacity of many. Furthermore, there is the site of the Acropolis itself, and the pleasantness, as it were from a gentle breeze, which strikes one everywhere. And the following among these features 353 should also be noted. For it has befallen to other cities, whatever their general climate, to have a somewhat worse one than their countrysides; but

Athens and Piraeus, the northern built in 458 the other in 445 ; and another wall running S.S.W. to Phalerum in 468 or 467.—E.H.W.]

249

(305 D.)

δὲ τῆς πάσης Ἀττικῆς ἀέρος οὕτως ἔχοντος ἄριστος
καὶ καθαρώτατός ἐστιν ὁ τῆς πόλεως ὑπερέχων.
γνοίης δ᾽ ἂν αὐτὴν ἐπὶ τῇ πόρρωθεν ὥσπερ αὐγῇ[1]
τῷ ὑπὲρ κεφαλῆς[2] ἀέρι.

354   Καὶ τὰ μὲν παρὰ τῆς φύσεως τοιαῦτα, πολλὰ τῶν
306 D. ὄντων ἀφελόντι. τῶν δ᾽ αὖ τῆς τέχνης τί χρὴ
μέγιστον θεῖναι ἢ τί πρῶτον εἰπεῖν; νεώ τε γὰρ
ἐνταῦθα οἱ αὐτοὶ μέγιστοι καὶ κάλλιστοι τῶν πάντα-
χοῦ, καὶ ἀγάλματα ἄνευ τῶν οὐρανίων τῆς πρώτης
τέχνης τὰ πρῶτα, καὶ παλαιὰ καὶ καινά· πρὸς δὲ
τούτοις βιβλίων ταμιεῖα οἷα οὐχ ἑτέρωθι γῆς
φανερῶς,[3] καὶ μάλα τῶν Ἀθηνῶν κόσμος οἰκεῖος,
καὶ οἷα δὴ τῆς παρούσης ἐξουσίας καὶ διαίτης,
λουτρά τε σεμνότητι καὶ τρυφῇ νικῶντα καὶ δρόμοι
καὶ γυμνάσια· ὥστε εἴ τις τῆς πόλεως περιέλοι
τοὺς Ἐριχθονίους, τοὺς Κέκροπας, τὰ μυθώδη, τὰ
τῶν καρπῶν, τὰ τρόπαια τὰ ἐν τῇ γῇ καὶ τῇ θαλάττῃ,
τοὺς λόγους, τοὺς ἄνδρας, πάντα δι᾽ ὧν τὸν αἰῶνα
διεξελήλυθεν, σκοποῖτο δ᾽ αὐτήν, ὥσπερ τὰς νῦν
φρονούσας ἐφ᾽ αὑταῖς, ἐξαρκεῖν αὐτὴν τοῖς ὁρωμένοις νικᾶν.

355   Καὶ μὴν τὰ μὲν ἔσχηκεν, τὰ δὲ ἔχει, καὶ οὔτε οἷς
ὑπερεῖχεν ἀφῄρηται τὴν μνήμην οὔτ᾽ αὖ τῆς παρούσης εὐδαιμονίας ἀπολέλειπται, εἴ τῳ καὶ τούτων
φίλον μεμνῆσθαι, ἀλλὰ μόνη δὴ πόλεων τὰ μὲν
307 D. παλαιὰ τοῖς παλαιοῖς νικᾷ, τὰ δὲ καινὰ τοῖς καινοῖς,
εἰ δὲ βούλει, τὰ μὲν παλαιὰ τοῖς καινοῖς, τὰ δὲ
καινὰ τοῖς παλαιοῖς, τοῖς ἑαυτῆς λέγω τὰ τῶν

---

[1] ὡς περιαυγῇ ci. Wordsworth, Athens and Attica, I, 244.
[2] κεφαλὴν TQ.
[3] codd. dett. : φανερᾶς TQVA.

although the air of all of Attica is perfect, that over the city is the best and purest. You could recognize the city at a distance by the air overhead, which is like a crown of light.

And such are the natural phenomena, and I omit 354 most of these. Again in the matter of art, what should we judge greatest or speak of first ? For the temples here are both the greatest and the fairest of those anywhere, and the statues, apart from those which fell from heaven, hold the highest place in the highest form of art, both the ancient and modern ones. Besides, the libraries are such as clearly nowhere else on earth, and are a particularly proper ornament for Athens; and characteristic of its present power and way of life are the baths, stadiums, and gymnasiums which are surpassingly decorous and luxurious ; so that if one should strip from the city the Erichthonii and the Cecropes, the mythical element, and the sharing of the crops, and the trophies on land and sea, the literature, and the men, and all the events of its history, and would consider it like those cities which are now proud of themselves, it is quite capable of taking first place by means of its appearance.

Indeed, some features it had in the past, and 355 others it has now ; and neither has it been deprived of the memory of its former excellence, nor again has it been wanting in the present felicity, if someone wishes to mention these points too. Alone of cities, it surpasses the ancient deeds of others by its own ancient deeds and the modern deeds of others by its own modern deeds, and if you wish, it surpasses ancient deeds by modern deeds and modern deeds by ancient deeds, I mean those of others by its own.

(307 D.)

356 ἄλλων. κατίδοι δ' ἄν τις κἀκεῖθεν τὰς ὑπερβολὰς
αὐτῆς· ὅσοι γὰρ καὶ μικροῦ τινος μέρους τῇ πόλει
κεκοινωνήκασιν, ὡς ἄριστοι τῶν ἄλλων ἀγάλλον-
ται· ἡ δ' οὐδεμιᾶς μὲν φιλοτιμίας ὑστερεῖ τῶν οἰστισινοῦν ὑπαρχουσῶν,[1] τῶν δὲ ἑαυτῆς οὐδένα κοινω-

357 νὸν ἔχει διὰ τέλους· οἷον Ἀργεῖοι παλαιότατοι τῶν
Ἑλλήνων ἀξιοῦσιν εἶναι, οὐκοῦν καὶ ἡ τῶν Ἀθηναίων πόλις· καὶ ὅλως οὐχ ὅμοια ⟨τὰ⟩[2] τῶν Ἀργείων παλαιὰ τοῖς τῶν Ἀθηναίων οὐδ' ἂν εἷς φήσαι

358 δικαστὴς κοινός. Ἀρκάδες αὐτόχθονες, μετά γε
Ἀθηναίους, καὶ τοῖς δευτέροις αὖ νικῶνται τῇ τῶν
καρπῶν εὑρέσει καὶ δόσει. δῆλον δ' ἐκ τῶν
ἐνταῦθα φερόντων Ἑλλήνων τὰς ἀπαρχάς, ἀλλ' οὐκ

359 ἐκεῖσε. ἄριστοι Λακεδαιμόνιοι τὰ πρὸς τὸν πόλεμον,
ἀλλὰ καὶ ἡ τῶν Ἀθηναίων πόλις· καὶ τά γε δεύτερα

360 ἐκείνοις ἐν φιλοτιμίᾳ καθέστηκεν. ἔχει ταῖς Θήβαις
χάριν καὶ τιμὴν ἡ τῶν θεῶν γένεσις· τούτων τοίνυν
ὁ μὲν ἐν τῇ Ἀττικῇ τὴν δωρεὰν ἔφηνεν, τὸν δὲ
πρῶτοι τῶν Ἑλλήνων Ἀθηναῖοι θεὸν ἤγαγον,
χωρὶς τῶν διὰ Θησέως πρὸς αὐτὸν κοινωνιῶν.
ἀλλὰ καὶ τῆς τελευταίας Θηβαίων ῥώμης ἅπαντες
μέμνηνται, ταύτης ἡ πόλις αἰτία, καὶ ὅτε ἔδει τἀναν-

361 τία πράττειν, οὐκ ἔδεισεν. ἐπαινεῖν ἄν τις ἔχοι
Κορινθίους δικαιοσύνης ἕνεκα· ἡ τοίνυν πόλις οὐ

308 D. βεβούλητα μόνον τὰ δίκαια, ἀλλὰ καὶ βραβεύουσα

362 τοῖς ἄλλοις διαγέγονεν. ἐνδοξότατοι πάντων οἱ
κατὰ τὴν Ἑλλάδα ἀγῶνες· καὶ μὴν τούτων πρεσβύτατος ὁ τῶν Παναθηναίων, εἰ δὲ βούλει, ὁ τῶν
Ἐλευσινίων. ἔπειτα καὶ πάντας αὐτοὺς ἡ τῆς
πόλεως δωρεὰ συγκροτεῖ, λέγω γὰρ οὖν τῆς πόλεως

---

[1] ὑπαρχόντων codd. dett.   [2] add. codd. dett.

Its superiority is also clear from the following. 356
For all who share with the city even in a small part
of its attributes, pride themselves as being best of all
other people. But the city can match the glory of
any people ; yet no one fully shares in its own. For 357
example, the Argives think that they are the most
ancient of the Greeks. So does the city of Athens.
And the ancient history of the Argives is not in any
way equal to that of the Athenians, nor would any
impartial judge say so. The Arcadians are sprung 358
from the soil, but after the Athenians, and again are
worsted in the second round, the discovery and
sharing of agriculture. This is clear from the fact
that the Greeks bring their first fruits here and not
there. Well, the Lacedaemonians are very good in 359
warfare ; but so also is the city of Athens. And
in the matter of glory, the former take second place.
The birth of certain Gods brings grace and honour to 360
Thebes. Then of these Gods, one revealed his gift in
Attica ; and the Athenians were the first Greeks to
regard the other as a God,[a] apart from the ventures
which they shared with him through Theseus. Also
everyone remembers the final strength of Thebes ;
the city was the cause of this, and when opposition
was necessary, it was not afraid. The Corinthians 361
could be praised because of their justice.[b] Your city
has not only desired justice, but also has always acted
as an arbitrator for others. The games in Greece 362
are the most famous of all. And of these, the oldest
is that of the Panathenaea, and if you wish, that of
the Eleusinia. The gift of the city also forges
them all together, I mean the city's gift from

---

[a] Dionysus and Heracles.
[b] Cf. xlvi. 27.

ARISTIDES

363 τὴν παρὰ τῆς Ἀθηνᾶς. Σαμοθρᾷκες ἀγάλλονται
τοῖς ἱεροῖς, καὶ ταῦτα πάντων ὀνομαστότατά ἐστιν,
πλὴν τῶν Ἐλευσινίων· ἀλλὰ καὶ Δῆλος ἀνεῖται τοῖς
θεοῖς· ἡ δέ ἐστι τῆς πόλεως. τὸ δὲ δὴ καὶ τὴν εἰς
Δελφοὺς ὁδὸν ἔργον εἶναι τῆς πόλεως καὶ τὴν θεωρίαν τὴν Πυθιάδα Ἀθηναίων μόνων πάτριον τί ἂν
εἴποις ἢ τῶν θεῶν ἅπαντα ταῦτ' εἶναι, βουλομέ-
νων πανταχῇ τὰς Ἀθήνας πρεσβεύειν καὶ πᾶσιν ὥσ-
364 περ χεῖρα τοῖς καλοῖς ἐπιβάλλειν τὴν πόλιν; ἔτι
τοίνυν εἰσὶν αἱ τῶν κατὰ τὴν Ἀσίαν πόλεων μεγέθει
νεῶν φιλοτιμοῦνται, αἱ δὲ κατασκευῇ λουτρῶν τῆς
χρείας κρείττονι· καὶ ταῦτ' ἐστὶ παρὰ τῇ πόλει
πρὸς ὑπερβολήν, καθάπερ πρῴην συνῳκισμένῃ. καὶ
τὸ κάλλιστον· ἃ γὰρ τοῖς ἄλλοις ἐν ἀγάλμασι δεῖξαι
309 D. σπουδὴν ἔχει, τούτων ὑμεῖς τοὺς νεὼς καὶ τὰ θέα-
τρα κέκτησθε. ἀγάλματα θαυμάζεται καὶ τούτων
πρῶτον εἶναι κρατεῖ τὸ παρ' ὑμῖν[1] ἐν τῇ πόλει,
χωρὶς τοῦ καὶ τὰ ἄλλα πανταχοῦ κάλλιστα προσήκειν τρόπον δή τινα τῇ πόλει. ἁπάντων γάρ, ὡς
ἔοικεν, τῶν ἀρίστων αὕτη πατρὶς καὶ σοφίας πάσης
καὶ τέχνης ἡγεμών, ὥστε οὐ μόνον τοῖς ἀγάλμασιν,
ἀλλὰ καὶ τοῖς ἀγαλματοποιοῖς αὐτοῖς περίεστιν.
365 Ἀλλὰ μὴν ἑπτά γε ἀνδρῶν, ἵνα μηδὲ τοῦτο
παρῶμεν, ἐνδόξων ἐπὶ σοφίᾳ γενομένων, εἷς ἀπὸ
τῆς πόλεως γέγονε, καὶ δυοῖν ἀρίστοιν νομοθέταιν
366 ἅτερος αὐτὸς οὗτος. δύο τοίνυν ἀνδράσι τῶν πρόσθεν ἐκ θεῶν ψῆφον δεδόσθαι παρειλήφαμεν, Λυ-
κούργῳ τε τῷ Λακεδαιμονίῳ καὶ Σωκράτει τῷ
παρ' ὑμῶν· ὥστε καὶ τῆς ἐπὶ τοῖς κοινοῖς[2] καὶ τῆς

---

[1] codd. dett. : ἡμῖν TQVA.
[2] κοινοῖς VAT a. corr.

[a] The olive ; and all athletes rubbed themselves with oil.

254

Athena.[a] The Samothracians are proud of their 363
sacred ceremonies, and these are the most famous of
all except for the Eleusinia. Well, Delos has been
dedicated to the Gods ; but it belongs to the city.
What would you say of the fact that the road to
Delphi is the work of the city and that the Pythian
Mission is native only to the Athenians, except that
all this comes from the Gods who wish in every way
to honour Athens and for the city to have a hand as
it were in all fair things ? Further, some of the cities 364
in Asia take pride in the greatness of their temples,
others in the construction of baths which is greater
than necessary. And the city has these things in
abundance, as if it had been recently settled. And
the fairest of all is that what others think a serious
matter to have portrayed in statues, you possess
temples and theatres to these. There are admired
statues, and that one of yours in the city is the best
and first of these,[b] apart from the fact that all those
which are the fairest everywhere in a certain way
belong to the city.[c] For this, as it seems, is the
home of everything which is best, and the leader of
all knowledge and art, so that it is not only superior in
statues, but also in statuaries themselves.

Of the seven men—so that we may not even omit 365
this—who were famous for wisdom, one came from
the city ; and one of the two best lawgivers was this
self-same man.[d] Then we have a tradition that Gods 366
approved of two men of old, Lycurgus the Lacedae-   [885];
monian and Socrates, who is one of your citizens ;   C. 469–
so that the city shares in the honours for both ordin-   399.

---

[b] The Athena of Phidias.
[c] Because of its marble quarries ; cf. § 21.
[d] Solon. The other lawgiver was Lycurgus of Sparta.

(309 D.)

ἐπὶ τοῖς ἄκροις φιλοτιμίας μετέχειν τὴν πόλιν καὶ
μηδὲν εἶναι τῶν ὀνομαστῶν ὅτῳ μὴ ⟨τὸ⟩[1] τῶν
367 Ἀθηνῶν ὄνομα ἐπιφημίζεται. εἰ τοίνυν τις ἐρωτῴη
ποῖον τῶν ἐν τοῖς Ἕλλησι δικαστηρίων ἐντιμότατον
310 D. καὶ ἁγιώτατον, τὸ ἐν Ἀρείῳ πάγῳ πάντες ἂν φή-
368 σαιεν. ἤθεσιν[2] δὲ τίνες κοινοτάτοις καὶ δημοτικω-
τάτοις ἐχρήσαντο; ἡ τῶν Ἀθηναίων πόλις ὁμοίως
Ἀθηναίοις τε καὶ πᾶσιν ἀναγκαῖον εἰπεῖν, εἰ τἀληθῆ
λέγειν ἐθέλοιεν. καὶ τὸ μὲν διὰ πάντων ἀπο-
δεικνύναι συχνοῦ καὶ λόγου καὶ χρόνου, μόνοι δ᾽
ἁπάντων ἀνθρώπων τρία ταῦτα ἐνομίσατε· τῶν
μὲν ὑπὲρ τῆς πόλεως τελευτησάντων αὐτῶν μὲν
ἐπαίνους ἐπὶ ταῖς ταφαῖς καθ᾽ ἕκαστον ἔτος λέγειν,
τοὺς δὲ παῖδας δημοσίᾳ τρέφειν ἄχρι[3] ἥβης, καὶ
τηνικαῦτα ἀποπέμπειν ἐπὶ τοὺς πατρῴους οἴκους
μετὰ τῶν πανοπλιῶν· τοὺς δ᾽ ἀδυνάτους τῶν πολιτῶν
δημοσίᾳ τρέφειν. ὥστε καὶ τὴν δύναμιν καὶ τὴν ἀ-
δυναμίαν τιμῶντες ἐδείξατε ὡς ἑκάτερον προσῆκεν.
369 ψηφίσματα τοίνυν πόθεν ἢ λαμπρότερα ἢ φιλανθρω-
πότερα; ὧν ἃ μὲν ἐν τοῖς εἰρημένοις ἐστὶν παραλείπω, ἓν δ᾽ ὡσπερεὶ δείγματος χάριν ἔστω μοι
κατὰ παντὸς τοῦ περὶ ταῦτα λόγου, τὸ κατ᾽ Ἀρθ-
μίου τοῦ Ζελείτου νικῆσαν· ὅν, ἐπεὶ τῷ βασιλεῖ
διακονῶν χρυσίον ἤγαγεν εἰς Πελοπόννησον, πολέ-
μιον τοῦ δήμου τοῦ[4] Ἀθηναίων ἐψηφίσαντο αὐτὸν
καὶ γένος καὶ ἀτίμους. καίτοι μόνου τούτου πάνθ᾽
370 ὁμοῦ τὰ τῶν ἄλλων ἀπολείπεται. πρεσβείας τοίνυν
πλείστας μὲν ἐδέξατο, πλείστας δὲ ἐξέπεμψεν. καὶ
τοῦτο εἰ μὲν ὅλως ὁμολογεῖται· εἰ δὲ μή, τῇ προσθήκῃ μεῖζον γίγνεται, πλείστας γὰρ ὑπὲρ τῶν

---

[1] add. codd. dett.   [2] ἔθεσιν VA.
[3] ἄχρις TQ.   [4] τῶν TQ.

ary and superior things and there is nothing of
importance to which the name of Athens is not
attached. Then if someone would ask which of the 367
courts among the Greeks was the most revered and
holy, all would say the Areopagus. And who be- 368
haved in the most public spirited and popular
fashion ? 'The city of Athens,' it is equally necessary for Athenians and all men to say, if they should
wish to speak the truth. And to prove this fully
needs much argument and time. But alone of all
men you have followed these three practices :
praising at their graves each year those who died in
behalf of the city ; publicly raising their children to
the time of manhood, and then sending them to their
fathers' houses with a suit of armour ; and publicly
maintaining those citzens unable to care for themselves, so that you have shown that you honour
strength and weakness in a way that is fitting for
each. Where are to be found more glorious or 369
generous decrees ? I omit those which are included
in what has been said. But let one, as it were for the
sake of proof, answer for the whole discussion on this
subject, that which was passed against Arthmius
of Zelea.[a] When in the service of the king, he
brought gold to the Peloponnesus, they decreed him a
public enemy of the Athenian people, himself and
his family, who were both disfranchised. Yet all the
decrees of the other Greeks taken together are less
than this one alone. The city received the largest 370
number of embassies, and sent out the largest
number. And let this bare statement stand if you
wish. But if not, it becomes a greater accomplishment if we add the following. For it sent out the

---

[a] Cf. iii. 334 (p. 287 Ddf.) ; Demosthenes IX. 42-43.

371
311 D. δεομένων[1] ἀπέστειλεν. ὅσα μὲν οὖν ἢ κοινῇ τοὺς
Ἕλληνας μὴ πολεμεῖν ἀλλήλοις ἑκάστοτε πείθουσα,
ἢ τοὺς ἐν χρείᾳ παραμυθουμένη διεπρεσβεύσατο,
ἀναγκαῖον παραλιπεῖν διὰ πλῆθος. δυοῖν δὲ κἀνταῦθα μνησθήσομαι· Ἀργείους μὲν γὰρ στασιά-
ζοντας ἐν αὑτοῖς[2] ἔπαυσεν, Κρῆτας δὲ πολεμοῦντας
372 πρὸς ἀλλήλους διήλλαξεν. εὐσεβείας τοίνυν ἅμα καὶ
φρονήματος καὶ πρᾳότητος τίς ἂν εἰπεῖν ἔχοι δεῖγμα
κάλλιον; Κορινθίων γὰρ ψηφισαμένων ποτὲ μὴ
δέχεσθαι τῇ πανηγύρει τὴν ἐνθένδε θεωρίαν, ἀλλὰ
καὶ διὰ πρεσβείας ἀπειπόντων τῇ πόλει μὴ πέμπειν,
κοσμήσαντες ὁμοῦ τούς τε θεωροὺς καὶ τοὺς
ὁπλίτας ἀπέστειλαν, ὡς δ᾽ ἦσαν Ἐλευσῖνι, Κορίνθιοι
μὲν ἧκον σπενδόμενοι, οἱ δὲ τὴν θεωρίαν πέμψαντες
373 τοὺς ὁπλίτας ἐπανήγαγον. ἀλλὰ μὴν τῶν γε μυστη-
ρίων τὰ μὲν ὡς ἀρχαῖα τετίμηται, τὰ δ᾽ ὡς ἀναγκαῖα, τὰ δ᾽ ὡς πλείστοις γνώριμα. πάσαις τοίνυν
ταῖς ψήφοις προφέρει τὰ Ἐλευσίνια. καὶ περὶ μὲν
τῶν ἄλλων οὐχ ἡμῶν ὁ λόγος· μόνοι δὲ τῶν Ἑλλήνων καθ᾽ ἕκαστον ἔτος ποιεῖτε πανήγυριν οὐδεμιᾶς πεντετηρίδος φαυλοτέραν καὶ δέχεσθε τῷ
Ἐλευσινίῳ πλείους ἢ ἕτεροι τῇ πάσῃ πόλει· καὶ
πάντες ἐρίζουσιν ἀεὶ τὴν παροῦσαν ἑορτὴν νικᾶν
374 πολυανθρωπίᾳ. ἀλλὰ μὴν Ἡρακλέα γε καὶ Διοσ-
κούρους[3] ἅπαντες δήπου θεοὺς εἶναι[4] νομίζουσιν·

---

[1] codd. dett. : δεξομένων TQVA. [2] αὑτοῖς TQ.
[3] codd. dett. : Διοσκόρους TQVA. [4] εἶναι om. TQV.

---

[a] The scholiast cites Demosthenes III. 20, but the circumstance is unknown, as also are those in § 371.
[b] The same thought is found in xxii. 9. " Quinquennial

258

largest number on behalf of those in need. We 371
must omit because of their large number all of the
embassies in which on each occasion it persuaded
the Greeks in common not to wage war against one
another, or in which it comforted those in need.
But even here I shall mention two acts. For it
stopped the internal faction of the Argives, and it
reconciled the Cretans when they were waging war
against one another. Who could offer a fairer proof 372
of both piety, intelligence, and gentleness than the
following ? When the Corinthians passed a decree
not to receive the sacred mission from here into their
national assembly, but by means of an embassy
forbade the city to send one,[a] they arrayed and
dispatched both envoys for the sacred mission and
hoplites. And when they were at Eleusis, the
Corinthians came and made peace, and they sent
on their sacred mission and brought back their
hoplites. But indeed, some of the mysteries have 373
been honoured because they are ancient, others
because they are necessary, others because they are
well known to most men. Then the Eleusinian
mysteries are superior on every count. And our
speech is not concerned with the others. But you
alone of the Greeks each year hold a national assembly which is inferior to no quinquennial festival and
you receive more people in the Precinct of Eleusis
than others do in their whole city.[b] And all men are
eager that the then current festival has a larger
attendance than the preceding ones. Everybody of 374
course believes that Heracles and the Dioscuri are

festival." Aristides calls it πεντετηρίς " five yearly " according to the strange idiom whereby fifth year inclusive equals
every fourth year.

(311 D.)

τούτοις δέ γε, ἕως ὡμίλουν ἀνθρώποις, πρώτοις
312 D. ξένων ἡ πόλις δείκνυσι τὰ ἱερά· ὥστε οἷς νῦν ἱερὰ
375 δρῶμεν, τούτους ἱεροποιήσασα αὐτὴ φαίνεται. καὶ
μὴν ἀγῶνάς γε τοῦ πρώτου τέλους μία δὴ πόλις
αὐτὴ πλείστους ἁπάντων ἔτι νῦν ἄγει. ὡς δὲ
εἰπεῖν, ἅπαντα ἢ παρ' ὑμῖν ἐστιν μόνοις, ἢ καὶ παρ'
ὑμῶν, καὶ τριῶν ἕν γέ τι συμβέβηκεν· τὰ μὲν γὰρ
παρ' ὑμῶν ἤρξατο, τὰ δ' ὡς κάλλιστα παρ' ὑμῖν
ἐστιν, τὰ δὲ ὡς πλεῖστα.

376   Εἰσὶ τοίνυν οἳ μηδὲν ἔχοντες φανερὸν δεῖξαι μηδὲ
εἰπεῖν ἔργον ἑαυτῶν, μηδὲ ἐφ' ὅτῳ δικαίως ἂν
φρονοῖεν, ἐπὶ τοὺς Τρωικοὺς καταφεύγουσι χρόνους
καὶ φιλοτιμίας ἀμφισβητοῦσιν, οὐδ' οὕτω λέγοντες
οὐδὲν κοινὸν ἑαυτῶν, ἀλλ' ἑνὸς ἀνδρὸς δόξης ἐξαρ-
τώμενοι, οἷον Φθιῶται καὶ Πύλιοι καὶ Ἰθακήσιοι,
ὥσπερ τινὲς γεωπεῖναι, δι' ἑνὸς τῶν πλουσίων ἑαυ-
377 τοὺς ποιούμενοι. ἡ πόλις δὲ πρὸς τῷ[1] μηδὲν δεῖσθαι τοιαύτης καταφυγῆς οὐδὲ τούτου στέρεται τοῦ
ἡδύσματος. ἀλλ' ὁ κοινὸς τῶν Ἑλλήνων ποιητὴς
ἐν τῷ καταλόγῳ τῶν νεῶν τε καὶ πόλεων τὸν
Ἀθηναίων στρατηγὸν εἰς ἄκρον φησὶν ἐλθεῖν,

Κοσμῆσαι ἵππους τε καὶ ἀνέρας ἀσπιδιώτας.

378 καὶ τό γε πλείονος ἄξιον καὶ καθαρὸν τῆς εὐφημίας,
τοὺς μὲν γὰρ ἄλλους οὓς ἐπαινεῖ κατὰ τὴν τοῦ
σώματος ἕξιν ἢ καὶ ἄλλως πως ὡς ἀρίστους, ἂν οὕτω τύχῃ, τῶν Ἀχαιῶν, ἢ τῶν δεινῶν, οὕτως ἐπ-
αινεῖ· φησὶ γοῦν " Αὐτῶν ἠδὲ καὶ[2] ἵππων, οἳ ἅμ'
Ἀτρείδῃσιν ἕποντο," καὶ ἑτέρωθι λέγει, τῶν τότε
ἐπὶ τοῦ Ἰλίου λέγων, ὡς ἄρα ἦν κράτιστος τὴν το-

―――――――

[1] τὸ VA.   [2] καὶ om. VA.

Gods. But they were the first strangers to whom the city revealed its sacred ceremonies, while they still lived among mankind, so that it clearly has initiated into the mysteries those to whom we now sacrifice. This single city still celebrates the largest 375 number of first class contests. One might say that everything is either in your possession alone, or owes its origin to you, with one of three results. Of some things you are the originator, and of others you possess the fairest possible, and of others the most numerous.

Some people who can neither point to nor speak 376 of any clear accomplishment of their own, or anything over which they would justly be proud, take refuge in Trojan times, and argue over their honours, not even then speaking of anything in which they participated, but depending on the reputation of a single man, as the Phthiotians, Pylians, and Ithacesians do, like certain land-poor people who include themselves among the rich because of a single rich man. Besides needing no such refuge, the city is not 377 even deprived of this garnish. But the common poet of the Greeks in the catalogue of ships and cities says that the Athenians' general was an expert " in marshalling horses and shield-bearing men." [a] And 378 the following aspect of his praise is more valuable and unqualified. For the others whom he praises, perhaps of the Achaeans or whomever it may be, because they are the best in respect to their physical condition or for some other reason, he praises as follows. He says : " Best of them and the horses who followed the sons of Atreus." [b] And in another place he says that someone was best in archery of those

[a] *Iliad* II. 554.　　　　　[b] *Iliad* II. 762.

(312 D.)

ξικήν. καὶ Νέστωρ αὐτῷ λέγει πρός τινας τῶν ἐφ᾽ αὐτοῦ λαμπρῶν

313 D. Ἤδη γάρ ποτ᾽ ἐγὼ καὶ ἀρείοσιν ἠέπερ ὑμῖν
ἀνδράσιν ὡμίλησα.

καὶ ἑξῆς ἀπαριθμεῖ πολλούς τινας, ὡς αὖ κἀκείνους παραπλησίους ἀλλήλοις ὄντας καὶ οὐδένα ὑπερ-
379 έχοντα ἐπιφανῶς αὐτῶν. τοῦ δὲ Μενεσθέως μνησθεὶς ὁ ποιητὴς οὐδεμιᾷ τοιαύτῃ προσθήκῃ κέχρηται, ἀλλὰ ταῦτα πάντα περικόψας εἰσάπαξ φησὶν

Τῷ δὲ οὔπω τις ὅμοιος ἐπιχθόνιος γένετ᾽ ἀνήρ·

ἐν δέ γε τοῖς ἄνω μικρὸν τούτων διηγεῖται περὶ τοῦ Ἐρεχθέως ὡς θρέψειε[1] μὲν αὐτὸν ἡ θεός, τέκοι δ᾽ ἡ
380 γῆ. οὐκοῦν ἴσως οὐδὲν ἀπεικὸς τοὺς μὲν ἄλλους, οὓς ἐφ᾽ ἑκάστων κρατίστους ὡρίσατο μετὰ προσ-θήκης, ἢ τῶν χρόνων, ἢ τῶν γενῶν, αὐτοὺς[2] ἀναγο-ρεύειν· ὃν δὲ τῶν ἀπ᾽ αὐτῆς τῆς γῆς φύντων ὡς ἄριστον ἐπαινεῖ, τοῦτον ὡς διὰ πάντων τῶν ἐν τῇ[3]
381 γῇ φύντων ἄριστον ἐπαινέσαι. δύο τοίνυν ἀρί-στους τὰ πρὸς τὸν πόλεμον τιθεὶς τῶν Ἀχαιῶν, Σαλαμίνιον δήπου λέγει τὸν ἕτερον τῶν ἐπωνύμων.
382 Ἔν τι δήπου καὶ τοῦτο λέγεται σεμνὸν κατὰ τὴν Λακεδαιμονίων[4] πολιτείαν, ὅτι αὐτοῖς ὁ θεὸς
314 D. συνέταξε τὸ κατ᾽ ἀρχὰς τοὺς νόμους· ὁ δέ γε αὐτὸς οὗτος θεὸς τάς τε φυλὰς φαίνεται διελὼν τῇ πόλει καὶ τὰ γένη καὶ τὰς ἑκάστοις προσηκούσας θυσίας θύειν ἀναθείς, ὥσπερ οὖν καὶ βασιλέας καὶ ἄρχοντας καὶ τὴν ἄλλην πολιτείαν σχεδὸν ἅπασαν διορίσας

---

[1] A corrector : θρέψε TQVA.   [2] αὐτῶν TQ.
[3] τῇ om. VA.   [4] τῶν Λακεδαιμονίων TQ.

then at Ilium.[a] And his Nestor says in respect to
some of those who were famous in his time : " For
in times gone by I have associated with better men
than you." [b] And next he lists many of them, but as if
they were similar to one another and no one of them
was clearly superior. But when the poet mentioned 379
Menestheus, he employed no such qualification, but
sheared off all that, and said simply : " Nor was any
mortal man his equal yet." [c] And in the verses a
little before, he narrates how the Goddess nourished
Erechtheus but the earth bore him.[d] Perhaps it was 380
not unreasonable for him to proclaim the others,
whom he defined as best in each particular, with the
qualification of either time or race, yet to praise this
man as best in every way of those born upon the
earth, when he praises him as best of those born from
the earth. When he described two of the Achaeans 381
as being best in warfare, he called the second of
these eponymi a Salaminian.[e]

One distinctive point is indeed made in respect 382
to the Lacedaemonian constitution, that the God [885.]
originally drew up their laws.[f] But this same God
clearly divided up our city's tribes and families,
and prescribed for each the proper sacrifices
to make, as indeed he clearly arranged for their
kings, archons, and almost all the rest of their con-

---

[a] *Iliad* XIII. 313.   [b] *Iliad* I. 260-261.
[c] *Iliad* II. 553.
[d] *Iliad* II. 547-548.
[e] *Cf. Iliad* II. 557. The meaning of " eponymi " is
rather uncertain. The scholiast explains it from the fact
the Ajax gave his name to the Athenian tribe Aiantis. If it
were possible, one would like to understand it as Canter :
" Salaminium nominat cognominum duorum alterum."
[f] Apollo.

(314 D.)

αὐτοῖς. ὥστε οὐχ ἧττον ἂν εἴη τῆς πόλεως ὁ θεὸς νομοθέτης ἢ ἐκείνων.

383 Βούλομαι δὲ καὶ περὶ τῆς πολιτείας αὐτῆς μνησθῆναι διὰ βραχέων, ὡς ἂν οἷός τε ὦ· καὶ γὰρ ἅπαντες μὲν αὐτὴν ἐγκωμιάζουσιν, οὐ μὴν διηρευνήσατό γε ἅπαν τὸ ἑνὸν σχεδὸν οὐδείς· ἐγὼ δὲ ἁπλοῦν τε καὶ οὐχ ἁπλοῦν λέγω. τριῶν γὰρ οὐσῶν, ὡς ἀνωτάτω διελέσθαι, τῶν πολιτειῶν, ἣ τις ἂν τίθηται,

384 τίθεται τῇ πόλει. βασιλείαις μέν γε τὸ ἐξ ἀρχῆς φανεῖται χρωμένη, γεν· ὰς οὐκ ὀλίγας τινάς, οὐ μόνον τῶν Ἐρεχθειδῶν, ἀλλὰ καὶ τῶι ὕστερον ἀξίων ὀφθέντων. δημοκρατία δ' αὖ καὶ παιδὶ γνώριμος καὶ καθαρωτάτη δὴ καὶ μεγίστη τῶν πασῶν ἡ παρ'

385 ὑμῖν γεγενημένη. καὶ μὴν εἰς τὴν ἐξ Ἀρείου πάγου βουλὴν βλέψαντα πάντα ἂν ἡγοῦμαι φῆσαι μὴ εἶναι καλλίω λαβεῖν ἀριστοκρατίας εἰκόνα μηδ' ἥτις[1]

386 σῴζει μᾶλλον τοὔνομα. οὕτω πάντα τὰ τῶν πολιτειῶν παραδείγματα ἐνθένδε ὥρμηται· καθάπερ γὰρ νομοθετοῦσα τοῖς ἀνθρώποις ἡ πόλις πρὸς τοὺς αὐτῶν[2] τρόπους ἑκάστοις ἐκλέγεσθαι τὸ πρόσφορον, οὕτω πάντα ἐξεῦρέν τε καὶ προὔθηκεν εἰς κοινόν, βοηθοῦσα τῇ φύσει πανταχῇ· ὅπερ καὶ κατὰ τοὺς καρποὺς καὶ πολλὰ ἕτερα ἐπιδείκνυμεν αὐτὴν βεβουλευμένην.

387 Ὁ δέ γε ἔτι μεῖζον καὶ τελεώτερον, οἵ τε γὰρ
315 D. βασιλεῖς αὐτοὶ φανοῦνται διαφερόντως τῶν ἄλλων τὴν κοινότητα ἀγαπήσαντες, καὶ μάλιστα δήπου πρὸς τοὺς πολλοὺς ἐξ ἴσου ταῖς γνώμαις καταστάντες, ὅ τε δῆμος, εἴ τινα εὕροι που τῶν πολλῶν ὑπερέχοντα, ἐθελοντὴς ἑαυτοῦ προϊστάμενος καὶ χρώμενος οἷον ἄρχοντι διηνεκεῖ, τὸ δ' αὐτὸ τοῦτο

---

[1] εἴ τις TQA. [2] αὐτῶν VA.

stitution, so that the God would be as much the law-giver of this city as of theirs.

I also wish to mention the constitution itself as 383 briefly as I can. For everyone praises it ; hardly anyone, however, has investigated all of its qualities. I say what is both simple and not simple. For there are three kinds of constitutions, to define them in the most general way, and whichever of these one favours, he favours the city. In the be- 384 ginning it will clearly have employed a monarchy for no few generations, and not only for the Erech-theids, but also of those who later appeared worthy. And the democracy which has arisen among you is well known to every child, and is the most un-qualified and the greatest of all of them. I believe 385 that everyone would admit with reference to the Areopagus that no fairer image of aristocracy can be conceived nor one which more preserves the meaning of its name. Thus exemplars of all the constitutions 386 have come from here. As if the city were legislating for mankind, for each people to select that form which was appropriate to their character, so it discovered and made all of these public, assisting nature in every way, an intention of the city which we have also demonstrated in the matter of agricul-ture and in many other actions.

Still greater and more perfect is the fact that 387 beyond all others their kings will clearly have been content with an absence of privilege, and have been of the same mind surely as the masses ; and that if the people ever found someone who was superior to the masses, they will clearly have volun-tarily made him their leader and have employed him like a perpetual archon ; and that they will

(315 D.)

καὶ τοῖς ὀλίγοις φυλάττων, εἰ τῶν ἄλλων ἀμείνους ὄντας αἴσθοιτο, ἐφαμίλλους δὲ ἐν σφίσιν αὐτοῖς.

388 ὡσαύτως δὲ καὶ ἡ βουλὴ τὸν δῆμον ὅπως μείζω καταστήσῃ σκοποῦσα ἀεί, τὸ δὲ αὑτῆς[1] οὐδεπώποτε ἰδίᾳ λογισαμένη, ἀλλὰ ταύτην καὶ καλὴν καὶ γιγνομένην πλεονεξίαν ἑαυτῆς κρίνουσα, τὸ τῶν πολλῶν ἐπὶ σωτηρίᾳ μετ᾽ εὐδοξίας προΐστασθαι. ὥστ᾽ εἰκότως οὐ μόνον κατὰ τὴν πολιτείαν ἑκάστην, ἀλλὰ καὶ κατὰ τὴν κρᾶσιν τῶν πολιτειῶν παρὰ πάντας τοὺς ἄλλους εὐδοκιμεῖν εἶναι τῇ πόλει. ὥσπερ γὰρ ὁ πᾶς οὑτοσὶ κόσμος οἶμαι συνέστη μὲν ἐκ τεττάρων, ὡς ὁ παλαιὸς λόγος, αὐτὸ δ᾽ ἕκαστον αὖ τούτων μετέχει τῇ φύσει καὶ τῶν λοιπῶν, τῷ δ᾽ ὑπερβάλλοντι τὴν ἐπωνυμίαν χωρὶς ἕκαστον εἶδος εἴληφεν, οὕτω καὶ τὰς πολιτείας, εἰ καὶ ὅτι μάλιστα κεχωρισμέναι τυγχάνουσιν, μετέχειν ἀμωσγέπως ἀλλήλων εἰκός ἐστιν, εἴπερ βασιλείαν ὀρθὴν καὶ δικαίαν ὄψεσθαι μέλλομεν, ἢ τῶν ὀλίγων ὡσαύτως

389 δὲ[2] πολλῶν ἀρχήν. γνοίη δ᾽ ἄν τις, εἰ τὰς μὲν βασιλείας τὰς ἐν τῇ πόλει πρὸς τὰς ἑτέρωθί που βασιλείας ἐπὶ τῶν αὐτῶν χρόνων, ἢ τῆς Ἑλλάδος ἢ τῆς βαρβάρου γεγοννυίας ὁρῴη, τὴν δ᾽ αὖ δημοκρατίαν τὴν Ἀθήνησιν πρὸς τὰς ἑτέρων δημοκρατίας, καὶ μὴν τό γε τῆς βουλῆς συνέδριον πρὸς τὰ ἑτέρωθί

316 D. που κύρια καὶ ἡγούμενα. εἰ γὰρ δεῖ τῶν ἄλλων ἀποστάντα ὑπὲρ τῆς δημοκρατίας μόνης εἰπεῖν, φανήσονται τοῖς μὲν βουλήμασι καὶ ταῖς ἐπιθυμίαις πολλῷ προπετέστεροι καὶ ὑβριστότεροι πάντες οἱ τοῦ σχήματος τούτου μετασχόντες, τῷ δ᾽ ἀξιώματι καὶ τῇ λαμπρότητι μηδ᾽ ⟨ἐγγὺς⟩[3] τοῖς ἀπὸ τῆς

---

[1] αὑτῆς TQV.   [2] δὲ ⟨καὶ τῶν⟩ ci. Reiske.
[3] add. codd. dett.

clearly have preserved this principle in respect to the few, if ever they perceived them to be better than the rest, but equal among themselves. In the 388 same way, the council will always clearly have been considering how to make the people greater, and will never have shown any private regard for its own position, but will have decided that the fair and proper use of its power lay in leading the masses for their security and glory. Therefore with good reason the city is distinguished beyond all other peoples not only in respect to each particular constitution. but also in the mixture of these constitutions. For just as this Universe arose, to be sure, from four elements, according to the old theory,[a] and each of these elements naturally partakes of the remaining three, but each species has received a separate classification through that element which predominates, so it is probable that even if the constitutions happened to have been as diverse as possible, in some way they partake of one another, if we shall ever behold a fair and just monarchy, or oligarchy, or democracy. One would understand 389 this, if he would compare the monarchies which arose in the city with those monarchies elsewhere of the same time, in Greece or in barbarian lands, and if he would compare the democracy at Athens with those of other peoples, and the Board of the Council with the ruling and leading bodies elsewhere. If we must ignore the other constitutions and speak in defence of democracy alone, all those who have participated in this form of government, will clearly have been much more unstable and unjust in their wishes and desires, and have not even approached

[a] *Cf.* Plato, *Timaeus* 32 c ff. ; also xliii. 11 ff.

(316 D.)

390 πόλεως γεγενημένοι. καὶ μὴν ἐκεῖνό γε ἡ πόλις
πρώτη κατέδειξεν, μὴ τίθεσθαι πλούτῳ μηδὲ θαυμάζειν. οὔτε γὰρ τοὺς ὑπερέχοντας ταῖς οὐσίαις
οὐδεπώποτε ἐπῆρεν, ἀλλ' ὅσον μὴ ἀδικεῖσθαι διὰ
τοῦτο, τοσοῦτον αὐτοῖς ἠξίου παρ' αὐτῆς[1] ὀφεί-
λεσθαι, οὔτε τοῖς ἀρετῇ μὲν ὑπερφέρουσι, χρήμασι
δ' ἡττημένοις, οὐδαμοῦ πώποτ' ἔλαττον ἔνειμεν,
αἰσχρὸν οἶμαι νομίζουσα τῶν μὲν οἰκετῶν οὐ τοὺς
εὐπορωτάτους, ἀλλὰ τοὺς πιστοτάτους βελτίστους
νομίζειν, τῶν δ' ἐλευθέρων φασκόντων εἶναι τὴν
ἀξίαν ὡρίσθαι χρήμασιν, ἀλλὰ μὴ ὁποῖός τις ἂν
αὐτὸς ἕκαστος ᾖ, τοιοῦτον καὶ νομίζεσθαι. καὶ
γάρ τοι μόνη πόλεων οὐ μετέθηκε τὸν θεσμόν, οὐδὲ
ἐποίησεν τὰ τῇ φύσει τρίτα τῷ νόμῳ πρῶτα· οὐδὲ
ὥσπερ τῶν φασκόντων φιλοσοφεῖν ἔστιν ἰδεῖν
ἐνίους λέγοντας μὲν οὕτω περὶ τούτων, ἔργῳ δὲ
ὑποπίπτοντας καὶ συγχωροῦντας ἀεὶ τούτοις οὓς
ἂν αἴσθωνται δυνατωτέρους, ἀλλὰ καὶ εἰς ἀρχὰς
ἄγουσα καὶ πιστεύουσα καὶ πασῶν ἀξιοῦσα τῶν
τιμῶν ἑωρᾶτο οὐ τοὺς ἀπὸ τῶν μεγίστων τιμημάτων,
ἀλλὰ τοὺς ἐπιεικεστάτους τὰς φύσεις· ὡς ὅστις εἰς
ἀρετῆς λόγον νικῴη, τοῦτον τοῖς πᾶσι νικῶντα.
391 ἔδειξε δ' οὐχ ἥκιστα, ἡνίκα ἴσχυσε τὰ μέγιστα.
ὄντων γὰρ κατὰ τοὺς αὐτοὺς χρόνους ἐπιφανῶν
ἀνδρῶν παρ' αὐτῇ τῶν μὲν πλουσίων ὑπὲρ τὰ
πρῶτα τῶν Ἑλληνικῶν οἴκων, τῶν δ' ὡς οἷόν τε
πενεστάτων, ἐπὶ τὴν προστασίαν τῶν Ἑλληνικῶν
317 D. ἕνα τῶν ἀπὸ τούτων εἵλετο· καὶ γάρ τοι ὁ μὲν οἷς
ἔταξεν εὐδοκίμησεν, ἡ πόλις δ' οἷς ἔκρινεν.

---

[1] Ddf. : αὐτῆς TQVA.

the dignity and glory of those in this city. The 390
city was the first to teach that wealth should not be
favoured or admired. For it never exalted the very
rich, but it thought that it owed them only the
privilege of not being wronged on this account;
nor did it ever slight those of superior virtue, but
inferior wealth, with the idea, I think, that it was
shameful, while believing that not their richest,
but their most trustworthy servants were the best,
when men claim to be free, for their worth to be
defined by possessions, and for each one not to
be regarded in the light of what he is. This city alone
has not changed the natural order of things, nor
has it made what is third in the rank of nature first in
that of law, nor did it act as it can be seen that some
of those who claim to be philosophers act, when they
speak in this way concerning these matters, but in
fact always bow low and yield to whomever they
perceive to be richer than themselves.[a] It was not
seen to install in office, to confide in, and to think
worthy of every honour those of the highest property
classes, but those who had the best character, as if
whoever was superior in regard to virtue, would be
superior in every way. It showed this most of all, 391
when it enjoyed its greatest power. For of its
distinguished citizens who were then alive, some
rich beyond the first houses of Greece and others as
poor as might be, it selected one from the latter
class as the leader of Greek affairs.[b] And he was 478.
respected for his assignment of the tribute, but the
city for its choice.

[a] An allusion to Aristides' *bête noire*, the Cynics; *cf.* iii.
663-693 (pp. 397-414 Ddf.) and Behr, *Aelius Aristides*, p. 94.
[b] Aristides, son of Lysimachus. See note on § 282.

(317 D.)

392 Πολλῶν δ' ὄντων ἅ τις ἂν περὶ τῆς πολιτείας
εἰπεῖν ἔχοι, τὰ μὲν πολλὰ καὶ προκατείληπται καὶ
ὁ καιρὸς ἀφαιρεῖται, καὶ οὐ πᾶσα ἀνάγκη λέγειν· ἓν
δέ τι προσθεὶς καταλύσω καὶ τὸν περὶ τούτου λόγον.
τὸ γὰρ εἶναι τό τε βέλτιστον καὶ τὸ κατ' ἐξουσίαν
συμπεπτωκὸς ἐνταυθοῖ, καὶ τὴν μὲν δίαιταν κοι-
νοτάτην ἅπασιν, τὰς δὲ τιμὰς τοῖς ἐπιεικεστάτοις
ἀνεῖσθαι, πῶς οὐκ ἐλευθέρας πόλεως καὶ πολιτείας
ὡς ἀληθῶς, ἐν ᾗ ζῆν μὲν ἔξεστιν, ὡς ἄν τις βούληται, τιμᾶσθαι δὲ καὶ ἰσχύειν οὐ τοῖς βουλομένοις
393 ἔστιν, ἀλλὰ τοῖς ἐξητασμένοις; καὶ γάρ τοι κἂν
τοῖς τῶν πολέμων ἀγῶσι κἂν ταῖς[1] χρείαις τὸ εἰκὸς
διεσώσαντο, οὐ γὰρ[2] ἐξ ἡμισείας οὐδ' αὖ[3] ἐλάττονος
ἔτι μοίρας ἐσπούδαζον ὑπὲρ τῶν πραγμάτων, ἀλλὰ
πάντες ἐξ ἴσου ταῖς προθυμίαις κατὰ δύναμιν
ἡμιλλῶντο, ὡς ὑπὲρ κοινῆς τῆς πατρίδος καὶ κοινῶν
τῶν ἄθλων ἀγωνιζόμενοι, καὶ οὐχ ἑτέροις μὲν τοῦ
κινδυνεύειν, ἑτέροις δὲ τοῦ δεσπόζειν, ἂν κρατήσωσι,
προκειμένου. ἐξ ὧν ὁμόνοια μὲν καὶ πίστις ἀλλήλων
ἤνθει κατὰ τὴν πόλιν, εἰ δέ που καὶ διασταῖεν, οὐ
χαλεπῶς ἀλλήλους ἐγνώριζον· ἀνδρείας δ' εἴ που
318 D. δεήσαι, λῆρος ἅπαντα τὰ ἄλλα πρὸς ἐκείνους ἦν,
ἐμοὶ μὲν οὐδὲ πένταθλοι δοκοῦσιν οἱ πάντα νικῶντες
τοσοῦτον τοῖς πᾶσι κρατεῖν.

394 Ἐν ποίοις δ' ἄν τις καιροῖς οὐχὶ βελτίων εἴη τῆς
πόλεως μεμνημένος; πότερα ἐπὶ στρατείαις; καὶ
πόθεν ἂν λάβοι καλλίω παραδείγματα; ἢ ποίοις
ἂν λόγοις χρησάμενος βέλτιον ἂν παρακελεύσαιτο;
395 ἀλλ' ἐν ταῖς πανηγύρεσιν; ἀλλ' αὐτὴ τούτων ἡγε-
396 μών. ἀλλ' ἐν ταῖς ἐκκλησίαις καὶ τῇ τῶν κατὰ

---

[1] ταῖς ⟨ἄλλαις⟩ ci. Reiske.
[2] Canter: τὰς TQVA; οὔτ' ἄρ' ci. Reiske; οὔτ' ἂν Oliver.
[3] Canter: ἂν TQVA.

Although there are many things which could be 392
said about this constitution, many have already been
anticipated by others and time does not permit, and
there is no great necessity to mention them. When I
have added one point, I shall conclude the discussion
of this subject. When what is finest and the right of
free choice coincide here, when the styles of life are
unrestricted, while public honours have been left
open for the best element, do we not have the signs
of a truly free city and constitution, in which it is
possible to live as one wishes, yet in which honours
and power do not go to those who desire them,
but to those who have been proved worthy? And in 393
the struggles of war, and in times of need, they maintained what was to be expected. For they did not
show a half way or still lesser degree of concern over
public affairs, but all competed as far as they could
with equal enthusiasm, since they contended on
behalf of their common country and for common
prizes, and it was not prescribed for one party to
run the risks and another to rule in the event of
success. Therefore concord and trust in one another
flourished throughout the city. If ever there was
dissension, mutual recognition came easily. If ever
there was need of courage, all was vain compared to
them. Not even the contestants in the pentathlon
who win every event seem to me to be so entirely
victorious.

On what occasions would one not be better off 394
for remembering the city? On campaigns? And
where else would one find fairer examples? Or
using what examples in any public speech, would he
make a better exhortation? In national festivals? 395
The city is a guide for these. In assemblies and in 396

271

(318 D.)

τὴν πόλιν διοικήσει; καὶ τίς δῆμων αὐτὸς ὀξύτερος
καὶ πραότερος, ἢ τίνες δημαγωγοὶ μᾶλλον ἄξιοι
397 θαυμάσαι; ἀλλ' ἐν τῇ τῶν λόγων ἀσκήσει καὶ τῆς
λοιπῆς σοφίας; ἀλλ' ἔτι καὶ νῦν ἐνταῦθα πάντες
συνέρχονται· καὶ τὰ γένη τῶν φιλοσόφων οὐ τέθνηκε
τῇ τῆς πόλεως ἀγαθῇ τύχῃ, χωρὶς τοῦ καὶ τοὺς
ὅπου δὴ γῆς ἀναγκαίως ἔχειν ἅμα τῶν τε λόγων καὶ
τῶν Ἀθηναίων μεμνῆσθαι, καὶ μηδέποτε ἐκβαλεῖν
ἂν ἐκ τῆς ψυχῆς τὸ εἴδωλον, ὥσπερ ἐν κατόπτρῳ
398 τοῖς λόγοις ἐμβλέποντας. καὶ γάρ τοι πᾶσι μὲν ἀνθρώποις οὕτως αἰδέσιμον τοὔνομα καὶ τοὔδαφος
τῆς πόλεως ὡς οὐδὲν ἄλλο ἓν καὶ τὸ αὐτὸ καὶ οὔτ'
ἰδιῶται οὔτε βασιλεῖς μικρὰ ἄττα ἐτίμησαν, ἀλλ'
οὕτως ὥστ' αὐτοὺς ἀγάλλεσθαι ταῖς ὑπερβολαῖς
399 τῶν τιμῶν αἷς ἐπεδείκνυντο. φανερὰ δὲ καὶ ἡ παρ'
αὐτῶν τῶν θεῶν εὔνοια καὶ ψῆφος καὶ διὰ τοῦ κοινοῦ μάντεως καὶ ἐξηγητοῦ τοῦ πατρῴου τῇ πόλει,
319 D. θύειν τε ὑπὲρ τῶν Ἑλλήνων τὴν προηροσίαν κε-
λευόντων καὶ μητρόπολιν τῶν καρπῶν αὐτὴν ἐπ-
ονομαζόντων, ἔτι δὲ στεφανηφορεῖν ἀξιούντων, ὡς
διὰ βίου νικῶσαν. ἀετόν τε ἐν νεφέλαις αὐτὴν ὁ
400 θεὸς καλεῖ πρὸς τἆλλα πολίσματα. μόνη δ', ὡς
ἔοικε, ταύτῃ πόλεων δύο τἀναντία συμβέβηκεν·
πλεῖστά τε γὰρ καὶ κάλλιστα ἀνθρώποις εἴρηται περὶ
ταύτης καὶ οὐκ ἔστιν ἥτις ἐλαττόνων τετύχηκεν.
πρὸ μὲν γὰρ τῶν ἄλλων τεθαύμασται, ἄξιον δ' αὐτῆς[1]
401 οὐδὲν ἤκουσεν. πρότερον μὲν οὖν ἠγάμην ἀκούων

---

[1] codd. dett. : αὐτῆς TQVA.

[a] Apollo Pythius.

the administration of city-affairs ? And what people are either keener or more gentle, what popular leaders more worthy to be admired ? In the practice 397 of oratory and the remaining branches of knowledge ? Everyone still comes here to learn. And the sects of philosophy have not perished through the good fortune of the city, apart from the fact that men anywhere on earth must of necessity think of oratory and of the Athenians simultaneously and that they would never expel from their soul the city's image, perceiving it in oratory as it were in a mirror. And indeed the name and ground of 398 this city is revered by all, as if no other were the same. And kings and commoners have honoured it in no small way, but so that they themselves are proud of the great honours which they have presented. The 399 goodwill and favour of the Gods themselves is also evident through the medium of the common seer of the race and the ancestral interpreter of the city,[a] when the Gods ordered it to offer the pre-plowing sacrifice [b] on behalf of the Greeks and named it "the mother city of the crops,"[c] and also thought that it should wear a crown, as if it were a life-long victor. And the God called it an "eagle in the clouds" compared to other towns.[d] To this city 400 alone, as it seems, two contradictory circumstances have befallen. For men have given the largest number and the fairest compliments to it, and no city has received less of what was due to it. It has been admired before all other things, but never was spoken of as it deserved. Formerly I heard with 401

[b] *Cf.* scholium to Aristophanes' *Knights* 729.
[c] Also quoted above, § 37.
[a] *Cf.* scholium to Aristophanes' *Knights* 1013.

(319 D.)

τὸ τῆς σοφίας πρυτανεῖον καὶ τὴν τῆς Ἑλλάδος
ἑστίαν καὶ τὸ ἔρεισμα καὶ ὅσα τοιαῦτα εἰς τὴν πόλιν
ᾖδετο, νῦν δέ μοι δοκεῖ πάντα ταῦτα εἴσω πίπτειν.
ἀλλ᾽ εἴ τινα χρὴ πόλιν θεῶν ὕπαρχον ἢ συγγενῆ
προσειπεῖν ἢ τῆς φύσεως τῆς ἀνθρωπείας εἰκόνα
καὶ ὅρον, ἥδ᾽ ἄν μοι δοκεῖ¹ δικαίως κληθῆναι.

402 Ἀνθ᾽ ὧν, ὦ ἄνδρες Ἕλληνες, οὔτε φθόνον εἰκὸς
ἔχειν τῇ πόλει οὔθ᾽ ὑποχωροῦντας αἰσχύνεσθαι, ἀλλὰ
συναύξειν ἐκ τῶν ἐνόντων καὶ φιλοτιμεῖσθαι. τῶν
γὰρ Ἀθηναίων νικώντων, παρ᾽ ὑμῖν ἐστι τὸ νικᾶν.
πάντας μὲν γὰρ ἁπάντων ἂν εἶναι ἀρίστους ἀδύνα-
320 D. τον. ὥσπερ δὲ ὅταν στρατηγὸς προέχῃ, μετέχει τῆς
δόξης ἡ πόλις, οὕτω τῆς ἡγουμένης πόλεως τὰ εἰ-
κότα τιμωμένης ἅπασι μέτεστιν τῆς φιλοτιμίας.

403 οἶμαι δὲ οὐδ᾽ αὐτοῖς Ἀθηναίοις φέρειν αἰσχύνην, ἄν
τις αὐτοῖς πρεσβεύῃ τὴν ἀκρόπολιν. χρὴ τοίνυν καὶ
ὑμᾶς, ὥσπερ ἀκρόπολίν τινα ἢ κορυφὴν νομίσαν-
τας τῆς Ἑλλάδος καὶ τῶν ὁμοφύλων τὴν πόλιν καὶ
ἔργῳ καὶ λόγῳ κοσμεῖν, καὶ μετέχειν τῆς δόξης,

404 ἀλλ᾽ οὐκ ἀποστερεῖσθαι νομίζοντας. εἴργασται καὶ
ἡμῖν ὁ λόγος ἀντὶ τοῦ πέπλου κόσμος Παναθηναίων
τῇ θεωρίᾳ· δοῦναι δὲ χάριν τῆς αὐτῆς θεοῦ ἧσπερ
καὶ ὁ λόγος καὶ ἡ πόλις.

¹ δοκοῖ TQ.

ᵃ Plato, *Protagoras* 337 D.
ᵇ From a Delphic oracle, so the scholiast; *cf.* Athenaeus
254 b.

admiration, "the town hall of knowledge,"[a] and "the hearth of Greece,"[b] and "its bulwark,"[c] and all such things which were written in praise of the city. But now all these things seem to me to fall short of the mark. If it is fitting to call a city "the lieutenant of the Gods" or their "kinsman," or "the image and model of human nature," I think that this city would have been justly so named.

Therefore, O men of Greece, it is reasonable that 402 you neither are envious of the city nor feel shame in giving precedence to it, but that you aid in its increase as far as you can and feel pride therein. For when the Athenians prevail, the victory is yours. It would be impossible for all men to be the best of mankind. But just as whenever a general is superior, his city shares in his glory, so when the leading city is properly honoured, all men participate in its sense of pride. But I think that the Athenians themselves 403 are not ashamed, if someone prefers their Acropolis. It is fitting that you too honour the city in deed and word, in the belief that it is as it were a sort of Acropolis or summit of Greece and its kindred races, and with the view that while you participate in its glory, you are not deprived of your own. Our speech 404 has been fashioned like the robe of Athena as an adornment for the festival of the Panathenaea.[d] But to show favour to it lies in the power of the Goddess to whom this speech and this city belong.

[c] Pindar, frg. 76 Schroeder, 92 Turyn.
[d] The peplos, which each year was woven by Athenian girls and carried in procession at the Panathenaic festival to the wooden statue of Athena on the Acropolis.

II

TO PLATO
IN DEFENCE OF
ORATORY

INTRODUCTION

The Defence of Oratory was written in Pergamum
between A.D. 145 and 147, at the height of Aristides'
incapacitating illness and his almost total absorption
in the practice of incubation at the Asclepieion.[a]
Pergamum was the site of the revival of Platonism
through the efforts of the school of Caius, but Aristides' defence was prompted more, it seems, by
Cynic philosophers who used the arguments of
Plato's *Gorgias* for indiscriminate attacks upon
oratory.[b] Indeed, Caius and his disciples appear to
have been mainly interested in the cosmological
aspects of Plato's philosophy as it is presented
principally in the *Timaeus*. Aristides' refutation
consists of bringing to light the contradictions in
Plato's own position, particularly in the *Gorgias*
itself, *Phaedrus*, seventh *Epistle*, *Laws*, *Menexenus*,
Politicus, and *Euthydemus*. Aristides' thorough
knowledge of Plato, which is apparent in his easy
citation, innumerable allusions, and stylistic borrow-
ings, made any dependence on former discussions of
these discrepancies unnecessary.[c] Further, Aristides

[a] *Cf.* Behr, *Aelius Aristides and the Sacred Tales*, pp.
54-56. [b] § 464.
[c] There is a possibility that Apollonius Molon, Cicero's
teacher, composed a similar work against Plato; *cf.*
scholium on Aristophanes' *Clouds* 144; Diogenes Laertius
III. 34; U. v. Wilamowitz, *Aristoteles und Athen*, vol. 1,
p. 298, n. 16.

278

buttresses his arguments with his own deep commitment to oratory, especially in §§430-438. The tone, style, and use of citations are parallel to or. xxviii, which was also composed at the same time.

The work aroused immediate criticism, which Aristides answered in or. iv. The lasting effects of this rather absurd controversy can be seen in Porphyry's composition of seven books *Against Aristides*, a few fragments of which still survive.[a]

OUTLINE OF THE CONTENTS OF THE ORATION

A. Proem. Truth before precedence. Defence of oratory : §§ 1-20.
B. The charge in the *Gorgias* : §§ 21-31.
C. Result of conceding that oratory is not an art : §§ 32-134.
D. Refutation of the charge that oratory is not an art : §§ 135-177.
E. Refutation of the charge that oratory fawns over the masses : §§ 178-203.
F. Oratory is truly representative of justice and all the virtues : §§ 204-318.
G. The virtue of the Four : §§ 319-343.
H. The argument of the two oratories : §§ 344-361.
I. The power of the true orator : §§ 362-437.
J. Plato honours oratory : §§ 438-445.
K. The fallacy of the two oratories : §§ 446-461.
L. Peroration : Attack on Cynics : §§ 462-466.

[a] *Cf.* Behr, A.J.P. lxxxix (1968), pp. 186-199.

II

ΠΡΟΣ ΠΛΑΤΩΝΑ ΥΠΕΡ ΡΗΤΟΡΙΚΗΣ

ΛΟΓΟΣ ΠΡΩΤΟΣ

II 1 D.
[1] Οἶμαι δεῖν ὅστις μέλλει τὰ δέοντα ἐρεῖν, ἢ ψή-
φου κύριος ὀρθῶς ἔσεσθαι, μὴ τοῦτο σκοπεῖν μηδὲ
βασκαίνειν εἴ τινι τῶν πρότερον καὶ δόξαν ἐχόντων
ἑτέρως εἰρῆσθαι περὶ τῶν αὐτῶν συμβέβηκεν, ἀλλ'
οὗ πανταχοῦ πλεῖστον εἰκός ἐστι λόγον εἶναι, τοῦτο
κἂν τῷ παρόντι ζητεῖν, ὁποτέρωθι τἀληθές, καὶ
[2] τοῦτο συμβούλεσθαι νικᾶν. ἄτοπον γὰρ ἐν μὲν ταῖς
ἐκκλησίαις μὴ τὸν πρῶτον εἰπόντα πιστεύεσθαι μηδ'
ἐν τοῖς δικαστηρίοις, ἀλλὰ τοῦτό γε εὖ εἰδέναι
πάντας, ὅτι εἰ ταύτῃ ταῦτα κριθήσεται, τῶν φευ-
γόντων οὐδεὶς ἀποφεύξεται· πάντες γὰρ ὕστεροι δήπου[1] τοῦ διώκοντος λέγουσιν· ἐν δὲ τοῖς λόγοις
αὐτοῖς καὶ τῇ περὶ τούτων κρίσει τοὺς τῷ χρόνῳ
προλαβόντας κρατεῖν, ἀλλὰ μὴ τοὺς ἀποδείξοντας
περὶ ὧν ἀγωνίζονται, καὶ τραγῳδοὺς μὲν καὶ κιθα-
ριστὰς καὶ τοὺς ἄλλους τοὺς ἐπὶ τῆς μουσικῆς μὴ

---

[1] δήπουθεν ὕστεροι Phot.

---

[a] The division of this work into two books (the second
commences at § 319) seems to be as old as Sopater of Apamea
(c. A.D. 300) if he was indeed the author of the Hypothesis to
or. iii (pp. 435 ff., vol. 3 of Dindorf's edition), as F. W. Lenz

280

2

TO PLATO:
IN DEFENCE OF ORATORY

BOOK I[a]

I THINK that whoever will make a correct pro- 1
nouncement, or will rightly cast his vote, must not
invidiously consider whether someone of past
renown happens to have held a different opinion
on the same subject, but rather now must seek and
wish to prevail the question which reasonably is
everywhere most significant: on which side is the
truth to be found. It is strange that neither in the 2
assemblies nor in the courts is the first speaker
believed,[b] but that all realize that if judgements
will be made in this way, no defendant will be
acquitted—for they all speak after the prosecutor—
but that on the other hand in oratory itself and the
judgement about it those antecedent in time prevail,
not those who will prove their points of contention.
Tragic poets, lyre players, and others in the musical

contends, *The Aristeides Prolegomena* (1960), p. 23. It is
possible that Porphyry knew nothing of this unnatural
division, *cf.* Behr, A.J.P. lxxxix (1968), p. 198.

[b] Aristides (a very sick man at this time) writes somewhat
carelessly here. He means that a first speaker's arguments
are not accepted without proof.

(1 D.)

ταὐτὸν φέρεσθαι τῆς τε ἀξίας ὄνομα καὶ τῆς τάξεως,
ἢ κληροῦν γε ἂν ἧρκει μόνον, ἀλλ' ὅστις ἂν κάλλιστ'
ἀγωνίσηται, τοῦτον στεφανοῦν καὶ πρῶτον ἀναγορεύ-
ειν, κἂν ὕστατος εἰσελθὼν τύχῃ, τοὺς δὲ τῶν ἀστει-
οτέρων ἀγωνισμάτων ἀξιοῦντας ἀγωνιστὰς ἢ κριτὰς
εἶναι οὕτω σφόδρα τὸν χρόνον σεμνύνειν ὥστε μὴ

2 D. μόνον τοῖς ὅλοις χείρους τοὺς ὑστέρους ἡγεῖσθαι,
ἀλλὰ μηδ' ἂν τυχεῖν εὑρόντας βέλτιον τῶν εἰρημέ-

3 νων μηδέν. ὁρῶ δὲ ὅτι κἂν τοῖς γυμνικοῖς ἀγῶσιν
οὐχ ὅστις πρῶτος τὴν ἀπογραφὴν ἐποιήσατο, οὗτος
ἀπέρχεται νικῶν, ἀλλ' ὅστις οὗ τὴν ἀπογραφὴν πε-

4 ποίηται, τοῦτο ἐπὶ τῆς πείρας ἄριστα δείκνυσιν. καὶ
τοῦθ' οὕτως ἰσχύει διὰ τέλους ὥστε καὶ ἐν αὐτοῖς
τοῖς ἄθλοις, προσθήσω δ' ὅτι καὶ τοῖς αὐτοῦ τοῦ
τάχους, οὐ τοῖς ἐπὶ τῆς ἀρχῆς ἐξενεγκοῦσιν ἀποδίδο-

5 ται τὸ σύμβολον, ἀλλὰ τοῖς παρελθοῦσιν. καίτοι πῶς
οὐκ ἀλογία πολλὴ τοὺς μὲν ἃ τῆς τοῦ σώματος
τύχης ἔχεται μελετῶντας ἢ τιμῶντας οὕτω σφόδρα
⟨καὶ νῦν⟩[1] καὶ πρότερον τὸ τοῦ λόγου καλὸν καὶ
δίκαιον τετιμηκέναι,[2] τοὺς δ' ἐπὶ τῶν λόγων ἀνέ-
χοντας καὶ χωρὶς τῆς ἐν τούτοις διατριβῆς οὐδ' ἂν
ζῆν δεξαμένους οὕτως ἀργῶς, μᾶλλον δ' ἀδίκως
ἔχειν, ὥσθ' ἑνὶ πιστῷ χρῆσθαι περὶ ἁπάντων, ἄν τις
φθάσῃ γενόμενος, καὶ τὰ ὀνόματα ἀντὶ τῆς ἀληθείας
θαυμάζειν αἱρεῖσθαι, ὥσπερ νομίσαι δέον, οὐχ εὑρεῖν τὸ βέλτιον· καὶ τοὺς μὲν νόμους αὐτούς, ἂν συμ-
φέρῃ, κινεῖν, τοὺς δὲ περὶ τῶν ἀεὶ μενόντων τῇ
φύσει λόγους ἐπὶ τοῖς πρώτοις μὴ δέχεσθαι, ἀλλ'
ὥσπερ ὅρους ἢ στήλας τοὺς προκατεσχηκότας πρεσβεύειν, καὶ ταῦτα οὐ λύειν ὥσπερ ἐν τοῖς νόμοις τοὺς
προτέρους διὰ τῶν ἐναντίων δέον, ἀλλὰ τῆς αὐτῆς

---

[1] add. codd. dett.   [2] om. A, secl. Lenz.

arts are not ranked in worth according to the order of their appearance—or the drawing of the lots would be enough—, but whoever is the best contestant, he is crowned and proclaimed the victor, even if he happens to appear last. But on the other hand those who claim to be contestants and judges of more urbane contests, so very much esteem time that they not only regard those who come afterwards as totally inferior, but even incapable of any argument better than the ones already presented. I note that in gymnastic contests, the first entrant 3 does not go off the victor, but he who in trial has proved the best in that which he has entered. And 4 this practice is so universal that in the competitions themselves, I shall add even in those of speed, the token of victory is not awarded to those who hold the lead at the start, but to those who overtake and pass them. Yet how is it not most odd for those 5 who practise and honour physical attainments, now and in the past, to have respected the fairness and rightness of reason, while those who excel in the attributes of reason and could not live without such study, are so slothful, nay unjust, as to employ as a single trustworthy test in all matters, precedence, and to prefer respect for titles instead of truth, as if they must believe in tradition but not discover any improvements ? And men even change the law, if it is expedient, while they do not at all admit discussion about what is naturally immutable [a]; but like boundaries or markers they show preference for the original arguments, although it is unnecessary, unlike the law, to repeal the older through a contrary point of view, but only to give the other side

[a] *i.e.* oratory.

(2 D.)

χώρας καὶ ἑτέρους ἀξιοῦν αὐτοῖς· καὶ τοῖς μὲν ὅρ-
κοις τοῖς κοινοῖς προσπαραγράφειν ἐξεῖναι ἀνελεῖν
3 D. καὶ προσθεῖναι ὅ τι ἂν σκοπουμένοις ὕστερον συν-
δοκῇ, οὓς δὲ ἀπὸ τῆς αὐτῆς ἐξουσίας ἀεὶ καὶ διὰ
παντὸς ἐξετάζειν δεῖ λόγους, τῷ παρελθόντι χρόνῳ μόνῳ προσθεῖναι, ὥσπερ ἂν εἴ τις καὶ ὑγιαίνειν
χρῆναι φάσκοι μόνους τοὺς πρώτους γενομένους, καὶ
μηδὲ ἐκεῖνο ὁρᾷ ὅτι ἡ τοιαύτη κρίσις καὶ ὁ τοιοῦτος λογισμὸς αὐτοῖς πρώτοις οὓς τιμῶσιν οὐ
λυσιτελεῖ.

6   Εἰ γὰρ τῷ χρόνῳ δεῖ συγχωρεῖν καὶ τὴν ἀξίαν ἀπὸ
τούτου μετρεῖν, οὐκέτ' ἔχει τόπον ἡ νῦν παρὰ
7 πάντων εἰς ἐκείνους αἰδώς. Ἴασος γὰρ ἂν οὕτω γε
νικῴη περὶ λόγους καὶ Κρίασος καὶ Κρότωπος καὶ
Φορωνεὺς καὶ εἴ τις Ἀργεῖος ἐκ μύθου καὶ Δευκα-
λίων ἢ εἴ τις ἔκ τε ἄλλων ⟨ἄλλος⟩[1] καὶ Λυκάων ἐξ
Ἀρκαδίας καὶ Κέκροψ Ἀθήνηθεν ἀντὶ τῶν νῦν
βεβοημένων· ἐν δὲ τοῖς ἔθνεσι Φρύγες διὰ τὴν παρὰ
τοῦ βέκους,[2] οἶμαι, μαρτυρίαν. καὶ παρῆκα Καλ-
λαίθυιαν ἀρίστην γυναικῶν ἅμα καὶ ἀνδρῶν γενο-
8 μένην. ἐὰν οὕτω κρίνωμεν, ὡς οὐ Κόδρῳ γε μετέσται
τῆς φιλοτιμίας, ἀλλὰ καὶ οὗτος παῖς οἷς εἶπον
συμβάλλειν καὶ οὐκ[3] ἀρχαῖος, καὶ κατὰ μικρὸν οὕτω
9 ζητήσομεν εἴ τις ἦν πρὶν σελήνην εἶναι. Ὁμήρου δὲ
καὶ Ἡσιόδου καὶ τῶν εἰς ἡμᾶς νενικηκότων, Πλάτωνος, εἰ βούλει, καὶ Δημοσθένους καὶ τῶν ὀλίγον
πρὸ τούτων, οὐδ' εἰς πολλοστὸν χρόνον ἐλπὶς ὁμοίαν
ἐγγενέσθαι δόξαν, συμπροϊόντος ἴσου τοῦ πρὸ

---

[1] add. Reiske.   [2] Ddf. : βαίκους TQVA.
[3] codd. dett. : οὔτ' TQVA.

284

the same scope which they had. And they append clauses to public oaths, that it is permissible to add or subtract as we may decide after a later scrutiny ; but they leave to the past alone arguments which must ever and in every way be examined with the same privilege, as if someone should proclaim that only the first born were fated to enjoy good health ; and they do not even recognize that such a verdict and judgement is unprofitable to those first of all whom they honour.

If we must yield to time and take our values from 6 it, the current respect which all men have toward those ancients is out of place. For Iasus, Criasus, 7 Crotopus, Phoroneus, any mythic Argive, Deucalion, or someone else from another nation, Lycaon from Arcadia, Cecrops of Athens, would thus hold first place in literature instead of those who are now re-nowned, and among the provincials, the Phrygians, I suppose, by the evidence of " bekos." [a] And I have omitted Callaethyia,[b] the best of both women and men. If we so decide, even Codrus will be 8 without honour, but he too is a mere boy and not ancient in comparison with those whom I have lis-ted ; so we shall gradually seek out whoever lived in pre-lunar times. Homer, Hesiod, those who 9 have remained pre-eminent to our day, Plato, if you will, and Demosthenes, and those a little before them, can have no expectation of an equal fame even after the longest time, since the age of their predecessors will ever increase concurrently with

---

[a] *Cf.* Herodotus II. 2. " Bekos " is Phrygian for "bread." The persons mentioned in this section are legendary.
[b] Synonymous with Pandora, according to the scholiast ; for Codrus, last king of Athens, *cf.* or. i. 87.

(3 D.)

10 αὐτῶν ἐκείνοις ἀεί. εἰ δὲ τοῦτο εὔδηλον ἅπασιν ὅτι
καὶ οὗτοι φύσει καὶ δυνάμει διενεγκόντες τοὺς πρὸ
αὐτῶν ἀπέκρυψαν, οὐδὲ τοὺς ὕστερον παντάπασιν
ἅπαντας ἀπείργειν εἰκός, οὐδ' ἀπιστεῖν εἴ τις καὶ
τοῦ νυνὶ χρόνου μετεσχηκὼς ἔχει συμβαλέσθαι

4 D. γνώμην περὶ ὧν πρόκειται λόγος, ἀλλὰ παρ' αὐτῶν,
ὡς ἔοικεν, ὧν τιμῶμεν ὑπάρχειν εἰδότας τὸ προσ-

11 ίεσθαι καὶ προσέχειν ὁπόσον διαφέρει. ἅπαντας
μὲν οὖν ἴσως τοὺς παλαιοὺς αἰδεῖσθαι μὲν δίκαιον,
φρίττειν δὲ οὐκ ἄξιον, εἴπερ μὴ τοὺς ἐπὶ τοῖς λόγοις
ὀνομασθέντας μᾶλλον ἢ τοὺς λόγους αὐτοὺς δεῖ
δοκεῖν τιμᾶν· ὅτι δ' εἰ πρὸς ἄλλον τινὰ χρὴ γνώμης
οὕτως ἔχειν, καὶ πρὸς Πλάτωνα, οὐκ ἄλλου δέομαι
μάρτυρος, ἀλλ' αὐτὸς ἐξαρκεῖ οὐ μόνον οἷς ἀπαντα-
χοῦ βοᾷ καὶ παρακελεύεται μηδὲν πρότερον ποιεῖσθαι τῆς ἀληθείας, ἀλλὰ καὶ ὀλίγου[1] τῷ παραδείγ-

12 ματι. εἰ γὰρ ἐκεῖνος Ὁμήρῳ τῷ τοσοῦτον πρὸ
αὐτοῦ περὶ πολλῶν ἐπιτιμῶν οὐκ ἀπεστέρηται λόγου, ἀλλ' ἔχει πρὸς τοὺς ἀγανακτοῦντας ὅ τι εἴπῃ,
κατ' αὐτόν, ὡς ἔοικε, Πλάτωνα καὶ τοὺς ἐκεῖνον
ἐπαινοῦντας καὶ πάσης αἰτίας ἀφιέντας ἔστι, κἂν
ἄλλος τις ἐκείνῳ δοκῇ τι λέγειν ὑπεναντίον, τολ-
μᾶν ἀκροάσασθαι, μή που τοῦτ' ἔγκλημα ποιουμέ-
νους, ἀλλ' ἐὰν τοῖς περὶ τῶν πραγμάτων λόγοις
ἀπολειφθῇ.

13 Ἃ τοίνυν εἴρηκεν περὶ ῥητορικῆς φιλονικότερον
τοῦ δέοντος, Γοργίου καὶ Σωκράτους ὑποθέμενος
συνουσίαν Ἀθήνησι φέρε ἐπισκεψώμεθα καὶ δεί-

14 ξωμεν ὅπως ἔχει. καὶ γὰρ ἂν εἴη δεινόν, εἰ ἐκεῖνος
μὲν ὑποστὰς κατηγορεῖν ἐκ προφανοῦς οὐκ ἀπε-
στέρησε τρόπον γέ τιν' αὐτὴν τῶν ὑπὲρ αὐτῆς λόγων,

---

[1] Reiske : ὀλίγῳ TQVA.

their own. But if it is clear to all that these men, 10 through the excellence of their natural faculties, thrust into the shade those before them, it is unreasonable to bar the way for absolutely all later men, and to be incredulous if a man of the present has an opinion to offer on the subject at hand, but reasonable to understand surely from the very ones whom we honour, how important it is to remain receptive and attentive. Perhaps it is right to respect all of the 11 ancients, but it is unworthy to be scared by them, unless we must appear to honour more those famed for their ideas than the ideas themselves. Moreover, as to the fact that so must we feel toward Plato if toward anyone, I need no other witness, but he is sufficient not only in his ubiquitous claims and exhortations to place nothing above the truth,[a] but almost by his own example also. For if he on 12 many counts censured Homer who was far older and if he was not deprived of the right to speak, but could do so in the face of those annoyed at his remarks, then in imitation of Plato himself, as it seems, and those who praise him and exonerate him from every charge, if someone else seems to oppose Plato, we can dare to listen to him without invoking this complaint, unless his substantive arguments are deficient.

Let us now consider and evaluate his over-conten- 13 tious remarks about oratory, when he used the literary contrivance of a meeting of Gorgias and Socrates at Athens. For it would be terrible if 14 on the one hand he, in openly making his accusation, did not indeed in a sense deprive oratory of its

[a] *Cf. Phaedo* 91 c.

(4 D.)

ἀλλ' ἀπέδωκεν δυσὶν καὶ τρισὶν ἀντειπεῖν, ὡς γοῦν
ἐν σχήματι διαλόγων, ἡμεῖς δὲ οἱ τὸ ὅλον βοηθεῖν
ἔχοντες καὶ προῃρημένοι μὴ τολμήσομεν,[1] ὥσπερ
τοσαῦτ' ἀντιλέγειν Πλάτωνι δέον, ὁπόσα ἂν αὐτὸς
15 πρὸς αὑτὸν βουληθείη. ἄλογον δέ μοι φαίνεται, εἰ
Πλάτων μὲν οὐκ ᾐδέσθη ψέγων ῥητορικήν, ἧς ἴσως
5 D. τι καὶ αὐτῷ μετῆν, ἡμεῖς δ' αἰσχυνούμεθα ὑπὲρ
ῥητορικῆς λέγοντες μή τις δι' ἐκεῖνον ἀχθεσθείη.
16 χωρὶς δὲ τούτων εἰ μὲν μηδὲν ἀντειπεῖν δεῖ, ἀλλ'
ἐρήμην ἑαλωκέναι καθάπερ ἐν δικαστηρίῳ, καὶ
ταῦτα λόγων τέχνην οὖσαν, ἄλλο τι τοῦτ' ἂν εἴη
τοὐπίταγμα· εἰ δ' ἔσθ' ὅντινα δεῖ, σχεδὸν ἡμῖν ἂν
πρέποι, ἵνα καὶ τὸ δίκαιον εὐθὺς ἐν αὐτῷ τούτῳ
πρώτῳ δείξωμεν οὗ προεστήκαμεν· ὡς ἔστιν οὐ
λόγον σῷζον παρ' ἧς τὸ τοῖς ἄλλοις συναγορεύειν
ἐστίν, ταύτῃ τῶν παρ' αὑτῆς μὴ μεταδοῦναι, ἀλλὰ
δυοῖν θάτερον, ἢ τοιοῦτον εἶναι δοκεῖν αὐτὴν οἷον
Πλάτων βεβούληται, ἢ τοιοῦτόν γ' εἶναι δοκεῖν
17 ποιῆσαι. οὐ γάρ ἐστιν ἓν τοῦτο ὃ πανταχοῦ, ὅτι τὰς
αἰτίας ἡ σιωπὴ βεβαιοῖ, ἀλλ' ἅμα τῶν τε δικαίων
οὐ τεύξεται καὶ τὸ σεμνὸν αὐτῆς ἐπ' αὐτῆς ἐξελήλεγκται. δόξει γὰρ οὐχ οἷά τ' εἶναι σῴζειν τὰ
18 δίκαια. ἐγὼ δὲ μάλιστα μὲν καὶ πρῶτον αἰδοῖ τῶν
λόγων αὐτῶν καὶ τῷ νομίζειν χρῆναι καθάπερ
γονεῦσι βοηθεῖν, ὡς ἕκαστος ἔχει τῆς ἐν αὐτοῖς
δυνάμεως, εἶτα καὶ τῶν ἄλλων ἕνεκ' ἀνθρώπων,
ὅπως μὴ περὶ τῶν μεγίστων φαύλως ὑπαχθεῖεν
μηδ' ἀγνοήσαιεν ὅσῳ λαμπρότερος καὶ μείζων
ἀνήρ, τοσούτῳ προχειρότερον πιστεύσαντες αὐτῷ,
μηδὲ ἣν οὐ[2] θέμις οὐδὲν φλαῦρον ἀκοῦσαι, ταύτην

---

[1] codd. dett. : τολμήσωμεν TQVA.   [2] οὐδὲ VA.

defence, but did grant to two or three people the chance to take the opposite side as he did at least in the guise of a dialogue ; but on the other hand we, who can and have chosen to help in every way, shall lack the courage to do so, as if the arguments against Plato ought only to be those which he wished to make against himself. It seems to me 15 senseless for Plato to feel no shame in criticizing oratory, in which perchance he had some part, but for us to feel embarrassment speaking in defence of oratory, since someone might be annoyed because of him. Besides if oratory must offer no arguments 16 in opposition, but as in court be convicted in absentia, although it is the art of words, this limitation would be something else again. But if anyone must do so, it would be more or less incumbent on us forthwith and in this very aspect first to prove the right which we champion. For it is irrational not to give to that, by the use of which others are defended, a part of its own means. The result is that it either seems such as Plato wished or that we make it seem such. For there is not only the generality that 17 silence confirms an accusation, but oratory will not obtain its due, and its very dignity is refuted in its own concern. It will seem to be incapable of protecting its own rights. I have undertaken the discourse 18 for the sake of the right and for a practical reason, particularly out of respect for oratory and the belief that it must be aided like one's parents by each as best he can, and secondly on behalf of other men, that they may not be badly misled or form incorrect opinions about the most important matters, being the more readily credulous, the more a man is great and distinguished, and although they think that they

(5 D.)

οἰόμενοι κακίζειν αὐτοὺς τῶν καλλίστων ἀποστερή-
σαιεν ἑκόντες, ἐν ἴσῳ δὲ ἄκοντες ⟨ὡς⟩[1] εἰπεῖν,
ὑπέστην τὸν λόγον τοῦ τε δικαίου χάριν καὶ τῆς
19 χρείας. τὸ μὲν οὖν ἀξίωμα τοσοῦτον τοῦ παρόντος
ἀγῶνος. καλῶ δ' ἐπὶ τούτῳ τῷ τολμήματι καὶ
Ἑρμῆν λόγιον καὶ Ἀπόλλωνα μουσηγέτην καὶ
6 D. Μούσας ἁπάσας ἡγεμόνας γενέσθαι, μάλιστα μὲν
καὶ δι' αὐτὸ τὸ ἴδιον τῆς νῦν κλήσεως, ὅτι τούτων
ἡ δωρεὰ ὑπὲρ ἧς ἅμα καὶ δι' ἧς ἀγωνιζόμεθα,
ἔπειθ' ὅτι καὶ δύο συμπέπτωκεν. οὔτε γὰρ πρὸς
τὸν φαυλότατον τῶν Ἑλλήνων οὔθ' ὑπὲρ τῶν φαυ-
λοτάτων οἱ λόγοι.
20 Εἰσὶ δὲ οἳ καὶ τῶν ἐκείνου λόγων τῶν εἰς μνήμην
ἡκόντων τούτους μάλιστα θαυμάζουσιν οἷς ἐνταῦθα
καὶ περὶ τούτων κέχρηται. ὥστε πανταχῇ θείας
21 δεῖν τῆς βοηθείας ὡς ἀληθῶς. ὥσπερ οὖν οἱ τὰς τῶν
παρανόμων γραφὰς εἰσιόντες ἀπ' αὐτῶν ὧν εἴρηκε
22 τὴν ἀρχὴν ποιησόμεθα. ἔστι δὲ ταυτὶ " Δοκεῖ τοίνυν μοι, ὦ Γοργία, εἶναι ἐπιτήδευμα τεχνικὸν μὲν οὔ,
ψυχῆς δὲ στοχαστικῆς καὶ ἀνδρείας καὶ φύσει δεινῆς προσομιλεῖν τοῖς ἀνθρώποις. καλῶ δὲ αὐτοῦ
ἐγὼ τὸ κεφάλαιον[2] κολακείαν. ταύτης μοι δοκεῖ
τῆς ἐπιτηδεύσεως πολλὰ μὲν καὶ ἄλλα μόρια εἶναι,
ἓν δὲ καὶ ⟨ἡ⟩[3] ὀψοποιική, ὃ δοκεῖ μὲν εἶναι τέχνη,
ὡς δὲ ὁ ἐμὸς λόγος, οὐκ ἔστι τέχνη, ἀλλ' ἐμπειρία
καὶ τριβή· ταύτης μόριον καὶ τὴν ῥητορικὴν ἐγὼ
καλῶ καὶ τήν γε κομμωτικὴν καὶ τὴν σοφιστικήν,
τέτταρα ταῦτα μόρια ἐπὶ τέτταρσι πράγμασιν. εἰ
οὖν βούλεται Πῶλος πυνθάνεσθαι, πυνθανέσθω, οὐ
γάρ πω πέπυσται ὁποῖόν φημι ἐγὼ τῆς κολακείας
μόριον εἶναι τὴν ῥητορικήν, ἀλλ' αὐτὸν λέληθα

are only reviling oratory which ought to be sanctified from silly slander, that they may not willingly, and equally, one might say, unwillingly, deprive themselves of what is fairest in the world. Such 19 then is the magnitude of the present contest. In this bold act, I invoke Hermes, God of Oratory, Apollo, Leader of the Muses, and all the Muses, to be my guides, particularly because of the propriety of the present summons, since it is their gift on behalf of which and by means of which we contend, and because of the two following circumstances : we argue neither against the meanest of the Greeks nor in defence of the meanest of subjects.

Of all Plato's words which are remembered, some 20 most admire those in which he treated this subject. Therefore in every way we truly need divine help. Just as those who go to prosecute the charge of an 21 illegal proposal, we shall begin with his own statements. They are as follows [a] : " ' It seems to me, 22 Gorgias, not to be an artistic practice, but that of a soul taking aim, courageous, and naturally clever in associating with men. Its total effect I call flattery. It seems to me that there are many other parts of this activity. One is cookery, which seems to be an art, but in my reasoning is no art, but a matter of experience and familiarity. A part of this I also call oratory, beautification, and sophistry, these being four parts concerned with four actions. If Polus wishes to inquire, let him, for he has not inquired as to what part of flattery I say that oratory is. Yet

---

[a] *Gorgias* 463 A—465 C.

---

[1] add. Behr.   [2] τὸ κεφάλαιον ἐγὼ TQ.
[3] Plato : om. TQVA.

(6 D.)

οὔπω ἀποκεκριμένος. ὁ δὲ ἐπανερωτᾷ εἰ οὐ καλὸν
ἡγοῦμαι εἶναι· ἐγὼ δ' αὐτῷ οὐκ ἀποκρινοῦμαι πρότερον εἴτε αἰσχρὸν εἴτε καλὸν ἡγοῦμαι τὴν ῥητορικὴν πρὶν ἂν πρῶτον ἀποκρίνωμαι ὅ ἐστιν. οὐ γὰρ
δίκαιον, ὦ Πῶλε. ἀλλ' εἴπερ βούλει πυνθάνεσθαι,
ἐρώτα ὁποῖον μόριον τῆς κολακείας φημὶ εἶναι τὴν
ῥητορικήν. Ἐρωτῶ δή, καὶ ἀπόκριναι[1] ὁποῖον
7 D. μόριον. Ἆρ' οὖν ἂν μάθοις ἀποκριναμένου; ἔστι
γὰρ ἡ ῥητορικὴ κατὰ τὸν ἐμὸν λόγον πολιτικῆς
μορίου εἴδωλον. Τί οὖν; καλὸν ἢ αἰσχρὸν λέγεις
αὐτὴν εἶναι; Αἰσχρὸν ἔγωγε. τὰ γὰρ κακὰ αἰσχρὰ
καλῶ, ἐπειδὴ δεῖ σοι ἀποκρίνασθαι ὡς ἤδη εἰδότι
ὃ λέγω. Μὰ τὸν Δία, ὦ Σώκρατες, ἀλλ' ἔγωγε
οὐδὲ αὐτὸς[2] συνίημι ὅ τι λέγεις. Εἰκότως γε, ὦ
Γοργία. οὐδὲν γάρ πω σαφὲς λέγω. Πῶλος δὲ
ὅδε νέος ἐστὶ καὶ ὀξύς. Ἀλλὰ τοῦτον μὲν ἔα, ἐμοὶ
δὲ εἰπὲ πῶς λέγεις πολιτικῆς μορίου εἴδωλον εἶναι
τὴν ῥητορικήν. Ἀλλ' ἐγὼ πειράσομαι φράσαι ὅ γέ
μοι φαίνεται εἶναι ἡ ῥητορική· εἰ δὲ μὴ τυγχάνει ὂν
τοῦτο, Πῶλος ὅδε ἐλέγξει. σῶμά που καλεῖς τι
καὶ ψυχήν; Πῶς γὰρ οὔ; Οὐκοῦν καὶ τούτων οἴει
τινὰ εἶναι ἑκατέρου εὐεξίαν; Ἔγωγε. Τί δαί;
δοκοῦσαν μὲν εὐεξίαν, οὖσαν δ' οὔ; οἷον τοιόνδε
λέγω· πολλοὶ δοκοῦσιν εὖ ἔχειν τὰ σώματα, οὓς οὐκ
ἂν ῥᾳδίως αἴσθοιτό τις ὡς οὐκ εὖ ἔχουσιν ἀλλ' ἢ[3]
ἰατρός τε καὶ τῶν γυμναστικῶν τις. Ἀληθῆ λέγεις. Τὸ τοιοῦτον λέγω καὶ ἐν σώματι εἶναι καὶ ἐν
ψυχῇ, ὃ ποιεῖ μὲν δοκεῖν εὖ ἔχειν τὸ σῶμα καὶ τὴν
ψυχήν, ἔχει δὲ οὐδὲν μᾶλλον. Ἔστι ταῦτα. Φέρε
δή σοι ἐὰν δύνωμαι σαφέστερον ἐπιδείξω ὃ λέγω.

[1] ἀπόκριναί μοι TQ.

he has not noticed that I have not answered him. He asks me again whether I do not think that it is fair. I shall not answer him whether I believe oratory to be shameful or fair, until I first answer what it is. For it would not be right, Polus. But if you wish to inquire, ask to what part of flattery I say that oratory belongs.' 'Well, I ask this ; answer what part.' 'Then would you understand me, if I answered ? According to my reasoning oratory is a shadow of the part of politics.' 'Well ! Do you say that it is fair or shameful ?' 'I call it shameful. For I call evil things shameful, since I must answer you as if you now understood what I mean.' 'No indeed, Socrates. I certainly do not comprehend what you mean.' 'Reasonably, Gorgias. For my remark is not clear. But Polus here is young and sharp.' 'Ignore him, and tell me how you mean oratory to be a shadow of the part of politics.' 'I shall try to make clear what oratory seems to me to be. If it does not happen to be this, Polus here will refute me. Is, would you say, the body and soul something ?' 'Of course.' 'Then do you think that there is a state of well being for each of these? ' 'I do indeed.' 'Well ? An apparent, but not a real state of well being ? For example : many seem to be of sound body, and one would not easily perceive that they are not sound, except for a doctor or a gymnast.' 'True.' 'I say that there exists such a quality in the body and soul, which causes the body and the soul to seem to be sound, but they are none the more sound for that.' 'That is so.' 'Come, if I can, I shall show you more clearly what I mean. For

---

² codd. dett.: αὐτὸ TQVA.   ³ om. TQ.

δυοῖν ὄντων ⟨τῶν⟩[1] πραγμάτων δύο λέγω τέχνας.
τὴν μὲν οὖν ἐπὶ τῇ ψυχῇ πολιτικὴν καλῶ, τὴν δ' ἐπὶ
τῷ σώματι μίαν μὲν οὕτως ὀνομάσαι οὐκ ἔχω σοι,
μιᾶς δὲ οὔσης τῆς τοῦ σώματος θεραπείας δύο
μόρια λέγω, τὴν μὲν γυμναστικήν, τὴν δὲ ἰατρικήν.
τῆς δὲ πολιτικῆς ἀντίστροφον μὲν τῇ γυμναστικῇ
τὴν νομοθετικήν, ἀντίστροφον δὲ τῇ ἰατρικῇ τὴν
δικαιοσύνην. ἐπικοινωνοῦσι μὲν δὴ ἀλλήλαις ἅτε
περὶ τὸ αὐτὸ οὖσαι ἑκατέρα τούτων, ἥ τε ἰατρικὴ τῇ γυμναστικῇ καὶ ἡ δικαιοσύνη τῇ νομοθετικῇ. ὅμως δὲ διαφέρουσίν τι ἀλλήλων. τεττάρων
δὲ τούτων οὐσῶν καὶ ἀεὶ πρὸς τὸ βέλτιστον θερα-

8 D. πευουσῶν, τῶν μὲν τὸ σῶμα, τῶν δὲ τὴν ψυχήν, ἡ
κολακευτικὴ αἰσθομένη, οὐ γνοῦσα λέγω, ἀλλὰ
στοχασαμένη, τέτραχα ἑαυτὴν διανείμασα, ὑποδῦσα
ἕκαστον τῶν μορίων προσποιεῖται εἶναι τοῦτο[2]
ὅπερ ὑπέδυ, καὶ τοῦ μὲν βελτίστου οὐδὲν φροντίζει,
τῷ δὲ ἡδίστῳ θηρεύει τὴν ἄνοιαν καὶ ἐξαπατᾷ, ὥστε
δοκεῖν πλείστου ἀξίαν εἶναι. ὑπὸ μὲν οὖν τὴν ἰατρικὴν ἡ ὀψοποιικὴ ὑποδέδυκεν καὶ προσποιεῖται
τὰ βέλτιστα σιτία τῷ σώματι εἰδέναι, ὥστε εἰ δέοι
ἐν παισὶ διαγωνίζεσθαι ὀψοποιόν τε καὶ ἰατρὸν ἢ
ἐν ἀνδράσιν οὕτως ἀνοήτοις ὥσπερ οἱ παῖδες,
πότερος ἐπαΐει περὶ τῶν χρηστῶν σιτίων καὶ πονη-
ρῶν, ὁ ἰατρὸς ἢ ⟨ὁ⟩[3] ὀψοποιός, λιμῷ ἂν ἀποθανεῖν
τὸν ἰατρόν. κολακείαν μὲν οὖν αὐτὸ καλῶ καὶ
αἰσχρόν φημι εἶναι τὸ τοιοῦτον, ὦ Πῶλε, τοῦτο
γὰρ πρὸς σὲ λέγω, ὅτι τοῦ ἡδέος στοχάζεται ἄνευ
τοῦ βελτίστου. τέχνην δὲ αὐτὴν οὔ φημι εἶναι,
ἀλλ' ἐμπειρίαν, ὅτι οὐκ ἔχει λόγον οὐδένα ᾧ προσ-
φέρει, ὁποῖα ἄττα τὴν φύσιν ἐστίν, ὥστε τὴν αἰτίαν

these matters, which are two in number, I say there
are two arts. That pertaining to the soul I call politics. That pertaining to the body, I cannot name as a
unit. But although there is a single service of the
body, I say that there are two parts of this, gymnastics and medicine. In politics, legislation is the
opposite of gymnastics, justice the opposite of medicine. Each of these pairs has a community of interests,
since they are concerned with the same thing ; medicine with gymnastics, justice with legislation. Still
they differ somewhat from one another. These are
four in number and ever serve aiming at the best,
the one the body, the other the soul. Then flattery,
through a feeling, I mean, not through understanding, but guesswork, has divided itself into four, surrep-
titiously entered into each of the parts, and pretends
to be that into which it has entered. It cares nothing
for the best, but hunts out folly by means of what is
most pleasant, and uses deception so that it seems
to be very valuable. Cookery has entered into
medicine, and pretends to know the best foods for
the body, so that if a cook or a doctor had to contend
before boys or men as foolish as boys, as to which,
the cook or the doctor, understands about good or
bad foods, the doctor would starve to death. I call
this flattery, and I say that it is a shameful quality,
Polus—I am talking to you—because it conjectures
at the pleasant without regard for the best. I do
not call this an art, but a matter of experience,
because it has no understanding by which it tests
the nature of a characteristic, with the result that it

---

¹ add. codd. dett. ² codd. dett. : τοιοῦτο TQVA.
³ add. codd. dett.

(8 D.)

ἑκάστου μὴ ἔχειν εἰπεῖν· ἐγὼ δὲ τέχνην οὐ καλῶ ὃ
ἂν ᾖ ἄλογον πρᾶγμα. τούτων δὲ πέρι εἰ ἀμφισβη-
τεῖς, ἐθέλω ὑποσχεῖν λόγον. τῇ μὲν οὖν ἰατρικῇ,
ὥσπερ λέγω, ἡ ὀψοποιικὴ κολακεία ὑπόκειται, τῇ
δὲ γυμναστικῇ κατὰ τὸν αὐτὸν τρόπον ἡ κομμωτική,
κακοῦργος καὶ ἀπατηλὴ καὶ[1] ἀγεννὴς καὶ ἀνελεύθε-
ρος, σχήμασι καὶ χρώμασι καὶ λειότητι καὶ ἐσθῆτι
ἀπατῶσα, ὥστε ποιεῖν ἀλλότριον κάλλος ἐφελκο-
μένη τοῦ οἰκείου διὰ τῆς γυμναστικῆς ἀμελεῖν. ἵνα
οὖν μὴ μακρολογῶ, ἐθέλω σοι εἰπεῖν, ὥσπερ οἱ
γεωμέτραι, ἤδη γὰρ ἂν ἴσως ἀκολουθήσαις, ὅτι ὃ
9 D. κομμωτικὴ πρὸς γυμναστικήν, τοῦτο σοφιστικὴ
πρὸς νομοθετικήν, καὶ ὃ[2] ὀψοποιικὴ πρὸς ἰατρικήν,
τοῦτο ῥητορικὴ πρὸς δικαιοσύνην."

23 Ἐνταῦθα ἀπόδειξις μὲν οὐδ' ἡτισοῦν ἔνεστιν οὐδ'
ἔλεγχος ἀνάγκη προεληλυθώς, ὑπόκειται δ' ἁπλῶς
ὥσπερ ἐξόν, οὐ πολὺς ἦν ἱδρὼς πρότερον· οὐδὲν
διαφερόντως ἢ εἰ χάριν ᾔτει τοὺς ἀκούοντας ταῦτα
24 συγχωρῆσαι. καίτοι εἰ τὰ ζητούμενα ὡς ὁμολογού-
μενα ὑποτίθεσθαι γέλως, πῶς εἰκὸς ἅ γε ζητεῖν
γέλως, ταῦτ' ἐξ ἀρχῆς ὑποτίθεσθαι; πῶς γὰρ οὐ
γέλως εἰ τῆς αὐτῆς φύσεως ῥητορικὴ καὶ ὀψοποιικὴ
ζητεῖν· ὁ δ' ὥσπερ ὁμολογούμενον εἴληφεν αὐτό.
25 γνοίη δὲ ἄν τις ἐκείνως, εἰ τὸ τῆς ῥητορικῆς ὄνομα
ἐξελὼν τὸ τῆς φιλοσοφίας ἀντ' ἐκείνου μεταλάβοι
26 καὶ ἐπὶ τούτῳ πᾶσι τοῖς αὐτοῖς χρήσαιτο. καὶ
μηδεὶς μήτε ἀγροικίαν μήτε ψυχρότητα καταγνῷ
τοῦ λόγου. μάλιστα μὲν γὰρ οὐ δήπου δυοῖν ἐπι-
στήμαιν ἢ δυνάμεοιν τοῖς μὲν τὴν ἑτέραν προΐστα-
μένοις, οὐδ' ἂν ὁτιοῦν βλασφημῶσιν εἰς τοὺς ἑτέρους,

---

[1] om. TVA. [2] codd. dett. : καὶ ὅτῃ TQVA.

cannot supply a reason for each action. I do not
call an art, whatever is an unreasoning matter. If
you dispute this, I wish to be examined. Therefore,
as I say, the flattery of cookery belongs to the classification of medicine, and in the same fashion beautification belongs to gymnastics, vicious, deceptive,
ignoble, and servile, deceiving by forms, colours,
smoothness, and clothing, so that by introducing a
foreign beauty it causes neglect of natural beauty
derived through gymnastics. So as not to make a
long story of this, I wish to speak in the terms of
geometry, for perhaps you might then follow what I
say. What beautification is to gymnastics, sophistry
is to legislation, and what cookery is to medicine,
oratory is to justice.' "

Here there is no proof at all nor a chain of reason- 23
ing which had to be arrived at. An assumption is
simply made, as if he had the power to do so, on a
subject which formerly caused much difficulty. It
is no different than if he asked his hearers to make
these concessions as a favour. Yet if it is farcical to 24
hypothesize the object of an investigation as a
matter agreed upon, how is it reasonable to hypothesize at the outset, what it is farcical even to
investigate ? For how is it not farcical to investigate
whether oratory and cookery are of the same nature ?
But he has assumed this as a matter agreed upon.
The case might better be understood, if the word 25
" oratory " were removed, and " philosophy " were
put in its place, and all the same arguments were
used in regard to this. Let no one condemn the 26
argument for boorishness and frigidity. Indeed, if
the defenders of one of two sciences or faculties in any
way slander the other side, we shall not admit that

(9 D.)

οὐδὲν ἄγροικον ὑπεῖναι φήσομεν, τοῖς δ᾿ οὐδὲ τοῖς
27 αὐτοῖς ἀμύνεσθαι δώσομεν. ἔπειτ᾿ οὐ τοῦ φορτικοῦ
χάριν εἰρήσεται, ἀλλὰ τῆς ἀποδείξεως, ἣν οὐδαμοῦ
28 τούτοις εἶναι φαμέν. οὐκοῦν ὡδὶ γίγνεται " Δοκεῖ
τοίνυν μοι, ὦ Γοργία, εἶναι ἐπιτήδευμα τεχνικὸν μὲν
οὔ, ψυχῆς δὲ στοχαστικῆς καὶ ἀνδρείας, καὶ φύσει
δεινῆς προσομιλεῖν τοῖς ἀνθρώποις. καλῶ δὲ αὐτοῦ
ἐγὼ τὸ κεφάλαιον κολακείαν. ταύτης μοι δοκεῖ τῆς
10 D. ἐπιτηδεύσεως πολλὰ μὲν καὶ ἄλλα μόρια εἶναι, ἓν δὲ
καὶ ἡ ὀψοποιική, ὃ δοκεῖ μὲν εἶναι τέχνη, ὡς δὲ ὁ
ἐμὸς λόγος, οὐκ ἔστι τέχνη, ἀλλ᾿ ἐμπειρία καὶ τριβή·
ταύτης μόριον καὶ τὴν ῥητορικὴν ἐγὼ καλῶ καὶ τήν
γε κομμωτικὴν καὶ τὴν σοφιστικήν, τέτταρα ταῦτα
29 μόρια ἐπὶ τέτταρσι πράγμασιν." καὶ διὰ πάντων
δὴ τῶν εἰρημένων, εἴ τις οὕτως ἅπαντα τἆλλα κατὰ
χώραν ἐῶν τὴν¹ ῥητορικὴν εἰς τὴν φιλοσοφίαν μετα-
λαμβάνοι, συμβαίνει δήπου μηδὲν ἐμποδίζεσθαι τά
λε ῥήματα. ἀλλ᾿ οὔτε τοῦτο ὑγιαίνοντος, οἶμαι,
30 οὔτ᾿ ἐκεῖνο ἀποδεικνύντος. οὔτε γὰρ φιλοσοφίας²
τῶν ὀψοποιίας ὀνειδῶν οὐδὲν ἅψεται δήπουθεν, ἕως
ἂν ἄλλο τι τὴν φύσιν ᾖ, οὔθ᾿ οἷς ὀψοποιικὴν κακίζει τις ἐξελέγχει ῥητορικήν, ἕως ἂν μὴ δείξῃ τὴν
ἀνάγκην, ὑφ᾿ ἧς ταῦτα ὁμοίως ἔχει, πλὴν εἰ τοῦτ᾿
αὐτὸ ἱκανὸν ἡγήσατο εἰς ἀνάγκην περιστῆσαί τινα
τοῦ πῶς ὀψοποιικὴ ῥητορικῆς κεχώρισται λέγειν.
31 καίτοι τοῦτο ὀκνῶ μὲν εἰπεῖν, οὐκ ἔχω δὲ μαθεῖν
ὡς οὐχ ὑβρίζοντός ἐστιν.
32 Ὅμως δ᾿ ἔγωγε ὑποστήσομαι τοῦτο τὸ ἄτοπον.
καὶ γὰρ ὡς ἀληθῶς ἐστι δεινότερον καὶ ἀτοπώτερον,
εἰ μᾶλλον ὁ πειρώμενος ὡς οὐκ αἰσχρὸν ῥητορικὴ

their behaviour is boorish, while not even granting
the other side to defend themselves in the same way.
Then my argument will be made not from lack 27
of taste, but for proof, which we claim is lacking in
these arguments. This is what he says[a]: " It seems 28
to me, Gorgias, not to be an artistic practice, but
that of a soul taking aim, courageous, and naturally
clever, in associating with men. Its sum I call
flattery. It seems to me that there are many other
parts of this activity. One is cookery which seems
to be an art, but in my reasoning is no art, but a
matter of experience and familiarity. A part of this
I also call oratory, beautification, and sophistry,
these being four parts concerned with four actions."
And in this whole statement, if one should leave the 29
rest alone and change " oratory " to " philosophy,"
the tenor of the words is in no way impeded. But
neither is this the act of a sane man, I think, nor that
the act of a man proving his point. For surely 30
neither will any of the criticism of cookery touch
philosophy, at any rate so long as its nature is different, nor do the arguments which are used to vilify
cookery refute oratory, so long as no necessity is
proven, by which these are equal, unless it is thought
sufficient to impose on someone the necessity of saying
in what way cookery is separate from oratory. I 31
hesitate to say this, but I cannot conceive how this
is not the act of a slanderer.

Still I shall not eschew this odd predicament. 32
For truly it is more terrible and odd if he who tries to
show that oratory is not shameful feels a greater

[a] *Gorgias* 463 A—463 B.

---

[1] τὴν δὲ VA.   [2] φιλοσοφία VA.

(10 D.)

διδάσκειν αἰσχύνεται ἢ ὁ τολμήσας πρῶτον ἐν
33 αἰσχροῦ μοίρᾳ ψέγειν. πρῶτον μὲν οὖν εἰ τὰ
μάλιστα μὴ τέχνην εἶναι δοίημεν αὐτήν, ὅπερ ὡς
ἕρμαιον στρέφει παρ' ὅλον τὸν λόγον, τί μᾶλλον
αἰσχρόν γ' εἶναι συγχωρησόμεθα; εἰ μὲν γὰρ ἦν
ἀναγκαίως ἅπαν τὸ μὴ τέχνῃ γιγνόμενον κακόν, ἢ
34 τοῦ μηδενὸς ἄξιον, ἦν τι προὔργου[1]· νῦν δ' οὐδείς
11 D. ἐστιν ὅστις οὐκ ἂν συμφήσαι τὸ μὴ οὐ τὰ μέγιστα
ἀνθρώποις καὶ κάλλιστ' ἐκ θεῶν ἅμα τε ἔξω τέχνης
εἶναι καὶ τέχνης κρείττω, καὶ τοῦθ' οὕτω παρὰ πᾶσιν ἀνθρώποις καὶ δεξιοῖς καὶ πολλοῖς κεκράτηκεν
ὥσθ' ὅσα μὲν τῶν ἑπτὰ σοφῶν κληθέντων οὕτως
ἐν τοῖς πᾶσιν ὄντων εὐαριθμήτων εἶπέ τις ἢ συν-
εβούλευσεν, ἢ τῶν ἄλλων οὓς ἐπὶ παιδείᾳ θαυμάζο-
μεν ὡς πρώτους, οὐδεὶς προστίθησι θεῷ, ἀλλὰ τὸ
τοῦ ἀνδρὸς ὄνομα ἑκάστοις ἐπιφημίζεται· ἃ δ' ἂν αἱ
Πυθοῖ προμάντεις φῶσιν, ἐπειδὰν ἐκστῶσιν ἑαυτῶν,
ταῦθ' ὡς ὁ Πύθιος εἶπε καὶ Πλάτων καὶ ἅπαντες
35 λέγουσιν. καὶ[2] τίνα ἐπίστανται δήπου τέχνην τότε,
αἵ γε οὐχ οἷαί τέ εἰσι φυλάττειν οὐδὲ μεμνῆσθαι;
καίτοι μικρὰ μὲν ἡ πάντας εἰδυῖα λόγους ἀνθρωπί-
νους ἰατρικὴ καὶ κρείττων ὀψοποιικῆς πρὸς τὰς ἐκ
Δελφῶν, οἶμαι, δύναται λύσεις, ὅσαι καὶ ἰδίᾳ καὶ
κοινῇ καὶ νόσων καὶ παθημάτων ἁπάντων ἀνθρώποις ἐφάνθησαν, μικρὰ δ' ἡ κατ' αὐτὴν ἑστηκυῖα
δικαιοσύνη, κρίσεως ἕνεκα πραγμάτων καὶ συμ-
36 βουλῆς. τί δὲ ἐροῦσι σύμπαντες οἱ γυμνασταί; δυοῖν
καὶ τριῶν λογίων οὐχ ἡττᾶσθαι σφῶν πᾶσαν τὴν
ἐπιστήμην, εἴπερ ἕν γε τοῦτ' ἐπίστανται βραχὺ
37 σωφρονεῖν; τί δὲ ἡ σεμνή σοι νομοθετικὴ καὶ τὰ

---

[1] post προὔργου add. τῆς σπουδῆς V.
[2] καὶ TQVA : καίτοι codd. dett. (prob. Ddf.).

sense of shame than he who first dared to criticize
it as a kind of shameful thing. Therefore, to begin 33
with, if we should grant that it is not an art, which
point like some lucky find traverses the whole argument, why shall we any more concede that it is a
shameful thing ? For if of necessity everything which
takes place without art were evil or worthless, there
was some profit in the argument. As things are, no 34
one would deny that men's greatest and fairest
possessions come from the Gods and are also apart
from art and greater than art. And this view has so
prevailed among all men, both the cultured and the
masses, that no one attributes to God whatever
was said or advised by any of the seven wise men so
called, being few among all mankind, or by any of
the others whom we admire as being pre-eminent
in education, but they append the man's name to
each saying. But as to the pronouncements of the
priestesses at Pytho, when they are ecstatic, both
Plato [a] and all men declare that the Pythian has said
these things. What art do these priestesses know, 35
who are incapable of preserving and memorizing
their predictions ? Medicine which has studied all
human science and which is greater than cookery,
is feeble, I think, in contrast to the cures from Delphi,
which privately and publicly have been revealed to
men for all diseases and sufferings. Feeble is a
similarly constituted justice, in respect to judgement
and advice in affairs. What will all the gymnasts 36
say ? Not that their whole science is inferior to two
or three oracles, at least if they know just this one
thing—how to act with a little moderation ? What 37
then of your proud legislation which has made great

[a] *Cf.* §§ 38-41.

(11 D.)

μεγάλα ἀνθρώποις εὑρίσκουσα; οἶμαι μὲν παραχω-
ρήσεται, μᾶλλον δὲ πάλαι παρεχώρησεν ταῖς ἀπὸ
38 τοῦ τρίποδος γυναιξί. βαδίζουσί γε εἰς Δελφοὺς καὶ
πυνθάνονται περὶ τῶν πολιτειῶν. καὶ τότε τοὺς
νόμους τίθενται πρὸς τὴν ἐλθοῦσαν παρὰ τῆς Πυθίας
φωνὴν ἀπὸ Λυκούργου πρώτου, τὸν μετὰ πολλοὺς
39 εἰ δεῖ πρῶτον εἰπεῖν χάριν τοῦ λόγου. οὔκουν
12 D. φασί γ᾽ ἐκεῖνον οὐδὲν θεῖναι Λακεδαιμονίοις ἄνευ
τῆς παρὰ τοῦ θεοῦ φωνῆς, ἀλλ᾽ ὅμως οὐκ ἐπειδὴ
Λυκοῦργος ὁ τῶν Ἑλλήνων ἄριστος ἔθηκεν, οὐ διὰ
τοῦθ᾽ ὁ θεὸς δόξαν εἴληφεν τεθεικέναι τοὺς νόμους, ἀλλ᾽ ὁ μὲν Λυκοῦργος ἄριστος ὢν τῶν Ἑλλήνων ἐμαρτύρει τὰ τῆς οὐδὲν ἰδίᾳ γιγνωσκούσης
Πυθίας νικᾶν, ἡ δὲ ἀπεκρίνατο[1] ὡς ἐδόκει τῷ θεῷ,
ὁ δὲ τῷ παρὰ τὴν Πυθίαν μέρει τὴν δόξαν εἴληφεν
40 τὴν ἐπὶ τοῖς νόμοις. καίτοι οὔτ᾽ ἐπιστήμην τιν᾽
ἔχουσιν περιττοτέραν παρὰ τοὺς ἄλλους ἀνθρώπους
αὗται αἱ γυναῖκες οὔτ᾽ εἴ τι καὶ γιγνώσκουσιν, ἀφ᾽
ὧν πεπαίδευνται καὶ προΐσασι λέγουσιν, ἀλλ᾽ ὡς
ἂν κινηθῶσιν ἑκάστοτε ὑπὸ τοῦ κρείττονος, πέμπουσι πανταχοῖ γῆς, εἰς Ἰωνίαν, εἰς Πόντον, εἰς
Κυρήνην, ἐπ᾽ ἔσχατα τῆς[2] γῆς· οὐδ᾽ εἴ τις εἴσεισιν
ὡς αὐτὰς ἢ πεύσεται προΐσασι πρὸ τῆς ἑσπέρας
καὶ τῆς ἐπὶ τοῦ τρίποδος καθέδρας, ὡς ἔπος εἰπεῖν.
41 ἀλλ᾽ ἀρτίως ἀγνοοῦσαι καὶ τὰ[3] τῶν γειτόνων ἐξαί-
φνης τὰ πάντων ἀνθρώπων ἴσασιν καὶ δημηγοροῦ-
σιν παρὰ τῷ θεῷ καὶ πολιτεύονται τὰ κοινὰ τῆς γῆς
καὶ πάσαις ταῖς ἐπιστήμαις καὶ τέχναις ἡγεμόνες

---

[1] ἀπεκρίνατο post θεῷ TQ.
[2] om. TQ. [3] codd. dett. : τὸ TQVA.

discoveries for mankind ? It will yield, I think.
Moreover, it has long ago yielded to the women on
the tripod. Men go to Delphi and inquire about 38
constitutions. And then they legislate according
to the voice which comes from the Pythian priestess,
beginning with Lycurgus, who came after many
others, but must be called first for the sake of
argument. Therefore they say that that man 39
legislated nothing for the Lacedaemonians without
the God's voice. Still not because Lycurgus, the
best of the Greeks, proposed legislation, was the C. 885-825.
God on that account thought to have legislated the
laws.[a] But Lycurgus, since he was the best of the
Greeks, attested to the superiority of the Pythian
priestess, who had no special knowledge. She
answered as the God decided, and he got the glory
for his laws because of the Pythian. Yet these 40
women neither have any deeper knowledge than
other men, nor, if they do know anything, do they
speak from training and prescience. But, as they
are moved each time by the God, they dispatch men
throughout the earth, to Ionia, Pontus, Cyrene, to
the ends of the world. And they have no fore-
knowledge, one might say, before that evening and
their sitting [b] upon the tripod, whether anyone will
come and make inquiry of them. But at the very 41
moment when they are ignorant even of the affairs of
their neighbours, suddenly they know those of all
men. They make public speeches in the presence
of the God, administer the governments of earth,
and become instructors in all sciences and arts, of

[a] Cf. Laws 632 D. Lycurgus : the law-giver of Sparta.
[b] Possibly " on the evening before, and when sitting."
So Reiske.

(12 D.)

τοῦ τί δεῖ ποιεῖν ἢ λέγειν καθίστανται. καὶ οὐδὲ
Πλάτων αὐτὰς παρέρχεται. ἀλλὰ καὶ οὗτος ἀξιοῖ
τὴν Πυθίαν ἐρωτᾶν ὁπόταν πολιτεύηται καὶ νομο-
θετῇ, καὶ τότε φησὶ δεῖν ποιεῖν, ἐὰν καὶ ἡ Πυθία
συναναιρῇ, πρότερον δὲ οὐ θαρρεῖ.

42 Εἶεν· αὕτη μὲν ἐκ Δελφῶν ἡ μαρτυρία τῷ λόγῳ
καὶ παρὰ Ἀπόλλωνος ⟨τοῦ⟩¹ Πυθίου· τὰς δ' ἐν
13 D. Δωδώνῃ τί φήσεις ἱερείας, αἳ τοσαῦτα ἴσασιν ὅσ'
ἂν τῷ θεῷ δοκῇ καὶ μέχρι τοσούτου μέχρις ἂν δοκῇ;
43 καίτοι οὔτε πρότερόν τινα τοιαύτην εἶχον ἐπιστήμην,
πρὶν εἰσελθεῖν ἐπὶ τὴν τοῦ θεοῦ συνουσίαν, οὔθ'
ὕστερον οὐδὲν ὧν εἶπον ἴσασιν, ἀλλὰ πάντες
μᾶλλον ἢ ἐκεῖναι. ὥσθ' οἱ μὲν ἀγνοοῦντες καὶ
πυθόμενοι παρ' αὐτῶν μεμαθήκασιν, αἱ δὲ εἰποῦσαι
τί χρὴ ποιεῖν οὐκ ἴσασιν οὐδ' αὐτὸ τοῦτο ὅτι εἰρήκα-
σιν. οὐκοῦν ἐκ Διὸς ἂν ταύτην τὴν μαρτυρίαν
44 τιθεὶς οὐκ ἂν ἁμαρτάνοις. ταῦτα δὲ ταῦτα λέγω
καὶ περὶ τῶν ἐν Κλάρῳ καὶ περὶ τῶν ἐν Ἄμμωνος
καὶ πάντων ὅσοι περὶ χρηστήρια ὁμοίως ἄνδρες καὶ
γυναῖκες. καίτοι πότερον² τούτους ἅπαντας καὶ
ταύτας πάσας ἐρωτήσομεν τὸν λόγον, ᾧ χρώμενοι
ταῦτα συμβουλεύουσιν; καὶ πῶς σωφρονεῖν δόξο-
μεν; ἢ τοῦ μηδενὸς ἄξια καὶ κολακείαν ταῦτ' εἶναι φήσομεν, ἐπειδήπερ οὐκ ἔχομεν τοὺς εἰπόντας
ἀπαιτῆσαι ⟨τὸν⟩³ λόγον; πολλῷ μέντἂν πλέον
45 ἐλλείποιμεν⁴ τοῦ σωφρονεῖν. οὐκοῦν παρὰ πάντων
ὡς εἰπεῖν τῶν θεῶν μαρτυρία καὶ ψῆφος ἐπῆκται

¹ add. codd. dett.
² codd. dett. : πρότερον TQVA.
³ add. codd. dett.
⁴ codd. dett. : ἐλείπομεν TQVA.

ᵃ Republic 540 c.

what must be said and done. And not even Plato
ignores them. But he also asserts that he inquires of
the Pythian priestess whenever he draws up constitutions or legislates ; and he says that then he must
act, " if the Pythian priestess assents," but before
that he does not dare.[a]

So be it ! Here is the evidence for our argument, 42
from Delphi and Pythian Apollo. What will you say
of the priestesses in Dodona,[b] who know as much as
the God approves, and for as long as he approves ?
Yet neither had they any such knowledge until they 43
entered into communion with the God, nor afterwards do they know anything which they have said,
but all inquirers understand it better than they. So
those who were ignorant and made inquiry have
learned from them, but those who told what must be
done do not even know the very fact that they have
spoken at all. Therefore you would not be wrong in
adding this evidence from Zeus. My point is the 44
same in regard to those at Clarus, and the oracle of
Ammon, and similarly in regard to all the men and
women who deal in oracles. Yet shall we ask all
these men and women for the reason behind their
counsels ? How shall we seem to act with propriety ?
Or shall we call these things worthless and flattery,
since we cannot demand a reasoning principle from
the speakers ? But then we would be behaving with
far less than propriety. Therefore evidence and 45
support has come, one might say, from all the Gods,

[b] [The oracle of Zeus at Dodona in remote Epirus had to
take second place to the more central one of Apollo at Delphi ;
there was a famous oracle-shrine of Apollo at Clarus (§ 44)
in Ionia, Asia Minor ; and one of Ammon (The Egyptian
Amūn) in the oasis of Siwa, in Libya.—*E.H.W.*]

(13 D.)

τοῦ μηδενὸς ἄξιον εἶναι τὸν τοιοῦτον λόγον, ὅστις
ἢ τὴν τέχνην ζητεῖ, ἢ φαυλίζει τὸ μὴ σὺν ταύτῃ
46 πανταχοῦ. ὅσοι δ' αὖ καὶ καθάπαξ ὑποδύντες θεῷ
καὶ τέχνης οὐδὲ μικρὸν μετασχόντες οὐ μόνον τοῖς
ἐφ' αὑτῶν, ἀλλὰ καὶ τοῖς ὕστερον πολλὰ δὴ καὶ
θαυμάσια προεῖπον, οἷον εἰ βούλει, Βάκις, Σίβυλλα,
ἕτεροι μετὰ τούτων, εἰ δὲ μὴ πολλοί, καὶ τοῦτ'
ἐστὶν ὑπὲρ τοῦ λόγου· τὰ γὰρ μέγιστα ἐκπέφευγε
τοὺς πολλούς· τίς οὕτω τεχνίτης τοῦ κακῶς λέγειν
47 ἐστὶν ὅστις καὶ τούτους κακίσειεν ἄν; ὅταν δ' εἰς
ποιητὰς ἴδω τοὺς κοινοὺς τῶν Ἑλλήνων τροφέας καὶ
14 D. διδασκάλους, οἳ διαρρήδην ὁμολογοῦσιν περὶ αὑτῶν μηδ' ὁτιοῦν ἐπίστασθαι, μηδὲ νεῶν ἀριθμόν, ἀλλ'
ἀεὶ καὶ περὶ παντὸς τὰς Μούσας ἐνοχλοῦσιν δεόμενοι φράσαι σφίσιν, ὡς αὐτοὶ μὲν προφητῶν σχῆμα
καὶ τάξιν ἔχοντες, ἐκείνας δὲ μάντεις ἀληθεῖς οὔσας
περὶ ἁπάντων, μᾶλλόν μοι δοκεῖ προσήκειν τὸ μὴ
σὺν τέχνῃ κοσμεῖν ἐνίοτε ἢ δυοῖν θάτερον, ἢ τοὺς
ποιητὰς ἐπιστήμῃ φάσκειν ἀποχρώντως ποιεῖν, ὃ
μηδ' αὐτοὶ δέχονται, ἢ τοῦ μηδενὸς ἀξίαν τὴν τῶν
48 Μουσῶν ἡγεῖσθαι δωρεάν. εἶτ' οὖν, ὦ πρὸς Διός,
ἐν μέτρῳ μὲν εἰπεῖν ἄνευ τέχνης οὐ δεινόν, ἀλλὰ καὶ
θεῖον πολλάκις, οὑτωσὶ δ' εἰπεῖν τὰ βέλτιστα δεινὸν
ἐὰν μὴ σὺν τέχνῃ; ἐγὼ μὲν οὐχ ὁρῶ τὴν ἀνάγκην.
πῶς γὰρ οὐκ ἄτοπον, εἰ ὁ μὲν ποιητὴς ἄνευ τέχνης
ποιῶν ὀρθῶς τὸν ῥήτορα μιμήσεται καὶ τὰ βέλτιστ'
ἐρεῖ, ὁ ῥήτωρ δ' αὐτὸς οὐκ ἐρεῖ τὰ βέλτιστα, ἐὰν μὴ
49 ⟨σὺν⟩¹ τέχνῃ; καὶ μὴν οἵ γε ποιηταὶ φιλόδωρον
τὸν Ἑρμῆν οὐδενὸς ἧττον θεῶν, οἶμαι δὲ καὶ διαφερόντως, κεκλήκασιν. οὐκοῦν εἰ δι' Ἀπόλλωνος

¹ codd. dett. : om. TQVA.

that such an argument is worthless, which either
seeks art or belittles whatever does not have it.
Again as to all who had all together entered into 46
God, without even a little share of art, and have
foretold many marvels not only to those of their
time, but also to future generations, for example,
if you wish, Bacis, Sibyl, and others besides—if few,
this advances my argument ; for the greatest things
are beyond the masses—, as to all of them, who is
such an artist of slander that he would malign them ?
Whenever I consider the poets, the common foster- 47
fathers and teachers of the Greeks, who openly
confess their complete ignorance, even about the
number of ships at Troy,[a] but are always and in
every way bothering the Muses with their requests
for information, as if they had the rank and position
of heralds, and the latter were the true seers for all
things, I think that sometimes it is better to adorn
one's writings without art than either for the poets to
claim that they write sufficiently through knowledge,
which even they do not admit, or for them to believe
the gift of the Muses to be worthless. So then, by 48
Zeus, it is not terrible to speak in metre without art,
but often divine to do so. But is it terrible to speak of
the most important things, unless with art ? I do not
see the necessity of the argument. For how is it not
strange if the poet, writing properly, yet without
art, can imitate the orator and discuss the most
important things, but if the orator himself cannot
discuss the most important things unless with art ?
Indeed, the poets have called Hermes a " Lover of 49
Gifts," no less than any God, I think, and especially
so. Therefore if prediction comes by way of Apollo

[a] *Iliad* II. 491.

(14 D.)

μαντικὴ καὶ διὰ Μουσῶν ποιητικὴ χωρεῖ, καὶ
τούτων ἄνευ ψυχρὰ τὰ τῆς τέχνης, τί κωλύει καὶ
ῥητορικὴν τῆς Ἑρμοῦ τιθέναι δωρεᾶς, ἥν γε τῷ
ὄντι χρὴ θείαν καλεῖν καὶ τέχνης κρείττω;

50 Μέχρι μέντοι τῶν νῦν τούτων ὑπ' αὐτῶν τῶν
λόγων ἐξελέγχεσθαι Πλάτωνα φαίη τις ἄν· βούλομαι δ' αὐτὸν καὶ ὑπὸ τῶν αὐτοῦ[1] λόγων ἐξελεγχό-
μενον φανῆναι. τρόπον μὲν οὖν τινα καὶ τοῦτ' ἤδη
γέγονεν. ἐν οἷς γὰρ αὐτὸν ἐδείκνυμεν καταφεύγοντα
ἐπὶ τὴν Πυθίαν πολλαχοῦ τῶν Νόμων οὐ διέφυγεν
51 τοῦτον τὸν ἔλεγχον. οὐ μὴν ἀλλὰ καὶ παντελῶς
διὰ πάντων ἑξῆς ὧν εἴρηκα βούλομαι δεῖξαι ταὐτὰ
15 D. φθεγγόμενον. φανήσεται γὰρ ἃ νῦν ἡμεῖς λέγομεν
αὐτὸς πρόσθεν εἰρηκώς, εἰ καὶ μὴ τούτοις τοῖς ῥήμασιν μηδ' εἰς τοσοῦτον τῆς ἀναγκαίας ἀποδεί-
52 ξεως, ἀλλ' οὖν τῷ γε ὅλῳ λόγῳ. ὑπομνήσω δ' αὐτὸν Φαίδρου τοῦ καλοῦ. ὃ γὰρ αὐτὸς ἐκεῖ ποιεῖ τὰ
Λυσίου τιθεὶς μεταξὺ τῶν αὐτοῦ, τοῦτο κἀγὼ νῦν
ποιήσω, αὐτὰ τἀκείνου παρέξομαι καθάπερ νόμον.
'' ποῦ δή μοι,''[2] φησίν, '' ὁ παῖς;'' ποῦ δή μοι καὶ ὁ
λόγος ὁ πρὸς τὸν παῖδα; οὑτοσὶ μάλα πλησίον.
φέρε δὴ τί λέγει; '' Εἰ μὲν γὰρ ἦν ἁπλοῦν τὸ μανίαν
κακὸν εἶναι, καλῶς ἂν ἐλέγετο· νῦν δὲ τὰ μέγιστα
τῶν ἀγαθῶν ἡμῖν γίγνεται διὰ μανίας, θείᾳ μέντοι
δόσει διδομένης.[3] ἥ τε γὰρ ἐν Δελφοῖς προφῆτις[4]
αἵ τ' ἐν Δωδώνῃ ἱέρειαι μανεῖσαι μὲν πολλὰ δὴ καὶ
καλὰ ἰδίᾳ τε καὶ δημοσίᾳ τὴν Ἑλλάδα εἰργάσαντο,
σωφρονοῦσαι δὲ βραχέα ἢ οὐδέν. καὶ ἐὰν δὴ λέγωμεν Σίβυλλάν τε καὶ ἄλλους ὅσοι δὴ μαντικῇ
χρώμενοι ἐνθέῳ πολλὰ δὴ πολλοῖς προλέγοντες εἰς

---

[1] αὐτοῦ QVA.　　　　[2] δήπου TQ.
[3] codd. dett. : διδομένη TQVA.
[4] codd. dett. : αἵ—προφῆτις TQ, αἵ—προφήτεις VA.

and poetry by way of the Muses, and apart from these art is frigid, why not presume oratory to be a gift of Hermes, indeed a gift which ought to be called divine and greater than art?

Up to this point it might be said that Plato is 50 refuted by the general argument itself. But I wish him to be obviously refuted by his own statements. In a certain way, this has already happened. For when we proved that he has taken refuge with the Pythian priestess in many places in the *Laws,*[a] he did not escape this refutation. However, I wish to 51 show that he says the same things entirely and in every way, point by point, as I have said myself. For it will be obvious that formerly he said himself, what we now state, if not in these exact words, or with such compelling proof, still in the tenor of his argument. I shall remind him of the handsome 52 Phaedrus. What he does there in inserting the words of Lysias among his own, I also shall do now. I shall present his words like the citation of a law. " Where please," he says, " is my boy ? "[b] Indeed, where please is the speech to the boy ? Here it is at hand. Come, what does he say ?[c] " If madness were simply an evil, it would be well said. But now the greatest good comes to us through madness, which moreover is given by a divine gift. For the prophetess in Delphi and the priestesses at Dodona in their madness have done much good for Greece publicly and privately, but when sane, little or nothing. And if we speak of Sibyl and all the others who in their mantic inspiration often have predicted many things to many people and aided them in the

[a] *Cf.* § 39.   [b] *Phaedrus* 243 E.
[c] *Phaedrus* 244 A—245 B.

(15 D.)

τὸ μέλλον ὤρθωσαν, μηκύνοιμεν ἂν δῆλα παντὶ
λέγοντες. τόδε μὴν ἄξιον ἐπιμαρτύρασθαι, ὅτι καὶ
τῶν παλαιῶν οἱ τὰ ὀνόματα τεθειμένοι οὐκ αἰσχρὸν
ἡγοῦντο οὐδ᾽ ὄνειδος μανίαν. οὐ γὰρ ἂν τῇ καλλίστῃ
τέχνῃ, ᾗ τὸ μέλλον κρίνεται, αὐτὸ τοῦτο τοὔνομα
ἐμπλέκοντες μανικὴν ἐκάλεσαν, ἀλλ᾽ ὡς καλοῦ
ὄντος ὅταν θείᾳ μοίρᾳ γίγνηται, οὕτω νομίσαντες
ἔθεντο. οἱ δὲ νῦν ἀπειροκάλως τὸ ταῦ ἐπεμβαλόντες
16 D. μαντικὴν ἐκάλεσαν. ἐπεὶ τήν γε τῶν ἐμφρόνων
ζήτησιν τοῦ μέλλοντος διά τε ὀρνίθων ποιουμένων
καὶ τῶν ἄλλων σημείων, ἅτε ἐκ διανοίας ποριζομένων ἀνθρωπίνῃ οἰήσει, οἰονοϊστικὴν ἐπωνόμασαν,
ἣν νῦν οἰωνιστικὴν τὸ ω σεμνύνοντες οἱ νέοι καλοῦσιν. ὅσῳ δὴ οὖν τελεώτερον καὶ ἐντιμότερον
μαντικὴ οἰωνιστικῆς, τό τε ὄνομα τοῦ ὀνόματος τό
τε ἔργον τοῦ ἔργου, τόσῳ κάλλιον μαρτυροῦσιν οἱ
παλαιοὶ μανίαν σωφροσύνης τὴν ἐκ θεοῦ τῆς παρὰ
ἀνθρώπων γιγνομένης. ἀλλὰ μὴν νόσων τε καὶ
πόνων τῶν μεγίστων, ἃ δὴ παλαιῶν ἐκ μηνιμάτων
ποθὲν ἔν τισι τῶν γενῶν, ἡ μανία ἐγγενομένη καὶ
προφητεύσασα, οἷς ἔδει, ἀπαλλαγὴν εὕρετο,[1] καταφυγοῦσα πρὸς θεῶν εὐχάς τε καὶ λατρείας. ὅθεν
καὶ καθαρμῶν τε καὶ τελετῶν τυχοῦσα ἐξάντη
ἐποίησε τὸν αὐτὴν ἔχοντα πρός τε τὸν παρόντα καὶ
τὸν ἔπειτα χρόνον λύσιν τῷ ὀρθῶς μανέντι τε καὶ
κατασχομένῳ τῶν παρόντων κακῶν εὑρομένη. τρίτη
δὲ ἀπὸ Μουσῶν κατοχή τε καὶ μανία λαβοῦσα

---

[1] codd. dett. : εὕρατο TQVA a. corr.

_a One of Plato's fanciful and humorous etymologies;

310

future, we should be long winded about what is
obvious to everyone. This is worthwhile to offer in
evidence, that those ancients who designed our
language did not believe madness a shameful thing
or a term of abuse. For they would not have in-
twined this word into the fairest art, through which
the future is judged, and used the word ' manic.'
But since it is a fair thing whenever it comes to pass
through divine fate, in this belief they designed
the word. Men nowadays have ignorantly added a
' t ' and call it ' mantic.' Moreover, they named
οἰονοϊστική, or ' haruspicy,' the investigation of the
future by thinking men through birds and other
signs, being transmitted to human thought from
notion, which now modern man calls οἰωνιστική
by lengthening the ' o '.[a] As much more perfect,
then, and honourable the mantic is than the " oionis-
tic,' the name than the name and the practice than
the practice, so much fairer do the ancients attest is
madness than moderation, that which comes from
God than that which comes from man. When madness entered in and prophesied, taking refuge in
prayers and the service of the Gods, it found release,
for those for whom it was necessary, from disease
and the greatest sufferings, which arose from some
source out of ancient curses among certain races.
Then through the means of purification and ritual,
it made sound its possessor for both present and
future, and found freedom from the present evil for
him who was rightly mad and inspired. A third
spiritual possession and madness, from the Muses,

οἰωνιστική (the taking of omens from the flight of birds), of
which the actual root is οἰωνός " bird," is taken as derived
from οἴομαι, οἴησις " idea," " notion."

(16 D.)

ἀπαλὴν καὶ ἄβατον ψυχὴν ἐγείρουσα κἀναβακχεύ-
ουσα κατά τε ᾠδὰς καὶ κατὰ τὴν ἄλλην ποίησιν
μυρία τῶν παλαιῶν ἔργα κοσμοῦσα, τοὺς ἐπιγιγνομένους παιδεύει. ὃς δὲ ἂν ἄνευ μανίας Μουσῶν
ἐπὶ ποιητικὰς θύρας ἀφίκηται, πεισθεὶς ὡς ἄρα
ἐκ τέχνης ἱκανὸς ποιητὴς ἐσόμενος, ἀτελὴς αὐτός
τε καὶ ἡ ποίησις ὑπὸ τῆς τῶν μαινομένων ἡ τοῦ
17 D. σωφρονοῦντος ἠφανίσθη. τοσαῦτα μέν σοι καὶ
ἔτι πλείω ἔχω μανίας γιγνομένης ἀπὸ θεῶν λέγειν
καλὰ ἔργα."

53 Εἰ τοίνυν, ὦ Ζεῦ καὶ θεοί, μανία τίς ἐστιν ἀμείνων σωφροσύνης καὶ παρὰ θεῶν ἀνθρώποις γιγνομένη, πῶς ἄξιον πᾶν γε τὸ μὴ τέχνῃ γιγνόμενον ψέ-
54 γειν, ἢ πῶς ῥητορικὴν ἁπλῶς αἰσχρὸν ἡγεῖσθαι;[1] εἰ
δὲ δὴ τὴν μὲν καλλίστην τῶν τεχνῶν προσείρηκεν
τῷ μανικὴν εἶναι, τὴν δ᾽ ἁπλῶς οὐδ᾽ εἶναι τέχνην,
τὴν ποιητικήν, ἀλλ᾽ ἐπίπνοιαν ἐκ Μουσῶν, ὃς δ᾽ ἂν
ἄνευ μανίας Μουσῶν ἐπὶ ποιητικὰς θύρας ἀφίκηται,
πεισθεὶς ὡς ἄρα ἐκ τέχνης ἱκανὸς ποιητὴς ἐσόμενος,
ἀτελὴς αὐτός τε καὶ ἡ ποίησις ὑπὸ τῆς τῶν μαινομένων ἡ τοῦ σωφρονοῦντος ἠφανίσθη, πῶς οὐκ ἐξ
ἀμφοῖν δείκνυται τὸ μὴ τὴν τέχνην νικᾶν, ἀλλ᾽ ἔστιν
οὗ καὶ λαμπρότερον καὶ θεοφιλέστερον εἶναι τὸ μὴ
δουλεῦον[2] τέχνῃ; σαφῶς γὰρ οὑτωσὶ Πλάτων ἤδη
διορίζεται τὸ μὴ δεῖν ἐπὶ τῶν μεγίστων τέχνην ζη-
55 τεῖν. ὥστ᾽ εἰ μὲν βούλει, τὸ τοῦ Εὐριπίδου καὶ τῶν
αὐτοῦ νὴ Δία συμβαίνει, σοῦ τάδε, οὐκ ἐμοῦ κλύ-
εις, ὦ τοσοῦτον ἐνθυμηθείς· εἰ δ᾽ αὖ βούλει, τὸ τοῦ

---

[1] post ἡγεῖσθαι add. καὶ μὴ συγχωρεῖν δύναμίν γέ τιν᾽ εἶναι
τέχνης κρείττονα codd. dett. (prob. Ddf.).
[2] δουλεύειν TQ.

---

[a] Some Byzantine editor, apparently feeling that the

taking a tender and untrodden soul, awakes and makes it revel in song and other poetry, and adorning in writing the countless deeds of the ancients, educates future generations. But whoever without the madness of the Muses comes to the doors of poetry, persuaded that he will be a satisfactory poet from art, he is uninitiated and his poetry, that of the sane man, is eclipsed by that of mad men. All these, and still more, fair deeds, can I tell you of madness arising from the Gods."

If then, O Zeus and you other Gods, there is a 53 certain madness better than sanity which comes from the Gods to men, how is it worthy to censure everything which does not occur with art, or how simply to believe that oratory is shameful ?[a] If he has 54 called the mantic art the fairest of arts from its madness, and has said that poetry is simply not even an art, but an inspiration from the Muses, and whoever without the madness of the Muses comes to the doors of poetry, persuaded that he will be a satisfactory poet from art, he is uninitiated and his poetry, that of a sane man, is eclipsed by that of mad men, how is it not in both ways proved that art is not best, but that what is not subservient to art is sometimes more glorious and dearer to the Gods than anything ? For Plato now clearly establishes that art need not be sought in the greatest things. Therefore, if you wish, by Zeus, a quotation from 55 Euripides perfectly suits his own arguments, " You hear this from your lips, not mine,"[b] you who have these great conceptions. Again, if you wish, a

sentence was incomplete, added : ". . . and not to concede that there is a certain power greater than art ? "

[b] *Hippolytus* 352.

(17 D.)

Αἰσχύλου, τάδ᾽ οὐχ ὑπὸ ἄλλων, ἀλλὰ τοῖς αὐτοῦ
18 D. πτεροῖς, ἃ θρυλεῖς ἐν ἐκείνοις τοῖς λόγοις, ἁλίσκῃ.
56 καὶ μὴν εἰ μαντικὴν μὲν ἐξ Ἀπόλλωνος ἢ καὶ Διός,
τελετὰς δὲ ἐξ ἄλλου του θεῶν τίθης, ποιητικὴν δ᾽ ἐκ
Μουσῶν, οὐδ᾽ ὁ τῶν μὲν ἀδελφός, τοῦ δὲ παῖς
Ἑρμῆς ἀπορήσει λόγων περὶ τῆς ἑαυτοῦ δωρεᾶς,
ἀλλ᾽ αὑτῷ τε καὶ τῷ πατρὶ προστιθεὶς τοὺς λόγους
57 ἀληθῆ τε καὶ δίκαια ἔρει. οἶμαι δὲ καὶ οἱ λογίους
τούτους προσειπόντες τοὺς θεούς, καὶ παλαιοὶ καὶ
νέοι, καὶ οὐδὲ περὶ ἓν γράμμα διενεχθέντες, πολλῷ
σαφέστερον ἢ περὶ μανίας μαρτυροῦσιν ὅτι εἰς
ἀξιόχρεως ἀνοίσομεν, ἄν τι μετῇ λόγων ἡμῖν, εἰ καὶ
μηδεμιᾷ προσφύγοιμεν τέχνῃ.

58   Εἶεν. τίνα δὴ τὰ ἐφεξῆς ἦν; '' ''Ωστε τοῦτό γε
αὐτὸ μὴ φοβώμεθα, μηδέ τις ἡμᾶς λόγος θορυβείτω
δεδιττόμενος, ὡς πρὸ τοῦ κεκινημένου τὸν σώφρονα
δεῖ προαιρεῖσθαι φίλον.'' ὅρα δὴ καὶ τάδε. ὥστε
τοῦτό γε αὐτὸ μὴ φοβώμεθα, μηδέ τις ἡμᾶς λόγος
θορυβείτω δεδιττόμενος, ὡς οὐ τὸν φύσει καὶ θείᾳ
μοίρᾳ κατορθοῦντα δεῖ νικᾶν, ἀλλ᾽ ὅστις τεχνικῶς
μικρῶς[1] ἐστίν. '' Ἀλλὰ τόδε '' φησὶν '' πρὸς
ἐκείνῳ[2] δείξας φερέσθω τὰ νικητήρια, ὡς οὐκ ἐπ᾽
ὠφελείᾳ ⟨ὁ⟩[3] ἔρως τῷ ποθοῦντι καὶ τῷ ἐρωμένῳ ἐκ
θεῶν ἐπιπέμπεται.'' καὶ τόδε τοίνυν πρὸς ἐκείνῳ
δείξας φερέσθω τὰ νικητήρια, ὡς οὐκ ἐπ᾽ ὠφελείᾳ
τῇ πάσῃ καὶ μεγίστῃ λόγοι παρὰ θεῶν ἀνθρώποις
γίγνονται. '' ἡμῖν δὲ ἀποδεικτέον αὖ τοὐναντίον ''
19 D. φησίν, '' ὡς ἐπ᾽ εὐτυχίᾳ τῇ μεγίστῃ παρὰ θεῶν ἡ
59 τοιαύτη μανία δίδοται.'' τὸν δὲ Τήλεφον οὐκ οἴει

---

[1] Iunt. : τεχνικῶς μικρὸς T (a. corr. τεχνικὸς) QVA.
[2] T p. corr. Q : ἐκεῖνο VA.   [3] Plato : om. TQVA.

quotation from Aeschylus : you are convicted " in this not by another, but with your own plumage," [a] *i.e.* by what you reiterate in those discourses. Indeed, if you presume that prophecy comes from 56 Apollo or even Zeus, and other rituals from other Gods, and poetry from the Muses, Hermes, who is their brother and his son, will not be mute about his gift, but claiming oratory for himself and his father, he will speak truthfully and justly. Those, I think, 57 who addressed these as the Gods of Oratory, both ancient and modern men, differing not even by one letter, give much clearer testimony than they did about madness, that our reference to these Gods will be sufficient, if we have any sense, even if we should take refuge in no art.

Well ! What comes next ? [b] " Therefore let us not 58 fear this, nor let any argument frighten and terrify us, that the sane man must be preferred as a friend before the ecstatic. " Consider this too : therefore let us not fear this, nor let any argument frighten and terrify us, that he who succeeds by his nature and divine portion must not prevail, but whoever is trivially artistic. " But," he says, " in addition to that, having proved that love is not sent from the Gods for the benefit of the smitten and the beloved, let him have the prize of victory." Then, in addition to that, having proved that men have not received oratory from the Gods for every great benefit, let him have the prize of victory. "But it must be proved by us on the contrary," he says, " that such madness is given by the Gods for the greatest good fortune." " Do you not think that 59

---

[a] *Myrmidons* frg. 135 N². *Cf.* iii. 424 (p. 319 Ddf.).
   Phaedrus 245 B.

(19 D.)

τὰ αὐτὰ ταῦτα; εἰ δὲ ἄρα μηδὲν ἐκεῖνος προτιμᾷ,
ἀλλ' ἡμῖν γε ἀποδεικτέον ὡς ἐπ' εὐτυχίᾳ τῇ μεγίστῃ
καὶ τὸ ἐξ ἀρχῆς ἡ τῶν λόγων δύναμις παρὰ θεῶν
ἧκεν εἰς ἀνθρώπους, καὶ νῦν ἐν καλοῦ μοίρᾳ τῇ
πρώτῃ καὶ εἰς τὸν ἔπειτα χρόνον καὶ δίδονται καὶ
60 δοθήσονται. καὶ μὴν εἰ μὲν ἀξιόπιστος Πλάτων,
⟨οὗτος⟩[1] αὐτός ἐστιν ὁ μὴ διδοὺς τῇ τέχνῃ τὰ
πρεσβεῖα· εἰ δὲ οὐδὲ[2] τοῦτό τις συγχωρεῖ, πῶς
ῥητορικὴ διὰ τοὺς ἐκείνου λόγους αἰσχρόν; ἐγὼ
δ' ἀξιόπιστον μὲν[3] τοῖς ὅλοις οὐδενὸς ἧττον Ἑλλήνων ἡγοῦμαι, ἡδέως δὲ ἂν ἐροίμην τοὺς πρὸς
ἐκείνου πότερ' αὐτῷ μᾶλλον πιστεύειν ἄξιον, ταῦτα
ἢ 'κεῖνα. καὶ μὴν εἰ τὰ μάλιστα σεμνός ἐστιν,
φαίνεται μαρτυρῶν ἡμῖν, ὥστε ὑπὲρ ἡμῶν σεμνός
ἐστιν. ὅταν γὰρ ἡμεῖς μὲν καὶ ἡμῖν αὐτοῖς ταὐτὰ
λέγωμεν κἀκείνῳ, ἐκεῖνος δὲ μήθ' αὑτῷ μήθ'[4] ἡμῖν,
οὐκ ἀντιλέγει μᾶλλον ἢ μαρτυρεῖ κατ' αὐτὸ τοῦτο
⟨τὸ⟩[5] μὴ τἀληθῆ λέγειν.

61 Φέρε δὴ καὶ ἑτέραν ἐκ τοῦ αὐτοῦ γυμνασίου, ἔφη
Πλάτων, μαρτυρίαν ἀντ' εἰκόνος παράσχωμαι. οὐ
20 D. γάρ που δυσχερανεῖ Πλάτων, ἐὰν Αἰσχίνης ἐπι-
ψηφίσῃ Πλάτωνος εἰπόντος '' Ἐγὼ δ' εἰ μέν τινι
τέχνῃ ᾤμην δύνασθαι ὠφελῆσαι, πάνυ ἂν πολλὴν
ἐμαυτοῦ μωρίαν κατεγίγνωσκον· νῦν δὲ θείᾳ μοίρᾳ
ᾤμην μοι τοῦτο δεδόσθαι ἐπ' Ἀλκιβιάδῃ. καὶ
62 οὐδέν γε τούτων ἄξιον θαυμάσαι.'' ἀκούεις ἀνδρὸς
ἑταίρου καὶ τὸν αὐτόν σοι σοφώτατον νομίζοντος,
προσθήσω δ' ὅτι καὶ τῷ αὐτῷ τοὺς λόγους ἀνατιθέν-
τος, ᾧπερ καὶ σὺ τούτους. οὐ χρή, φησίν, θαυμάζειν, ὦ Πλάτων, εἴ τις καὶ τέχνην μὴ κτησάμενος

---

[1] om. VA, add. s.l. T.
[2] Phot. : οὐδὲν TQVA.   [3] om. VA.
[4] corr. codd. dett. : μὴ δὲ TQVA.   [5] om. VA.

Telephus will say the same ? " [a] But if Telephus recks not, then it must be proved by us that right from the start the power of oratory came to men from the Gods for the greatest good fortune, and now is bestowed as constituting the highest degree of beauty and will be bestowed in the future. Indeed, 60 if Plato is trustworthy, it is he who does not grant the highest honours to art. But even if someone does not concede this, how then is oratory shameful through his arguments ? I believe that he is wholly trustworthy no less than any Greek. I should gladly ask his followers, whether he is more credible in the former or latter statements. If indeed he is serious, he obviously testifies for us, so that his serious side is in our favour. For when we are consistent and agree with him, but he is neither consistent nor agrees with us, he no more disputes, but confesses in this very act that he is not speaking the truth.

Come now let me provide another testimony, not 61 just the Platonic metaphor, " from the same school." [b] For Plato will not be angry, if Aeschines gives his approval to Plato's words [c] : " If I thought that I could be helpful through my art, I should find myself guilty of much stupidity. But as it is I thought that this had been granted to me by a divine portion in respect to Alcibiades. And none of this should be wondered at." You hear a comrade, who believed 62 the same man, as you did, to be the wisest of men, and I shall add, who also dedicated his discourses to the same man as you did these. We must not, he says, Plato, marvel, if someone who has possessed

[a] Aristophanes, *Acharnians* 555.
[b] *Gorgias* 493 D.   [c] Frg. 11a Dittmar.

(20 D.)

οἷός τ᾽ ἐστὶν ὠφελεῖν ἀνθρώπους. '' πολλοὶ γὰρ καὶ
τῶν καμνόντων ὑγιεῖς γίγνονται οἱ μὲν ἀνθρωπίνη
⟨τέχνῃ⟩,[1] οἱ δὲ θείᾳ μοίρᾳ. ὅσοι μὲν οὖν ἀνθρωπίνη
τέχνῃ, ὑπὸ ἰατρῶν θεραπευόμενοι, ὅσοι δὲ θείᾳ
μοίρᾳ, ἐπιθυμίᾳ αὐτοὺς ἄγει ἐπὶ τὸ ὀνῆσον· καὶ τότε
ἐπεθύμησαν ἐμέσαι, ὁπότε αὐτοῖς ἔμελλε συνοίσειν,
καὶ τότε κυνηγετῆσαι, ὁπότε συνοίσειν ἔμελλεν
63 πονέσαι.'' Ἡράκλεις, ὡς διαρρήδην καὶ περιφανῶς
Αἰσχίνης ὁ τοῦ Πλάτωνος συμφοιτητὴς μαρτυρεῖ
Πλάτωνι ταῦθ᾽ ἃ μικρῷ πρόσθεν παρεσχόμεθα αὐτοῦ
πολλῷ καὶ ἀνθρωπινώτερα καὶ πρὸς θεῶν εἶναι καλ-
λίονα ὧν ἕνεκα τοῦ παραδόξου συνεσκεύακεν.
64 οὐκοῦν αὐτός τε μαρτυρῶν ἡμῖν ὥσπερ ὑπὸ κήρυκος
ἀνήρ[2] φαίνεται καὶ τὴν τοῦδε μαρτυρίαν ὥσπερ
ἐπισφραγίζεται· τοὺς γὰρ πρὸς ἡμῶν αὐτοῦ λόγους
65 κυροῖ. καὶ μὴν εἰ πολλοὶ τῶν καμνόντων ὑγιεῖς
γίγνονται χωρὶς ἰατρῶν καὶ τέχνης, καὶ ταῦτ᾽ οὐδ᾽
ἐφ᾽ ἑνὶ ἄλλῳ τῆς τῶν ἰατρῶν τέχνης οὔσης ἢ τῷ
21 D. ποιεῖν ὑγιεῖς, οὐδὲν ἀπεικὸς οὐδὲ ἔξω τῆς ἀνθρωπίνης τύχης χρὴ[3] εἰπεῖν εἴτε θείας μοίρας κἂν τοῖς
λόγοις τοῦ βελτίστου τυγχάνειν μηδεμιᾷ τέχνῃ
χρωμένους, εἰ καὶ ὅτι μάλιστα τῆς τέχνης ἦν τὸ τοῦ
βελτίστου τυγχάνειν περὶ αὐτοὺς τοὺς λόγους.
66 Περί γε ⟨μὴν⟩[4] τούτου τοῦ μέρους οὐκέτι [οὐκ][5]
ἐκ λόγου πρὸς Πλάτωνα ἀγωνιοῦμαι, ὡς ἄρα πολλοὶ
διὰ θείας μοίρας ἐσώθησαν, οὐδέ μοι νεμεσήσει
δήπουθεν οὔτ᾽ Αἰσχίνης ὁ Λυσανίου οὔτ᾽ ἄλλος

---

[1] add. codd. dett.   [2] Ddf. : ἀνὴρ TQVA.
[3] χρὴ post ἀνθρωπίνης TQ, secl. Keil.

no art is capable of helping mankind. " For many of
the sick become well, some by human art, some by a
divine portion. Those by human art, cured by
doctors ; those by a divine portion, desire leads to
what will profit them. They desired to vomit, when
to do so was going to be expedient for them, and to
hunt, when physical exertion was going to be
expedient." [a] Heracles ! How clearly and lucidly 63
Aeschines, the fellow pilgrim [b] of Plato, attests to
Plato, that those arguments of his which we produced
a little before are more humane and in the eyes of
the Gods fairer than what he concocted for a para-
dox. Therefore the man himself clearly gives evi- 64
dence for us, as it were through the medium of a
herald, and as it were sets a seal of confirmation on
Plato's testimony. For he confirms those arguments
of his which favour our position. Indeed, if many of 65
the sick are cured without doctors and art, and at
that while the art of doctors exists for no other purpose than to cure, it is not improbable, nor must it
be said that it is beyond human fortune or divine
portion, that in oratory also those who use no art
achieve what is best, even if the achievement of the
best in oratory itself were particularly the province
of art.

On this subject I shall no longer use the arguments 66
of literature against Plato, that many have been
saved through a divine portion ; nor, I think, will
Aeschines the son of Lysanias or anyone else be

[a] Frg. 11b Dittmar.
[b] συμφοιτητής is also a technical term used of incubants at
the temple of Asclepius, cf. Behr, *Aelius Aristides*, p. 42, n. 5.

---

[4] add. codd. dett. [5] om. codd. dett.

(21 D.)

67

22 D.

68

69

70

οὐδείς, εἰ φαίην αὐτὸς ἔχειν μαρτυρῆσαι μᾶλλον
τοῖς ῥήμασιν ἢ τῆς παρ' ἐκείνου πρὸς δὴ ταῦτα
προσδεῖσθαι μαρτυρίας. ἀλλ' ὡς ἀληθῶς ὥσπερ
οἱ θεομάντεις οἱ τοῖς τῶν πραγμάτων ἐπωνύμοις
τετελεσμένοι παρ' αὐτῶν τῶν θεῶν ἔχω τὸ μάθημα,
ὑφ' ὧν ἃ μηδεὶς ἰατρῶν μήτε οἶδεν ὅ τι χρὴ προσειπεῖν, οὐχ ὅπως ἰάσασθαι, μήτε εἶδεν ἐν ἀνθρώπου
φύσει συμβάντα, ἄλλοτε ἄλλαις παραμυθίαις τε καὶ
συμβουλαῖς ἐκ τοῦ θεοῦ[1] διαφεύγων ζῶ[2] παρὰ πᾶν
τὸ ἐκ τῶν παρόντων εἰκός. πολλοὶ δ' ἔμοιγε καὶ
ἄλλοι κοινωνοί τε καὶ μάρτυρές εἰσι τῶν λόγων, οὐ
μόνον τῶν Ἑλλήνων, ἀλλὰ καὶ βαρβάρων, αἵ τ' ἐν
Ἀσκληπιοῦ τῶν ἀεὶ διατριβόντων ἀγέλαι καὶ ὅσοι
τῷ κατ' Αἴγυπτον θεῷ συνεγένοντο. καίτοι τέχνης
μὲν ἡμῶν οὐδ' ὁτιοῦν εἰς ταῦτα μέτεστιν οὐδενὶ
δήπουθεν, ἀλλὰ καὶ τοῦ καταφυγεῖν ἐπὶ τοὺς θεοὺς
σχεδὸν ἀρχὴ τὸ τῆς τέχνης ὑπεριδεῖν ἐστίν· ὅμως
δὲ σὺν αὐτοῖς εἰπεῖν οὔθ' οἱ θεοὶ τὸν τοιοῦτον ἡμῶν
λογισμὸν ἀτιμάζουσιν οὔτε πολλοὶ μετέγνωσαν τῶν
πρὸ τῆς τέχνης τὴν παρὰ τοῦ θεοῦ τύχην ἑλομέ-
νων. ἀλλὰ καὶ ὀνείρασι χρώμεθα οὐ προειδότες,
οἶμαι, τῆς ἑσπέρας ὅ τι μέλλομεν ὄψεσθαι, καὶ τί
χρὴ ποιήσαντας[3] σωθῆναι γιγνώσκομεν, ἀγνοοῦντες
μέχρις ἐκείνου τοῦ μέρους τῆς ὥρας, ἐν ᾧ παρὰ
τῶν θεῶν ἧκεν τἀγαθόν, καὶ πάλιν γὰρ ὥσπερ ἐπ-
ᾴδων ἐν μέλει ταὐτὸν ἐρῶ, τέχνης οὐδὲ ὁτιοῦν
ἐπαΐοντες οὐ μόνον περὶ τῶν ἡμῖν αὐτοῖς συμφερόν-

---

[1] ἐκ τοῦ θεοῦ secl. Reiske et Keil.
[2] codd. dett. : διαφεύγω ζῶν TQVA, φεύγω solum Phot.
[3] Iunt. : ποιήσαντα TQVA.

---

[a] i.e. θεομάντεις, "seers of god." As a scholium on

320

angry if I should say that I can bear witness to his words rather than that I require his evidence on these matters. Truly just as the seers, initiated 67 into the service of the Gods who have given their name to their speciality,[a] I have knowledge from the Gods themselves.[b] Through their aid, contrary to the likelihood of the circumstances, I am alive, having escaped at different times through various kinds of consolation and advice on the part of the God from things which no doctor knew what to call, to say nothing of cure, nor had seen befall the nature of man. There are many others like me and they 68 can bear witness to these tales, not only Greeks, but barbarians, both the flocks of those who dwell at times in the Temple of Asclepius and all who attend upon the God of Egypt.[c] Yet no one of us, I think, has 69 any share of art in regard to these matters, but the scorn of art is, one might almost say, the beginning of taking refuge with the Gods. Still, to speak by their grace, neither do the Gods dishonour our judgement such as it is, nor have many of those who have preferred fortune from the God to art repented. But we employ dreams, not knowing in advance of 70 the evening, surely, what we are going to see, and we know what we must do to be saved, although we are in ignorance up to that minute in which the benefit has come from the Gods. For again as if singing a refrain, I shall repeat myself, knowing nothing of art, we can often speak not only about

---

another passage notes (vol. 3, p. 65. 31 Ddf.), the word is used in the sense of θεοφορούμενοι.

  [b] Cf. Behr, op. cit., p. 169, n. 24.

  [c] Sarapis, also a healing god, as popular as Asclepius, and much cultivated by Aristides, cf. Behr, op. cit., p. 149.

(22 D.)

τῶν, ἀλλὰ καὶ περὶ τῶν ἑτέροις ἔχομεν εἰπεῖν πολλάκις, ἂν δοκῇ τῷ θεῷ, ὥστε καὶ τοὺς ἰατροὺς
23 D. οὐδὲν κωλύει φρίττειν, ἐπειδὰν ἀκούωσιν πολλὰ
71 τῶν ἔργων. πότερ' οὖν τὰ ὀνείρατα ποιεῖ θεοῖς
ἀνακεῖσθαι τὰ ἀνθρώπεια, ἢ τὸ θεοὺς ἀνθρώπων
κήδεσθαι ποιεῖ καὶ δι' ὀνειράτων ἀνθρώπους σῴζε-
72 σθαι; ἐγὼ μὲν οἶμαι τοῦτο. τί οὖν, ὦ μεγίστη σὺ
γλῶττα τῶν Ἑλληνίδων, ἔφη Κρατῖνος ποιῶν, ἔσθ'
ὅ τι κωλύει καὶ ὕπαρ γιγνώσκειν τὰ βέλτιστα ἄνευ
τέχνης καὶ συμβουλεύειν ἑτέροις ἔχειν, εἴπερ γε καὶ
τὰ ὀνείρατα ποιεῖ καὶ ἑτέροις ἔχειν συμβουλεύειν;
ἢ σωθῆναι μὲν ἔστιν ἄνευ τέχνης καὶ ἕτερον σῶσαι δι' ὧν τις οὐκ οἶδεν, συμβουλεῦσαι δ' οὐκ ἔστιν
ἄνευ τέχνης οὐδέν, οὔτ' ἀπὸ τῆς αὑτοῦ τύχης οὔτ'
ἀπὸ τῆς θείας οὔτε, τὸ τοῦ Δημοσθένους, τῆς τῶν
ἀκροωμένων;

73 Καὶ ταυτὶ μὲν ὑπ' αὐτοῦ τοῦ λόγου κινηθεὶς [καὶ]¹
τοῦ τοῖς θεοῖς ὡσπερεὶ τετελεσμένου ἐπὶ πλεῖον
ἴσως ἐξήγαγον· καί μοι συγγνώμη καὶ παρ' αὐτοῦ
⟨τοῦ⟩² Πλάτωνος ἔστω καὶ παρ' ἄλλου παντὸς τοῦτ'
αὐτὸ παθόντι ὅπερ ἐν τοῖς λόγοις ἐνῆν· οὐ γὰρ ἦν
κατασχεῖν αὐτόν,³ ἐπειδὴ θεία μοῖρα καὶ σωτηρία
74 παρέπεσεν. διὸ καίπερ μαρτυρίᾳ χρώμενος ἠναγ-
κάσθην αὐτὸς μαρτυρεῖν τῷ λόγῳ, ἐπάνειμι δ' αὖθις
πρὸς τὰ λοιπὰ τῆς μαρτυρίας. "'Ἐγὼ δὲ διὰ τὸν
ἔρωτα ὃν ἐτύγχανον ἐρῶν Ἀλκιβιάδου οὐδὲν διάφορον τῶν Βακχῶν ἐπεπόνθειν. καὶ γὰρ αἱ Βάκχαι

---

¹ secl. Keil.
² add. codd. dett.
³ codd. dett.: αὐτὸν TQVA.

ᵃ All this is drawn from Aristides' current experience as an
incubant.

322

what is expedient for ourselves, but also for others, if the God approves, so that the doctors must shudder whenever they hear many of these practices.[a] So do dreams cause a concern for man to be 71 attributed to the Gods, or does the care of the Gods for mankind cause mankind to be saved through dreams ?[b] I think the latter. Well ! " O you 72 greatest of the Greek tongues," in Cratinus' poetic expression,[c] is there anything to prevent also in waking life the recognition without art of what is best and the counselling of others, if dreams enable the counselling of others ? Or can one be saved without art and save another through an action which he does not understand, but is it impossible to give counsel without art, either from one's own good fortune or from divine fortune, or to quote Demosthenes,[d] " from the fortune of the audience " ?

Moved by my very argument, which is, as it were, 73 a part of religion,[e] I have perhaps made this too long an excursus. Let Plato and everyone else pardon me for experiencing this feeling which was innate in the argument. I could not restrain myself, when " divine portion " and " salvation " entered into the discussion. Therefore although I was citing evidence, I 74 was forced myself to give evidence for the argument. But I shall return once more to the rest of the evidence[f] : " Through the love which I had for Alcibiades, I had felt no different from the Bacchants. For when-

---

[b] A question first posed by Aristotle, cf. De Divinatione 463 b 14, and cf. Behr, op. cit., p. 173, n. 9.

[c] Frg. 293 Kock. Comic poet of Athens.

[d] Or. i. 1.

[e] Because of the importance of dreams and the irrational cures of incubation. Literally : "... argument, ... as it were, consecrated to the Gods."   [f] Aeschines, frg. 11c Dittmar.

(23 D.)

ἐπειδὰν ἔνθεοι γένωνται, ὅθεν οἱ ἄλλοι [ἐκ τῶν
24 D. φρεάτων]¹ οὐδὲ ὕδωρ δύνανται ὑδρεύεσθαι, ἐκεῖναι
μέλι καὶ γάλα ἀρύονται. καὶ δὴ καὶ ἐγὼ οὐδὲν
μάθημα ἐπιστάμενος ὃ διδάξας ἄνθρωπον ὠφελή-
σαιμι ἄν, ὅμως ὤμην ξυνὼν ἂν ἐκείνῳ διὰ τὸ ἐρᾶν
βελτίω ποιῆσαι." ἐνταῦθα τελευτᾷ τῶν διαλόγων
οὐ διὰ αἰνιγμάτων, οὐδὲ ὑπονοίας, οὐδὲ τρόπον τινὰ
ταὐτὰ λέγων ἡμῖν, ἀλλ᾽ ὥσπερ ἐξεπίτηδες εἰς τὴν
75 χρείαν πεποιηκώς. εἰ τοίνυν ὄνειροι μὲν τὰς²
Ἀσκληπιοῦ συμμορίας τῆς τῶν ἰατρῶν τέχνης ἀπαλ-
λάττουσιν, Βάκχαι δὲ αἱ Διονύσου καὶ τὰ τῶν
Νυμφῶν δῶρα μεταβάλλουσιν ἡνίκ᾽ ἂν ἔνθεοι γένωνται, τί τῶν αἰσχρῶν ἢ τί τῶν ἔξω τῆς φύσεως καὶ
τοὺς ἐν τοῖς λόγοις ἐνθέους παραδέχεσθαι καὶ
νομίζειν εἰς προστάτας ἔχειν ἀνενεγκεῖν τούς γέ
76 που κρείττονας; καὶ μὴν οὐδὲ τοῦτ᾽ ἔστ᾽ εἰπεῖν
ὡς ἄρ᾽ ὁ μάρτυς οὐδενὸς ἄξιος, ἢ πόρρω τῶν πραγμάτων, ἢ καταφεύγομεν εἰς ὄνομα αὐτὸ δὴ τοῦτο.
ἀλλ᾽ εἴ γέ τινας ὥσπερ παῖδας οὕτως καὶ ἑταίρους³
χρὴ λέγειν γνησίους, ⟨γνήσιον⟩⁴ Αἰσχίνην Σωκρά-
77 τους παρειλήφαμεν. μαρτυρεῖ δὲ καὶ ἡ ψευδὴς
ἐνίων δόξα τῶν αὐτοῦ Σωκράτους εἶναι τὰ γράμματα ταῦτα ὑπειληφότων· οἷς εἰ μὴ τὸ ὅλον πιστεύειν ἄξιον, ὥσπερ ἐγὼ πρῶτος οὐκ ἂν φαίην, ἀλλ᾽
οὖν οὐκ ἐπὶ πάσης γε τῆς ἀλογίας ἡ πλάνη συμβέβηκεν, ἀλλ᾽ οὕτω σφόδρα ταῦτ᾽ οἰκεῖα τῷ Σωκρά-
25 D. τους ἤθει καὶ προσήκοντα ἐκρίθη, ὥστε καὶ ταύτῃ
τῇ δόξῃ γενέσθαι χώραν.
78 Δοκεῖ δέ μοι καὶ Σωκράτης αὐτὸς εἰ καὶ μηδεὶς
λόγος αὐτοῦ γραφῇ σῴζεται, οὐχ ἧττον οὔτε Πλάτωνος τοῦ σεμνοῦ οὔτ᾽ Αἰσχίνου τοῦ κομψοῦ μαρτυρεῖν, ἀλλ᾽ ἔτι κάλλιον καὶ ὡς ἀληθῶς εἰς τὸ μέσον.

ever the Bacchants become inspired, they draw milk
and honey from sources where others cannot even
draw water. And though I knew no study by which I
might usefully educate a man, still I thought that by
associating with him I would improve him through
love." He ends on this point of dialogue not in
riddles and hints nor only in a fashion in agreement
with us, but as if he wrote for this very purpose.
Then if dreams free the companies of Asclepius from 75
the art of medicine, and the Bacchants of Dionysus
transform the gifts of the Nymphs, whenever they
become inspired, why is it shameful or beyond the
realm of nature to accept the idea of men inspired
in oratory, and to believe that they can refer to the
Gods as patrons ? Indeed, it cannot be said that the 76
witness is worthless, or far removed from the matter,
or that we take refuge only in a name. But if, as is
the case with children, comrades ought to be called
legitimate, we have traditionally accepted the
legitimate relationship of Aeschines to Socrates.
Evidence is even forthcoming in the false belief of 77
certain people who have assumed that these are the
writings of Socrates himself. If no credence at all
must be given them, as I should first agree, still the
mistake was not completely senseless. But these
writings were adjudged so much akin and suitable
to the character of Socrates, that there was even
room for this belief.

But even if no writing of Socrates is preserved, he 78
himself seems to me to give his evidence no less than
the proud Plato or the clever Aeschines, but fairer
still and truly for all to see. It is agreed that he

---

¹ secl. Jacobs. ² Reiske : τῆς TQVA.
³ T p. corr. : ἑτέρους QVA. ⁴ add. Reiske.

(25 D.)

ὁμολογεῖται μέν γε λέγειν αὐτὸν ὡς ἄρα οὐδὲν ἐπίσταιτο, καὶ πάντες τοῦτό φασιν οἱ συγγενόμενοι. ὁμολογεῖται δὲ αὖ καὶ τοῦτο, σοφώτατον εἶναι Σωκράτη τὴν Πυθίαν εἰρηκέναι. πῶς οὖν ταῦτ᾽ ἔχει; οὐ γὰρ τόν γε τοῦ παντὸς ἐσφαλμένον ὡς ἀνέλοι σοφώτατον ἀνθρώπων πιστεῦσαι θεμιτὸν περὶ τοῦ θεοῦ. τέχνην δέ, ὡς ἔοικεν, ἔφασκεν[1] οὐκ ἀσκεῖν, ἀληθῆ λέγων. ᾧ γοῦν συνεγένετο Ἀναξαγόρᾳ, οὐ τἀκείνου
79 τιμήσας φαίνεται. ἐν μὲν δὴ τοῦτο μαρτυρεῖ Σωκράτης, οὐκ αἰσχρὸν εἶναι τὸ μὴ τέχνην κεκτῆσθαι, εἴπερ περὶ αὐτοῦ λέγων οὐκ ᾐσχύνετο. ἕτερον δὲ ἀκόλουθον. οὐ γάρ ἐστιν ὅστις οὐ λέγει περὶ Σωκράτους ὅτι φάσκοι τὸ δαιμόνιον αὐτῷ σημαίνειν.
80 οὐκοῦν[2] μηδὲν μὲν ἐπίστασθαι τῶν δεόντων ἀμήχανον ᾧ γε παρηκολούθει τὸ δαιμόνιον· ὅτι δ᾽ οὐδὲν ἐπίσταιτο αὐτὸς ἔλεγεν, λέγων δ᾽ οὐκ ἐψεύδετο, εἴπερ
81 γε μηδὲ ὁ θεὸς σοφώτατον αὐτὸν εἰρηκώς. λοιπὸν οὖν τί ποτε ἐστὶν τὸ φάσκειν οὐκ εἰδέναι; οἶμαί γε τὸ μὴ τέχνῃ. ἀλλὰ μὴν εἰ μηδετέρως γ᾽ ἂν[3] σοφώτατος ἦν ἔτι, μήτε ψευδόμενος περὶ αὐτοῦ, εἴπερ ἔν τι τῶν αἰσχρῶν τὸ ψεύδεσθαι, μήτ᾽ ἀληθῆ λέγων, εἰ τὸ μὴ χρῆσθαι τέχνῃ τῶν ἁπλῶς αἰσχρῶν ἦν, ἅμα Σωκράτης τε δι᾽ ἀμφοτέρων μαρτυρεῖ τῷ λόγῳ, καὶ ὧν ἔξαρνος ἦν καὶ ὧν ὡμολόγει, καὶ διὰ τοῦ Σωκράτους ὁ θεὸς μεμαρτύρηκεν περὶ ἀμφοῖν, χρήσας
26 D. ἐκεῖνον σοφώτατον εἶναι, ὥστε διπλῆν οὖσαν τὴν τοῦ Σωκράτους μαρτυρίαν ἑτέρᾳ κυρίᾳ τῇ παρ᾽ αὐ-
82 τοῦ βεβαιοῖ. μάθοι δὲ ἄν τις καὶ παρ᾽ αὐτοῦ τοῦ πράγματος συμβαίνοντα τῷ Σωκράτους λόγῳ καὶ βίῳ τὰ ἀπὸ τῆς μαντείας. τὸν γὰρ ζῶντα ὑπὸ θεῷ καὶ τῶν ἀνθρωπίνων πραγμάτων ἠμεληκότα πῶς

[1] om. VA. [2] οὔκουν Keil.

said that he knew nothing ; all his associates concur. Again it is agreed that the Pythian priestess proclaimed that Socrates was the wisest man. What does this mean ? For it is impious to believe of the God that he proclaimed the wisest of men one who had failed in everything. But Socrates, as it seems, truthfully claimed that he was trained in no art. While he studied with Anaxagoras, he obviously has not respected his doctrine. Socrates bears witness to this 79 one fact, that the failure to possess an art is not shameful, since he felt no shame in discussing himself. A second point follows. Everyone says that Socrates claims that his guiding spirit gave him signs. Then 80 he, who was attended by a guiding spirit, could not possibly be ignorant of anything important. But he said that he knew nothing. He did not lie, if the God did not who declared him the wisest of men. Then 81 what is the meaning of the claim that he did not know anything ? I think that he did not know anything through an art. Indeed, if Socrates would no longer be the wisest of men, either if he lied about himself, since a lie is shameful, or if he told the truth, if not to make use of an art is a simple matter of shame, then he bears witness to the argument in two ways, both in his denial and concurrence ; and through Socrates the God has borne witness about both points, when he gave the oracle that Socrates was the wisest of men. Therefore he confirms with his own testimony that twofold testimony of Socrates. One might also understand from the facts themselves 82 that the oracle agreed with the aims and life of Socrates. For is it not perfectly sensible that one who lived in the service of the God, in neglect of

---

[3] ad ἄν, cf. § 333.

(26 D.)

οὐκ εὔλογον ἐκ προχείρου παρὰ θεῷ κριτῇ σοφώ-
83 τατον ἀνθρώπων ἀνῃρῆσθαι; ἡ μὲν οὖν παρὰ τοῦ
Πλάτωνος ἡμῖν μαρτυρία τοσαύτη, δι᾿ αὐτοῦ καὶ
διὰ τῶν ἑταίρων ἀμφοτέρων τελευτῶσα εἰς τὸν θεὸν
τὸν ἐν Δελφοῖς, ὃς ἐπιψηφίζει Πλάτωνι ἃ μικρῷ
πρόσθεν ἔφην Αἰσχίνην.¹

84 Εἰ δὲ δεῖ καὶ ποιητῶν παρασχέσθαι μαρτυρίας,
ἔστι μὲν ἔργον ἢ τὰς ἁπάντων ἢ τὰς τῶν προκριθέν-
των διὰ πάντων παρασχέσθαι, ὅμως δ᾿ ὡς ἄν τις
ἔχοι τῶν γνωριμωτάτων ἐκλέξας εἰπεῖν ῥαθυμία
85 παραλιπεῖν. κοινῇ μὲν οὖν πάντες ποιηταὶ μαρτυροῦσιν τὴν ἔργῳ μαρτυρίαν, εἴπερ εἰσὶ ποιηταὶ τῷ
κρατοῦντι λόγῳ τῆς τέχνης. ἀλλ᾿ οὐ ταύτης δέομαι
τὰ νῦν, ἔστι γὰρ ἐν τοῖς εἰρημένοις, ἀλλὰ τῆς κατὰ
86 ῥῆμα. τοῦτο μὲν τοίνυν ὁ πρεσβύτατος αὐτῶν καὶ
πᾶσι συνηθέστατος Πάνδαρον μὲν τὸν Ζελείτην ἐπαινῶν εἰς τὴν τοξικὴν '' Ὧι καὶ τόξον Ἀπόλλων
27 D. αὐτὸς ἔδωκεν '' λέγει. τὸν δὲ τῶν Φαιάκων βασιλέα
ποιήσας εἰς ὑπερβολὴν φιλάνθρωπον καὶ θεοφιλῆ τῷ
ῥήματι τούτῳ τετίμηκεν

Ἀλκίνοος δὲ τότ᾿ ἦρχε θεῶν ἄπο μήδεα εἰδώς.

μή μου πύθῃ, φησίν, ποίαν τέχνην ἐκέκτητο, ἢ τίς
87 διδάσκαλος αὐτοῦ· θεῶν γὰρ ἄπο μήδεα ᾔδει. τὸν
δ᾿ αὖ Δημόδοκον ὡσαύτως τὸν κιθαρῳδὸν ἐπαινῶν
ὡς ἄκρον τὴν μουσικὴν οὕτω ποιεῖ

Τὸν πέρι Μοῦσ᾿ ἐφίλησε, δίδου δ᾿ ἀγαθόν τε κακόν
τε·
ὀφθαλμῶν μὲν ἄμερσε, δίδου δ᾿ ἡδεῖαν ἀοιδήν·

καὶ πάλιν

Μοῦσ᾿ ἄρ᾿ ἀοιδὸν ἀνῆκεν ἀειδέμεναι κλέα ἀνδρῶν.

328

human affairs, was readily proclaimed in the judgement of the God to be the wisest of men ? This is the 83
sum of our evidence from Plato, his own and both his
comrades, which ends with the God of Delphi, who
assents to Plato's judgement, just as I said, a little
before, Aeschines assented.

If evidence must be produced from the poets, it is 84
difficult either to produce that of all of them, or that
of those who are pre-eminent among all. Still it is
slothful to omit this, since a selection could be made
of the most distinguished. Poets as a class provide 85
actual evidence, since they are poets through a reason
which surpasses art. But now I do not need this
evidence, for it has been given, but that of direct
citation. Therefore the oldest of them, he who is 86
best known to all, when he praises Pandarus of
Zelea for his skill with the bow, says [a] : " To him
Apollo himself gave the bow." Describing the king
of the Phaeacians as extremely humane and pious, he
honoured him with this expression [b] : " Then did
Alcinous rule, who was wise from the Gods." Do not
ask me, he says, what art he possessed or who was his
teacher. He was wise from the Gods. Again in the 87
same way while praising the lyre-player Demodocus
as supreme in music, he writes [c] : " The Muse loved
him, but gave him good and evil. She deprived him
of his sight, but gave him sweet song." And again [d] :
" The Muse sent him as a bard to sing the glorious

[a] *Iliad* II. 827.
[b] *Odyssey* VI. 12.
[c] *Odyssey* VIII. 63-64.
[d] *Odyssey* VIII. 73.

---

[1] codd. dett. : Αἰσχίνῃ TQVA.

(27 D.)

ὁ δέ γε ᾿Αλκίνους αὐτὸς συνιστὰς αὐτὸν καὶ καλῶν εὐθὺς ἐν ἀρχῇ φησιν

Τῷ γάρ ῥα θεὸς πέρι δῶκεν ἀοιδήν,
τέρπειν ὅππῃ θυμὸς ἐποτρύνῃσιν ἀείδειν.

ταυτί φησιν ὁ ᾿Αλκίνους αὐτός, ᾧ φιλοτιμίαν εἶχεν δήπουθεν, εἴ τι καὶ διδασκάλοις ἀνήλωσεν ὑπὲρ αὐτοῦ, καὶ ταῦτα ὄντι λαμπρῷ καὶ μεγαλοψύχῳ καὶ δόξης ἐραστῇ. ἀλλ᾿ ὅμως ἐγώ σοι, φησίν, αὐτὸς 88 λέγω καὶ διορίζομαι, τοῦτον οὐκ ἐδιδαξάμην. καὶ οὐχ ὁ μὲν ᾿Αλκίνους οὕτως ὁ τῶν Φαιάκων βασιλεύς, ὁ δὲ τῶν ῾Ελλήνων σοφώτατος οὐχ ὁμοίως περὶ τῶν αὐτῶν, ἀλλ᾿ ἔτι μᾶλλον ἀγασθεὶς τοῦ Δημοδόκου τῆς ἐπιδείξεως καὶ ὥσπερ ἐπίτηδες ζητῶν ὅ τι εἴποι μέγιστον, ὦ Δημόδοκε, φησίν,

28 D.   ῎Εξοχα δή σε βροτῶν αἰνίζομ᾿ ἁπάντων·
ἢ σέ γε Μοῦσ᾿ ἐδίδαξε Διὸς παῖς, ἢ σέ γ᾿ ᾿Απόλλων·

ὡς τοῦ πράγματος κρείττονος ἢ τέχνῃ λαβεῖν.

λίην γὰρ κατὰ κόσμον ᾿Αχαιῶν οἶτον ἀείδεις.

οὐδὲ τοῦτο πάρεργον, οὐδ᾿ εἰκῇ προσθείς, οὐδ᾿ ἐφόλκιον ἄλλως ἐπὶ τοῖς ἄνω, ἀλλ᾿ ἐνδεικνύμενος καὶ πρὸς ἓν σημαινόμενος ὅτι τοῦτο τὸ ἐν κόσμῳ καὶ λαμπρῶς οὐκ ἐκ τέχνης, ἀλλ᾿ ἐπιπνοίᾳ θεῶν παρα- 89 γίγνεται. κομψὸν μὲν γάρ τι, φαυλότερον δὲ ἡ τέχνη πολλῷ· πάλιν δ᾿ ὥσπερ ἐπισφραγιζόμενος τὴν μαρτυρίαν, προβαλὼν αὐτῷ τὸν τοῦ ἵππου κόσμον ἀεῖσαι, τοσοῦτον ὑπισχνεῖται,

Αἴ κεν δή μοι ταῦτα (φησὶν)[1] κατὰ μοῖραν καταλέξῃς,

330

deeds of men." When Alcinous himself introduces
him and summons him, right at the start he says [a] :
" To him the Goddess gave song, to cause delight,
whenever his heart urges him to sing." So says
Alcinous to whom I think it would have been a point
of pride, since he was a resplendent, generous,
praise-loving man, if he had spent anything on his
education. However, I say and affirm to you, he
says, that I did not have him instructed. And not only 88
Alcinous, the king of Phaeacians, but the wisest
of the Greeks spoke likewise on the same subject.
Even more astounded at the display of Demodocus,
and as it were purposely seeking for the greatest
compliment, " Demodocus," he says [b] : " Beyond all
men I praise you. Either the Muse, child of Zeus,
or Apollo has taught you," since the matter was
beyond the capacity of art ; " for in a very orderly
fashion you sing the fate of the Achaeans." He has
not added this as a random aside, nor as a purposeless
addition to the above ; but he demonstrates and
particularly reveals that this glorious orderliness does
not come from art, but through the inspiration of the
Gods. For art is clever, but a far inferior thing. 89
Again, as it were confirming this evidence, he proposes to him to sing of the making of the horse, and
makes a promise [c] : " If you tell these things

[a] *Odyssey* VIII. 44-45.
[b] *Odyssey* VIII. 487-489. Odysseus speaks.
[c] *Odyssey* VIII. 496-498.

[1] φησὶ ταῦτα VA.

(28 D.)

αὐτίκα καὶ πᾶσιν μυθήσομαι ἀνθρώποισιν
ὡς ἄρα τοι πρόφρων θεὸς ὤπασε θέσπιν ἀοιδήν.

ὡς οὐκ ἔχων τί τούτου μεῖζον ὑπόσχοιτο αὐτῷ.
90 οὕτω τοίνυν ὁ ποιητὴς πεπεικὼς αὐτὸν ἐποίει περὶ
τούτων, ὥστε ὥσπερ δεδοικὼς μή τις αὐτὸν περὶ
Δημοδόκου μόνου λέγειν ταῦτα δόξειεν, ἀπὸ τοῦ
κοινοῦ τῶν ἀοιδῶν ἐποίησεν ἀρχόμενον τὸν Ὀδυσσέα
καὶ λέγονθ' οὕτω

Πᾶσι γὰρ ἀνθρώποισιν ἐπιχθονίοισιν ἀοιδοὶ
τιμῆς ἔμμοροί εἰσι καὶ αἰδοῦς, οὕνεκ' ἄρα σφᾶς
οἴμας Μοῦσ' ἐδίδαξε· φίλησε δὲ φῦλον ἀοιδῶν.

ὥσπερ δεδοικὼς Ὅμηρος ὑπὲρ ἑαυτοῦ μή τις αὐτὸν
29 D. φῇ¹ παρ' ἑτέρου τι μεμαθηκέναι, ἀλλὰ μὴ παρ'
91 αὐτῶν τῶν Μουσῶν. πῶς οὖν αἱ Μοῦσαι διδάσκου-
σιν; ἆρά γε ὥσπερ οἱ γραμματισταὶ διδασκαλεῖον
ἀνοιξάμεναι; οὐκ ἔστιν. ἀλλ' οἶμαι ἐπὶ νοῦν
ἄγουσιν καὶ τὴν εὕρεσιν κινοῦσιν, ὡς καὶ ἐν αὐτοῖς
τούτοις ἐμφαίνεται τοῖς ἔπεσιν· φησὶ γοῦν ἐπὶ πᾶσιν

Ὣς φάθ'· ὁ δ' ὁρμηθεὶς θεοῦ ἤρχετο, φαῖνε δ'
ἀοιδήν.

ταὐτὸν διὰ πάντων ἐμφανίζων, ὅτι ληρεῖ τέχνῃ πρὸς
92 θεὸν κινοῦντα. τὸν τοίνυν Φήμιον ἐν τῇ τῶν μνη-
στήρων σφαγῇ πεποίηκεν τὸ ὑπὲρ ἑαυτοῦ παραιτού-
μενον καὶ λέγοντα

Αὐτοδίδακτος δ' εἰμί· θεὸς δέ μοι ἐν φρεσὶν οἴμας
παντοίας ἐνέφυσεν, ἔοικα δέ τοι παραείδειν
ὥστε θεῷ· τῷ μή με λιλαίεο δειροτομῆσαι.

τοῦτο μὲν ὡς ταὐτὸν ὅ τε αὐτοδίδακτος καὶ ὁ τῶν
θεῶν μαθητὴς ἐγγύθεν οὑτωσὶ δηλῶν, τοῦτο δὲ ὡς
οὐδὲν ἄλλο εἰπόντος εἰς σωτηρίαν τοῦ Φημίου

properly," he says, " straightway I shall report to all
men how a gracious God has given you divine song,"
as if he could promise him nothing greater. With 90
such conviction did the poet write about these
matters, that as if in fear that someone might think
that he spoke about Demodocus alone, he made
Odysseus begin with poets in general and say [a] :
" Among all men on the earth, bards have a share of
honour and reverence, because the Muse has taught
them their lays. She has loved the race of bards,"
as if Homer were afraid on his own behalf that
someone might say that he learned from another,
and not from the Muses themselves. How then do 91
the Muses teach ? By opening a school like elementary teachers ? It is not possible. But I think they
move and excite conceptions in our minds, as even
appears in these verses. For he says at the end [b] :
" So he spoke. But he, moved by the God, began
and revealed his song." He always is stressing the
same point, that art is drivel compared to the inspiration of God. Therefore in the slaughter of the 92
suitors he has depicted Phemius pleading for himself
and saying [c] : " I am self-taught. God has inspired
various lays in my heart. I think that I sing beside
you as to a God. Therefore do not desire to cut
my throat." Thus on the one hand he makes it
immediately and clearly evident that to be self-
taught and the pupil of the Gods is the same, and
on the other, that Phemius had no greater argument

[a] *Odyssey* VIII. 479-481.   [b] *Odyssey* VIII. 499.
[c] *Odyssey* XXII. 347-349.

---

[1] ἑτέρου τι φῇ VA.

(29 D.)

μεῖζον ἢ ὅτι οὐδενὸς ἀνθρώπων ἐστὶν μαθητής.
εἰκότως· τὸν γὰρ ὑπὸ τῶν ἠδικῆσθαι δοκούντων
μέλλοντα σωθήσεσθαι εἰς τὴν παρὰ τῶν θεῶν τιμὴν
καταφεύγειν[1] εἰκὸς ἦν. δι' ἃ τούτοις αὐτὸν σῴζει
τοῖς λόγοις.

93 Ἔτι τοίνυν, ἀναλήψομαι γάρ, τὸν Τηλέμαχον ἀπο-
δημοῦντα πεποίηκε δήπου κατὰ πύστιν τοῦ πατρὸς
ἐν τοῖς πρώτοις, ὡς δὲ προσέσχεν τῇ Πύλῳ καὶ
συντυγχάνειν ἔδει τῷ Νέστορι ἀγωνιῶντα καὶ ἀπο-
ροῦντα ὅ τι χρὴ λέγειν πρὸς αὐτὸν διὰ τὸ συνει-
δέναι μὴ ὅπως τέχνην αὐτῷ τινα ἐπισταμένῳ περὶ
30 D. λόγους, ἀλλ' οὐδ' αὐτό, ὅ φησι Πλάτων, ἐμπειρίαν
ἔχοντί πω μέχρι τούτου. κατακέκλεικε γοῦν αὐτὸ
τοῦτ' εἰς ἔπος ἐξ ἀρχῆς εἰς τέλος

  Οὐδέ τί πω μύθοισι πεπείρημαι πυκινοῖσιν.

ὁ δ' αὐτὸν παραμυθεῖται καὶ λέγει, Μηδείς σε τῶν
σοφιστῶν ἐξαπατάτω, μηδ' ἀθυμήσῃς ἐπὶ σαυτῷ.
εἰ γὰρ καὶ τῆς τέχνης ἀπολέλειψαι καὶ τῆς ἐμπειρίας,

  Ἄλλα μὲν αὐτὸς ἐνὶ φρεσὶ σῇσι νοήσεις,
  ἄλλα δὲ καὶ δαίμων ὑποθήσεται· οὐ γὰρ ὀΐω
  οὔ σε θεῶν ἀέκητι γενέσθαι τε τραφέμεν τε,

συνάπτων κἀνταῦθα τρόπον τινὰ καὶ συντιθεὶς ἐφεξῆς τό τε αὐτὸν συνεῖναι καὶ τὸ ὑπειπεῖν τὸν
θεόν, καὶ πάλιν αὖ τὴν φύσιν καὶ τροφὴν τῇ θείᾳ
μοίρᾳ προστιθείς. καὶ ταῦτα οὐ Μέντωρ, οὐδ'[2]
Ἁλιθέρσης αὐτῷ λέγει, ἀλλὰ θεῶν ἡ σοφωτάτη καὶ
ᾗ τά τε τῆς φρονήσεως καὶ τὸ περὶ τὰς τέχνας ἀνά-
94 κειται. καὶ ὁ Τηλέμαχος πρῶτον τότε ῥητορεύων
εὔπορος γίγνεται καὶ λόγους ἀποχρῶντας εὑρί-

---

[1] codd. dett. : φεύγειν TQVA.
[2] codd. dett. : οὐκ T in ras. QV, οὖν A.

for saving himself than that he is the pupil of no man. Reasonably so. For it was reasonable for one who is going to be spared by those who think that they have been wronged to seek safety in his honour from the Gods. Thus he saves him with this argument.

He also wrote about Telemachus, for I shall go 93 back to the beginning, going abroad primarily to learn about his father; and when he had put in at Pylus and had to meet Nestor, he is described as in a state of anxiety and despair over what he ought to say to him, because he was conscious that far from knowing any art of speaking, he did not even possess, at this time, that which Plato calls " experience." He has embodied this whole idea from beginning to end in a verse [a] : " Nor have I yet any experience in clever speech." But in consolation, he says, Let none of the sophists deceive you, nor be disheartened over yourself. For if you are deficient in art and experience [b] : " Some things you will conceive in your own heart, others God will suggest to you. For I do not think that you were born and raised without the will of the Gods." Here in a certain way he links and joins together knowledge and prompting by the God, and again assigns his nature and education to the divine portion. And neither Mentor nor Halitherses says this to him, but the wisest Goddess to whom the sources of both intelligence and the arts are attributed. And Telemachus, then first acting as an orator, 94 becomes articulate and finds words sufficient for his

[a] *Odyssey* III. 23.   [b] *Odyssey* III. 26-28.

335

(30 D.)

σκει τῇ χρείᾳ—ἃ γὰρ ἐν μνηστῆρσιν ἐδημηγόρησεν
ἐῶ λέγειν—[τῆς Ἀθηνᾶς],[1] καὶ τυγχάνει τοῦ σκοποῦ
οὕτως ὥστε ὅ γε Νέστωρ ἀκούσας, τοῦτο γὰρ ἐστι
τὸ ἥδιστον, ἐπαινεῖ τε καὶ φησὶν

Ἤτοι γὰρ μῦθοί γε ἐοικότες, οὐδέ κε φαίης
ἄνδρα νεώτερον ὧδε ἐοικότα μυθήσασθαι·

καίτοι τῶν ἄκρων[2] ῥητορικὴν καὶ λόγους εὑρεῖν καὶ
κρῖναι ὁ Νέστωρ αὐτῷ πεποίηται καὶ ἐν Ἰλιάδι καὶ
ἐν Ὀδυσσείᾳ· ἀλλ᾽ ὅμως ἐπαινεῖ καὶ λαμπρῶς. ὡς
δ᾽ ἧκεν ἐκ τῆς Πύλου πρὸς τὸν ἕτερον ῥήτορα καὶ
βασιλέα τὸν Μενέλαον, ὁ μὲν Τηλέμαχος ὡς θεοῦ
φησιν ἀκούων τέρπεσθαι τοῦ Μενελάου, ὁ δὲ τὴν
αὐτὴν αὖ περὶ ἐκείνου φέρει τῷ Νέστορι δόξαν, καὶ
φησὶν ἅτε καὶ αὐτὸς ἤδη πρεσβύτης ὢν

Αἵματός εἰς ἀγαθοῖο φίλον τέκος οἷ᾽ ἀγορεύεις·

οὐδὲν ἀλλ᾽ ἢ τοῦτο λέγων ὅτι πέφυκας πρὸς λόγους,
διὰ τοῦτο λέγεις τὰ βέλτιστα, καὶ παρ᾽ ἑτέροις
τοιούτοις εὐδοκιμεῖς· ὥστε εἰ καὶ μὴ τέχνην τιν᾽
ἔχεις περὶ τοὺς λόγους, ἔμοιγε, φησίν, ἐξαρκεῖ.
οὕτω δι᾽ ὅλου τοῦ δράματος ὥσπερ ἐξεπίτηδες καὶ
διὰ πάντων τῶν ἀξιόχρεων Ὅμηρος μαρτυρεῖ μὴ
τὴν τέχνην εἶναι κυρίαν ἐν τοῖς λόγοις, ἀλλὰ τὸ τῆς
φύσεως κράτος καὶ τὸ δοκοῦν τῷ θεῷ. αὐτὸς τοίνυν
ὁ τοῦ Τηλεμάχου πατήρ, ὃν τῆς εἰς τοὺς λόγους
παρασκευῆς ἐπὶ πλεῖστον ἐποίησεν ἥκοντα, παρ-
οξυνθείς τι πρὸς τὸν Φαίακα καὶ σωφρονίζων αὐτόν, πῶς λέγει καὶ παρρησιάζεται,

Ἄλλος μὲν γάρ τ᾽[3] εἶδος ἀκιδνότερος πέλει ἀνήρ,
ἀλλὰ θεὸς μορφὴν ἔπεσιν στέφει·

31 D.
95

96

---

[1] secl. Behr ; ⟨ὑφηγουμένης⟩ τῆς Reiske.
[2] codd. dett. : ἄκρως TQVA.　　　[3] del. Bentley.

needs—for I omit his harangue among the suitors—, and is so successful that when Nestor heard him—this is particularly charming—he praises him and says [a] : " Indeed, your speech is seemly. You would not say that a young man spoke such seemly things as these." Yet in both the *Iliad* and the *Odyssey* Homer has depicted Nestor as one of the experts in the performance and criticism of oratory. Still he gives him glowing praise. When he came from 95 Pylus to the other orator and king, Menelaus, Telemachus says [b] that he listens to Menelaus with pleasure, like a God, and Menelaus gives the same verdict about him as Nestor did, and says as he was now himself an old man [c] : " Dear child, you are of good stock, such are the things you say ! " He means only this, that you are naturally endowed for oratory, therefore you say what is best, and you have distinction in the eyes of other such men. Thus even if you do not possess any art of oratory, he says, *I* am content. So through the whole drama, 96 as it were intentionally, and with all credible witnesses, Homer attests that art is not paramount in oratory, but strength of nature and what the God approves. Therefore when the father of Telemachus, whom he has depicted as having made the farthest advance in the practice of oratory, became somewhat angered at the Phaeacian and castigates him, what bold free speech does he use ? [d] " One man is weaker in body, but God crowns his form with words." At the same time he emphasizes the dignity of

---

[a] *Odyssey* III. 124-125.
[b] *Odyssey* IV. 160. Aristides here errs. The speaker was not Telemachus, but Pisistratus.
[c] *Odyssey* IV. 611.   [d] *Odyssey* VIII. 169-170.

(31 D.)

ὁμοῦ μὲν τὸ ἀξίωμα τῆς ῥητορικῆς ἐμφανίζων καὶ
τὴν δύναμιν αὐτῆς ὁπόση τις καὶ ἡλίκη, ὁμοῦ δ'
αὐτὰ ταῦτα τῷ θεῷ προστιθεὶς ὡς ἐκεῖθεν ἥκοντα,
ὥσπερ Πλάτωνι ἀποκρινάμενος, οὐκ Εὐρυάλῳ.

97 Δοκεῖ δέ μοι καὶ Ἡσίοδος τῆς αὐτῆς ἔχεσθαι γνώμης Ὁμήρῳ καὶ τοῖς ῥήμασι μόνοις διαλλάττειν
ἐν τοῖσδε τοῖς ἔπεσιν

Κεῖνος[1] μὲν πανάριστος ὃς αὐτῷ[2] πάντα νοήσῃ·
ἐσθλὸς δ' αὖ κἀκεῖνος ὃς εὖ εἰπόντι πίθηται·
32 D. ὃς δέ γε μήτ' αὐτὸς νοέῃ μήτ' ἄλλου ἀκούων
ἐν θυμῷ βάλληται, ὁ δ' αὖτ' ἀχρήιος ἀνήρ·

πρῶτον μὲν ἔθετο τὸν αὐτὸν εὑρόντα τὰ βέλτιστα,
ἔσχατον δὲ ἀμαθίᾳ τὸν οὔτε συνιέντα οὔτε πειθό-
μενον, μέσον δὲ ἀμφοτέρων, ὥσπερ ἐν ἀριθμῶν
ὅροις, τὸν τῷ συνιέντι πεισθέντα, τοσούτῳ χείρω
τοῦ νοήσαντος, ὅσῳ βελτίω τοῦ μήθ' εὑρόντος[3]
98 μήτε πεισθέντος. οὐκοῦν ὁ μὲν αὐτὸς πάντα νοήσας
ἐστὶν ὁ εὖ εἰπών· εἰ δὲ βούλει ἐκείνως, ὁ μὲν εὖ εἰπών ἐστιν ὁ νοήσας αὐτὸς ἅπαντα. δῆλον δέ· προσθεὶς[4] γὰρ '' ὃς αὐτὸς πάντα νοήσῃ '' μετείληφεν
ἐν τῷ δευτέρῳ ἐπὶ τοῦ εὖ εἰπόντος τὸν αὐτὸν τοῦτον λέγων, ἀντὶ τοῦ νοήσαντος τὸν εὖ εἰπόντα θείς,
99 ὡς αὐτὸν τοῦτον ὄντα τὸν βέλτιστον ῥήτορα. οὕτω
δὲ τούτων κειμένων ὁ μέν, οἶμαι, νοήσας παντὶ
συμβαλεῖν ῥάδιος, ὅτι ὁ τῇ φύσει κρατῶν ἐστιν, ὃν
ἄριστον ὡρίσατο, ὃν καὶ εὖ εἰπόντα προσεῖπεν· ὁ

---

[1] ἐκεῖνος TQA, οὗτος libri Hesiodi.
[2] αὐτῷ VA, αὐτὸς libri Hesiodi.
[3] codd. dett. : μήτ' εἰπόντος TQVA.
[4] προθεὶς Keil.

338

oratory, and the greatness and extent of its power, and attributes these things to the God, as if this was their source, as it were answering Plato, not Euryalus.

Hesiod seems to me to hold the same view as 97 Homer and to differ only in expression, in the following verses [a]: "That man is wholly best, who has thought out all things for himself. Again that man is good who hearkens to him who speaks well. But who neither thinks out things for himself nor listens to another, and stores it in his heart, he is a useless man." He put in the first rank the discoverer of what is best, in the last him who through ignorance neither understands nor listens, and in the middle, as in a numerical progression, him who has listened to one who understands, and who is as much inferior to one who has thought out things for himself as he is better than he who has neither discovered nor listened to anything. Therefore " he 98 who has thought out all things for himself " is the same as " he who speak well." If you wish to put it the other way, " he who speaks well " is " he who has thought out all things for himself." It is quite clear. For when he had applied " who has thought out all things for himself," in the second verse he changed it to " he who speaks well," meaning the same man, having put " he who speaks well " in place of " he who has thought out all things for himself," as if this man were the best orator. For on these terms, I think, " he who 99 has thought out things for himself " is understood by everybody, that it is the man who is naturally excellent, whom Hesiod defined as best, and whom he also called " him who speaks well." On the other hand, he

[a] *Works and Days* 293, 295-297. Verse 294 is also omitted in other ancient citations of this passage.

(32 D.)

δὲ αὖ πεισθεὶς ἐν τῇ τοῦ μαθόντος γίγνεται μερίδι.
ἀκούσας γὰρ τοῦ[1] τὰ βέλτιστα λέγοντος οὕτω
100 χρῆται παρ' ἐκείνου λαβών. εὑρεῖν οὖν φησιν, ὦ
Πλάτων, κρεῖττον ἢ μαθεῖν, καὶ τέχνη φύσεως
δεύτερον, εἰκότως ὁ Ἡσίοδος καὶ φρονῶν οὕτω καὶ
λέγων, καὶ τῆς δάφνης οὐκ ἀμνημονῶν, ἣν ἅμα τῷ
101 λαβεῖν ποιητὴς ἦν γεγονὼς ἐκ ποιμένος. ἐπεὶ καὶ
τὰς τέχνας αὐτὰς καὶ τὰ ἐπιτηδεύματα φύσει δήπου
33 D. διενεγκόντες ἄνθρωποι καὶ νικήσαντες ἀνεῦρον τὸ
ἐξ ἀρχῆς. οὐ γὰρ αἱ τέχναι τὰς φύσεις ἐποίησαν,
ἀλλ' αἱ κράτισται φύσεις[2] τὰς βελτίστας τῶν
τεχνῶν εὗρον, ὥστε καὶ τῇ τάξει καὶ τῇ δυνάμει
102 παρὰ τῇ φύσει τὰ πρεσβεῖα εἶναι. εἰ δὲ δὴ μηδ'
ἁπλῶς ἀνθρώποις τὴν εὕρεσιν προστίθεμεν τῶν
τεχνῶν, ἀλλὰ θεοὺς ἡγήσασθαι φαμὲν αὐτοῖς καὶ
καταδεῖξαι, πῶς οὐκ εὔδηλον ὅτι πολλῷ τινος εἶναι
νικῶντος δεῖ προσθήκην τὴν τέχνην; καὶ μὴν εἰ
τοῦτο δῆλον ἅπασιν καὶ πάντες ἂν συμφαῖεν μὴ
θεοὺς παρ' ἀνθρώπων λαβεῖν τὰς ἐπιστήμας, ἀλλ'
ἀνθρώπους παρὰ θεῶν, καὶ διδασκάλων μὲν ἐκείνους,
μαθητῶν δὲ ἡμᾶς ἔχειν τάξιν, τοσούτῳ κρεῖττον,
ὡς ἔοικεν, εὑρεῖν ἢ μαθεῖν, ὅσῳ κρείττων[3] ἀνθρώπου θεός. οἱ μὲν γὰρ εὑρήκασιν ἅπαντα, ἡμεῖς δ',
103 οἶμαι, λαβόντες χρώμεθα. ὀρθῶς ἄρα καὶ δικαίως ὁ
τοῦ Ἑλικῶνος πρόσοικος καὶ ὡς εἰκὸς ἦν τὸν αὐτὸν
ἐκ θεῶν ἐπιπνοίας ταῦτα λέγειν εἰληφότα τὸν μὲν
τοιοῦτον ἄνδρα ὡς θεὸν καὶ θεῶν ἐγγὺς πρῶτον καὶ
κράτιστον ἔθετο ὃς αὐτὸς πάντα νοήσῃ, τὸν δ'
104 ἀκούσαντα καὶ μαθόντα δεύτερον. ποῦ[4] γὰρ ἄν τις

---

[1] codd. dett. : που TQVA.
[2] ἐποίησαν—φύσεις om. A.

340

who has listened to him has the part of a pupil. For
when he has heard the best advice from the speaker,
he takes it from him and uses it. Then, Plato, he 100
says that the conception of an idea is superior to
learning one, and art is inferior to nature. With
good reason Hesiod thinks and says these things,
and he has not forgotten the laurel which he once
received and so at once became a poet from a
shepherd.[a] Indeed, in the beginning, naturally 101
outstanding and superior men invented the arts
themselves and their practice. For the arts did
not create men's natures, but the best natures
invented the best arts, so that pre-eminence belongs
to nature both in order and power. But if we do not 102
simply attribute the invention of the arts to men,
but we say that the Gods led and guided them, is it
not quite clear that art is only an appendage of
something far superior ? Indeed, if this is clear to all,
and all would agree that the Gods have not taken
the sciences from men, but men from the Gods, and
that they have the place of teachers, but we of
pupils, invention, it seems, is as much better than
learning, as a God is better than a man. For they
have invented all things, but we, I think, take their
inventions and use them. Then rightly and justly, 103
and as was reasonable for one who learned and spoke
under the inspiration of the Gods, did that neighbour
of Helicon [b] make such a man like a God and near
to the Gods, first and best, who has " thought out
all things for himself," and him who has listened
and learned, only second. For how and in what way 104

[a] *Theogony* 30.   [b] Hesiod.

---

[3] κρεῖττον TVA.   [4] codd. dett. : ὅπου TQVA.

(33 D.)

καὶ κράτιστον θείη τὸν μαθόντα καὶ πῶς; οὐκ ἔστιν
οὐδὲ βουλομένῳ, ἀλλὰ φύσει κεκώλυται, δικαίως,
105 ὅτι καὶ νικᾶν πανταχοῦ φαμὲν τὴν φύσιν. εἰ γὰρ
ἦν τὸ μαθεῖν ἄριστον καὶ πρῶτον, οὐδὲ ἂν αὐτὸ
πρῶτον τὸ μαθεῖν ἦν. ἐχρῆν γὰρ δήπου μαθεῖν
παρ' ἑτέρου. ὥστε οὐκ ἂν ἦν ὁ διδάσκων πρῶτος,
34 D. εἰ τὸ μαθεῖν κρεῖττον καὶ πρῶτον ἦν. παρὰ τοῦ[1]
γάρ, ὦ καὶ σὺ τὴν Ποικίλην κοσμήσας, ἀκούσῃ, τίσι
πεισθῇ, εἰ κρείττων ὁ μαθών ἐστι τοῦ τὸ πρῶτον
εὑρόντος, καὶ μὴ ἀνάγκη δεύτερος, εἴπερ τι μέλλει
106 μαθήσεσθαι. πᾶς γὰρ ὁ μανθάνων ὡμολόγηκε δήπουθεν εἶναι χείρων αὐτῷ γε τῷ δεῖσθαι μαθεῖν·
ὡς εἴ γε μὴ πείσειεν αὐτὸν δεῖσθαι πρότερον, πῶς
107 ἂν μάθοι, ἢ πῶς ἄλλῳ γ' ἂν εἰπόντι πεισθείη; οὐκοῦν
ἄτοπον τόν γε αὐτὸν ὡμολογηκότα εἶναι χείρω,
τοῦτον ἀμείνω καλεῖν, καὶ ταῦτα δι' αὐτὸ τοῦτ' ἐπ-
αινούμενον, ὅτι ὡμολόγηκεν χείρων εἶναι. ἢ κατὰ
μὲν τὰς δωρεὰς οὐδαμοῦ κρείττων ὁ λαβὼν τοῦ δόν-
τος αὐτῷ τῷ λαβεῖν, ἀλλὰ τὸ δοῦναι τοῦ κρείττονος εἶναι δοκεῖ, ἐν δὲ τοῖς μαθήμασιν κρείττων ὁ
προσέχων τὸν νοῦν τοῦ νοήσαντος αὐτοῦ καὶ παρα-
108 σχόντος; καὶ μὴν ἐφ' οἷς ὁ λαβὼν ἄριστος πῶς οὐ
πρῶτος ὁ ταῦτ' ἔχων ἐξ ἀρχῆς, καὶ διὰ τὸν χρόνον
γέ που καὶ παρὰ τὴν αἰτίαν;
109   Ἔτι τοίνυν ἑνὸς ποιητοῦ τῶν ἀπὸ Βοιωτίας καὶ
Ἑλικῶνος παρασχήσομαι μαρτυρίαν, ᾧ καὶ Πλάτων
αὐτὸς τὰ πλείστου, φασίν, ἄξια χρῆται. οὗτος δέ,

---

[1] τοῦ TQA.

---

[a] Decorated metaphorically by his teaching there.

342

could the learner be made best? It is impossible even if you wished it; indeed, it is prohibited by nature, and rightly so, because everywhere we say that nature is superior. For if learning was best 105 and first, to begin with there would not even be any learning. For learning must surely come from another. Therefore the teacher would not be first, if learning were superior and first. For from whom, you who have also decorated the Painted Porch,[a] will he learn, whom will he listen to, if the learner is superior to him who has first conceived the idea, and not necessarily second if he intends to learn something? For everyone who is in the process of 106 learning has agreed, I think, that he is inferior by the very fact that he needs to learn. So that if he should not first persuade himself that he has this need, how could he learn, or how could he heed any other speaker? Then it is strange to call superior 107 the very man who has agreed that he is inferior, and that too when he is approved of for the reason that he has agreed that he is inferior. In the giving of gifts the recipient is by no means superior to the giver by the act of receiving, but the act of giving seems to be the part of the superior person. But in learning is the attentive student superior to the conceiver and transmitter of the idea? Indeed, 108 as regards those qualities whereby the recipient is presumed to be best, does not the highest rank belong to him who possessed these from the start, both because of length of time and as being the cause of their transmission?

I shall also present the evidence of a poet from 109 Boeotia and Helicon, whom Plato himself, they say, used as being of the greatest worth. This man, O

(34 D.)

ὦ θεοί, καὶ μάλ' ἀποκαλύψας καὶ τῆς αὐτοῦ φύσεως
καὶ Μούσης ὡς ἀληθῶς βοᾷ Στεντόρειον εἰς τοὺς
ἀνθρώπους ὥσπερ σιωπὴν κηρύξας

> Σοφὸς ὁ πολλὰ εἰδὼς φυᾷ·
> μαθόντες δὲ λάβροι

35 D.
> παγγλωσσίᾳ κόρακες ὡς ἄκραντα γαρύετον
> Διὸς πρὸς ὄρνιχα θεῖον.

κοράκων φησὶν εἶναι φωνὰς τὰς τῶν μαθόντων καὶ
παρ' ἄλλων εἰληφότων πρὸς ἀετὸν γιγνομένας τὸν
110 φύσει νικῶντα καὶ ἐκ θεοῦ ῥήτορα καὶ σοφόν. ἑτέρωθι δ' αὖ βραχύτερον μέν, γνωρίμως δ' οὐχ ἧττον
διαμαρτύρεται

> Τὸ δὲ φυᾷ κράτιστον ἅπαν.
> πολλοὶ δὲ διδακταῖς
> ἀνθρώπων ἀρεταῖς κλέος
> ὤρουσαν αἱρεῖσθαι,

σφόδρ' ἀκολούθως ἀμφότερα εἰπών. ἐπειδὴ γὰρ τὸ
μὲν κράτιστον ἐν τοῖς ὀλίγοις, τὰ δὲ φαυλότερα ἐν
τοῖς πολλοῖς, ἀντιτέθεικε τῷ κρατίστῳ τὸ [πολλῷ][1]
χεῖρον διὰ τοῦ τῶν πολλῶν ὀνόματος, ὡς ἐκεῖνο μὲν
παντάπασιν τινῶν ὀλίγων ὄν, τοῦτο δὲ εἰς τοὺς πολλοὺς ἀφικνούμενον. καὶ ἔτι πρὸ τούτων " 'Αγαθοὶ
δὲ φύσει[2] καὶ σοφοὶ κατὰ δαίμονα ἄνδρες ἐγένοντο,"
ὅμοιον καὶ[3] τοῦτο τῷ ἑτέρῳ ῥήματι καὶ ταὐτὸν
λέγων. οὗ μὲν γὰρ διδακταῖς εἶπεν ἀρεταῖς, προσέθηκεν ἀνθρώπων, οὗ δὲ τὴν φύσιν πρεσβεύει, κατὰ
δαίμονα, τούτους εἶναι τοὺς τῷ ὄντι ἀγαθοὺς καὶ
111 σοφούς. εἰκότως· εἰ γὰρ ἐν αὐτοῖς τοῖς λόγοις τοὺς
τὰ ὑφ' ἑτέρου εἰρημένα καὶ προκατειλημμένα κλέπ-
τοντας καὶ διεξιόντας ὡς αὐτῶν οὐδεὶς οὕτω μαίνε-
ται ὥστε βελτίους ἡγεῖσθαι τῶν οἴκοθεν εὐπόρων

Gods, in revealing that from his nature and Muse, truly shouts out in a Stentorian voice to mankind, like a herald calling for attention [a] : " He is wise who knows many things naturally. But those who have learned, impetuous in their garrulity, like crows, they chatter vain things against the divine bird of Zeus." He says that the voices of those who have learned and received knowledge from others are those of crows compared to an eagle, compared to the naturally superior man, who is an orator and a wise man from God's inspiration. In another place 110 more briefly, but no less clearly he attests [b] : " Everything which is natural is best. But many through the taught virtues of mankind have been eager to win glory." Both statements are consistent. For since the best belongs to the few, and the worse to the many, he has contrasted the inferior to the best by using the word " many," as if the former were the possession of a very few, but the latter applied to the many. And still earlier [c] : " Men became " naturally " brave and wise through God." He means just the same as in the other quotation. For when he spoke of " taught virtues," he added " of mankind," but when he praises nature, he adds that they who are truly brave and wise are so through God. Reasonably. For if in oratory no one 111 is so mad as to believe that those who plagiarize and narrate as their own what has been said and anticipated by another are superior to those naturally

---

[a] *Olymp.* II. 94-96.   [b] *Olymp.* IX. 107-110.
[c] *Olymp.* IX. 30-31.

---

[1] secl. Reiske.
[2] om. libri Pindari, secl. Keil.   [3] δὲ TQ.

(35 D.)

καὶ γονίμων εἰς τοὺς λόγους, ἀλλ' οὗτος κράτιστος
παρ' ὅτῳ πλεῖστον ἔστιν εὑρεῖν τὰ δέοντα, πῶς
36 D. οὐ γελοῖον καὶ πάσης ἀλογίας μεστὸν τὸν ἐξ ἀρχῆς
παρ' ἄλλων ἀκούσαντα καὶ μαθόντα ὅ τι χρὴ λέγειν
112 θεῖναί ποτ' ἔμπροσθεν τοῦ φύσει κρείττονος. οὐκ
ἔξω δ' ἵσταται τῆς ὅλης μαρτυρίας οὐδὲ τόδε '' Ἐν
ἔργμασι[1] δὲ νικᾷ τύχα, οὐ σθένος''· ⟨τὸ μὲν σθένος⟩[2]
πρὸς τῆς τέχνης[3] τῆς ἀνθρωπίνης, τὴν δὲ τύχην πρὸς
τῆς θείας μοίρας εἰ λάβοις.

113   Καίτοι εἰ ποιηταὶ μὲν οὐ τέχνῃ ποιοῦντες, ὥς
φησιν ὁ Πλάτων, ἀλλ' ἐκ θεοῦ τυγχάνοντες[4] παιδεύουσι τοὺς ἐπιγιγνομένους, οὐ μόνον τοὺς καθ' ἑαυτούς, παιδεύοντες δὲ μαρτύρονται καὶ διορίζον-
ται τοῦ μηδενὸς ἀξίαν εἶναι τὴν τέχνην πρὸς τὸ τῆς
φύσεως κράτος καὶ τὰ ἀπὸ τῶν θεῶν· καὶ ἐν ἔργοις
καὶ ἐν λόγοις διὰ τῶν ποιητῶν μαρτυρεῖ Πλάτων,
προσθήσω δὲ ὅτι καὶ δι' ἀμφοτέρων οἱ θεοί, καὶ
Πλάτωνος καὶ τῶν ποιητῶν, ὅτι ῥητορικὴ καλὸν
καὶ θεῖον, εἰ καὶ τέχνῃ μὲν ἀνθρώποις μὴ παρα-
γίγνεται, φύσεως δ' ἐστὶν ἔργον ἀνδρείας καὶ
114 βλεπούσης νικᾶν. εἰ τοίνυν μήτε ποιητῶν μηδένα
μηδὲν εἰρηκέναι τοιοῦτον μήτ' αὐτὸν Πλάτωνα
μαρτυρεῖν ἡμῖν θείη τις μήτε δι' αὐτοῦ[5] μήτε διὰ
τῶν ποιητῶν, ὃ σαφῶς οὑτωσὶ[6] φαίνεται ποιῶν,
εἰς αὐτόν γ' ἄν τις βλέψας τὸν τοῦ πράγματος
λόγον οὐ χαλεπῶς ἴδοι συκοφαντίαν, ἀλλ' οὐκ
ἔλεγχον οὐδὲ πίστιν ἐνοῦσαν τῇ παρ' αὐτοῦ βλα-
37 D. σφημίᾳ. τίς γὰρ οὐκ οἶδεν ὅτι κἂν τοῖς σώμασιν
οὔτε τὸ κάλλος οὔτε τὸ μέγεθος οὔτε ἡ χάρις τέχνης
ἔργον ἢ ποίημά ἐστιν, οὐδ' ἀπὸ χειρῶν ἢ λόγου

---

[1] codd. dett. : ἔρμασι TQVA.   [2] add. Q.
[3] τύχης codd. dett. (prob. Ddf.).

articulate and eloquent but that that man is best
who is most able to conceive of necessary ideas,
is it not silly and absurd to rank before the naturally
superior him who at the start has heard and learned
from others what must be said ? Even the following 112
is not irrelevant to the body of the testimony[a] :
" In deeds, fortune, not strength, prevails," if you
would understand " strength " in the sense of human art, and " fortune " in the sense of the divine
portion.

Yet if the poets do not write through art, as 113
Plato says, but through divine inspiration educate
future generations, not only their own, and, in the
process of education, bear witness and affirm that art
is worthless against the force of nature and divine
inspiration, then in word and deed, through the
poets, Plato bears witness—and I shall add the Gods
themselves bear witness through both Plato and the
poets—that oratory is a fair and divine thing,
even if it does not come to men through art, but is the
work of a bold nature, having an eye to victory.
Then if one should assume that no poet had said any 114
such thing, nor that Plato had given evidence to us,
either through himself or the poets, which he clearly
seems to do, considering only the tenor of the argument, he would easily see that slander but not
refutation or proof resides in his insults. For who
is unaware that in bodies neither beauty, size, nor
grace is the work or product of art, and that these
qualities do not come from manufacture or any

[a] Frg. 38 Schroeder, 167 Turyn.

---

4 post τυγχάνοντες add. κάτοχοι codd. dett. (prob. Ddf.).
5 codd. dett. : αὐτοῦ TQVA.   6 codd. dett. : οὑτοσὶ TQVA.

(37 D.)

τινός, ὡς ἂν εἴποιμεν, ἀπαντᾷ; ἀλλ' ἐπαλεῖψαι μὲν
ταῦτα καὶ θεραπεῦσαι τῆς τέχνης εἶναι δοκεῖ,
συστήσασθαι δ' ἐξ ἀρχῆς οὐδεμία οὕτω τέχνη ἂν
115 εἴη δεινή. οὐκοῦν διακόνου καὶ θεραπαίνης τάξιν
ἔχειν προσήκει τῇ τέχνῃ, τὴν φύσιν δ' ἐν σχήματι
δεσποίνης τετάχθαι, εἰ μὴ καὶ τοὺς σκευοφόρους
πρὸ τῶν ὁπλιτῶν τάττοιμεν ἄν. ἀλλ' οὐκ ἄξιον.
πῶς γὰρ οὐκ ἄτοπον τοὺς μὲν γονέας τιμᾶν καὶ τοῖς
πρεσβυτέροις ὑπανίστασθαι νομίζειν, τὴν δὲ φύσιν
τὴν τοσοῦτον προτέραν φαύλου λόγου νομίσαι παρὰ
τὴν τέχνην, ὥσπερ ἂν εἴ τις τὰ ὑποδήματα κρείττω
τῶν ποδῶν, τὴν δ' ἐσθῆτα τοῦ σώματος κρίνοι
116 τιμιωτέραν; καὶ ὡς ἔοικε τὰ μὲν χρήματα τῶν
ποριζόντων αὐτὰ καὶ κτωμένων ἀτιμότερα ἡγούμεθα, ἡ δὲ τέχνη κρείττων[1] τῆς εὑρούσης φύσεως
117 καὶ ἧς ἔργον ἐστὶ νομισθήσεται. ἄλογον μέντἂν
εἴη κατ' αὐτὸ τὸ παράδειγμα ἐπὶ μὲν τῶν κτημάτων
καὶ τῶν οὐσιῶν βελτίω νομίζειν χρηματιστὴν τὸν
αὐτὸν πορίσαντα καὶ συλλέξαντα τοῦ κληρονομή-
σαντος ἕτερον, ἐν δὲ τοῖς λόγοις καὶ τοῖς πράγμασι
μὴ τὸν φύσει προέχοντα πρεσβεύειν, ἀλλ' ὅστις
38 D. παρ' ἄλλου φαίνεται μετειληφώς, καὶ μηδ' ἐκεῖν'
ὁρᾶν, ὅτι οὐ μόνον ἐξ ἀρχῆς αἱ φύσεις τὰς τέχνας
συνεστήσαντο, ἀλλὰ καὶ περὶ αὐτὰς τὰς τέχνας οἱ τῇ
118 φύσει νικήσαντες διενηνόχασιν. ἕνεκα μὲν γὰρ τῆς
τέχνης πάντας ἔδει παραπλησίους εἶναι τοὺς ταὐτὰ
μαθόντας, οἶμαι δὲ καὶ χείρους τοὺς δευτέρους ἀεὶ
τῶν προτέρων, ἕως εἰς τὸ λυθῆναι τὴν τέχνην
ἀφίκετο· οὐ γὰρ ἂν[2] ἦν πάντα λαβεῖν ἀκριβῶς παρ'
ἑτέρου λαμβάνοντα, ἀλλ' ἔδει διαφυγεῖν ἀεί τι·
ῥώμῃ δέ, οἶμαι, φύσεως καὶ περιουσίᾳ τὴν δόξαν οἱ

---

[1] T a. corr. V: κρεῖττον QA.   [2] om. VA.

exercise of reason, as we should call it. But to prepare and tend these seems to belong to art, but no art would be clever enough to compose these things to begin with. Therefore art ought to have the 115 position of servant or maid ; but nature to be put in the rank of mistress, unless we should place the sutlers before the infantry. But this is unfitting. For how is it not strange to believe in honouring one's parents and in giving way to one's elders, but to consider nature, which is so greatly superior, of no account compared to art, as if someone should judge shoes better than feet and clothing more valuable than the body ? And as it seems, we think that 116 money is of less value than those who make or possess it, but art will be believed to be superior to the nature which conceived it and whose product it is. Yet it would be senseless, to follow the analogy 117 of possessions and property, to believe that the business man, who both made and acquired his wealth, is superior to him who inherited from another, but in oratory and other endeavours not to prefer the natural leader, but whoever clearly has got his share from another, and not to recognize that not only did man's nature form the arts at the start, but also that the naturally superior have excelled in the arts themselves. For as far as art is concerned, 118 all who have learned the same things must be alike. And I think that the following generation must always be inferior to the preceding, until the art reaches the point of disintegration. For one who learns from another could not learn everything exactly, but something must always escape him. But the best men got their reputation, I think, through the strength and greatness of their nature.

(38 D.)

κρατήσαντες εἰλήφασιν· καὶ οὐδεὶς τὸν Δαίδαλον
οὐδὲ τοὺς ἄνω θαυμάζει παρὰ τὸν Φειδίαν, ἀλλὰ
τοὐναντίον ἐκ μικρῶν καὶ φαύλων τὸ κατ᾽ ἀρχὰς εἰς
τὸ μεῖζον καὶ τελεώτερον αἱ τέχναι κατέστησαν.
119 αὐταῖς τοίνυν, ὡς ἔοικε, ταῖς τέχναις οὐ λυσιτελοῦν
φαίνεται τὴν τέχνην πρὸ τῆς φύσεως τετιμῆσθαι.
οὔκουν προελθεῖν[1] γ᾽ ἂν αὐταῖς ἦν, οὐδὲ τυχεῖν τοῦ
νῦν σχήματος οὐδὲ σεμνύνεσθαι. ἀλλ᾽ οἶμαι, οὐχ
αἱ τέχναι τοὺς ἄνδρας ἦραν μεγάλους, ἀλλ᾽ οἱ τῇ
δυνάμει πρωτεύσαντες ἐντίμους τὰς τέχνας ἐποίη-
120 σαν, οὐ μείναντες ἐφ᾽ ὧν παρέλαβον. εἰ δὲ τοῦθ᾽
ἅπασιν εὔδηλον, εἰ καὶ μὴ πρότερον, ἀλλὰ νῦν γε
εἰρημένον, οἱ μέγιστοι τῶν ἐν ταῖς τέχναις οὐχ ᾧ
μετεσχήκασι τῆς τέχνης μέγιστοι γεγόνασιν, ἀλλ᾽
ᾧ τὴν τέχνην παρεληλύθασιν. διὰ ταῦτα καὶ
συμφοιτητῶν οἱ μὲν χείρους, ἀλλὰ καὶ κρείττους, ὁ
Φειδίας, ὁ Ζεῦξις, ὁ Ἱπποκράτης, ὁ Δημοσθένης,
ὅντινα βούλεται θαυμάζειν τις. οὐ γὰρ ὥσπερ ὅροις
τακτοῖς ἐνέμειναν, οὐδ᾽ ἐν μικρῷ τὰ σφέτερ᾽ αὐτῶν
ἤγαγον, οὐδ᾽ ὡμολόγησαν ὑπὸ τῆς τέχνης ἄρχεσθαι,
39 D. ἀλλ᾽ ἐνιδόντες τῇ φύσει ⟨τὸ ἄρχειν οἱ μὲν⟩[2] τῶν
λόγων, οἱ δὲ τῶν πραγμάτων, παῖδας τοὺς πρὸ αὑτῶν ἀπέδειξαν, καὶ μάλ᾽ ἀναγκαίως καὶ κατ᾽ αὐτὴν
τὴν φύσιν. ἐπειδήπερ καὶ λόγων καὶ πραγμάτων
ἁπάντων καὶ θεῶν καὶ ἀνθρώπων ⟨ἡγεμών⟩[3] ἐστιν
φύσις, οὐ τέχνη, καὶ τὰ πράγματα οὕτως ἔχει,
121 ὡς ἡ φύσις αὐτῶν ἔχει, οὐχ ὡς ἡ τέχνη. ἀλλὰ καὶ
ἡ τέχνη τῆς φύσεώς ἐστιν, οὐχ [ὡς][4] ἡ φύσις τῆς
τέχνης ἔργον· νὴ Δί᾽ ἔγωγ᾽ ἂν εἴποιμι καὶ εὕρημα
καὶ κτῆμα τὴν τέχνην εἶναι τῆς φύσεως. ἅ τις εἰ
μὴ παραδέξεται, τοὺς πρώτους εὑρόντας αὐτὰς τὰς
τέχνας τοῦ μηδενὸς ἀξίους εἶναι κρινεῖ. καὶ πρε-

And compared with Phidias no one marvels at Daedalus nor those before ; on the contrary, from small and insignificant beginnings, the arts became greater and more perfect. Then, as is likely, it is 119 clearly unprofitable to the arts themselves that art be preferred to nature. They would have made no progress, nor pridefully have reached their present state. But, I think, the arts have not made men great, but those, who were most talented, made the arts honoured, by not having kept to tradition. If 120 this is clear to all, now that it has been said, even if it was not clear before, the greatest names in the arts did not become greatest because they participated in art, but because they surpassed art. Therefore some of the fellowship are inferior, but also some are superior ; Phidias, Zeuxis, Hippocrates, Demosthenes, whomever one wishes to admire. For they did not, as it were, keep to set bounds, nor humble their professions, nor admit that they were ruled by art, but they recognized in their nature that they ruled, the one group matters of reason, the other practical affairs, and they made those before them appear as children, both necessarily and naturally, since in all matters of reason and practical affairs, nature not art is the leader of Gods and men, and matters proceed according to the state of their nature, not of their art. Art is the product of nature, 121 not nature of art. By Zeus, I should say that art is the discovery and possession of nature. If someone will not accept this, he must judge that those first discoverers of the arts themselves were worthless.

---

¹ προσελθεῖν TVA. ² add. Behr.
³ add. codd. dett. ⁴ secl. Keil.

(39 D.)

σβεύων τὴν τέχνην ἀτιμάσει τοὺς πατέρας τῶν
122 τεχνῶν. διὰ τί; ὅτι οὐ χαλκευτικὴ χαλκευτικὴν
εὗρεν οὐδὲ ἰατρικὴ ἰατρικήν, οὐδὲ ἁπλῶς εἰπεῖν
οὐδεμί᾽ εὗρε τέχνη τέχνην, ἀλλὰ πάσας τὰς τέχνας,
ὅπερ εἶπον, ἡ φύσις εὗρεν. εἰ γὰρ αἱ τέχναι τὰς
τέχνας ἔμελλον εὑρήσειν, οὐκ ἂν ἦν λαβεῖν τὴν
ἀρχήν. οὐ γάρ πω τεχνῶν οὐσῶν οὐκ ἂν ἦν τέχνην
123 εὑρεῖν· τῇ γὰρ μὴ οὔσῃ πῶς ἐνῆν εὑρεῖν; εἰ δ᾽ αὖ τὸ
φύσει γιγνόμενον φαυλότερον τῆς τέχνης, πάντες ἂν
οἱ πρῶτοι τὰς τέχνας εὑρόντες ἦσαν φαυλότατοι·
πάντες γὰρ φύσει τὰς τέχνας εὗρον τὸ¹ ἐξ ἀρχῆς.
οὐκοῦν καὶ κατὰ τοὺς εὑρόντας ἐξ ἀρχῆς καὶ κατὰ
124 τοὺς ὑπερέχοντας ἡ φύσις νικᾷ. καὶ μὴν εἴ τις
ἐξετάζοι τί ποτ᾽ ἐστὶν ᾧ στρατηγὸς στρατιώτου
διαφέρει, καὶ ὅλως ἄρχων ἰδιώτου, τοῦτ᾽ ἂν εὕροι
προφαινόμενον, ὅτι ἄρχοντος μέν ἐστι προστάξ’υι,
40 D. ἀρχομένου δ᾽ ἀκούσαντα ποιῆσαι. οὐκοῦν προστάττει μὲν ὁ εὑρών, ὁ δ᾽ ἀκούσας μανθάνει. εἰ γάρ
τις μὴ εὕροι ὅ τι χρὴ ποιεῖν, πῶς ἂν ἄλλῳ προστάξειεν ἃ χρὴ ποιεῖν; εἰ γὰρ αὐτὸς ἀκούσας
ἄλλου προστάξειεν ἃ χρὴ ποιεῖν, πείσεται πρότερον
ἢ προστάξει. τοῦτο δ᾽, ἕως ἂν ἄρχων ᾖ, τῶν ἀδυνάτων. προστάττειν μὲν γὰρ ἦν τοῦ γε ἄρχοντος,
οὐ πείθεσθαι, οὐδέν γε μᾶλλον ἢ καὶ διδασκάλου
125 πείθεσθαι τοῖς μαθηταῖς ἐστιν. φαίνεται τοίνυν καὶ
κατὰ τοῦτον τὸν λόγον ἡ μὲν φύσις ἄρχοντος χώραν ἔχουσα, ἡ δ᾽ ἐκ τοῦ μαθεῖν τέχνη διακόνου καὶ
126 πειθομένου τῷ κρείττονι. καὶ μὴν κἀκεῖνό γε ἐν
τοῖς ἄνω λόγοις ἦν, ὡς θεοὶ μὲν εὗρον καὶ κατέδει-
ξαν ἕκαστα, ἄνθρωποι δὲ λαβόντες παρὰ θεῶν

¹ codd. dett. : εὕροντο TQVA.

And preferring art, he must dishonour the fathers of the arts. Why? Because metal-working did not 122 discover metal-working, nor medicine medicine, nor in a word, did any art discover an art, but, as I said, nature discovered all the arts. For if the arts were going to discover the arts, it would be impossible to make a beginning. When the arts did not exist, it would be impossible to discover art. How could the possibility of discovery be innate in art when art did not exist? Again if what naturally comes into being 123 is inferior to art, all of those who first discovered the arts would be most inferior. For at the start, all men discovered art through nature. So both in respect to the initial discoverers and the pre-eminent practitioners, nature is superior. Indeed, if one 124 should examine in what way a general differs from a soldier, and any kind of a ruler from a private citizen, he would quite clearly find that it is the part of a ruler to command, and of the ruled to do what he has heard. Then the discoverer commands, but the hearer learns. For if one should not discover what must be done, how would he command another what must be done? If he, who had heard it from another, should command what must be done, he will obey before he commands. But while he is a ruler, this is impossible. For to command was the part of the ruler, not to obey, no more than it is the part of a teacher to obey his pupils. Therefore on 125 this reasoning nature clearly has the position of the ruler, and art from its learning that of the servant and of him who is obedient to a superior. Indeed, it was said above that the Gods discovered 126 and revealed each thing, and that we men took these from the Gods for our use, employing different

(40 D.)

127 χρώμεθα, ἄλλοις ἄλλων ἑρμηνεῦσι χρησάμενοι. τίς
ἂν οὖν λόγος μᾶλλον σώσειε τὸ γιγνόμενον ἢ τῷ
πιστεῦσαι δικαιότερον ἢ ᾧ θεοὺς μὲν εὑρεῖν ἕκαστα
τίθεμεν καὶ νῦν ἔτι σημαίνειν; πάλιν δ' ἀρχῆς ἴδιον
φαμὲν εἶναι τὸ εὑρεῖν καὶ προστάξαι, τὸ δ' ἀκοῦσαι
καὶ μαθεῖν τοῦ χείρονος, οὔτε γὰρ δήπου θεῶν
ἅπανθ' εὑρόντων αἰσχρὸν ἄρχοντος θεῖναι τὸ εὑρεῖν,
εἴπερ ἄρχουσιν οἱ θεοὶ πάντων, οὔτ' ἀρχῇ τοῦ προστάξαι προσήκοντος αἰσχρὸν εἰς θεοὺς ἀνενεγκεῖν
τὴν εὕρεσιν, εἴπερ εὑρόντος μέν ἐστι σημῆναι, εὑρί-
σκει δὲ ὁ κρείττων ἀεί.

128 Εἶεν. δεσπότης δ' οἰκέτου τῷ διαφέρει πρὸς θεῶν;
οὐ δεσπότου μὲν προστάξαι, δούλου δ' ὑπακοῦσαι
πᾶς τις ἂν φήσειεν εἶναι; οὐκοῦν ὁ μὲν οἶδεν ἐφ'
129 ἑαυτοῦ τί χρὴ ποιεῖν, ὁ δὲ ἀκούσας μανθάνει. τί
δὲ ὁ τῶν παρθένων ἐπαινέτης τε καὶ σύμβουλος
λέγει ὁ Λακεδαιμόνιος ποιητής;

41 D. Πολλαλέγων[1] ὄνυμ' ἀνδρί, γυναικὶ δὲ Πασιχάρηα.

πολλά, φησίν, ὁ ἀνὴρ λεγέτω, γυνὴ δὲ οἷς ἂν
ἀκούσῃ χαιρέτω. ἆρ' οὖν οὐκ εὔδηλον ὡς ὁ μὲν
αὐτὸς εὑρηκὼς καὶ προειδὼς ἐρεῖ πολλά, ᾗ δ'
ἄρχεσθαι προσήκει, στέρξει τοῖς λεγομένοις; οὐ
γὰρ δήπου τῆς γε γυναικὸς ἀκοῦσαι περιμένων,
εἶτ' ἐρεῖ πρὸς τὴν γυναῖκα αὐτὸς τί δεῖ ποιεῖν· οὐδ'
ὡς ἐκέλευσεν Ἡσίοδος, ἵνα ἤθεα κεδνὰ διδάξῃ, τοῖς
ἐκείνης λόγοις ἀκολουθῶν. ἀλλ' εἴπερ διδάξει,
προστάξει· εἰ δὲ προστάξει,[2] τῆς ἑαυτοῦ φύσεως

---

[1] Hermann : πολλὰ λέγων TQVA.
[2] προστάξει—προστάξει om. VA.

354

men as interpreters for each matter. What argument 127 then would better preserve the proprieties, or to what is it more right to trust, than that in which we assume that the Gods discovered each thing and still now reveal these, and in which we also claim that discovery and command are peculiar to rule, and listening and learning to the inferior? For neither is it shameful to assume that discovery is the part of a ruler, since the Gods have discovered all things, if the Gods rule all, nor is it shameful to refer the act of discovery to the Gods, since the giving of commands is the duty of ruling, if revelation is the part of the discoverer, and the superior is always the discoverer.

Well! In what way, by the Gods, does master 128 differ from servant? Would not everyone say that it is the part of a master to command, but of a servant to obey? Then the one knows of himself what must be done, but the other hears and learns. What does the Lacedaemonian poet say, the adviser 129 and counsellor of the maidens? [a] " The man's name is Much-Talk, the Wife's Pleased-With-All." Let the man, he says, talk much, but let the wife be pleased with whatever she hears. Then is it not clear that he will say many things, in discovery and foresight, but she, whose role is to be ruled, will be content with what is said? For not waiting to listen to his wife, he will tell his wife what must be done; nor does he attend to her words, so that, as Hesiod commanded,[b] " he may teach her good ways." But if he will teach her, he will command her. If he will command her, he will make his wife conform as

---

[a] Alcman, frg. 27 Bergk, 107 Page.
[b] *Works and Days* 699.

(41 D.)

ἐγγύτατα ἄξει τὴν γυναῖκα, ὡς ἀμείνων χείρονα.
130 ὅσῳ τοίνυν θεὸς μὲν ἀνθρώπου, ἄρχων δ᾽ ἰδιώτου,
δεσπότης δ᾽ οἰκέτου, γυναικὸς δ᾽ ἀνὴρ κρείττων καὶ
τελεώτερος, τοσούτῳ κρεῖττον καὶ ἱκανώτερον φύσις
ἢ τέχνη, ἢ κομιδῇ πάντα ἄνω καὶ κάτω γένοιτ᾽ ἄν.
131 Ἔτι τοίνυν κἂν ἀπὸ τῶν ἐναντίων τις αὐτὸ[1]
λόγων ἴδοι. εἰ μὲν γὰρ ἅπαντας τοὺς ἐπὶ τῶν
τεχνῶν ὡμολογεῖτο εἶναι σπουδαίους, ἢ πᾶσαν πάντως τέχνην ἀγαθόν, τάχ᾽ ἄν τις ὥσπερ ἔλεγχον εἶναι
ταῦτα ᾠήθη. νῦν δὲ τίς οὐκ οἶδεν πολλοῖς ὄνειδος
τὴν τέχνην οὖσαν; οἷον τοὺς σκυτοδέψας καὶ
σκυτοτόμους καὶ γναφεῖς καὶ νευρορράφους τίς ἂν
132 εὐδαιμονίσειεν τῆς τέχνης; καὶ μὴν οὐκ ἐμὸς ὅ[2]
μῦθος, ἔφη ὁ Πλάτων, τὸ τοῦ Εὐριπίδου προσπαί-
ζων, ἀλλ᾽ ὑμέτερος, ὦ Πλάτων, καὶ τοῦ σοῦ νὴ Δία
42 D. ἐργαστηρίου, καὶ τὰς τέχνας ταύτας βαναύσους καὶ
133 τοὺς ἐπ᾽ αὐτῶν ἀνδραποδώδεις εἶναι. οὐκοῦν ἄτοπον καὶ περιφανὴς συκοφαντία[3] τοῖς μὲν ἃς εἶπον
τέχνας εἰδόσιν καὶ τοῖς ἄλλας μυρίας μηδενὸς ἀξιοῦν μετεῖναι χρηστοῦ παρὰ τὴν τέχνην, εἰ δέ τις
μὴ τέχνῃ τι μετέρχεται, διὰ τοῦτ᾽ αὐτὸν[4] ψέγειν ὡς
ἑνὸς τῶν βεβαίως καλῶν στερόμενον, καὶ τοὺς
αὐτοὺς ὑμᾶς ἅμα μὲν μηδένα ποιεῖσθαι τῆς τέχνης
λόγον, ἀλλὰ καὶ προφέρειν αὐτὸ τοῖς πολλοῖς, ἅμα
δὲ ὡς καθαρῶς ἀγαθὸν τὸ αὐτὸ τοῦτο σεμνύνειν, ὅ τι
134 ἂν μὴ τέχνῃ γίγνηται κακίζοντας. καὶ μὴν ἑλοῦ γε

[1] αὐτῷ T a. corr. VA.
[2] om. VA.
[3] συκοφαντία περιφανὴς VA.
[4] codd. dett. : αὐτὸ TQ, αὐτὰ A, αὖ V.

356

closely as possible to his own nature, as a better person would treat an inferior one. Then by as much as God is superior and more perfect than man, and the ruler than the private citizen, and the master than the slave and the husband than the wife, so much more superior and sufficient is nature than art, or everything would be topsy-turvy. 130

Moreover, one might realize this from the opposite argument. For if it were agreed that everyone engaged in the arts practised a serious profession, or that every art was honourable, possibly someone would think that this fact alone as it were refuted my position. But as it is, who is unaware that what is an art brings opprobrium to many ? For example, tanners, cobblers, fullers, leather-repair men, who would felicitate them for their art ? Indeed, it is not my tale, as Plato said playing on Euripides,[a] but yours, O Plato,[b] and your school's by Zeus, that these arts are menial and those engaged in them servile. Then it is strange and a manifest act of slander to assert that those who know the arts which I have ennumerated and many others besides have no share in anything worthwhile because of their art ; but if someone does not pursue something with art, on that account to criticize him as if he were wanting in one of the absolutely fine qualities of life ; for you and your school at the same time to have no regard for art, but to cast this practice in the teeth of the common people, and again by belittling whatever does not take place through art, to glorify this same practice as completely honourable. Indeed, choose 131 132 133 134

---

[a] Plato, *Symposium* 177 A ; Euripides, *Melanippe the Wise* frg. 484 N² ; *cf. Hippolytus* 352.
[b] *Gorgias* 512 C.

(42 D.)

δυοῖν θάτερον, εἴποι δικαίως ἂν ἡ ῥητορική, ἢ καὶ
τοὺς χειροτέχνας ὡς καλοὺς κἀγαθοὺς τιμᾶν, ἢ τούς
γε ῥήτορας μὴ ψέγειν, εἰ μὴ τέχνην κέκτηνται περὶ
ὧν λέγουσιν.

135 Ἆρ᾽ ἔχει τινὰ καὶ ἡ ῥητορικὴ τὸν ἐροῦνθ᾽ ὑπὲρ
αὐτῆς παρασχέσθαι, ἢ ταῦτα ἴσα ἀντ᾽ ἴσων; οὐκ

136 ἂν, οἶμαι, φήσειεν ὁ Ὁμηρικὸς Ἰδομενεύς. ἃ μὲν
οὖν, εἰ καὶ μὴ τέχνην εἶναι δοίημεν αὐτήν, ἔχοι τις
ἂν λέγειν ὑπὲρ αὐτῆς πολλὰ ἀφελόντι τῶν ἐπιόντων
τοσαῦτα καὶ τοιαῦτά ἐστιν. ἴσως δέ τις οἰήσεται
τούτων οὕτως ἀποδεδειγμένων τὸ φαυλότερον σπεύ-
δειν ἡμᾶς λοιπόν, ἐὰν ὅτι καὶ τέχνη διδάσκειν

137 πειρώμεθα. ἐγὼ δὲ οὔτε τῶν εἰρημένων οὐδὲν μετα-
τίθεμαι οὔτε Πλάτωνι συγχωρῶ τὸ μηδὲν μετεῖναι
ῥητορικῇ τέχνης, ἀλλ᾽ ὅσον αὐτοῦ τέχνη,[1] χρήσομαι
γὰρ τοῖς Πλάτωνος αὐτοῦ ῥήμασι, τοῦτ᾽ ἐπέξειμι.
ὅπερ δὲ ἐν τοῖς ἄνω, τοῦτο κἀνταῦθα ποιήσω,

138 αὐτοῖς οἷς εἴρηκε Πλάτων ἀκολουθῶν ἐπιδείξω
43 D. μετέχουσαν τέχνης. καίτοι τί ἂν ἄλλο τις βούλοιτο·
φησὶ γὰρ δήπου διαβάλλων αὐτὴν ὅτι στοχάζεται
καὶ προσάγει[2] τοὺς λόγους οὕτως ὅπως ἂν στοχά-

139 ζηται. καίτοι πῶς οὐχ ὑπεναντίον φάσκειν μὲν στοχάζεσθαι, λέγειν δ᾽ ὡς οὐ χρῆται λόγῳ δι᾽ αὐτὸ
τοῦτο; πάντες γὰρ οἱ στοχαζόμενοι δήπου τῷ λόγῳ
προσάγοντες αὑτοὺς οὕτως στοχάζονται. οὐ γάρ
ἐστιν μὴ λόγῳ χρώμενον στοχάζεσθαι, ἀλλ᾽ ὁ τοῦ
πράγματος λόγος οὗτός ἐστιν ὁ ποιῶν στοχάζεσθαι.
οἷον οἱ τῶν πόρρωθεν ὁρωμένων στοχαζόμενοι καὶ
τυγχάνοντες ἀναφέροντες οἶμαι πρὸς τὴν φύσιν οὕτως στοχάζονται, καὶ τούτῳ χρώμενοι τῷ λόγῳ,

---

[1] Behr ex Plat. : αὐτῇ τέχνης TQVA.
[2] προάγει codd. dett. (prob. Ddf.).

one or the other, oratory might justly say, either to honour craftsmen as gentlemen, or not to criticize orators if they do not possess artistic competence in the subject of their discourse.

Then can oratory provide anyone who will speak 135 in its defence, or is this tit for tat ? Homer's Idomeneus,[a] I think, would not say so. Although 136 omitting much which occurred to him, these are some of the many things which one could say in oratory's defence, if we should grant that it is not an art. Perhaps someone will think, now that this has been demonstrated, that it is left for us to support the worse side of the case, if we try to teach that it is an art. I neither retract anything which has been said 137 nor do I concede to Plato that oratory has no share of art, but I shall now discuss " the extent of its art "—for I shall use Plato's own expression.[b] I shall also do here what I did above [c] ; using Plato's own statements I shall demonstrate that it shares in art. Yet what more would one wish ? In his slander 138 he says that it aims at things [d] and guides its words, according to its aim. Yet how is it not a contra- 139 diction to claim that it aims at things, but to say that on that account it does not use reason ? For all who take aim at things, aim surely by guiding themselves by means of reason. It is impossible to take aim at a thing without using reason, but it is the reason involved in the object aimed at which causes taking aim at it. For example, those who aim at things seen from afar and hit the mark, take aim, I think, by referring to nature, and by employing this kind

---

[a] *Iliad* XIII. 447.　　[b] *Phaedrus* 269 D.　　[c] § 51.
[d] The following argument is based on the double meaning of στοχάζεσθαι, " to take aim " and " to use conjecture."

(43 D.)

καὶ ὡσπερεὶ σκοπῷ τούτῳ στοχάζονται. ὡς οἵ γ᾽
ἀποτυγχάνοντες ἀρχὴν οὐδὲ στοχάζονται, ἀλλ᾽ αὐτὸ
τοὐναντίον τῷ στοχάζεσθαι ποιοῦσιν. τὸ γὰρ στοχ-
140 άζεσθαι τοῦτ᾽ ἐστὶ τυχεῖν τοῦ πράγματος. οὐκοῦν
οὐχ ᾧ στοχάζεται ἁμαρτάνει τις, ἀλλ᾽ ᾧ διήμαρτεν
οὐκ ἐστοχάσατο. εἰκότως· οὐδεὶς γὰρ ἁμαρτάνει
λόγῳ χρώμενος, ἀλλ᾽ ἅμα ἐσφάλη καὶ τὸν λόγον
οὐ διεσώσατο. ὁ γὰρ λόγος ταύτην εἶχε τὴν
δύναμιν, μὴ διαμαρτάνειν, καὶ τοῦθ᾽ οὕτως ἀληθές
ἐστιν ὥστε οἱ φρονιμώτατοι τῶν ἀνθρώπων καὶ
λόγου πλείστου μετέχοντες ἄριστα στοχάζονται.
ὥστε εἰ τὸ στοχάζεσθαι τῆς ῥητορικῆς ἐστιν, ἐπὶ
πλεῖστον ἡ ῥητορικὴ σῴζει λόγον.

141 Τοῦτο μὲν οὖν ἐξ αὐτῶν ὧν εἴρηκε συγκρουόμενον
44 D. οὕτω φαίνεται. θαυμάζω δὲ ὅπως οὔτ᾽ ἔγνω οὔτ᾽
ἐστοχάσατο ὅτι καὶ χωρὶς τοῦ τἀναντία συνθεῖναι
καὶ χρήσασθαι σημείῳ τοῦ μὴ τέχνην εἶναι, ὃ τοῦ
τέχνην μᾶλλον[1] εἶναι σημεῖόν ἐστιν, δι᾽ ἑνὸς καὶ[2]
μόνου τούτου δώσει λαβήν, εἰ δοίη τῆς ῥητορικῆς
142 εἶναι ⟨τὸ⟩[3] στοχάζεσθαι. φέρε γὰρ πρὸς θεῶν εἴ
τις αὐτὸν ἤρετο ὡδὶ λέγων κατ᾽ αὐτὸν ἐκεῖνον,
Τοξικὴν δέ τινα, ὦ Πλάτων, οἶσθα τέχνην, ὅσον
εἰπεῖν, ἢ καλεῖς; τὴν μὲν γὰρ πολιτικὴν ἐπιστήμην πᾶσαν διελήλυθας καὶ τὰ μόρια αὐτῆς εὕρηκας
ἀκριβῶς. Ἔγωγε, εἶπεν ἄν, οἶδα καὶ καλῶ. Τίς
οὖν ἐστιν αὕτη καὶ τί ἐπαγγέλλεται; Τοῦ σκοποῦ
τυχεῖν ἐν τῇ τῶν βελῶν ἀφέσει. Καλῶς. οὐκοῦν
ὁπόταν στοχάσηται, τότε τυγχάνει. Πῶς γὰρ οὔ;
Πότερον οὖν οὐκ ἔστι τέχνη διὰ τὸ στοχάζεσθαι, ἢ
τούτου καὶ ἔστι τέχνη τοῦ στοχάζεσθαι; Ἐγὼ μὲν
οἶμαι τούτου.

---

[1] μὲν VA.   [2] Reiske: καὶ δι᾽ ἑνὸς TQVA

of reason and, as it were, target, so take aim. So
those who miss the mark, do not at all take aim, but
they do the opposite of taking aim. For to take aim
is to have hit the mark. Then one does not err in 140
the fact that he takes aim ; but in the fact that he has
erred, he has not taken aim. With good reason.
No one errs when he uses reason, but in the act of
failing, he has not at the same time maintained
reason. Reason is the faculty of not erring ; and
this is such a simple truth that those men, who are
wisest and have the largest share of reason, aim the
best. Thus if taking aim is an attribute of oratory,
oratory preserves reason to the fullest extent.

So his argument is obviously shattered from his 141
own statements. But I wonder how he neither knew
nor took aim that apart from combining contradictory arguments and using as a sign of not being an art
what is rather a sign of being an art, he will offer
his opponent a hold through this one point alone, if
he should grant that taking aim is part of oratory.
Come, by the Gods, suppose someone interrogated 142
him, speaking in his fashion : Do you know, Plato, or
call by its name a certain art of archery, as far as the
term is concerned ? For you have recounted the
whole science of politics, and with precision have
discovered its parts. I know and so call it, he would
say. What is this and what does it claim ? To hit the
mark, in the dispatch of missiles. Good ! Then
when it takes aim, it hits the mark. Of course.
Then does this fail to be an art through taking aim,
or is it even the art of taking aim ? I believe the
latter.

---

[3] add. codd. dett.

(44 D.)

143 Εἶεν. τί δ' ἡ κυβερνητική; ἐμοὶ μὲν γὰρ δοκεῖ
τοῦτο ὅπερ ἡ τοξικὴ καὶ αὐτὴ πράττειν, κατὰ γοῦν
τὸν λόγον ᾧ χρῆται. στοχάζεται γάρ, οὐ μὴν
ὡς βέλει τυχεῖν, οἶμαι, ἀλλ' ὡς ἐκ τῆς θαλάττης
σῶσαι. ὅσα μὲν γὰρ δεῖ μαθεῖν ἐν παιδείᾳ τὸν
κυβερνήτην οἶδεν καὶ ἀκήκοεν. σῴζει δὲ οὐ τούτοις

45 D. τὸ σύμπαν εἰπεῖν τὴν ναῦν, ἀλλ' οἷς εὖ τίθεται τὸ
144 παρόν. τοῦτο δὲ ἀμήχανον αὐτῷ χωρὶς τοῦ στοχάζεσθαι. σκόπει γὰρ πρῶτον μέν, εἰ βούλει, τοὺς εἰς
Αἴγιναν διακομίζοντας, ὅτι[1] ὁρῶσι τὴν Αἴγιναν·
πρὸς ὃ οὖν ὁρῶσι στοχάζονται· ἔπειτα τοὺς εἰς τὸν
Πόντον, εἰ δὲ βούλει, τοὺς εἰς Αἴγυπτον καὶ τὴν
οὐδὲ σοί ποτε ἀήθη Σικελίαν· τούτους γὰρ καὶ
παντάπασιν εὑρήσεις στοχαζομένους. πρῶτον μὲν
γὰρ αὐτοῦ δεῖ τοῦ ποῦ ποθ'[2] ὁ σκοπὸς στοχάσασθαι,
καὶ ὃ τότ' ἦν παρὰ τῶν ὀφθαλμῶν, τοῦτ' εἰκάσαι
τῷ λογισμῷ· ἔπειτα φανέντος αὖθις στοχάζεσθαι

145 πρὸς τὸ ὁρώμενον. φέρε γὰρ τὸν Ὀδυσσέα παρὰ
τῆς Καλυψοῦς ἀκηκοότα [πλεῖν][3] ὅτι χρὴ τηρεῖν
τὴν ἄρκτον ἐπ' ἀριστερὰ χειρὸς ἔχοντα. οὔκουν[4] τὰ
καθ' ἔκαστα καὶ δι' ὧν εἰσιν ἡ ναῦς αὐτὸν ἤδη δεῖ
συλλογίζεσθαι· πολλὰ γὰρ ἂν πελάγη περάσαις καὶ
πολλοὺς ἂν εἰς τόπους καὶ λιμένας κατάραις ἐπ'
ἀριστερὰ τὴν ἄρκτον ποιησάμενος, ὡς δ' αὖ καὶ

46 D. ἐπὶ δεξί',[5] ὥστε[6] Φάρου τυχεῖν ⟨οὐκ ἔχοις ἂν χωρὶς
τοῦ στοχάζεσθαι πλέων οὔτε διὰ τοῦ πελάγους⟩

[1] om. VA.   [2] πῶς VA.   [3] secl. Keil.

362

Well ! What is the art of navigation ? For I think 143
that this functions in the same way as archery, at
least in the reason which it employs. For it takes
aim not indeed so as to hit the mark with a missile,
I suppose, but so as to save men from the sea.
As much as the helmsman must learn in his training,
he knows and has studied. But in sum, he does not
save his ship through these means, but according
to how well he disposes of present circumstances.
But this is impossible for him without taking aim. 144
Consider first of all, if you wish, those who carry
passengers to Aegina ; they have Aegina in sight.
Then they take aim at what they see. Next consider those who carry passengers to the Pontus, and,
if you wish, to Egypt, and to Sicily, with which you
were once not unacquainted.[a] You will find these
taking aim in every possible way. First it is necessary
to take aim as to where the target is, and to conjecture through the exercise of reason that which in
the former example was plainly visible. Next when
this has come into view, to take aim at what is
seen. Consider Odysseus with these instructions 145
from Calypso : that he must observe the north star,
"keeping it on his left."[b] Must he not now calculate the particulars and through what regions his
ship will go ? For you would cross many seas and
put into many places and harbours by keeping the
north on your left, and so also on your right. Therefore without conjecture you could not reach Pharus,
either sailing through the sea or even through an

---

[a] See §§ 280 ff.   [b] *Odyssey* V. 277.

---

⁴ Canter : οὐκοῦν TQV, οὐκοῦν—ἕκαστα om. A.
⁵ δεστι sine acc. V, δ////// A.   ⁶ om. VA.

(46 D.)

οὐδὲ διὰ Λιβυκοῦ πορθμοῦ[1]· ἀλλ' ἀνάγκη τὰ ἐπὶ
146 μέρους στοχάζεσθαι. φέρε γάρ, τί μαθόντες νῦν
μὲν εἴσω τοὺς οἴακας ἄγουσι, πάλιν δὲ εἰς τὸ ἔξω
τῆς αὐτῆς ἡμέρας; οὐχὶ τοῦ ὁρωμένου στοχαζόμενοι, ἢ τοῦ μέλλοντος ὀφθήσεσθαι; τοῦ δὲ χάριν
παρὰ τῶν ἐντυχόντων ποῦ θαλάττης εἰσὶν ἢ πρὸς
τίνι γῇ πολλάκις πυνθάνονται; οὐχ οἵ γε ἀκριβεῖς,
147 ἐρεῖς. τίς δ' ἀνθρώπων ἀκριβὴς ἢ διαρκής; οὐκοῦν
οὐδὲ τεχνίτης οὐδεὶς τῷ λόγῳ τούτῳ. εἰ δὲ τοῦθ'
οὕτως ἔχει, τί δεινόν, εἰ μηδὲ ῥήτωρ τεχνίτης
148 διαρκὴς μηδείς; καὶ μὴν εἰ μὲν τὸ κυβερνᾶν τέχνη,
κἂν ἐπὶ τοῦ κεκλημένου κυβερνήτου μὴ σῴζηται, τί
κωλύει καὶ ῥητορικὴν τέχνην εἶναι, κἂν παρὰ τοῖς
ῥήτορσιν εἶναι φάσκουσι μὴ σῴζηται; εἰ δὲ δὴ καὶ
περὶ τούτων διαλέγῃ τῶν κυβερνητῶν ὧν τις
πυνθάνεται παρ' ἑτέρου τι καὶ ζητεῖ, οὐ γὰρ περί
γε τοῦ Ποσειδῶνος, οὐδὲ τῶν Νηρηίδων,[2] οὐδὲ τῶν
Διοσκούρων, ὅμως δ' αὐτοῖς ἀποδίδως εἶναι κυβερνήταις, ὡς ἄνθρωπος ἀνθρώποις, καὶ τέχνην ἔχειν
τὴν κυβερνητικήν, τούτοις ἅπασίν ἐστι τὸ στοχάζεσθαι, οἵ γε καὶ πρὶν ἀπαίρειν εὐθὺς κάθηνται
στοχαζόμενοι περὶ τῶν πνευμάτων· οὐ γὰρ παρὰ
τοῦ γε Διὸς ἤκουσαν ἐπὶ τῆς Ἴδης ἢ τοῦ Γαργά-
ρου, ἀλλ' οἶμαι ἐξ ἀρχῆς εἰς τέλος στοχάζονται
47 D. ἀνέμων λιμένων εἰ φθήσονται πάντων ὡς ἔπος εἰπεῖν.

---

[1] add. et corr. Behr : οὐδὲ πορθμοῦ διὰ βιβλίου TQVA.
[2] codd. dett. : ἡρωίδων TQVA.

African strait.*a* Aim must be taken at specific
details. Well, for what possible reason during 146
the same day do they now turn the rudders inwards,
and again outwards ? Are they not taking aim at
what is seen or going to be seen ? Why do they often
inquire from those they meet about their position
on the sea or near what land they are ? At any rate
the accurate do not do this, you will say. But what
man is sufficiently accurate ? Well then, on this 147
argument no one is an artist. If this is the situation,
why is it terrible if no orator is a satisfactory artist ?
Indeed, if to be a helmsman is an art, even if it is not 148
preserved in him who is called a helmsman, what
prevents oratory from being an art, even if it is not
preserved among those who claim to be orators ?
But if you are discussing any of these helmsmen
who inquire of and seek information from others—
and not, of course, about Poseidon, the Nereids, or the
Dioscuri *b*—, and if you still grant them to be helmsmen, as one mortal to another, and to possess the
art of navigation, all of these are involved in taking
aim, since even just before they put out, they sit
down and conjecture about the winds. For they have
heard nothing from Zeus on Ida or Gargarus,*c* but from
beginning to end, I think, they aim in their conjecturing about the breezes, harbours, if they will get
there first, about everything, one might say. There-

---

a The allusion is not to *Odyssey* IV. 355, but to *Gorgias*
511 D. For the straits on the African side of Pharus, *cf.*
Bellum Alexandrinum 14 : " vada transitu angusto quae
pertinent ad regionem Africae."
b All deities connected with the sea and sailors.
c [Gargarus is the highest peak of Mt. Ida in N.W. Asia
Minor. But Aristides may be thinking also of Mt. Ida in
Crete where in legend Zeus was born.—*E.H.W.*]

(47 D.)

ὥστε σοι τὸ τοῦ μορίου εἴδωλον σκιᾶς ὄναρ εἰς
ἔλεγχον κατὰ Πίνδαρον γίγνεται.

149 Πρὸς Διός, ἡ δὲ τῇ δικαιοσύνῃ ἀντίστροφος ἰατρική σοι καὶ δεύτερον ἀγαθὸν τῷ σώματι, εἰ δὲ
βούλει, καὶ ἡ γυμναστική, πότερον οὐ στοχάζονται
τῆς φύσεως τῶν σωμάτων; νὴ Δία, ἐάν τε εἴπῃς
γε, ἐάν τε μή. ἢ πρόοιδεν ὁ γυμναστὴς εὐθὺς καὶ
ἐξ ἀρχῆς ὅπως ἡμῶν ἕκαστος ἔχει σώματος, οὐ
150 παρὰ τῆς πείρας μανθάνει; τί δ' ἐπειδὰν πρὸς
τοῦτο γυμνάζῃ, πρὸς ὃ πειρᾶται, πότερ' ὥσπερ ὁ
Ἀπόλλων ὁ ἐν Δελφοῖς, οὕτως ἐξεπίσταται τὸ
μέλλον, καὶ διισχυρίζεται τὸν ἄνδρα τόνδε ἐκ τῶνδε
πανταχῇ καὶ πάντως ἀπαθῆ καταστήσειν ἢ καθάπαξ
151 ἢ ποσόν τι χρόνου; οὐκοῦν ἢ[1] μὴ στοχαζόμενον
μαινόμενον τὸν γυμναστὴν λέγεις, ἢ σωφρονῶν αὐτὸς
ὁμολογήσει στοχάζεσθαι τοῦ βελτίστου, τοιοῦτον δ'
152 οὐδὲν ἔχειν προειπεῖν[2] οὐδὲ ἐπαγγείλασθαι. εἶεν.
ὁ δὲ δὴ τῆς μὲν πείρας εἰς πίστιν ἰσχύσας καὶ τοῖς
48 D. φαρμάκοις καὶ ταῖς διαίταις ἤδη χρώμενος τούτοις[3] ἰατρός, ὅπως δ' ἕκαστος ἡμῶν ἔχει φύσεως
ἢ συγκρίσεως ἀγνοῶν, ἆρ' οὐ στοχαζόμενος προσάγει πάνθ' ὅσα ἂν ποιῇ περὶ τὸν κάμνοντα ἀναφέρων
153 εἰς τὸ εἰκός; ἐγὼ μὲν οἶμαι. ἢ δύναιτ'[4] ἄν τις
αὐτῶν ἀποτόμως εἰπεῖν ὅτι τούτοις οὑτοσὶ χρώμενος ἔξω παντὸς ἔσται κινδύνου καὶ δυσχερὲς οὐδ'
ὁτιοῦν πείσεται; οὐ μέντἂν τοσοῦτον ἐλείποντο τοῦ
τὴν Ἐπίδαυρον ἔχοντος θεοῦ, φαίης ἄν, καὶ μάλα
ἐμοὶ γοῦν κατὰ νοῦν. ἀλλ' ἀπὸ τῶν πολλῶν καὶ κοινῶν, οἶμαι, καὶ τὰ ἴδια εἰκάζουσιν. εἰ δ' ἄρα καὶ
ἰδίᾳ τισὶ παρηκολούθησαν, πρὸς αὐτὴν τὴν πεῖραν

---

[1] Reiske: εἰ TQVA.   [2] codd. dett.: προσειπεῖν TQVA.
[3] secl. Keil.   codd. dett.: δύναται TQVA.

fore your shadow of a part becomes, as a proof, in Pindar's words,[a] " a phantom dream."

By Zeus, take medicine, according to you, the 149 opposite of justice and second ranking good for the body, and if you wish, gymnastics. Do they not conjecture at the nature of the body ? Yes by Zeus, whether you say so or not. Or has the trainer foreseen right at the start the state of each of our bodies ? Does he not learn by trial ? Well ! when- 150 ever he is training someone for the purpose which he is attempting, then like Apollo in Delphi, does he know the future and assert that he will make this man wholly and in every way free from these symptoms, either once and for all or for some length of time ? Then either you think the trainer a madman, 151 if he does not conjecture, or he himself will agree, if he is in his right senses, that he conjectures at what is best, but that he can predict and promise no such thing. Well then ! this doctor who has achieved a 152 credible experience and now employs these various drugs and regimens, but is ignorant of one's physical state or constitution, does he not apply all of his treatment for the sick person, by conjecturing and referring to probability ? I think so. Or could 153 any one of them say off-hand that by using these things this sick man will be free from all danger and have no trouble at all ? Then they would not be so inferior to the God who holds Epidaurus,[b] you would say, and indeed I at least agree. But they form a picture of one's particular physical state from many common characteristics, I think. But if they have privately attended any people, they conjecture

[a] *Pyth.* VIII. 99.
[b] Asclepius.

(48 D.)

στοχάζονται, τὸ μέλλον ἑκάστῳ συνοίσειν ἐκλέ-
154 γοντες. καὶ ταῦτα, ὦ Πλάτων, ταῖς σαῖς ἀδαμαν-
τίναις ἀνάγκαις ἀποδείκνυται. ὅτι μὲν γὰρ οὐ
ταὐτὰ πᾶσι λυσιτελεῖ τοῖς σώμασιν οὔτε νοσοῦσιν
οὔτε ὑγιαίνουσι λέγω, ἀλλ' ὥσπερ οὐ ταὐτὰ νοσοῦσί
τε καὶ ὑγιαίνουσιν,¹ οὕτω καὶ ἔτι μᾶλλον οὔτε ἐν
ταῖς νόσοις ἅπασι ταὐτὰ οὔτ' ἐπὶ τῆς ὑγιείας αὐτῶν
πεύσῃ² τῶν ἰατρῶν. τὰς δ' ἁπάντων αὖ διελέσθαι
φύσεις ἀδύνατον. ὥσπερ γὰρ ταῖς ἰδέαις διαφέρειν
ἀλλήλων ἐν πᾶσιν ἀνθρώποις ἐστίν, οὕτως κἂν τῇ
49 D. δι' ὅλου φύσει τοῦ σώματος ἄλλος ἄλλου κεχώρι-
155 σται διὰ παντὸς τοῦ γένους. ἀλλὰ μὴν τόν γε συν-
τυχόντα καὶ δεηθέντα κελεύει θεραπεύειν ἡ τέχνη,
156 κἂν ἐκ περάτων ἥκῃ τις ἀρτίως. τί οὖν δεῖ λοιπὸν
ἢ στοχάζεσθαι; εἰ γὰρ μήτ' εἴσεται πάντας καὶ
θεραπεύσει τὸν προσελθόντα, καὶ τοσοῦτον εἴσεται
δήπου, μὴ πᾶσι δεῖν τῶν αὐτῶν, ὃ λέγω λείπεται.
ἢ σὺ τἀναντία δείξας μὴ σφυρήλατος σταθεὶς ἐν
Ὀλυμπίᾳ μόνον, ἀλλὰ καὶ πομπείου τυχὼν Πανα-
θηναίοις τοῖς μεγάλοις περίιθι.
157 Σκόπει δὴ καὶ περὶ τῆς γραφικῆς, ἣν εἰ καλεῖς
τέχνην, οὐκέτ' ἐρήσομαι· καλεῖς γὰρ ἐν αὐτοῖς γε
158 τούτοις τοῖς Γοργιείοις λόγοις. ἆρ' οὖν ἄλλο τι
ταύτης κεφάλαιόν ἐστιν πλὴν στοχάζεσθαι τῶν ἀεὶ
παρόντων καὶ ὧν ἂν τὴν μίμησιν δέῃ ποιήσασθαι;
159 καὶ μὴν εἰ μὴ τοῦτο, τί ἕτερον; αὕτη γοῦν ἐστιν
ἡ καὶ τὸ ῥῆμα πεποιηκυῖα τῷ πράγματι· αἱ γὰρ τῶν
γραφέων εἰκόνες εἰκάζειν ἐποίησαν καὶ περὶ τῶν

¹ λέγω—ὑγιαίνουσιν om. VA.   ² σπεύσει VA.

according to their experience, selecting what will be
expedient for each. And this is proved, Plato, by 154
your " adamantine " [a] necessities. I say that the
same things do not profit all bodies, either when they
are sick or well. But just as they are not sick and
well in the same way, so still more neither when they
have the same diseases nor when they are healthy,
will the doctors tell you the same things for all.
But again it is impossible to classify the natures of
all men. For just as all men differ in appearance
from one another, so throughout every race each
man is separate in the nature pervading his whole
body. Indeed, a doctor's art commands him to treat 155
whatever chance person has requested his aid, even
if someone has just now come from the ends of the
earth. What of necessity is left, other than conjec- 156
ture ? If he will not know all men and will treat
whoever approaches him, and he will also know
this much at any rate, that all do not need the same
treatment, there is left what I say. Or *you* prove the
opposite, and your bronze statue will not only be
erected at Olympia,[b] but you will obtain a triumphal
carriage and be carried about at the Great Panathenaic Games.

Consider the art of painting. I shall not bother to 157
ask whether you call it an art. For you call it one
actually in this Gorgon-like discourse.[c] Then is the 158
sum of this anything other than taking aim at whatever is the subject and what must be imitated ?
Indeed, if it is not, what else ? This is the art which 159
has even created the word for the action. For the
pictures of painters have caused " to form a picture "

---

[a] *Gorgias* 509 A.   [b] *Phaedrus* 236 B.
[c] *Gorgias* 450 C.

(49 D.)

ἄλλων λέγεσθαι. εἰ δ' ἄρα πρότερον ἦν τὸ ῥῆμα
τῆς τέχνης, ἔτι κάλλιον μαρτυρεῖται μόνου τοῦ εἰκάζειν εἶναι τὴν τέχνην, εἴπερ τὸ ἔργον αὐτῆς εἰκὼν
160 εἶναι κρατεῖ. οὐ μὴν οἶμαι λόγου χωρὶς εἰκάζει, ἀρχὴν γὰρ οὐδ'[1] ἂν εἴκαζεν, εἰ μὴ εἶχε δι' ὅτου, ἀλλ'
161 εἰκάζει πρὸς τὸν τῆς φύσεως λόγον. εἰ δέ σοι φίλον
50 D. καὶ περὶ τούτου φιλονικεῖν, ἔχε τὰ ἄλλα ἡμετέραν
χάριν, ἀλλ' ὡς οὐχ ᾗ γε τῶν χρωμάτων κρᾶσις στο-
χαζομένης ἐστὶ τῆς τέχνης, καὶ οὐ τέχνης μόνον,
ἀλλὰ καὶ φύσεως ἱκανῆς. ταυτὶ μόνον δείξας κατα-
162 γέλα τῆς ῥητορικῆς. καὶ μὴν τό γε[2] κάλλιστον τῆς
τέχνης καὶ τελεώτατον καὶ ᾧ γραφικὴν ἢ πλαστι-
κὴν εἶναι διαφέρει, τοῦτ' ἐστὶν ἡ τοῦ χρώματος δήπου
μίξις. ἐγγὺς γὰρ ἄγει τὸ εἰκασθὲν τῆς ἀληθείας.
οὐκοῦν ᾧ μεγίστῳ προέχει, τοῦτ' ἀφαιρεῖς, ἐὰν μὴ
λίπῃς τὸ εἰκάζειν.

163   Καὶ τί δεῖ τὰς ἄλλας ἐξετάζειν τέχνας[3] ὅσαι διὰ
τοῦ στοχάζεσθαι χωροῦσιν; αὐτὴ γὰρ ἡ μαντικὴ
κινδυνεύει τοῦτ' εἶναι μόνον εἰκάσαι· καίτοι φαίη
τις ἂν οὑτωσὶ σκοπῶν καὶ διαιρῶν ὅτι τούτῳ καὶ
μόνῳ μάντιν ἢ ἰδιώτην εἶναι διαφέρει, τῷ τὸ μὲν
εἰκάζειν ἁπάντων, τὸ δ' ἐπίστασθαι τοῦ μάντεως
εἶναι· ἐγὼ δέ φημι τὸν μάντιν αὐτὸ τοῦτο ἐπίστασθαι
164 εἰκάσαι, πλέον δὲ οὐδ' ὁτιοῦν. καὶ τούτου Πλάτωνα
παρέξομαι μάρτυρα, κἂν μὴ φαίνηται μαρτυρῶν,
ἔμοιγε πιστεύσῃ μηδείς. τὸ δὲ ἥδιστον τῆς μαρτυρίας, οὐ γὰρ ἐν ἄλλοις τισὶ δράμασιν ἢ λόγοις, ἀλλ'
ἐν αὐτοῖς οἷς ἀρτίως εἰς ἑτέρων ἀπόδειξιν ἐχρώμεθα
ἔνεστι διαρρήδην, " ἐπεὶ τήν γε τῶν ἐμφρόνων ζήτησιν τοῦ μέλλοντος διά τε ὀρνίθων ποιουμένων καὶ

---

[1] οὐκ VA.   [2] om. TQ.   [3] ἄλλας τέχνας λέγειν VA.

[a] *Phaedrus* 244 c. See pp. 310-311.

to be used of other things. But if the word was older than the art, there is still better evidence that there is an art whose sole action is " forming a picture," if its product proves to be a picture. It does 160 not, I think, form a picture without reason, for it could not even have formed a picture at all unless it had some means, but it forms a picture by reasoning about nature. If you want to argue even about this, 161 maintain your other points for all we care. But prove only that the blending of colours is not the act of an art which takes aim, and not only of art, but also of a great nature, and then make fun of oratory. Indeed, this mixture of colours is the fairest and most 162 perfect part of the art, and that in which painting differs from sculpture. For it approximates the picture, which has been formed, to truth. Then you deprive it of its greatest feature, if you do not leave its action of forming a picture.

And why must all the other arts be examined which 163 proceed through taking conjectural aim ? For the mantic art may be only this, the forming of a picture. Yet upon consideration and classification of this matter, one might say that in this alone lies the difference between seer and private individual : all men can form a picture, but a seer can make this into a science. I claim that the seer knows this very science, how to form a picture, and nothing more. And I shall provide Plato as a witness of this, 164 and may no one believe me if he does not clearly give this evidence. This is the sweetest kind of testimony. For it is not in any other dramas or discourses, but expressly in the very one which we just now used to prove another point [a] : " Moreover, they named οἰονοϊστική, or ' haruspicy,' the

(50 D.)

51 D.

165

166

167

168

τῶν ἄλλων σημείων, ἅτε ἐκ νοῦ καὶ[1] διανοίας ποριζομένων ἀνθρωπίνη οἰήσει, οἰονοϊστικὴν ἐπωνόμασαν, ἣν νῦν οἰωνιστικὴν τὸ ω σεμνύνοντες οἱ νέοι καλοῦσιν.'' οὐκοῦν ὅτε τὴν οἰωνιστικὴν εἰκαζόντων εἶναι φῂς τῶν ἀνθρώπων, οὐκ ἐκφεύγει μαντικὴ τὸ μὴ εἰκάζειν κατὰ τοῦτο, εἴπερ μέρος οἰωνιστικὴ μαντικῆς. καὶ μὴν ὅτι καὶ διὰ τῶν ἄλλων σημείων προστίθης αὐτός. τοῦτο δ' ὅταν προσθῇς, ἅπασαν δίδως τὴν μαντικὴν εἰκασίαν εἶναι, καὶ μάλα ὀρθῶς κατὰ γοῦν τὴν γνώμην τὴν ἐμήν. οὐ γὰρ ὁμοίως, οἶμαι, οἵ τε θεοὶ τὰ μέλλοντα ἴσασιν καὶ τῶν ἀνθρώπων ὅσοι φάσκουσιν. οἱ μὲν γὰρ ἃ μέλλουσι ποιεῖν ἐπίστανται, καὶ πρόκειται τὰ πράγματ' αὐτοῖς ὥσπερ ἐν ὀφθαλμοῖς. διὰ τοῦτο '' Ζεὺς ἐν θεοῖσι μάντις ἀψευδέστατος,'' καὶ ὅτι γε δι' αὐτὸ τοῦτο ὁ αὐτὸς οὗτος ποιητὴς μαρτυρεῖ. τὸ γὰρ δεύτερόν ἐστιν αὐτῷ '' καὶ τέλος αὐτὸς ἔχει.'' οἱ δ' ὥσπερ ἐν σκότῳ τὰ πράγματα κρίνουσι, πρὸς τὸν ψόφον ἤ τι τῶν ἐκφανέντων, διηνεκὲς δ'[2] οὐδὲν ἔχουσι προειπεῖν. τεκμήριον δέ· εἰ γὰρ μὴ φράσαις τὸ ἐρώτημα, οὐδὲν ἔχει σοι λέγειν περὶ ὧν εἶδεν σημείων. ἀλλ' ἀντὶ τοῦ περὶ τοῦ μέλλοντος ἔχειν εἰπεῖν οὐδὲ αὐτὸ τοῦτο οἶδεν ὅτου χάριν ἥκεις, εἰ μὴ πύθοιτο. οὐ γὰρ ἔγκειται τὰ πράγματα αὐτῷ προφαινόμενα, ἀλλὰ τὰς πύστεις[3] τοῖς σημείοις προσάγων εἰκάζει πρὸς τὸν λόγον. καὶ οὐ μόνον κατὰ τοῦτ' ἐλέγχεται στοχάσασθαι τοῦ μέλλοντος ὂν τὸ μαντεύεσθαι,

---

[1] νοῦ καὶ desunt apud Platonem et § 52.
[2] om. VA.
[3] codd. dett. : πίστεις TQVA (prob. Ddf.).

---

[a] Of doubtful provenance : cf. Archilochus, frg. 84 D ; Euripides, frg. 1110 N[2] ; also Plato, *Epinomis* 985 A.

investigation of the future on the part of thinking men through birds and other signs, being transmitted to human thought from mind and notion, which now modern man calls οἰωνιστική, by lengthening the ' o '." Then when you say that haruspicy is the 165 act of men who form a picture, on these terms the mantic art does not escape the forming of a picture, if haruspicy is a part of the mantic art. Indeed, you 166 yourself add that it forms a picture through other signs. When you add this, you grant that the whole mantic art is the action of forming a picture, and quite rightly so in my estimation anyhow. For not in the same way, I think, do the Gods know the future as all those men who make this claim. The former know that which they intend to do, and the matters are set before them, as it were in sight. Therefore [a] " Zeus among the Gods is the most truthful seer." And that it is for this reason, this same poet [b] bears witness. For the second verse is : " He holds the outcome." But men judge matters, 167 as it were, in darkness, by sound or some manifestation, and they cannot predict details from beginning to end. Here is proof. If you should not make your question clear, the seer can tell you nothing about the signs which he has seen. But instead of being able to talk about the future, he does not even know without asking, why you have come. For him matters are not fixed and apparent in advance, but by relating one's inquiries to the signs, he forms a picture which has regard for reason. And not only 168 in this way is being a seer proved to be taking aim

[b] Probably Archilochus. The second verse is a catalectic dactylic trimeter (suitable for lyrics), not the beginning of a dactylic hexameter.

(51 D.)

ὅπερ καὶ τῶν ποιητῶν ἤδη τις ἐμαρτύρησεν, ἀλλὰ
κἂν ἀποκρίνηται τὸ ἐρωτηθέν, εἰκάζει τὰ κύκλῳ
52 D. πρὸς τὸ πρᾶγμα. νίκη πολέμου, καὶ τίνος συμβάντος
οὐκ οἶδεν, οὐδ' ἁπλῶς τῶν περὶ τὴν μάχην οὐδέν,
ἀλλ' εἰκάζει. πάλιν ἢ πολιτῶν, ἤ τινων ἄλλων
ἐπιβουλή, καὶ τὸν τρόπον οὐκ ἔχει φράσαι, ἀλλ'
169 ὥσπερ τὰ ὀνείρατα οὗτος[1] οὕτω συμβάλλεται. τὴν
δ' Αἰγυπτίων σοφίαν τίς οὐκ οἶδεν τῶν ἐντετυχη-
κότων; ὡς ἄ γ' ἂν ἢ φοβήσῃ περὶ τοῦ μέλλοντος
ἢ ὑπόσχηται, τόν γε τρόπον καὶ τοὺς τόπους καὶ
τὸ μέτρον, οὐκ ἔχει διορίσασθαι ἀλλ' ἢ πλοῦτον, ἢ
πενίαν, ἢ λύπην, ἢ χαράν, ἢ θάνατον, ἢ πράξεις, ἢ
τὰ τοιαῦτα λέγει, αὐτὰ δ' ἕκαστα οὐ συνείληφεν,
ἀλλὰ τὰ μὲν πρὸς τὸ μέγεθος τῶν φαινομένων, τὰ
δὲ πρὸς τὰ νόμιμα εἰκάζει τὰ ἑκάστων, τὰ δὲ πρὸς
τὰ ὅμοια, ἔστι δ' ἃ καὶ πλεῖστον ἀλλήλων κεχωρι-
170 σμένα. πανταχοῦ δὲ τὴν ἐπίνοιαν παρακαλεῖ, ὅτι
ταύτης[2] μόνης καὶ μόνον εἶναι δοκεῖ τὸ εἰκάζειν,
ἀλλὰ μὴ ἁπλῶς εἰπεῖν. οὐδὲν οὖν ἀλλ' ἢ εἰκάζουσα
τῇ ἀληθείᾳ φαίνεται διὰ πάντων.

171 Τί δὲ περὶ ῥητορικῆς εἰ στοχάζεται θαυμάζεις;
φαίνεται γὰρ ὁμοίως διακειμένη τῇ μαντικῇ, πλὴν
ὅσον μαντικὴ μὲν ἀπήλλακται στοχασαμένη, ῥητορικὴ δὲ οὐ στοχάζεται μόνον τῶν πραγμάτων, ἀλλὰ
53 D. καὶ πράττει διὰ τῶν ὑπηρετῶν ἅττ' ἂν εὑρίσκῃ
βέλτιστα. ὥστε καὶ τὸν τῆς μαντικῆς ἐπέχει λόγον
καὶ τὸν τῆς στρατηγικῆς, ἣν μηδὲν τῇ πολιτικῇ
172 προσήκειν Πλάτων οὐκ ἐρεῖ. πῶς οὖν ῥητορικὴ

---

[1] οὕτως οὕτω VA : οὗτος secl. Reiske (prob. Ddf.).
[2] post ταύτης add. καὶ codd. dett. (prob. Ddf.).

---

[a] Cf. Euripides, frg. 973 N²; Menander, frg. 224 Kock.
[b] These are four subclassifications used in aiding the

at the future, a fact which a certain poet already has attested.[a] But even if the seer answers one's question, he forms only a general picture in regard to the matter. Victory in war ; but he does not know the circumstances, nor simply any of the details of the battle ; he merely forms a picture. Again the citizens are plotting, or someone else ; and this seer cannot tell how, but interprets these things just like dreams. Who of those who have met them is 169 unaware of the wisdom of the Egyptians ? In their warnings or promises about the future, they can define neither methods, place, nor degree, but they talk about wealth, poverty, pain, joy, death, activities, or such things. They have not included details. Some of their pictures are formed according to the size of the manifestation, some according to the customs of individuals, some according to similarities, and some according to direct contrarieties.[b] Every- 170 where they invoke cleverness, because the forming of mental pictures, although not in a simple sense, seems to belong to this alone. Their wisdom in everything is in truth clearly nothing but the act of forming pictures.

Why then do you wonder about oratory, if it uses 171 conjecture ? It is obviously in the same situation as the mantic art ; except that the mantic art having made its conjecture is done, while oratory not only conjectures about matters, but also accomplishes through its servants whatever it finds to be best. Therefore it maintains both the underlying theory of the mantic art and that of strategy, which Plato will not deny is connected with the art of politics.[c]

interpretation of dreams and omens ; *cf.* Behr, *op. cit.*, p. 193, n. 71a.   [c] *Politicus* 304 E ff.

(53 D.)

πολιτικῆς μορίου εἴδωλον, εἰ μὴ οὕτως;   ἀλλὰ μὴν
173 οὕτω γε οὐκ εἴδωλον. εἶεν. αὐτοὶ δὲ οἱ στρατηγοὶ
τί πράττουσιν, ὦ θαυμάσιε; οἶμαι μὲν οὐδὲν ἄλλο
ἢ στοχάζονται οἵ γέ που βέλτιστοι καὶ φρονιμώτατοι καὶ τῆς τῶν πολεμίων διανοίας καὶ φύσεως
τῶν σφετέρων στρατιωτῶν, καὶ τόπων γε οἶμαι καὶ
καιρῶν. ἆρ' οὖν τοῦ μηδενός εἰσιν ἄξιοι χρῆσθαι;
174 οὐκ οἶμαί γε. ἀλλὰ μὴν εἰ διὰ τοσούτων γε ὧν εἶπον
τεχνῶν—τὰς γὰρ πλείους ἀφίημι—τὸ στοχάζεσθαι
φαίνεται τῶν ἔργων ἡγούμενον καὶ διὰ τούτου
πάντα χωροῦντα, πῶς ἄξιον τούτῳ τὴν ῥητορικὴν
ψέγειν; ἢ πῶς ὃ μόνον κοινόν ἐστιν τῶν τεχνῶν
ὡς εἰπεῖν, εἰς ἔλεγχον τοῦτο φέρειν, ὡς οὐ μετέχει
ῥητορικὴ τέχνης; οὐδὲν γὰρ ἄλλο ἢ τοῖς συμβό-
λοις, [καὶ]¹ δι' ὧν ἔδει γνωρίσαι καὶ παραδέξασθαι,
τούτοις διαφθείρειν αὐτήν ἐστιν, ὅταν ταὐτά τις
175 ἐγχειρῇ λέγειν. οὐκοῦν οὐχ ὅτι στοχάζεται, διὰ
τοῦτο οὐ μέτεστι τέχνης αὐτῇ, ἀλλ' εἰ καὶ μὴ δι' ἕν²
τῶν ἄλλων πάντων, δι' ἓν τοῦτο μέτεστι τὸ στοχάζεσθαι, εἰ τοῦτ' ἀληθές³ εἴρηκεν Πλάτων ὅτι δὴ
176 στοχάζοιτο. τί δὲ τἆλλα λέγοι τις ἄν, ἀλλ' αὐτὴν
τὴν πολυτίμητον εἴτ' ἐπιστήμην εἴτε σοφίαν χρὴ
προσειπεῖν, οὐκ αὐτός, ὦ πρὸς θεῶν, εἰκάζειν περὶ
τῶν μεγίστων ὁμολογεῖς, ὅταν γέ που φῇς μὴ εἶναι
54 D. διισχυρίσασθαι, ἀλλ' ἀφίης τῷ θεῷ τἀκριβές, εὖ
177 ποιῶν καὶ φιλοσοφῶν ὡς ἀληθῶς; ἀλλ' ἐγώ, τοῦτ'
εἰπέ μοι, πεισθῶ μηδὲν εἶναι τὸν Δία βελτίω τοῦ
Σολέως σοφιστοῦ; ὦγαθέ, σκόπει μὴ πάντα τἀν-

¹ secl. Reiske.
² cod. det., Iunt.: μηδὲν TQVA.
³ codd. dett.: τοῦτο τ' ἀληθὲς TQVA.

Then how is oratory a " shadow of a part of the art of 172
politics," except in this way ? But indeed, in this
way it would not be a shadow. Well then ! What do 173
these generals do, my fine friend ? I think the best
and wisest of them at any rate do nothing other
than conjecture at the plan of the enemy and the
nature of their own troops, and I think at the terrain
and the opportunities. Then are they worthless and
useless ? I don't think so. Indeed, if in all the arts 174
which I have enumerated—and I omit the majority
—obviously conjecture precedes action and everything takes place through this, how should oratory
be blamed for this ? Or how should the only thing,
one might say, which is common to the arts, be
used as a proof that oratory has no share in art ?
This is nothing other than to destroy it by those very
tokens through which it must be accepted and
recognized, whenever someone undertakes this
argument. Then it does not fail to have a share in 175
art because it uses conjecture ; but if not through
any other reason, through its use of conjecture alone,
it does have a share, if Plato's statement is true,
that it uses conjecture. What else would one say ? 176
Except that in this most honoured—should I say
science or wisdom—, do you not yourself, by the
Gods, confess that you form a picture about the
highest matters, when you admit that " a firm
assertion " is impossible,[a] but remit such precision to
God, in a truly proper and philosophic way ? But tell 177
me this, am I to be persuaded that Zeus is no better
than the sophist of Soli ?[b] Dear sir, consider. Perhaps
the capacity of man is limited to forming pictures,

[a] *Phaedo* 63 c, 114 D.
[b] The Stoic philosopher Chrysippus.

(54 D.)

θρώπεια ὅσον εἰκάσαι ᾖ, ἡ δὲ ἐπιστήμη καθ᾽
Ὅμηρον ἐν Διὸς οὔδει μόνου.

178 Ὅτι τοίνυν ὅλως ἐστὶν σόφισμα τὸ φάσκειν τὰ
δοκοῦντα τοῖς πλήθεσι ταῦτα συμβουλεύειν τοὺς
ῥήτορας καὶ τούτου μόνου στοχάζεσθαι, εἰ καὶ μὴ
παῖς ἐξελέγξειεν, ἀλλ᾽ ὅστις γ᾽ εὖ φρονεῖ. ἐμοὶ μὲν
γὰρ τοὐναντίον πᾶν φαίνεται, μήτ᾽ ἐν τῇ τῆς ῥητορικῆς φύσει πλεῖον εἶναι μηδὲν ἢ τὸ μὴ τὰ δοκοῦντα
τοῖς πλήθεσιν εὐθὺς ἐᾶν γίγνεσθαι μήθ᾽ οἱ ῥήτορες
ἄλλο τι μᾶλλον σκοπεῖν ἢ τὰ βέλτιστα, μήτε τοὺς
δήμους αὐτοὺς τοῦτό γε ἐκφυγεῖν, ὡς οὐκ ἀμείνους
σφῶν οἱ ῥήτορες λογίσασθαι περὶ τῶν πραγμάτων,
καὶ πᾶσαν ὅλως τὴν τοῦ βίου σχέσιν καὶ τὴν τύχην.

179 καὶ τοῦτ᾽ ἐξ αὐτῶν τῶν τιμῶν εἶναι δῆλον ὧν αὐτοῖς
ἀπονέμουσιν. εἰ γὰρ ἦν ἀληθὲς τοῦτο, ὃ Πλάτων
αἰτιᾶται, καὶ μὴ τοὺς δήμους ἦγον οἱ ῥήτορες, ἀλλ᾽
οὗτοι τῶν δήμων ἦσαν, πρῶτον μὲν τίς ἂν αὐτοῖς
αἰδὼς καὶ τιμὴ παρὰ τῶν δήμων ἦν; ποῦ δ᾽ ἂν
προεδρίας ἢ τῶν ὑπὲρ τοὺς πολλοὺς ἔτυχον; οὐδεὶς
γὰρ τοὺς διακόνους ὡς κρείττους αὑτοῦ θαυμάζει,

55 D. οὐδὲ οὗ πρότερος περὶ τῶν πραγμάτων ἐντεθύμηται,
τούτῳ τὴν αὑτοῦ γνώμην προστίθησιν.

180 Ἔπειτα τίς ἢ κῆρυξ ἢ πρεσβεία δεηθήσεσθαί ποτε
ἔμελλεν ἀνδρὸς ῥήτορος, εἰ τὰ δοκοῦντα τοῖς
πλήθεσι συμβουλεύειν τῶν ῥητόρων εἶναι κατε-
δέδεικτο; τίς γὰρ ἂν ἡ πόλις πέμπουσα τὸν τοῦ
μηδενὸς ἄξιον θεραπεύειν εἵλετο, ἢ πρεσβευτὴς
ἥκων προσῆλθεν ἄν ποτε τούτῳ τοῦ πεῖσαι χάριν
τὸν δῆμον, εἰ τοῦ βίου κεφάλαιον ὂν ἠπίστατο ἅττ᾽
ἂν ὁ δῆμος βούλοιτο, ταῦτα συμβούλεσθαι, καὶ
περιμένειν τὴν ἐκείνου φωνήν, ὥσπερ τὴν τῶν

181 διδασκάλων οἶμαι παῖδες; τοὐναντίον μέντἂν ἢ

but science, to quote Homer,[a] rests " upon the floor of Zeus alone."

As to the claim that orators advise and only aim at 178 what the multitudes approve, that it is entirely a sophism, " even if a child would not prove this," [b] still whoever has good sense would. It seems to me to be wholly the opposite, that the predominant feature of the nature of oratory is at the outset not permitting the occurrence of what the multitude approves, nor do orators consider anything more than what is best, nor does it escape the notice of all peoples, that orators are their superiors in judging matters, in respect to both the entire state and fortune of their life. And this is clear even from the 179 honours which they bestow on them. For if Plato's charge were true, and orators did not lead all the peoples, but were owned by them, first of all what respect and honour would they have from all the peoples ? Where would they obtain precedence or privilege beyond the commons ? For no one admires his servants as his superiors, nor when he has formed an opinion on a matter in advance of someone else, does he attribute his judgement to him.

Next what herald or embassy would ask help 180 from an orator, if it were regarded as a fact that it was the part of orators to advise what the multitude approved ? What city would dispatch and choose to serve its needs a worthless man, or what newly arrived ambassador would approach him to persuade the people, if he knew that the sum of his life was to concur in the wishes of the people, and to await their pronouncements, just as to be sure children await the pronouncements of their teachers ? It 181

[a] *Iliad* XXIV. 527.   [b] *Gorgias* 470 c.

(55 D.)

ἐπὶ τῶν χορῶν εἶχεν, εἰ μὴ οἱ πλείους ἔμελλον τὸν
ῥήτορα ἀναμένειν, ἀλλ' ὁ ῥήτωρ ἐπεῖχεν ἕως ἂν ὁ
182 δῆμος ἐπισημήνῃ. τίς δ' ἂν ἰδίαν[1] ἢ δημοσίαν δίκην
φεύγων δι' ὅτου νικήσει τῶν ῥητόρων ἐζήτησεν, εἰ
τὰ δοκοῦντα τοῖς δικασταῖς ταῦτ' ἐρεῖν ἔμελλεν ὁ
ῥήτωρ καὶ μηδ' ὁτιοῦν ἕτερον; οὕτω μέντἂν οἱ
μάλιστα κινδυνεύοντες καὶ περὶ τῶν μεγίστων ἀγω-
183 νιζόμενοι πλεῖστον ῥητόρων ἠμέλουν. εἰσὶ μὲν γὰρ
οἱ μάλιστα δήπου κινδυνεύοντες οἷς χαλεπῶς ἔχει
τὰ τῶν ἀκρωμένων καὶ οἱ ταῖς διαβολαῖς προ-
κατειλημμένοι. εἰ δὲ ἃ δοκοίη τοῖς ἀκρωμένοις,
ταῦτ' ἔργον ἐπεποίηντο λέγειν οἱ ῥήτορες καὶ ταῦτα
ἐπηῦξον, Ἡράκλεις, ἦν αὐτῷ οἴκοθεν[2] φέρειν τὸν ὄλε-
θρον, εἴ τις ἦγεν ῥήτορα πρὸς τοιοῦτον πρᾶγμα
184 ὥσπερ ἂν εἴ τις αὐτῷ τὸν δήμιον συνεισῆγεν. ἆρ'
οὖν ταῦθ' οὕτως ἔχει καὶ οἱ μάλιστα ἀποθανεῖσθαι
56 D. προσδοκῶντες καὶ οἷς πλεῖστος ἔπεστι φόβος μὴ
τῶν ἴσων τεύξεσθαι, οὗτοι καὶ διαφερόντως ἀμε-
λοῦσι τῶν ῥητόρων; οὐκ ἔστι ταῦτα. οὐχ οὕτω
παράδοξα ἐρεῖ Πλάτων. ἀλλ' ἐπὶ θύρας ἔρχονται,
δέονται, προκυλινδοῦνται,[3] πάντων φάρμακον τὴν
ῥητορικὴν εἶναι[4] νομίζοντες, θανάτου, φυγῆς, αὑτῶν
τῶν φόβων, δικαστῶν ὀργῆς, δήμου φιλονικίας,
185 πάντων. διὰ τί; ὅτι οὐ τὰ δοκοῦντα τοῖς καθημένοις ἴσασι λέγειν μελετῶντας τοὺς ῥήτορας,—οὐ
γὰρ ἂν οὐδὲ αὐτὸ τοῦτ' ἐνῆν λέγειν μελετᾶν αὐτοῖς,
εἰ τοῦτο ἔμελλον[5]—ἀλλ' ἴσασιν αὐτοὺς πόρρωθεν
προσέχοντας τοῖς πράγμασι καὶ μελετῶντας λέγειν
ὡς ἡ τῶν πραγμάτων τάξις ἀπαιτεῖ, καὶ τῆς τούτων

---

[1] codd. dett. : ἂν ἐπ' ἂν ἰδίαν TQ, ἂν ἐπὶ ἂν VA.
[2] οἴκοθεν ἦν αὐτῷ TQ.

would be the reverse of the situation in choruses, if
the majority were not going to await the orator, but
the orator held back until the people gave the sign.
What defendant in a private or public suit would have 182
sought for some orator to win him acquittal, if the
orator intended to say what the jurors approved,
and not anything else? Then those who are in the
greatest danger and contend over the greatest
matters would have shown the most disregard for
orators. For indeed it is those who are in the greatest 183
danger and those who have been subjected to the
prejudice of calumnies to whom the audience is
harsh. Sure, if orators had made it their task to say
and to enlarge upon what seemed best to the audience, the defendant would have provided his own
destruction, if he had brought an orator for such a
purpose, as if someone should bring with him the
public executioner. Then is this the case? Do those 184
who most expect to be condemned to death and are
most afraid of not receiving a fair hearing particularly disregard orators? It is not so. Not even
Plato will speak such absurdities. They go to their
doors, beseech them, grovel, believing that oratory
is a curative for everything, death, exile, their
terrors, the wrath of the jurors, the contentiousness
of the people, everything. Why? Because they 185
know that orators do not practise to say what their
seated audience approves—for they could not even
say that they practise, if such was their intent—
but they know that they give attention to these
matters from afar and practise to speak as the
situation demands, conjecturing its nature, not that

---

³ Behr; προσκυλινδοῦνται TQVA.   ⁴ om. VA.
    ⁵ codd. dett.: ἔμενον TQVA.

(56 D.)

φύσεως στοχαζομένους, οὐ τῆς τῶν ἀκροωμένων,
εἰ δ' ἄρα καὶ τῆς τῶν ἀκροωμένων, οὐχ ὥστε τὰς
ἐκείνων ἐπιθυμίας θεραπεύειν, οὐδ' ὅσα βουλομένοις
ἐστὶν ἀκούειν λέγειν, ἀλλ' ὅσα βέλτιον εἰπεῖν, ταῦτ'
εἰπόντας πεῖσαι δυνηθῆναι· ὥσπερ γε καὶ τοὺς ἰατροὺς στοχαζομένους ὁρῶμεν τῆς φύσεως τῶν σωμάτων, οὐ μὴν ὥστε χαρίζεσθαι ταῖς ἐπιθυμίαις
ἁπλῶς, ἀλλ' ὥστε τὸ βέλτιστον μὴ εἰκῇ προσενεγ-
186 κεῖν, ἀλλ' ὡς μάλιστ' ἂν ὁ κάμνων παραδέξαιτο. ἄχρι
τούτου φημὶ κἀγὼ τὸν ῥήτορα τῶν ἀκροωμένων στοχάζεσθαι, καὶ τοῦτό γε εἰ λέγεις, συγχωρῶ, ἀλλ' οὐ
δουλεύων οἶμαι τοῖς πλήθεσιν οὐδὲ ὑπὲρ τοῦ χαρίζεσθαι παρατηρεῖ τὰς φύσεις, ἀλλὰ τὸ τοῦ Δημοσθένους, ὅπως τὰ βέλτιστα εἰς δέον εἴποι. '' Ἐγὼ
δ' οὐχ ὅ τι χρὴ λέγειν περὶ τῶν παρόντων ἀπορῶ ''
57 D. φησὶν '' ἀλλ' ὅντινα χρὴ τρόπον πρὸς ὑμᾶς περὶ αὐτῶν εἰπεῖν.'' εἶτα παρρησιάζεται, καὶ μάλα γε,
ὡς ἐγῷμαι, λαμπρῶς. '' Πέπεισμαι γὰρ ἐξ ὧν
παρὼν καὶ ἀκούων σύνοιδα τὰ πλείω τῶν πραγμάτων ὑμᾶς ἐκπεφευγέναι τῷ μὴ βούλεσθαι τὰ δέοντα
187 ποιεῖν, οὐ τῷ μὴ συνιέναι.'' εἰ τοῦτ' ἔστιν, ὦ
Πλάτων, τὸ[1] στοχάζεσθαι καὶ προσομιλεῖν τὰς φύσεις τηροῦντα, οὐκ ἐκφεύγομεν[2] τὰς αἰτίας, πάντες
ἐροῦσιν οἱ ῥήτορες. εἰ δ' ὑπείκειν αὐτοὺς τοῖς πλήθεσι φῂς καὶ ποιεῖν τὰ κελευόμενα, ἀλλ' οὐ κελεύ-
ειν, τὴν θεράπαιναν εἴληφας ἀντὶ τῆς δεσποίνης,
καὶ τοὺς δημοσίους ψέγων δοκεῖς τοὺς ῥήτορας.
188 ἀλλ' οὔθ' οἱ δημόσιοι μέγα φρονοῦσιν ἐφ' ἑαυτοῖς,
ὅτι δουλεύουσι τοῖς τῆς πόλεως βουλήμασιν, καὶ
τοῖς ῥήτορσι τοῦ φρονεῖν αὐτὸ τοῦτο αἴτιόν ἐστι τὸ
μὴ τὰ δοκοῦντα τοῖς δήμοις λέγειν, ἀλλ' ἃ δοκοῦσιν

---

[1] om. TQ.　　　　[2] codd. dett. : οὐ φεύγομεν TQVA.

of the audience, and if that of the audience too, not so as to serve their desires, nor to say all that they wish to hear, but by saying all that is better to be said, so as to have the power of persuasion ; just as we see doctors conjecturing the nature of the body, not indeed so as simply to gratify the desires, but so as not at random to apply the best treatment, but in what way the patient would be most receptive. To this degree, I admit that the orator conjectures 186 about his audience ; and if you mean just this, I yield. But he does not, I think, serve the multitudes, nor observe their natures to gratify them, but in the words of Demosthenes,[a] so that he may say what is best for the situation. " I am not at a loss about what must be said concerning present matters," he declares, " but in what way to speak to you about them." Then he speaks boldly, and indeed, as I think, gloriously. " For I am persuaded, from what I understand by being present and listening to the arguments, that the majority of your opportunities have escaped you because you do not wish to do what is necessary, not because you do not comprehend them." If this, Plato, is to conjecture men's natures 187 and to address them after observing them, then we have not escaped the charge, all orators will say. But if you say that they yield to the multitudes and do what they are commanded, but do not command, you have taken the servant-girl for the mistress, and in blaming the public slaves, you think you blame the orators. The public slaves are not proud 188 because they serve the will of the city, while it is a source of pride for orators that they do not say what the people approve, but what they think is the best.

[a] Or. III. 3.

(57 D.)

αὐτοὶ βέλτιστα εἶναι. εἰ δὲ ἦσαν διάκονοι τῆς τῶν
ὄχλων ἐπιθυμίας καὶ τὰ δοκοῦντα τοῖς καθημένοις
ἐδημηγόρουν, οὐδ' ἂν παρρησιάσασθαί ποτ' αὐτοῖς
189 ἐξῆν, οὐχ ὅπως ὑπὲρ τοὺς ἄλλους φρονεῖν. ἀλλ'
οἶμαι συνίσασιν αὐτοῖς οὐ τὰς ἡδονὰς θεραπεύουσιν,
ἀλλὰ τὰς ἐπιθυμίας σωφρονίζουσιν, οὐδὲ ὁρῶσιν
εἰς τοὺς πολλούς, ἀλλὰ ⟨τοῖς⟩¹ πολλοῖς ὁρῶσιν εἰς
τούτους, οὐδ' ἀρχομένοις ὑπὸ τῶν ἰδιωτῶν [ἑαυ-
τοῖς],² ἀλλ' ἄρχουσιν αὐτοῖς³ τῶν πολλῶν. καὶ
τὴν ἐπωνυμίαν διὰ τοῦτο εἰλήφασι παρ' αὐτῶν ἀντ'
ἄλλου συμβόλου μαρτύριον τῆς ἐξουσίας, λέγω τὴν
58 D. τῶν δημαγωγῶν, οὐκ ἐπειδήπερ ὑπὸ τῶν δήμων
ἄγονται, ὦ πάντ' ἄνω καὶ κάτω ποιῶν, ἀλλ' ὅτι
τοὺς δήμους ἄγουσιν· ὥσπερ γε δὴ καὶ τοὺς παι-
δαγωγούς, οἶμαι, καλοῦμεν, οὐκ ἐπειδήπερ ὑπο-
πεπτώκασιν τοῖς παισίν, ἀλλ' ὅτι αὐτοῖς ἡγοῦνται.
190 ὅ τι γὰρ ἂν φαίης ἁρμόττει τὸ τοιοῦτον ἀκοῦσαι τῷ
ῥήτορι, ἄρχων, προστάτης, διδάσκαλος, πάντα ταῦτ'
ἐστὶ τοῦ ῥήτορος τὰ ὀνόματα. ὅπερ γάρ εἰσι τοῖς
παισὶν οἱ διδάσκαλοι, τοῦτο τοῖς δήμοις εἰσὶν οἱ
ῥήτορες· δεικνύουσιν ἃ χρὴ πράττειν καὶ παιδεύουσι
191 ταῖς γνώμαις καὶ τοῖς ψηφίσμασιν. καὶ ἡ φύσις
οὕτω ταῦτ' ἔταξεν. οὐ δουλεύει ταῖς τῶν χορευτῶν
ἐπιθυμίαις ὁ κορυφαῖος, ἀλλ' εἴ τί που καὶ χαρίζεται, τὸ μηδὲν ἅπασι συμπαρατηρῶν τῷ χαρίζεσθαι. ἀλλ' οὐχ ὑποβάλλουσίν γε αὐτῷ τὰ ἐνδόσιμα
οἱ χορευταί, οὐδ' ὅπως ἂν ἐκεῖνοι κελεύσωσιν,⁴
οὕτω προσάγει τὸ μέλος καὶ τὸν ῥυθμόν, οὐδὲ τί
χρὴ διδάσκειν αὐτοὺς παρ' ἐκείνων μανθάνει, οὐ
μᾶλλόν γε ἢ παρὰ τῶν ναυτῶν ὁ κυβερνήτης μανθάνει τί χρὴ πράττειν. ἀλλ' ἀκούουσι μὲν οἱ ναῦται ἃ
προστάττει, λέγει δὲ ὁ κυβερνήτης οὐκ εἴ τι καὶ

If they were servants of the desire of the mobs and harangued what the audience approved, it would be impossible for them to have spoken boldly, not to mention to be proud beyond other men. But I 189 think they know in their hearts that they do not serve pleasures, but chastise desires, nor look to the multitude, but the multitude looks to them, nor are ruled by ordinary citizens, but themselves rule the multitude. And therefore they have got this name from them, like a token, as an evidence of their power, I mean that of demagogues, not because they are led by the peoples, O you who make all things topsy turvy, but because they lead the peoples; just as, to be sure, we call men pedagogues, not because they are subservient to children, but because they lead them. Any of the following titles which 190 you might use is fitting for an orator : ruler, patron, teacher. All these are the titles of the orator. For just as teachers are to children, so are orators to the peoples. They show what must be done, and educate by their opinions and decrees. And nature has so 191 ordered. The leader does not serve the desires of the members of the chorus ; but if in any way he gratifies them, he carefully guards against any dissonance through his gratification. The members of the chorus do not suggest the keynote to him, nor does he treat the melody and rhythm as they command, nor does he learn from them what he must teach them, no more than the helmsman learns from his sailors what must be done. But the sailors hear what he enjoins, and the helmsman says not

---

¹ add. Reiske.　　² om. Phot., secl. Reiske.
³ Phot. : αὐτοῖς TQ, ἑαυτοῖς VA.
⁴ κελεύωσιν codd. dett. (prob. Ddf.).

(58 D.)

δοκοῦν τοῖς ναύταις, ἀλλ᾽ οὖν αὐτὸς ὢν κύριος ἐν
192 τῇ νηὶ τῶν ναυτῶν. πανταχοῦ πάντ᾽ ἐστὶ πρὸς τοὺς
59 D. ἡγεμόνας, καὶ τὰ τούτων ἡγεῖται βουλήματα.
ἕπεται δὲ τὰ μὲν ἑκουσίως, τὰ δὲ ἀκουσίως τὰ
τῶν πολλῶν. κορυφαῖος χοροῦ, ναυτῶν κυβερνήτης,
στρατιωτῶν στρατηγός, δήμου ῥήτωρ ἡγεῖται.
193 πάντες μὲν οὖν ἄρχοντες φύσει κρείττους τῶν ὑφ᾽
αὑτοῖς· εἰ δέ τις μετ᾽ ἐξουσίας καὶ χαρίζεται,
πείθων, οὐκ ἀναγκάζων, καὶ πρὸς τῷ σῴζειν τὴν
ἑαυτοῦ τάξιν στοχάζεται καὶ τῆς ἐπιθυμίας τῶν[1]
ὑφ᾽ αὑτῷ, οὗτος ἐκεῖνός ἐστιν ὁ τῷ ὄντι πολιτικὸς
καὶ ὃν Ὅμηρος ἔφη πατέρα ὡς ἤπιον εἶναι. οἶμαι
δὲ τὸν αὐτὸν καὶ ῥήτορα ἄριστον πεποίηκεν, ᾧ
194 τοῦτο ἀνέθηκεν. μὴ δὴ τοῦτο λέγε ὡς ὄνειδος κατὰ
τῶν ῥητόρων εἰ χαρίζονται, ἀλλ᾽ εἰ μετὰ τοῦ βελτίστου καὶ τῆς χάριτος στοχάζονται. καὶ κατὰ
τοῦτ᾽ ἀπόδος τῇ ῥητορικῇ τὴν πρέπουσαν εὐφημίαν,
195 ἵνα τοῖς ὁμοίοις αὐτὴν ἀμειβόμενος φανείης. εἰ δὲ
λέγεις ὡς ἁπλῶς χαρίζονται καὶ δουλεύουσι ταῖς
ἐπιθυμίαις, τίς ἡ πίστις; ἐγὼ μὲν γὰρ παρ᾽ αὐτῶν
τῶν πραγμάτων τὴν ἑτέραν παρέχομαι. εἰ γὰρ
μήθ᾽ ὑπὸ τῶν δήμων ἔμελλον οὕτω γε θαυμασθή-
60 D. σεσθαι μήθ᾽ ὑπὸ τῶν ἰδιωτῶν μήθ᾽ ὑπὸ τῶν πολιτῶν[2]
μήθ᾽ ὑπὸ τῶν ξένων μήτ᾽ αὐτοὶ μηδαμῶς ἅπερ
νυνὶ σεμνύνεσθαι, συνελόντι δ᾽ εἰπεῖν, εἰ μήτ᾽ εὐδο-
ξήσειν μήτε χρηματιεῖσθαι μήτε ἰσχύσειν μήτε
ἐρεῖν, πῶς ἐγχωρεῖ τοιαύτην αἰτίαν κατ᾽ αὐτῶν
παραδέξασθαι, δι᾽ ἧς ταῦτ᾽ ἀπήντησεν ἄν;

196 Ἔτι τοίνυν καὶ ὅλως ἀδύνατα ἐγκέκληκεν. ἴσως
μὲν γὰρ οὐδὲ τοῖς ἱπποκενταύροις χαρίσασθαι ῥᾳ-

386

whatever the sailors approve, but speaks as master of the sailors in his ship. Everywhere everything is 192 done according to the leaders, and their wishes lead, and those of the multitude follow, some willingly, some unwillingly. The leader leads the chorus, the helmsman the sailors, the general the soldiers, the orator the people. Then all rulers are naturally 193 superior to those beneath them. If someone, who has power, also uses gratification, by persuading and not compelling, and in addition to preserving his rank, conjectures the desires of those beneath him, he is the truly political man, and who, Homer said,[a] was " like a gentle father." I think, he has also depicted the same man, to whom he attributed this quality, as a very fine orator. Do not speak, as if it 194 were an insult to orators, if they use gratification. But say, if, along with what is best, they also aim at gratification. And on these terms give oratory the praise which is due it, so that you may be seen to requite it fairly. If you say that they simply gratify 195 and serve the desires, what proof is there ? For I provide proof for the other side from the matter itself. If they will not be admired by the peoples, nor by ordinary individuals, nor by their fellow citizens nor by strangers, nor enjoy the pride which they have now, and to sum up, if they will neither have fame nor transact business, nor have influence, nor open their mouths, how can we accept such a charge against them, through which all this would occur ?

Again his accusations are entirely impossible. 196 Perhaps it was not easy to gratify the hippocentaurs,

[a] *Odyssey* II. 47 ; said of Odysseus.

---

[1] τῆς VA a. corr.   [2] μήθ' ὑπὸ τῶν πολιτῶν om. TQ.

διον, εἴ τις ἐδημηγόρει παρ' αὐτοῖς, οὐχ ὅτι κοινῇ
λέγω πᾶσιν, ἀλλ' οὐδὲ καθ' ἕνα οἶμαι, εἴπερ ἦσαν
[οἱ]¹ διπλοῖ τὴν φύσιν· δήμου δὲ βουλήματα γνῶναι
καὶ θεραπεῦσαι διὰ τέλους τίς μηχανή; καὶ ποῦ
δυνατόν; οὐδεὶς γάρ ἐστιν εἷς δῆμος, οὐδὲ μιᾶς
ἐπιθυμίας, οἶμαι δ' οὐδ' ἔσται· ἀλλ' ὥσπερ ῥεύματα
ἄλλος ἀλλαχόθεν φέρονται τοῖς πᾶσι μεμερισμένοι,
ταῖς ἡλικίαις, τοῖς ἐπιτηδεύμασι, ταῖς φύσεσι, τῇ
τύχῃ, ταῖς ἐπιθυμίαις, ἄλλος ἄλλα γιγνώσκων, εἴ γε
γιγνώσκειν χρὴ καλεῖν τὸ μηδ' ὁτιοῦν εἰδέναι περὶ
τῆς ἀληθείας. καὶ νὴ Δί' οἱ μὲν νυνὶ πάρεισιν, οἱ δ'
αὖθις ὥσπερ τὰ φύλλα δοκεῖ μὲν εἶναι ταὐτὰ καὶ
τῶν αὐτῶν δένδρων, ἔστιν δ' οὐδέποτε ἃ πρὸ τοῦ.
197 ποίαις οὖν ἐπιθυμίαις ὁ ῥήτωρ μέλλει δουλεύσειν, ἢ
τὰ τίσιν δοκοῦντα ἐρεῖν, ἢ τίνων στοχάσεσθαι, οἵ
γ' οὕτως ἀτόπως ἔχουσιν, ὥστ' οὐδ' αὐτοὶ γνῶναι
δύνανται τί βούλονται; ἀλλὰ τοσοῦτ' ἀπέχουσι τοῦ
ταὐτὰ φρονεῖν ἀλλήλοις ὥστ' οὐδεὶς αὐτῶν ὡς ἔπος
εἰπεῖν αὐτὸς αὑτῷ περὶ τῶν αὐτῶν ταὐτὰ φρονεῖ
διὰ τέλους, ἀλλὰ πάντες ὥσπερ χειραγωγοῦ τοῦ
198 ῥήτορος [χρώμενοι]² ἀεὶ δέονται. εἰς τίνας οὖν εἰπέ
61 D. μοι βλέψει; πάλιν γὰρ ταὐτὸν ἐρήσομαι. καὶ πῶς
διακονήσεται ταῖς ἐπιθυμίαις; ὅταν γὰρ δέῃ μὲν
διακονεῖν πολλοῖς, οὗτοι δ' ὦσι μὴ κατὰ ταὐτὰ
γιγνώσκοντες, πᾶσι δὲ ἀμήχανον ἐκ τῶν αὐτῶν
ταὐτὰ χαρίζεσθαι, πῶς ὁ ῥήτωρ θεραπεύσει τὰς
ἐπιθυμίας αὐτῶν; ἅμα γὰρ χαριεῖται τοῖς ἑτέροις
καὶ τοὺς ἑτέρους ἀνιάσει. ὥστε οὐ μᾶλλον πρὸς
ἡδονὴν ἢ πρὸς ἀηδίαν ἐρεῖ.

if someone spoke in their midst, not to mention all in common, but not even singly, I think, if they were of a double nature. What method can be contrived to know and continuously serve the will of the people? And where is it possible? For there is no unified people with but one desire, and, I think, there never will be. But as streams, they each are borne along from different sources, entirely separated, by age, profession, nature, fortune, and desire, each having different opinions, if indeed understanding nothing about truth should be called having an opinion. And by Zeus, some now are present, some later, just as leaves seem to be the same and from the same trees, but are never what they formerly were. Then what desires does the orator intend to serve, 197 or who are those who will find the words which he will speak acceptable, about whose moods will he conjecture, when the people are in so strange a state that they cannot even know what they wish? But they are so far from being all of the same opinion that none of them, one might say, persistently holds the same opinion about the same things, but all are ever in need of the orator as if he were a guide. Tell 198 me then, to whom will he look? For I shall repeat the question. And how will he serve their desires? For whenever it is necessary to serve many people and they are not of the same opinion, and it is impossible to gratify all on the same subject in the same way, how will the orator serve their desires? At the same time he will gratify one group and offend the other. Therefore he will speak no more to please than to pain.

---

¹ om. codd. dett., secl. Reiske.
² secl. Keil; Reiskio iam suspectum.

(61 D.)

199 Πῶς οὖν καλεῖς διακόνους τούτους; οὐ γὰρ ἐγχωρεῖ. ὅτι τοίνυν αὐτὸς Πλάτων ὡμολόγηκε μὴ τὰ
δοκοῦντα τοῖς πολλοῖς λέγειν τοὺς ῥήτορας ἔξεστιν
ἴσως εἰπεῖν τοῦτό γε ὡς κἂν παῖς προσέχων φωρά-
σειεν, ἵνα μὴ ἐλέγξειεν λέγω. δίδωσι γὰρ δήπου
τοσοῦτον, πειθοῦς εἶναι δημιουργὸν τὴν ῥητορικήν·
εἰ δὲ πιστευτικῆς ἢ διδασκαλικῆς οὐ διαφέρομαι τὸ
νῦν εἶναι, ἀλλ' οὖν τό γε πείθειν αὐτῇ προστίθησιν.

200 ὅτε τοίνυν τὸ πείθειν ἐστὶ τῆς ῥητορικῆς, οὐ λέγουσι
τὰ δοκοῦντα τοῖς πολλοῖς οἱ ῥήτορες. εἰ γὰρ τὰ
δοκοῦντα λέγουσιν, οὐ πείθουσιν· οὐδεὶς γὰρ ἐφ'
αὑτοῦ γιγνώσκων ἑτέρῳ περὶ τούτου πείθεται. ἀλλὰ
τούτῳ κεχώρισται τό τ' ἐφ' αὑτοῦ βεβουλεῦσθαι

201 καὶ τὸ πεισθῆναι. ἀλλ' εἰ καὶ τοῦτ' ἄρα εἰπεῖν
δεῖ, αὐτοῖς, οὐ τοῖς ῥήτορσι πείθονται οἱ τὰ δοκοῦντα αὑτοῖς ποιοῦντες. πείθει δὲ οὐδεὶς ὅστις μὴ
τὴν αὑτοῦ γνώμην εἰπὼν ἐνίκησεν. ὥστ' αὐτὸ τοὐναντίον τῷ Πλάτωνος λόγῳ συμβαίνει, εἰ τὰ τοῖς
πολλοῖς δοκοῦντα λέγουσιν οἱ ῥήτορες. ἃ γὰρ οἱ

62 D.
202 βουλόμενοι λέγουσι,[1] ταῦτα πείθονται λέγειν. οὐκοῦν εἰ μὲν ⟨ἡ⟩[2] ῥητορικὴ πειθοῦς δημιουργὸς καὶ τὸ
πείθειν τῶν ῥητόρων, οὐ κολακεύουσιν οἱ ῥήτορες·
οὐ γὰρ διακονοῦσιν τοῖς πολλοῖς, ἀλλὰ πείθουσιν·
εἰ δ' οἱ ῥήτορες τὰ δοκοῦντα λέγουσιν τοῖς πολλοῖς, οὐ δημιουργὸς ἡ ῥητορικὴ πειθοῦς· πειθο-
μένους γὰρ τοῖς πολλοῖς, ἀλλ' οὐ πείθοντας παρ-

203 έχεται. πρὸς ταῦτα ἑλοῦ ὁποτέρωθι τὸ ψεῦδος.
Πλάτων γὰρ ἡμῖν ἐλέγχει Πλάτωνα, καὶ τὸ κάλ-

How do you call them servants? It is not pos- 199
sible. Perhaps this can be said, that if even a
child paid attention he would detect, not to say
refute, that Plato himself has admitted that orators
say what the people do not approve. For he grants
thus much, that " oratory is the maker of persuasion." [a] For the present I do not dispute whether
it is persuasive or instructive persuasion. But
at any rate he attributes persuasion to it. When 200
persuasion is a part of oratory, orators do not say
what the people approve. If they say what they
approve, they do not persuade. For no one having
his own opinion is persuaded by another about any
matter. But this is the difference between reaching a
conclusion by oneself and being persuaded. If this 201
must also be said, those who do what they themselves approve, are persuaded by themselves, not by
orators. But no one persuades who has not prevailed
in stating his opinion. Therefore a conclusion
opposite to Plato's reasoning is reached, if orators
say what the people approve. For they are persuaded to say what the people wish and tell them to say.
Then if oratory is the maker of persuasion and 202
persuasion belongs to orators, orators do not fawn ;
for they do not serve the people but persuade them.
But if orators say what the people approve, oratory
is not the maker of persuasion ; for it shows orators
being persuaded by the people, not persuading them.
In respect to this, choose where the falsehood is. 203
Plato refutes Plato as far as we can see, and most

[a] *Gorgias* 455 A.

---

1 κελεύουσι VA.
2 add. Phot. ; ἡ μὲν ῥητορικὴ VA.

(62 D.)

λιστον, οὐ πόρρωθεν, ἀλλ' ἐκ τῶν αὐτῶν καὶ τοῖς
αὐτοῖς [τούτοις]¹ λόγοις ἀναμίξ.

204   ῾Ως τοίνυν οὔτ' ἄλογον ⟨ἡ⟩² ῥητορικὴ οὔθ' οἷον,
ὡς οὑτωσὶ φάναι, στοχάζεσθαι, οὐδ', εἰ μετέχει
τέχνης, εὕρημα ποιεῖσθαι, οὐδὲ μεθ' ὧν ἀρτίως διεξ-
ήειν τεχνῶν εἶναι τῶν πολλῶν, ⟨οὐ μόνον ἀποδει-
κτέον⟩³ ἀλλὰ καὶ πλεῖστον λόγου μετέχον, μᾶλλον
δὲ ἅπαν ἐν λόγοις, καὶ μέγιστον καὶ πρῶτον τῶν
ἐν ἀνθρώποις καὶ τελεώτατον καὶ πέρας, εἰ οἷόν τ'
63 D. εἰπεῖν, εὐχῆς ἄξιον δεῖξαι.

205   Γνοίη δ' ἄν τις εἰ σκέψαιτο τὴν φύσιν αὐτῆς καὶ
ὑπὲρ τίνων καὶ πηλίκων τὸ κατ' ἀρχὰς εὑρέθη καὶ
206 τί πράττει καὶ ποιεῖ διὰ τέλους. οἶμαι τοίνυν
ἅπαντας ἂν οἷς δυνατὸν συμφῆσαι τὸ μὴ κατὰ
ταὐτά⁴ φῦναι τοὺς ἀνθρώπους, ἀλλὰ δυοῖν μερίδοιν
τὴν μὲν οἵαν βιάζεσθαι καὶ πλεονεκτεῖν εἶναι, ἣν
τῶν κρειττόνων τις ἂν εἴποι, λέγω δ' οὐκ ἀρετῇ
βελτιόνων, ἀλλ' ἰσχυροτέρων, τὴν δ' οἵαν ἐλαττοῦσθαι καὶ παρὰ γνώμην συγχωρεῖν ἀπορίᾳ τοῦ
κωλύειν, ἣν τῶν ἀσθενεστέρων οὖσαν γιγνώσκομεν.

207 τοῦτο οὖν εἶναι τὸ ποιῆσαν εὑρεῖν τι τοιοῦτον ἀνθρώπους ὑπὲρ αὐτῶν, ἢ θεούς γε ὑπὲρ τῶν ἀνθρώπων,
ὃ τὴν μὲν ἰσχὺν ἐπισχήσει, τοῦ δὲ ἴσου καὶ δικαίου
πᾶσιν ὥσπερ ἐνέχυρον γενήσεται ταὐτὸν τοῖς τε
πολλοῖς συμφέρον καὶ τοῖς πρὸς τὸ βιάζεσθαι
πεφυκόσιν αὐτοῖς. οὐδὲ γὰρ ἐκεῖνοι ἔμελλον⁵
ἐκφεύξεσθαι τῶν ἀδίκων καὶ κακῶν ἔργων τἀπί-
χειρα, ἀλλὰ τῶν ἀσθενεστάτων πρώτων ἀναιρεθέν-
των ἄλλων ὑπ' ἄλλων⁶ κατὰ μικρόν, οὕτως ἀεὶ τῶν

---

¹ τούτοις TQ Phot.: om. VA (prob. Ddf.); secl. Behr.
² add. codd. dett.   ³ add. Behr.
⁴ codd. dett.: κατ' αὐτὰ TQVA Phot.
⁵ codd. dett.: ἐκεῖνος ἔμελλεν TQVA.

fairly, not in far different passages, but on the same subject and right in the same arguments.

Then not only must it be proved that oratory is not 204 without the use of reason, nor, so to speak, a thing that only uses conjecture, nor that it is to be thought a great discovery, if it has a share of art, and belongs with the many arts which I have just now enumerated, but also it should be shown that it has the greatest share of reason, moreover is entirely involved in the action of reason, and that of all human things, it is greatest, first, and most perfect, and if it is possible to say so, the greatest thing to be prayed for.

One might understand this if he would consider 205 its nature, and for what and what great purposes it was first discovered, and what it unceasingly does and accomplishes. I believe that all, who could, would 206 agree that men are not born equal ; but that they fall into two categories, one which uses force and gets the larger share, which might be called the superior—I do not mean those better in virtue but I mean the stronger—, and one which is inferior and yields contrary to its wish through an inability of stopping the other, which we recognize to be the weaker. I think that it was this state which caused 207 men, or the Gods on their behalf, to discover, in their defence, that which would curtail force, and would be as it were a surety of equality and justice for all, both expedient for the people and for those whose disposition is toward violence. For not even the latter would escape the wages of their unjust and evil acts ; but when the weakest first had been gradually destroyed by the others, and in this way

---

[6] ὑπ' ἄλλων om. VA.

(63 D.)

λοιπῶν ὑπεξαιρουμένων ἔμενεν τελευτῶντας αὐτοὺς
ἐφ' ἑαυτοὺς ἐλθεῖν, ὥσπερ φασὶ τοὺς σπαρτούς, εἰ
ἄρα καὶ ὁ μῦθος τοῦτο αἰνίττεται. ἐμοὶ μὲν γάρ, εἴ
τι δεῖ καὶ παραβῆναι, θαυμαστῶς δοκεῖ τοῦτο
βούλεσθαι δηλοῦν. πεποίηκέ γε τὴν ἀρχὴν αὐτοῖς

64 D. τῆς γενέσεως ἐκ δράκοντος ὀδόντων, αὐτοὺς δ'
ἀναβῆναί φησι τοὺς ἄνδρας ἐνόπλους, Ἄρει δὲ ἀνθ'

208 Ἑρμοῦ μελῆσαι τοῦ θέρους. ὅπερ οὖν ἔφην, οὐδ'
αὐτοῖς τοῖς ὑπερέχουσι ταῖς δυνάμεσιν εἰς τέλος
λυσιτελήσειν ἔμελλεν ἡ δοκοῦσα κατ' ἀρχὰς εὐτυχία,
ἀλλ' ὑφ' οὗ καὶ κρείττους ἦσαν, μᾶλλον δ' ᾤοντο
εἶναι, ὑπὸ τούτου κατελείπετο αὐτοῖς ἀπολωλέναι,

209 ὥστ' ἔρρειν κομιδῇ τὰ πάντων ἀνθρώπων. ἔδει δή
τι κοινὸν εὑρεθῆναι φάρμακον τῷ γένει ταὐτὸν
ἅπασιν συμφέρον, τοῖς ἰσχυροῖς, τοῖς ἥττοσιν, τοῖς
ἐπιεικέσιν· ὡς τοὺς μὲν ἢ κωλῦσαι πρὸ τῶν ἀδικη-
μάτων, ἢ παρ' αὐτὰ τιμωρήσασθαι, τοῖς δ' ἄδειαν
τοῦ βίου παρασκευάσαι, τοῖς δὲ χάριν τὴν πρέπου-

210 σαν, ὅσοι τὸ δίκαιον ἐτίμων ἑκόντες. εὑρέθη τοίνυν
ἐκ τούτων ῥητορικὴ καὶ παρῆλθεν φυλακτήριον δικαιοσύνης καὶ σύνδεσμος τοῦ βίου τοῖς ἀνθρώποις,
ὅπως μὴ ταῖς χερσίν, μηδὲ τοῖς ὅπλοις, μηδὲ τῷ
προλαβεῖν, μηδὲ πλήθει καὶ μεγέθει, μηδ' ἄλλῳ τῶν
ἀνίσων μηδενὶ κρίνοιτο τὰ πράγματα, ἀλλ' ὁ λόγος

211 τὸ δίκαιον ἐφ' ἡσυχίας διαιροῖ. ἀρχὴ μὲν οὖν αὕτη
καὶ φύσις ῥητορικῆς καὶ βούλημα τοῦτο σῶσαι
πάντας ἀνθρώπους καὶ τὴν βίαν διὰ τῆς πειθοῦς
ἀπώσασθαι. εὑρεθεῖσα δὲ ὑπὲρ τοιούτων καὶ τηλικούτων μόνη βιωτὸν ἡμῖν πεποίηκε τὸν βίον, τούς

394

those left were always being removed, it remained that in the end they turn against themselves, just as they say the Sown-men did, if the myth hints at this.[a] If I must here digress, it seems to me very much to have this meaning. It has depicted their original birth from dragon's teeth, and says that they arose as fully armed men, and that their reaping was the care of Ares instead of Hermes. Then as I said, what at the start seemed to be good 208 fortune in the end was not going to profit those who excelled in power, but it was left for them to perish by that very attribute in which they were superior, or rather thought that they were. So human affairs were going to ruin. Some general curative must be 209 found for the race, expedient alike for all, the strong, the inferior, and the decent : thus to restrain the first before acts of injustice or to punish them because of these ; to provide for the second the power to live without fear, and for the last, all who have voluntarily honoured justice, a fitting reward. From those causes then oratory was 210 discovered and entered on the scene as an amulet for justice and as the bond of maintaining life for mankind, so that matters should not be decided for anyone by force, weapons, anticipation, numbers, size, or any other inequality ; but that reason should calmly determine justice. This is the 211 beginning and nature of oratory, the desire to save all men and to repel force through persuasion. It was discovered for the sake of human affairs of the sort and magnitude such as I have described, and alone has made life livable for us, bringing into

[a] Sown by Cadmus from the dragon's teeth in the myth of the founding of Thebes.

(64 D.)

τε ἰδίους οἴκους καὶ τὰ κοινὰ τῶν πόλεων εἰς
ὁμόνοιαν τὸ καθ' αὑτὴν ἄγουσα καὶ τὸ διδάξαι καὶ
μαθεῖν ἅπασιν ἀεὶ καθιστᾶσα καλόν, τὴν δὲ ἀλογίαν
καὶ τοὺς θορύβους πανταχοῦ φεύγειν τε καὶ μισεῖν
πρώτη διδάξασα.

212   Σκεψώμεθα δὴ καὶ τοὺς νόμους τί ποτε ἔστι τὸ
ποιῆσαν, κἂν ἄλλην τις εὕρῃ νόμων ἀρχήν, ἀλλ'
οὐχὶ τὴν αὐτὴν ἥνπερ καὶ ῥητορικῆς, λῆρον τοῦτο
65 D. εἶναι λέγων, νικάτω.   ἀλλὰ μὴν τοῦτό γε πάντες
ἂν εἴποιεν, ὡς οὐδὲ πρὸς ἓν τῶν πάντων ἐδέησεν
νόμων ἡμῖν, ἢ τὸ μηδὲν ὑπ' ἀλλήλων πάσχειν
δυσχερές, μηδὲ τοὺς φαύλους καὶ θρασεῖς τῶν
χρηστῶν κρατεῖν, ἀλλὰ τοὺς χρηστοὺς τῶν φαύλων
213 περιεῖναι μετὰ τοῦ δικαίου.   ταυτὶ δύ' ἔστιν ὡς
εἰπεῖν τῶν νόμων κεφάλαια, τιμωρία τῶν ἀδικούν-
των καὶ τιμὴ τῶν ἐπιεικῶν.   εἰ γὰρ ἕκαστοι τῆς
ἀξίας τυγχάνοιεν, οὐκ ἔστιν ὅπως ἂν ἄμεινον σωθείη
τὸ δίκαιον οὐδ' ὅπως ἂν ἀσφαλέστερον τὸ κοινὸν
214 τῶν ἀνθρώπων σῴζοιτο.   οὐκοῦν ταῦτα ἐνόντα ἐν
τῇ τῆς ῥητορικῆς φύσει φαίνεται.   οἷς μὲν γὰρ
ἤρκει σιγῇ πλεονεκτεῖν, οὐκ ἔμελλον δήπου δεή-
σεσθαι λόγου, οὔθ' ὥστε εἰπόντες αὐτοὶ νικῆσαι,
ἑτέρωθι γὰρ ἦσαν ἰσχυροί, οὔθ' ὥστε ἑτέρων ἀκούειν, αὐτὸ γὰρ τοῦτ' ἦν αὐτοῖς τὸ βούλημα ἀκούειν
μηδενός.   οἷς δ' οὐκ ἦν ἄλλως τῶν ἴσων τυχεῖν,
τοῦ πείθοντος ἔδει λόγου· τοῦτο δ' ἦν[1] εὐθὺς ὑπὲρ
τῆς δικαιοσύνης.   ὁ μὲν γὰρ αὑτῷ[2] καὶ ταῖς παρα-
σκευαῖς ἐπιτρέπων τὸ δοκοῦν ἑαυτῷ ἀξιοῖ κρατεῖν,
ὁποῖόν ποτ' ἂν ᾖ, ὁ δ' ἀφ' ὧν καὶ τοὺς ἔξω δεῖ
πεῖσαι ταῦθ' ὁρῶν καὶ ταῦτ' ἀξιῶν μελετᾶν, οὐ
φεύγει τὴν τοῦ ποῖα ἅττ' ἐστὶν ἃ βούλεται βάσα-

---

[1] αὖ Ddf. nescio ex quo.   [2] codd. dett. : αὑτῷ TQVA.

harmony through its power both private households and the assemblies of cities, and ever making teaching and learning an acceptable good to all men, being the first to teach them everywhere to eschew and hate lack of reason and tumult.

Let us now consider what it is which created the 212 laws ; and if someone finds another beginning of the laws, and one not the same as oratory's, and says my argument is nonsense, let his view prevail. Indeed, all would agree that our need for laws was for no other single purpose than that men should not be badly treated by one another, and that the evil and bold should not prevail over the good, but that the good, with justice on their side, should overcome the evil. The two main points, one might 213 say, of the laws are to punish wrongdoers and to honour the decent. If each should obtain their deserts, there is no better way in which justice might be preserved or in which the commonwealth of mankind might be more secure. Therefore these 214 qualities are clearly inherent in the nature of oratory. Those who were satisfied with quietly having a greater share, were of course not going to need oratory, neither so that their arguments might prevail, for they were strong in other ways, nor so that they might listen to others, for their actual desire was to listen to no one. But those who could not otherwise obtain equality, had need of persuasive argument. And the following directly advanced the cause of justice. He who grants all power to himself and his devices, demands that his view prevail, whatever it is ; but he who recognizes and thinks that it is necessary to practise that by which outsiders must be persuaded, does not escape examin-

(65 D.)

215 νον. φαίνεται τοίνυν ἡ ῥητορικὴ τῇ νομοθετικῇ τῆς
αὑτῆς φύσεως μετειληφυῖα, εἴπερ τό γε ἀκριβὲς
ἐπ᾽ ἀμφοτέρων δεῖ θεωρεῖν, μᾶλλον δὲ μέρος οὖσα
τῆς ῥητορικῆς ἡ νομοθετικὴ καὶ τοῖς πᾶσι δευτέρα
πως, πρῶτον μὲν ὅτι καὶ[1] περὶ αὐτῶν ἔδει τῶν
66 D. νόμων λόγου τοῦ πείθοντος. εἰ γάρ ἐστιν εὔδηλον
ὅτι οἱ νόμοι μὲν ὑπὲρ τοῦ πάντας τὸ προσῆκον ἔχειν
ἔμελλον τεθήσεσθαι, τοῦτο δ᾽ οἱ τῇ χειρὶ κρείττους
οὐκ ἔμελλον συμβουλήσεσθαι, πῶς οὐκ ἀναγκαίως
ἔδει λόγου τοῦ πείσοντος ἤδη; οὐ γὰρ βιάσασθαί γε
ἐνῆν τοὺς πρὸς αὐτὸ τοῦτο πεφυκότας, οὐδ᾽ ἦν αὕτη
νόμων ἀρχή· ὑπὲρ γὰρ αὐτοῦ τοῦ μὴ βιάζεσθαι
216 τοὺς νόμους ἔδει θέσθαι. οὔκουν ἦν τιθέναι βιασάμε-
νον, ἀλλὰ τοῦτ᾽ ἦν πρῶτον παρὰ τοὺς νόμους. ἔδει
δὴ πεῖσαι μάλιστα μὲν καὶ τοὺς ἀντιπράττοντας
αὐτούς, καὶ βελτίους γε εὐθὺς αὐτῷ τούτῳ ποιῆσαι·
εἰ δὲ μή, τούς γε πολλοὺς καὶ ὑπὲρ ὧν ἐτίθει τις. οἱ
μὲν γὰρ τῇ σφετέρᾳ φύσει χρώμενοι πρὸς τοὺς
πολλοὺς ἀδικεῖν ἔμελλον τοὺς ἄλλους, οἱ δὲ τῇ τῆς
ῥητορικῆς καὶ σφετέρᾳ πρὸς ἐκείνους[2] εὖ ποιήσειν
ἔμελλον κἀκείνους, εἴπερ σωφρονεῖν ἔμελλον. εἰ δ᾽
ἄρα ἐκεῖνοι μὴ ἐδέχοντο, λοιπὸν ἦν πεῖσαι τοὺς
πολλοὺς καὶ ὑπὲρ ὧν ἐτίθει τις αὐτὸ τοῦτο, ὅτι ὑπὲρ
217 αὐτῶν τίθησιν. ἔδει δὴ λόγων καὶ πειθοῦς. δι᾽ ἓν
μὲν τοῦθ᾽ οὕτως ἀναγκαίως ἡ ῥητορικὴ νόμων
πρότερον καὶ ἡγούμενον, δεύτερον δὲ τί χρὴ τοὺς
νόμους αὐτούς, ὦ πρὸς θεῶν, εἶναι φῆσαι πλὴν
λόγους, τοσοῦτον τῶν ἄλλων ἐξηλλαγμένους ὅσον
εἰσὶ γεγραμμένοι; εἰ μὲν ἐγώ τι[3] μέμνημαι, καὶ

[1] om. TQ.   [2] ἀλλήλους VA.

ation of the quality of his wishes. Therefore oratory 215
clearly has the same nature as legislation if a precise
examination must be made of both ; moreover
legislation clearly is a part of oratory, and in every
way inferior : first because the laws themselves
needed a persuasive argument. For if it is quite
clear that laws were going to be passed so that all
men have their rights, and those physically stronger
would not concur, how then was there not great
need of persuasive argument ? For it was not
permissible for those to use force who were naturally
disposed to this, nor was this how law began. For
it was to prevent the actual use of force, that it was
necessary to pass laws. Then it was not possible to 216
pass them by force, but this was first of all against
the law. It was most necessary to persuade those
who were opposed and to improve them by these
very means ; if not them, then the multitude, and
those on whose behalf one had established the laws.
They who used their own nature against the multitude, intended to wrong other men ; they who used
the nature of oratory as well as their own against
those, intended to benefit even those, if they would
behave with moderation. But if they were not
receptive, it remained to persuade the multitude
and those on whose behalf one had legislated, of
this fact that he was legislating on their behalf.
There was of course need of argument and persua- 217
sion. Through this one reason oratory thus necessarily takes precedence over and comes before laws.
Secondly, what must we say that laws are, by the
Gods, if not arguments, differing only from the rest
in that they are written down ? If I remember,

---

³ τοι TQ.

(66 D.)

218 Σωκράτει συνδοκεῖν Αἰσχίνης μαρτυρεῖ. χωρὶς δὲ
67 D. τῆς μαρτυρίας καὶ τοῦ Σωκράτους εἰς αὐτό τις ἂν
σκοπῶν ἴδοι. λέγουσι γάρ πως καὶ τί δεῖ ποιεῖν καὶ
τίνων ἀπέχεσθαι καὶ ἐν εἰρήνῃ καὶ ἐν πολέμῳ καὶ
καθ᾽ ἕνα καὶ κοινῇ, καὶ πολιτεύονται διηνεκῶς ἐν
219 ταῖς πόλεσιν. οὐκοῦν ταῦτα ἃ ἐν ταῖς δημηγορίαις
τῶν ῥητόρων ἐστίν, ταῦθ᾽ οἱ νόμοι λέγουσιν, πλὴν
ὅσον οὐ διαλείπουσιν οἵ γε νόμοι λέγοντες, ἀλλὰ δι᾽
220 αἰῶνος ῥητορεύουσιν, ἅτ᾽ οἶμαι γεγραμμένοι. ὅτε
τοίνυν ῥητορικῆς οἱ περὶ τούτων λόγοι, ῥητορικῆς
μέρος οἱ νόμοι. καὶ γὰρ τὸ γεγράφθαι γιγνόμενον
μέρος τοῖς λόγοις ἐστίν, εἴ γε οἱ μὲν αὐτῶν ἀπὸ
221 στόματος λέγονται, οἱ δὲ γράφονται. καὶ μὴν τά
γε ψηφίσματα οἱ ῥήτορες δήπου συγγράφουσιν.
οὐκοῦν ὅτε τὰ ψηφίσματα[1] τῆς αὐτῆς φύσεώς ἐστι
τοῖς νόμοις καὶ τῶν αὐτῶν πολιτειῶν, ἀμφότερά γ᾽
ἐστὶ τῶν ῥητόρων, ὥσθ᾽ οἵ γε νόμοι μέρος τῆς
ῥητορικῆς.

222 Φέρε δὴ σκεψώμεθα καὶ περὶ τῆς δικαστικῆς τοῦ
χάριν αὐτῆς ἐδεήθημεν καὶ τί ποθ᾽ ἡμῖν βούλεται. ἢ
τοῦτο καὶ ῥᾷστον ἁπάντων ἰδεῖν, ὅτι τοῖς νόμοις
ἐπικουρεῖ; τοὺς γὰρ παραβαίνοντας ἃ προστάττου-
σιν ἐκεῖνοι, τούτους ἀναζητεῖ καὶ τιμωρεῖται· καὶ
οὐδ᾽ αὐτὸ τοῦτο ἁπλῶς, ἀλλὰ κἀνταῦθα ἀκολου-
θεῖ τοῖς νόμοις. ὡς γὰρ ἐκεῖνοι κελεύουσιν, οὕτω
223 κολάζει. εἶεν. τίνος οὖν δεῖ τῇ δικαστικῇ πρὸς
ταῦτα; πόθεν εὑρήσει τὸ δίκαιον ἢ[2] παρὰ τῆς ῥητορικῆς; ἡ μὲν γὰρ ἐλέγχει τὰ γιγνόμενα, ἡ δ᾽ ἐπὶ
224 τοῖς ἐλέγχοις ψηφίζεται. φαίνεται τοίνυν κἀνταῦθα
68 D. ἡ ῥητορικὴ βουλομένη μὲν ταὐτὰ[3] τῇ δικαστικῇ,

---

[1] οἱ ῥήτορες—ψηφίσματα om. VA.

Aeschines bears witness that Socrates agrees on
this point.[a] But apart from the evidence even of 218
Socrates, by considering the matter one might
understand. In a certain way the laws tell what
must be done and from what we must abstain both
in war and peace, individually and in common, and
they govern without ceasing in the cities. Therefore 219
the laws say those things which are in the speeches of
the orators, except that the laws never stop speaking,
but eternally play the orator, I think, since they have
been written down. When the arguments about 220
these matters belong to oratory, then the laws are a
part of oratory. For to be written down is a proper
division of arguments, since some of them are verbally
stated, and some written down. Indeed, orators 221
compose decrees. So, since decrees are of the same
nature and governance as laws, both belong to the
orators. Therefore the laws are a part of oratory.

Come now, let us consider the art of justice, why 222
we needed it and what it means for us. Or is this
even the easiest of all to understand, that it succours
the laws ? It seeks out and punishes the transgressors of the laws' commandments. Nor does it do
this on its own, but even here it follows the laws.
For as they order, so it punishes. Well! What 223
does the art of justice need for this purpose ? By
what means will it find what is just, if not through
oratory ? Oratory examines what takes place, and
the art of justice renders a decision after the examination. Even here oratory clearly desires the same 224
ends as the art of justice, but surpasses it by as

[a] Frg. 51 Dittmar.

---

[2] om. VA.   [3] μὲν ταὐτὰ om. VA.

(68 D.)

τοσοῦτον δὲ νικῶσα ὅσον ἀμφοτέρας συνέχει μόνη
βεβαίως. βουλομένη γὰρ ἡ δικαστική, καθάπερ ἐν
μάχῃ τῇ νομοθετικῇ βοηθῆσαι, ταὐτὸν ἔπαθεν αὐτῇ
τῇ νομοθετικῇ. ἐκείνη τε γὰρ ῥητορικῆς πρότερον ἐδέησεν, ὥστε ταύτῃ ἔχειν πάροδον ⟨ἐπὶ⟩[1]
τοὺς νόμους, ἥ τε δικαστικὴ σχῆμα ἐπικούρου λαβοῦσα τοῖς νόμοις αὐτὴ πρότερον προσεδεήθη τῆς
παρὰ τῆς ῥητορικῆς βοηθείας. ἔδει γὰρ αὐτὴν δυνηθῆναι βοηθῆσαι· τοῦτο δὲ οὐκ ἦν ἄνευ ῥητορικῆς.
225 τοσούτῳ δὴ σεμνότερον καὶ τιμιώτερον [ἡ][2] ῥητορικὴ δικαστικῆς ὅσῳ μικροῦ δέω λέγειν δικαστὴς
δημίου. ὁ μὲν γὰρ ἐλέγχει τἀδικήματα ὁ ῥήτωρ
καὶ παραδίδωσι τῷ δικαστῇ, ὁ δ' ἀκούσας καὶ
μαθὼν παραδίδωσιν αὖ τοῖς ὑπηρέταις, καὶ μέσος
226 ἔσθ' ὁ δικαστὴς διακόνου καὶ ῥήτορος. αὖθις δὲ ἐπειδὰν τέλος ἡ δίκη λάβῃ, τῇ μὲν δικαστικῇ πλέον
οὐδ' ὁτιοῦν περίεστιν, ἀλλ' ὥσπερ ἡ νομοθετικὴ
θεῖσα τοὺς νόμους ἀπήλλακται, οὕτως ὁ δικαστὴς
μετὰ τὴν κρίσιν. εἰσδεξαμένη δὲ ἡ ῥητορικὴ τοὺς
ἤτοι δι' ἄγνοιαν ἢ δι' ἀγνωμοσύνην ἀγανακτοῦντας
τοῖς δεδικασμένοις καὶ πρὸς θορύβους ἢ στάσεις τὰ
πράγματα ἐξάγοντας κατέχει καὶ νουθετεῖ, πείθουσα
στέργειν τοῖς νόμοις καὶ τῇ ψήφῳ τῶν δικαστῶν,
οὐ τὸν Πινδάρου νόμον τιμῶσα, ᾧ τἀναντία αὐτὰ
λέγων τῇ φύσει τῆς ῥητορικῆς, οὐδὲ ταῦτ' ἐπάδουσα
" Νόμος ὁ πάντων βασιλεὺς θνατῶν τε καὶ ἀθανάτων
69 D. ἄγει[3] δικαιῶν τὸ βιαιότατον ὑπερτάτᾳ χειρί. τεκμαίρομαι ἔργοισιν Ἡρακλέος, ἐπεὶ ἀπριάτας ..."
οὐ γὰρ φῂς ὅλου μεμνῆσθαι, ἐχρῆν δὲ ἴσως οὐδὲ[4]
227 τούτων, μὴ οὖν ἐπὶ ῥητορικήν γε. ἀλλ' ἄχρι μὲν

---

[1] add. Behr. [2] om. edd.; secl. Keil.
[3] Plato : λέγει TQVA.
[4] μηδὲ TQ.

much as it alone firmly maintains both arts. While
the art of justice wished, as it were in a battle,
to come to the aid of legislation, it was subject to
the same deficiency as legislation itself. That first
had need of oratory, so that by this it had access to
the laws, and the art of justice, having taken the
form of a succourer of the laws, itself first needed
aid from oratory. It was necessary that it have the
power to help, but this was impossible without oratory. Oratory is so much a more important and 225
valuable thing than the art of justice by as much—
I am close to saying—as a juror is better than a public
executioner. The orator examines crimes and passes
the matter over to the juror ; but he, having listened
and learned, in turn passes the matter over to the public servants, and the juror is between servant and
orator. Again whenever a case is concluded, nothing 226
more is left to the art of justice ; but just as legislation is done with when it has established laws, so
too the juror after the verdict. But oratory thereafter takes on those who either through ignorance or
cruelty are angry at the verdict and bring matters to
tumult and faction, and it restrains and admonishes
them, persuading them to be satisfied with the laws
and the vote of the jurors, not honouring the law of
Pindar, O you who speak contrary to the nature of
oratory, nor singing this refrain [a] : " Law, the king of
all mortals and immortals, leads with a most mighty
hand, justifying the utmost violence. I judge by the
deeds of Heracles, since unbought . . ." For you say
that you do not remember all of it. Perhaps you
ought not even to have remembered this, not at any

[a] *Gorgias* 484 B ; Callicles is meant ; Pindar, frg. 169
Schroeder, 187 Turyn.

(69 D.)

τούτου καὶ ἡ ῥητορικὴ λέγει, νόμος ὁ πάντων βασιλεὺς θνατῶν τε καὶ ἀθανάτων· τὰ δὲ ἑξῆς οὐκέτι ταὐτά—πόθεν; οὐδέποτε ἡμέρα καὶ νὺξ ταὐτὰ
συμφήσουσιν—ἀλλὰ πᾶν τοὐναντίον ἄγει τὰ δίκαια

70 D. πρεσβεύων καὶ τοὺς ἐν ὕβρει θρασεῖς νουθετῶν.
εἰ γὰρ ἀξιώσει τὸ βιαιότατον νόμον εἶναι τὸν
δικαιοῦντα καὶ τὴν ὑπερτάτην χεῖρα κρατεῖν
Ἡρακλέους, ᾧ μετὰ τῆς χειρὸς τῶν δικαίων

228 ἐμέλησεν, αὐτὴ τοῖς ἑαυτῆς λόγοις ἀπολεῖται. τίς
γὰρ τόπος λοιπὸν ἢ χρεία[1] ῥητορικῆς ἢ λόγων, εἰ τὸ
δίκαιον ἡ χεὶρ ὁριεῖ καὶ μηδὲν πλέον ἔσται τῷ δυ-
ναμένῳ διδάξαι περὶ τοῦ πράγματος; ποῦ δὲ τὸ πείθειν, εἰ τὸ βιάζεσθαι κρατήσει; καὶ ταῦτα αὐτῆς,

229 ἧς ἔργον πείθειν, δούσης βιάζεσθαι; δοκεῖ δέ μοι
καὶ Πίνδαρος, εἴ τι δεῖ[2] περὶ τοῦ ᾄσματος εἰπεῖν,
οὐκ εἰσηγούμενος οὐδὲ συμβουλεύων σπουδῇ ταῦτα
λέγειν τοῖς ἀνθρώποις, ἀλλ' ὡσπερεὶ σχετλιάζων.
τεκμαίρομαι ἔργοισιν Ἡρακλέος αὐτοῖς τούτοις,
ὅτι καὶ ἑτέρωθι μεμνημένος περὶ αὐτῶν ἐν διθυράμβῳ
τινί, " Σὲ δ' ἐγὼ παρ' ἁμὶν " φησὶν " αἰνέω μὲν
Γηρυόνᾳ, τὸ δὲ μὴ Δὶ φίλτερον σιγῷμι πάμπαν."
οὐ γὰρ εἰκός, φησίν, ἁρπαζομένων τῶν ὄντων

230 καθῆσθαι παρ' ἑστίᾳ καὶ κακὸν εἶναι. καίτοι τό[3]
γε πρὸς νόμον καὶ ταῦτα ἀνθρώπων ἅμα καὶ θεῶν
βασιλέα μάχεσθαι οὐκ ἦν ἐπαινεῖν πρὸς Πινδάρου,
οὐδὲ συμβουλεύειν πρὸς κέντρα λακτίζειν. αὐτὸς

71 D. γοῦν τὸ[4] τοιοῦτον κέκληκεν " Ὀλισθηρὸν οἷμον "

231 καὶ κελεύει φυλάττεσθαι. ἀλλὰ τί, φησί, τούτων
ἐμοὶ νῦν; εἴτε γὰρ δοκοῦντα Πινδάρῳ ταῦτ' ἦν

---

[1] ἢ χρεία λοιπὸν VA.   [2] δεῖ καὶ VA.
[3] τοῦτό TQ.   [4] Iunt. : τοῦτο TQVA.

rate against oratory. Thus far oratory speaks, " Law, 227
king of all mortals and immortals." But the rest is
no longer the same. How could it be ? Never will
night and day agree. Law acts in a wholly opposite
fashion, always honouring justice and reproving
those who dare to commit crimes. If oratory will
assert that there is a law which justifies the utmost
violence and that the most mighty hand of Heracles
ought to prevail, who with his hand cared for justice,
it will perish by its own arguments. What place 228
or use is left for oratory or words, if force will define justice, and he who has the power of teaching
about some matter will have no advantage ? Where
is persuasion, if force will prevail, and that too when
that very art, whose product is persuasion, grants
the use of force ? If anything ought to be said about 229
this lyric, Pindar seems to me to say these things to
mankind, not seriously proposing and advising
them, but, as it were, indignantly. I judge by these
very deeds of Heracles because elsewhere remembering them in a certain dithyramb he says [a] : " Compared to him, I praise you, Geryon ; and I would not
say at all what does not please Zeus." For it is not
reasonable, he says, to sit by your hearth and be
cowardly when your possessions are being stolen.
Yet it was not Pindar's part to praise fighting against 230
law, and at that, king of both men and Gods,
nor to counsel kicking against the pricks. Indeed
he himself called such a thing,[b] " a slippery path,"
and bids us guard against it. But what, oratory 231
says, has this to do with me now ? Whether Pindar
approved these things or not, still Plato will not

[a] Frg. 81 Schroeder, 88 Turyn.
[b] *Pyth.* II. 96.

(71 D.)

εἴτε μή, ἀλλ᾽ οὐ τῇ γε ῥητορικῇ δείξει τὸ τοιοῦτον δοκοῦν. οὐ δεῖ γὰρ ἁρπάζειν ἕκαστον κατὰ δύναμιν καὶ τοῦτο νόμον καλεῖν, ἀλλ᾽ ἕκαστον τῶν δικαίων τυγχάνειν, καὶ τὸν ταῦτα διαιροῦντα νόμον τιμᾶν, καὶ καλεῖν γε μόνον τὸ τοιοῦτον νόμον καὶ

232 τοὐναντίον παρανομίαν. τοῦτ᾽ ἔστι τὸ δόγμα τῆς ῥητορικῆς καὶ τούτῳ σύνεστι τῷ νόμῳ καὶ περὶ τούτου πείθει τηροῦσα ὅπως μηδεὶς ὑπερβήσεται, τοὺς ὑπερβαίνοντας σωφρονίζουσα. μέγιστον δὲ μαρτύριον· οὗ μὲν γὰρ νόμος καὶ δίκαι, ἐνταῦθα καὶ ῥητορικὴ καὶ λόγοι, οὗ δ᾽ ὑπερτέρα χεὶρ ἀφαιρεῖται τὸ δίκαιον, οὐδὲν ἴδοις ἂν ἐκεῖ ῥητορικῇ διοικούμε-

233 νον. ἀλλ᾽ ἔστι μιᾶς ὡσπερεὶ μοίρας καὶ φύσεως οἱ νόμοι, ἡ δίκη, οἱ λόγοι. τριῶν δ᾽ οὐσῶν τούτων δυνάμεων, ὅπερ λέγων ἐξέβην, ἁπάσας τὰς χώρας ἡ ῥητορικὴ μόνη καταλαμβάνει. προτέρα γὰρ οὖσα τῆς νομοθετικῆς κατὰ τὴν ἐκείνης χρείαν, προτέρα δ᾽ αὖ καὶ τῆς δικαστικῆς, ὅτε κἀκείνη[1] ἔδει, λαβοῦσα μέσην πρότερον τὴν νομοθετικήν, εἶτ᾽ αὖ τὴν δικαστικὴν ὡσαύτως διχόθεν περιέχουσα, πρώτη καὶ μέση καὶ τελευταία γίγνεται, ὁμοῦ μὲν [γὰρ][2] ἀμφοῖν αὐτὴν μέσην, ὁμοῦ δ᾽ ἄμφω μέσας αὑτῆς καθιστᾶσα, ὡς μάλιστ᾽ ἔμελλον ἅπασαι συμμένειν, ἀντὶ

234 συνδέσμου τῇ ῥητορικῇ χρώμεναι.

72 D. Πότερον οὖν πολιτικῆς μορίου εἴδωλον ἡ ῥητορική, ἢ τὰ τῆς πολιτικῆς ὡς σὺ φῂς μόρια ὑπὸ τῆς ῥητορικῆς συνέχεται; ἐμοὶ μὲν γὰρ ὡς ἀληθῶς οὐ ῥητορικὴν ἐν τούτοις κακίζειν φαίνεται οὐδὲ πολιτικῆς μορίου εἴδωλον δεικνύναι, ἀλλ᾽ οὕτως ὥσπερ εἴδωλον ῥητορικῆς ἀπειληφὼς ἐπὶ τούτῳ σπουδάζειν, αὑτῆς δ᾽ οὐδ᾽ ἅπτεσθαι, ὥσπερ οἱ Στησιχόρου

show that oratory approves any such thing. Each
must not plunder as much as he can, and call this
law, but each must obtain justice, and honour law
which defines these things, and call such alone law,
and the opposite illegality. This is the opinion of 232
oratory, with this law it consorts, concerning this
law it uses its powers of persuasion, carefully guard-
ing that no one will transgress it, and moderating the
behaviour of the transgressors. Here is the greatest
proof. Where there is law and justice, here there is
oratory and speeches. Where a mighty hand removes justice, there you would see nothing administered by oratory. The laws, justice, and speeches 233
are as it were of one portion and nature. But of
there three faculties, in discussing which I have
digressed, oratory alone occupies all positions.
For it precedes legislation when it is needed by
legislation ; it also precedes the art of justice, when
that has need of it ; and oratory first surrounds
legislation, and next encompasses the art of justice
in the same way. It becomes first, middle, and last ;
at the same time putting itself between both, and
putting both in its midst, so that all three were going
to cohere firmly, using oratory like a bond.

Then is oratory a shadow of a part of politics, or 234
are the parts of politics, as you express it, held
together by oratory ? In these arguments he seems
to me not really to abuse oratory, nor to prove that
it is a shadow of a part of politics ; rather as if he
had caught a shadow of oratory, he appears to devote
serious attention to this, but does not touch oratory,
like the Trojans of Stesichorus who hold the shadow

---

¹ Behr : κἀκείνης TQVA.　　² om. codd. dett.

(72 D.)

Τρῶες οἱ τὸ τῆς Ἑλένης εἴδωλον ἔχοντες ὡς αὐτήν. διαφέροι δ᾽ ἂν τοσοῦτον, ὅτι οὐδὲ ὅμοιον τῇ
ῥητορικῇ τὸ εἴδωλον.

235 Ἀλλὰ μὴν τῆς γε ἀρετῆς τέτταρα δήπου φασὶν
εἶναι μόρια, φρόνησιν, σωφροσύνην, δικαιοσύνην,
ἀνδρείαν. ῥητορικὴ τοίνυν εὑρέθη μὲν [ἐν]¹ φρονήσει καὶ ὑπὲρ δικαιοσύνης, σωφροσύνῃ δὲ τῶν
ἐχόντων καὶ ἀνδρείᾳ τὰς πόλεις σῴζει· σωφροσύνη
μέν, ἐπεὶ τὸν ἐν κόσμῳ βίον πρὸ τῆς ἀταξίας αἱ-
ροῦνται, ἀνδρείᾳ δ᾽ ὅτι τοῖς ἐναντίοις οὐχ ὑπείκουσιν.
ἂν γὰρ εἴξωσιν, οὐ φυλάξουσι τὴν ῥητορικήν,
236 ὥστε ἕως ἂν φυλάττωσιν, οὐκ εἴκουσιν. οὐκοῦν
οὐ τεττάρων ὄντων μορίων τῆς κολακείας τοῦτό ἐστι ῥητορικὴ πρὸς δικαιοσύνην ὅπερ ὀψοποιικὴ
πρὸς ἰατρικήν, ἀλλὰ τεττάρων ὄντων μορίων τῆς
ἀρετῆς ἅπαντα δι᾽ αὑτῆς πεποίηται, ⟨καὶ⟩² ὅπερ
ἐν σώματι γυμναστικὴ καὶ ἰατρική, συναμφότε-
ρον λέγω, τοῦτ᾽ ἐν τῇ³ ψυχῇ καὶ τοῖς τῶν πόλεων
73 D. πράγμασι ῥητορικὴ φαίνεται. τὰ μὲν γὰρ ἄδηλα
εἰ καὶ γενήσεται προορᾷ, ἐπειδὰν δημηγορῇ· τὰ δὲ
ὅπως μὴ γενήσεται προορᾷ, ἐπειδὰν νομοθετῇ· τὰ
δὲ διατηρεῖ καθ᾽ ὅσον⁴ δύναται· τὰ δὲ πραχθέντα
ἐπανορθοῖ, ἐπειδὰν τοὺς ἀδικοῦντας τοῖς δικασταῖς
237 παραδιδῷ. τί οὖν εἰ Ἀρχέλαος τὸν αὑτοῦ δεσπότην
καὶ θεῖον ἀποκτείνας κατέσχε τὴν ἀρχήν, ἢ τὸν
ἑπταετῆ ἐκείνου παῖδα εἰς τὸ φρέαρ ἐμβαλὼν ἔφη
πρὸς Κλεοπάτραν διώκοντα τὸν χῆνα ἐμπεσεῖν,
ἢ μανίᾳ τινὶ παρελήρησεν ἐπὶ τῆς μύλης, τί ταῦτ᾽
ἐστὶ πρὸς ῥητορικήν, ὦ πάντα λόγον καὶ μονονοὺ

---

¹ secl. Reiske (prob. Keil).   ² s.l. add. A.
³ om. TQ.   ⁴ ὃ TQ.

ᵃ Cf. frg. 32 Bergk, 15 Page.

of Helen as if it were herself.[a] There would still be a great difference, because the shadow is not even like oratory.

Indeed, they say that there are four parts of virtue, 235 intelligence, moderation, justice, and courage.[b] Oratory was discovered by intelligence and for the sake of justice. The moderation and courage of those who have oratory preserve cities : moderation, when they choose a life of decency instead of disorder ; courage because they do not yield to the enemy. If ever they yield, they will not keep the tenets of oratory. Therefore so long as they keep them, they do not yield. Then of the four parts of 236 flattery, oratory is not to justice, what cookery is to medicine. Rather of the four parts of virtue, every one is accomplished through oratory ; and what gymnastics and medicine are in the body—I mean both of them together—, this oratory appears to be in the soul and in the conduct of city life. Whenever it speaks in public, it employs foresight in respect to things which doubtfully will come to pass ; whenever it legislates, it employs foresight so that other things shall not come to pass ; other matters it preserves as far as it can ; whenever it hands the unjust over to the jurors, it rectifies deeds already done. What 237 of it then if Archelaus slew his master and uncle, and held the kingdom ; or threw that man's seven year old son into a well, and then told Cleopatra that he fell in while chasing a goose,[c] or in a kind of madness babbled by the mill ?[d] What has this to do with oratory, O you who have stirred up every

---

[b] Cf. § 382, or. xxviii. 144–145.
[c] Gorgias 471 B-C. See note b, p. 413.
[d] Cf. Menander frg. 943 K.

(73 D.)

τοὺς λίθους κεκινηκὼς ὡς ἀληθῶς αὐτούς; τί
βούλεταί σοι τὰ μηδὲν προσήκοντα ἐπεισόδια; οὐ
γὰρ ἔγωγε ταῦτ᾽ ἔπειθον, φήσειεν ἂν ἡ ῥητορική.
οὐδ᾽ εἴ τις ἐπείθετο ἐμοὶ σφάττων καὶ ἀποπνίγων,
οὔτε ταῦτα οὔτ᾽ ἄλλ᾽ οὐδ᾽ ὁτιοῦν ἂν διεπράττετο,
ἀλλὰ πείσας καὶ φανερῶς ἀποδείξας ὅτι τῶν αὐτῷ[1]
238 προσηκόντων ἀντιποιεῖται. ἐπὶ γοῦν τῶν βραχυτέ-
74 D. ρων, φησίν, τούτῳ χρῶμαι καὶ τοὺς κλήρους οὐ
τοῖς ἁρπάσασιν, ἀλλὰ τοῖς ἀποδείξασι δίδωμι. καὶ
τὸν Ἀρχέλαον αὐτόν, φησίν, οὐχ ὅπως τούτων ἄν
ποτε ἠξίωσα, ἀλλ᾽ εὐθὺς ἂν εἰσήγαγον οὗ δίκην ἂν
ἔδωκεν καλὴν καὶ πρὶν τὸν παῖδα ἴσως ἀποπνῖξαι,
ἔτι τῶν πρώτων φόνων ὄντων ἐν χερσίν, εἴ τινα
εἶχεν ἡ ῥητορικὴ χώραν ἐν Μακεδονίᾳ· νῦν δ᾽
ἀπούσης ἐμοῦ ὁ μὲν ἠδίκει, οἱ δ᾽ ἠτύχησαν οἵ τε
διαφθαρέντες καὶ οἱ τοιοῦτον ἄρχοντα δεξάμενοι.
ὥστ᾽ εἰ μηδαμόθεν ἄλλοθεν, ἔκ γε τῶν Ἀρχελάου
κακῶν γνῶθι ὡς καλὸν ῥητορικὴ καὶ ἀναγκαῖον καὶ
[τῇ]² πόλει καὶ ἔθνει παρεῖναι [τῷ]³ μέλλοντι
σωθήσεσθαι καὶ μὴ τοῖς ἐναγέσι κακῶς δουλεύειν.
ταυτὶ μᾶλλον ἄν, οἶμαι, πείθοι λέγουσα ἡ ῥητορική,
οἰκεῖά τε καὶ δίκαια καὶ προσόντα ἑαυτῇ λέγουσα.
239   Οὐ μὴν ἀλλ᾽ εἰ Πλάτων οἴεται τούτοις ἐλέγχειν
αὐτήν, ὥρα καὶ τὰ Γύγου τοῦ Λυδοῦ προσεγκα-
λεῖν αὐτῇ οἶμαι—ταῦτα μέν ἐστι καὶ ἀτοπώτερα
—ὅτι τὸν δεσπότην ἀποκτείνας ἔσχε τὴν ἀρχήν· ἢ
δὲ συνῄδει καὶ συνέπραττεν ἡ τοῦ μὲν γυνή, τοῦ

---

[1] Iunt. : αὐτῷ TQVA.   [2] om. codd. dett.
        [3] om. Jebb, Ddf.

---

[a] Herodotus I. 8-15. Gyges ruled c. 687–652.

argument and truly almost the stones themselves ?
What do these unrelated episodes mean to you ?
I did not persuade those people to do these things,
oratory would say. If anyone, while he butchered
and strangled, had listened to me instead, he would
not have completed either these things or anything else evil. Rather he would have achieved his end
through persuasion and a clear demonstration that he
claims that which is properly his. Even in minor 238
matters, oratory says, I employ this procedure, and I
give inheritances not to those who have stolen them,
but to those who have proved their case. As for
Archelaus himself, it says, far from having approved
of his actions, I should have immediately haled him
into court, where he would have paid a proper
penalty, perhaps even before he strangled the boy,
while he was still committing his first murders, if
oratory had any place in Macedonia. But as it is, he
committed those wrongs while I was absent, and the
unfortunate ones were both those who were slain
and those who got such a ruler. Therefore if in no
other way, from the evil deeds of Archelaus, learn
how fair a thing oratory is and how its presence is
necessary for both the city and the race which is
going to survive and not disgracefully serve cursed
men. In making this statement, I think, oratory
would be the more persuasive, since its remarks
would be natural, just, and proper to it.

Moreover, if Plato thinks that he refutes it with 239
these arguments, it is time, I think, to blame it as
well for the acts of Gyges the Lydian [a]—these were
even more extraordinary, because he slew his master
and held his kingdom ; and she who was both wife
to one and queen to the other connived and aided

411

(74 D.)

240 δὲ δέσποινα. τί οὖν οὐ κἀκεῖνα λέγομεν, ὅτι Κῦ-
ρος τὸν Ἀράξην διαβὰς Μασσαγέταις συνέβαλεν,
Δαρεῖος δὲ τὸν Βόσπορον ζεύξας ἐπὶ Σκύθας διέβη,
Ξέρξης δὲ τὸν Ἑλλήσποντον ζεύξας ἐπὶ τὴν Ἑλλάδα, Νίνος[1] δὲ ὑπὸ Μήδων ἑάλω, ὁ δὲ Σαρδανά-
παλλος[2] ἐκαύθη ζῶν ἀναβὰς ἐπὶ τὴν πυρὰν αὐτός;

241
75 D. καὶ τί ταῦτ᾽ ἐστὶν πρὸς ἔπος; ἢ πότ᾽ ἂν σταίη τις
κατηγορῶν ῥητορικῆς, εἰ πάνθ᾽ ὅσα πώποτε ἢ
ἰδιώταις ἢ πόλεσι συνέβη κατὰ συμφοράς, ταῦτα

242 ῥητορικῇ λογίζοιτο; καίτοι γε περὶ Ἀρχελάου καὶ
τοῦτ᾽ ἔχοι τις ἂν εἰπεῖν, ὅτι Σωκράτην οὗτος ἦν ὁ
καλῶν ὡς αὑτόν,[3] οὐ τῶν ῥητόρων οὐδένα· ἀλλ᾽ ἐῶ
τοῦτο. ἀλλ᾽ οἶμαι γέλως ἐστίν. ἕως γὰρ ἄν τις
μὴ δείξῃ τούτων αἰτίαν τὴν ῥητορικὴν οὖσαν, μηδὲ
τῇ ταύτης φύσει ταῦτα συμβαίνοντα, οὐ ῥητορικὴν
δίδωσιν ἁμαρτῆσαι, τοῦτο δέ ἐστι ἐλέγξαι τὸ

243 ζητούμενον. πρὸς δὲ κἀκεῖνο εὔηθες, εἰ αὑτῷ[4] μὲν
νομίζοι πᾶσαν ἄδειαν καὶ ἃ μὴ ταύτης ἔστιν ἔργα
ῥητορικῇ προσάπτειν ἐξεῖναι, τὸν δ᾽ ἀντικείμενον
λόγον οὐχ ὁρᾷ, οὐδ᾽ οἰήσεται καὶ τὸν ὑπὲρ ταύτης
λέγοντα καὶ σεμνύνοντα πάνθ᾽ ὅσα πώποτ᾽ ἐπράχθη
χρηστὰ κατ᾽ ἀνθρώπους ἐπὶ ῥητορικὴν ἄγειν δυνήσεσθαι.

244 Ἡμεῖς τοίνυν ἀποδείκνυμεν οὗ χάριν εὑρέθη ῥητορική, ἵν᾽ εἰ μὲν εἴη τοῦτο καλόν, καὶ τὴν ῥητορι-

---

[1] Stephanus : Νῖνος TQVA.
[2] T p. corr. : Σαρδανάπαλος QVA.
[3] codd. dett. : αὐτὸν TQVA.
[4] codd. dett. : αὐτῷ TQVA.

---

[a] [Cyrus the Persian subdued the Massagetae, across the
river Jaxartes or perhaps the Oxus, near the Sea of Aral, in

412

in this. Why do we not also say that Cyrus crossed 240
the Araxes and attacked the Massagetae, and Darius
bridged the Bosporus and crossed over against the
Scythians, and Xerxes bridged the Hellespont
against Greece, and Ninus was captured by the
Medes, and Sardanapallus ascended his own pyre
and was burned alive ? [a] How are these things to the 241
point ? Or when would someone stop accusing
oratory, if he would charge to oratory all the misfortunes of private individuals and cities ? Yet 242
concerning Archelaus one could say that he himself
invited Socrates to visit him, not any orator.[b] But I
let this pass. I think that this is ridiculous. So long
as no one can prove that oratory is the cause of these
things, nor that they take place through its nature,
he does not show that oratory is at fault, that is,
prove what is being investigated. Besides, it is also 243
silly, if he should think that he has complete freedom and power to ascribe to oratory things which are
not its work, but does not see the opposite reasoning,
and will not think that one who speaks in its defence
and honours it, will not be able to attribute to it
every good deed throughout the world.

So we show why oratory was invented, so that 244
we may believe oratory to be a good thing if this

---

[a] 530 or 529 B.C., on an expedition during which he met his
death in 528 ; Darius I bridged the Bosporus c. 512, Xerxes
the Hellespont in 480. According to Greek story, Sardanapallus is not here Assurbanipal, King of Assyria c. 668-626,
but a lazy predecessor under whom Arbaces, a governor of
Media, rebelled. Ninus, Nineveh, was taken, and Sardanapallus burnt himself with his wives and treasures in his
palace, 880.—E.H.W.]

[b] Archelaus was King of Macedonia 413-399 B.C., the year
when the philosopher Socrates was put to death at Athens.

(75 D.)

κἂν χρηστὸν ἡγώμεθα,[1] εἰ δ' αἰσχρὸν καὶ φευκτόν,
τοῖς αὐτοῖς ὀνόμασι καὶ λογισμοῖς καὶ περὶ τῆς ῥη-
245 τορικῆς χρώμεθα. φαίνεται τοίνυν ἐξ ἀρχῆς ὑπὲρ τοῦ
δικαίου συστᾶσα καὶ νομισθεῖσα, ὥσπερ ἀφ' ὧν, ὅπερ
εἶπον, τοῦτο ἴσχυσεν[2] ὄνομα οἱ νόμοι. ἔδει γὰρ
τοῖς ταῖς χερσὶν ἐλαττουμένοις λόγου καὶ νόμου βοη-
246 θοῦ. οὐκοῦν ὅσ' ἄν τις ἐκλέξας ἀδικήματα εἰς τὸ
μέσον φέρῃ, πρὸς τῷ μηδὲν προὔργου πράττειν εἰς
τοὺς κατ' αὐτῆς ἐλέγχους καὶ τοὺς ὑπὲρ αὐτῆς
λόγους κομιεῖ. ταῦτα γὰρ καὶ τὰ τοιαῦτα ὥστε
μισεῖν καὶ κωλύειν εὑρέθη.
247
76 D. Νὴ Δί' ἀλλὰ συκοφαντοῦσί τινες τῆς ῥητορικῆς
προϊστάμενοι. καὶ κατ' αὐτό γε τοῦτο σεμνότερον[3]
ἡ ῥητορική. πῶς; ὅτι καὶ τῶν ἰατρικῆς, οἶμαι,
τινὲς προϊσταμένων ἀπέκτειναν φαρμάκῳ τινὰς ἤδη
καὶ τιν' ἴσως ἄλλον τρόπον, ἀλλ' οὐ διὰ τοῦτο
πονηρὸν ἡ ἰατρική, ἢ τοσοῦτον ἀπέχει τοῦ κτείνειν
ἀνθρώπους ὥστ' ἐστὶ θανάτου φάρμακον ὡς εἰπεῖν
248 τό γε ἐφ' ἑαυτῇ. [οὐκοῦν ὅστις μάλιστα μισεῖ καὶ
δυσχεραίνει τοὺς ἀποκτιννύντας, οὗτος μάλιστα
249 τοὺς σῴζοντας ἀσπάζεται καὶ τιμᾷ.][4] οὐκοῦν καὶ
ἐπὶ τῆς ῥητορικῆς εἰ μὲν πέφυκεν ὥστε ὑβριστὰς καὶ
κόλακας ποιεῖν, ἐξ ἀνάγκης αἰσχρὸν καὶ ἀγεννὲς καὶ
ἀνελεύθερον καὶ οὐ πρέπον ἀνδρὶ καλῷ καὶ ἀγαθῷ.[5]
εἰ δὲ ὑπὲρ τοῦ λόγῳ σῴζειν τοὺς ἀνθρώπους καὶ τὸ
δίκαιον, ὑπὲρ τούτου κατεδείχθη, ὅπερ κατὰ σῶμα
ἰατρική, τοῦτ' ἐν ψυχῇ ῥητορικὴ προϊόντος ἑξῆς τοῦ
λόγου πέφηνεν ἡμῖν οὖσα, ἐῶ γὰρ τὰ νῦν γυμναστι-

---

[1] codd. dett. : ἡγοίμεθα TQ, ἡγούμεθα VA.
[2] ἴσχυσαν TQ.

were a fair reason ; but if the reason be shameful
and one to be avoided, we may likewise speak and
think about oratory. From the beginning it was 245
clearly composed and believed in for the sake of
justice, like the laws from which this word, which I
used,[a] has its force. For those of inferior strength
needed argument and law as an aid. Then all the 246
crimes which one selects and brings to light, besides
contributing nothing of value for the refutation of
oratory, will even supply arguments in its defence.
For oratory was invented to hate and prevent these
and other such acts.

Yes by Zeus, but certain men who champion ora- 247
tory, use their art to slander others. · Even on these
grounds oratory is more honoured. How ? Because
also certain of those who champion medicine, I think,
have killed people with drugs or perhaps in some
other way. But medicine is not thereby evil, for
it is so far from killing men, that in itself it is a drug
against death, one might say. [Then he who most 248
hates and detests murderers, most welcomes and
honours those who save life.]. Then also as to 249
oratory, if its nature is such as to create criminals
and flatterers, it is necessarily shameful, degenerate,
ignoble, and unbefitting a gentleman. But if it has
been discovered for the purpose of preserving mankind and justice through argument, then according
to the development of our argument, what medicine
is in the body, this oratory clearly is for us in the
soul. For the present I omit consideration of gym-

---

[a] νομίζειν " believe in " is derived from νόμος, law.

---

³ codd. dett. : σεμνὸν TQVA.   ⁴ secl. Behr.
    ⁵ καὶ ἀγαθῷ καὶ καλῷ VA (prob. Lenz).

(76 D.)

κήν. [⟨ὥσθ'⟩]¹ ὅστις μάλιστα τοὺς συκοφαντοῦντας
ἢ κολακεύοντας δυσχεραίνει, τούτῳ μάλιστα προσήκει τὴν ὑπὲρ τοῦ βελτίστου νομισθεῖσαν καὶ
τούτων οὖσαν φάρμακον τιμᾶν.]² ὥσπερ γὰρ ὅστις
ἀποκτιννύει³ ἰατρικὴν ὑπισχνούμενος οὐχ ἅμα ἰατρός τέ ἐστιν καὶ ἀποκτίννυσιν, ἀλλ' ἕως μὲν ἰατρός, οὐδαμῶς συμπράξει ταῦτα, ἀλλὰ κἂν ἄλλου
πατάξαντος αὐτὸς ἰῷτο, ἅμα δὲ ἀποκτίννυσί τε καὶ
τὴν τέχνην συνδιέφθαρκεν, οὕτω κἀνταῦθα οὐχ ἅμα
ῥήτορές τέ εἰσι καὶ συκοφαντοῦσι καὶ κολακεύουσιν,
ἀλλ' ἕως μὲν ῥήτορες, οὐδέτερα τούτων, οὐδέ γ'
77 D. ἄλλο τι αἰσχρὸν οὐδέν ἐστι παρ' αὐτοῖς οὐδὲ παρὰ
πολύ, ἀλλὰ τοὺς μὲν ἀδικοῦντας ἐξελέγχουσιν, τοὺς
δ' ἀγνοοῦντας διδάσκουσι περὶ τῶν πραγμάτων, ἅμα
δ' ἔξω τούτων τε καὶ τῆς ῥητορικῆς ἔσονται.
250 οὔκουν ὄνειδος ποιήσουσι τῇ ῥητορικῇ, ὁπόταν πλημ-
μελῶσιν. ἁμαρτήσονται γὰρ τοσοῦτον αὐτῆς ὅσονπερ τοῦ δικαίου, ἐπεὶ καὶ ἡ κυβερνητικὴ τοῦ
σῴζεσθαι δήπου τοὺς ἐμπλέοντάς ἐστι τέχνη, καὶ
μὴν ἔχοι γ' ἄν τις τῶν ἐπὶ πρύμναν καθημένων
ἀναγαγὼν εἰς τὸ πέλαγος καὶ καταδῦσαι καὶ ἄλλο τι
χρήσασθαι τοιοῦτον. ἀλλ' οὔτε τὴν κυβερνητικὴν
δεῖ ψέγειν διὰ ταῦτα οὔτε λέγουσιν ἄνθρωποι ὅτι τῇ
τῶν ἐμπλεόντων σωτηρίᾳ πάντων ἐναντιώτατόν
ἐστι κυβερνήτης συνεμβάς, οὔτε τοὺς καταποντιστὰς
εἰς ἕν, οἶμαι, τοῖς κυβερνήταις οὐδεὶς τίθησιν.
ἀνάγκη μὲν γάρ, οἶμαι, καὶ τὰ βλάψοντα τὴν ναῦν
καὶ τὰ διατηρήσοντα εἰδέναι τόν γε⁴ κυβερνήτην,
78 D. ὥσπερ οἶμαι καὶ τὸν ἰατρὸν ἀνάγκη καὶ τὰ σφαλερὰ
τῷ σώματι γιγνώσκειν καὶ τὰ σωτήρια· χρῆσθαι δ'
ἑκατέρωθι τοῖς χρηστοῖς ἡ τέχνη βούλεται, εἰκότως

---

¹ add. codd. dett. et Reiske.   ² secl. Behr.

416

nastics. [Whoever most detests slanderers or flatterers, it is most proper for him to honour that which is believed in for the sake of what is best and is as a drug against these]. Just as whoever while promising medicine murders instead, is not a doctor when he is a murderer—while he is a doctor, he will never so conspire, but would heal the blows caused by another—and just as in the act of murder, he has destroyed his art with it, so here also men are not at the same time orators, slanderers, and flatterers ; but while they are orators, they possess neither of these qualities, nor anything else which is shameful. Far from it. But they convict criminals, instruct the ignorant about affairs, and if they abandon these qualities, they will abandon oratory. They will 250 bring no shame to oratory, whenever they err. For they will stray from oratory as much as from justice. Navigation is of course the art of preserving those who sail, and indeed the man who sits at the stern, having put out to sea, could sink his ship or use it in any other such way. Navigation must not be blamed thereby nor do men say that when a helmsman boards a ship it is most inimical to the safety of those who sail aboard her, nor does anyone, to be sure, put murderous pirates in the same class as helmsmen. For it is necessary, to be sure, that the helmsman know what will harm his ship and what will keep it safe, just as, of course, it is also necessary for a doctor to know what is dangerous and safe for the body, and each of these arts naturally wishes to employ what is useful in accord with their names.

---

³ codd. dett.: ἀποκτιννύειν TQ a. corr. VA a. corr., at -ειν-(ν)ύειν.

⁴ τε TQVA a. corr.

(78 D.)

251 καὶ κατ' ἐπωνυμίαν. καὶ τοσοῦτόν γ' ἀπέχει τοῦ περὶ ταῦτα κακουργῶν τις φυλάττειν τοὔνομα τῆς τέχνης, ὥστε κἂν ἄκων ἐξαμάρτῃ, φησὶν ⟨ὁ⟩[1] Πλάτων, οὐκ ἀκριβεῖ τῷ λόγῳ χρώμεθα, ἐπειδὰν φῶμεν ὅτι ὁ ἰατρὸς ἐξήμαρτεν ἢ ὁ κυβερνήτης. ἕως γὰρ ἂν ἡ τέχνη κρατῇ, ἁμάρτημα οὐκ ἔστιν, οὐ γάρ ἐστιν ἁμαρτεῖν κατ' αὐτήν· τὸ γὰρ ἁμαρτεῖν[2] οὐκ
252 ἔστιν τέχνη. κομιδῇ ἄρα ἐάν τις ἐξεπίτηδες τἀναντία οἷς ἡ τέχνη βούλεται ποιῇ, τοῦτον ᾧ μετέχει τῆς τέχνης ἀδικεῖν φήσομεν, ἢ τῇ τέχνῃ ποιεῖν ὄνειδος, ἀλλ' οὐ τὴν τέχνην τούτῳ διπλοῦν ποιεῖν τοῦ-
253 νειδος. καὶ τί δεῖ παραδειγμάτων ἑτέρων ἀλλ' οὐ μικρῷ πρόσθεν ἡμεῖς τε ἐμεμνήμεθα καὶ Πλάτωνα σύμψηφον ἐδείκνυμεν; οἱ νόμοι σωτηρίας δήπου τῶν πόλεων ἕνεκα καὶ τοῦ τὰ δίκαια βεβαιοῦν ἅπασι τίθενται, καὶ ἡ νομοθετικὴ καὶ[3] κατ' αὐτὸν ἐκεῖνον καὶ καθ' ἡμᾶς καὶ κατὰ πάντας ἀνθρώπους χρηστὸν καὶ καλὸν καὶ σὺν δικαιοσύνῃ καταριθμεῖ-
79 D. σθαι τοῦτ' αὐτὸ δήπου τὸ δικαίως οὐκ ἐκπεφευ-γός, Πλάτων δὲ αὐτὸ καὶ πρότερον τίθησιν.

254 Ἐὰν οὖν τις ἡμᾶς ἔρηται λέγων ὡδί, Πόσοι δὲ ἤδη νόμους ἤνεγκαν οὐδὲν ὑγιὲς καὶ πάντ' ἔχοντας τὰ δεινότατα; πόσοι δ' ἐν γραφαῖς ἑάλωσαν παρα-νόμων; ἢ πόσοι τῶν κυρίων ὄντες νόμων ἐλύθησαν ὡς οὐκ ἄμεινον αὐτοῖς χρῆσθαι; τί οὖν; πότερον τὴν νομοθετικὴν οὐ πάντῃ καλὸν φήσετε διὰ τοὺς τοιούτους νόμους, ἢ πάντας τοὺς πώποτε γραφέντας ἢ μέλλοντας γραφήσεσθαι νόμους εἶναι καλοὺς καὶ δικαίους, ἐπειδὴ δεῖ πάντως καλὸν εἶναι τὴν νομο-
255 θετικήν; ἆρ' ἄφυκτα ἐρωτᾶν αὐτὸν φήσομεν καὶ

---

[1] add. codd. dett.

And if someone does wrong in these matters, so far 251 is he from preserving the name of his art, that even if he errs unwillingly, according to Plato, our language is imprecise when we say that the doctor or the helmsman erred.[a] While the art prevails, error is impossible ; for in its terms there can be no error. Error is not an art. Indeed, if someone purposely 252 acts contrary to the intentions of his art, we shall say that he wrongs his art by the fact that he participates in it, or that he disgraces his art, but not that his art brings him disgrace twice over. And what 253 need is there of other examples than the one which we called to mind a little before and in which we showed Plato in agreement ? Laws were established for the sake of the safety of the cities and to secure justice for all ; and legislation, according to him, to us, and to all men is a good and fair thing and rightly has not escaped being classified with justice, and Plato even ranks it higher.

So, if someone asks us the following : How many 254 have so far passed laws embodying nothing sound and everything which is most terrible ? How many men have been convicted in suits for proposing an illegal law ? Or how many actual laws have been repealed, since it was better not to use them ? Well ? Then will you say that legislation is not wholly a good thing because of such laws or that all the laws which have ever been written or are going to be written are good and just, since legislation must be in every way a good thing ? Then shall we say that 255 his questions are unanswerable and shall we hide

---

[a] Cf. Plato, Republic 340 D.

² κατ'—ἁμαρτεῖν om. VA.   ³ om. VA.

419

(79 D.)

συγκαλυψόμεθα; ἢ τίνος ἐστὶν εὐπορῆσαι μετρίας
ἀποκρίσεως καὶ ἢ τὴν νομοθετικὴν καὶ τοὺς τῷ
ὄντι νόμους καλόν τε καὶ δίκαιον εἶναι φήσει;
τούτου γὰρ χάριν ἐλθεῖν εἰς ἀνθρώπους τὸ πρῶτον,
τὰ δὲ τοιαῦτα οὐ νόμους εἶναι μᾶλλον ἢ τὸ τοῦ
Δημοσθένους ἀνομίαν, καὶ ἃ κωλύουσιν οἱ νόμοι καὶ
256 ὑπὲρ ὧν εὑρέθησαν ὅπως μὴ γίγνοιτο. προσθείην
δ' ἂν ἔγωγε ὅτι ὦ ὧδὶ σὺ¹ ἐρωτῶν οὐ φοβεῖ με
τοῦτο, ὅτι ἑάλωσαν παρανόμων νόμους ἤδη τινὲς
80 D. γράψαντες.   ἀλλὰ καὶ τοῦτο ἐμοὶ μαρτυρεῖ. τοὺς
γὰρ παρανόμων ἁλόντας οὐκέτ' εἶναι νόμους τό γε
ἀκριβές· οὐ γὰρ ἂν εἶεν νόμοι τε ἅμα καὶ παρὰ
τοὺς νόμους. ὥστε παρανόμοις ἀκούειν οὐ νομίμοις
προσήκει γράμμασιν αὐτοῖς.

257 Ταῦτά μοι καὶ ὑπὲρ ῥητορικῆς ἔστω πρὸς Πλάτωνα. ἣν δὲ ἂν τότε κοινὴν ἐποιησάμεθ' ἀπόκρισιν, αὕτη νῦν ἐμοὶ πρὸς τὸ παρὸν γιγνέσθω. οὐκ
ἂν ὁμοῦ κόλακές τε καὶ ῥήτορες εἶεν, οὐδὲ ὁμοῦ
συκοφάνται καὶ ῥήτορες, εἴπερ ὄντως² ἡ ῥητορικὴ
τοῦ δικαίου χάριν εἰσῆλθεν καὶ σωτηρίας ⟨τοῖς⟩³
258 ἀνθρώποις, ὥσπερ οἱ νόμοι. ἀλλ' ἕως ἂν ἰατρικὴ
σῴζῃ τοὺς κάμνοντας καὶ κυβερνητικὴ [σῴζῃ]⁴ τοὺς
πλέοντας καὶ νόμοι τοὺς χρωμένους, οἱ ῥητορικῆς
λόγοι σῴζουσιν οὓς χρὴ καὶ τὸ δίκαιον φυλάττουσιν·
ἐπεὶ καὶ τὴν ὑφ' ἡμῶν⁵ ταύτην κληθεῖσαν φιλοσοφίαν,
εἴ τις βούλοιτο κακίζειν, πόλλ' ἂν ἔχοι παράγειν ἐν
τοῖς λόγοις· οἷον εἰ Διαγόρου κατηγοροίη καὶ
Ἀναξαγόρου καί τινας ἄλλους ἐκλέξας ὕστερον ἢ⁶ τὸ
πρότερον γενομένους ἀτόπους ἀνθρώπους· ὧν οἱ

---

¹ Ddf. : ὧδε ἴσως σε TQ, ὁ δίς σε V, ὡδιωσσε A, ὦ διττῶς σὺ
Keil.   ² Canter : οὕτως TQVA.   ³ add. codd. dett.
⁴ secl. Keil.   ⁵ codd. dett. : ὑμῶν TQVA.
⁶ post ἢ add. καὶ codd. dett. (prob. Ddf.).

our heads ? Or can a reasonable answer be found which will say that legislation and real laws are good and just, that these first of all appeared among mankind for this reason, but that those other acts are no more laws than, to quote Demosthenes,[a] " illegality," and that the laws prevent those acts and were discovered so that they might not occur ? *I* would add 256 that it does not frighten me, my questioner, that some men who have written laws have been convicted of illegal proposals. But even this is evidence for my side : that they are not laws, in the precise sense of the term, which have been convicted of being illegal proposals. For they could not at the same time be laws and contrary to the laws. Therefore these writings ought to be called illegal, not legal proposals.

Let this also serve me in defence of oratory against 257 Plato ; and let our general answer then serve me now for the present. They could not at the same time be flatterers and orators, nor at the same time slanderers and orators, if truly oratory, like the laws, has entered the scene for the sake of justice and for the safety for mankind. So long as medicine 258 saves the sick, and navigation those who sail, and the laws those who use them, the words of oratory save the deserving and preserve justice. Indeed, if someone would wish to defame what we call philosophy, he could cite many examples in his arguments. He could accuse Diagoras or Anaxagoras,[b] or could select certain other peculiar men, who lived afterwards or even before. Of these some were

---

[a] Or. XXIV. 152.
[b] Both contemporaries of and popularly associated with Socrates, and both tried for impiety.

(80 D).

μὲν διέφθειραν δήπου τινάς, οἱ δ' ἐβλασφήμησαν
περὶ θεούς, οἱ δὲ λόγους ἄλλους τινὰς εἶπον, οὓς οὐκ
ἄμεινον ἦν ὅλως, οἱ δὲ αὐθαδείας πλέον ἢ φρονήσεως
259 εἰσηνέγκαντο. ἀλλὰ μὴ οὕτω βέλτιον ἢ λέγειν, ὅτι
οὔκ, εἴ τινες φιλοσοφίας προβλήματι χρώμενοι φαῦλοι καὶ μηδὲν βελτίους τῶν πολλῶν γεγόνασιν, ἢ
81 D. νὴ Δία καὶ δεινότεροι κακουργεῖν, οὐ διὰ ταῦτα
ἀτιμαστέον φιλοσοφίαν, ἕως ⟨ἂν⟩[1] φιλοσοφία μὴ τὸ[2]
⟨τὰ⟩[3] τοιαῦτα ποιεῖν ᾖ, ἀλλ' αὐτοῖς τούτοις τεκμη-
ρίοις χρηστέον κατ' ἐκείνων, ὅτι διημαρτήκασι φιλοσοφίας. οὐδὲ εἴ τινες, οἶμαι, κολακεύουσιν ἢ συκο-
φαντοῦσιν, χείρω τοῦτο ποιεῖ ῥητορικήν, ἀλλ'
ἡμαρτηκότας αὐτοὺς ῥητορικῆς ταύτῃ γε ταῦτα δεῖ
δοκεῖν, ὥσπερ ἐκείνους φιλοσοφίας, ἐπὶ τῷ τοῦ
καλλίστου προσχήματι τὴν τοῦ κακουργεῖν ἄδειαν
260 ἑαυτοῖς ἐκπορίζοντας. ἄτοπον δ' ἂν εἴη, εἰ τὰ μὲν
τῶν σκυτοτόμων καὶ τῶν τεκτόνων ἔργα μὴ ἐξ ὧν
ἂν διαμάρτωσι κρινοῦμεν, ἀλλ' ἐξ ὧν ἂν ὡς δυνατὸν
μάλιστα τύχωσιν, ῥητορικὴν δ' οὐ μόνον οὐκ ἐκ τῶν
κάλλιστα αὐτὴν ἀποτελεσάντων κρινοῦμεν, ἀλλὰ
καὶ ἐκ τῶν αὐτὰ τὰ ἐναντία πραττόντων οἷς ἡ[4]
ῥητορικὴ βούλεται.

261 Ναί. ἀλλ' ἀδικεῖσθαι βέλτιον ἢ ἀδικεῖν. ἔστω
ταῦτα. ἆρα οὖν ὥσπερ βέλτιον, οὕτω καὶ καθάπαξ
αἱρετόν; οὔ. φησὶ γοῦν οὐδέτερον βούλεσθαι,
δῆλον ὅτι καὶ τὸ ἀδικεῖσθαι κακὸν ἡγούμενος,
262 ὀρθῶς, οἶμαι,[5] καὶ γιγνώσκων καὶ λέγων. οὐκοῦν
εἰ Πλάτων αὐτὸς ἡμῖν ἀποκρίναιτο, πλείστου
γένοιτ' ἂν ἄξιον τῷ λόγῳ. ὑπάρχει δὲ[6] καὶ τοῦτο.
πῶς; ὡς αὐτῷ Σωκράτης ἀποκρινόμενος[7] πεποίη-

422

corrupters, some blasphemed about the Gods, some made statements which were wholly better unsaid, and some displayed more stubborn pride than intelligence. But perhaps it is better to say that if 259 certain men, under the cover of philosophy, have been bad and no better than the common people, or, by Zeus, even more adept in wrong doing, not on this account must philosophy be dishonoured, so long as such actions are not the part of philosophy, but this very evidence must be used against them, that they have failed in philosophy. Nor if certain men, I think, are flatterers or slanderers, does this make oratory worse, but on this account they must seem to have failed in oratory in their conduct, just as those in philosophy, acquiring for themselves the freedom to do wrong under the cover of a thing most fair. It would be strange, if we shall judge the works 260 of shoemakers and carpenters not from their blunders but from their most successful accomplishments ; but shall not only not judge oratory from those who have most fairly perfected it, but even from those who act contrary to oratory's intentions.

Yes ! But it is better to be wronged than to do 261 wrong. Let this be so. Then as it is better, is it once and for all to be chosen ? No. He says that he wishes neither, clearly believing that to be wronged is an evil, a correct judgement and statement, I think. If Plato would answer us, it would be most valuable 262 for the argument. And the answer is at hand. How ? He has described Socrates' answer. It is so

---

¹ add. codd. dett.　　² τῷ TQ.　　³ add. codd. dett.
　　⁴ om. VA.　　⁵ codd. dett. : εἶναι TQVA.
⁶ τοίνυν TQ.　　⁷ codd. dett. : ἀποκρινάμενος TQVA.

(81 D.)

ται. ἔστι γὰρ καὶ αὐτὸ οὑτωσὶ διακείμενον. ἐρωτᾷ
Πῶλος Σωκράτη, Σὺ δ' ἄρα ἀδικεῖσθαι βούλοιο ἂν
μᾶλλον ἢ ἀδικεῖν; καὶ ὃς ἀμείβεται, Βουλοίμην
82 D. μὲν ἂν ἔγωγε οὐδέτερον, εἰ δὲ ἀναγκαῖον εἴη ἀδικεῖσθαι ἢ ἀδικεῖν, ἑλοίμην μᾶλλον ἀδικεῖσθαι.
263 οὐκοῦν ὁπότε μηδέτερόν φησι βούλεσθαι, δῆλον ὅτι
καὶ τὸ ἀδικεῖσθαι κακὸν ἡγούμενος οὔ φησι βούλεσθαι, ἀλλὰ τοῦ μὲν ἀδικεῖν ἄμεινον τὸ ἀδικεῖσθαι,
οὐ μὴν ἐκείνου γε τοῦ μήτε ἀδικεῖν μήτε ἀδικεῖσθαι,
264 ὀρθῶς, οἶμαι, καὶ γιγνώσκων καὶ λέγων. εἰ μὲν
τοίνυν ἡ ῥητορικὴ ἀδικεῖσθαι μὲν ἐκώλυεν, ἀδικεῖν
δὲ προσηνάγκαζεν, οὐδ' οὕτω μὲν ἴσως ἂν καθάπαξ
πονηρὸν ἦν, πονηρόν γε ὂν κωλύουσα τὸ ἀδικεῖσθαι,
χεῖρον δὲ ἂν ἴσως βελτίονος, εἴπερ[1] ἀδικεῖσθαι
κρεῖττον ἢ ἀδικεῖν. εἰ δ' οὔτ' ἐκεῖνο ἐπαναγκάζει
καὶ τοῦτο κωλύει, κατ' ἐκεῖνο μὲν οὔτε ἀγαθὸν
οὔτε κακόν πω, δῶμεν γὰρ ὡς ἐν τῷ παρόντι, κατὰ
τοῦτο δὲ κυρίως ἀγαθὸν καὶ τοσούτῳ βέλτιον ἢ
χεῖρον, ὅσῳ τοῦ βελτίονος μετείληφεν, ἀλλ' οὐ τοῦ
χείρονος, εἴπερ βέλτιον τὸ μήτε ἀδικεῖν μήτε ἀδι-
265 κεῖσθαι, ἢ δυοῖν ἐκείνοιν τὸ ἕτερον. καὶ μὴν ὁ μὲν
μὴ ἀδικεῖν ἐγνωκὼς οὐχ ἅμα αὐτός τε τοῦ κακουργεῖν ἀπέχεται καὶ τὸ ἀδικεῖσθαι πέφευγεν. αὐτὸ
γὰρ τοῦτο ἦν ἀδικεῖν τὸ κακῶς ὂν οὐ προσῆκεν
ποιεῖν. ὥσθ' ἕως ἂν ἐν ἀνθρώποις ᾖ τὸ κακουργεῖν,
266 ἀδικήσεται. ὁ δὲ τὴν τοῦ μὴ ἀδικεῖσθαι φυλακὴν
ἔχων ἅμα καὶ τὸ ἀδικεῖν που κωλύει. ὥσπερ γὰρ
ἅμα ⟨τε⟩[2] ἠδίκηται καὶ ἠδίκηκεν ἕτερος, οὕτως ὁ
τὴν τοῦ μὴ ἀδικεῖσθαι δύναμιν ἔχων τὴν αὐτὴν τοῦ

[1] codd. dett.: ὅπερ TQA, ᾧπερ V.
[2] add. codd. dett.

contrived [a] : Polus asks Socrates, " Then you would prefer to be wronged than to do wrong ? " And he answers, " I should wish neither ; but if it were necessary to be wronged or do a wrong, I should choose to be wronged." When he says that he 263 wishes neither, it is clear that, believing to be wronged also to be an evil, he denies that he wishes it. But he states that to be wronged is better than to do wrong, not however than neither to do wrong nor to be wronged, a correct judgement and statement, I think. If oratory has prevented being wronged, but 264 has compelled the commission of wrong, perhaps it would not be even then an absolutely bad thing, since it prevents being wronged which is a bad thing ; but perhaps it would be more bad than good if to be wronged is better than to do wrong. If it does not compel wrong and prevents injustice, in the former case it is neither good nor evil—for let us grant this for the present ; but in the latter case, properly good, and so much better than not, by as much as it has shared in what is better, not worse, if not to do wrong nor to be wronged is better than one of these two states. Indeed, he, who has deter- 265 mined not to do wrong, does not, while he refrains from doing evil, avoid being wronged. To do wrong was to mistreat someone improperly. Therefore as long as the commission of evil exists among men, he will be wronged. But he who has a means of protec- 266 tion against being wronged, at the same time prevents the commission of wrong. For just as when he is wronged, another has committed a wrong, so he who has means against being wronged, has the same means for not allowing the commission of

[a] *Gorgias* 469 b-c ; more a paraphrase than a quotation.

(82 D.)

μὴ ἐᾶν ἀδικεῖν ἔχει. ὥστε εἰ τὸ μὲν μὴ ἀδικεῖσθαι
τῆς ῥητορικῆς τίθησιν, τὸ δὲ μὴ ἀδικεῖν τῆς φιλοσοφίας, τοσούτῳ χείρων φιλοσοφία ῥητορικῆς, ὅσῳ
267 τοῦ ἀδικεῖσθαι τὸ ἀδικεῖν. ὁπότε δ' αὖ πρὸ τούτου τίθησι τὸ μήτε ἀδικεῖν μήτε ἀδικεῖσθαι, τούτῳ
83 D. βελτίων αὖ γίγνεται ῥητορικὴ φιλοσοφίας, ἐπειδή
γε ὁμοῦ τῷ¹ ἀδικεῖσθαι καὶ τὸ ἀδικεῖν ἀναιρεῖ.
ἐπεὶ καὶ οἱ νόμοι κωλύοντες ἀδικεῖσθαι, ἅμα καὶ²
ἀδικεῖν δήπου κωλύουσιν. οὐ γὰρ ἔστιν οὐκ ὄντων
τῶν ἀδικουμένων τοὺς ἀδικοῦντας εἶναι, μηδενὸς
ὄντος ἐφ' ὃν τοῦτ' ἔρχεται. ὥσθ' ἡ ῥητορικὴ τὸ
ἀδικεῖσθαι κωλύουσα συγκωλύει ⟨καὶ⟩³ τὸ ἀδικεῖν
268 αὐτῷ τούτῳ ᾧπερ⁴ τὸ ἀδικεῖσθαι. εἰ δὲ δὴ καὶ ὅλως
βοηθείας ἕνεκα τῷ δικαίῳ τὴν ῥητορικὴν δείκνυμεν
εὑρεθεῖσαν καὶ τὴν αὐτὴν καθαρῶς τάξιν ἔχουσαν
τοῖς νόμοις, οὐ μόνον, ὡς ἔοικεν, ὁ ῥήτωρ οὐ τὸ
μὲν ἀδικεῖσθαι φεύξεται, τὸ δὲ ἀδικεῖν βεβαιώσει,
ἀλλ' οὐδὲν οὕτως ὡς τὸ ἀδικεῖν⁵ κωλύσει. οὐ γὰρ
μόνον τῶν εἰς αὐτὸν⁶ σχήσει πρόνοιαν, ἀλλ' ὅπως
μηδ' ἄλλος πείσεται κακῶς, εἴπερ ὧν τοὺς νόμους
χάριν, τούτων καὶ τὴν ῥητορικὴν εὑρέσθαι νενίκηκεν.
269 Ἀλλὰ μὴν ὅ γε ἑτέρους τὰ δίκαια πράττειν
ἐπαναγκάζων πολύ που πρῶτον αὐτός γε παρε-
σκεύασται. οὐ γὰρ ἐγχωρεῖ βοηθεῖν μὲν τῷ δικαίῳ,
τοῦ δὲ καταλύειν τὸ δίκαιον αὐτὸν πρῶτον ὑπάρχειν.
270 οὐκοῦν ὁ ῥήτωρ οὐ μόνον αὐτὸς οὐκ ἀδικήσει, ἀλλ'
οὐδ' ἕτερον ἐάσει· οὐδ' αὖ μόνον⁷ αὐτὸς οὐκ ἀδικηθή-
σεται, ἀλλ' οὐδ' ἕτερος τό γε τούτου μέρος. εἰ δὲ

¹ τὸ TQ Phot.   ² codd. dett. : τε TQV, τὸ ex τῷ corr. A.
³ add. codd. dett.   ⁴ ὥσπερ TQVA a. corr.
⁵ βεβαιώσει—ἀδικεῖν om. VA.
⁶ codd. dett. : αὐτὸν TQVA Phot.
⁷ Reiske : μόνος TQVA.

wrong. Therefore if he classifies not to be wronged as the part of oratory, and not to do wrong as the part of philosophy, philosophy is so much inferior to oratory, as to do wrong is to being wronged. Again 267 when he ranks, as more important than doing wrong, neither to do wrong nor to be wronged, in this also oratory is better than philosophy, since along with being wronged it does away with doing wrong. Indeed, those laws which prevent being wronged, also at the same time prevent the commission of wrong. For when there is no one who is being wronged, there can be no one who commits wrong, there being no one to whom this applies. Therefore oratory in preventing being wronged, also prevents the commission of wrong by the same act by which it prevents being wronged. If we prove that oratory was 268 invented wholly for the sake of aiding justice and that it has precisely the same position as the laws, the orator will not only, as it seems, escape being wronged, while not strengthening the commission of wrong, but will prevent nothing as much as the commission of wrong. He will not only be concerned for himself, but so that no one else will be mistreated, if it is proved that oratory was invented for the same purpose as the laws.

Indeed, the man who compels others to act justly, 269 is, I suppose, fully prepared to do so himself first. It is impossible to aid justice, and be the first to subvert justice. Then the orator will not only 270 himself not do wrong, but will not even permit another to do so ; and again he will not only not be wronged himself, but no other will be either as far as he is concerned. If he will neither do wrong nor

(83 D.)

μήτ' ἀδικήσει μήτε ἕτερον ἐάσει, κατὰ πάντας τοὺς
τρόπους ἡ ῥητορικὴ καλὸν κἀγαθόν [τε] καὶ ⟨καθ'
84 D. ὃν⟩¹ αἰσχρὸν τὸ ἀδικεῖν καὶ καθ' ὃν κρεῖττον τὸ
ἀδικεῖσθαι ἢ ἀδικεῖν καὶ καθ' ὃν ὅλως βέλτιστον
μήτε ἀδικεῖν μήτε ἀδικεῖσθαι, καὶ πέφηνεν ὁ τῷ
ὄντι ῥήτωρ ἀνδρὸς ἁπλῶς εἰπεῖν ἀγαθοῦ τοσούτῳ
κρείττων, ὅσῳ ὁ μὲν τὸ καθ' αὑτὸν μόνον παρέχεται,
ὁ δὲ καὶ τοὺς ἄλλους ὅπως τοιοῦτοι γενήσονται
παρασκευάζει. ὁ μὲν γὰρ καλός τε κἀγαθὸς οὐ
πάντῃ ῥήτωρ, ὁ δὲ ῥήτωρ καλὸς κἀγαθός, ὅς γε καὶ
271 τοὺς ἄλλους ἐπὶ ταῦτ' ἄγει. οὐ μὴν ἀλλ' εἰ τούτῳ
Πλάτων ἰσχυρίζεται ὡς οὐ πολλήν τινα οὐδ' ἀξίαν
σπουδῆς οὐδὲ λόγου χρείαν ἡ ῥητορικὴ παρέχεται,
ὅτι οὐ τηλικοῦτόν ἐστιν τὸ ἀδικεῖσθαι κακὸν ἡλί-
κον τὸ ἀδικεῖν, τί κωλύει καὶ τοὺς νόμους αὐτὸν
ἅπαντας τοῖς αὐτοῖς τούτοις διαγράφειν; οὐ γὰρ
ἄλλο γ' οὐδὲν ἢ τοῦτο βούλονται, μάλιστα μὲν
μηδένα μηδὲ ὑφ' ἑνὸς πάσχειν κακῶς, εἰ δὲ μή,
δίκην τοῖς παθοῦσιν παρὰ τῶν πραξάντων ἢ τῶν
αἰτίων γίγνεσθαι. ὥστ' οὐ μόνη² ἄπεισιν ἐκ τῶν
πόλεων ἐκκηρυχθεῖσα ὑπὸ τοῦ Πλάτωνος, ἀλλ' ὥσπερ ἑταιρείας καταγνωσθείσης μετὰ τῶν ταῦτα³
συμβουλομένων [τῶν]⁴ νόμων ἐξελαθήσεται· καὶ
τότε ῥητορικὴν ἐκπέμψομεν καὶ προπηλακιοῦμεν,
ὅταν καὶ τοὺς νόμους συνεκπέμψαι καλῶς ἡμῖν ἔχῃ.
272 πότ' οὖν τοῦτο ἂν γένοιτο; τίς ὁ καιρὸς αὐτοῦ;
τῶν Πλάτωνος ἑταίρων ἀποκρινάσθω⁵ τις, ἐπειδήπερ
αὐτὸν οὐκ ἔχομεν παραστήσασθαι.
273 Καὶ μὴν οὐδ' ἐνταῦθα ἔξω μαρτυρίας ἡμῖν παν-

---

¹ τε καὶ TQVA : τε omisso καθ' ὃν add. codd. dett.
² μόνον VA.
³ codd. dett. : ταῦτα TQVA.

permit another to do wrong, in every way oratory is a fair and good thing,[a] in that it is shameful to do wrong, in that to be wronged is better than to wrong, and in that it is wholly best neither to do wrong nor to be wronged. And the true orator appears to be so much better than a good man, to put it simply, by as much as the good man's action affects only himself, but the orator even makes others become good. The fair and good man is not always an orator, but the orator is a fair and good man, who even leads others to this state. Moreover, 271 if Plato asserts firmly that oratory provides a use worthy of no serious consideration or regard on the grounds that it is not as great an evil to be wronged as to do wrong, why does he not erase all the laws for the same reason ? The laws have no other purpose than this : principally that nobody be mistreated by anyone ; but if not, that the sufferers receive justice from the doers or those responsible. Therefore oratory will not leave the cities by itself when it is solemnly expelled by Plato, but as if a political club had been condemned, it will be driven out together with the laws, which are in sympathy with it. Then we shall expel oratory and revile it, whenever it is good for us to expel the laws as well. When would this be ? What is the right moment ? 272 Let one of Plato's comrades answer, since we cannot produce him as a witness.

Indeed, not even here will he stand outside the 273

---

[a] Or " a gentlemanly thing." To a Greek a καλὸς κἀγαθός meant a physically handsome or at least a morally good man of social standing, " a fine gentleman."

⁴ om. codd. dett.
⁵ codd. dett. : ἀποκρινέσθω TQVA.

(84 D.)

τελῶς στήσεται, ἀλλὰ καὶ ἔτι μᾶλλον ἐν τούτοις
ἤπερ ἐν οἷς ἄρτι διέξεισιν φαίνεται μαρτυρῶν. οὐ
85 D. γὰρ περὶ τῶν ἄλλων νόμων οὐδὲ πολιτειῶν δια-
λέξομαι, οὐδ' οὓς ὁ δεῖνα ἔθηκεν, ἀλλ' εἴ τις αὐτὸν
ἔροιτο, ὦ δαιμόνιε καὶ πάντα σὺ θαυμαστὰ εὑρίσκων,
εἰ μηδέν ἐστιν πρᾶγμα τὸ ἀδικεῖσθαι, μηδ' ἡ τοῦτο
κωλύουσα δύναμις μηδενὸς ἀξία λόγου, μηδ' ὁπόσα
ἐστὶν καὶ γίγνεται μηδὲν χρηστόν, ἀλλ' οὕτως ἄ-
τιμον καὶ ἀνελεύθερον ὥστ' εἶναι μόριον κολακείας
καὶ σκιᾶς, τοῦ χάριν οἰκίζων ταύτην τὴν ἐν τῇ
βίβλῳ πόλιν καθίστης αὐτῇ πολιτείαν, ἀφ' ἧς μηδ'
ὁτιοῦν πείσεται, καὶ τὸ μάχιμον χωρὶς τῶν ἄλλων
ἱδρῦσθαι κελεύεις, τιμὴν τὴν πρώτην ἀποδούς, ἵνα
μή τι πάθῃ, μηδὲ ὑπὸ ποίων ἀδικηθῇ πολεμίων; εἰ
γὰρ ἐξήρκει μὴ ἀδικεῖν, τί δέδοικας, εἰ πρὸς τοῦτό
γ' αὐτὴν παρεσκεύακας; εἰ δὲ δὴ καὶ χεῖρον τοῖς
ἀδικοῦσιν ὅταν μὴ διδῶσι δίκην καὶ χρὴ δὴ κατὰ σὲ
καὶ αὐτὸν ἑαυτοῦ κατήγορον ὅταν ἀδικήσῃ γίγνεσθαι
καὶ παιδίων καὶ πατρὸς αὐτοῦ, τοὺς δ' ἐχθροὺς ἐᾶν,
τί οὐ συνεύχῃ τοῖς πολεμίοις ἐπελθεῖν καὶ λαβεῖν
τὴν πόλιν καὶ νὴ Δία τοὺς μὲν ἐν ἡλικίᾳ πάντας
κατακόψαι καὶ ταῦτα πρὸς τοῖς βωμοῖς, παῖδας δὲ[1]
καὶ γυναῖκας ἐξανδραποδίσασθαι πέρα, εἰ βούλει,
Γαδείρων, τὰ δὲ ἱερὰ συλήσαντας κατασκάψαι
πάντα, μὴ λιπεῖν δὲ μηδὲ τοὺς τάφους ἀθῴους τῆς
ἑαυτῶν πλεονεξίας, ἵν' ἀδικήσαντες τὰ μέγιστα ἐν
τοῖς μεγίστοις δὴ κακοῖς ὦσιν μὴ δόντες δίκην,

[1] Phot. : τε TQVA.

range of giving testimony for us, but he clearly gives still more evidence in these matters than he does in those which he has just now recounted. I shall not discuss other laws or constitutions, or those which so-and-so set down. But if someone should ask him, you extraordinary fellow who discovers all these wonderful things, if to be wronged is of no consequence, and the power which prevents this is worth no consideration, and in all that exists and comes into being, is nothing useful, but it is so dishonoured and servile that it is a part of flattery and of a shadow, why in settling your bookish republic do you establish a constitution for it, by which it will be protected, and why do you command that the fighting force be settled apart from the others,[a] paying them the highest honour, so that the city may be safe and not be wronged by any sort of enemy? For if not to do wrong were enough, what fear have you, if you have prepared your city for this at least? And if it is worse for those who do wrong whenever they are not punished and it is fitting according to you [b] for one to denounce himself whenever he does wrong, as well as his children and his father, but to let his enemies go, why do you not pray to your enemies to attack and seize the city, and by Zeus cut down all the grown men, even at the altars, and carry off the women and children as slaves, beyond Gadira,[c] if you wish; and plunder the temples and tear down everything, nor even leave the tombs untouched by their greed, so that having committed the greatest wrongs by not being punished they may suffer the greatest evils. But

---

[a] *Republic* 415 D.   [b] *Gorgias* 480 A ff.
[c] Cadiz in Spain, at the limit of the known world.

(85 D.)

ἀλλὰ τοσοῦτον ἀπέχεις τοῦ ταῦτα συμπράττειν
86 D. ὥστε κωλύεις, προσκόπτεις, βίον ἐν τοῖς ὅπλοις εὔ-
ρηκας, ἵνα μή τι τοιοῦτον γένοιτο· κἄν τις ἐγγένηται προδότης, τοῦτον οὐ στεφανοῦν κελεύεις οὐδὲ κηρύττειν, ἀλλὰ ταὐτὰ τοῖς ἄλλοις περὶ τούτων
274 νομίζεις. καίτοι κατὰ τούτους τοὺς λόγους τίνας
μᾶλλον ἢ τοὺς προδότας ἔδει τιμᾶν, ὅτι τοὺς
οἰκείους καὶ τὴν χώραν καὶ τὰ ἱερὰ καὶ πάντα τὰ
ὄντα ὅπως ὑπὸ τοῖς πολεμίοις ἔσται παρασκευάζου-
σιν, ἵν᾽ ἐκεῖνοι τὰ μέγιστα ἀδικήσαντες τοῖς
275 μεγίστοις ἐνέχωνται[1] κακοῖς; εἰπὲ πρὸς Διὸς τερα-
στίου, τί χρὴ περὶ τούτων ἡμᾶς νομίζειν; εἶεν, ὦ
γενναῖε, νόμους δὲ δὴ τοῦ χάριν ἡμῖν ἐτίθης χωρὶς
αὖ τοσούτους τὸ πλῆθος, οἳ τοῖς τ᾽ εὖ βεβιωκόσι
τιμὰς ὁρίζουσι καὶ τοὺς ὁτιοῦν ἀδικοῦντας ἃ δεῖ πάσχειν λέγουσιν· καὶ ῥητορεύεις καθ᾽ ἕκαστον αὐτῶν
σπουδῇ καὶ τιμᾷς τὰ προοίμια, καὶ παραδείγματα
διττὰ ὥσπερ οἱ πλάσται προτίθης, ὁ τῶν λόγων
καταφρονῶν. εἰ γάρ, ὦ τᾶν, τὸ δίκην λαμβάνειν
καὶ τὸ μὴ ἐᾶν ἀδικεῖν οὐχ ἕν τι τῶν σπουδαίων ἦν,
τοῦ χάριν ταῦτα πραγματεύῃ καὶ σκοπεῖς ὅπως μη-
276 δεὶς ἀδικήσεται; οὐκοῦν ἢ ταῦτα πάντα τοσαῦτα
τὸ πλῆθος ὄντα ἡμαρτῆσθαι δεῖ τούτου ἑνὸς ὀρθῶς
ἔχοντος αὐτῶν, ἢ τάδ᾽ ἐκείνοις ἐξελήλεγκται.

277   Καὶ μὴν ἐν μὲν οἷς ἡμεῖς λέγομεν καὶ τοῖς ἄλ-
87 D. λοις συνδοκοῦν ἐστιν καὶ τῷ Πλάτωνι πρόσεστιν·
ἃ δ᾽ οὗτος ἐνταῦθα εἴρηκεν, οὐ μόνον τοῖς τῶν
πραγμάτων λόγοις, ἀλλὰ καὶ τοῖς αὐτοῦ Πλάτωνος
ἐξελέγχεται καὶ λόγοις καὶ βουλήμασιν. ἐκείνων
μὲν οὖν ὀρθῶς ἔχειν συγχωρουμένων καὶ ἡ παρὰ τῶν

you are so far from doing this, that you block it, fight against it, have invented a life in arms, in order that no such thing may happen. If someone is a traitor, you do not order that this man be publicly honoured, but you hold the same views as other men about these matters. Yet according to these 274 arguments, who ought to be more honoured than traitors? Because they bring it about that their family, land, temples, and all their possessions will fall into the hands of the enemy, so that having committed the greatest wrongs he may suffer the greatest evils. Tell me, by the Zeus of Prodigies, 275 what must we think about these things? Well, noble sir, why have you made so many laws for us besides, which define the honours for those who have lived well, and tell what those who do any wrong must suffer? And why do you orate over each of these so seriously and show a high regard to the preambles, and like the statuaries, display twin examples of them,[a] you who scorn arguments? If sir, receiving justice and not permitting wrong doing were not matters of importance, why do you concern yourself with these things and consider how no one will be wronged? Then all these many points 276 must be mistaken, if this one point is correct, or the latter is refuted by the former.

Indeed, our arguments agree both with others and 277 with Plato as well. His statement here is not only refuted by consideration of the facts, but also by the words and intentions of Plato himself. If those points are conceded to be correct, evidence in support is

---

[a] *Laws* 721 a—723 d.

---

[1] συνέχωνται V, συνέχονται A.

(87 D.)

ἄλλων μαρτυρεῖ δόξα καὶ ψῆφος ὀρθή· ταῦτα δ' εἰ
δοίημεν κρατεῖν, ἄπεστιν τὸ ὁτῳοῦν συνδοκεῖν τῶν
ἄλλων. ἰσχυρότερον δὲ τὸ καὶ ἅπασι καὶ Πλάτωνι
τοῦ μηδενὶ καὶ μηδὲ Πλάτωνι συνδοκεῖν, ὡς οὗτος[1]
278 ἀλλαχοῦ. οὐκοῦν οὐ τὴν παρὰ τούτου μαρτυρίαν
διὰ τὴν παρὰ τῶν ἄλλων φευξούμεθα, ἀλλὰ τῇ τῶν
ἄλλων τὴν παρὰ τούτου προσθήσομεν.[2] ἡγοῦμαι
μὲν τοίνυν κἂν τούτοις τὴν ἔργῳ μαρτυρίαν παρέχεσθαι. [τὸ γὰρ δὴ λόγοις πρὸς λόγους ἀγωνι-
ζόμενον λόγοις ἑτέροις σπουδαίοις μαρτυροῦντα
ἀποφαίνειν τὸν ἀντίπαλον τὴν ἔργῳ παρέχεσθαι
μαρτυρίαν ἐστίν.][3]

279   Οὐ μὴν ἀλλ' ἔτι καὶ προσωτέρω προελθεῖν βούλομαι, ἵνα ἐπειδὴ τιμᾷ τὸ ἕνα ἐπιψηφίζειν καὶ αὐτόν,
πρὸς ὃν ἂν οἱ λόγοι γίγνωνται, καὶ λόγῳ καὶ ἔργῳ
280 σύμψηφον ὄντα αὐτόν μοι δείξω. φέρε δὴ προσέστω
κἂν τούτοις ἐρώτησις, οἷον εἴ τις ἤρετο αὐτόν,
ἡνίκα εἰς Σικελίαν ἔπλει τὸ δεύτερον ἢ τρίτον, ἤτοι
σύμπλους ἢ καὶ αὐτὸς ὁ κυβερνήτης, σὺ δὲ δὴ τοῦ

---

¹ οὗτως TQA.   ² codd. dett. : προσθήσομαι TQVA.
³ secl. Behr.

ᵃ *Gorgias* 471 ε—472 d.

ᵇ [The tradition about Plato's visits to Sicily may be
largely if not wholly a legend :—In the reign of the unconstitutional monarch (" tyrant ") Dionysius II at Syracuse from
367 B.C. onwards, Dion, kinsman of Dionysius II by mar-
riages, and minister of the " tyrant " Dionysius I (who ruled
from 405 to 367 B.C.), wished to transform the " tyranny "
into something in accord with the philosophical theories of
Plato, and so to see Syracuse ruled by a constitutional
monarch—a king—preferably Dionysius II himself.   So
Dion invited Plato, who *c.* 388 B.C. had already made an
unhappy visit to Sicily under Dionysius I, to come from
Athens on a second visit.   Plato reluctantly did so and was at
first acceptable to Dionysius II ; whose enthusiasm soon

forthcoming in the opinion and correct verdict of others. If we should grant these points to be right, there is no agreement with anyone else. Agreement with all and Plato is more convincing than agreement with none and not even Plato, as he appears elsewhere. So we shall not avoid his testimony because of that 278 of others, but shall add his to the others. I believe that even in these matters actual testimony is provided. [For in contending by argument against another argument, to show an opponent bearing witness to the serious arguments of the other side is to provide actual testimony.]

Indeed, I wish to go still further, so that I may 279 show him in agreement both in word and in deed, since he shows a high regard for the approval of the individual with whom the argument takes place.[a] Here let us also add a question : for example if 280 someone asked him, either a fellow passenger or the helmsman himself, when he was sailing to Sicily for the second or third time [b] : please, why are you

wore off. Dion was shortly banished through the hostility of his political enemies, and Plato returned to Athens, only to come yet again to Sicily before 357 B.C. on the entreaties of Dionysius and with hopes of reconciling him to Dion ; without, however, any real results. But Dion himself, after a stay in Athens, returned with forces, and in the troubles which followed had periods of supremacy (more or less), becoming even a " tyrant " himself. He was murdered in 354 B.C. and Dionysius II began a second " tyranny " in 346 B.C. When Timoleon came from Corinth and freed Greek Sicily from its various tyrants in 344 B.C., Dionysius went to live in Corinth. Of the main sources for Plato's relations with Sicily (*Epistles* attributed to Plato, especially VII and VIII ; Plutarch, Cornelius Nepos, Diogenes Laertius, Diodorus) the *Epistles* are usually regarded as forgeries, and the other authorities depend on them.—*E.H.W.*]

(87 D.)

χάριν ἡμῖν ὦ Πλάτων εἰς Σικελίαν πλεῖς;[1] ἢ εἰ μὴ
τότε, ἀλλ' εἴ τις οἴκαδε αὐτὸν ἐπανελθόντα ἤρετο
τὰς τῆς ἀποδημίας καὶ πλάνης αἰτίας καὶ τί δὴ
88 D. μαθὼν[2] τὸ τρίτον αὖθις περὶ τὴν Χάρυβδιν ἐπραγ-
ματεύσατο, περὶ ἣν Ὀδυσσεὺς οὐ πλέον ἢ δίς, τί ἂν
ἀπεκρίνατο αὐτῷ; εἰ γὰρ τὸ βέλτιστον ἀληθὲς
εἶναι δοίημεν, ἔφη Δημοσθένης, ὥσπερ ἀνάγκη
δοῦναι Πλάτωνί γε, ἑτέραν αὐτῷ περὶ ὧν ἀμφισβη-
281 τοῦμεν οὐ λείπει τοῦτο ἀπόκρισιν. διὰ τί; ὅτι,
οἶμαι, ἂν φῆσαι, μᾶλλον δ' εἶπεν,[3] Δίωνος χάριν
ἀνδρὸς ἑταίρου καὶ ξένου πλεῦσαι, θέσθαι βουλόμενος
τὰ πρὸς Διονύσιον αὐτῷ καὶ μὴ περιιδεῖν. εἶτ'
ὦ πλέων καλῶς καὶ δικαίως ἀποδημῶν, σὺ μὲν
ξένου Συρακοσίου[4] κοινοῦ τῆς πατρίδος ἐχθροῦ τῆς
σεαυτοῦ,—οὐ γὰρ προεδρία γ' ἦν Ἀθηναίοις ἐν
Συρακούσαις, ἀλλ' ἃ μηδ' εἰπεῖν ἔστ' ἀδακρυτί,
ταῦθ' ὑπὸ τῶν Δίωνος ἑταίρων καὶ πολιτῶν ὀλίγοις
πρότερον χρόνοις ἐπεπόνθεσαν—ἀλλ' οὖν ἐπειδή γε
ἅπαξ αὐτὸν ἐδέξω φίλον νομίσας, ἔπλεις ἐκείνου
χάριν ἐν γήρᾳ πέλαγος τοσοῦτον, καὶ ταῦτα πρὸς
ἄνδρα παρ' ᾧ πάλιν κινδυνεύειν ἔδει καὶ οὗ συμ-
μαχίαν ὑπισχνουμένου συνῄδεις οὐ δεξαμένην τὴν
σαυτοῦ πατρίδα· καὶ τὸ τυράννῳ συνεῖναι δοκεῖν
οὐκ ἔφευγες, ὡς ἔχων παραμυθίαν τὸ σχῆμα τῆς
διατριβῆς, ὃ[5] Δίωνα μένειν οἴκοι καὶ τῆς οὐσίας
282 κρατεῖν ἦν. τὴν δ' αὐτοῦ[6] τις οἰκῶν καὶ τοῖς αὐτοῦ[7]

---

[1] codd. dett. et Reiske : ἔπλεις TQVA.
[2] παθών codd. dett. (prob. Ddf.).
[3] ἂν φῆσαι—εἶπεν Behr : φῆσαι—εἶπεν ἂν TQVA.
[4] Ddf. : Συρακουσίου TQVA.   [5] ᾧ Reiske, ὅτι Keil.
[6] codd. dett. : αὑτοῦ TQVA.
[7] codd. dett. : αὑτοῦ TQVA.

sailing to Sicily, Plato ? Or if not then, if someone asked him when he had returned home, the cause for his journey abroad and his wandering and what possessed him to be bothered with Charybdis three times, while Odysseus did it no more then twice, what would he answer him ? " For, if we should grant that his best answer were the true one," said Demosthenes,[a] as it is surely necessary to grant to Plato, still no other answer is left to him in the matter of our dispute. Why ? Because, I think, he 281 would say, moreover he *did* say that he sailed for the sake of Dion, a comrade and guest, wishing to set in order his affair with Dionysius and not to neglect it. Next, you who have sailed in a good cause and have travelled abroad for a just reason, did you sail for the sake of a Syracusan stranger, the common enemy of your country—for the Athenians had no special privilege in Syracuse but a few years before suffered at the hands of the comrades and fellow citizens of Dion that which cannot be said without tears [b]—anyhow, since you once had welcomed him and believed him a friend, did you sail for his sake in old age on a great sea, and that too against a man, from whom you must again face danger and whose proffered alliance you knew your country did not receive ? And you did not avoid the appearance of associating with a tyrant, as if consoled by the dignity of your profession, according to which you should have waited for Dion at home and cared for your own property. If someone 282

[a] *Or.* X. 71.
[b] A reference to the terrible imprisonment in the stone-quarries of Syracuse of those Athenians who were captured in the defeat at Syracuse in 413 B.C.

ARISTIDES

89 D. πολίταις καὶ γονεῦσιν καὶ ἀδελφοῖς εἰ τὴν ὅπως μὴ
ἀδικήσονται φυλακὴν ἔχοι καὶ σῴζοι καὶ τούτους
καὶ ἑαυτόν, καὶ νὴ Δία γε, εἰ τοῦτ᾽ αὐτὸ τύραννον
ἔσεσθαι μέλλοντα καὶ Διονυσίῳ προσόμοιον οἷός τ᾽
εἴη κωλῦσαι καὶ παρελέσθαι λόγῳ τὰς πράξεις καὶ
τὴν ἐκ τῶν νόμων ἄδειαν ἅπασι βεβαιῶσαι, ἔπειτ᾽
οὐδὲν σπουδαῖον τοῦτ᾽ εἶναι φήσομεν; οὐδ᾽ ἐπαινεῖν
ἐχρῆν τὴν τοιαύτην εἴτε τέχνην εἴτε μηδὲ τέχνην
εἰπεῖν δεῖ, ὅτι νὴ Δία ἓν μέγα τοῦτ᾽ ἦν κακὸν τὸ
283 ἀδικεῖν, τὸ δὲ ἀδικεῖσθαι πρᾶγμα οὐδέν; ἆρά γε[1]
καὶ μειζόνως τις ἀμύνεται τὸν ἐχθρὸν ἐῶν ἀδικεῖν,
καὶ σκοπούμενος ἐξ ὅτου τρόπου μηδ᾽ ἄλλος δίκην
284 παρ᾽ αὐτοῦ λήψεται; καὶ μὴν ἄχρι μὲν τούτων τῶν
λόγων αἰνίγματ᾽ ἂν εἴποι τις ταῦτ᾽ εἶναι, ἐπηγμένων
δὲ τούτων καὶ ὑπὸ τοῦ Πλάτωνος[2] καὶ ἐξεληλέγχθαι
καὶ λελύσθαι γ᾽, οὐ τὸν εἰωθότα καὶ τὸν αὐτὸν τρόπον τοῖς ἄλλοις αἰνίγμασι δῆλα ἐξ ἀδήλων γεγονότα,
90 D. ἀλλ᾽ ὡς ἀληθῶς δῆλα[3] οὗ τὸ σαθρὸν ἦν αὐτῶν.
285 Φέρε δὴ καὶ ταῦτα σκεψώμεθα. οἶμαι γὰρ ἡμῖν
ὥσπερ ἀπόντος ἐκμαρτυρίαν εἶναι. ἔστι δ᾽ ἐκ τῆς
μακρᾶς ἐπιστολῆς. ''Ταύτῃ μὲν τῇ διανοίᾳ τε καὶ
τόλμῃ ἀπῆρα οἴκοθεν, οὐχ ᾗ τινες ἐδόξαζον, ἀλλ᾽
αἰσχυνόμενος μὲν ἐμαυτὸν τὸ μέγιστον μὴ δόξαιμί
ποτε ἐμαυτῷ παντάπασι λόγος μόνον ἀτεχνῶς εἶναί τις, ἔργου δὲ οὐδενὸς ἄν ποτε ἑκὼν ἀνθάψασθαι,
κινδυνεύειν δὲ προδοῦναι πρῶτον μὲν τὴν Δίωνος
ξενίαν τε καὶ ἑταιρίαν ἐν κινδύνοις ὄντως γεγονότος
οὐ μικροῖς, εἴτ᾽ οὖν πάθοι τι εἴτ᾽ ἐκπεσὼν ὑπὸ
Διονυσίου καὶ τῶν ἄλλων ἐχθρῶν ἔλθοι πρὸς ἡμᾶς

[1] Iunt.: δὲ TQV, om. A.   [2] καὶ ὑπὸ—Πλάτωνος secl. Ddf.
[3] codd. dett.: ἀλλήλων pro ἀδήλων TQ, ἐξ—δῆλα om. VA.

[a] Epist. VII, 328 c—329 A. See Note on § 280.

438

staying at home had a means of protection for his fellow citizens, parents, brothers, so that they might not be wronged, and saved both these and himself, and, by Zeus, if in this way he could even block someone who was going to be a tyrant and like Dionysius, and could do away with his acts through argument and by means of law confirm freedom to all men, then shall we say that this is not a serious matter? And was it not fitting to praise such a practice, whether or not it must be called an art, because by Zeus the commission only of wrong was a great evil, but to be wronged was nothing? Then 283 does anyone more effectively defend himself against his enemy by permitting him to do wrong, and by considering how no one will get justice from him? Indeed, the statements up to this point one might 284 say were riddles, but when these further statements have been introduced, that they have been solved and refuted by Plato himself, not in the customary and same fashion as other riddles, becoming clear after being unclear, but truly making clear where their rottenness lies.

Come now, let us consider the following. For I 285 believe that we have as it were the deposition of an absent witness. It is from the long epistle [a]: "With this intention and daring, I put out from home, not as some thought, but with the feeling of greatest shame over my conduct, lest I ever seem to myself to be in every respect simply talk, but would never willingly apply myself to any action, and to be in danger first of all of betraying the hospitality and comradeship of Dion when he was in no small danger. Then if he should suffer something or having been expelled by Dionysius and his enemies

(90 D.)

φεύγων καὶ ἀνέροιτο εἰπών, Ὦ Πλάτων, ἥκω σοι
φυγὰς οὐχ ὁπλιτῶν δεόμενος οὐδὲ ἱππέων ἐνδεὴς
γενόμενος ἀμύνεσθαι τοὺς ἐχθρούς, ἀλλὰ λόγων καὶ
πειθοῦς, ᾗ σὲ μάλιστα ἠπιστάμην ἐγὼ δυνάμενον
ἀνθρώπους νέους ἐπὶ τὰ ἀγαθὰ καὶ δίκαια προτρέ-
ποντα εἰς φιλίαν τε καὶ ἑταιρίαν ἀλλήλοις καθιστά-
ναι ἑκάστοτε. ὧν ἐνδείᾳ κατὰ τὸ σὸν μέρος νῦν
ἐγὼ καταλιπὼν Συρακούσας ἐνθάδε πάρειμι. καὶ
τὸ μὲν ⟨ἐμὸν⟩[1] ἔλαττον ὄνειδός σοι φέρει· φιλοσοφία
δέ, ἣν ἐγκωμιάζεις ἀεὶ καὶ ἀτίμως φὴς ὑπὸ τῶν
λοιπῶν ἀνθρώπων φέρεσθαι, πῶς οὐ προδέδοται[2]
τὰ[3] νῦν μετ' ἐμοῦ μέρος ὅσον ἐπὶ σοὶ γέγονεν; καὶ
Μεγαροῖ μὲν εἰ κατοικοῦντες ἐτυγχάνομεν, ἦλθες
ἂν δήπου μοι βοηθὸς ἐφ' ἅ σε παρεκάλουν, ἢ πάντων
ἂν φαυλότατον ἡγοῦ σαυτόν· νῦν δ' ἄρα τὸ μῆκος
τῆς πορείας καὶ τὸ μέγεθος δήπου τοῦ πλοῦ καὶ τοῦ

91 D. πόνου ἐπαιτιώμενος οἴει δόξαν κακίας ἀποφεύξεῖ-
σθαί ποτε; πολλοῦ γε καὶ δεήσει. λεχθέντων δὲ
τούτων τίς ἦν μοι ἂν πρὸς ταῦτα εὐσχήμων ἀπόκρι-

286 σις; οὐκ ἔστι." ταῦτα οὐχ ἕτερος περὶ αὐτοῦ
γεγράφηκεν, οὐδὲ εἰκάζων τὴν ἐκείνου γνώμην, ἀλλ'
ὁ κάλλιστα εἰδὼς αὐτὸς περὶ αὐτοῦ τούτων φησὶν
χάριν ἐλθεῖν, τοὺς ὑπὸ τοῦ Δίωνος ἂν λεχθέντας
τούτους λόγους πρὸς αὐτὸν αἰσχυνθείς. καὶ ἔγωγε

287 πιστεύω. μαινοίμην γὰρ ἄν, εἰ μή. οὐκοῦν ἐν
τούτοις ἐστίν, ἥκω σοι, ὦ Πλάτων, οὐχ ὁπλιτῶν
⟨δεόμενος⟩[4] οὐδ' ἱππέων ἔρημος γενόμενος, ἀλλὰ
λόγων καὶ πειθοῦς· ταῦτα δ' ᾤμην παντὸς μᾶλλον

---

[1] add. Behr ex Plat.   [2] προδόται T a. corr. VA.

should come to us in exile, and should put a question to us, saying, ' Plato, I come to you an exile, not wanting hoplites nor being in need of horsemen to ward off my enemies, but of argument and persuasion, by which I knew that you were most able in your encouragement of young men in good and just conduct always to bring them into friendship and comradeship with one another. In need of these things as far as you can help, I have now left Syracuse and am here. My situation brings less shame to you. But as for philosophy which you are always praising and of which you say that it is dishonoured by other men, how is it not betrayed now along with me, as far as you are concerned ? And if we happened to live in Megara, you would come to aid me for whatever purpose I summoned you, or you would believe yourself to be the worst of all men. But as it is, by complaining of the length of the journey and the greatness of the voyage, I suppose, and of the effort, do you think that you will ever escape a reputation for cowardice ? Far from it ! ' When all this has been said, what seemly answer could I make ? None."
Another did not write this about him, conjecturing 286 his attitude, but he who knew best about himself says that he went for these reasons, ashamed of these words which would have been said by Dion to him. And I at least believe him. I should be insane, if I did not. Well, in these words of Dion are found : 287 " I come to you, Plato, not wanting hoplites, nor being bereft of horsemen, but of argument and persuasion. I thought that you had this more than

---

³ om. VA.

⁴ add. codd. dett. : δεόμενος om. TQ, οὐχ—δεόμενος om. VA.

(91 D.)

εἶναι παρὰ σοί. καλῶς γε, ὦ Πλάτων, αὐτός τε
λέγων καὶ τὸν Δίωνα ταῦτ᾽ εἰπεῖν ἂν νομίζων πρὸς
288 σέ. οὐκοῦν εἰ τὸ μὲν ἐκπεσεῖν ἢ παθεῖν τι Δίωνα
δεινὸν περιφανῶς, τὸ δ᾽ ὅπως μὴ ἐκπεσεῖται πρᾶξαι
καλὸν καὶ δίκαιον, οὕτω δ᾽ ἔχων λόγων[1] καὶ πειθοῦς
ἐδεῖτο, σὺ δὲ τῷ ταῦτ᾽ ἔχειν ἔπλεις, ὡμολόγηκας
ἅπαντα, καὶ δεῖν σπουδάζειν ὅπως τις ἐκ τῶν
δυνατῶν μὴ ἀδικήσεται, καὶ τὴν τῶν λόγων τοῦ
πείθειν δύναμιν οὐ φαύλην εἶναι, καὶ τοὺς πείθοντας
ὑπὲρ τούτων οὐ μόνον παρ᾽ ἀνθρώποις ἐπαίνων
ἀξίους, ἀλλὰ καὶ παρὰ θεοῖς ἀμέμπτους, εἴπερ τοὺς
ἐλλείποντας οὐδὲ ὁσίους. ἔτι δ᾽ αὖ τὸ πλέον τῷ
παντὶ πεποίηκας, εἴ γε μὴ μόνον δῆμον μηδὲ δικα-
στάς, ἀλλὰ καὶ τυράννους ὑπὲρ τούτων μὴ δεῖ[2]
92 D. φεύγειν μεταπείθειν καὶ τοσοῦτον ὑπερορίους. αὐτὴν
289 τοίνυν ὅλως τὴν ἐπιστολὴν τοῦ χάριν ἢ πειθοῦς
γέγραφεν; καὶ μὴν αὐτό γε δηλοῖ τὸ πρᾶγμα καὶ
τῆς ἐπιστολῆς αὐτὸς πολλαχοῦ. καὶ γὰρ τὸ ὦν
χάριν ἦλθεν διεξιέναι καὶ προσομολογεῖν ὅτι διὰ
τοῦτο διεξέρχεται ὅπως τὴν ἀληθῆ δόξαν περὶ
290 αὐτοῦ[3] παραστήσειε πείθοντός ἐστιν. οὐκοῦν καὶ
ἵνα πείσῃ γέγραφεν καὶ γράφων τοῦ πεῖσαι χάριν
φησὶν ἀπελθεῖν, μή τι πάθοι Δίων ἔρημος λόγων.
291 πῶς οὖν αἰσχρὰ ποιοῦσιν οἱ ῥήτορες; ἢ καθ᾽
ὁπότερον τούτων φαῦλον ἡ ῥητορική; πότερον καθ᾽
ὃ τοῖς ἀδικουμένοις πέφυκε βοηθεῖν, κἂν ἀδοξία τις
καὶ κίνδυνος προσῇ; ἀλλ᾽ ὅτι τοῦ γε λόγῳ πείθειν
καταφρονητέον; ἀλλ᾽ αὐτὸς ὡς λόγῳ πείσων, ἔργῳ
292 φῂς κινδυνεῦσαι. καὶ Μεγαροῖ μὲν εἰ κατοικοῦντες

---

[1] codd. dett. : λόγου TQVA. [2] Canter : δεῖν TQVA.
[3] codd. dett. : αὐτοῦ TQVA.

anyone." Well done, Plato! Both in what you said and in what you believed that Dion would have said to you. If Dion's expulsion or his suffering some- 288 thing was clearly terrible, and it was fair and just to have acted so that he would not be expelled, and in this state he had need of argument and persuasion, and you sailed because you possessed these, then you have confessed all, that serious action must be taken so that as far as possible someone will not be wronged and that the power of words to persuade is no mean thing, and that those who use persuasion for these ends are not only worthy of praise among men, but also are blameless among the Gods, since those who fail in this are impious. You have also brought this about all the more, if for these ends it is necessary not to avoid winning over not only the people and jurors, but also even very distant tyrants. For 289 what reason did he write the letter at all, other than for persuasion? Indeed, both the subject matter and he himself make this clear in many places in the letter. For it is the act of one using persuasion to recount the reasons for which he went and to admit besides that he gives this narration so that he may present the true opinion about himself. Thus he 290 wrote so that he might persuade, and in his writing he says that he went for the sake of persuasion, lest Dion, bereft of argument, suffer in some way. How then do orators do shameful things? Or in 291 which of these two ways is oratory bad? In that its nature is to aid those who are wronged, even if loss of reputation and danger are attendant? Or because the use of persuasion in argument must be scorned? But you yourself to persuade in argument say that you faced danger in fact. "And if we happened to 292

(92 D.)

ἐτυγχάνομεν, ὁ Δίων σοι λέγει, ἦλθες δήπου ἂν
μοι βοηθὸς ἐφ' ἅ σε παρεκάλουν, ἢ πάντων ἂν
φαυλότατον ἡγοῦ σαυτόν· νῦν δ' ἄρα τὸ μῆκος τῆς
πορείας καὶ τὸ μέγεθος δὴ τοῦ πλοῦ καὶ τοῦ πόνου
ἐπαιτιώμενος οἴει δόξαν κακίας ἀποφευξεῖσθαι[1]
293 ποτε; πολλοῦ γε καὶ δεήσει. τί οὖν; εἴ τις μεταστρέψας ὡδὶ φαίη πρὸς αὐτόν σε, Καὶ πλεῖν μὲν εἰς
Σικελίαν καὶ πάσχειν ὁτιοῦν οἴει δεῖν ὑπὲρ τοῦ τινὰ
πεῖσαι ὡς χρή τινα τῶν ἐπιτηδείων οἴκοι μένειν· εἰ
δέ τις μηδ' ὅσον Ἀθήνηθεν Μέγαράδε, ἀλλὰ μηδ'
ἐλθεῖν ποι τὸ παράπαν δέον, ἀλλ' οἴκοι μένοντα
τοὺς ἑαυτοῦ σῶσαι, τὴν ἐπὶ τούτῳ[2] δύναμιν μετα-
χειρίζεται, οὐκ οἴει τοῦτον δόξαν κακίας ἀποπεφευ-
93 D. γέναι πᾶσαν; πάλαι γε καὶ παρ' αὐτῷ σοι, εἴπερ
294 γέ τι τῶν προειρημένων ὄφελος. πῶς οὖν ὁμοῦ μὲν
ὁ μὴ βοηθῶν τῷ λόγῳ δόξαν κακίας ἐξοίσεται, ὁμοῦ
δ' ὁ βοηθῶν δόξαν κακίας[3] οὐ φεύξεται; οὐ τοίνυν
τοῦτο λέγεις ὅταν καλῇς κολακείαν τὴν ῥητορικὴν ᾗ
ταῦτα ἀνάκειται; τίς ἂν ἦν μοι, φησί, πρὸς ταῦτα
εὐσχήμων ἀπόκρισις; πρὸς δ' ἅ νῦν ἡμεῖς ἐρωτῶ-
μεν, τίς ὦ πρὸς θεῶν;

295   Μικρὸν δέ τι βούλομαι διαλαβεῖν, μή τις ὅλως
οἰηθῇ με τοῖς λόγοις κατηγορεῖν Πλάτωνος, ἢ λέγειν κακῶς μετὰ ἀφορμῆς. ἐγὼ γὰρ οὔτ' αὐτὸς
[ἐπ'][4] ἔγκλημα δήπου τοῦτο ποιοῦμαι εἴ ποι καὶ
ὁπωσοῦν ᾠήθη δεῖν Πλάτων ἐλθεῖν ἡστινοσοῦν
ἕνεκα αἰτίας οὔθ' ὅστις ἄλλος προφέρει τι τοιοῦτον
εὖ φρονεῖν ἡγοῦμαι, οὔθ' ὅλως ἔξω τῶν εἰς τὸν

---

[1] codd. dett. : ἀποφεύξεσθαί TQVA.
[2] codd. dett. : τούτων TQVA.
[3] codd. dett. : κακίας δόξαν TQVA.   [4] secl. Reiske.

live at Megara," Dion says to you, " you would have come to aid me for whatever purpose I summoned you, or you would have believed yourself to be the worst of all men. But as it is, by complaining of the length of the journey and the greatness, I suppose, of the voyage and the effort, do you think that you will ever escape a reputation for cowardice ? Far from it." Well ? Suppose someone changed this 293 around and said to you yourself, Do you think that you must sail to Sicily and suffer anything so as to persuade someone that it is fitting that one's friends should remain at home ? But if it were unnecessary to go as far as from Athens to Megara, or even to go anywhere at all, but by staying at home one could save his family, and someone employs a power which has this faculty, do you not think that he has entirely escaped a reputation for cowardice ? You long ago set the example, if there is any significance in what has been just said. How 294 then will he, who does not assist with his art of oratory, get a reputation for baseness, while he, who does assist, will not escape one for baseness ? Do you not say this when you call oratory, to which these matters refer, flattery ? " What seemly answer could I make," he says. But what answer, by the Gods, to our present questions ?

I wish to make one small distinction, so that no one 295 at all may think that in these arguments I am using this occasion to accuse or slander Plato. For, I do assure you, neither do I make a charge of this if in some way Plato thought that he must go abroad for any reason, nor do I believe that whoever proposes something of this kind is sensible, nor am I unnecessarily concerned with anything entirely

(93 D.)

λόγον ἡκόντων οὐδὲν περιεργάζομαι, μὴ τοσούτου
μηδὲν ἄξιον ἔστω νικητήριον, ἀλλ' ἃ αὐτὸς ἔπραξεν
καὶ τίνων¹ ἔπραξεν χάριν αὐτὸς καθαρῶς εἴρηκεν,
ταῦτα συμβαίνειν φημὶ τοῖς ὑπὲρ τῆς ῥητορικῆς
94 D. λόγοις· καὶ τοσούτῳ² δέω κακίζειν ἐκεῖνον τούτοις,
ὥστ' εἰ δεῖ καὶ τοῦτο εἰπεῖν, καὶ ἐν αὐτοῖς τούτοις
σεμνύνειν αὐτὸν ἡγοῦμαι, εἰ τούτων ἐκείνοις ὑπεναντίως ἐχόντων μὴ τὰ ἔργα μηδὲ τὰς πράξεις αὐτοῦ
διαβάλλω, ἀλλ' ἐκ τοῦ βίου καὶ τῶν ἔργων ἃ μεθ'
ἡμῶν καὶ ὧν ἡμεῖς ἀξιοῦμεν εἶναι τίθημι,³ ταῦθ'
296 ἑτέρως ἔχοντα ἢ ὥς τις⁴ πιστεύσειεν ἀποφαίνω. ὅτε
τοίνυν ἑώρα Δίωνα παρασκευαζόμενον καὶ πράττοντα ὅπως δίκην ὧν ἔπαθεν λήψεται, πότερόν ποτε
ἐᾶν καὶ παρ' οὐδὲν ἄγειν ἐπιστέλλων αὐτῷ φαίνεται
καὶ ὡς, εἰ μισεῖ τὸν Διονύσιον καὶ κακόνουν ⟨εἶναι⟩⁵
ὑπολαμβάνει, χρὴ περιορᾶν καὶ συγχωρεῖν ὅπως τὰ
μέγιστ' ἀδικῶν ἐν τοῖς ἐσχάτοις ᾖ κακοῖς, ἢ πολὺ
τοὐναντίον προτρέπων καὶ θεραπευτικὸν ἀξιῶν εἶναι ὅπως ὡς πλείστους⁶ τοὺς συμπράττοντας ἐπ'
αὐτὸν ἔχοι· καὶ τὸν μὲν Διονύσιον πάντως⁷ ἐχθρὸν
τιθείς, τὸ δὲ ὅπως ἀμυνεῖται συμβουλεύων σκοπεῖν
καὶ τό γ' ἐφ' αὑτῷ συμπράττων, τὸ συμπλεῖν καὶ
συστρατεύειν μόνον ἐξαρνούμενος· ὡς ἐπειδήπερ
αὐτὸν ἔχων ὁ Διονύσιος ἠδέσθη τότε καὶ οὐκ ἀπέ-
95 D. κτεινεν, οὐχὶ καλῶς ἔχον ἐλθεῖν ἐπ' αὐτόν; καίτοι
297 εἴ γε τοὺς ἐχθροὺς καὶ οὓς καθ' ὑπερβολὴν μισεῖ τις
ἐατέον ἦν ἀδικοῦντας, καὶ ἡ ῥητορικὴ φαῦλον καὶ

---

¹ Ddf. ex or. iv, p. 420 D. : ἃ τινῶν TQ, ἃ τίνων codd. dett.,
ἃ τιν' ὧν VA.
² codd. dett., cf. or. iv, p. 420 D. : τοσούτου TQVA.
³ Canter ex or. iv, p. 421 D. : τίθησι TQVA.
⁴ codd. dett. : ὅστις TQVA.
⁵ add. codd. dett.   ⁹ εἶναι—πλείστους om. VA.

outside the realm of the argument—let no victory-prize be so valuable— ; but I claim that what he did and the clear reasons he gave for doing it, are in agreement with these arguments in defence of oratory. And I am so far from reviling him with these arguments, that if even this must be said, I believe that I honour him even in making them, if, while his two positions contradict one another, I traduce neither his deeds nor actions, but I show from his life and acts, which I hold to be in agreement with us and our beliefs, that his position is otherwise than one would believe. When he saw 296 Dion preparing and working to get justice for what he suffered, then is he clearly commanding him[a] to ignore the matter and do nothing ?—and advising that, if he hates Dionysius and apprehends him to be hostile, it is fitting to ignore him and give way, so that by committing the greatest wrongs, Dionysius may suffer extreme evil ? Or is his encouragement far different, and does he deem it salutary that he raise as many fellow conspirators as possible against him ? And while regarding Dionysius in every way an enemy and counselling the plan for revenge and aiding within his power, does he refuse only to join the expedition and campaign, because it is not fair to attack him since when Dionysius had him in his power he respected him and did not kill him ? Yet if 297 enemies and those whom one thoroughly hates, must be left free to do wrong, and oratory which

---

[a] The account is in *Epist.* VII, 350 B ff. Aristides' use of the verb ἐπιστέλλειν, " to write to " or " to command," may have been intentional.

---

⁷ Iunt. : πάντων TQVA.

(95 D.)

ἄχρηστον ἡ δίκην ποιοῦσα παρ᾽ αὐτῶν εἶναι λαμβάνειν καὶ μὴ ἐῶσα προχωρεῖν ὡς ἐπὶ πλεῖστον, χρῆν
δήπουθεν αὐτὸν μάλιστα μὲν διακωλύειν τὸν Δίωνα,
ἑταῖρόν γε αὐτοῦ καὶ μαθητὴν ὄντα, καὶ ὑπομιμνή-
σκειν ὧν ποτ᾽ ἤκουσεν, εἴπερ ἤκουσεν, εἰ δὲ μή,
τότε[1] ἐπὶ τῶν ἔργων διδάσκειν ὅτι χρὴ φέρειν σιγῇ
καὶ σκοπεῖν ὅπως μὴ μόνον αὐτὸς στερήσεται τῆς
πατρίδος καὶ τῶν αὐτοῦ[2] ὑπὸ Διονυσίου,[3] ἀλλὰ καὶ
ἄλλοι πολλοὶ καὶ ταῦτα καὶ τοιαῦθ᾽ ἕτερα πείσονται
διὰ τέλους καὶ μὴ διαλείψει πάντας ἀνθρώπους
ἀδικῶν Διονύσιος· καὶ ὅπως γε μὴ μόνον Σικελίας
ἔσται τύραννος, ἀλλὰ καὶ Καρχηδόνος καὶ Λιβύης,
εἰ οἷόν τε, καὶ συμπάσης [καὶ][4] νὴ Δία τῆς γε
Εὐρώπης, εἰ δέ τις εἴη μηχανή, καὶ τῆς Ἀσίας συν-
εύξασθαι· καὶ μὴ μόνον αὐτὸν μηδὲν ἐνθυμεῖσθαι
περὶ καταλύσεως τοῦ τυράννου, ἀλλ᾽ ὅπως μηδ᾽
ἄλλος μηδεὶς ἐπιθήσεται μήτε ἐπ᾽ ἀναιρέσει μήθ᾽
ὥστ᾽ ἐκβαλεῖν, ἀλλὰ τοὐναντίον φυλακὴν τοῦ σώματος Διονυσίῳ φροντίσαι, ὅπως ἀθάνατος ᾖ πονη-
ρός, καὶ πάντας πάντ᾽ ἀδικῶν ἐν ἅπασι τοῖς χρόνοις
298 ἐν ἅπασι τοῖς κακοῖς ᾖ. μάλιστα μὲν ταῦτα ἐχρῆν
96 D. προδιδάσκειν[5] τὸν Δίωνα καὶ νουθετεῖν, εἴπερ τούτοις τοῖς λόγοις ἐπίστευεν, εἰ δὲ μή, σκοπουμένῳ
γε περὶ τιμωρίας μὴ συμπράττοντα φαίνεσθαι· ὃ
πολλοῦ δεῖ ποιήσας, ἔργῳ μάρτυς ἡμῖν περὶ ὧν
ἀπιστοῦμεν γεγένηται τοῦ[6] μὴ ληρεῖν.
299 Βούλομαι τοίνυν αὐτὸν καὶ πανοικησίᾳ τρόπον
τινὰ μαρτυροῦντα ἐπιδεῖξαι. ὁ γὰρ ἐν Ποτιδαίᾳ
παραταττόμενος Σωκράτης καὶ πάλιν γ᾽ ἐπὶ Δηλίῳ[7]

---

[1] τό γε VA.   [2] Reiske : αὐτῶν TQVA, αὐτοῦ codd. dett.
[3] ὑπὸ Διονυσίου secl. Keil.   [4] om. codd. dett.

causes them to be punished and does not let them get away with as much as possible is a bad and useless thing, he ought certainly to have restrained Dion, who was his comrade and pupil, even reminding him of his lectures, if he heard them ; and if not, then he ought to have taught him at the moment of action that these things must be borne in silence and he must make plans so that not only will he be deprived of his country and possessions by Dionysius, but also many others will unceasingly suffer this and more, and so that Dionysius will never stop wronging all mankind ; and so that he will be tyrant not only of Sicily, but also of Carthage and Africa if possible and, by Zeus, of all Europe, and if there should be some means, that he must include Asia in his prayers ; and that he must not only consider nothing about overthrowing the tyrant, but he must take care that no one else attacks him to kill or expel him, but on the contrary, he must be concerned with Dionysius' physical protection, so that he may be immortally evil, and wronging everybody in every way through all time be involved in every evil. It was especially fitting to have given this instruction 298 and admonition to Dion, if he believed in these arguments and if not, at least not to be clearly acting with him in his deliberations for vengeance. Far from doing this, he has become in fact a witness for us, that our doubts were not foolish.

I wish to show him in a way bearing witness for 299 our case with his whole household. Socrates in the ranks at Potidaea and again at Delium, retreating

---

⁵ codd. dett. : προσδιδάσκειν TQVA.
⁶ codd. dett. : τὸ TQVA.   ⁷ codd. dett. : Δήλῳ TQVA.

(96 D.)

καὶ τῆς τροπῆς συμβάσης ἀναχωρῶν, δῆλος ὢν
παντὶ καὶ πάνυ πόρρωθεν ὅτι εἴ τις ἅψεται τούτου
τοῦ ἀνδρός, μάλα ἐρρωμένως ἀμυνεῖται, πῶς οὐ
σαφῶς οὑτοσὶ¹ μαρτυρεῖ τοῖς ἀδικεῖν ἐπιχειροῦσιν
μὴ δεῖν ἐπιτρέπειν; οὐδεὶς ἀντερεῖ δήπουθεν. οὐ
γὰρ ἃ² καὶ τελευτᾶν ὡραῖον ἤδη νομίζων εἶναι καὶ
χαλεπὸν τὰς πολλὰς διαβολὰς ἐξελεῖν ἐκ πολλοῦ καὶ
ὑπὸ πολλῶν συνειλεγμένας ὕστερον εἶπεν, [ἢ οὐ ἐν
γήρᾳ]³ οὐ ταῦτ' ἐστὶν ἰσχυρὰ τεκμήρια τῆς ἐκείνου
γνώμης, ἀλλ' ἃ κωλύειν ἢ μὴ κύριος ὢν ἐφαίνετο
ποιῶν. διὸ δὴ καὶ ἀσφαλῶς, φησίν, ἀπῄει καὶ
οὗτος καὶ ὁ ἑταῖρος· σχεδὸν γάρ τι τῶν οὕτω
διακειμένων οὐδὲ ἅπτονται ἐν τῷ πολέμῳ, ἀλλὰ
τοὺς προτροπάδην φεύγοντας μᾶλλον⁴ διώκουσιν.

97 D. [τουτὶ γὰρ⁵ προσγέγονεν πλέον ἐκ τούτων αὐτῷ,
πάλιν σὺν τῷ Σωκράτει Πλάτωνος Πλάτωνα αὐτὸν
συμμαρτυρῆσαι τῷ λόγῳ· τῶν οὕτω διακειμένων οὐ
πάνυ τι ἅπτονται, ἀλλὰ τοὺς προτροπάδην φεύγοντας
μᾶλλον διώκουσιν. δηλονότι κἂν ταῖς πολιτείαις
τῶν μὲν οὕτω διακειμένων ὡς ἀμύνεσθαι οὐ πάνυ τι
ἅπτονται οἱ τὰ τοιαῦτα τηροῦντες, τοὺς δ' ὑπείκοντας
διώκουσιν. ὥστ' εἰ τοὺς ἐν τοῖς πολέμοις ἀνδρείους
ἐπαινεῖν εἰκός, καὶ τοὺς ἐνταῦθα τοιούτους.]⁶ ὥστ'
εἰ μηδὲ δι' ἓν ἄλλο, διὰ τοὺς συκοφάντας ἡ ῥητορικὴ
300 καλόν. καὶ μὴν εἰ μὴ θαρροῦσι τοὺς τοιούτους ἀδικεῖν, ἄμφω χρηστὰ συμβαίνει καὶ τοῖς ἄρτι λόγοις
ἀκόλουθα, μήτ' αὐτὸν ἀδικεῖσθαι μήθ' ἕτερον ἀδικεῖν ἐᾶν.

---

¹ codd. dett.: οὑτωσὶ TQVA.   ² ἂν TQVA a. corr.
³ secl. Ddf.   ⁴ codd. dett.: μᾶλλον φεύγοντας TQVA.
⁵ om. VA.   ⁶ secl. Behr.

when the rout occurred, " made it clear to all even
from afar that if someone touched him, he would
fiercely protect himself." [a]   Does he not clearly
bear witness that we should not let those who attempt
to commit wrong have their way ? No one surely
will dispute it.   For his later remarks, when he
thought that it was time to die and difficult to remove
the many calumnies which long had gathered from
many sources,[b] are not strong evidence of his belief,
but the evidence is rather in what he clearly did,
when he had the power to prevent these things or
not.   " So," he says, " he and his comrade went
off in safety.   For in war time those so disposed
are usually not troubled, but rather those in headlong
flight are pursued."   [For he has gained this advantage from the passage, that Plato himself together
with the Socrates of Plato has again testified for his
argument.   Those so disposed are not at all troubled,
but rather those in headlong flight are pursued.
Clearly also in government, men who observe such
things do not at all trouble those so disposed to
defend themselves, but prosecute those who give
way.   Therefore if it is reasonable to praise the
courageous in war, we should also praise such men
here.]   Therefore if for no other reason, oratory is a
fair thing because of slanderers.   Indeed, if they 300
lack the courage to wrong such men, both advantages result, consistent with the present argument,
that neither he himself is wronged nor does he permit
another to do wrong.

---

[a] Socrates served as a soldier at Potidaea in 432 B.C. and
at the Battle of Delium in 424 B.C. ; *cf.* Plato, *Symposium*
220 E—221 B.   His comrade was Alcibiades.

[b] Plato, *Apology* 19 A.

(97 D.)

301 Ὁ τοίνυν καὶ μέχρι τοῦ Βαβυλωνίου πεδίου
Κύρῳ συνανιὼν Ξενοφῶν ἐπὶ τὸν ἀδελφὸν αὐτοῦ
στρατεύοντι ἀδικήσαντα πρότερον, πῶς οὐ καὶ οὗτος
οἴκοθεν ὢν Πλάτωνι μάρτυς ἡμῖν ἐστιν εἰς τοὺς
παρόντας τουτουσὶ λόγους; οὐ γὰρ ἐκεῖνό γε
ἔστιν εἰπεῖν, ὡς ἐν μὲν τοῖς ὅπλοις καὶ ὑπὲρ τῶν
ἀλλοτρίων εἰκός ἐστιν ἀμύνεσθαι τοὺς ἀδικεῖν ἐπιχειροῦντας, εἰ δέ τις λόγῳ ταὐτὸν τοῦτο ποιοίη,
φαυλίζειν, κἂν ὑπὲρ ὧν αὐτὸς πέπονθεν ἐπεξίῃ·
οὐδέ γ' ἐκεῖνο μᾶλλον οὐκ ἔστιν εἰπεῖν, ὡς τὸ μὲν
τοῖς ὅπλοις ἀμύνεσθαι τοῖς ἐν τοῖς λόγοις βεβιωκόσι
τῶν προσηκόντων ἐστίν, τὸ δὲ αὐτοῖς τοῖς λόγοις
ἀμύνεσθαι ἐν ἀλογίᾳ θετέον. οὐδ' ἂν εἷς εἴποι
302 ταῦτα. καὶ μὴν ὅσῳ κάλλιον φρόνησις ἀνδρείας,
98 D. τοσούτῳ ῥητορικὴ τῆς κατὰ πόλεμον εὐψυχίας. εἰ
γὰρ δεῖ συνελόντα εἰπεῖν, οὐδέν ἐστιν ἄλλο ῥητορικὴ
ἢ φρόνησις λόγων δύναμιν προσειληφυῖα, ὡς μὴ
μόνον αὐτός ⟨τις⟩ εὑρεῖν[1] τὰ βέλτιστα, ἀλλὰ καὶ
303 ἑτέρους πείθειν ἔχοι. ἡγοῦμαι μὲν τοίνυν καὶ ταῦτ'
ἔχειν πίστεις ἱκανὰς τῆς ἀληθείας, εἰ μὴ καὶ
πλείους ἄρα τῶν ἱκανῶν.

304 Εἶμι δ' ἐπ' αὐτὸν ἤδη τὸν κολοφῶνα τῶν[2] Πλάτωνος, ὡς ἄν τις εἴποι, ῥημάτων.[3] οὐ γὰρ μόνον ἐξ
ὧν ἐλέγχεται βούλομαι φανῆναι μαρτυροῦντ' αὐτόν,
ἀλλὰ καὶ ὥσπερ ἂν εἰ παραστὰς αὐτὸς ἐμαρτύρει τῇ
ἑαυτοῦ φωνῇ. Ἐκ τῶν Νόμων[4]· ''Τοῖς δὲ εὐδαι-
μόνως ζῶσιν ὑπάρχειν ἀνάγκη πρῶτον τὸ μήτε
ἀδικεῖν ἄλλους μήτε ὑφ' ἑτέρων αὐτοὺς ἀδικεῖσθαι.

---

[1] Behr : ἔρδειν TQVA.
[2] cod. det. : τοῦ VA, om. TQ Phot., τῶν τοῦ plerique codd.
dett.
[3] codd. dett. : ῥήματι TQVA Phot.
[4] Ἐκ—Νόμων om. edd.

Xenophon accompanied Cyrus up-country as far as 301 the plain of Babylon, when he warred against his brother who had first wronged him.[a] Is he not also, being of the same stock as Plato, a witness for us in these present arguments? For it cannot be said that it is reasonable to fight under arms and for a cause not one's own against those who endeavour to commit wrong, but to belittle someone if he should do the same thing through argument, indeed if he prosecutes in a cause in which he has suffered. Still less can it be said that to fight with weapons is a proper thing for those who have spent their lives in the practice of oratory, but that fighting even with oratory must be regarded as senseless. No one would say this. Indeed, by as much as intelligence is a finer thing 302 than courage, to this degree oratory is finer than valour in war. For if I must speak briefly, oratory is nothing other than intelligence which has combined the faculty of argument, so that not only can someone himself find what is best, but also can persuade others. I believe that these points have sufficient 303 proof of their truth, if not even more than sufficient.

I shall come now to " the summit," as one might 304 say [b] of Plato's argument. For I not only wish for him clearly to bear witness in points where he is refuted, but also as if present he bore witness with his own voice.[c] From *The Laws* : " For those who live a happy life first of all it is necessary neither to wrong others nor to be wronged by others. Of these two the

---

[a] 401 B.C.; *cf. Anabasis* I. 7. 1 ff.
[b] *Cf. Laws* 673 D.
[c] *Laws* 829 A. " From *The Laws* " is used in imitation of the passages where evidence is cited in the texts of the Attic orators.

(98 D.)

τούτοιν δὲ τὸ μὲν οὐ πάνυ χαλεπόν, τοῦ δὲ μὴ
ἀδικεῖσθαι κτήσασθαι δύναμιν παγχάλεπον· καὶ οὐκ
ἔστιν αὐτὸ τελέως ἔχειν ἄλλως ἢ τελέως γενόμενον
ἀγαθόν.'' ἰοῦ ἰοῦ τῆς μαρτυρίας. τούτων ἐδεόμην.
ταῦτα λέγει Πλάτων, ὁ τοῦ ἐπιγράμματος μετέχων
καὶ δι' ὃν τὸ 'Αρίστωνος γένος θεῖον ὡς ἀληθῶς.
305 τελέως ἄρα, ὦ δαιμόνιε, ῥητορικὴ καλὸν καὶ οὐ
πρὸς παντὸς οὔτε λαβεῖν οὔτε κεκτῆσθαι. φαίνῃ
γὰρ καὶ σὺ τοῦτό γε συγχωρῶν, ὅτι ἐπὶ τῷ μὴ
ἀδικεῖσθαι τέτακται. οὐκοῦν ὅτ' ἀδικεῖν μὲν οὐκ
ἐπηνάγκαζεν, ἀδικεῖσθαι δ' οὐκ ἐᾷ, ὡς δ' ἐκ τοῦ λόγου συνέβαινεν, οὐδέτερον τούτων ἐᾷ, οὔτ' ἀδικεῖν
οὔτ' ἀδικεῖσθαι, εἰ μὲν καὶ τῆς φιλοσοφίας ὁ αὐτός
ἐστιν ὅρος, φιλοσοφία τις οὖσα ἡ ῥητορικὴ φαίνεται.
εἰ δ' ἐξαρκεῖ τῇ φιλοσοφίᾳ μὴ ἀδικεῖν, ἡ ῥητορικὴ
99 D. τελεώτερον· τὸ γὰρ χαλεπώτερον κτήσασθαι καὶ
μεῖζον ἤδη προστίθησιν, ὅπως μηδ' αὐτὸς ὑπ' ἄλλων
306 ἀδικήσεται. πῶς οὖν τὸ αὐτὸ ἅμα μὲν τελέως
ἀγαθὸν καὶ μέγιστον τῶν ἀγαθῶν, ἅμα δ' ἔσχατον
τῶν κακῶν καὶ κολακεία; ἢ¹ πῶς ἐλάχιστον οἱ
ῥήτορες δύνανται, εἴ γε οὗ καὶ παγχάλεπον κτήσασθαι δύναμιν, τοῦτ' αὐτοῖς περίεστιν; ἐγὼ μὲν οὐκ
ἔχω συμβαλεῖν. εὐδαίμονες ἄρα, οὐκ ἄθλιοι, κατὰ
τὸν Πλάτωνος λόγον οἱ ῥήτορες, εἴ γε ὁ μὲν τελέως
ἀγαθὸς εὐδαίμων, τὸ δ' οὐκ ἔστιν κτήσασθαι μὴ τελέως ἀγαθὸν γενόμενον.

307 Εἶτ' ἐλέγχειν μὲν βούλεται ῥητορικήν, κατηγορεῖ
δὲ τῶν τυράννων καὶ δυναστῶν, τὰ ἄμικτα μιγνύς,
ὥσπερ ἂν εἰ ὁ 'Ηρακλῆς, ἵλεως δ' εἴη τῷ παρα-

¹ καὶ codd. dett. (prob. Ddf.).

former is not very difficult, but to possess the power of not being wronged is very difficult. And it is impossible to possess this completely, otherwise than by being completely good." Hurrah, hurrah for the testimony! I needed this, and it is said by Plato, who shares in that epigram and through whom the race of Ariston is truly "divine."[a] Then, my dear sir, 305 oratory is wholly a fair thing, and it is not for everyone to take or possess it. You yourself clearly concede that its task is not to permit being wronged. Therefore since it has not compelled the commission of wrong, and does not permit being wronged, and according to the result of this argument, permits neither of these, doing wrong or being wronged, if the definition of philosophy is the same, oratory is clearly a kind of philosophy. But if it is enough for philosophy not to do wrong, oratory is more perfect. For he now adds what is a more difficult and greater thing—possession of the power of not being wronged by others. Then how is the same thing at the same 306 time completely good and the greatest of goods, and the extreme of evil and flattery? Or how do orators possess the least power,[b] if they have in abundance that whose power is very difficult to possess? I cannot understand. Orators are happy, not wretched, according to Plato's argument, if the completely good man is happy and it is impossible to possess this power if one is not completely good.

Next he wishes to refute oratory, but he accuses 307 tyrants and potentates,[c] combining the uncombinable, as if Heracles—may he pardon the example—,

---

[a] *Cf. Republic* 368 A. The epigram was in part, "O sons of Ariston" (Plato's father), "divine race of a famous man."
[b] *Gorgias* 466 B.   [c] *Gorgias* 523 A ff.

(99 D.)

δείγματι, προσταχθὲν αὐτῷ τὸν ἐν τῇ Νεμέᾳ ἀνελεῖν λέοντα, εἶτ᾽ ὄνῳ τινὶ συμπλακεὶς καὶ πνίγων
τὸν λέοντα ἄγχειν ᾤετο καὶ τοῦθ᾽ ὅπερ προὔθετο
πράττειν. τοσοῦτον δὲ λείπεται τὸ παράδειγμα
ὅσον οὗτός γε οὐχ ἕτερον ἀνθ᾽ ἑτέρου ποιεῖ τοῦτον
τὸν τρόπον τῷ λόγῳ χρώμενος, ἀλλὰ καὶ τοῖς ἐναντίοις περιπίπτει. τίς γὰρ οὐκ οἶδεν ὅτι ῥητορικὴ καὶ τυραννὶς τοσοῦτον ἀλλήλων κεχώρισται
ὅσον τὸ πείθειν τοῦ βιάζεσθαι; ἀλλὰ μὴν ταῦτά
γε οὐδείς ἐστιν ὅστις ἂν τὴν ἐναντίαν φύσιν εἰπὼν ἔχειν αἰσχυνθείη. ὥστ᾽ εἰ δεινὸν τὸ βιάζεσθαι
καὶ πλεονεκτεῖν, τό γε πείθειν καὶ τοῦ δικαίου προ-
308 εστάναι καλὸν καὶ προσῆκον. οὐκοῦν οὐχ οὕτω
100 D. ῥητορικὴ κακὸν ὡς τυραννίς, ἀλλ᾽ εἰ κακὸν ἡ τυραννίς,[2] ἡ ῥητορικὴ χρηστὸν ἐκ τῶν αὐτῶν· ἡ μὲν
γὰρ βιάζεσθαι πανταχοῦ ζητεῖ, ἡ δὲ τὸ πείθειν
τετίμηκεν. ὥσθ᾽ ὅμοιον ποιεῖ τούτοις ἐκεῖνό γ᾽
ἐλέγχειν νομίζων ὥσπερ ἂν εἴ τις τὸν ἐν τῇ νυκτὶ
σκότον[3] καταμεμφόμενος καὶ τὰς ἄλλας ἀτοπίας
309 τῆς ἡμέρας ἡγοῖτο κατηγορεῖν. καὶ τοτὲ μὲν κολακείαν εἶναί φησι τὴν ῥητορικήν, πάλιν δ᾽ εἰς ταὐτὸν
τοὺς δυνάστας καὶ τοὺς ῥήτορας τίθησιν, οὐ μόνον οὐδέτερον προσὸν τῇ δυνάμει ταύτῃ λέγων, πρὸς
δὲ τῷ μὴ προσεῖναι καὶ παντελῶς ἀλλότριον αὐτῆς,
ἀλλὰ καὶ αὐτὰ τὰ ἐναντιώτατα δύο συντιθεὶς ἐγκλήματα. πῶς γὰρ ὁμοῦ μὲν κολακεύουσιν οἱ ῥήτορες,
ὁμοῦ δ᾽ ἐν τοῖς δυνάσταις εἰσίν; οἱ μέν γέ που
κόλακες οἱ μέγιστοι δήπου καὶ τελεώτατοι αὐτῶν
⟨εἰσὶ τῶν τυράννων πάντῃ θεραπευταί·⟩[4] εἰσὶ δ᾽,
οἶμαι, καὶ τῶν τυχόντων τινές· ὥσθ᾽ ὅπερ δοῦλος
πρὸς δεσπότην, τοῦτο κόλαξ πρὸς τύραννον συμ-

when ordered to slay the Nemean lion, wrestled with an ass and, choking it, thought that he was strangling the lion, and that he was doing what he intended. The example is so far deficient in that he in his argument does not treat one thing for another in this fashion, but falls into exact opposites. Who is unaware that oratory and tyranny are as far separate as the use of persuasion and the use of force ? Indeed no one would be ashamed to say that these have an opposite nature. Therefore if the use of force and unfairness is terrible, the use of persuasion and the defence of what is just is fair and proper. So oratory 308 is not an evil like tyranny ; but if tyranny is an evil, on the same grounds oratory is good. For the former everywhere seeks the use of force, but the latter has honoured the use of persuasion. Therefore, believing that he refutes that by this, he does the same as if someone by blaming the darkness and the other oddities of night would believe that he accused the day. And sometimes he says that oratory is 309 flattery, and again he classifies potentates and orators together, not only naming two qualities neither of which is appropriate to the faculty of oratory, and besides being inappropriate, even totally foreign to it, but also combining two most contradictory accusations. How at the same time are orators flatterers and among the potentates ? As for flatterers, the greatest and most perfect of them are in every way the servants of tyrants ; and some also, I think, of common men. Therefore as the slave is to the master, so it turns out to be that the flatterer

---

¹ om. VA. ² ἀλλ'—τυραννίς om. VA.
³ codd. dett. : σκοπὸν TQVA. ⁴ add. codd. dett.

457

(100 D.)

βαίνει· οἱ δ' αὖ τύραννοι τοσοῦτον ἀπέχουσι τοῦ
κολακεύειν ὥστε βίᾳ πάντας ὠθοῦσιν καὶ οὐδὲ τῶν
μετρίων οὐδενός ἐστιν παρ' αὐτῶν τυχεῖν, μή τί γε
δὴ τῆς ὑπὲρ τὸ προσῆκον θεραπείας· [ὥσθ' ὁ τύραννος μικροῦ δεῖν καὶ τὸ τοῦ δεσπότου μέτρον παρελήλυθεν. κόλακος μὲν γὰρ οὐδέν ἐστι δήπου[1] ταπεινό-

101 D. τερον οὐδ' ὅ τι μᾶλλον ᾑρῆσθαι δουλεύειν, τυράννου
δὲ οὐδὲν ἂν εἴποις ἀγριώτερον οὐδ' ὅ τι μᾶλλον πρὸς
τὸ δεσπόζειν ἐθέλειν ἐστίν.][2] ὥστ' εἰ μὲν κολακεία
ἡ ῥητορική, τὰ τῶν τυράννων ἐγκλήματα οὐ πρὸς
αὐτήν ἐστιν, εἰ δ' ὁμοῦ τῇ τυραννίδι, τὴν κολακείαν

310 μεγάλοις τοῖς ὁρίοις παρελήλυθεν. οὐκοῦν τά γε
ἕτερα πάντως ἤδη ψευδῆ. ἐμοὶ μὲν τοίνυν, εἰ καὶ
μηδὲν ἔχοιμι χρηστὸν εἰπεῖν περὶ αὐτῆς, ἱκανὸν
τοῦτο, εἰ δείκνυμι καὶ οὑτωσὶ μὴ τἀληθῆ λέγοντα·
τῷ δέ, εἰ καὶ θάτερα ὀρθῶς ἐγκέκληκεν, περὶ τῶν
ἑτέρων λόγος οὐ λείπεται. ἀλλὰ μὴν ὡς οὐκ ὀρθῶς
ἅμα ἀμφότερα ὑπὸ τῶν αὐτὸς αὑτοῦ λόγων ἐξελέγχεται συγκρουόντων, ὡς δ' οὐδέτερον ὀρθῶς
ἡμεῖς ἀρτίως ἐπεδείξαμεν, ἰδίᾳ μὲν ὡς οὐ κολακεία
δείξαντες, πάλιν δὲ ὡς οὐ κοινωνεῖ τῇ τυραννίδι.

311 πῶς οὖν οὐ τρὶς[3] ἥττᾶται, τῷ τε τοῦ συναμφοτέρου
λόγῳ καὶ τῷ καθ' ἕτερον χωρίς; ταὐτὸν δὲ ἡμῖν ἐν
ἅπασιν σῴζεται. περί τε γὰρ ἀμφοτέρων ὁμοῦ
τοῖς αὐτὸς αὑτοῦ λόγοις περιωθεῖται καὶ πάλιν καθ'
ἕτερον αὐτὸς αὖ μαρτυρεῖ, τῷ τε τὸ πείθειν φανῆναι
τῶν χρησίμων ἕν τι παρ' αὐτῷ καὶ τῷ[4] τῶν βιαζο-

102 D. μένων καὶ ὑβριζόντων κατηγοροῦντα παρ' ὅλον τὸν
λόγον φαίνεσθαι. τοσοῦτον γὰρ ἡ ῥητορικὴ κεχώ-

---

[1] om. codd. dett.
[2] secl. Behr.
[3] codd. dett.: εἰ τρὶς T p. corr. (τρεῖς a. corr.) Q : ἢ τρεῖς VA.
[4] καὶ τῷ om. VA.

is to the tyrant. On the other hand, tyrants are so far from being flatterers that they push everyone around by force, and it is impossible to get any moderate treatment from them, to say nothing about service beyond their duty. [Therefore the tyrant has nearly passed even beyond the measure of the master. For there is nothing more humble than a flatterer, nor what is more the sort to have chosen to serve ; but you would not say that there was anything fiercer than a tyrant, nor what is more the sort to wish to be the master]. Therefore if oratory is flattery, the accusations against tyrants are not appropriate to it. If it is classed with tyranny, it has passed beyond flattery by a great distance. Then already one of the two statements is completely 310 false. It is enough for me, even if I should have nothing good to say about it, if I prove that even in this way he does not speak the truth. He is left with no argument about one of his accusations, even if the other is correct. Indeed, he is refuted by his own conflicting arguments since both accusations are not at the same time correct. That neither is correct, we have just now demonstrated, particularly showing that it is not flattery, and again that it has nothing in common with tyranny. How is he 311 not worsted in three ways, in the combined argument and in each separate one ? Our position is safely and consistently maintained in all of them. In the matter of the two together, he is dislodged by his own arguments and again in each separate point he bears witness for our side, by the fact that persuasion clearly was something useful in his estimation, and that he clearly in his whole argument condemns those who use force and violence. Oratory is as

(102 D.)

ρισται δυναστείας ὅσον, εἰ καὶ τοῦτ' εἰπεῖν δεῖ,
Πλάτων Διονυσίου.

312   Ἔστι τοίνυν μαθεῖν καὶ παρ' αὐτοῦ τοῦ πράγματος
καὶ τῶν συμπεπτωκότων ὅσον τὸ διάφορον τούτων
ἑκατέρου, καὶ καθ' ὅσην τινὰ τὴν ἀνάγκην ἐστίν.
φανήσεται γὰρ οὔθ' ὅπου ῥητορικὴ σώζεται τύραννος ἐγγιγνόμενος, μέχρις ἂν σώζηται λόγῳ, οὔτ'
αὖ ῥητορικὴ περιοῦσα ἔνθα¹ τυραννὶς κρατεῖ, ἀλλ'
ὅ τε ῥήτωρ πάντα πράττων ὅπως μηδεὶς τύραννος
ἐγγένηται τό τε αὑτοῦ καὶ τὸ κοινὸν ὁμοῦ προορῶν,
ὅπως μηδεὶς αὐτὸν τὸ λόγῳ πείθειν παρελόμενος
αὐτὸς ἄγῃ κατ' ἀρχὴν τὰ πράγματα, οἵ τε τύραννοι
σκοποῦντες καὶ φοβούμενοι τῶν πάντων οὐδὲν
μᾶλλον ἢ μή τις ἐγγένηται λέγειν καὶ πείθειν
δυνατός, ὅστις συναγαγὼν τὰ πλήθη καὶ σύμβουλος
καὶ μηνυτὴς τοῦ προσήκοντος γενόμενος ὁμοῦ τῆς
τε ἀρχῆς καὶ τῆς ἐξουσίας ἀκύρους² καταστήσει.

313 διόπερ τὴν ἔχθραν ἀλλήλοις ἀναγκαίως ἔχουσιν· ἡ
γὰρ τῶν ἑτέρων σωτηρία καὶ δύναμις μὴ εἶναι τοὺς
ἑτέρους ἐστὶν τὴν ἀρχήν. ὥστε πόσου ποτ' ἂν
πρίαιντο οἱ ῥήτορες, εἰ οἷόν τ' εἰπεῖν, φανῆναί τινα
ὥσπερ ἐν μάχῃ σφίσιν, ἢ Πλάτωνα λέγω, ἢ καὶ
ὁντινοῦν ἐπίκουρον καὶ βοηθὸν [ὄντα],³ τὰ τῶν
τυράννων κακὰ εἰς μέσον οἴσοντα καὶ δείξοντα καὶ
μηδὲ νύκτωρ ἀνήσοντα λέγοντ' αὐτοὺς κακῶς.
[σχεδὸν γὰρ ἤδη τοὺς τῆς ῥητορικῆς αὐτῆς ἀναλώ-
σει καὶ δείξει λόγους ὁ ταῦτα δεικνύς,]⁴ καί τινα
τρόπον οἴκοθεν τοῖς ῥήτορσιν ἡ βοήθεια ἀφίξεται.

314 οἱ δ' αὖ τυραννεῖν ἐπιθυμοῦντες πόσου ποτ' ἂν
103 D. πρίαιντο ἀπιστηθῆναι τὸ τῶν ῥητόρων ἔθνος ἐν ταῖς
πόλεσιν καὶ κόλακας καὶ μαγείρων οὐδὲν βελτίους

―――――――――――――
¹ om. VA.   ² ἀκύρους αὐτοὺς V Phot.

far separate from dynasty, as, if this must be said, Plato is from Dionysius.

It is possible to learn from the matter itself and 312 the circumstances concerning it how great is the difference of each and how necessary this difference is. Where oratory is preserved, a tyrant will clearly never arise, as long as regard for it is preserved ; nor again does oratory survive and rule where there is tyranny. But the orator does everything so that no tyrant may arise, providing for his own and the common welfare, so that no one may deprive him of his power to persuade by argument and assume authority ; and the tyrants consider and fear nothing more than that someone may arise able to speak and persuade, who in gathering together the populace and revealing their duty, will deprive the tyrants of their right to office and power. Thus of 313 necessity they hate one another. For the safety and power of the one lies in the absolute non-existence of the other. Therefore what price would orators have paid, if it can be so expressed, for the appearance on their side, as in a battle, of someone, I mean either Plato or some other supporter and helper, to bring to light and reveal the evils of tyrants, and not even at night to stop abusing them ? [For one might say that he who reveals these things will thereby more or less expend and reveal the arguments of oratory itself]. And in a way the orators will be helped by their own side. Again what price 314 would those who desire to be tyrants have paid for the race of orators to be distrusted in the cities, and for those who try to persuade through argument

---

³ om. codd. dett., del. Reiske.   ⁴ secl. Behr.

(103 D.)

ὑποληφθῆναι, τοὺς τῷ λόγῳ πείθειν ἐπιχειροῦντας,
ἵνα μὴ μάτην ἡ παροιμία τὰς ἐρήμους τρυγᾶν
ἀγορεύῃ. εἶθ' ἃ τοῖς ἀδικεῖν ἐπιχειροῦσι λυσιτελεῖ,
πῶς ταῦτα συγχωρητέον τοῖς τὰ δίκαια τιμῶσιν;

315   Πῶς οὖν τἀναντία λέγουσιν ἀλλήλοις οἱ ῥήτορες;
—ἔστιν μὲν οὐκέτι τοῦτ' ἐν τοῖς εἰρημένοις ὑπὸ
Πλάτωνος, ὅμως δὲ ὑπὲρ τοῦ πανταχῇ διακαθᾶραι
τὸν λόγον μηδὲ τοῦθ' ἡμῖν ἀνεξέταστον ἀφείσθω,
καὶ ταῦτ' ἰσχυρότατον πάντων ὂν ⟨σχεδὸν⟩[1] ὡς ἐν
ψεύδεσιν ὧν ἐκεῖνος εἴρηκεν.—ὅτι, οἶμαι, καὶ ἡμῖν
αὐτοῖς ἀπαντῶμεν ἐν τοῖς λόγοις, αὐτὸ τοῦτο ⟨ὃ⟩[2]
κἀγὼ νῦν πεποίηκα· ἀλλ' οὐδὲν μᾶλλον ὅ γ' ἐξ
ἀρχῆς λόγος διαφθείρεται, ἐπεὶ καὶ οἱ φιλοσοφεῖν
οὕτω λεγόμενοι οὐ τοῖς αὐτοῖς λόγοις[3] ἅπαντες δήπου χρῶνται, ἀλλὰ καί[4] τοῖς ἐναντιωτάτοις ἀλ-
316 λήλοις. ἀλλ' οὐδὲν κωλύει κατὰ τοὺς τυγχάνοντας
τῆς ἀληθείας φιλοσοφίαν εἶναι καλόν, οὐ δήπου δι-
317 πλοῦν ἐστιν οὐδ' ἐναντίον αὐτὸ ἑαυτῷ. πῶς οὖν ἂν
φαίη τις; ἢ φιλοσοφεῖν ἀμφοτέρους φήσομεν τἀναντία λέγοντας; ἢ τὸ φιλοσοφεῖν εἶναι καλὸν οὕτως
ὡς ἔφη; ἴδοις δ' ἂν καὶ κυβερνήτας ἐναντία ἀλλήλοις ναυμαχοῦντας, ἀλλ' ὅμως τῆς κυβερνητικῆς
318 ἐστιν σῴζειν τὴν ναῦν. οὕτω τοίνυν καὶ ὅταν οἱ
ῥήτορες ἐναντία ἀλλήλοις, ὡς ἄν τις φαίη, λέγωσιν,
οὐ κωλύεται τὸ ἐξ ἀρχῆς κεφάλαιον τῆς ῥητορικῆς,
ἀλλὰ τὸ συμβαῖνον τῷ λόγῳ χρὴ σκοπεῖν μεμνη-
μένους ὧν ἕνεχ' εὑρέθη. ὁ μὲν οὖν ὑπὲρ ῥητορικῆς
λόγος οὗτος.

---

[1] om. TQ Phot.   [2] add. Reiske.
[3] λόγοις post δήπου TQ.   [4] om. TQ.

to be thought of as flatterers and no better than cooks, so that not in vain the proverb might announce the harvesting of unwatched vines ? [a] Next how must what is profitable to those who endeavour to do wrong be attributed to those who honour justice ?

Then why do orators disagree with one another ? 315 This is no longer found in the statements of Plato. Still it must not be passed by unexamined by us so that our argument may be purged in every way, especially since it is nearly the strongest point of all, among, as it were, his false statements. The reason is, I suppose, that we take opposite sides in our arguments, the very thing I have just now done. But no more thereby is the original argument destroyed, since even those who are said to be philosophers do not, of course, all use the same arguments, but even arguments which are most opposed to one another. Yet in the eyes of men who attain to 316 the truth, nothing prevents philosophy from being a fair thing, and it does not have a double or self-contradictory nature.[b] Then what would one say ? 317 Shall we say when both disagree that they are both philosophers ? Or that philosophy is a fair thing on the terms which I said ? You would see helmsmen engaged in sea fights against one another. Still it is the part of the art of navigation to preserve one's ship. Thus whenever orators disagree with one another, as 318 one might say, the original goal of oratory is not impeded, but it is necessary to consider the result of the argument, and to remember for what reason oratory was discovered. This then is our argument in defence of oratory.

[a] *Cf.* scholium to Aristophanes' *Wasps* 634.
[b] *Cf. Gorgias* 503 A-B.

ΥΠΕΡ ΡΗΤΟΡΙΚΗΣ

ΛΟΓΟΣ ΔΕΥΤΕΡΟΣ

319 Ἐπεὶ δὲ καὶ Μιλτιάδου καὶ Θεμιστοκλέους καθ-
ήψατο καὶ Κίμωνος καὶ Περικλέους, οὐ πρὸς τὸ
βέλτιστον φάσκων προστῆναι τῆς πόλεως, ἔστι μὲν
οὐδὲν ἴσως κατεπεῖγον περὶ τούτων νῦν διαφέρεσθαι.
οὗτοι μὲν γάρ, εἰ δίκαια Πλάτων αὐτῶν κατηγόρηκεν, δικαίως ἂν φαῦλοι νομίζοιντο· ῥητορικὴ δ᾽, εἰ
καὶ πάντων μοχθηροτάτους τούτους θείημεν, οὐδὲν
320 μᾶλλον ἐλέγχεται. συγχωρούντων μὲν οὖν ἡμῶν ὅ
γε ὑπὲρ ῥητορικῆς οὐκ ἀπόλωλε λόγος. εἰ δὲ δὴ καὶ
περὶ τούτων ἐλέγχοιτο οὐ παντάπασιν εὐγνωμόνως
τῷ λόγῳ κεχρημένος, πανταχῇ δειχθήσεται φιλο-
νικῶν. τοῦτ᾽ ἔστιν προὔργου [τὸ][1] καὶ περὶ τούτων
321 εἰπεῖν. φέρε δὴ πρὸς Διός, εἴ πως ἀναστάντες ἢ
λαβόντες αἴσθησιν, ὥσπερ Πλάτωνι Δίων ὑπόκειται
πρὸς Συρακοσίους[2] λέγων, ταυτὶ πρὸς αὐτὸν εἴποιεν, ἡμεῖς, ὦ Πλάτων, ἄλλο μὲν οὐδὲν χρηστὸν
105 D. τὴν Ἀθηναίων πόλιν εἰργασάμεθα· οὐ γὰρ ἦμεν τῆς
σῆς ἀρετῆς καὶ σοφίας ἐπιστήμονες, πάντα δ᾽ οὐ
πᾶσιν οἱ θεοὶ διδόασιν· ἃ δ᾽ εἰς ἡμᾶς ἧκεν, εὔνοια,

---

[1] secl. Keil. [2] Ddf. : Συρακουσίους TQVA.

---

[a] See note a to page 280.

[b] *Gorgias* 503 c, 515 b ff. Miltiades was famous chiefly for
his leadership of Athens in the Marathonian campaign
(490 B.C.) ; Themistocles for his creation of Athenian sea-

IN DEFENCE OF ORATORY

BOOK II [a]

ALTHOUGH he attacked Miltiades, Themistocles, Ci- 319
mon, and Pericles,[b] alleging that they did not govern
the city for the best ends, there is perhaps now no
urgent reason to dispute about these men. They
would justly be believed to be bad, if Plato has justly
accused them. But oratory is no more refuted, even
if we should regard them as the most wicked men
of all. So through our concession the argument 320
in defence of oratory is not ruined. But if even in
the question of these men Plato should be shown
not to have used a very sensible argument, he will be
proved querulous in every way. So it is worthwhile
to discuss these men as well. Come now, by Zeus, 321
let us suppose that they were somehow resurrected
or became sentient, just as Dion is made by Plato
to talk to the Syracusans,[c] and were to say to him :
We did no other good for the city of Athens, Plato.
For we did not know the science of your virtue and
wisdom. The Gods do not give everything to every-

power, and for his leadership in the campaign of Salamis in
480 B.C. ; Cimon for his leadership of Athens' confederacy of
Delos in warfare against the Persians (478–449 B.C.) ;
Pericles for his consolidation of the Athenian Empire and his
renowned leadership (461–429 B.C.).

[c] *Epist.* VIII, 355 A.

(105 D.)

προθυμία, πίστις, ἀνδρεία, τὰ τοιαῦτα παρεσχόμεθα, ὥσθ᾽ ὑπερβολὴν ἑτέρῳ μὴ λιπεῖν, ἐν τοῖς τοιούτοις καιροῖς, ὦ Πλάτων, ἐν οἷς ἦν ἐν μὲν τῷ κρατεῖν ἅμα δόξα καὶ σωτηρία καὶ τὰ ἐκ τῶν εὐχῶν, ἡττηθέντας δὲ μηδ᾽ εἶναι τὸ παράπαν. λαβόντων δὲ ἡμῶν τούτους τοὺς λογισμοὺς καὶ τῶν θεῶν εὐμενῶς συναιρομένων ἐλευθέρα μὲν ἡ σὴ καὶ ἡμετέρα πατρὶς καὶ σῷα καὶ ἀθῷος τῆς τῶν βαρβάρων ὕβρεως καὶ παρανομίας, ἐλευθέρα δὲ καὶ πᾶσα ἡ Ἑλλάς, ἐξουσία δὲ καὶ σοὶ φιλοσοφεῖν καὶ τοῖς σοῖς ἑταίροις ἐγένετο καὶ πλεῖν ἐλευθέρως ὅποι ἐβούλεσθε[1] καὶ ἔχειν ἡμῶν μνησθῆναι καὶ ἔπειτα[2]—

322 εὔγνωμον δ᾽ ἦν, ὡς ἐπὶ τὰ βελτίω. ὡς εἰ τότε ἡμεῖς ἀπειπόντες παρεδώκαμεν ἡμᾶς αὐτοὺς τοῖς βαρβάροις ἀμαχητί, τίς ἂν ὑμῶν[3] λόγος κατ᾽ ἀνθρώπους ἐγένετο; ἀλλ᾽ οὔτε αὐτοὶ τοιοῦτον οὐδὲν ἐπάθομεν οὔτε τοὺς ἄλλους ἠνεσχόμεθα, οὐδ᾽ ἐκολακεύσαμεν οὐδετέρους, οὔτε τὸν βασιλέα δι᾽ οὐδέτερον τούτων, ἢ φόβον, ἢ κέρδους ἐλπίδα, οὔτ᾽ αὖ τὸν δῆμον τῶν Ἀθηναίων. οὐ γὰρ ἦν, εἰ κολακεύειν ἐβουλόμεθα, αὐτοὺς σῶσαι, οὐδ᾽ ὅπως τι

106 D. πρὸς ἡδονὴν ἀκούσονται παρεδίδου τόθ᾽ ὁ καιρός, ἀλλὰ τοσοῦτον ἀπείχομεν τοῦ κόλακες τοῦ πλήθους εἶναι ὥστ᾽ οὐδὲ βουλομένοις ἡμῖν κολακεύειν ἐνῆν. ἀλλ᾽ οὔτε προῃρούμεθα οὔτ᾽ ἦν δυνατὸν οὔθ᾽ οὕτω τὴν Ἑλλάδα ἐσώσαμεν χαριζόμενοι καὶ ψυχαγωγοῦντες, ὥσπερ ἂν σὺ μέμνησαι τῶν κιθαρῳδῶν, ἀλλ᾽ ἐπεγείροντες, διδάσκοντες, αὐτοὶ παράδειγμα τοῖς ἄλλοις γιγνόμενοι τοῦ πῶς δεῖ καρτερεῖν ἐν αὐτοῖς τοῖς δεινοῖς καὶ ταῖς ἀκμαῖς τῶν κινδύνων, τὴν

one. But what was ours, goodwill, eagerness, faith, and courage, these qualities we displayed, so that no one could surpass us, and in such times, Plato, when glory, safety, and the objects of our prayers lay in victory, and in defeat not even to exist at all. By our calculations and the kindly assistance of the Gods, your and our country is free, safe, untouched by the wanton and unlawful acts of the barbarians, and all Greece is also free, and there has been given to you and your comrades the power to be philosophers, and to sail in freedom wherever you wish, and to be able to remember us afterwards, though out of consideration, in a better way. For if then we 322 had given up our course and handed ourselves over to the barbarians without a struggle, what regard would men have for you? But neither did we suffer any such thing, nor did we allow others to, nor did we fawn over either side : not over the king either through fear or hope of gain, and not over the people of Athens. If we wished to fawn over them, we could not save them, nor did the time then permit them to hear pleasant speeches. But we were so far from being flatterers of the multitude, that not even if we wished, could we have been flatterers. Neither did we choose to do so nor was it possible, nor in this way did we save Greece by gratifying and charming it, like the lyre players you mention,[a] but by arousing it, teaching it, being ourselves an example for the others of how it is necessary to persevere when terrors actually beset us and in the height of danger,

---

[a] *Gorgias* 502 A ff.

---

[1] Reiske : βούλεσθε A, βούλεσθαι TQV.
[2] distinxit Keil.   [3] ἡμῶν TQ.

(106 D.)

ἡμετέραν αὐτῶν, εἰ συγχωρεῖς εἰπεῖν, ἀρετὴν ἐπι-
323 δεικνύμενοι. τί οὖν ἡμῖν προφέρεις κολακείαν καὶ
διακονίαν, καὶ τοὺς ἰδίᾳ τροφεῖα μὴ ἐκτίνοντας
φαύλους ἂν εἶναι συμφήσας αὐτὸς ἡμῖν οὐ καλὴν
χάριν ἐκτίνεις τῆς κοινῆς τῶν Ἑλλήνων σωτηρίας
καὶ τροφῆς, ἣν σύ τε καὶ οἱ ἄλλοι δι' ἡμᾶς ἐν ἐλευθε-
324 ρίᾳ τέθραφθε;[1] εἰ ταῦτα λέγοιεν οἱ ἄνδρες, ποίους
λαβυρίνθους σοφίας ἀνελίττων ἢ τί λέγων τῶν
πάντων οἷός τε γένοιτ' ἂν ἀντειπεῖν; πᾶσι τοίνυν
προτέροις ἐστὶ λόγος πρὸς ταῦτα ἢ Πλάτωνι. διὰ
τί; ὅτι ἐν αὐτοῖς τούτοις ἃ πρὸς τοὺς Δίωνος
γέγραφεν ἑταίρους καὶ ἐν οἷς ὁ Δίων αὐτῷ τετε-
λευτηκὼς ὑπόκειται λέγων ὡς ἔμπνους ἔνεστι
ταυτὶ " Δεξάμενοι δὲ τοὺς τοιούτους νόμους, ἐπειδὴ
κατέχει κίνδυνος Σικελίαν, καὶ οὔτε κρατεῖτε ἱκανῶς οὔτ' αὖ διαφερόντως κρατεῖσθε, δίκαιον ἂν ἴσως
καὶ συμφέρον γένοιτο ἡμῖν πᾶσιν μέσον τεμεῖν[2]
τοῖς τε φεύγουσι τῆς ἀρχῆς τὴν χαλεπότητα ὑμῖν
καὶ τοῖς τῆς ἀρχῆς πάλιν ἐρῶσι τυχεῖν· ὧν οἱ
πρόγονοι τὸ μέγιστον ἔσωσαν ἀπὸ βαρβάρων τοὺς
Ἕλληνας, ὥστ' ἐξεῖναι περὶ πολιτείας νῦν ποιεῖσθαι
107 D. λόγους· ἔρρουσιν δὲ τότε οὔτε λόγος οὔτ' ἐλπὶς
325 ἐλείπετ' ἂν οὐδαμῇ οὐδαμῶς." ἡμῶν δέ γε οὐχ οἱ
πρόγονοι, φαῖεν ἄν, ἀλλ' ἡμεῖς αὐτοὶ τοῖς ἡμετέροις
αὐτῶν[3] ἔργοις καὶ βουλεύμασι καὶ λόγοις ἀπὸ τῶν
βαρβάρων τοὺς Ἕλληνας ἐσώσαμεν, οὐ τὸ ἐν
Σικελίᾳ κατοικοῦν μέρος αὐτῶν, ἀλλὰ τοὺς σύμπαντας καὶ τοὺς τῆς ἁπάσης οἰκουμένης τὸ ἕτερον μέρος
νομισθέντας, ἐξ οὗ τότε τοῖς βαρβάροις ἀντάραντες

---

[1] codd. dett. : τέτραφθε TQVA.

by displaying our virtue, if you permit us to say it.
Why do you charge us with flattery and servitude ; 323
and while you would agree that individuals, who do
not pay back the care taken in raising them, are
evil men, will you not give thanks to us for the general
safety and care of the Greeks, which you and others
had in freedom through us ? If the men should say 324
these things, by the unfolding of what labyrinths of
wisdom or with what statement at all would he be
able to answer ? Anyone sooner than Plato has an
argument against this. Why ? Because in those
very remarks which he wrote to the comrades of
Dion and in which the dead Dion is made by him to
speak as if " with breath in him," is the following [a] :
" Having accepted such laws, when Sicily is now in
danger, and you are neither sufficiently victorious
nor again particularly defeated, perhaps it would be
just and expedient for us all to take a middle course,
both for you who recoil from the harshness of empire
and for you who desire again to obtain empire, both
of whose ancestors in the greatest way saved the
Greeks from the barbarians, so that it is possible
now to discuss a constitution. Had they failed then,
no talk and no hope would anywhere at all remain."
Not our ancestors, they would say, but we our- 325
selves by our own deeds, counsels, and words, saved
the Greeks from the barbarians, not the part which
dwells in Sicily, but all the Greeks, who are regarded
as one half of the world. After this deed then they
faced and repulsed the barbarians, so that it is

[a] *Epist.* VIII, 355 c-d.

---

2 Ddf. ex Plat. : τε μένειν TQVA.
3 codd. dett. : ἑαυτῶν TQVA.

(107 D.)

ἐώσαντο, ὥστε ἐξεῖναί σοι περὶ πολιτείας νῦν ποιεῖσθαι λόγους, καὶ περὶ αὐτῶν ἡμῶν, ἔρρουσιν δὲ τότε
οὔτε λόγος οὔτ᾽ ἐλπὶς ἐλείπετ᾽[1] ἂν οὐδαμῇ οὐδαμῶς.

326 " Νῦν οὖν " φησὶν ὁ Δίων " τοῖς μὲν ἐλευθερία γιγνέσθω μετὰ βασιλικῆς ἀρχῆς, τοῖς δὲ ἀρχὴ ὑπεύ-
θυνος βασιλική, δεσποζόντων νόμων τῶν τε ἄλλων
πολιτῶν καὶ τῶν βασιλέων αὐτῶν, ἄν τι παράνομον
πράττωσιν. ἐπὶ δὲ τούτοις ξύμπασιν ἀδόλῳ γνώμῃ
καὶ ὑγιεῖ μετὰ θεῶν βασιλέα στήσασθε,[2] πρῶτον
μὲν τὸν ἐμὸν υἱὸν χαρίτων ἕνεκα διττῶν, τῆς τε
παρ᾽ ἐμοῦ καὶ τῆς παρὰ τοῦ ἐμοῦ πατρός· ὁ μὲν
γὰρ ἀπὸ βαρβάρων ἠλευθέρωσεν ἐν τῷ τότε χρόνῳ
τὴν πόλιν, ἐγὼ δὲ ἀπὸ τυράννων νῦν δίς, ὧν[3] αὐτοὶ
μάρτυρες ὑμεῖς[4] γεγόνατε. δεύτερον δὲ δὴ ποιεῖσθε[5]
βασιλέα τὸν τῷ μὲν ἐμῷ πατρὶ ταὐτὸν κεκτημένον
ὄνομα, υἱὸν δὲ Διονυσίου, χάριν τῆς τε δὴ νῦν
βοηθείας καὶ ὁσίου τρόπου· ὃς γενόμενος τυράννου
πατρὸς ἑκὼν τὴν πόλιν ἐλευθεροῖ, τιμὴν αὐτῷ καὶ

108 D. γένει ἀΐδιον ἀντὶ τυραννίδος ἐφημέρου καὶ ἀδίκου
κτώμενος. τρίτον δὲ προκαλεῖσθαι[6] χρὴ βασιλέα
γίγνεσθαι Συρακουσῶν,[7] ἑκόντα ἑκούσης τῆς πόλεως, τὸν νῦν τοῦ τῶν πολεμίων ἄρχοντα στρατο-

---

[1] codd. dett. : ἐλίπετ᾽ TQVA.
[2] codd. dett. Plat. : στήσασθαι TQVA.
[3] codd. dett. Plat. : δ᾽ ἴσων TQVA.
[4] codd. dett. Plat. : ὑμῖν VA, ἡμῖν TQ.
[5] codd. dett. Plat. : δεῖ ποιεῖσθαι TQVA.
[6] codd. dett. Plat. : προσκαλεῖσθαι TQVA.
[7] Ddf. ex Plat. : Συρακουσίων TQVA.

---

[a] *Epist.* VIII, 355 D—356 B.
[b] [Dion, son of Hipparinus, named his own son Hipparinus,
who was about twenty years old at this time. Dion was
also son-in-law as well as brother-in-law of Dionysius I, tyrant
of Syracuse 405–367 B.C., and had as a nephew a third

possible now for you to discuss a constitution and us as well, but had we failed then, no talk and no hope would anywhere at all remain. " Now then," 326 says Dion,[a] " let the former have freedom under royal rule, and the latter royal rule subject to examination, the laws having absolute power both over the other citizens and the kings themselves if ever they do a lawless thing. To all these ends, with a guileless and sound intent, with the help of the Gods, create a king, first my son in repayment of a double favour, mine and my father's. He freed the city then from the barbarians and I now twice from tyrants, of which acts you have been witnesses. Secondly, make king him who has the same name as my father, the son of Dionysius, because of his present aid and pious character, who being born the son of a tyrant, voluntarily frees his city, earning for himself and his race eternal honour in place of an ephemeral and unjust tyranny.[b] Thirdly, it is fitting to invite to be king of Syracuse, willingly over a willing city, the present commander of the army of the enemy, Dionysius, the son of

Hipparinus who was also a son of Dionysius I. The " barbarians " are the Carthaginians who tried to extend their power so as to include Sicily. After a patched-up peace with the Carthaginians in 405 B.C., Dionysius I warred with them in 398–395 ; 392 ; 383–378 : and 368 B.C. ; and, despite some double dealing and much imperialism, did save Greek civilization in Sicily. Plato indicates that Dion's father Hipparinus helped Dionysius I in the Carthaginian campaigns. " Him who has the same name as my father " refers to the Hipparinus who was a nephew of Dion, and also son of Dionysius I. This Hipparinus was helping Dion's party. The idea is that the successive monarchs should be not unconstitutional " tyrants " ruling by force, but constitutional kings.—E.H.W.]

(108 D.)

πέδου, Διονύσιον τὸν Διονυσίου, ἐὰν ἐθέλῃ ἑκὼν εἰς
βασιλέως σχῆμα ἀπαλλάττεσθαι, δεδιὼς μὲν τὰς
τύχας, ἐλεῶν δὲ πατρίδα καὶ ἱερῶν ἀθεραπευσίαν
καὶ τάφους, μὴ διὰ φιλονικίαν πάντως πάντα ἀπολέσῃ, βαρβάροις ἐπίχαρτος γενόμενος.''

327   Εἰ τοίνυν καὶ τοιαῦτα γέρα τοὺς τῶν ἠλευθερωκό-
των τὴν πόλιν ἐκγόνους λαμβάνειν εἰκός, ὥστ'
αὐτοὺς γίγνεσθαι δυνάστας καὶ βασιλέας ἀντὶ τῶν
προτέρων ἐκείνων, ἢ που τούς γε αὐτοὺς ἐλευθερώ-
σαντας ἅπαν τὸ τῶν Ἑλλήνων γένος οὐχὶ δίκαιον
πρὸς τῷ μηδενὸς πλείονος ἀξιοῦν μηδ' ἐλευθέρους
τὸ κοινὸν ἐᾶν εἶναι δοκεῖν. εἰ δὲ δὴ καὶ τὸν τοῦ
τῶν πολεμίων ἄρχοντα στατοπέδου δίκαιον βασιλέα
ποιεῖσθαι, ἐὰν ἐθελήσῃ πατρίδα καὶ ἱερῶν ἀθεραπευσίαν καὶ τάφους ἐλεῆσαι, καὶ ὅπως μὴ διὰ φιλονικίαν πάντως πάντα ἀπολέσῃ βαρβάροις ἐπίχαρτος
γενόμενος, τούς γε οὐ μετὰ πολεμίων ταξαμένους,
ἀλλὰ πρὸς τοὺς ἐξ ἁπάσης γῆς πολεμίους ἀντιταξα-
μένους, ποῦ θήσομεν, οἳ πρὸς τῇ σφετέρᾳ πατρίδι
καὶ ἄλλοις πολλοῖς ὤρθωσαν τὰς πατρίδας, καὶ ἱερὰ
καὶ τάφους διετήρησαν, καὶ οὔτε αὐτῶν οὐδεὶς βαρβάροις ἐπίχαρτος ἐγένετο οὔθ' ἡ Ἑλλὰς δι' αὐτούς;
ἆρά γε φαῦλα ἢ φαύλης χάριτος ταῦτ' ἄξια τοῖς
328   ἀνδράσιν; εἶθ' οὕς, εἰ δεῖ πείθεσθαι τοῖς Πλάτωνος
λόγοις, τιμῶν ἀξιοῦν δεῖ καὶ πολὺ μειζόνων ἢ κατὰ
τὰς συνήθεις, τούτους τοῖς Πλάτωνος λόγοις πει-
σθέντες κόλακας καὶ διακόνους καὶ τοῦ μηδενὸς
109 D.   ἀξίους προσεροῦμεν; οὐ μέντἂν δίκαια ποιοῖμεν.
329   τὸ δὲ πάντων ἀτοπώτατον, ὅτι χρῆται μὲν τούτοις
ἐν ἐλέγχῳ τοῦ κολακείαν εἶναι τὴν ῥητορικήν, ὡς
δὴ τούτους ὄντας ῥήτορας, πάλιν δ' αὐτὸς αὐτοὺς

Dionysius, if he voluntarily wishes to change to the status of king, in fear of fortune, and in pity of his country, and its tombs, and the neglect of the temples, so that through strife he may not utterly destroy everything, and become a source of joy to the barbarians."

If then it is reasonable for the descendants of 327 those who have freed their city to get such prizes, so that they become potentates and kings in the place of those former men, it is indeed unjust not to allow those who freed the whole race of the Greeks even to seem to be free in the common sense of the word, beside not holding them in any higher esteem. And if it is just to make the commander of the camp of the enemy a king if he wishes to pity his country, and its tombs, and the neglect of the temples, and so, that through strife he may not utterly destroy everything and become a source of joy to the barbarians, where then shall we put those who did not join the enemy's ranks, but arrayed themselves against the enemy of the whole world, who set to rights the countries of many other men in addition to their own country, and preserved their temples and tombs, and of whom none became a source of joy to the barbarians, nor Greece because of them? Then are these trifling things, and do they merit trifling gratitude toward these men? Next as to 328 those men, who must be esteemed worthy of much greater honours than usual, if Plato's arguments must be believed, shall we believe in Plato's arguments and call them flatterers, servants, and worthless? We should indeed not act justly. But it is 329 strangest of all, that he uses them in his proof that oratory is flattery, as if they were orators, and again

(109 D.)

ἀφίησιν τῆς κολακείας. οὔκουν[1] φησί γ᾽ αὐτοὺς
330 ταύτῃ χρῆσθαι ἐν οἷς περὶ ὧν ἔπαθον λέγει. κἂν
τούτοις οὖν ἀνάγκη θάτερα ἐψεῦσθαι. εἰ μὲν γὰρ ἡ
ῥητορικὴ κολακεία, πάντως κόλακας δεῖ τούτους
εἶναι, ῥήτοράς γε ὄντας, ὥς φησιν· εἰ δὲ οὐδὲν
οὗτοι κολακείᾳ προσήκουσι, πῶς ῥητορικὴ κολακεία
διὰ τούτους ἢ τί τούτων ἔδει τῶν παραδειγμάτων;
ᾤμην δὲ οὐδὲ τοῦτο τῶν δικαίων εἶναι, τὰς προαιρέ-
σεις τὰς ἐκείνων ἐξετάζοντας τὰς συμφορὰς αἷς
ἐχρήσαντο ὑπολογίζεσθαι. οὐ γὰρ εἰ μὴ κατὰ νοῦν
ἀπήλλαξαν, φαῦλοι γεγόνασιν, ἀλλ᾽ εἰ μὴ τὰ βέλτιστα ἐβουλεύοντο τοῖς πράγμασιν. ἐκεῖνο μὲν γάρ
ἐστιν τῆς τύχης κατηγορεῖν, τοῦτο δὲ τὴν γνώμην
ἐλέγχειν.

331 Φέρε γὰρ σὺ πρὸς τὸ βέλτιστον, ὦ Πλάτων, προὔστης Ἀθηναίων ἤ τινος ἄλλου δήμου τῶν ἐν τοῖς
Ἕλλησιν ἢ τοῖς βαρβάροις; ἐκείνων φαίη τις ἂν
ἡδέως. οὐκ ἔχοις ⟨ἂν⟩[2] εἰπεῖν· οὐδὲ γὰρ προὔστης
ὅλως. τί δὲ[3] ὁ σὸς διδάσκαλος καὶ ἑταῖρος Σωκράτης; οὐδ᾽ οὗτος. τί δὲ[3] Σπεύσιππος ἢ Χαιρεφῶν;
332 οὐκ ἂν φαίης. πότερ᾽ οὖν ἔστι δῆμον καθάπαξ ἀποφῆναι χρηστὸν καὶ ἄμεμπτον καὶ δίκαιον, ἢ τοῦτο
μὲν οὐδ᾽ ἐπ᾽ ἀνδρὸς οἷόν τε διισχυρίζεσθαι; καὶ
μὴν εἰ μὲν ἐγχωρεῖ, τί παθὼν οὐκ ἀπέδειξας[4] αὐ-
110 D. τός, οὐδ᾽ ἐπ᾽ αὐτῶν τῶν πραγμάτων ἐφάνης βελτίων
πολίτης ἡμῶν; εἰ δ᾽ ἀμήχανόν ἐστι, τί προφέρεις
ἡμῖν εἴ τι καὶ προσεκρούσαμεν, φαῖεν ἂν αὖθις ἐκεῖ-

---

[1] codd. dett. : οὐκοῦν TQVA.
[2] add. codd. dett.

frees them from the charge of flattery. Indeed, he denies that they used flattery where he speaks about their misfortunes. Then here also one of the two 330 arguments must be false. If oratory is flattery, these men must be in every way flatterers, granting that they are orators, as he says. If they have nothing to do with flattery, how is oratory flattery because of them, or what need was there of these examples ? I did not even think that this was fair, in examining their professions, to take into account the misfortunes which they experienced. For they have not become bad men, if their lives did not turn out as they wished, but if they did not advise what was best in the circumstances. That is to accuse fate, this to refute a policy.

Come, Plato, did you ever lead the Athenians or 331 any other people among the Greeks or barbarians toward what is best ? Any one of those men would be glad to ask this. You could not say so. You were not even a leader at all. What about your teacher and comrade Socrates ? Not even he. What about Speusippus or Chaerephon ?[a] You would deny it. Then is it possible to make a people 332 good, blameless, and just, once and for all, or is this not even possible to affirm in the case of a single man ? Indeed, if it is possible, why in the world have you not done it yourself, and in the conduct of affairs also appeared as a better citizen than we ? If it cannot be done, why blame us, if we have stumbled, those men would say again, and

---

[a] Speusippus was Plato's nephew and disciple ; Chaerephon was Socrates' inseparable companion.

---

[3] δαὶ bis TQA.   [4] ἐπέδειξας VA. (prob. Keil).

(110 D.)

νοι, καὶ τί τῶν ἀδυνάτων αἰτεῖς εὐθύνας; [εἰ]¹
τοσούτῳ γὰρ ἡμεῖς λυσιτελέστεροι σοῦ τῷ δήμῳ
γεγόναμεν ὅσῳ σὺ μὲν οὔτε χεῖρον οὔτε βέλτιον οὐδὲν οὔτ᾽ εἶπας οὔτ᾽ ἔπραξας, ἀλλ᾽ ἀπώκνησας ἁπλῶς,
ἡμεῖς δ᾽ ὅσον ἧκεν ἐφ᾽ ἡμᾶς οὐ καθυφεῖμεν,² ἀλλ᾽
ὥσπερ χρημάτων εἰσφορὰν πλήρη τὴν ἀπὸ τῶν λο-
γισμῶν καὶ τῶν λόγων παρεσχόμεθα³ τῇ πατρίδι,
καὶ οὔτε πλῆθος τῶν τἀναντία ἐρούντων ὠκνήσαμεν
οὔτ᾽ ἰσχὺν πλουσίων κατεδείσαμεν, οἷς ἀναγκαῖον
ἦν τὸν ὑπὲρ τῶν κοινῶν πράττοντα προσκρούειν,
οὔτε δικαστὰς οὔτε κινδύνους οὔτε τοὺς οἴκοι οὔτε
τοὺς ἔξω πρὸς τοὺς πολεμίους οὔθ᾽ ὅλως τὰ τῆς
τύχης καὶ τοῦ μέλλοντος ἄδηλα. ἃ φυγεῖν μὲν δήπου
ῥᾷον⁴ ἢ ὑποστῆναι παντί. τοῦτο δ᾽ εἰ πάντες ἐν
ταῖς ἀνάγκαις λογίσαιντο, οἴχεται τὰ τῶν πόλεων
333 πράγματα. ταῦτ᾽ ἄν, οἶμαι, φαῖεν, μετρίως, ⟨ὡς⟩⁵
ἐγᾦμαι, λέγοντες. εἶεν. τί δὲ εἰ βελτίστους μὲν
μὴ ἀπέφηναν καθάπαξ Ἀθηναίους, βελτίους δ᾽
ἔστιν ᾗ; τί δ᾽ εἰ μείζω καὶ περὶ τούτους καὶ περὶ
ἄλλους ἐξήμαρτον ἄν, εἰ μὴ τοῖς ὑπ᾽ ἐκείνων λόγοις
334 κατείχοντο; ἔπειτα τὸν μὲν ἰατρὸν φῂς λιμῷ ἂν
ἀποθανεῖν, εἰ πρὸς τὸν ὀψοποιὸν ἀγωνίζοιτο ἐν
παισὶν ἢ τοιούτοις ἀνθρώποις, οἳ μὴ δύνανται
γνῶναι τἀληθές· εἰ δὲ Μιλτιάδης καὶ Κίμων καὶ
Περικλῆς πρὸς τὸ βέλτιστον ἄγοντες τὰ πράγματα
ἔσθ᾽ ἃ καὶ προσέπταισαν, τοῦτο θαυμάζεις;
335 Ἐνθυμοῦμαι δὲ ἔγωγε πῶς ἀνέχεσθαι χρὴ ὅτ᾽⁶
111 D. Ἀλκιβιάδην μὲν καὶ Κριτίαν Σωκράτει συγγενο-
μένους, οἳ τοσαύτας καὶ τηλικαύτας αἰτίας ἐσχή-

¹ om. edd.
² καθυφείκαμεν codd. dett. (prob. Ddf.).
³ codd. dett. : παρεχόμεθα TQVA.
⁴ codd. dett. et Reiske : ῥᾴδιον TQVA.

why demand an accounting of what is impossible ?
We have been so much more profitable than you for
the people, to the degree that you have said and
done nothing, either better or worse, but have simply
shirked, while we, as far as we could, did not yield,
but presented to our country from our calculations
and arguments, as it were, a full return of moneys
owing and neither shirked in the face of the multitude
of those who opposed us nor feared the power of the
rich, whom one acting in behalf of the general good
must offend, nor did we fear jurors, nor dangers at
home or abroad against the enemy, nor in general the
uncertainties of fortune and the future. All of
which it is easier for everyone to run from than to
oppose. If every man would calculate this way in
times of need, the affairs of their cities are ruined.
They would, I think, say these things, speaking 333
with moderation as I think. Well then ! What
if they did not make the Athenians best once and
for all, but in some way improved them ? What if the
Athenians would have made even greater mistakes
in regard to these and other men, if they had not
been restrained by their arguments ? Next you say [a] 334
that a doctor would die of starvation if he should
compete against a cook before boys or similar persons
who cannot recognize the truth. If Miltiades,
Cimon, Pericles, in guiding affairs toward the best
end, sometimes stumbled, do you wonder at this ?

I ponder as to how the following is to be endured. 335
Alcibiades and Critias, the associates of Socrates,
have been accused so much and so thoroughly both

[a] *Gorgias* 464 D.

---

5 add. codd. dett.   6 codd. dett. : ὅταν TQVA Phot.

(111 D.)

κασιν καὶ ὑπὸ τῶν πολλῶν καὶ ὑπὸ τῶν ἐπιεικῶν,
ὥστε Κριτίου γε οὐδ' ἐπινοῆσαι ῥᾴδιον ἐξωλέστερον,
ὃς ἐν τριάκοντα τοῖς πονηροτάτοις τῶν Ἑλλήνων
πρῶτος ἦν, τούτους μὲν οὔ φασιν δεῖν ἐν τεκμηρίῳ
ποιεῖσθαι ὅτι Σωκράτης τοὺς νέους διέφθειρεν, οὐδ'
εἶναι τἀκείνων ἁμαρτήματα οὐδ' ὁτιοῦν πρὸς Σωκράτη τὸν οὐδὲ αὐτὸν ἔξαρνον ὄντα τὸ μὴ οὐ διαλέγεσθαι τοῖς νέοις· εἰ δ' Ἀθηναίων ⟨ὁ⟩[1] δῆμος
ἐν πολλοῖς καὶ μεγάλοις οἷς καὶ ὑπὲρ αὑτοῦ[2] καὶ
ὑπὲρ τῶν Ἑλλήνων διεχείρισεν ἔσθ' ἃ μὲν ὀρθῶς
καὶ προσηκόντως ἐβουλεύσατο, ἔστιν δὲ ἃ καὶ ἐξήμαρτεν εἰς τοὺς προεστηκότας, ταῦτ' ἀξιοῦσιν αὐ-
336 τοῖς τοῖς προστάταις λογίζεσθαι. καὶ Λεσβίοις μὲν
Τέρπανδρος οὐχ οἷός τε ἐγένετο πάντας ποιῆσαι
μουσικούς, οὐδ' Ἀρίων, οὐδ' εἴ τις ἄλλος ἐν Λέ-
σβῳ μουσικὴν ἐποιήσατο[3]· εἰ δὲ Θεμιστοκλῆς καὶ
Περικλῆς μὴ καθάπαξ ἐπαίδευσαν Ἀθηναίους τὴν
πολιτικὴν ἀρετήν, τοῦτ' ἐκείνους, ὡς ἔοικεν, ἐλέγχει
τοῦ μηδενὸς ἀξίους ὄντας, ὥσπερ ἂν εἴ τις καὶ
θεῶν κατηγοροίη τοῖς αὐτοῖς λόγοις, ὅτι χρῆν
αὐτῶν τὴν πρόνοιαν εἶναι τοιαύτην ὥστ' ἀδικίαν καὶ
ἀγνωμοσύνην ἀνελεῖν παντάπασιν ἐξ ἀνθρώπων καὶ
μηδὲν ἁμαρτάνειν μηδένας ἀνθρώπων μηδαμῇ. νῦν
δὲ πῶς ἢ[4] προνοεῖν αὐτοὺς χρὴ νομίζειν, ὅταν μὴ
παύωνται πλημμελοῦντες ὧν ἄρχουσιν ⟨ἢ⟩[5] μὴ

---

[1] add. codd. dett. [2] codd. dett. : αὑτοῦ TQVA.
[3] ἐγένετο VA. [4] εἰ VA.
[5] add. codd. dett. et Canter.

---

[a] [For Miltiades, Cimon, and Pericles, see n. on § 319.
Alcibiades (c. 450–404 B.C.), wealthy, handsome, insolent,
unscrupulous but able " democratic " politician, was active
in Athenian affairs after 425 B.C. ; Critias was an " oligarch "
and the chief among the " Thirty Tyrants " set up in Athens

478

by the "democrats" and by the "moderates," that it is not even easy to conceive of anything more pestilential than Critias, who was first among the Thirty, themselves the wickedest of the Greeks.[a] These men they say must not be used as evidence that Socrates corrupted the young nor have their faults anything whatever to do with Socrates, who himself does not deny that he spoke to the young. But if the people of Athens in its many great accomplishments on its own behalf and on behalf of the Greeks, while making some of its plans rightly and properly, in some respects erred against its leaders, they demand that these faults be accounted to the leaders themselves. Terpander was unable to make 336 all the people of Lesbos musical nor could Arion, nor whoever else composed music in Lesbos.[b] But if Themistocles and Pericles did not once and for all educate the Athenians in political virtue, this fact, as it seems, proves that they are worthless, as if someone on the same grounds should accuse the Gods, because their care ought to be of such sort that injustice and cruelty are entirely removed from mankind and no men ever err in any way. But now how is it fitting to believe that they exercise care when those over whom they rule do not stop making mistakes? Or that they are not justly regarded as

in 404 after her defeat at Aegospotami. " Moderates " is a translation-term not ineptly applied to a " party " in Athens of that time which was neither extremely " democratic " nor extremely " oligarchic," and was led by Theramenes.—*E.H.W.*]

[b] Arion is legendary, but Terpander lived in the early part of the seventh century B.C. Lyric poet and musician of Lesbos, he went to live at Sparta. For Themistocles and Pericles see note on § 319.

(111 D.)

337 δικαίως ὑπ' ἐνίων ἀμελεῖσθαι; οὔκουν οἵ γ' ἵπποι
τοὺς μὲν οὐδεπώποθ' ἁψαμένους αὐτῶν γνωρίζουσι
112 D. προσβλέποντες, τοὺς δ' ἐφεστῶτας μισοῦσι καὶ
φεύγουσιν· ἀλλὰ τοῦτό γε καὶ τοῖς ὄνοις ἀπέδωκεν
ἡ παροιμία, τὸν ξύοντα ἀντιξύειν· ἄνθρωποι δ' ἄρα
ὑπὸ θεῶν ἀγόμενοι θεοὺς οὐ νομίζουσιν, ἢ περὶ αὐτούς τι φαῦλον τοὺς θεοὺς λέγουσι καὶ πράττουσιν.

338 καὶ ὁ μὲν ἡνίοχος παραλαβὼν λακτίζοντας τοὺς
ἵππους πραΰνει καὶ τιθασεύει καὶ τελευτῶν ἐπ'
αὐτῶν ἀσφαλῶς καὶ κατὰ πολλὴν ῥᾳστώνην εἴσιν
ὅποι βούλεται· οἱ θεοὶ δὲ οὔπω καὶ νῦν ἐξῃρήκασιν
ἐξ ἀνθρώπων ἀδικίαν ἐκ τοσούτου, καὶ ταῦτα ἐκ
τοῦ παντὸς αἰῶνος πολιτευόμενοι, καὶ προσέτι εἰς
ἑαυτοὺς ἁμαρτάνοντας ὁρῶντες ἔστιν οὓς αὐτῶν.

339 ἀλλὰ μὴν ὅτε ταῦτα οὐδ' ἂν εἷς ὑγιαίνων εἴποι
σπουδῇ πλὴν ὡς ἡμεῖς νῦν εἰς ἔλεγχον λόγου, πῶς οὐ
κομιδῇ Πλάτων συκοφαντεῖ; εἰ γὰρ ἃ μηδ' οἱ θεοὶ
πώποτε πεποιήκασι, μηδὲ παρ' αὐτῆς τῆς Ἀθηνᾶς
τῆς πολιάδος εἶχεν ἀπαιτῆσαι, ταῦτα παρὰ Θεμιστοκλέους καὶ Περικλέους ἀπαιτεῖ, αὐτὸν ἐρωτῶ[1]

340 πῶς οὐ συκοφαντεῖ. ἀλλ' οἶμαι τὴν μὲν ⟨τοῦ⟩[2]
δήμου φύσιν οὐκ ἠδυνήθησαν μεταποιῆσαι οὐδ' ἀφα-
νίσαι· ἔστιν δ' αὕτη μηδέποτε γενέσθαι πάντα χρηστὸν μηδ' ἀναμάρτητον· ὅσα δ' ἢ[3] κινδυνεύοντας
ἔδει προνοήσασθαι, ἐν οἷς ἅμα καὶ τῶν πολλῶν καὶ
τῶν ἐπιεικῶν ἦν εὐεργέτας εἶναι, ἢ κατ' ἐξουσίαν
πράττοντας ἀπάγειν ἀπὸ τῶν δυσχερεστάτων ἀεὶ καὶ
⟨εἰς⟩[4] ὡς ἐλάχιστον τρέπειν τὰ τῆς φύσεως ἁμαρτήματα, ταῦτ' οὐκ ἔστιν ὅπως οὐ παρὰ τούτοις ὄντα
φανήσεται, καὶ ταῦτα πρὸς τῷ λόγῳ τῷ παρ' ἡμῶν

---

[1] ἐρῶ VA. [2] add. Phot.
[3] codd. dett. : δὴ V, δὲ TQA Phot.
[4] add. Reiske ; pro ὡς habet εἰς Phot.

negligible by certain men ? Horses do not recog- 337
nize at sight those who have never touched them,
while hating and fleeing those who have charge of
them. There is even a proverb about asses, " Scratch
me, while I scratch you." [a] But men who are
guided by the Gods do not believe in the Gods, or
they say and do evil things in respect to the Gods.
When a charioteer has acquired horses who kick,[b] 338
he calms and tames them, and finally rides them
safely and comfortably wherever he wishes. But
after all this time even now the Gods have never
removed injustice from mankind, although they have
governed for all eternity, and besides they see some
men erring even against them. Indeed, when no 339
one who is sane would seriously say these things,
except as we do now to refute an argument, how is
not Plato very much a slanderer ? For if what the
Gods themselves have never done, and what he
could not demand from Athena Holder of the City,
this he demands from Themistocles and Pericles, I
ask him how he is not a slanderer. But, I think, they 340
were unable to change and eliminate the nature
of the people. The " nature " of the people is such
that never does a man arise who is altogether good
and faultless ! But unquestionably obvious will be
all the foresight which they had to exercise at their
own peril, when they could at the same time be
the benefactors of both the common people and
" moderate " men, or in the limits of their power
ever deflect them from the greatest difficulties and
make the faults of nature as small as could be. And
in addition to our argument and proofs, Plato himself

[a] The proverb recurs in or. iii. 365 (p. 300 Ddf.).
[b] *Cf. Gorgias* 516 A.

(112 D.)

113 D.

341

342

καὶ ταῖς ἀποδείξεσιν Πλάτων αὐτὸς ἐπισφραγίζεται καὶ ἔστιν ἡμῖν κἀνταῦθα μάρτυς ὑπὸ τῆς αὐτῆς δεξιότητος ἧσπερ κἂν τοῖς ἄνω κατὰ τὴν χρείαν ἀεὶ καὶ τὸ[1] λοιπόν, ἐὰν αὐτὸς αὐτοὺς ἐπαινῶν ἐπιδειχθῇ. πῶς οὖν ἄν τις περιφανέστερον ἢ λαμπρότερον τοὺς ἄνδρας ἐπήνεσεν ἢ ὡς οὗτος τὸν ἐπιτάφιον λόγον αὐτοῖς ποιήσας; ἐν ᾧ καὶ τοῖς ἄλλοις προξενεῖν φησι καὶ προμνᾶσθαι, εἰς ᾠδάς τε καὶ τὴν ἄλλην ποίησιν θεῖναι, κοσμήσαντας ἀξίως τῶν πραξάντων, λέγω δὴ τὰ τούτων ἔργα. τοῦτο γάρ ἐστιν ⟨τὸ⟩[2] χαριέστατον, ὅτι καὶ πάντα τἆλλα παρεὶς καὶ παριδὼν ἐπ' αὐτὰ τὰ τούτων ἴδια καὶ τὴν τούτων πολιτείαν ἐλήλυθεν, ὡς μάλιστα ἐκ τούτων ἐμφανιῶν τὴν τῶν τετελευτηκότων ἀρετήν, μέγιστον μὲν θεὶς[3] ἁπάντων τῶν ἔργων τὸ Μαραθῶνι, δεύτερον δὲ τὸ Σαλαμῖνι, κεφάλαιον δ' ἐπιθεὶς ὡς τοῖς βαρβάροις ἐπέδειξαν ὅτι πᾶς πλοῦτος καὶ δύναμις ἀρετῇ ὑπείκει.

Οὐκοῦν ὅτε τοὺς ταῦτα βουλευσαμένους καὶ πράξαντας ἐπαινεῖ, τὸν Θεμιστοκλέα καὶ τὸν Μιλτιάδην ἐπαινεῖ. οὗτοι γὰρ ἦσαν οἱ τούτων ἡγούμενοι. καίτοι πῶς οὐκ ἄτοπον ὧν τὰ ἔργα κοσμεῖ,[4] τούτων τὴν πολιτείαν[5] φαυλίζειν, καὶ ἃ τῆς τῶν πεισθέντων ἀρετῆς τίθεται δείγματα, ταῦτα μὴ τῆς τῶν πεισάντων πρῶτον ὑπάρχειν ἡγεῖσθαι; καὶ γὰρ ὅσοι μὲν ὑπὸ τῆς βουλῆς αἱρεθέντες ἐπὶ[6] τοῦ πλήθους τοὺς ἐπιταφίους τούτους διεξέρχονται ἔχουσιν ἴσως ἀποφυγὴν ὡς ἐξ ἀνάγκης ἐκόσμησαν καὶ οὐκ ἄν τις πρᾶγμα ποιοῖτο τοὺς λόγους αὐτῶν· ὅστις δ' ἐξεπίτηδες καὶ καθ' ἑαυτὸν ἐποίησεν περὶ αὐτῶν, εὔδηλον

---

[1] Iunt. : καίτοι τὸ TQVA.
[2] add. codd. dett.
[3] codd. dett. : τιθεὶς TQVA.

sets his seal of approval on this, and even here is a witness for us, with the same literary skill as in the above passages, which always is and will be useful, if ever he has been shown to praise them. How 341 would anyone more clearly or gloriously praise these men than he did when he wrote that funeral oration for them ? Here he says [a] that he advises and " suggests to others to make this the theme of lyric and other poetry, with adornment worthy of the doers," I mean their deeds. This is most charming, that he omitted and ignored all other history, and dealt with their own acts and government, as if from these he would make most clear the virtue of the dead. He ranks highest of all the deeds those at Marathon, second those at Salamis, and adds in conclusion [b] that they showed to the barbarians " that all wealth and power yields to virtue."

Then when he praises those who counsel and act 342 thus, he praises Themistocles and Miltiades. For they were their leaders then. Yet how is it not strange to belittle the administration of those whose deeds he adorns, and to believe that these things are not signs of the virtue of those who first persuaded them, while he makes them signs of the virtue of those who were persuaded ? And all who by the election of the Council narrate these funeral orations before the multitude, perhaps have an excuse in that their adornment was required and one should not take their speeches seriously. But it is quite clear that he who has intentionally and on his own written

---

[a] *Menexenus* 239 c. [b] *Menexenus* 240 D.

---

[4] codd. dett. : ἦν τὰ ἔργα κοσμεῖν pro ὧν κτλ. TQVA.
[5] τὴν δὲ πολιτείαν TQ. [6] Iunt. : ὑπὸ TQVA.

114 D. ὡς οὐκ ἄν, εἰ μὴ καὶ αὐτοὺς ἀξίους λόγου καὶ τὰ
ἔργα ἡγοῖτο. οὐ γὰρ κολακεύων γε Ἀθηναίους
ταῦτα εἰρηκέναι φησίν, οὐδ᾽ ἂν αὐτὸς λέγῃ πιστεύ-
σομεν ἡμεῖς. εἰ γὰρ αὖ λόγου χάριν καὶ δύναμιν
δεικνὺς ἐνεχείρησεν, πῶς ἔνεστιν αὐτῷ ῥητορικὴν
343 ψέγειν ἐν ᾗ ταὐτὸν ἦν; περὶ μὲν τοίνυν τούτων τῶν
ἀνδρῶν οὕτω μεμαρτύρηκεν, ὅτι οὐ πρὸς τὸ χείριστον
ἦγον τοὺς πολίτας, οὐδὲ τὰς ἐπιθυμίας αὐτῶν
διετέλουν ἀποπληροῦντες, ἀλλὰ τοιούτων ἔργων
ἡγεμόνες αὐτοῖς ἐγένοντο, ἃ καὶ Πλάτων οὐκ ἂν
αἰσχυνθείη κοσμῶν, καὶ προστιθεὶς ἀρετὴν τοῖς
εἰργασμένοις· οὐχ ὡς κατὰ Μίθαικον τὸν ὀψοποιὸν
καὶ Θεαρίωνα τὸν ἀρτοποιὸν τὴν φύσιν γενομένων,
ἀλλ᾽ ὡς χαλεπὸν τοῖς ἄλλοις καὶ εἰπεῖν πρεπόντως
περὶ αὐτῶν.

344 Εἰς δὲ τὸν καθάπαξ λόγον πῶς αὖ καὶ ποῦ
μαρτυρεῖ οὑτοσί;[1] ἐν αὐτῷ Γοργίᾳ τούτῳ ἐν τοῖς
Σωκράτους καὶ Καλλικλέους λόγοις. ἐλθὼν γὰρ
ἐπ᾽ αὐτὸ τὸ λῦον τὸν λόγον καὶ φανερᾶς τῆς κρίσεως
γενομένης[2] σχίζεται περὶ αὐτό, καὶ ὁ μὲν οὕτως
ἐρωτᾷ, ὁ δὲ ἀποκρίνεται ἀναμὶξ ὡδί. " Πότερόν
σοι δοκοῦσιν πρὸς τὸ βέλτιστον ἀεὶ λέγειν οἱ ῥήτο-
115 D. ρες, τούτου στοχαζόμενοι ὅπως οἱ πολῖται ὡς βέλτιστοι ἔσονται διὰ τοὺς αὐτῶν λόγους, ἢ καὶ οὗτοι
πρὸς τὸ χαρίζεσθαι [αὖ][3] τοῖς πολίταις ὡρμημένοι
καὶ ἕνεκα τοῦ ἰδίου τοῦ αὐτῶν[4] ὀλιγωροῦντες
τοῦ κοινοῦ ὥσπερ παισὶ προσομιλοῦσι τοῖς δήμοις,
χαρίζεσθαι αὐτοῖς πειρώμενοι μόνον· εἰ δέ γε βελ-

---

[1] codd. dett. : οὑτωσί TQVA.
[2] codd. dett. : γινομένης VA, γιγνομένης TQ.
[3] αὐτοῖς VA a. corr., αὖ secl. Ddf. ex Plat.

about these things would not have done so, unless
he believed both them and their deeds worthy of
consideration. For he does not claim that he said
these things in fawning over the Athenians, nor if
he says so, will we believe him. If he undertook
them as a demonstration of the power and grace
of his prose-style, how can he blame oratory, which
embodies the same impulse ? So he has borne 343
witness concerning these men that they did not
guide their fellow citizens to what is worst, nor pass
their time in satisfying the citizens' desires, but that
they led them in such deeds, which not even Plato
would be ashamed to adorn and to attribute virtue
to their accomplishment. For they were not like
Mithaecus, the cook, and Thearion, the baker,[a]
but it is difficult for others even to speak suitably
about them.

Again how and where does this our Plato bear 344
witness in respect to the principal argument ? In the
Gorgias itself, in the discussion of Socrates and
Callicles. For when he has come to the conclusion
of the dialogue, and his verdict has already been
made clear, he has divided opinions about this point.
Thus in turn does the one pose the question and the
other give his answer [b] : " ' Then do orators seem
to you always to speak for the best ends, aiming
at this, how the citizens will be as good as possible
through their speeches ; or intending to please the
citizens, and disregarding the public welfare for the
sake of their private affairs do they address the
people as children, trying only to please them, not

---

[a] *Gorgias* 518 B. [b] *Gorgias* 502 E—503 A.

[4] codd. dett. : αὐτῶν TQVA.

(115 D.)

τίους ἔσονται ἢ χείρους διὰ ταῦτα οὐδὲν φροντίζου-
σιν; Οὐχ ἁπλοῦν ἔτι τοῦτο[1] ἐρωτᾷς. εἰσὶ ⟨μὲν⟩[2]
γὰρ οἳ κηδόμενοι τῶν πολιτῶν λέγουσιν ἃ λέγουσιν,
εἰσὶ δὲ καὶ οἵους σὺ λέγεις. Ἐξαρκεῖ. εἰ γὰρ
καὶ τοῦτό ἐστιν διπλοῦν, τὸ μὲν ἕτερόν που τούτων[3]
κολακεία ἂν εἴη καὶ αἰσχρὰ δημηγορία, τὸ δὲ
345 ἕτερον καλόν.'' οὐκοῦν καὶ παρ' ἡμῶν ἐξαρκεῖ. εἰ
γάρ ἐστιν διπλοῦν καὶ μὴ ἀεὶ μὲν τὰ βέλτιστα
λέγουσιν οἱ ῥήτορες, ἔστιν δ' ὅτε καὶ τὰ βέλτιστα, ἢ
νὴ Δί' οἱ μὲν οὕτως, οἱ δὲ ἐκείνως λέγουσιν, ὁ κολακείαν ὁριζόμενος τὴν ῥητορικὴν εἶναι λόγος ἐν
346 βραχεῖ λύεται. ἔτι τοίνυν σαφέστερον ἐπὶ τελευτῆς
τοῦ διαλόγου τὸ πᾶν ἀποκαλύψας ἐκπέφαγκεν· οὐ
γὰρ ὑφ' ἡμῶν γε ταῦτα παρεμβέβληται '' Ἀλλὰ γάρ,
ὦ Καλλίκλεις, ἐκ τῶν αὐτῶν[4] εἰσὶ καὶ οἱ σφόδρα
πονηροὶ γιγνόμενοι ἄνθρωποι· οὐδὲν μὴν κωλύει καὶ
ἐν τούτοις ἀγαθοὺς ἄνδρας ἐγγίγνεσθαι, καὶ σφόδρα
γε ἄξιον ἄγασθαι τῶν γιγνομένων. χαλεπὸν γάρ,
ὦ Καλλίκλεις, καὶ πολλοῦ ἐπαίνου ἄξιον ἐν μεγάλῃ
ἐξουσίᾳ τοῦ ἀδικεῖν γενόμενον δικαίως διαβιῶναι·
ὀλίγοι δὲ γίγνονται οἱ τοιοῦτοι, ἐπεὶ καὶ ἐνθαδὶ καὶ
ἄλλοθι γεγόνασιν, οἶμαι δὲ καὶ ἔσονται καλοὶ
κἀγαθοὶ ταύτην τὴν ἀρετὴν τοῦ δικαίως διαχειρίζειν
⟨ἃ⟩[5] ἄν τις ἐπιτρέπῃ· εἷς δὲ καὶ πάνυ ἐλλόγιμος
116 D. γέγονεν καὶ εἰς τοὺς ἄλλους Ἕλληνας Ἀριστείδης ὁ
Λυσιμάχου· οἱ δὲ πολλοί, ὦ ἄριστε, κακοὶ γίγνονται
347 τῶν δυναστῶν.'' ἐνταῦθα τοσοῦτον αὖ περαιτέρω
προβέβηκεν, ὅσον οὐ μόνον ὡς ἐγχωρεῖ γίγνεσθαι
προσωμολόγηκεν, ἀλλὰ καὶ ἕνα γε αὐτὸς ὠνόμακεν,
Γεγόνασι δέ, φησί, καὶ ἕτεροι καὶ ἐνταῦθα καὶ

---

[1] τοῦτο δ Plato.   [2] add. codd. dett. ex Plat.
[3] τούτου Plato.   [4] δυνάμεων Plato.

caring whether they will be better or worse thereby ? ' ' You are no longer asking a simple question. For some out of care for their fellow citizens say what they say, and some are as you describe them.' ' It is enough. For even if this thing has two natures, one of them would be flattery and shameful harangue, and the other fair.' " It is also enough from our 345 point of view. If it has a double nature, and orators do not always say what is best, but even sometimes what is best, or by Zeus, some speak thus and some the other way, the argument which defines oratory as flattery is quickly undone. Still more clearly 346 at the end of the dialogue he has uncovered and revealed everything. For these things have not been inserted by us[a]: " ' But, Callicles, from this same group are men who become very evil. Yet nothing prevents good men from also arising among them, and we should admire those who do arise. For it is hard, Callicles, and worth much praise to have passed one's life justly, while having great power to do wrong. Such men are few. But they have existed here and elsewhere, and, I think, in the future there will be " fair and good men " with this virtue of justly handling whatever one entrusts to them. One very honourable man, even in the view of the other Greeks, was Aristides,[b] the son of Lysimachus. But the common run of potentates, dear sir, are bad.' " Here he has gone so far that he has not only admitted 347 that it can happen, but even has named one. And there have been others, he says, here and elsewhere.

---

[a] *Gorgias* 525 E—526 B.
[b] See note on or. i. 282.

---

[5] Ddf. in apparatu ex Plat.

(116 D.)

348 ἄλλοθι. ἐγὼ τοίνυν ἀφαιρῶ τοῦτο τὸ καὶ ἕτεροι καὶ
εἴ τις ἑτέρωθι· ὃν δὲ καὶ πάνυ ἐλλόγιμόν φησι γε-
γενῆσθαι καὶ οὐ μόνον εἰς τοὺς πολίτας, ἀλλὰ καὶ εἰς
τοὺς ἄλλους Ἕλληνας, τοῦτον τίθημι μόνον. ἔγκειται μὲν γάρ που ταῦτα[1] μεταξὺ τοῦ μύθου οὐκ ἀσκέ-
πτως[2] ἐμοὶ δοκεῖν οὐδὲ φαύλως οὐδὲ ὡς ἐξέπεσεν,
ἀλλ' ὅπως συγκρυφθείη τε ὡς δυνατὸν μάλιστα, καὶ
εἴ τις εὑρὼν χρῷτο, μηδ' αὐτὸς δοκοῖ[3] παρελ-
349 θεῖν, ἀλλ' ἐνείη. οὕτω μέσην τινὰ εὗρεν ⟨τάξιν⟩[4] καὶ
ἅμα πρὸς τῇ τελευτῇ τοῦ λόγου τοῦ παντὸς ἃ θεὶς
ἐν ἀρχῇ τοῖς ἐφεξῆς οὐκ ἔμελλεν ἕξειν οἶμαι χρῆ-
350 σθαι. οὐ μὴν τούτου γε ἕνεκα καὶ ἡμᾶς ⟨εἰκὸς⟩[5]
117 D. παρήσειν, ἕως ἂν τοῦ γε αὐτοῦ καὶ περὶ τῶν αὐτῶν
ὄντος τοῦ λόγου, προσθήσω δ' ὅτι κἂν τοῖς αὐτοῖς
351 τούτοις ἐνόντα φαίνηται.[6] οὐκοῦν εἰ ὅτι μάλιστα
ἕτερος μὲν ἐν τοῖς πᾶσιν μήτ' Ἀθήνησιν μήτ' ἄλλοθι
μηδαμοῦ ῥήτωρ ἐλλόγιμος, μηδ' ἔξω τῆς τοῦ κολακεύειν αἰτίας, γεγένηται δὲ εἷς [Ἀριστείδης][7]
Ἀθήνησιν, τί μᾶλλον τό γε πρᾶγμα κακιστέον ὡς
ἀναγκαίως φαῦλον; οὐ γὰρ εἰ ῥᾴδιον ἢ μὴ τῷ ὄντι
γενέσθαι ῥήτορα προὔκειτο σκοπεῖν, ἐπεὶ τοῦτό γε
καὶ ἡμεῖς, εἰ βούλει, μαρτυρούμεν, κἂν εἰ τὴν Στέν-
τορος φωνὴν κτησαίμεθα, φθεγξαίμεθ' ἂν[8] ὡς οὐ[9]
ῥᾴδιον, κἂν ὁ Νεῖλος, ὦ μακάριε, τοῖς ἑπτὰ στόμα-
σιν εἰ λάβοι φωνήν, ὥσπερ ὁ Σκάμανδρος κατὰ

---

[1] ταῦτα τά TQ. [2] codd. dett. : ἀσκήπτως TQVA.
[3] codd. dett. : δοκεῖ TQ Phot., δοκῇ VA.
[4] add. Phot. [5] add. Reiske.

I disregard the " others " and if there was anyone 348
" elsewhere." I consider only him who, he says, was
very honourable not only in the eyes of his fellow
citizens, but also in the eyes of the other Greeks.
These things are placed in the middle of the myth [a]
not unintentionally, it seems to me, nor clumsily,
nor by chance, but that they might be concealed as
much as possible, and so that if someone should hit
on this argument and use it, Plato would not seem
to have overlooked it, but it would be in his work.
So he found a certain middle ground, and that at the 349
end of the whole dialogue ; for if he had put it at the
beginning, he would not have been able, I think, to
use the arguments which follow. It is not likely 350
that we shall omit it for this reason at any rate, so
long as the argument and topic remains the same,
and I shall add, these things are clearly present in
this same dialogue. Then if absolutely no other 351
orator among all men, either at Athens or anywhere
else, has been honourable and free of a charge of
flattery, but there has been one man at Athens,
why must the practice be abused any longer as
necessarily bad ? For it was not under consideration
whether or not it is easy to become a real orator—
since here we can be witnesses, if you wish, and if we
had the voice of Stentor, we should cry out that it is
not easy, and the Ni¹e too would cry out, dear sir,
with its seven mouths, if it could become vocal like
the Scamander in Homer.[b] But the consideration

[a] *Gorgias* 523 A—527 A.
[b] *Iliad* XXI. 213.

---

[6] codd. dett. : φαίνεται TQVA.   [7] om. Ddf., secl. Behr.
       [8] om. V.   [9] om. TQ.

(117 D.)

Ὅμηρον, ἀλλ᾽ εἰ δυνατὸν ἢ μὴ καὶ φύσιν ἔστ᾽ ἔχον
συμβῆναι, τοῦτ᾽ ἦν ἐκ τοῦ λόγου.

352 Φέρε γὰρ πρὸς Διός, εἰ πρὶν Ἀριστείδην γενέσθαι,
τοὺς κατὰ τῆς ῥητορικῆς λόγους τούτους ἐποιεῖτο,
προθυμούμενος ἐκ παντὸς τρόπου δεικνύναι φαῦλόν
τι καὶ φυγῆς ἄξιον, λέγων ὡς ἀδύνατον χρηστόν
ποτε ἄνδρα ἢ δίκαιον γενέσθαι λόγων τοιούτων προσ-
αψάμενον, οὐκ ἂν ἐψεύδετο; δηλοῖ τό γε Ἀριστείδην φανῆναι τοιοῦτον, εἴπερ μὴ ψευδῆ Πλάτων
353 εἴρηκεν περὶ αὐτοῦ. οὐκοῦν δεινὸν εἰ¹ πρὶν μὲν
Ἀριστείδην γενέσθαι προσδοκᾶν ἔδει γενήσεσθαί
118 D. τινα καὶ μὴ νομίζειν καθάπαξ ἀδύνατον, ἐπεὶ δ᾽
οὗτος² ἐμφανὲς παράδειγμα ὑπάρχει, μήθ᾽ ὡς γενομένου τούτου μήθ᾽ ὡς ἐγχωροῦν ὅλως ἐγκαλεῖν.
354 καὶ μὴν οὐδ᾽ ἐκεῖνο ἴσον, μὴ γενομένου μὲν ὅλως
χρηστοῦ μηδενὸς τοῦτ᾽ ἂν ποιεῖσθαι τεκμήριον κατὰ
τῆς ῥητορικῆς ὡς ἄφυκτον, ὁμολογουμένου δ᾽ ὑπ᾽
αὐτοῦ τοῦ κακῶς ἀγορεύοντος αὐτὴν καὶ γεγενῆσθαί
τινας ἀξίους λόγου καὶ ἔσεσθαι, τουτὶ γάρ ἐστιν
ὑπερφυὲς τὸ καὶ περὶ τῶν μελλόντων προλέγειν ὡς
355 ἔσονται, εἶτ᾽ οἴεσθαι μηδὲν εἶναι πλέον. ἕτερον³
τοίνυν, ὅπερ ἐστὶν ἐκ τῆς τελευταίας ταυτησὶ μαρτυρίας, ὅτι καὶ πολλῷ μειζόνων εἶναι τοὺς τοιούτους
ἐπαίνων ἀξίους προσωμολόγηκεν αὐτός. χαλεπὸν
γάρ, φησίν, ὦ Καλλίκλεις,—οὐκοῦν καὶ ὦ Πλάτων
—ἐν μεγάλῃ ἐξουσίᾳ τοῦ ἀδικεῖν γενόμενον δικαίως
356 διαβιῶναι. εἰ τοίνυν ῥητορεύειν μέν ἐστιν ⟨ἀδικεῖν⟩⁴
δύνασθαι κατ᾽ αὐτόν σε, δυνατὸν δ᾽ ἐστὶ καὶ δικαίως
διαβιῶναι ῥητορεύοντα, μεῖζον δὲ τεκμήριον δικαιοσύνης τὸ δυνάμενον ἀδικεῖν ἡσυχάζειν ἢ τὸ μή, πῶς

¹ om. VA.   ² codd. dett. : οὕτως TQVA.
³ ἔτι TQ.   ⁴ add. Reiske.

according to the argument was whether or not it was possible and within the bounds of nature to take place.

Come, by Zeus, if he had written these works against 352 oratory before the birth of Aristides, eager in every way to prove that it was bad and to be avoided, saying that it was impossible for any man to be good and just who involved himself with such speeches, would he not have lied? That Aristides was obviously such a man, shows this clearly. Unless Plato lied about him. It is terrible therefore if, before Aristides' 353 birth, it ought to have been suspected that some such man would be born and not to have been believed once and for all impossible; but when he exists as a clear example, to find fault as if he were not born and as if it were entirely impossible. Indeed it is not at all fair that the absence of any 354 good orator would be used as an inescapable argument against oratory, but that when it is even admitted by the slanderer of oratory that there have been and will be certain worthwhile men— and this prediction about the future, that such men will exist, is an extraordinary thing—it is thought that no point is scored in oratory's favour. There is 355 another matter, which comes from the conclusion of this testimony, the admission by himself that such men are worthy of much greater praise. " For it is hard, Callicles," he says—and we might say, it is hard, Plato—, " to have passed one's life justly while having great power to do wrong." If according 356 to your definition to be an orator is to have the power to do wrong, and it is possible even being an orator to have passed one's life justly, and it is a greater evidence of justice to refrain from action when one

(118 D.)

οὐ πολὺ τῶν κολάκων ἀπέχουσιν οἱ τοιοῦτοι, οἵ γε
καὶ τῶν ἀναγκαίως δικαίων τοσοῦτον προέχουσιν;
357 ἔοικεν οὖν τὸ τοῦ Ὁμήρου συμβαίνειν

119 D.   Καί τι ἔπος προέηκεν¹ ὅπερ τ᾽ ἄρρητον ἄμεινον.

τὸν γὰρ Ἀριστείδην οὐ μόνον οὐ κακῶς εἰπεῖν
δυνηθείς, ἀλλὰ καὶ διαφέροντα ἀναγκαίως θείς,² καὶ
Μιλτιάδου καὶ Θεμιστοκλέους τοῦτο δ³ κατηγόρηκεν αὖθίς ἐστι διεφθορώς. ἀνδρῶν γὰρ ἂν εἴη
τοῦτό γε ἤδη κατηγορεῖν, οὐ ψέγειν ῥητορικήν, ὡς
358 αἰτίαν τοῦ λέγειν ἢ πράττειν κακῶς. ὥσπερ τοίνυν
αὐτὸς τὰ μὴ ἀναγκαῖα κατηγόρηκεν ἐκείνων, τί
κωλύει καὶ ἡμᾶς αὖ τὰ⁴ μὴ ἀναγκαῖα ὑπὲρ αὐτῶν
ἀντιθεῖναι; καίτοι διά γε τοῦτον ἐξ ἡμισείας ἀναγκαῖα. φανήσεται γὰρ οὐχ ἁπλῶς οὐδ᾽ ὡς νῦν μόνον
δείκνυμεν εἰς τοὺς ἐναντίους λόγους ἐληλυθὼς αὐτὸς
αὑτῷ, ἀλλὰ καὶ ἐξ ὧν ἐκείνους ᾐτίαται τοῦτον
ἐπαινεῖν οὐκ ἔχων, ἢ εἴπερ ὀρθῶς ἐπαινεῖ τοῦτον,
359 δι᾽ αὐτὸ τοῦτο οὐδ᾽ ἐκείνους ἔχων αἰτιάσασθαι. πῶς;
ὅτι σύμβολον οἶμαι ποιεῖται τοῦ κακῶς Ἀθηναίων
ἐκείνους προστῆναι τὸ παθεῖν αὐτοὺς ὑπ᾽ Ἀθηναίων
κακῶς, ὡς οὐκ ἂν τούς γε βελτίους ὑπ᾽ αὐτῶν
γενομένους ἁμαρτόντας εἰς τούτους ὑφ᾽ ὧν μηδ᾽ εἰς
τοὺς ἄλλους ἁμαρτάνειν ἐπαιδεύθησαν. ταῦτα δ᾽
οὕτω θεὶς καὶ ἡνιόχους καὶ τοιαῦτα ἐπεισαγαγὼν
ἐνταυθοῖ τόν γε Ἀριστείδην οὐ μόνον οὐδὲν φλαῦρον
εἴρηκεν, ἀλλὰ καὶ σαφῶς ἐξαίρετον τῶν ἄλλων
360 πεποίηται. καίτοι εἰ τὸ παθεῖν κακῶς ὑπ᾽ Ἀθη-

¹ codd. dett. : προσέθηκεν TQVA.
² ἀλλὰ—θείς om. VA.
³ τούτῳ ᾧ VA a. corr., τούτῳ ᾧ A p. corr.

can do wrong than when one cannot, surely such
men are far from being flatterers since they even
very much surpass those who are just by necessity.
Homer's remark seems appropriate [a] : " And he has 357
emitted a word which were better unsaid." For
not only by having been unable to slander Aristides,
but also by necessarily having counted him an
exception, he has again destroyed the meaning of
his accusation against Miltiades and Themistocles.
Now his accusation would be against the men, and
there would be no blame of oratory as being the cause
of their speaking or faring badly. Just as his accusa- 358
tions against them were not inevitable, what prevents
us also from counterposing a defence which is not
inevitable ? Yet because of Aristides, it is partly
inevitable. For he will clearly have proceeded to
contradict himself not in a simple sense, nor as we
now only are proving, but also by being unable to
praise Aristides where he finds fault with the others,
or if he rightly praises Aristides, thereby being unable to find fault with them. How ? Because, I 359
believe, he uses as a proof of their poor leadership
of the Athenians the fact that they suffered at the
hands of the Athenians, as if, had the Athenians
been improved by them, they would not have erred
against these by whom they were even taught not to
err against others. Having established this and
added charioteers and such things,[b] here not only
did he say nothing insulting of Aristides, but even
clearly set him apart from the others. Yet if to 360
suffer at the hands of the Athenians is a sign of

---

[a] *Odyssey* XIV. 466.   [b] *Gorgias* 516 E.

---

⁴ Reiske : αὐτὰ τὰ TQVA.

(119 D.)

ναίων δεῖγμα τοῦ μὴ καλῶς Ἀθηναίων προστῆναί
120 D. ἐστιν, οὐδ᾽ Ἀριστείδης προὖστη καλῶς· οὐδὲ γὰρ
οὗτος ἀθῷος δήπου διέφυγεν, ἀλλ᾽ ἐξέπεσεν, προσθήσω δ᾽ ὅτι οὗτός γε οὐδὲ ἐν δικαστηρίῳ δυσ-
τυχήσας ὥσπερ Μιλτιάδης καὶ Περικλῆς οὐδ᾽ ὑπὸ
τούτων οἷς προσέκρουσεν ὑπὲρ τῶν πολλῶν, ἀλλ᾽
361 ἐξοστρακισθεὶς ὑπ᾽ αὐτοῦ τοῦ δήμου. οὐκοῦν εἰ
μὲν μηδέν ἐστι τοῦτο σύμβολον κακίας, εἴ τις ῥήτωρ ἠτύχησεν πρὸς τούτους ὧν προυστήκει, οὔτε
Μιλτιάδης οὔτε¹ Θεμιστοκλῆς, οὐδ᾽ εἴ τις ἄλλος,
ἅμα τ᾽ ἔπταισαν καὶ δικαίως ἂν φαῦλοι νομίζοιντο·
εἰ δ᾽ ἐκεῖνοι τούτοις ἐξελέγχονται, τί κωλύει μηδ᾽
Ἀριστείδην ἐλλόγιμον μηδ᾽ ἔξω τῆς ἐκείνων αἰτίας
τιθέναι; ὥστ᾽ οὐ μόνον τοῖς κατὰ ῥητορικῆς
λόγοις, ἀλλὰ καὶ τοῖς ἰδίᾳ κατὰ τῶν ἀνδρῶν, ὅ γε
Ἀριστείδης ὑπεναντίως ὑπ᾽ αὐτοῦ τιμηθεὶς ἐκείνοις
οὓς κακίζει βοηθῶν φαίνεται, ὥσπερ ἐπεισόδιον
παρὰ δόξαν προχωροῦν.

362 Ἔπειτ᾽ εἰσάγει² τὸν κυβερνήτην, καὶ τίνος ἕνεκα,
φησίν, οὐ φρονεῖ μέγα οὐδὲ ἴσον τῷ ῥήτορι, σῴζων
ἐκ θανάτου καὶ οὗτος ἀνθρώπους καὶ αὐτοὺς καὶ
χρήματα; ἐγὼ δὲ ὁρῶ μὲν κἀκεῖνο ὑπάρχον ἀντ-
ερωτῆσαι, τίνος οὖν ἕνεκα οὐδὲ αὐτὸς τῷ κυβερνήτῃ παραχωρεῖς; εἰ γὰρ φιλοσοφίας ἕνεκα ἀτίμως
ὑπὸ τῶν πολλῶν ἀγομένης πλεῦσαι φὴς εἰς Σικελίαν τῷ Δίωνι βοηθός, οὐχ ἧττον ὁ κυβερνήτης
ἐκεῖνον ἔσῳζεν ὁ σὲ ἄγων, καὶ ταῦτα μέντοι διὰ
τοῦ μεγίστου τῶν πελαγῶν, ἀλλὰ τοσούτῳ σοῦ
πλέον εἰπεῖν ἔχει, ὅσῳ καὶ αὐτὸν τὸν μέλλοντα σώ-
363 ζειν τὸν Δίωνα ἔσῳζεν. ἀλλ᾽ ἐῶ ταῦτα. ἀλλὰ πῶς

poorly leading the Athenians, even Aristides did
not lead them well. For he did not escape unscathed,
but was expelled. And I shall add that his misfortune did not even take place in a court, like that of
Miltiades and Pericles, nor at the hands of those
whom he offended on behalf of the common people,
but he was ostracized by the people itself. Then if 361
this is not a proof of evil, if some orator has been
unfortunate in respect to those whom he led, neither
Miltiades, nor Themistocles, nor anyone else, when
they stumbled, would justly be believed bad. If they
are refuted by these arguments, what prevents us
from including the honourable Aristides in the accusation of those men? Therefore Aristides, who has
been honoured by him inconsistently not only with
the arguments against oratory, but also with those
particularly against the men themselves, clearly aids
those whom Plato demeans, just as an episode in a
play which proceeds contrary to expectation.

Next he brings in a helmsman,[a] and why, he says, 362
is he not equally proud as an orator, since he too saves
men from death and their property as well? But I see
that this too can be asked in rejoinder. Why then
do not you yourself give way to the helmsman? If
you say that you sailed to Sicily to help Dion because
philosophy was being held in contempt by the common
people, the helmsman, who brought you, indeed
through the greatest of seas, no less saved that man,
and can claim this so much more than you, to the
degree that he saved him who was going to save Dion.
But I dismiss this argument. But how is it not truly 363

---

[a] *Gorgias* 511 B ff.

---

¹ Μιλτιάδης οὔτε om. VA.   ² **Reiske :** ἄγει TQVA.

(120 D.)

οὐκ ἄτοπον ὡς ἀληθῶς, εἰ αὐτὸς μὲν ὁ κυβερνήτης μὴ ἀξιοῖ τὸ ἴσον φρονεῖν τῷ ῥήτορι μηδ' ἀμφισ-
βητεῖ, σὺ δὲ χρῇ[1] τούτῳ παραδείγματι, ὥσπερ

121 D. ταπεινοτέρους τι ταύτῃ ποιήσων τοὺς ῥήτορας, εἰ
364 πάντες εἴκουσιν αὐτοῖς. καὶ μὴν ὅτι γε οὐχ ὑπ'
ἀνοίας ὁ κυβερνήτης ὑποχωρεῖ τῷ ῥήτορι οὐδὲ
ἔχοι τις ἂν αὐτὸν νουθετῶν εἰπεῖν, ὥσπερ ἐν ἀγῶνι
παρ' ἀξίαν εἴκοντα. ὦ οὗτος, ὅρα τί ποιεῖς· ὁ
ῥήτωρ οἰχήσεται τὸν στέφανον λαβών· οὐ μέγα
ἀγώνισμα τῆς ῥητορικῆς τοῦτο ἐπιδεῖξαι. καὶ[2] γὰρ
οἶδεν καὶ οὐ δεῖται τοῦ διδάξοντος, τοσοῦτόν
γε νοῦ μετέχων, ὅτι αὐτὸς τῶν μὲν ναυτῶν ἐστιν
ἄρχων, τῶν δὲ ἐμπλεόντων διάκονος καὶ ὑπηρέτης.

365 καὶ τῶν γε καιρῶν τοσοῦτον αὐτῷ μέτεστιν, ὅσον
τοῖς ἐγνωκόσιν πλεῖν σημῆναι, καὶ νὴ Δία ὁρμοῦν-
τας ἐπ' ἀκτῆς ἀναστῆσαι προσάγοντος τοῦ πνεύ-
ματος· τὸ δὲ ὁπότε πλεῖν ἄμεινον καὶ ὁπότε[3] οἴκοι
μένειν καὶ ὅποι καὶ ὑπὲρ ὧν πλεῖν οὐδὲν οὔτε ἰδεῖν
ὧν ἑτέρου μᾶλλον δυνατὸς οὔτε συμβουλεῦσαι

366 κύριος. τὸ δὲ τοῦ ῥήτορος οὐ τοιοῦτόν ἐστιν, ἀλλ'
ὥσπερ οἱ κυβερνῆται τῶν ναυτῶν ἄρχουσιν, οὕτως
αὖ τῶν κυβερνητῶν οἱ ῥήτορες ἄρχουσιν, ὅταν τὰ
κράτιστα δεήσῃ νεῶν. καὶ τοσούτῳ γέ τι τῶν κυβερνητῶν οἱ ῥήτορες κυριώτεροι ἢ τῶν ναυτῶν ἐκεῖνοι, ὅσον οἱ μὲν πλεόντων[4] εἰσὶ κύριοι τῶν ναυτῶν,
οἱ δὲ καὶ αὐτοῦ τοῦ πλεῖν ἢ μὴ τοὺς κυβερνήτας.

367 μᾶλλον δὲ ἀμφοτέρων εἰσὶ κύριοι, καὶ τῶν κυβερνητῶν καὶ τῶν ἐμπλεόντων,[5] οἱ ῥήτορες. διδάσκουσί
γε καὶ πείθουσιν ἐξ ἀρχῆς πότε καὶ ποῖ πλευστέον·

---

[1] codd. dett. : χρᾷ TQVA.   [2] οὐ VA.

strange if the helmsman neither demands nor disputes with the orator for the right to be equally proud, yet you use this example as if thus you were going to make orators somewhat more humble when all men yield to them ? Indeed, it is not much 364 trouble for oratory to show that the helmsman wisely yields to the orator, nor could anyone admonish him and say, as if he unworthily yielded in some game, My man, see what you are doing ; the orator will go off with the prize. For he knows and needs no teacher, since he has this much sense, that he is the ruler of the sailors, but the attendant and servant of the passengers. And his share in these occasions 365 is limited to the extent of giving the signal for setting sail to those who have determined to do so, and, by Zeus, to taking out the ship at anchor by the beach, when the breezes come. But he has no more power than any other to know nor authority to counsel when it is better to sail, when to stay at home, and where and for what reason to sail. The orator is 366 not in this position. Just as helmsmen rule the sailors, so in turn orators rule the helmsmen, as to when ships will be most needed. And orators have so much more authority over helmsmen than they do over sailors, to the extent that their authority is over the sailors when they sail, but orators have authority over whether the helmsmen sail or not. Moreover, 367 orators have authority over both groups, the helmsmen and those who sail on board. First they teach and use the power of persuasion as to when and where the sailing must be made. And again when-

---

[3] ἄμεινον—ὁπότε om. VA.
[4] Reiske : ἐμπλεόντων TQVA, secl. Keil.
[5] πλεόντων VA.

122 D. καὶ πάλιν ἡνίκα ἂν τούτου δέῃ κωλύουσιν. ὥστε
οὐκ ἴσον μισθώσαντα ὑπηρετεῖν καὶ νικήσαντα ἀπο-
στεῖλαι, οὐδὲ τὸ σεσωκέναι τὴν ναῦν οὐδὲ τοὺς ἐν
τῇ νηὶ σκοπεῖν οἴεται δεῖν ὁ κυβερνήτης, ἀλλὰ τὸ
σχῆμα προσεξετάζειν τοῦ πράγματος, ὥσπερ ὁ
δήμιος οὐκ ἀξιοῖ μεῖζον τοῦ δικαστοῦ φρονεῖν οὐδὲ
ἴσον, ὅτι δὴ αὐτὸς ἀποκτιννύει, εἰ δὲ μή, ἀλλ᾽ ὅτ
καὶ αὐτός, ἀλλ᾽ οἶδεν αὐτὸς μὲν ὑπηρέτης ὤν, τοῦτο
ἀνάγκη ποιῶν, τὸν δὲ μετ᾽ ἐξουσίας κρίνοντα τὸ
368 δίκαιον ἐξεπίτηδες. ἔτι δὲ ὁ μὲν κυβερνήτης ἐξ
ἡμισείας τὴν ἰσχὺν ἔχει. τὸ γὰρ σῴζειν μόνον ἐστὶν
αὐτοῦ, ἀπέκτεινεν δὲ οὐδεὶς οὐδένα πω τῷ λόγῳ
τῆς τέχνης, ἀλλ᾽ ἐάν τινες καὶ ναυαγίας συμβάσης
διαφθαρῶσιν, παραιτεῖται καὶ οὐ σεμνύνεται. ὁ δὲ
ῥήτωρ οὐ σῴζειν οἶδεν μόνον, ἀλλὰ καὶ ἀποκτιννύειν
καὶ ἐκβάλλειν οὓς ἄμεινον· ὥστε τέλειον ἐξ ἀμφοτέ-
369 ρων τὸ κράτος τῷ ῥήτορι. καὶ ὁ μέν γε κυβερνήτης
οὐδὲ οὓς σῴζει πρὸς ἀξίαν σῴζει, ἀλλ᾽ ὥσπερ καὶ
τὸ παράδειγμα λέγει, οὐκ ἀπεικὸς ἡγεῖται τοιούτους ἐνεῖναί τινας οἷς τεθνάναι κρεῖττον ἢ ζῆν· ὁ δὲ
370 ῥήτωρ καὶ τὴν τοῦ σῴζειν μερίδα σὺν τῷ δικαίῳ πλη-
123 D. ροῖ. οὐκοῦν οὐχ ὅμοιον γίγνεται τὸ παράδειγμα,
ὅταν δυοῖν ὄντοιν ὁ μὲν ἀμφοῖν ᾖ σὺν τῷ δικαίῳ
κύριος, ὁ δὲ καὶ θάτερον ἐξ ἡμισείας ἔχῃ. διὰ
ταῦτα ὁ κυβερνήτης δύο ὀβολοὺς πραξάμενος, ἐὰν
ἐξ Αἰγίνης, ἐὰν δὲ¹ ἐξ Αἰγύπτου, φής, ἢ τοῦ² Πόν-

---

¹ Ddf. ex Plat. : τε TQVA.
² om. TQ.

ᵃ Cf. Gorgias 466 ʙ.   ᵇ Gorgias 511 ᴇ ff.

ever there is need of this, they prevent it. Therefore hiring out one's ship and being a servant is not on the same level as prevailing in debate and dispatching the ship. Nor does the helmsman think that he must consider in this context his saving of the ship and those in it, but that he must examine besides the character of the task, just as the public executioner does not lay claim to the right to be more proud than or as proud as the juror, because he himself performs the act of killing, and if not himself alone, because he participates in it, but he knows that he is a servant and must so act, while the juror of a purpose and with full authority judges what is just. Also the helmsman's power is limited by half. His **368** competence is only to save, but no helmsman has killed anyone by reason of his art. If ever some people are lost in the course of a shipwreck, he makes excuses and feels no pride. But the orator knows not only how to save, but also how to kill and expel those for whom this is required.[a] Therefore the orator has full power in both respects. And the helms- **369** man does not save according to their deserts those whom he saves ; but just as the example says,[b] he believes that it is not unlikely that there are such among them for whom it were better to die than to live. But the orator fulfils even the part of saving with an eye to justice. Then the example is inappropriate, when, given two elements, one man is master **370** of both together with the concept of justice, and the other man possesses only one of the two in a half-way measure. For this reason when the helmsman " has earned his two obols, if from Aegina, or if from Egypt," as you say,[c] " or from Pontus, two

[c] *Gorgias* 511 D—512 B.

(123 D.)

του, δύο δραχμάς, ἐὰν πάμπολυ, ἐκβὰς παρὰ τὴν θάλατταν καὶ τὴν ναῦν περιπατεῖ ἐν μετρίῳ σχήματι.
λογίζεται γάρ, φῄς,[1] ὅτι ἄδηλόν ἐστιν οὕστινας ὠφέ-
ληκεν τῶν ⟨συμπλεόντων⟩[2] καὶ οὕστινας ἔβλαψεν, καὶ
διὰ ταῦτα οὐ νόμος ἐστὶ σεμνύνεσθαι τὸν κυβερνήτην
371 καίπερ σῴζοντα ἡμᾶς. ὁρᾷς τί λέγεις; οὐ νόμος
ἐστί, φῄς· ἀλλὰ τόν γε ῥήτορα νόμος, οὐκοῦν καὶ δίκαιον. ἀλλ᾽ ὁ κυβερνήτης ἐκεῖνά τε οἶδεν καὶ πρὸς
ἐκείνοις εἰ μὲν καὶ ταῦτα λογίζεται οὐκ ἂν ἔχοιμι
εἰπεῖν, ἔστι δὲ καὶ κυβερνήτῃ καὶ παντὶ συνιδεῖν
124 D. ὅτι κυβερνήτης μὲν ὅστις πλείστους ἀθρόους ⟨οὐκ⟩[3]
ἔσωσεν ὑπὲρ χιλίους, τὸ δὲ τοῦ ῥήτορος πλήρωμα
ὃ σῴζει οὐ κατὰ ναῦν ἐστιν Αἰγυπτίαν, οὐδέ γε
ὅλως μετρεῖται στόλῳ, ἀλλὰ καὶ λιμένες αὐτοὶ καὶ
πόλεις, οὐ μυριάνδροι μόνον ἀντὶ τῶν μυριοφόρων,
ἀλλὰ καὶ μετρῆσαι χαλεπαὶ τῇ τῆς ῥητορικῆς ὑπο-
πίπτουσι τύχῃ τε καὶ προστασίᾳ. καὶ ὁ μέν γε κυβερνήτης κατάρας οὐκ ἔχει τί χρήσεται τῇ τέχνῃ, τοῦ
372 δὲ ῥήτορος οὐδέν ἐστιν χωρίον ἐξαίρετον. κατα-
χώσει, φησίν, ἡμᾶς[4] ὁ μηχανοποιὸς τοῖς λόγοις.
ποίοις, ὦ Γοργεία κεφαλή; μέχρι μὲν γὰρ ἁπλῶς
μηχανοποιός ἐστιν, μὴ ὅτι κοσμεῖν ἔχει λόγῳ τὴν
τέχνην, ἀλλ᾽ οὐδὲ τἀκ τῆς τέχνης παρέχειν ἕως ἂν
μὴ νικήσωσιν οἱ ῥήτορες· εἰ δὲ μέλλει καταχώσειν
τοῖς λόγοις, τίς ἡ τούτων προεστηκυῖα δύναμις;
373 οὐκοῦν ὅτε καὶ μηχανοποιῷ ῥητορικὴ χρήσιμον, εἰ

---

[1] Ddf.: φησὶ TQVA.
[2] Behr ex Plat.: τῶν TQVA: αὐτῶν Ddf. ex codd. dett.
[3] add. cod. det. et Canter.   [4] ὑμᾶς Plato.

[a] *Gorgias* 512 B.

drachmas, at the very most, having disembarked, he walks about alongside his ship and the sea with no haughty demeanour. For he calculates," you say, " that it is unclear whom of the passengers he has helped and whom he has harmed. Therefore there is no approved custom for the helmsman to feel proud, although he saves us." Do you see what you are say- 371 ing ? " There is no approved custom," you say. But it is an approved custom for the orator ; therefore it is also right for him to do so. That much the helmsman knows ; I could not say whether in addition to that he also calculates the following. But it is possible for a helmsman and everyone else to realize that the helmsman who has saved the largest number of men in a group has not saved more than a thousand, while the complement which the orator saves is beyond the capacity of an Egyptian ship, and is not at all measured by a convoy, but it is the very harbours and cities, not only those of ten thousand men instead of ten ton ships, but those cities hard even to assign a measurement fall under the fortune and protection of oratory. And when the helmsman has made port, he does not know what to do with his art, but no place is exempt from the orator. " The 372 engineer will bury us under an avalanche of argu- ments," he says.[a] " Arguments " indeed, O Gorgon head ![b] For while he is simply an engineer, far from being able to adorn his art with words, he cannot even provide the use of his art, so long as the orators' proposals do not prevail. If he is going to bury us with an avalanche of arguments, what is the faculty which professes these ? When oratory is even useful 373

[b] A pun on Gorgias' name ; cf. §157; or. iv. 38 (p. 430. 11, Ddf.), or. xxviii. 101, and Plato, *Symposium* 198 c.

(124 D.)

γέ τι μέλλει περὶ τῆς τέχνης ἕξειν εἰπεῖν, πῶς οὐ
πανταχῇ ῥητορικὴ χρήσιμον;

374 Ἧττον μὲν οὖν[1] ἴσως τούτων ἄτοπα, ἀκόλουθα
δὲ ὅμως ποιεῖ καὶ παιδοτρίβας ἰατρῶν ἐντιμοτέρους
ἄγων. εἰ μὲν γὰρ οὐ ταύτην λέγεις γυμναστικήν,
ἀλλ' ἁπλῶς τὴν ὁπωσοῦν τὸ σῶμα κινοῦσαν, πάντες ἄνθρωποι μετέχουσι γυμναστι ῆς· πάντες γὰρ
375 ὁπωσοῦν[2] κινοῦνται. καίτοι θαυμάσαιμ' ἂν εἰ πάν-
125 D. τας ἀμείνους εἶναι συγχωρητέον τῶν ἰατρῶν καὶ
τεχνικωτέρους χρῆσθαι σώματι. εἰ δὲ ᾗς οἱ παιδο-
τρίβαι προεστᾶσι περὶ ταύτης λέγει, πῶς γε ἔνι
ταύτην εἰς ταὐτὸν ἄγειν ἰατρικῇ; πᾶσι γὰρ ὑπάρχον
ἰδεῖν τοῦθ' ὅτι χωρὶς μὲν παιδοτριβῶν πολλὰ γένη
τῶν ἀνθρώπων ἄγεται καὶ σῴζεται, ἰατρικὴν δὲ
εἶναι καὶ μὴ πᾶσι τὸ πᾶν ὡς εἰπεῖν διαφέρει. ἀλλ'
ἵνα μὴ λόγος ἡμῖν λόγον ἐκδέξηται, ἀγαπητὸν ὂν εἰ
καὶ τοῖς ἐπικαίροις ἐξαρκέσαιμεν, ἐῶ τὸ νῦν εἶναι
τὴν ὑπὲρ τούτου διαφοράν.

376 Καὶ ἡ τοῦ νεῖν ἐπιστήμη, φησίν, ἐκ θανάτου
σῴζει. ὥστε τί οὐ καὶ ταύτην σεμνύνομεν; ὅτι, ὦ
βέλτιστε—οὐδὲν γὰρ οὐδ' ἡμεῖς ὑποστελούμεθα
αἰσχύνῃ τὸ περὶ τῶν φανερῶν λέγειν—ὁ μὲν κάλλιστα νεῖν εἰδὼς αὐτὸς ἀρκούντως ἔχει[3] [σωθείς][4]—
ἕτερον δ' οὐδεὶς πώποτε ἐπινέοντα ἔσωσεν αὑτῷ,
ὅτι μὴ ὁ δελφὶς λέγεται τὸν Μηθυμναῖον Ἀρίονα.
ὁ δὲ ῥήτωρ οὐχ αὑτὸν μόνον οὐδὲ ἄλλον ἕνα συσ-
σῴζειν, ἀλλὰ καὶ φίλους καὶ πόλιν καὶ συμμάχους
377 δυνήσεσθαι μεμελέτηκεν. καὶ ὅστις μὲν ἄριστος

---

[1] om. TQ.   [2] τὸ σῶμα—ὁπωσοῦν om. VA.
[3] codd. dett. : ἔχοι TQVA.   [4] secl. Behr.

---

[a] Cf. Gorgias 520 B.   [b] Gorgias 511 C.

to the engineer, if he is going to be able to say anything about his art, how is oratory not in every way useful ?

His arguments are perhaps less strange than 374 these, but still consistent with them, when he holds gymnastic trainers in more esteem than doctors.[a] If you do not mean the generally understood art of gymnastics, but simply that which moves the body in any way, then all men participate in the art of gymnastics. For all men move themselves in some way. Yet I should wonder if it must be conceded 375 that all men are more competent and endowed with greater art in the use of the body than doctors. But if he means what the gymnastic trainers champion, how is it possible to rank this together with medicine ? All can see that many races of men are guided and saved without gymnastic trainers, but it makes all the difference, one might say, to everyone whether the art of medicine exists or not. But so as to avoid a succession of arguments, since it is enough if we have satisfactorily dealt with the major points, for the present I forego to dispute this matter.

The knowledge of swimming, he says,[b] saves men 376 from death. Therefore why do we not also honour this ? Because, dear sir—for we shall not shrink through modesty from discussing the obvious—he, who knows how to swim the best, will be well enough off. But no one has ever saved another by letting him swim on his rescuer's back, except in the story of the dolphin and Arion of Methymne. The orator has trained so that he will be able not only to save himself or one other besides, but also his friends, city, and allies. The best diver does not 377

(125 D.)

κολυμβητής, τριῶν καὶ τεττάρων πλέθρων οὐκ
ἐπινεῖ περαιτέρω, πλὴν εἰ Σκύλλαν εἴποις· οὐδὲ ὅταν
ἐκβῇ τῆς θαλάττης ἢ τῆς λίμνης ἢ τοῦ ποταμοῦ,
χρήσιμον οὐδὲν τὸ νεῖν αὐτῷ· τῷ δὲ ῥήτορι καὶ
λίμνας καὶ πελάγη καὶ ποταμοὺς ἐπελθεῖν[1] δυνατὸν
τῇ τέχνῃ· καὶ μένων οἴκοι καὶ πλέων καὶ καθεζό-
378 μενος καὶ βαδίζων ⟨ὁ⟩[2] αὐτός ἐστιν. ἆρ' ἴσα πρὸς
ἴσα ἀμειβόμεθα; καὶ οὔπω τὸ κυριώτατον εἴρηκα,
ἀλλὰ νῦν προσαποκρινοῦμαι, ὅτι, ὦ θαυμάσιε, νεῖν
μὲν καὶ σύες καὶ αἱ κύνες αἱ φαυλόταται πάντων
126 D. ἐπίστανται,[3] καὶ πολύ γε ἱκανώτερον ἀνθρώπου,
καὶ τάς γε ἐλάφους φασὶν ἐπινεῖν ἐπὶ πλεῖστον τῆς
θαλάττης ἐχομένας ἀλλήλων, πρώτην καὶ τελευ-
379 ταίαν ἀεὶ γιγνομένην τὴν αὐτὴν ἐκ διαδοχῆς. τὴν
δὲ τοῦ λόγου φύσιν καὶ δύναμιν οὐ λαγωοῖς οὐδὲ[4]
πιθήκοις οὐδὲ ἐλάφοις ἐνέθηκεν ὁ πάντα δημιουργή-
σας θεός, οἶμαι δὲ οὐδὲ τοῖς λέουσιν οὐδὲ τῶν
ἄλλων ζῴων οὐδέσιν, οὔθ' ὅσα ἐν θαλάττῃ οὔθ' ὅσα
κατ' ἤπειρον οὔθ' ὅσα ὑπερπέταται, ἀλλ' ἐν δυοῖν
γένεσι μόνοις τοῦτο ἵδρυται, προτέρῳ μὲν καὶ
τελεωτάτῳ τῷ πάντων[5] ἀρίστῳ, δευτέρῳ δὲ τῷ
πάντων τῶν λοιπῶν ἀρίστῳ, δι' ἓν τοῦτο ὃ ῥητορικὴ
παραλαβοῦσα ἄγει καὶ κοσμεῖ τὸν ἔχοντά τε καὶ
τοὺς χρωμένους αὔξουσα τὸ προσῆκον αὔξεσθαι
380 κατὰ τὴν φύσιν ἀνθρώπῳ. καίτοι εἰ τοσαῦτα
Πλάτων ἐπέδειξεν ὑπὲρ τοῦ κολακείαν εἶναι ῥητορικήν, ὅσα νῦν ἡμεῖς ὑπὲρ παντὸς τοῦ ἐναντίου
δείκνυμεν, οὐκ οἶδ' ὅπως ἄμεινον ἐπιστώσατο
τὸν λόγον. εἰ δὲ οἴεται παραδειγμάτων φαυλότητι
καταισχύνειν αὐτῆς τὴν ἀξίαν, ἐμοὶ μὲν οὐκ ἔτι

[1] Reiske: ὑπελθεῖν TQVA. [2] add. Iunt.
[3] πάντων ἐπίστανται om. VA. [4] καὶ TQ (prob. Ddf.).
[5] codd. dett.: πάντα TQVA.

swim over more than three or four plethra,[a] except
perhaps Scylla. And whenever he emerges from the
sea, lake, or river, swimming is of no use to him.
It is possible for the orator to reach lakes, seas,
and rivers through his art ; and he is the same man
whether he stays at home, sails abroad, sits, or walks.
Then are we really offering like for like in the ex- 378
change of arguments ? And I have not yet given
the most authoritative argument. But now, my
fine fellow, I shall offer an additional answer, that
even pigs and the meanest curs know how to swim,
and much more satisfactorily than man. And they
say [b] that deer swim over much of the sea clinging
to one another, taking turns at being first and last.
But the God who fashioned everything did not place 379
the nature and faculty of reason in rabbits, monkeys,
and deer, nor, to be sure, in lions and any other
animal, either all that are in the sea or on land, or
fly above the earth. But this is established in only
two races, the best of all, which is the older and most
perfect race ; and that which came second, and is
best of all the remaining races because of this one
quality.[c] Oratory is the inheritor of this quality
and it guides and adorns its possessor, and causes
those who use it to grow in a way that is proper and
natural for a man to grow. If Plato produced as 380
many demonstrations of the fact that oratory is
flattery, as we now produce for the opposite conclusion, he would have somehow better proved his argument. But if he thinks to shame oratory's value by
the cheapness of his examples, the arguments

---

[a] A surface area of 10,000 sq. feet,
[b] *Cf.* Oppian, *Cyn.* II. 218 ff. ;   Maximus of Tyre XII. 3
(ed. Didot).   [c] Gods and mankind ; *cf.* or. xliii. 17.

(126 D.)

τἀπὶ τούτοις ῥητά· δύναιτο δ' ἄν τις τὸ τοῦ Ὁμήρου
σῴζων ἔπος πρὸς ἔπος τὸ ὅμοιον ἀνταποδιδοὺς
ὑπολαμβάνειν, τί δαί; οὐχὶ καὶ αἱ τίτθαι τοῖς
παιδαρίοις ταῦτα λέγουσιν καὶ οἱ γραμματισταὶ καὶ
οἱ παιδαγωγοί; ὑπερεμπίπλασθαί σε οὐ χρὴ καὶ
βαδίζειν ἐν ταῖς ὁδοῖς [ὅτι χρὴ]¹ κοσμίως καὶ τοῖς

127 D. πρεσβυτέροις ὑπανίστασθαι καὶ τοὺς γονέας φιλεῖν
καὶ μὴ θορυβεῖν μηδὲ κυβεύειν μηδ' ἴσχειν, εἰ
βούλει, τὼ πόδ' ἐπαλλάξ· ἀλλ' ὅμως οὐ διὰ ταῦτα
μέγα φρονοῦσιν αἱ τίτθαι οὐδὲ ἀξιοῦσι πρὸ τῶν
φιλοσόφων εἶναι. ὥστε ἢν ἂν πλείστου τῆς ἀξία²
δυοῖν ἐστιν³ ἴσως ἢ τριῶν μνῶν. οἱ δὲ παιδαγωγοὶ
καὶ ὑποβαρβαρίζοντες ταῦτα νουθετοῦσιν οἱ πολλοὶ
καὶ φέρουσιν ἐνίοτε ἀντὶ παιδαγωγῶν θυρωροὶ
γιγνόμενοι τοῖς αὐτῶν δεσπόταις, ὁπόταν κατα-
λύσωσι τὴν τέχνην· ⟨καὶ⟩⁴ οὐ μὰ Δία οὐκ εἰ τῶν
ἑτέρων⁵ ἔλαττον ἕξουσιν, δυσκολαίνουσιν, οὐδέ γε
ἐκεῖνο λέγουσιν, τί δή ποτε αὐτοὶ μὲν ὁσημέραι
βοῶντες καὶ κονδυλίζοντές γε ἐνίοτε καὶ οὐχ ὅσον
ἀφοσιώσασθαι νουθετοῦντες οὐκ ἀνεσπάκασιν τὰς
ὀφρῦς, οὐδὲ εἰς τὴν προεδρίαν ὠθίζονται, οὐδὲ τὴν
τοῦ τὰ μέγιστα τῶν ἀνθρωπείων πραγμάτων
ἐπίστασθαι δόξαν οὐδέπω καὶ νῦν εἰλήφασιν· οἱ δὲ
φιλόσοφοι σεμνύνονται καὶ γαυριῶσιν καὶ πρωτείων
ἀντιποιοῦνται καὶ μεγάλους αὑτοὺς⁶ ἄγουσι ταῦτα⁷

128 D. λέγοντες ἐν αὑτοῖς, καὶ οὔτε τοῖς ῥήτορσιν ὑπείκουσιν οὔτε τοῖς παιδαγωγοῖς ἴσον οἴονται δεῖν φρονεῖν.

381 ἀλλ' οὔτε ταῦτα ἔχει λόγον ὑγιᾶ κἀκεῖνα τούτοις

---

¹ secl. Behr.   ² codd. dett. : ἄξιον TQVA.
³ om. Ddf.   ⁴ add. codd. dett.
⁵ Behr : ῥητόρων TQVA.   ⁶ codd. dett. : αὐτοὺς TQVA.
⁷ ταὐτὰ Keil.

thereafter are no longer utterable by me. In keeping with the verse of Homer,[a] one could give back the same, word for word, and interrupt with : What then ? Do not nurses, elementary teachers, and slaves who take children to school, say the following to little children ? " It is not proper to stuff yourself full," and " walk on the street in a seemly way, and rise for your elders, love your parents, do not be noisy, or play dice, or " (if you wish to add this) " cross your legs." [b] Still on that account nurses are not proud nor do they demand to be ranked before philosophers. Therefore whatever nurse you value most, is worth perhaps two or three minae. Most slaves who take children to school give this advice in a rather barbarous Greek, and whenever they are done with their art, sometimes they have put up with being door-keepers for their masters instead of slaves who take children to school. And by Zeus, they are not angry if they are fated to be less important than their counterparts, and they do not say, Why did we not frown scornfully, since we shout every day and sometimes administer a beating and give admonitions beyond mere duty, and why " do we not force our way to the best seats "[c] and why have we not now even earned a reputation for knowledge of the highest human affairs, while philosophers are proud and prance and claim pre-eminence, and extol themselves privately, and neither yield to orators nor think that they should feel no more proud than the slaves who take children to school ? But these examples are senseless and Plato's examples are like 381

  [a] *Iliad* XX. 250.
  [b] Aristophanes, *Clouds* 964, 983, 993-994.
  [c] *Cf.* Aristophanes, *Acharnians* 42.

(128 D.)

ἔοικεν. ἔγραφον δ' ἂν καὶ τὴν τέχνην, εἰ μὴ μει-
ρακιῶδες.

382   Οὐ μὴν ἀλλ' ἔν γε τοῖς ἄνω λόγοις ἐπειρώμην
δεικνύειν ὅτι ῥητορικὴ διὰ πάντων τῶν τῆς ἀρετῆς
μορίων διήκει, φρονήσει μὲν εὑρεθεῖσα, εὑρεθεῖσα δὲ
ὑπὲρ δικαιοσύνης, σωφροσύνῃ δὲ καὶ ἀνδρείᾳ φυλατ-
τομένη. τοῦτο δὲ καὶ κατὰ τούτους τοὺς λόγους
αὐτῆς ἰδεῖν ἔστιν. ἔστι μὲν γὰρ δήπου ῥητορεύειν
τὸ τὰ δέοντα ἐξευρεῖν καὶ τάξαι¹ καὶ τὰ πρέποντα
ἀποδοῦναι μετὰ κόσμου καὶ δυνάμεως. φαίνεται δὲ
ἡ μὲν εὕρεσις κατὰ τὴν φρόνησιν ἔχουσα, εἴπερ ἀ-
μήχανον φρονήσεως ἀπολειπόμενον τῶν χρησίμων
εὑρεῖν ὁτιοῦν, ἡ δὲ σωφροσύνη κατὰ τὴν διαχείρισιν
οὖσα καὶ τὴν τῶν ἡγουμένων τε καὶ εἰκότων συμ-
φωνίαν· ἀντὶ δὲ αὖ τῆς² δικαιοσύνης τὸ πρέπον τίθει.
τοῦτο δέ ἐστιν ὁποῖα³ ἄττα καὶ ὁπόσα ἑκάστῳ
προσήκει τῷ πράγματι σῶσαι. ἀλλὰ μὴν ἀνδρείας
ἐκ τοῦ εὐθέος οὐδὲν οὕτω μετέχειν ὡς ὁ λόγος βούλεται. τὸ γὰρ ταπεινὸν καὶ ἀγεννὲς οὐδὲν οὕτως ὡς
ὁ λόγος ἐξορίζει καὶ ὑπερφρονεῖ.

383   Εἶεν. ἐχόντων δὴ τούτων οὕτως τίνος ὧν εἶπον
λαβόμενον κακίζειν ἔνεστι τὴν ῥητορικήν; ἢ τίς
ἄμεινον καὶ καθαρώτερον ἐκ τῶν εἰκότων ἀνθρώπῳ
129 D. προσφέροιτ' ⟨ἂν⟩⁴ ἢ ὅστις δύναιτο ὁποίους χρὴ καὶ
ὁπόσους καὶ πρὸς ὁποίους καὶ οὕστινας δεῖ ποιεῖσθαι
τοὺς λόγους, ἢ πῶς ἔξω τῆς τοιαύτης δυνάμεως
ἔνεστιν ἢ πολλοῖς ἢ ὀλίγοις ὀρθῶς διαλεχθῆναι; ἢ
πῶς ἀδελφῷ προσομιλεῖν, νεωτέρῳ ἢ πρεσβυτέρῳ
λέγω, ἢ πῶς γονεῦσιν, ἢ πῶς ἑταίροις, ἢ πῶς

---

¹ καὶ τάξαι om. VA.
² codd. dett. Reiske : αὐτῆς TQVA.

these. I would have even used the words "their servile art," if it were not childish.

Indeed, in the former arguments,[a] I tried to show 382 that oratory partakes of all the parts of virtue, discovered by intelligence, and discovered for the sake of justice, and preserved through moderation and courage. This can be seen even in these arguments. For to be an orator is to discover what is necessary, and to arrange and present it in a proper manner with adornment and force. Invention clearly depends on intelligence, since it is impossible for one deficient in intelligence to discover anything useful. Moderation clearly is in disposition and in the harmony between theme and probability. Again put propriety in place of justice, that is the maintenance of a nature and magnitude suitable to the matter. Indeed, nothing signifies so direct a participation in courage as an argument; for nothing so bans and scorns that which is humble and ignoble as an argument.

Well! This being the case, by criticizing which of 383 my statements is it possible to abuse oratory? Or who in all probability would make a better and finer contribution to mankind than he who could write speeches of the proper quality and number, addressed to what sort and whomsoever of mankind it is necessary? Or how is a proper discussion with many or few men possible without such a faculty? Or how is conversation possible with a brother, I mean younger or older, or with parents, or comrades,

[a] § 235.

---

[3] codd. dett. Stephanus: ἡ ποῖα TQVA, ποῖα Phot.
[4] Canter: προφέροιτο ἢ TQVA.

(129 D.)

εἰδόσιν, ἢ πῶς ἀγνοοῦσιν, ἢ πολεμίοις, ἢ συμμάχοις, ἢ τρυφῶσιν, ἢ δεομένοις,—[1] ἢ μυρία ἄν τις
ἕτερα ἐπιδιαιροῖ; ὁ γὰρ τὸ πρέπον τῶν λόγων
ἐξητακὼς πανταχοῦ καὶ τὸν καιρὸν εἰδὼς καὶ δυνάμενος ταῦθ᾽ ὥσπερ οἶδεν καὶ περαίνειν, οὗτός ἐστιν
ὁ μόνος πᾶσιν οἷς εἶπον χρῆσθαι δυνάμενος, οὗτος ὁ
νουθετῶν ἀνύτειν, οὗτος ὁ κατηγορῶν πιστεύεσθαι,
οὗτος ὁ πανταχοῦ κρείττων τοῦ κατὰ ταὐτὰ ἀπο-
384 λειπομένου. καὶ μὴν ὅ γε εἰδὼς τί δεῖ λέγειν οἶδεν
τί δεῖ σιωπῆσαι καὶ πότε ἄμεινον εἰπεῖν καὶ πότ᾽
ἐᾶσαι,[2] ὥσπερ καὶ ὅστις οἶδεν πότε πλεῖν καιρός,
οὐκ ἀγνοεῖ καὶ πόθ᾽ ὁρμεῖν· ὅστις δὲ λόγου καὶ
σιωπῆς καιρὸν ἐπίσταται, κατ᾽ οὐδέτερον τούτων
ἁμαρτήσεται, εἰ δὲ μήτε λέγων μήτε σιωπῶν, οὐδέ-
385 ποτε ἐκ τῶν εἰκότων κατὰ γοῦν τὴν τέχνην. οὐκ ἄρα
τοῦ φιλοσόφου μᾶλλον ἢ τοῦ ῥήτορος εἰδέναι πότε
χρὴ σιωπᾶν. καὶ μὴν ὅστις γε ἃ προσήκει λέγειν οἶ-
130 D. δεν οἶδεν[3] ἃ πράττειν προσήκει. οὐδεὶς γάρ ἐστιν
ὅστις ἃ προσήκει πράττειν εἰπεῖν εἰδὼς ἃ προσήκει
πράττειν ἀγνοεῖ, οὐδὲ ὅστις ἀγνοῶν ἃ προσήκει
πράττειν εἰπεῖν ἔχει. καὶ μὴν ὅ γε εἰδὼς ἑτέρῳ τί
πρακτέον οἶδεν καὶ τί αὑτῷ δήπου, ὥσπερ γε καὶ
ὅστις διψῶντα ἕτερον παύειν ἑαυτὸν οὐκ ἀγνοεῖ.
386 ὁ αὐτὸς ἄρα ἐκ τοῦ λόγου φαίνεται λέγειν τε ἃ δεῖ
καὶ πράττειν δυνάμενος καὶ ὁ αὐτὸς περὶ ἀμφοτέρων
κατὰ τὸ εἰκὸς ἁμαρτών.
387   Ταῦτ᾽ ἄρα καὶ οἱ παλαιοὶ συνῆπτον τὰς δυνάμεις

---

[1] aposiopesin distinxit Lenz.
[2] πότε ἆσαι TQA.   [3] om. V.

or the informed or the ignorant, or enemies or allies,
or the self-indulgent or the needy, or—, one could
make countless other distinctions ? For by having
examined in every way the propriety of the argument and by knowing the right occasions, and by
being able to accomplish these things, just as he
understands them, he alone is able to make use of
all that I have said, to succeed in his admonitions,
to be believed in his accusations, to be in every
way superior to him who is deficient in these respects.
And indeed, he who knows what must be said knows 384
what must be kept silent, and when it is better to
speak and when to let a thing pass, just as he who
knows when it is opportune to sail, is not ignorant
of when it is opportune to drop anchor. Whoever
knows the right occasion for speech and silence, will
err in neither of these. But if he will err neither
in speech nor in silence, he will never err in all
likelihood, at least in respect to his art. Then the 385
knowledge of when to be silent, no more belongs to
the philosopher than to the orator. And indeed
whoever knows what it is proper to say, knows what
it is proper to do. For no one who knows how to say
what it is proper to do, is ignorant of what it is
proper to do, nor can whoever is ignorant of what
it is proper to do say what this is. And indeed who
knows what must be done by another, also knows
what must be done by himself, just as whoever
knows how to quench another's thirst, is not ignorant
of how to quench his own. Then from this argument 386
the same man clearly is able to say and to do what is
necessary, and clearly the same man in all probability
errs in both respects.

Therefore the ancients also joined these faculties 387

(130 D.)

καὶ οὐ διέκρινον. ἀλλ' Ὅμηρος μὲν ἔφη τὸν Φοί-
νικα ὑπὸ τοῦ Πηλέως πεμφθῆναι τῷ Ἀχιλλεῖ

μύθων τε ῥητῆρ' ἔμεναι πρηκτῆρά τε ἔργων,

ὡς τὸν αὐτὸν εἰδότα ἅ τε δεῖ λέγειν καὶ ἃ πράττειν
ἄμεινον. καὶ πρό γε τούτου πρότερον αὐτὸς συν-
ῆψεν εἰπὼν

οὔπω εἰδόθ' ὁμοίου πολέμοιο,
οὐδ' ἀγορέων, ἵνα τ' ἄνδρες ἀριπρεπέες τελέθουσιν,

τὸ μὲν [γὰρ]¹ πρακτικὸν ἐξ ἑνὸς εἴδους τοῦ κατὰ τὸν
πόλεμον ἐμφανίζων, τὸ δ' αὖ λογικὸν ἐκ τοῦ κατὰ
τὰς ἀγοράς, μνησθεὶς δὲ ὅμως ἀμφοτέρων τὸ '' ἵνα
τ' ἄνδρες ἀριπρεπέες τελέθουσιν '' ταῖς ἀγοραῖς
προσέθηκεν, οὐ τῷ πολέμῳ, ὡς ἀμείνω τὸν ῥήτορα
ὄντα ὅταν λέγῃ περὶ τῶν πρακτέων, ἢ ὅταν αὐτὸς
πράττῃ τὴν πρᾶξιν. εἰκότως. ὅσῳ γὰρ βέλτιον ἄρχειν ἢ διακονεῖν, τοσούτῳ λέγειν τὰ δέοντα βέλτιον
ἢ πράττειν. ὁ μὲν γὰρ οἶμαι πολλοῖς σύμβουλος γί-
388   γνεται, ὁ δὲ ἀνθ' ἑνὸς ἄλλου τινὸς γίγνεται. ὥσπερ
131 D.   οὖν τοὺς ἀρχιτέκτονας τῶν τεκτόνων ἀνάγκη προέχειν, ὄντας ὅμως περὶ ταῦτα² ἃ τῆς τῶν τεκτόνων ἐστὶν ἐμπειρίας, οὕτω τοὺς ἐν ταῖς ἀγοραῖς
καὶ τοῖς λόγοις προέχοντας τῶν τούτοις ὑπηρε-
τούντων βελτίους ὁ ποιητὴς ἔθηκεν καὶ προσεῖπεν
ἀριπρεπεῖς, μάλα ὀρθῶς προσειπών. ὁ μὲν γὰρ ἐν
πολλοῖς πράττων οὐκ ἔκδηλος γίγνεται· πολλοὶ γὰρ
οἱ μετέχοντες· ὁ δὲ εἰς τὸ μέσον λέγων ἅπαντας
ἐφέλκεται καὶ πάντες εἰς αὐτὸν ὁρῶσιν·

389   Ὁ δ' ἀσφαλέως ἀγορεύει,
αἰδοῖ μειλιχίῃ, μετὰ δὲ πρέπει ἀγρομένοισιν.

512

together and did not discriminate between them. Homer said that Phoenix had been sent by Peleus to Achilles [a] " to be a speaker of words and doer of deeds," since the same man knew what ought to be said and what had to be done. And before this verse, he first joined these qualities together in saying [b] " unknowing of fair-matched war and of the council places, where men are famous." He stresses action from one of its forms, " war," and reason from " council places "; and nonetheless having mentioned both, he attributed " where men are famous " to the council places, not to war, as if the orator were a better man when he speaks about what must be done than when he himself performs the action. With reason. For by as much as it is better to rule than to serve, to this degree it is better to say than to do what is necessary. The former, I think, is the adviser of many, but the latter is only the equivalent of any other one man. Just as the master 388 carpenters must be superior to the carpenters, although they are still engaged in that which is a part of the practice of carpenters, so the poet has made those who are involved in the council places and are superior in argument better than those who serve them and has called them famous, and very rightly too. A man who acts among many men does not become noticeable, for there are many participants. But he who speaks out in their midst, attracts the attention of all men to himself and all gaze upon him. " He speaks with assurance, with a gentle 389 dignity, and is distinguished among those assem-

---

[a] *Iliad* IX. 443. [b] *Iliad* IX. 440-441.

---

[1] om. codd. dett., edd. [2] ταὐτὰ Phot. (prob. Keil).

(131 D.)

εἰς γὰρ ἕτερα αὖ παραπλήσια σχεδὸν αὐτομάτως
ἥκει φέρων ὁ λόγος· ἐν οἷς Ὅμηρος σαφῶς μαρτυρεῖ ὅτι οὐ κολακεύων ὁ ῥήτωρ λέγει οὐδὲ ὑποπε-
πτωκώς, οὐδὲ τὸν δεῖνα ἢ τὸν δεῖνα θαυμάζων, οὐδὲ
ἐπίκαιρον ἡδονὴν διώκων, ἄλλος[1] ἄλλοθι γιγνόμενος,
ὥσπερ ⟨οἱ⟩[2] ὀψοποιοὶ χάριν ἡδονῆς ἑτέρου, οὐδὲ σχη-
ματιζόμενος ὡς δοῦλος τῶν ἀεὶ δυναμένων, ἀλλ'
390 ἀσφαλῶς ἀγορεύει, φησίν. τὸ δὲ ἀσφαλῶς ἔστιν
ἀπταίστως. ἀμήχανον δὲ ἀπταίστως λέγειν ὅστις
μὴ ὑγιῶς λέγει. αἴτιον δὲ τούτου φησὶν ὅτι αἰδοῖ
μειλιχίῃ, οὐ τὸ ἀναιδέστατον ἦθος τὸ τοῦ κόλακος
λαμβάνων ἐν τῇ ψυχῇ καὶ ἀναματτόμενος, ἀλλ'
αἰδούμενος. τοῦ γὰρ τοιούτου καὶ τοὺς λόγους
ἀνάγκη κοσμίους εἶναι, κόσμον δὲ καὶ τάξιν ἔχοντα
391 κρατεῖν. Ἡσίοδος δ' αὖ φησιν καὶ τοὺς βασιλέας
θείᾳ μοίρᾳ καὶ δόσει γίγνεσθαι λόγων μετόχους,
λέγων ὅτι ἡ Καλλιόπη

καὶ βασιλεῦσιν ἅμ' αἰδοίοισιν ὀπηδεῖ.
ὅντινα τιμήσουσι Διὸς κοῦραι μεγάλοιο,
γιγνόμενόν τ' ἐσίδωσι διοτρεφέων βασιλήων,
132 D.   τῷ μὲν ἐπὶ γλώσσῃ γλυκερὴν χείουσιν ἀοιδήν,
τοῦ δ' ⟨ἔπε'⟩[3] ἐκ στόματος ῥεῖ μείλιχα· οἱ δέ τε
λαοὶ
πάντες ἐς αὐτὸν ὁρῶσι διακρίνοντα θέμιστας
ἰθείῃσι δίκῃσιν· ὁ δ' ἀτρεκέως ἀγορεύων
αἶψά τε καὶ μέγα νεῖκος ἐπισταμένως κατέπαυσεν·

σχεδὸν οὐ μόνον κατὰ ταὐτά,[4] ἀλλὰ καὶ ταὐτὰ
ἄντικρυς Ὁμήρῳ λέγων, μᾶλλον δὲ πολὺ κυριώτε-
ρον καὶ λαμπρότερον οὗτος τῇ ῥητορικῇ συναγο-
ρεύων, ὁπότ' οὐ μόνον πράττειν τὰ δέοντα τὸν

---

[1] codd. dett. : ἄλλοτε TQVA.   [2] add. codd. dett.
[3] add. Ddf. ex Hesiodo.

bled." [a] Again the argument brings us more or less
of its own accord to other related points where Homer
clearly bears witness that the orator does not speak
fawningly and abjectly, nor in awe over so-and-
so or so-and-so, nor pursuing the pleasure of the
moment, changing himself for the occasion, as cooks
do for the sake of another's pleasure, nor taking a
posture like a slave of the powerful men of the
moment. But he speaks with assurance, he says.
With assurance means without stumbling. But 390
one who does not speak soundly cannot speak without
stumbling. He says that the cause of this assurance
is that the orator speaks with gentle dignity, and
does not take the shameless manner of the flatterer
and mould it in his soul, but has dignity. The words
of such a man must be dignified, and the man of
dignity and of good order must prevail. Again, 391
Hesiod says that the kings participated in the power
of argument by a divine portion and gift, saying
that Calliope [b] : " attends the revered kings.
Whomever of the Zeus-cherished kings, at birth, the
daughters of great Zeus will honour and look upon,
upon his tongue they pour sweet song, and gentle
words flow from his mouth. All the people gaze
upon him when he decides suits with upright justice.
And he speaks the truth and straightway with skill
has stopped great strife." He speaks not only
almost in the same way, but also says precisely the
same things as Homer. And he pleads for oratory
even more authoritatively and honourably when
he not only makes the same man do what is necessary

[a] *Odyssey* VIII. 171-172. [b] *Theogony* 80-87.

[4] codd. dett. et Canter : ταῦτα TQVA.

(132 D.)

αὐτὸν ὅνπερ¹ λέγειν² τὰ δέοντα τίθησιν, ἀλλὰ καὶ
τοὺς ἀρίστους τῶν βασιλέων ῥητορικῆς φησι μετ-
ουσίᾳ γίγνεσθαι τοιούτους. καὶ προστίθησι

Τοὔνεκα γὰρ βασιλῆες ἐχέφρονες, οὕνεκα λαοῖς
βλαπτομένοις ἀγορῆφι μετάτροπα ἔργα τελεῦσι,
ῥηιδίως μαλακοῖσι παραιφάμενοι ἐπέεσσιν·

δι' ἐν τούτοις μαρτυρῶν, ὅτι τε ἡ ῥητορικὴ σύνεδρος
τῆς βασιλικῆς καὶ ὅτι περὶ τὸν αὐτόν ἐστι τό τε τοῦ
ἐχέφρονος πρόσρημα καὶ τὸ λέγειν καλῶς. ὁ γὰρ ἐν
μὲν τοῖς ἄνω ποιήσας ὡς ἄρα ἡ Καλλιόπη τοῖς αἰ-
δεσιμωτάτοις τῶν βασιλέων ἕπεται καὶ ποιεῖ δύνασθαι λέγειν, ἐνταῦθα δὲ προσθεὶς '' Τοὔνεκα γὰρ
βασιλῆες ἐχέφρονες,'' ὥστε διαιρεῖν τὰ τοῦ δήμου
διάφορα, δεικνύει ἐν ᾗ μοίρᾳ πρόσθεν ἔθηκεν τοὺς
133 D. λόγους, ἐν ταύτῃ τὴν σωφροσύνην, καὶ πάλιν αὖθις
ὡς οὐχ³ ὑπ' ἀνοίας τοὺς ῥήτορας ⟨λέγοντας, οὕτως⟩⁴
ὄντας καὶ ἐχέφρονας, ῥητορικῆς μὲν ἀρχὴν φρόνησιν
καὶ σωφροσύνην τιθείς, ταύτας δ' αὖ συνάψας πρὸς
ἀλλήλας, τήν τε βασιλικὴν καὶ δικαστικήν, ὀρθῶς
ἀγορεύων Ἡσίοδος καὶ τὰς Μούσας ἀμειβόμενος
δικαίως, παρ' ὧν καὶ τὸ δύνασθαι περὶ τούτων
392 λέγειν παρειληφὼς ἦν. οὐκοῦν οἱ μὲν ἐχέφρονες
περὶ τούτων λέγουσι τὰ δέοντα, οἱ δὲ βασιλεῖς
λέγειν εἰδότες εἰσὶν ἐχέφρονες, οὐ μόνον ἵνα αὐτοὶ
τὰ δέοντα πράττωσιν, ἀλλ' ἵνα καὶ ἑτέρους παρα-
σκευάζωσιν. ἔστιν ἄρα ῥητορικῆς ἔργον καὶ φρονεῖν ὀρθῶς καὶ μὴ μόνον αὐτὸν⁵ ἃ δεῖ πράττοντα,
ἀλλὰ⁶ καὶ ἑτέρους πείθοντα ἃ δεῖ πράττειν παρέχε-

¹ codd. dett. : τῶν αὐτῶν ὥσπερ TQVA a. corr.

and say what is necessary, but also says that the best kings become such through participation in oratory and adds[a] : " Therefore kings are wise, because when the people are being wronged in the assembly, they set matters aright, readily persuading them with gentle words." In these passages he bears witness to two things : that oratory is the coadjutor of the art of kingship and that the title of wise and the ability to speak well are attributes of the same man. For in the above passage he wrote that Calliope attends the most revered kings and gives them the ability to speak, and here he adds, therefore kings are wise so that they can settle the differences of the people. He shows that moderation is to be understood where he formerly used argument, and again that as orators do not speak through folly, so also are they wise, while he makes the beginning of oratory intelligence and moderation, and again has combined with one another both the art of kingship and that of being a judge. Rightly does Hesiod expound, and justly he requites the Muses, from whom he got his ability to speak about these matters. So, wise men say what is necessary 392 about these matters, and kings who know how to speak are wise not only that they may do what is necessary, but also that they may prepare others to do so. The product of oratory is the correct use of the mind, and not only the presentation of oneself doing what is necessary, but also persuading others to do what is necessary, and in sum it is a royal

[a] *Theogony* 88-90.

---

[2] τὸ λέγειν TQ. [3] om. V. [4] add. Behr.
[5] codd. dett. : αὐτὸν TQVA. [6] om. VA.

(133 D.)

σθαι, καὶ ὅλως εἶναι βασιλικόν. οὐκ ἀποστατεῖ δὲ
οὐδὲ[1] ἡ παροιμία τούτων ἡ λέγουσα οἷος ὁ τρόπος,
τοιοῦτον εἶναι καὶ τὸν λόγον· καὶ πάλιν τὸ ἕτερον
393 ὡσαύτως. οὕτω καὶ τοῖς παρ' ἡμῶν λόγοις, μᾶλλον
δὲ οἷς αὐτὸς ὑποτίθησιν ὁ λόγος, καὶ τῇ παρὰ τῶν
πραγμάτων μαρτυρίᾳ καὶ τῇ παρὰ τῶν ἐντιμοτάτων
ποιητῶν καὶ τῇ τῶν παροιμιῶν πίστει παρ' ἡμῖν
τἀληθές ἐστιν.

394 Εἰ δὲ δεῖ καὶ μῦθον λέγειν, δέδοικα μὲν ἐγὼ μὴ
καὶ ταῖς γραυσὶν ἡμᾶς ἐξούλης ὀφλεῖν[2] ἐπισκώπτων
φῇ τις ἀνὴρ κωμικός. ἐρῶ δὲ οὐ μῦθον ἄλλως
αὐτὸν εἰς αὑτὸν[3] τελευτῶντα, ἀλλὰ καὶ ἐνταῦθα ἡ
παρὰ τῶν πραγμάτων προσέσται πίστις, ἵν' ὡς
ἀληθῶς καὶ τὴν τοῦ Ἀμφίονος ῥῆσιν ἀνταποδῶ καὶ
⟨πρὸς⟩[4] τὸν Ζῆθον ἀναμνησθῶμεν εἰπεῖν, εἰ μὴ κατὰ
134 D. τὸν Εὐριπίδην εἷς[5] ἀμφοτέρους ποιήσει τοὺς λόγους,
395 ἀλλὰ κατ' αὐτοὺς ἐκείνους διελώμεθα. νεωστὶ γὰρ
τῶν ἀνθρώπων γεγονότων καὶ τῶν ἄλλων ζῴων
θόρυβος πολὺς ἦν κατὰ τὴν γῆν καὶ ταραχή. οὔτε
γὰρ αὐτοί σφισιν εἶχον ὅ τι χρήσωνται, οὐδὲ γὰρ
ἦν οὐδὲν τὸ συνάγον, ἀλλ' οἱ μείζους τοὺς ἐλάττους
ἦγον, οὔτε τοῖς ἄλλοις ζῴοις εἶχον ἀνταρκεῖν· πᾶσι
γὰρ πάντων ἀπελείποντο ἄλλοτε ἄλλων, τάχει μὲν
τῶν πτηνῶν ἀπάντων—ὅπερ οὖν Ὅμηρος ἔφη τοὺς
Πυγμαίους πάσχειν ὑπὸ τῶν γεράνων, πᾶσι τοῖς

---

[1] om. VA.   [2] Phot.: ὄφλειν TQVA.
[3] codd. dett.: αὐτὸν TQVA.   [4] add. Reiske.
[5] codd. dett. Reiske: εἰς TQVA.

518

thing. No different from this argument is the proverb which says[a] : " as the character is, such is the speech." And the reverse is also true. Thus truth 393 is on our side through our arguments, moreover through the reasoning which prompts them, and through the evidence of the facts and of the most distinguished poets, and through the proof of proverbial wisdom.

If a myth must be told, I am afraid that some 394 comical fellow may say in jest[b] that we lost a suit for illegal possession to the old ladies. Still I shall tell a myth which does not purposelessly end in itself—but even here will be further factual proof—so that I may truly present in turn the argument of Amphion[c] and we may remember to answer Zethus if one man will not write both arguments, as Euripides did; but let us divide these between them. When human beings and the other animals had just 395 been born, there was great disturbance and confusion upon the earth. Men neither knew what to do with themselves—for there was nothing which brought them all together, but the bigger led the smaller—, nor could they maintain themselves against the other animals. For in every way they were inferior to all of them, to some at one time, to others at another ; inferior to all the birds in swiftness,—thus it used to happen that all men then suffered

[a] Cf. or. xlvii. 49 ; a well-known saying : e.g. Plato, Republic 400 D ; Seneca, Epistles 114 and 115 ; Quintilian XI. 1. 30 ; Juvenal IV. 82 ; see Norden, Die antike Kunstprosa, vol. 1, p. 11, n. 2.

[b] Frg. 652 Kock ; cf. Gorgias 527 A. Plato had already narrated a similar myth in Protagoras 320 c ff.

[c] Gorgias 506 B ; from Euripides' Antiopê. Aristides here sarcastically equates Plato with the boorish Zethus.

(134 D.)

τότε ὑπὸ πάντων συνέβαινεν τῶν ἀλκίμων ὀρνίθων—
κατ' ἰσχὺν δ' αὖ πόρρω καὶ τῶν λεόντων καὶ τῶν
κάπρων καὶ πολλῶν ἄλλων ἦσαν· ὥστ' ἀπώλλυντο
396 σιγῇ. καὶ μὴν τῇ γε κατασκευῇ τοῦ σώματος οὐ
μόνον τῶν προβάτων, ἀλλὰ καὶ τῶν κοχλιῶν
ἀπελείποντο, οὐδεὶς αὐτῶν ὑπάρχων αὐτάρκης.
φθειρομένου δὲ οὕτω τοῦ γένους καὶ κατὰ μικρὸν
ὑπορρέοντος κατιδὼν ὁ Προμηθεὺς ἀεί πως ὢν
φιλάνθρωπος ἀνέρχεται πρεσβευτὴς ὑπὲρ τῶν ἀνθρώπων, οὐχ ὑπὸ τῶν ἀνθρώπων πεμφθείς, οὐδὲ
135 D. γὰρ πρέσβεις πέμπειν ἦν πω τότ'[1] εἰδέναι, ἀλλ'
αὐτὸς ἀφ' ἑαυτοῦ. ὁ δὲ Ζεὺς τοῦ τε Προμηθέως
ἀγασθεὶς δίκαια λέγοντος καὶ ἅμα καθ' ἑαυτὸν
εἰληφὼς λογισμὸν τοῦ πράγματος, τῶν αὐτοῦ παίδων Ἑρμῆν κελεύει ῥητορικὴν ἔχοντα ἐλθεῖν[2] εἰς
397 ἀνθρώπους. ὁ μὲν οὖν Προμηθεὺς καθ' ἕκαστον
ἅπασι τάς τε αἰσθήσεις καὶ τἆλλα μέλη τοῦ σώματος
ἦν συμπεπλακὼς πρότερον, τὸν δὲ Ἑρμῆν[3] οὐχ
οὕτως ἐκέλευσεν ὥσπερ θεωρικοῦ διάδοσιν διελεῖν,
ἵνα πάντες ῥητορικῆς ἐφεξῆς μετέχοιεν, ὥσπερ
ὀφθαλμῶν καὶ χειρῶν καὶ ποδῶν, ἀλλ' ἐπιλεξάμενον
τοὺς ἀρίστους, καὶ γενναιοτάτους καὶ τὰς φύσεις
ἐρρωμενεστάτους, τούτοις ἐγχειρίσαι τὸ δῶρον, ἵνα
ὁμοῦ σφᾶς τε αὐτοὺς καὶ τοὺς ἄλλους σῴζειν ἔχοιεν.
398 ἀφικομένης δὲ ῥητορικῆς εἰς ἀνθρώπους οὕτως ἐκ
θεῶν μὲν ἠδυνήθησαν ἄνθρωποι[4] τὴν μετὰ τῶν θη-
ρίων δίαιταν χαλεπὴν ἐκφυγεῖν, ἐπαύσαντο δὲ ἐχ-
θροὶ πάντες ὄντες[5] ἀλλήλοις ἐν κύκλῳ, κοινωνίας

---

[1] codd. dett. : πώποτ' VA, πώποτέ γ' TQ.
[2] codd. dett. : ἐλθεῖν ἔχοντα TQVA.

520

from the predatory birds what Homer said [a] the
Pygmies suffer from the cranes. Again in strength
they were far inferior to lions, boars, and many
other animals. Thus they quietly perished. Indeed, 396
in the fitting out of their body they were inferior
not only to sheep, but also to snails, since none of
them was self-sufficient. While the race was perishing in this fashion and gradually diminishing,
Prometheus beheld it, and ever being in some way
benevolent, he went up to heaven as an ambassador
on mankind's behalf, not dispatched by mankind,—
for then there was not even the knowledge of
sending ambassadors—but of his own accord. Zeus,
much impressed by Prometheus' just remarks, when
he had considered the matter by himself, ordered
Hermes, one of his sons, to go to mankind with the
art of oratory. Prometheus had formerly fashioned 397
the senses and the other limbs of the body for every
person, yet he ordered Hermes not to divide oratory
as if it were a distribution of the festival fund, so
that all in turn might share in it, as in eyes, hands,
and feet ; but to select the best, the noblest and
those with the strongest natures, and to hand the
gift to them, so that at the same time they could
save themselves and others. When oratory had come 398
in this way from the Gods to mankind, men were
able to escape their harsh life with the beasts, and
all men everywhere stopped being the enemies of
one another, and they discovered the beginning

---

[a] *Iliad* III. 6.

³ συμπεπλακώς—Ἑρμῆν om. VA.
⁴ Behr : ἄνθρωποι TQVA Phot. : οἱ ἄνθρωποι codd. dett.
⁵ om. TQ.

(135 D.)

δ' εὗρον ἀρχήν. καταβάντες δὲ ἐκ τῶν ὀρῶν ἄλλοι
κατ' ἄλλα μέρη τῆς οἰκουμένης ἐπλησίασαν, τό γε
πρῶτον ὕπαιθροι, μετὰ δὲ τοῦτο ἤδη λόγου νικήσαν-
τος πόλιν τε κατεσκευάσαντο καὶ διεκρίθησαν οὐχ
ὥσπερ πρότερον ὡς ἔτυχεν, ἀλλ' εἰς τὰς¹ συντάξεις
κοινωνιῶν, καὶ τοὺς πόλεων ἡγεμόνας νόμους ἔθεντο
136 D. καὶ ἄρχοντας καὶ πολιτείαν ἐνόμισαν, καὶ θεοῖς
χαριστήρια ἀνήγαγον, πρώτας ἀπαρχὰς [αὐτοῖς]²
ποιησάμενοι τὰς ἀπὸ τῶν λόγων, αἷς ἔτι καὶ νῦν
χαίρειν μάλιστα τοὺς θεοὺς λόγος αἱρεῖ, ὅτι καὶ
γνωρίσαι πρῶτον αὐτοῖς τοὺς θεοὺς ὑπῆρξεν ἐντεῦ-
399 θεν. οὕτως ἄνθρωπος ἤρθη μέγας ἐξ ἀσθενοῦς καὶ
σαθροῦ τοῦ κατ' ἀρχάς, καὶ πρόσθεν καταφρονού-
μενος ὡς οὐδὲν πρᾶγμα κύριός ἐστιν ἐξ ἐκείνου τοῖς
ἐν τῇ γῇ, τοῦτο ὅτι βούλεται χρῆσθαι, πρόβλημα
ποιησάμενος ἀντ' ἄλλου φυλακτηρίου τὸν λόγον.

400 Καὶ ὁ μῦθος μὲν ἡμῖν ταύτην ἐχέτω τὴν τελευτήν,
οἶμαι κεφαλὴν οὐδὲν ἄτιμον εἰληφώς. ὅτι δ' οὐκ
ἄλλως μῦθος ταῦτα οὐδ' ὄναρ, ἀλλ' ὕπαρ, καὶ ὁ τῶν
πραγμάτων αὐτῶν ἐστιν λόγος δῆλον ἐξ αὐτῶν.

401 οὐκοῦν οὐ μόνον ἐξ ἀρχῆς ῥητορικῆς δύναμις
διώρισε ταῦτα καὶ κατέστησεν, ἀλλὰ καὶ τὰς ἐκ
πλείστου τῶν πόλεων οἰκουμένας ἔτι ⟨καὶ⟩³ νῦν
ῥητορικὴ συνέχει τε καὶ κοσμεῖ, πρὸς τοὺς παρόντας
ἀεὶ κόσμους ζητοῦσα τὸ πρόσφορον. ὥσπερ γὰρ
ἔφην ἀρτίως, ἡ μὲν νομοθετικὴ θεῖσα τοὺς νόμους
εὐθὺς ἀπήλλακται, καὶ ἡ δικαστικὴ μετὰ τὴν
ψῆφον οὐδὲν πολυπραγμονεῖ, ἡ δὲ ὥσπερ τις ἄγρυ-
πνος φρουρὸς οὐ καταλύει τὴν φυλακήν, ἀλλ' ἐκεί-
ναις τε συνῆν ἐξ ἀρχῆς ἡγουμένη τε καὶ προδιδά-

---

¹ Behr, qui distinxit : τε TQVA.   ² om. Ddf.
³ add. codd. dett.

of the community. When they had descended from the mountains, they came together in various parts of the world, at first living in the open air; and afterwards, when reason prevailed, they built cities, and were not distinguished as formerly by chance, but according to the organizations of their communities, and they established laws as the governors and rulers of their cities, and developed a belief in political science. And they brought thank-offerings to the Gods, the initial ones being the first fruits of their speeches, in which, reason proves, even now the Gods much delight, because first from that source they came to recognize the Gods. So man was raised 399 up to be great from his weak and rotten beginnings; and, formerly scorned as nothing, from that time he has had the power to use the things on earth as he wishes, making reason his shield instead of some other means of protection.

Let our myth end here, with a conclusion, I think, 400 in no way dishonourable. From the matter itself it is clear that this is no vain myth or a dream, but reality and a factual account. So the power of 401 oratory arranged and established these things not only at the beginning, but even now oratory still holds together and adorns cities which have been settled for the longest time, searching out at any time what is appropriate for their present adornment. For as I just now said,[a] legislation is done with once it has established its laws, and the art of the juror has no more concern after the vote. But oratory, like some sleepless guard, never ends its watch. At the beginning, it was joined with those two arts, guiding and teaching, and now alone it

[a] § 226.

(136 D.)

σκουσα καὶ καθ᾽ αὑτὴν αὖθις ἕκαστα ἐπέρχεται,
εἰσηγουμένη, πρεσβεύουσα, ἀεὶ τὸ παρὸν συντιθε-
μένη· καὶ οὐδ᾽ ἂν πάντα τὰ ἀδικήματα καὶ ἁμαρτήματα ἐξ ἀνθρώπων ἀπέλθη, οὐδὲν μᾶλλόν ἐστιν
ἄχρηστον, ὥσπερ νόμων οὐδὲ δικαστῶν οὐδὲν ἄν
που δέοι[1] τούτου συμβάντος. ἀλλὰ ἕως ἂν ᾖ τὸ
402
137 D.
χρῆσθαι καὶ καθ᾽ αὑτοὺς ἀλλήλοις καὶ τοῖς ἄλλοις,
τὰ ἔργα τῇ ῥητορικῇ σώζεται.

403   Οὐ μόνον δὲ τῶν ἄλλων ζῴων τῇ τοῦ λόγου φύσει
προέχοντες τοσοῦτον ἐσμὲν πρότεροι, ἀλλ᾽ [οὐδὲ τῶν
ἄλλων ζῴων][2] οὐδὲν[3] τῶν ὁμοφύλων τοσοῦτον διαφέρει παρ᾽ οὐδὲν τῶν ἰδίων ὅσον[4] ἄνθρωπος ἀνθρώπου
404 παρὰ τὸν λόγον. οὐ τοίνυν οὐδὲ ἐν ἀνθρώποις αἵ γε
ἄλλαι δυνάμεις τοσοῦτον παραλλάττουσιν ἢ διαρκοῦ-
σιν. ὁ μὲν γὰρ χρήμασι νικῶν ἕνα καὶ δύο ἴσως νικᾷ,
τριῶν δὲ ὁμοῦ καὶ τεττάρων ἀναμιξάντων τὰς οὐσίας
οὐκ ἂν εἴη πλουσιώτερος· εἰ δὲ καὶ τεττάρων, ἀλλ᾽ οὐ
δὶς τοσούτων. εἰ δέ τοι καὶ πολλαπλασίων, ἀλλ᾽ οὐ
πάντων τῶν ἐν τῇ πόλει· εἰ δὲ καὶ πάντων τῶν ἐν τῇ
ἑαυτοῦ, ἀλλ᾽ οὐ δήπου καὶ τῶν ἀστυγειτόνων· εἰ δὲ
κἀκείνων, ἀλλ᾽ οὐκ ἀμφοῖν γε ὁμοῦ, πολὺ δὲ οἶμαι
καὶ μᾶλλον οὐ τῶν κατὰ πᾶσάν γε ὁμοῦ τὴν Ἑλλάδα, παντάπασιν δὲ ἀμήχανον τῶν κατὰ πᾶσαν τὴν
405 ἤπειρον. ὁ δὲ δὴ λόγῳ νικῶν ὁμοίως καθ᾽ ἕκαστον
καὶ πάντων ἀθροισθέντων ἐστὶν ἔμπροσθεν, καὶ
ὅσον κρατεῖ, μένει διηνεκὲς αὐτῷ, καὶ οὐκ ἀπόλλυσιν. οὐ γὰρ δὴ συνενεγκεῖν γε ἔστιν ὥσπερ
χρήματα, οὐδὲ ἐράνῳ τὸ ἔλλειμμα ἀναπληρῶσαι.
406 καὶ ὁ μέν γε κατ᾽ ἰσχὺν προφέρων εἰ καὶ ἑνὸς εἴη
524

peruses every matter, making proposals, acting in missions, ever arranging present circumstances. And even if all injustice and error departed from mankind, it is no more because of that without use, in the way that there would be no need of laws and jurymen if this happened. But work remains for 402 oratory so long as men have dealings with one another privately and publicly.

By excelling in the nature of reason we not only 403 rank far before other animals, but no animals of like class differ as much in particular characteristics as does man from man in the matter of reason. Nor even 404 among men are the other faculties so different or comprehensive. A man who is extremely wealthy, perhaps is worth more than one or two men, but he would be no richer than three or four men who had pooled their possessions. And if even richer than four, still not than twice that number. And if even richer than many times these, still not than every one in the city. And if even richer than every one in his city, still not than those of the neighbouring regions. And if even richer than those, still not than both together, and certainly not, I think, than everyone throughout Greece together, and it is wholly impossible to be richer than all men on the whole continent. But he who 405 ranks first in reason takes precedence both over individuals and over all men collectively, and his degree of superiority remains fixed, and he does not lose it. For it is impossible to bring in shares like tax-money, or to fill up the deficit by contributions. And as for him 406 who is very strong, even if he should be stronger than

---

¹ Ddf. : δέῃ TQVA. ² οὐδὲ — ζώων secl. Behr.
³ codd. dett. : οὐδὲ TQVA.
⁴ ὡς codd. dett. (prob. Ddf.).

(137 D.)

κρείττων, ὑπὸ δυοῖν γ' ἂν αὐτὸν κατείργεσθαί φη-
138 D. σιν καὶ 'Αρχίλοχος καὶ ἡ παροιμία. εἰ δ' οὖν καὶ
ἀμφοτέρων ὑπερέχοι, ῥᾴδιον εὑρεῖν ὁπόσοι κρείττους περιφανῶς γένοιντο. "Συμφερτὴ δ' ἀρετὴ
πέλει ἀνδρῶν" ἔφη Ὅμηρος, τὴν κατ' ἰσχὺν ὀνο-
407 μάζων. ἀλλ' οὐχὶ λόγους γ'[1] ἂν ἀμείνους σύμπαντες παράσχοιντο ἑνὸς τοῦ καθ' ἕκαστον ὑπερφέ-
ροντος, οὐδὲ συμφερτῇ ἀρετῇ τοῦτο κρίνεται, ἀλλ'
εἷς καὶ πολλοὶ τὸ ἴσον δύνανται, τὸ ἐπιβάλλον τῆς
ἥττης σῴζων ἕκαστος ὥσπερ ἐν κάλλει. ἕως γὰρ
ἂν μὴ παρ' αὑτοῦ τὸ κρεῖττον παρέλθῃ, ἥ γε κοινω-
νία καὶ τὸ πλῆθος οὐδενὸς ἄξιον, οὐδ' ἂν τὴν
Δαρείου στρατιὰν ἄγῃς. ᾧ καὶ μεγίστῳ δείκνυται
ὅση τις ἡ τῷ λόγῳ πρὸς τὸ καλὸν συγγένεια, καὶ
ὅτι τοῦτ' ἐν ψυχῇ λόγοι, ὅπερ[2] κάλλος ἐν σώ-
408 ματι. καίτοι καὶ περὶ τούτου τοῦ μέρους ἔχοι τις
ἂν εἰπεῖν ὅτι κάλλος μὲν χρόνος ἐξελέγχει ῥᾳδίως,
ἀμέλει καὶ τὸ τῆς ὥρας ὄνομα αὐτῷ συγκεκλή-
ρωται· οἱ δὲ λόγοι τῷ χρόνῳ συμπροβαίνουσιν,
καὶ τούς γε βελτίστους αὐτῶν οὐδὲν οὕτως ὡς χρόνος δείκνυσιν, ὥσπερ τὸν δίκαιον ἄνδρα ἔφη
Σοφοκλῆς μόνῳ τῷ χρόνῳ φαίνεσθαι· τὸ τῆς προσ-
139 D. θήκης ἀφαιρῶ, ὅτι οὐ μόνον τῷ χρόνῳ οἵ γε δὴ
λόγοι, ἀλλὰ καὶ παραχρῆμα ἅπτεσθαι πεφύκασιν,
καὶ μόνων τούτων[3] τὴν ὥραν ἀθάνατον εἶναι συμβέ-
409 βηκεν. καὶ ὁ μὲν χρήματα κεκτημένος οὓς ἂν εὖ
ποιεῖν οἴηται δεῖν, ἀφαιρῶν ὧν ἔχει ποιεῖ, ὥστ'
ἐλάττω τὰ λοιπὰ καθίστησι τοῖς προειμένοις· εἰ δὲ
δὴ καὶ συνεχῶς ἐμμεῖναι τῇ τοιαύτῃ φιλονικίᾳ,

[1] codd. dett. : τ' TQVA.
[2] Iunt. : ὅτι περ TQVA ; ὅτι περ—σώματι secludere possis,
cf. xxvi. 13.
[3] Canter et Reiske : μόνῳ τούτῳ TQVA.

one man, both Archilochus[a] and the proverb say that " he would be subdued by two." Even if he should be superior to both, it is easy to find the total number which would be manifestly stronger. " There is a united valour of men," said Homer,[b] referring to strength. But all men collectively would not make 407 their reasoning better than the one man who is individually superior, nor is this matter judged by united valour, but one man and many men have equal force, since each man preserves his own portion of inferiority, just as in beauty. For so long as his superiority does not leave him, combination and number are worthless, not even if you bring in the army of Darius. By this very important evidence is shown the great kinship between reason and beauty, and that what beauty is in the body, this reason is in the soul. Yet even concerning this 408 particular argument, one could say that time easily refutes beauty, indeed the name of " season " has been allotted to it.[c] But reason increases with time, and nothing reveals the best argument as does time, just as Sophocles said[d] " the just man is seen through time alone." I omit to add that reason has it in its nature to hit its target not only in time but also right away, and that it has befallen that the beauty of this alone is immortal. And as for him 409 who has amassed money, he benefits whomever he thinks he ought to benefit, by taking from his possessions, so that by his outlay he reduces the remainder. If he should persist in such an ambi-

---

[a] Frg. 144 Bergk.   [b] *Iliad* XIII. 237.
[c] ὥρα means both " season " and " beauty " ; for the theme, Keil compares Isocrates, *Demonicus* 6.
[d] *Oedipus Tyrannus* 614.

(139 D.)

ταχὺ δήπου τοῦ ταῦτα ἐπικουρήσοντος αὐτῷ προσ-
δεήσεται· ἡ δὲ τῶν λόγων κτῆσις καὶ δύναμις παρὰ
τὴν χρῆσιν οὐκ ἀναλίσκεται, ἀλλὰ εἰ οἷόν τε εἰπεῖν,
410 καὶ μάλιστα τούτῳ αὔξεσθαι πέφυκεν. τὸ δὲ αἴτιον
ὅτι χρήματα μὲν κάτωθεν λαμβάνομεν ἐκ τῶν μετάλ-
λων καὶ λιθοτομιῶν καὶ παρὰ σκυθρωπῶν τῶν
ἔργων, λόγοι δὲ ἡμῖν παρὰ τῶν οὐδὲν ἀπολλύντων
δι᾽ ὧν ἡμᾶς εὖ ποιοῦσιν ἥκουσιν. τῆς οὖν θείας φύ-
411 σεως εἰκότως μετέχουσι μόνοι. καὶ μὴν νόσους μὲν
εἴ τις ἐξ ἀνθρώπων ἀνέλοι τῷ λόγῳ, μηδὲν δεῖν
ἰατρικῆς ἔστ᾽ εἰπεῖν, ὥσπερ μηδὲν δεῖν κυβερνήτου
μὴ πλέοντι· ῥητορικῇ[1] δὲ οὐ μόνον εἰ καὶ πάντα τὰ
τῶν ἰδιωτῶν ἁμαρτήματα, ἀλλ᾽ εἰ καὶ πόλεμοι
πάντες ἐξ ἀνθρώπων ἀπέλθοιεν, οὐκ ἄπορα τὰ
πράγματα, οὐδὲ πέπτωκεν αὐτῆς ἡ δύναμις ὥσπερ
ῥίζης ὑφαιρεθείσης. ἔτι γὰρ μᾶλλον αἱ πανηγύρεις
καὶ τὰ τῆς εἰρήνης χαρίεντα τοῦ παρ᾽ αὐτῆς κόσμου
προσδεῖται, καὶ νὴ Δία αἵ τε θεῶν τιμαὶ καὶ ἡρώων
καὶ ὅσαι τοῖς ἀγαθοῖς τῶν ἀνδρῶν ὀφείλονται δικαίως εὐφημίαι. πάντα γὰρ ταῦτα ἐπέρχεται καὶ
140 D. κοσμεῖ καὶ πᾶσιν αὐτὴ πρέπουσα ὁμοίως φαίνεται.
412 Εἰ δὲ δὴ καὶ κοινωνήσειέν τινι τῶν ἄλλων τεχνῶν
καὶ δυνάμεως, Ἡράκλεις, ὡς οὐδ᾽ εἰπεῖν ἔστιν ὡς
ἐκφαίνει τὸ παρ᾽ αὐτῆς. οἷον ἰατρὸς εἰ προσλάβοι
ῥητορικήν, τῆς ἰατρικῆς αὐτῆς μάλιστα οὕτω τὴν χάριν εἴσεται. εἰ γὰρ προσέλθοι τὸ δύνασθαι πείθειν τοῖς ἄλλοις τοῖς ὑπάρχουσιν αὐτῷ κατὰ τὴν
τέχνην, τί κωλύει προθεραπεύειν τὰ πολλὰ τῇ ῥη-

tion, he will quickly be in need of someone to assist him in this. But the possession and power of reason is not expended by use ; if one can so express the matter, it is in its nature to increase by this very fact. The cause is that we get our money from 410 below ground, from mines and quarries, and by grim works, but reason comes to us from sources that cause no loss, and through these benefits us. Therefore it alone in all likelihood shares in the divine nature. Indeed, if someone should hypothetically 411 remove diseases from mankind, it can be said that there would be no need of medicine, just as there is no need of a helmsman if one does not sail. But if not only all of the errors of private individuals, but also all wars should pass from mankind, oratory's affairs would not be in difficulty, nor would its power collapse, as if its roots were pulled out. For still more the national assemblies and the charms of peace require adornment from it, and so do, by Zeus, the honouring of Gods and heroes and all of the laudations which are justly owed to good men. It deals with all these matters and adorns them and on all occasions is clearly and equally appropriate.

If it should make a common cause with some one 412 of the other arts and faculties, Heracles !—It could not be expressed how it would be put into high relief its own contribution. For example, if a doctor would add oratory to his art, then he would particularly know the charm of medicine itself. For if the power to persuade should be added to the other means available to him in his art, why would he not give much preliminary treatment through oratory,

---

¹ ῥητορικὴ T a. corr. VA.

(140 D.)

τορική, πρὶν τῶν τῆς ἰατρικῆς ὀργάνων ἅψασθαι,
τῷ σοφωτάτῳ τῶν φαρμάκων, ἔφη τις, χρώμενον;
413 μετὰ τοίνυν τῆς στρατηγικῆς γενομένη πολλῷ μᾶλλον σῴζειν αὐτὰ τὰ τῆς στρατηγικῆς πέφυκεν· ἃ
δὴ καὶ Ὅμηρος πανταχοῦ σαφῶς δηλοῖ

Ὣς εἰπὼν ὤτρυνε μένος καὶ θυμὸν ἑκάστου

καὶ

Ὣς ἔφαθ', οἱ δ' ἄρα μᾶλλον ἐπ' Ἀργείοισιν
ὄρουσαν

καὶ

Τοῖσι δ' ἄφαρ πόλεμος γλυκίων γένετ' ἠὲ νέ-
εσθαι
ἐν νηυσὶ γλαφυρῇσι φίλην ἐς πατρίδα γαῖαν.

414 τοιαῦτα ἀεὶ τοῖς λόγοις προστίθησιν. ἐκφανέστατα
δὲ αὐτὸ καὶ μόνον οὐχ ὑπὸ κήρυκος βεβαιοῖ, ποιήσας
τὸν Ἀγαμέμνονα τῶν μὲν

ἀσπίσι καὶ κορύθεσσι καὶ ἔγχεσι πεφρικυίας

τὰς τάξεις παρεχομένων Αἰάντων ἅπαντας λαβεῖν
τὸν θυμὸν εὐχόμενον

Τοῖος πᾶσιν θυμὸς ἐνὶ στήθεσσι γένοιτο·

[ἐποίησεν αὐτὸν εὐχόμενον, ἵνα τὴν Τροίαν ἕλῃ.][1]
τοῦ δὲ τὰ βέλτιστα συμβουλεύσαντος τῷ στρατοπέδῳ Νέστορος δέκα τοὺς πάντας συμβούλους μὴ
χείρους λαβεῖν.

141 D.   Τοιοῦτοι γάρ, ἔφη, δέκα μοι συμφράδμονες εἶεν,
Ἀχαιῶν·
τῷ κε τάχ' ἡμύσειε πόλις Πριάμοιο ἄνακτος
χερσὶν ὑφ' ἡμετέρῃσιν ἁλοῦσά τε περθομένη τε·

θεὶς τὴν ῥητορικὴν τῆς στρατηγικῆς τοσούτῳ κυ-

before touching the instruments of medicine, using, as someone said,[a] " the wisest of drugs ? " Combined 413 with strategy, it will maintain much more the very function of strategy. Homer everywhere makes this clear [b] : " So speaking, he aroused the might and spirit of each." And [c] : " So he spoke, and they rose up more against the Argives." And [d] : " To them straightway war was sweeter than to return in their hollow ships to their dear homeland." Such qualities he always attributes to argument. He most 414 clearly confirms this, almost as if having it proclaimed by a herald, when he wrote that when the two Ajaxes set out their battle lines [e] " bristling with shields, helmets, and spears," Agamemnon prayed that all take heart [f] : " Would that such courage were in the breasts of all " ; [he described him as praying in order that he might capture Troy] ; but that when Nestor had offered the best counsel to the army, Agamemnon prayed that he have ten counsellors in all who were no worse. For he said [g] : " Would that I had ten such advisers of the Achaeans. Then swiftly the city of King Priam would fall beneath our hands, taken and sacked." He ranks oratory so much higher than strategy, to the degree that ten

---

[a] *Cf.* or. i. 330 (p. 297 Ddf.) ; or. xxxiv. 26 ; Aeschylus, *Prometheus* 379-380 ; Euripides, frg. 1079 N[2] ; frg. Anon. 317 N[2] ; Menander, *Sententiae* 313 Kock ; Plato, *Critias* 106 B ; Seneca, *Epistles* 75 ; Tertullian, *Pall.* 6.
[b] *Iliad* V. 470.　　　　　　　　[c] *Iliad* XV. 726.
[d] *Iliad* II. 433-454.　　　　　　[e] *Iliad* VII. 62.
[f] *Iliad* IV. 289.　　　　　　　　[g] *Iliad* II. 372-374.

---

[1] om. edd.

ARISTIDES

ριωτέραν, ὅσῳ δέκα ἄνδρες δέκα μυριάδων ἐλάτ-
415 τους ἀριθμῷ· εἰκότως. οὐ γὰρ πόρρωθεν εἰλήφει
τὸν ἔλεγχον, ἀλλ᾽ εἰ τότε ὡρμημένους Ἀχαιοὺς
ἀνίστασθαι καὶ ὑφαιροῦντας ἤδη τὰ ἕρματα τῶν
νεῶν καὶ τὴν θάλατταν ὑπερβοῶντας μὴ κατέσχον
οἱ δύο οὗτοι ῥήτορες, τί πλέον τῶν τακτικῶν ἦν, τί
δὲ ἀσπίδων καὶ δοράτων καὶ νεῶν [καὶ]¹ πλήθους
καὶ χρημάτων καὶ σκευῶν; ἀλλ᾽ ὡς ἀληθῶς ὅπερ
οἱ σκευοφόροι τοῖς ὁπλίταις εἰσί, τοῦτο ἐφάνη τότε
πᾶσα οὖσα παρασκευὴ πρὸς τὴν ἐπιστατοῦσαν
416 ἅπασι τούτοις ῥητορικήν. κυβερνήτης δ᾽ αὖ προσλαβὼν μόριον ταύτης τῆς δυνάμεως, εἰδὼς καὶ
φοβεῖν ἡνίκα καιρὸς καὶ πάλιν θαρρεῖν παρασκευά-
ζειν, πόσῳ προφέρει πρὸς αὐτὰ τὰ τῆς κυβερνητικῆς
πράγματα;
417   Οὐκοῦν ἰδίᾳ τε [πανταχοῦ]² θαυμαστὴ καὶ οἷς ἂν
προσγένηται ῥοπὴν τοσαύτην παρέχεται. φημὶ δ᾽
ἔγωγε καὶ κάλλος τε καὶ ῥητορικὴν συνελθόντα τῇ
ῥητορικῇ κριθήσεσθαι, καὶ οὐδένα τὸν τοιοῦτον
ἡδέως ὄψεσθαι μᾶλλον ἢ ἡδέως ἀκούσεσθαι λέγοντος. ἔοικεν δὲ καὶ τοῦτο Ὅμηρος μαρτυρεῖν

142 D.   Οὐ τότε γ᾽ ὧδ᾽ Ὀδυσῆος³ ἀγασσάμεθ᾽ εἶδος ἰδόν-
τες,

ὥς,⁴ ἔφη, τὴν πυκνότητα τῶν νοημάτων καὶ τῶν⁵
ῥημάτων καὶ τῆς φωνῆς τὴν μεγαλοπρέπειαν, διο-
418 σημίᾳ παρεικάζων τὴν ῥητορείαν αὐτοῦ. μαρτυρεῖ
δὲ καὶ ἐν οἷς ἀρτίως ἐλέγομεν

Ἄλλος μὲν γάρ τ᾽ εἶδος ἀκιδνότερος πέλει ἀνήρ,
ἀλλὰ θεὸς μορφὴν ἔπεσι στέφει·

men are fewer than one hundred thousand. Reason- 415
ably. For his proof was ready at hand. If then those
two orators [a] had not restrained the Achaeans who
were eager to depart, and were already pulling the
blocks out from under the ships, and out-shouting
the sea, what good would there have been in tactics,
what in shields, spears, large numbers of ships,
money and equipment ? Truly just as sutlers are to
hoplites, so then was clearly all this preparation compared to oratory which kept charge over the whole 416
army. Again when the helmsman has added part of
this faculty to his art, and knows how to inspire fear
when it is opportune, and in the opposite way how to
make men brave, how superior is he compared to the
unadorned functions of the art of navigation ?

Then by itself oratory is wonderful, and it provides 417
a great advantage to whatever it is joined. I say
that when beauty and oratory compete, the verdict
will go to oratory, and that no one will view a handsome man with more pleasure than he will hear his
words. Here also Homer seems to bear witness [b] :
" Then having seen only his appearance, we did not
show such admiration for Odysseus," as, he said,
when we heard his many ideas and phrases, and the
loftiness of his diction, and he compares his style of
oratory to a storm. He also bears witness in a pas- 418
sage we just now cited in our discussion [c] : " One
man is weaker in body, but God crowns his form

---

[a] Nestor and Odysseus.
[b] *Iliad* III. 224.
[c] § 96, *cf.* or. xxviii. 40 ; *Odyssey* VIII. 169-170.

---

[1] om. Ddf.   [2] secl. Behr.
[3] Ddf. ex Hom. : γ' ὦδ' V, haec verba om. TQA.
[4] distinxit Lenz.   [5] om. VA.

(142 D.)

οὐκ ἀργῶς οὐδ᾽ ἁπλῶς εἰπὼν τὸ στέφει,[1] ἀλλ᾽ ἐνδεικνύμενος ὅτι οὐ μόνον τὰ ἐλαττώματα ἀναπληρ-
οῖ, ἀλλὰ[2] προσέτι νικᾶν ποιεῖ, ἐπειδή γε καὶ ὁ
419 στέφανος νίκης ἐστὶ σύμβολον. τὸν οὖν αἰσχρὸν
καλῶς δυνάμενον λέγειν ὅτε τοῦ καλλίστου, λέγειν
δὲ ἀδυνάτου, πρότερον τίθησι, τὸν ἅμα καλὸν καὶ
ῥήτορα εἰκότως καὶ ἀκολούθως φησὶ μᾶλλον θαυ-
μασθῆναι παρὰ τοὺς λόγους.

420   Πίνδαρος δὲ τοσαύτην ὑπερβολὴν ἐποιήσατο ὥστε
ἐν Διὸς γάμῳ καὶ τοὺς θεοὺς αὐτούς φησιν ἐρομένου
τοῦ Διὸς εἴ του δέοιντο αἰτῆσαι ποιήσασθαί τινας
αὐτῷ[3] θεούς, οἵτινες τὰ μεγάλα ταῦτα ἔργα καὶ
πᾶσάν γε[4] δὴ τὴν ἐκείνου κατασκευὴν κατακοσμή-
421 σουσιν λόγοις καὶ μουσικῇ. καὶ ταῦτα οὐ ποιηταὶ
μόνοι, ἀλλὰ καὶ πάντες ἄνθρωποι προσομολογοῦσι·
τὰ μὲν γὰρ[5] ἄλλα ἢ ψυχαγωγίαν ἢ χρείαν ὡς ἐπὶ πλεῖστον εἰπεῖν ἔχει, μόνον δὲ τοῦτο μάλιστά γε ἄμφω
143 D. πληροῖ καὶ μετὰ τῶν ὠφελειῶν τὴν χάριν θαυμαστὴν ἔχει, ὥστε καὶ ὅταν εἰς πολέμους ἀλλήλοις ἔλ-
θωσιν ἄνθρωποι,[6] τοὺς παρὰ τῶν αὐτοχείρων πρέσβεις ἀφικνουμένους δέχονται καὶ ἀποπέμπουσιν,
ἐνθυμούμενοι [τὸ τῶν ῥητόρων φῦλον ὑπεξαιρούμε-
νοι][7] τὴν[8] τοῦ λόγου φύσιν [αἰδούμενοι],[9] ὅτι ἐξ ἀρχῆς
ἐπὶ σωτηρίᾳ καὶ κοινῇ χρείᾳ τοῦ γένους εἰσῆλθεν.

422 καὶ ἡ μὲν ἐν τοῖς ὅπλοις ἕξις ἄχρηστος ἐπ᾽ εἰρήνης,
ἡ δ᾽ ἐν τοῖς λόγοις δύναμις ἐν τοῖς πολέμοις οὐκ
ἄτιμος, ἀλλὰ καὶ πολίταις χρήσιμος καὶ πολεμίοις αἰ-
δέσιμος, καὶ τῶν ὅπλων πολλάκις ἐν τῷ τῶν ὅπλων

---

[1] οὐκ—στέφει om. VA.
[2] ἀλλὰ καὶ codd. dett. (prob. Ddf.).
[3] Ddf. : αὐτῷ VA, αὐτῶν TQ.   [4] om. VA.
[5] om. VA ; τὰ μὲν οὖν Phot., ὡς τὰ μὲν codd. dett. (prob.
Ddf.).

with words." He says " crowns " not idly nor simply, but shows that it not only fills up the deficiency, but in addition causes him to prevail, since the crown is a token of victory. Then when he ranks the ugly 419 man who can speak well before the most handsome man who is unable to speak, he says with reason and consistency that the handsome orator was more highly regarded for his speeches.

Pindar wrote with such exaggeration [a] that he 420 says that in the marriage of Zeus, upon Zeus asking the Gods if they desired anything, they requested that he create for himself Gods who would honour in words and music these great deeds and all of his preparations. And not only poets, but also all men 421 agree. For other things, to speak most generally, provide pleasure or use, but this alone most fully satisfies both and has a wonderful charm along with its helpfulness, so that even when men go to war with one another, they receive and send back ambassadors who come from the murderers of their people, considering that the nature of reason from the beginning appeared on the scene for the safety and common use of the race.[b] And the state of 422 being under arms is useless in peace, but power in argument is not without honour in war. It is useful for one's fellow citizens and respected by the enemy, and often on the occasions when arms are

---

[a] Frg. 31 Schroeder, 20 Turyn.
[b] A very corrupt passage. It seems that the two phrases in the Greek text which I have bracketed, " exempting the race of orators " and " showing reverence to (*i.e.* the nature of reason)," are glosses.

---

[6] Ddf. : ἄνθρωποι TQVA.   [7] secl. Behr.
[8] τήν ⟨τε⟩ Keil.   [9] secl. Behr.

(143 D.)

423 καιρῷ περιγίγνεται. δοκοῦσι δὲ ἔμοιγε καὶ τὸν Ἑρμῆν οἱ ποιηταὶ τὸν τῆς σοφίας ταύτης ἡγεμόνα καὶ προστάτην τούτου χάριν τῷ κοινῷ τῶν θεῶν μόνον καλεῖν ὀνόματι. κοινῇ μὲν γὰρ ἅπαντας δωτῆρας[1]

144 D. ἐάων ὀνομάζουσιν, ἰδίᾳ δ᾽ οὕτως μόνον τοῦτον· καὶ ἀκάκητά γε καὶ ἐριούνιον, ὅτι κακὸν μὲν οὐδὲν ἡ παρ᾽ αὐτοῦ δωρεά, ἀγαθὰ δ᾽ ἑξῆς ἅπαντα πορίζει τοῖς ἀνθρώποις, ἐν πολέμοις, ἐν εἰρήνῃ, ἐν γῇ, ἐν θαλάττῃ, ἐν δυσκολίαις, ἐν εὐφροσύναις, πανταχοῦ.

424 δοκεῖ δ᾽ ἔμοιγε καὶ τὸ τῶν δαιμόνων γένος, εἰ δεῖ Πλάτωνι πιστεύειν, διαγγέλλον τε[2] τοῖς θεοῖς τὰ παρ᾽ ἀνθρώπων καὶ ἀνθρώποις τὰ παρὰ θεῶν.[3] ὥστε καὶ σύνδεσμον τὴν ῥητορικὴν τοῦ παντὸς ὀρθῶς ἂν καὶ ⟨κατὰ⟩[4] τοῦτο εἴποι τις.

425 Μέγιστον δὲ καὶ τοῦτό ἐστιν εἰπεῖν ὑπὲρ ταύτης τῆς δυνάμεως, ὅτι οὐδὲν ὁμοῦ τοῖς τε[5] πολλοῖς οὕτω κοινόν ἐστι καὶ τοσοῦτον αὖ τὴν τῶν πολλῶν ἕξιν καὶ φύσιν ἐκπέφευγεν. ἀεὶ δὲ ὂν ὡς εἰπεῖν ἐν ἀνθρώποις χαλεπώτατα εὑρίσκεται τό γε παντελές. ὥσπερ γὰρ οἱ λέοντες καὶ ὅσα ἐντιμότερα τῶν ζῴων σπανιώτερα τῶν ἄλλων ἐστὶ τῇ φύσει, οὕτω καὶ κατ᾽ ἀνθρώπους οὐδὲν οὕτω σπάνιον [ὡς][6] ὅσον ἄξιον

426 προσειπεῖν ῥήτορα. εἷς δὲ ἀγαπητῶς καὶ δεύτερος ὥσπερ ὁ Ἰνδικὸς ὄρνις ἐν Αἰγυπτίοις[7] ἡλίου περιόδοις φύεται. οἱ δὲ πολλοὶ μορίοις τισὶ τῆς τέχνης περιτυχόντες Ὁμήρου δέονται προσαγορεύοντος αὐ-

145 D. τούς, ὥσπερ ἐκεῖνος " ἔσκεν ὑφηνίοχος " φησὶν καὶ πάλιν " Ποσειδῶνος ὑποδμώς." τὸ μὲν ἀρχή

---

[1] Stephanus : δοτῆρας TQVA.
[2] Reiske : τι TQ, om. VA.
[3] post θεῶν cum δοκεῖν pro δοκεῖ add. ταύτῃ κεχρῆσθαί φησιν codd. dett.; eadem, sed cum φημί alii codd. (prob. Ddf.).
[4] add. codd. dett.　　　[5] Reiske : γε TQVA.

used surpasses arms. For this reason poets seem to 423
me to call Hermes, the leader and patron of this wisdom, alone by the epithet shared by all the Gods.
For they name them all in common as " the givers of
goods," but individually only him. And they call
him " Without Evil " and " Helper," because his gift
is without evil, but he provides in turn all good things
to mankind, in war, in peace, on land, on sea, in
trouble, in joy, everywhere. It seems to me, if Plato 424
is to be trusted, that there is a race of demons,[a] which
brings messages from men to the Gods and from
the Gods to men. Therefore in this respect one could
rightly call oratory the bond of the Universe.[b]

But this is the greatest thing that can be said on 425
behalf of its power, that nothing is at the same time so
common to the masses and again has so escaped the
condition and nature of the masses. Although it
always exists, one might say, among men, it is most
difficult to find its perfect form. For just as lions
and all the nobler animals are naturally rarer than
the others, so among men nothing is so rare as an
orator worthy of the name. It is enough if one or 426
two are born in a revolution of the sun, like the bird
of India in Egypt.[c] But most men, having fallen on
certain parts of the art, need a Homer to name them,
with verses such as [d] " he assisted him in the chariot,"
and again [e] " servant of Poseidon." The one is the

---

[a] *Symposium* 202 E ff.   [b] *Cf.* § 210.
[c] The phoenix.   [d] *Iliad* VI. 19.
[e] *Odyssey* IV. 386 (Ποσειδάωνος, which probably Aristides
also wrote).

---

[6] om. codd. dett. (prob. Ddf.); ὡς ὃν (pro ὅσον) Reiske.
[7] codd. dett. : Αἰγυπτίαις TQVA.

(145 D.)

που, τὸ δὲ ἀκροτελεύτιον ἔπους ἐστίν. οὕτω πολλοῦ δέουσιν κατὰ Μίθαικον καὶ Θεαρίωνα οἱ τῷ ὄντι ῥήτορες εἶναι τὴν φύσιν.

427 Καὶ ὅσα τοίνυν εἴδη λόγων ἕτερα, ἵνα μηδὲ τοῦτο παρέλθωμεν, ταὐτὸν[1] πέπονθεν πρὸς τοὺς τῆς ῥητορικῆς λόγους ὅ τί περ τὰ πέμματα πρὸς τὰ τῷ ὄντι σιτία καὶ κρέα. ὥστε καὶ τῶν περὶ ἔκαστα οὗτοι μάλιστα εὐδοκιμοῦσιν οἵτινες ἂν πλεῖστον ῥητορικῆς εἰσενέγκωνται, καὶ τούτων αὐτῶν μάλι

428 στα ὃς ἂν ἐγγύτατα ἥκῃ ῥητορικῆς. Ὅμηρος καὶ τῶν Ὁμήρου ταῦτα, Σοφοκλῆς καὶ τῶν Σοφοκλέους ταῦτα. Πλάτων δὲ αὐτὸς ἡμῖν τί φησιν; ἡμεῖς μὲν γὰρ αὐτὸν οὐκ ἀγνοοῦμεν, ἀλλ᾽ ἐν τῷ καλλίστῳ τοῦ χοροῦ τάττειν ἕτοιμοι.

429 Τί δῆτα αὐτή γε καθ᾽ ἑαυτὴν ἡ ῥητορικὴ καὶ ὁ ῥήτωρ; ἐγὼ μὲν γὰρ οὐκ ἀποκνήσαιμ᾽ ⟨ἂν⟩[2] φάναι τοῦτον ἄριστον εἶναι περὶ λόγους ὅστις ἀνὴρ

146 D.
430 [ῥήτωρ][3] ἄριστος. εἰ τοίνυν τις καὶ τοιοῦτος ἐγγένοιτο οἷος ῥητορικὴν ἔχων εἰς μὲν δήμους ῥᾳδίως μὴ εἰσιέναι, μηδὲ περὶ πολιτείας ἀμφισβητεῖν ὁρῶν ἑτέρως ἔχοντα τὰ πράγματα, καὶ ταῦτα οὐκ ἐν ὑστάτοις ὢν δόξης ἕνεκα καὶ τιμῶν καὶ τῶν ἐπικαίρων φιλοτιμιῶν, αὐτὸς δὲ ἐφ᾽ ἑαυτοῦ τοῖς λόγοις χρῷτο, τὴν αὐτῶν φύσιν καὶ τὸ ἐν αὐτοῖς καλὸν τετιμηκώς, καὶ θεὸν ἡγεμόνα καὶ προστάτην ἐπιγραψάμενος τοῦ τε βίου καὶ τῶν λόγων, οὐδὲ τούτῳ χαλεπὸν πρὸς Πλάτωνα ἀντειπεῖν, ἀλλ᾽ οὗτος ἂν καὶ πολὺ καλλίστων καὶ δικαιοτάτων εὐπορήσειεν

431 λόγων, ὅτι, ὦ θαυμάσιε, ἐγὼ ταύτην τὴν δύναμιν

---

[1] codd. dett. : ταῦτα A, ταῦτα TQV.   [2] add. Iunt.
[3] om. codd. dett., secl. Reiske.

beginning, the other the end of a verse. So far are
the true orators from the nature of a Mithaecus and
Thearion.[a]

And all of the types of literature, so that we may 427
not even pass this matter by, have the same relationship to the arguments of oratory as sweet cakes to
real bread and meat. Therefore the most distinguished in each particular genre are those who have
most employed oratory, and of these especially
whoever has come closest to oratory. Homer is 428
famous for those passages of Homer, Sophocles for
those passages of Sophocles. What of Plato's words
to us ? For we are not unaware of him, but are ready
to rank him in the fairest part of the chorus.[b]

What then is the real oratory and orator ? I 429
should not hesitate to say that he is the best speaker
who is the best sort of man. If someone should be 430
of such a nature so that he does not easily appear
before the people with his oratory and engage in
political disputes,[c] since he sees that the government
is now differently constituted,[d] although as far as
reputation, honour, and opportune ambition is
concerned, he is not among the last, but if he should
speak in solitude, and show honour to oratory's
nature and the beauty in it, and should enlist God
as the leader and patron of his life and speech, not
even this man would find it hard to answer Plato,
but he would be well supplied with the fairest and
most just arguments. My dear sir, I have honoured 431

[a] *Gorgias* 518 B.

[b] For the conceit *cf.* Galen, *Protrepticus* V.

[c] Aristides speaks of his own inactivity during his incubation, *cf.* Behr, *op. cit.*, p. 51.

[d] The Roman government is said to have put an end to
political oratory in the Greek cities.

(146 D.)

ἐξ ἀρχῆς ἐτίμησα καὶ περὶ πλείστου πάντων κερδῶν
καὶ πραγμάτων ἐποιησάμην, οὐχ ἵνα τὸν δῆμον
κολακεύω οὐδὲ ἵνα τῶν πολλῶν στοχάζωμαι οὐδὲ
ἀργυρίου χάριν, ἀλλὰ καὶ ὅστις πρὸς τοῦτο ὁρᾷ καὶ
τῶν διδόντων ἐστί, μισθωτὸν καλῶ τοῦτον, οὐ
ῥήτορα, καὶ πολλοῖς ἑτέροις φημὶ λελοιπέναι τόπον
ἀμφισβητεῖν εὐδαιμονίας, εἰ ταύτῃ σεμνύνονται,[1]
ἀλλ' ὑπ' αὐτῶν τῶν λόγων ἀχθεὶς καὶ νομίσας
εἶναι πρέπον ἀνθρώπῳ κτῆμα λόγους καλούς, οὕτως
432 ἐργάζομαι κατὰ δύναμιν τὴν ἐμαυτοῦ. τί οὖν μοι
προφέρεις κολακείαν, ὃς τοσοῦτον ἀπέχω τοῦ κολακεύειν ὥστε οὐδὲ ὅπως ἐμὲ ἕτεροι κολακεύσουσιν
σκοπῶ; οὐδὲ εἰ μὴ θαυμασθήσομαι παρὰ τοῖς
πολλοῖς, οὐδέν μοι διαφέρει, ἀλλ' ὥσπερ ὁ φίλοινος
οὐχ ἡγεῖται ζημίαν, εἰ μηδὲ εἷς[2] αὐτῷ πίνοντι
συνείσεται, καὶ ὁ παιδεραστὴς καὶ ὁ φιλογύνης οὐ
147 D. πρὸς τὴν ἑτέρων μαρτυρίαν τὴν ἐπιθυμίαν μετέρχονται, ἀλλὰ στέργουσιν ἂν ἔχωσιν οἷς χαίρουσιν, οὕτω
δὲ καὶ ἐγὼ λόγοις συνὼν καὶ τούτοις ἀνθ' ἑτέρων
χρώμενος τέρπομαι τὴν πρέπουσαν ἴσως μᾶλλον
ἐλευθέρῳ τέρψιν τε καὶ ἡδονήν· ὥστε μηδ' ἂν τῶν
433 γειτόνων μοι συνειδῇ μηδείς, οὐ τίθεμαι βλάβος. σὺ
μὴν καὶ τὸν ἔχοντα τὴν ἰατρικὴν ἐπιστήμην ἰατρὸν
καλεῖς, κἂν μὴ δημοσιεύῃ τὴν τέχνην, καὶ πολιτικόν
γε τὸν ταύτην τὴν ἐπιστήμην ἔχοντα, κἂν τὰ αὑτοῦ
πράττων, ⟨τί ἄρα κωλύει τὸν τῷ ὄντι ῥήτορα ἐφ'
434 ἑαυτοῦ⟩[3] τοιοῦτον εἶναι; διὰ ταῦτα οὐκ ἐγχωρεῖ
φῆσαι σοί γε μᾶλλον ἢ ἐμοὶ κολακείαν γε ἐπιτηδεύ-
ειν οὕτω διακείμενον πῶς ἔνεστιν εἰπεῖν, ἢ πῶς τῶν
αἰσχρῶν τινος εἶναι προστάτην, ὃν εἰ μηδὲ[4] δι' ἕτε-

---

[1] codd. dett. : σεμνύνεται (prob. Ddf.).
[2] μηδεὶς Stephanus (prob. Ddf.).

this faculty from the start, and have valued it above all
profit and all affairs, not so that I might be a flatterer
of the people nor so that I might conjecture at the
desires of the masses, nor for money—but whoever
looks to this and belongs to those who pay him, I call
a hireling not an orator, and I say that I have left
room for many others to dispute about felicity, if
they are proud of this. But guided by speech itself
and believing that good oratory is a fitting possession
for man, I work according to my ability. Why then **432**
do you accuse me of flattery, I who am so far from
being a flatterer that I do not even consider how
others will be flatterers toward me ? Nor does
it matter to me if I shall not be admired among the
masses. But just as the lover of wine does not feel
it a loss, if no one at all will know that he drinks,
and the lover of boys and the lover of women do not
pursue their passions for others to witness but are
glad if they have what delights them, so I in my
association with oratory and in my use of this in place
of those other practices, have a joy and pleasure
perhaps more fitting for a free man. Therefore I do
not count it an injury, even if none of my neighbours
knows of me. You call him a doctor who possesses **433**
the art of medicine, even if he does not publicly
practise his art, and him a politician who possesses
the art of politics, even if he remains in private life.
What then prevents the true orator in solitude
from being such a man ? Therefore you can no more **434**
say than I how one so disposed may be said to
practise flattery, or to be the patron of anything
shameful. If for no other reason, because of the

---

³ add. Behr.   ⁴ μηδὲν Keil.

(147 D.)

ρον, δι᾽ αὐτά γε ταῦτα ἃ τιμᾷ καὶ διώκει πλεῖστον
ἀνάγκη πάντων τῶν αἰσχρῶν ἀπηλλάχθαι. ἀγαπητὸν γάρ, εἰ πάντα ταῦτα[1] παριδών τις καὶ πόρρω
που θέμενος καὶ ταύτην μίαν ἡδονὴν προστησά-
μενος, μηδεμιᾷ δὲ ἑτέρᾳ δουλεύσας, εἶτα δύναιτο
ταύτης σὺν θεῷ βοηθῷ κατατυχεῖν. ὃ γὰρ περὶ
τῶν ναυτικῶν ἔφη Θουκυδίδης, περὶ ῥητορικῆς ὅδε
φήσει[2] καὶ λόγων[3] πολὺ μᾶλλον εἰπεῖν[4] ἁρμόττειν,

148 D. ὅτι οὐκ ἔστιν ὡς ἂν τύχῃ ταῦτα ἐκ παρέργου
μελετᾶν, ἀλλὰ μᾶλλον μηδὲν τούτοις πάρεργον ἄλλο

435 τι γίγνεσθαι. οὐ μόνον δὴ κολακείας αὐτὸν ἐφ᾽
αὑτοῦ καθαρεύειν ἀνάγκη καὶ μηδ᾽ ὁτιοῦν ἔχειν
κίβδηλον τῇ ψυχῇ, ἀλλὰ καὶ πόρρω κολάκων ἁπάντων εἶναι καὶ πασῶν αἰσχρῶν συνόδων τε καὶ ὁμι-

436 λιῶν. τί οὖν οὐ ποιεῖς, ὦ βέλτιστε, ἐρεῖ, παλιν-

437 ῳδίαν, εἴ τί σοι μέλει τῆς ἀληθείας; οὐκοῦν καὶ
κατὰ τοὺς ἐξ ἀρχῆς λόγους καὶ κατὰ τοὺς δευτέρους τούτους καὶ ὅποι στρέφοι τις ἂν καλὸν καὶ
γενναῖον κτῆμα καὶ ἔργον ἀνδρὸς ἡ ῥητορικὴ καὶ
φιλοτιμίαν δικαίαν ἔχον καὶ τῷ κεκτημένῳ καὶ ὅσοι
τούτῳ χρῶνται, καὶ οὐ μόνον παρὰ ἀνθρώποις, ἀλλὰ
καὶ παρὰ θεοῖς πλείστης ὥρας[5] καὶ τιμῆς ἐξ ἀρχῆς
τε τυχὸν καὶ διὰ παντὸς δικαίως τυγχάνον.

438 Λοιπὸν ἕν μοι δεῖξαι, ὅτι καὶ Πλάτων αὐτὸς ταὐτὰ ἐμοὶ περὶ ῥητορικῆς φθέγγεται. λέγει γὰρ ἐν
μὲν τῷ Πολιτικῷ δήπου λόγῳ ταυτὶ '' Κατὰ ταὐτὸν
τοίνυν ἔοικεν καὶ νῦν ἡμῖν τὰ μὲν ἕτερα καὶ ὁπόσα
ἀλλότρια καὶ τὰ μὴ φίλα πολιτικῆς ἐπιστήμης
ἀποκεχωρίσθαι, λε τὰ τίμια καὶ τπεσθα δὲ ιγ-ιά ξυ

---

[1] τἆλλα codd. dett. (prob. Ddf.).
[2] codd. dett. Canter : φησὶ TQVA.

542

very things which he honours and pursues, he must be farthest removed from all things shameful. For it is enough if having ignored and set aside all of this, and having professed this single pleasure and served no other, he would be able with God's help to achieve this art. For what Thucydides said about seamanship,[a] he will say is much more appropriate to say about oratory and speech, that it is impossible to practise this in a casual way, as a side-line, but rather it admits no side-line at all. Not only in himself must he be pure of flattery and have nothing counterfeit in his soul, but also he must be far apart from all flatterers and all shameful society and associations. Why then do you not, dear sir, he will say, write a recantation, if you have any regard for the truth ? So both in respect to our original arguments and these second arguments, and wherever one would turn, oratory is a fair and noble possession and work of man, in which its possessor and all that employ him can be justly proud and which from the beginning has obtained and through all time justly obtains the greatest care and honour not only among men, but also among the Gods.

One thing remains for me to prove, that Plato himself enunciates the same views as I about oratory. For he says, indeed, in the dialogue *Politicus* the following[b] : "On the same grounds, it now seems to us that the other matter, all that is foreign and hostile to political science, has been separated ; and that there is left what is precious and related.

---

[a] I. 142. 9.   [b] *Politicus* 303 E—304 A.

³ codd. dett. Canter : λόγῳ TQVA.   ⁴ om. TQ.
⁵ Ddf. : ὥρας TQVA.

543

(148 D.)

γενῆ. τούτων¹ δέ ἐστιν δήπου στρατηγία καὶ δικαστικὴ καὶ ὅση βασιλικῇ² κοινωνοῦσα ῥητορεία πείθουσα τὸ δίκαιον συγκυβερνᾷ³ τὰς ἐν ταῖς πόλεσι
πράξεις." ἃ μικρῷ πρόσθεν ἡμῖν Ἡσίοδος λέγων
ἐφαίνετο, ταῦτα ἄντικρυς καὶ σχεδὸν τὸ μέτρον λύ-
σας ἐν τούτοις Πλάτων ὁμολογεῖ, κοινωνὸν τῆς βασιλικῆς τὴν ῥητορικὴν ἀποφαίνων ὑπὲρ τοῦ δικαίου.

439   ἐν δὲ Σωκράτους ἀπολογίᾳ ταυτὶ πάλιν αὖ λέγει
149 D. "Δικαστοῦ μὲν γὰρ αὕτη ἀρετή, ῥήτορος δὲ τἀληθῆ
440 λέγειν." εἰπὲ δή μοι πρὸς θεῶν, εἴτε Πλάτων εἴτε
ἄλλος τις ὑπὲρ ἐκείνου βούλεται, ἔσθ' ὅ τι ἀλλο-
τριώτερόν ἐστιν τῷ κόλακι ἢ τἀληθῆ λέγειν; τί
δαί;⁴ τῷ τἀληθῆ λέγοντι ἄλλο τι τοῦ κόλακος ἐχ-
θρότερον; καὶ μὴν αὐτό γε τοῦτό ἐστιν ἡ κολα-
441 κεία, μὴ τἀληθῆ λέγειν. οὐκοῦν ἡ παλινῳδία καὶ
δὴ φανερά. ἣν γὰρ ἐνταῦθα εἶναι κολακείαν φησίν,
ἐκεῖ μὴ κολακείαν εἶναι, ἀλλὰ τοῦ τἀληθῆ λέγειν
προεστάναι σαφῶς οὑτωσὶ διορίζεται. ταὐτὰ ἄρα
Πλάτωνι νῦν ἡμεῖς λέγομεν περὶ ῥητορικῆς, δοκοῦν-
442 τες ἐναντία. ἐὰν τοίνυν ἔτι τούτων ἐγγυτέρω προσ-
αγάγω τὸν λόγον, ἦ που τρυφή τις ἂν εἴη τῆς
ἀποδείξεως καὶ οὔτε ἔννοιαν οὔτε ἐλπίδα ἐλέγχων
ἰσχυροτέρων οὐδ' ἂν εἷς ἔτι δήπου λάβοι. οὐ γὰρ
μόνον αὐτὸς Πλάτων, ἀλλὰ καὶ ἐν αὐτοῖς τούτοις
τοῖς λόγοις τῷ παραδόξῳ δὴ συγγράμματι διαρρήδην ὁμολογεῖ τῇ ῥητορικῇ τὰ κάλλιστα εἶναι
πράττειν, καὶ μὴ τὴν αὐτὴν χώραν ἔχειν αὐτὴν τῶν
αἰσχρῶν μηδενί, προσθεὶς ἐπὶ τελευτῆς⁵ τὸ βραχὺ
τοῦτο καὶ εὐμνημόνευτον " Καὶ τῇ ῥητορικῇ οὕτω

¹ Ddf. ex Plat. : τούτῳ VA, τοῦτο TQ.
² codd. dett. : βασιλικὴ TQVA.

To this belongs strategy and the art of the juror, and oratory to the extent that it participates in the kingly art, and by persuading what is just, joins in the direction of activities in the cities." What we saw Hesiod say a little before,[a] here Plato is almost in direct agreement with this, having reduced it to prose, showing oratory to be a partner of the kingly art for the sake of justice. In the *Apology* of Socrates 439 he again says the following [b] : "This is the virtue of a juror, but of an orator to speak the truth." Tell 440 me by the Gods, whether Plato will answer or some- one else on his behalf, is there anything more foreign to a flatterer than to speak the truth ? Well ? To a man who speaks the truth is there anything more hateful than a flatterer ? Indeed flattery means not to speak the truth. Then the recantation 441 is clear. For what he says here is flattery, there he denies is flattery, but clearly defines it to champion the speaking of the truth. So we now agree with Plato concerning oratory, although we seem to hold opposite positions. If I apply my argument still 442 closer than I have, we would in a way luxuriate in proof, and no one could still have a suspicion or expectation of stronger refutations. For not only Plato himself, but even in these very arguments in that strange treatise he explicitly agrees that it is possible for oratory to do what is most fair, and that it does not occupy the same place with anything shameful, and he adds at the end this brief and memorable remark [c] : " Thus oratory must always be

---

[a] § 391.   [b] *Apology* 18 A.   [c] *Gorgias* 527 c.

3 συνδιακυβερνᾷ Plato.   4 δὲ V.
5 τελευτῇ TQ.

(149 D.)

443 χρηστέον ἐπὶ τὸ δίκαιον ἀεί." εἶεν, ὦ γενναῖος,
ἔστιν ὅπου ἐγχωρεῖ κολακείᾳ χρῆσθαι πρὸς τὸ
δίκαιον ἀεί; οὐκ ἔστιν οὐδέποτε. καὶ μὴν ὑπὲρ
καλοῦ χρώμενοι τῇ ῥητορικῇ, καλὸν ἄν τι πράτ-
444 τοιμεν ὑπ᾿ αὐτῆς. οὐκοῦν καλὸν ἡ ῥητορικὴ μετὰ
τοῦ δικαίου γιγνομένη. καὶ μὴν κολακεία γε
445 σαφῶς αἰσχρὸν ἀεί. οὐκοῦν οὗτος ἐκεῖνος Πλάτων
ὁ τοῦ Ἀρίστωνός ἐστιν, ὁ φάσκων μὴ κολακείαν
εἶναι τὴν ῥητορικήν, μηδὲ τῆς αὐτῆς ἔχεσθαι φύσεως.
παραλείπω δὲ νᾶμά τε κάλλιστον πάντων[1] ναμάτων
150 D. καὶ τοὺς ἐκ τοῦ σωφρονοῦντος στόματος ἰόντας λόγους καὶ ὅσα τοιαῦτα ἄλλα ἄλλοθι ῥητορικὴν εἴρηκεν ἐπικοσμῶν.

446 Εἰ δέ τις ἡμῖν περὶ Πλάτωνος ὑπολάβοι ὅτι οὐ
ταύτην κακῶς εἴρηκε ⟨τὴν⟩[2] ῥητορικὴν ὑπὲρ ἧς νῦν
ἡμεῖς τοὺς λόγους ποιούμεθα, ἀλλὰ δύο οὐσῶν τὴν
ἑτέραν κακίζει, πρῶτον μὲν οὐδὲν μᾶλλον τά γε
ἡμῖν εἰρημένα φαύλως ἔχοντα ἐλέγχεται, ἀλλὰ
[κατ᾿][3] αὐτὸ τοῦτο καλῶς καὶ προσηκόντως ἅπαντα
ταῦτα ἠνύσθαι μαρτυρεῖ. ὥσπερ γὰρ ἐκεῖνος τὴν
φαύλην δικαίως ψέγει, τί κωλύει τήν γε ἐναντίαν
447 ἡμᾶς ἐπαινοῦντας ὀρθῶς ποιεῖν; ἔπειτα οὐκ ἀναιρεῖ τοὺς παρ᾿ ἡμῶν ἐλέγχους ἡ παραίτησις αὕτη,
ἀλλὰ καὶ οὕτως ἐναντία φαίνοιτο ἂν εἰρηκὼς αὐτὸς
ἑαυτῷ, εἰ διττὴν εἶναι τὴν ῥητορικὴν ἀξιῶν, εἶθ᾿
ὡς μιᾶς καὶ ἁπλῆς τινος οὕτως τὴν κατηγορίαν
πεποίηται. δῆλον γὰρ ὅτι εἰ τοῦτ᾿ ἐστὶν ἀληθές,
τὴν μὲν φαυλίζειν, τὴν δὲ ἐπαινεῖν αὐτῷ προσῆκε
διελομένῳ, ὥσπερ ἐν τοῖς περὶ ἔρωτος λόγοις φαίνεται πεποιηκώς, καὶ πολύ γε μειζόνων εὐφημιῶν

---

[1] codd. dett. Plato Tim. 75 E : ἁπάντων TQVA.
[2] add. codd. dett. ; τὴν ῥητορικὴν om. Phot., delet Keil.
[3] καὶ ταὐτὸ VA a. corr., καὶ αὐτὸ Ddf., secl. Behr.

used in the interests of justice." Well, then, honour- 443
able sir ! Is it in any way possible ever to use flattery toward the ends of justice ? It is not. Indeed
in using oratory for the sake of what is fair, we would
perform a fair act by means of it. So oratory com- 444
bined with justice is a fair thing. And flattery is
always clearly shameful. Therefore here is Plato, the 445
son of Ariston, who denies that oratory is flattery or
is a part of the same nature. But I leave aside " the
fairest stream of all " [a] streams and those words
which come from a temperate mouth, and all of his
other like statements in various places in praise of
oratory.

If someone should interrupt us in this discussion of 446
Plato, saying that he did not slander this oratory,
which we are now defending, but that there are two
oratories and he demeans the second of them,[b]
to begin with, our remarks are not any more shown
to be wrong, but this fact bears witness that all these
arguments have been fairly and properly made.
For just as Plato justly blames the bad oratory,
how do we not act correctly in praising its opposite
number ? Next this plea does not remove our re- 447
futations, but even on these terms he would obviously
have contradicted himself, if while claiming that
oratory is of two kinds, he accused it as if there were
only one single kind. For it is clear that if this is
true, he ought to have separated them and belittled
the one and praised the other, as he clearly has
done in his arguments about love,[c] where he has
deemed the good love worthy of praise much greater

---

[a] Plato, *Timaeus* 75 E.
[b] *Gorgias* 503 A-B, 517 A.
[c] *Symposium* 180 C.

(150 D.)

τὸν χρηστὸν ἠξιωκὼς ἢ οἵων τὸν ἕτερον βλασφη-
448 μιῶν. θαυμάζω δ᾽ ἔγωγε τί ἄν ποτε ἐποίησεν, μόνην ταύτην εἰδὼς οὖσαν ῥητορικὴν περὶ ἧς ταῦτα
διεξέρχεται, ὁπότε οὐσῶν, ὡς ἂν φαίη, δυοῖν καὶ
τοσοῦτον διαφερουσῶν τοσαύτην φαίνεται σπουδὴν πεποιημένος τοῦ καθάπαξ κακῶς εἰπεῖν. τί
γὰρ μᾶλλον φαῦλον[1] ἡ ῥητορικὴ ἢ χρηστόν, εἴπερ
449 ἐστὶ διττόν; οὐκοῦν οὐκ εἰς τὰς ἴσας λαβὰς
151 D. ἥκομεν, ἀλλὰ τὸ τῶν ἴσων κατ᾽ ἐκείνου γίγνεται.
ἔπειτα τί κωλύει κἀμὲ τῶν αὐτῶν τούτων λόγων
ἐχόμενον φάσκειν ὅτι καὶ ἡ διαλεκτικὴ διττὴ καὶ
οὐχὶ μία ἐστὶν ἁπλῶς, ἀλλ᾽ ἡ μὲν οἵα παρακρούε-
σθαι καὶ ἐξαπατᾶν καὶ χρόνους τρίβειν καὶ εἰς
ὑγιὲς οὐδὲν πάντῃ τὴν γλῶτταν ἄγουσα, ψυχρά τις
καὶ ἀγεννὴς καὶ κακοῦργος καὶ ἀπατηλὴ καὶ ἀνελεύ-
θερος, ἡ δὲ οἵα χαρίεντας παρέχεσθαι καὶ δεξιούς;
450 καὶ δὴ καὶ φαίη τις ἄν, εἴτ᾽ οὖν ὀρθῶς εἴτε μή, ὅτι
καὶ μέρος εἶναι κινδυνεύει τῆς ῥητορικῆς ⟨ἡ⟩[2] δια-
λεκτική, ὥσπερ τὰ ἐρωτήματα τοῦ λόγου παντός.
451 ἀλλ᾽ ἔστω ταῦτα χωρίς. ὁ δ᾽ οὖν αὐτὸς λόγος καὶ
περὶ πάσης φιλοσοφίας, καὶ περί γε τῶν τῆς ἀρετῆς ⟨μορίων⟩,[3] εἴ τις βούλοιτο διαιρούμενος πρῶτον μὲν σοφίας δύο προσαγορεύειν, τὴν μὲν ᾗ τὰ
βέλτιστα συνίεμεν, τὴν δ᾽ ἑτέραν ᾗ κακουργοῦσιν,
ἔπειτα σωφροσύνην διπλῆν, τὴν μὲν σπουδῆς ἀξίαν
καὶ πολιτικήν, τὴν δὲ νωθρῶν τε καὶ ὑπτίων, ἔτι
δ᾽ αὖ δικαιοσύνην ὀρθὴν καὶ ἑτέραν ταπεινήν, καὶ
διπλῆν ἀνδρείαν, τὴν μὲν σὺν νῷ καὶ φρεσίν, τὴν δὲ
452 ἀπόνοιαν καὶ μανίαν οὖσαν. ἀλλ᾽ οἶμαι πάντα
ταῦτα τῶν φυρόντων ἐστὶν τὰ ὀνόματα, καὶ διῄρη-

than the slander with which he describes the other.
I wonder whatever he would have done if he knew 448
that this oratory, concerning which he recounts
these arguments, was the only kind existing, since
when there are two kinds, as he would say, and
both so very different, he clearly has been most
eager to slander oratory once and for all. Why is
oratory more bad than good, if it has a double
nature? So we have not got equal holds, but even 449
this equality is against him. What prevents me also
from applying the same arguments and saying that
dialectic has a double and not a single, simple
nature? But that the one will mislead, deceive,
waste time, and use our tongues everywhere for no
sound purpose, a certain frigid, ignoble, roguish,
deceptive, low born kind of thing; and that the
other will make men charming and clever? And one 450
could say, whether rightly or not, that dialectic
might be a part of oratory, just as questions are a part
of speech in general. But let this be treated elsewhere. The same argument can be made about 451
all philosophy, and about all the parts of virtue: for
example, if first of all one should choose to speak of
two separate wisdoms, one by which we know what is
best, the other by which men do wrong; and next a
double moderation, one worthy of zeal and political,
the other belonging to the sluggish and inert; and
also an upright justice, and another humble one;
and a double courage, the one combined with sense
and intelligence, the other being folly and madness.
But, I think, all this is the part of those who muddy 452
the meanings of words, and a distinction has already

---

¹ om. VA.   ² add. codd. dett.   ³ add. Behr; cf. § 235.

(151 D.)

ται σοφία καὶ κακουργία, σωφροσύνη καὶ βλακεία,
δικαιοσύνη τε καὶ εὐήθεια, ἀνδρεία καὶ θρασύτης,
οὐδέτερον δέ¹ γε οὔτε καλὸν [οὔτε χαλεπὸν]² οὔτε
προσῆκον, οὔτε τὰς κακίας ὑποκορίζεσθαι τῷ τῆς
152 D. ἀρετῆς ὀνόματι οὔτε τὰς ἀρετὰς φαυλίζειν τὰ τῆς
453 κακίας ἑκάστῃ παρατιθέντα. οὕτω τοίνυν καὶ ῥητορικὴν κατὰ τοὺς ὀρθῶς μεταχειριζομένους καὶ τῷ
ὄντι τυγχάνοντας αὐτῆς, ἀλλὰ οὐ κατὰ τοὺς πρόσχημα ποιησαμένους τῆς ἑαυτῶν πλεονεξίας ἢ
φαυλότητος ἐξετάζειν εἰκός, κατ᾿ αὐτόν γε τὸν τοῦ
πράγματος λόγον, εἰ καὶ μηδεὶς τετύχηκε, καὶ διαιρεῖν συκοφαντίαν καὶ κολακείαν ἀπὸ τῆς ῥητορικῆς, ὥσπερ δὴ³ καὶ μαγγανείαν καὶ τερατείαν ἀπὸ
πάσης φιλοσοφίας.

454   Οὐκοῦν κολακείας, οὐ ῥητορικῆς, Πλάτων ἐν
τούτοις κατηγόρηκε, καὶ συκοφαντίας, οὐ ῥητορικῆς.
οὔτ᾿ οὖν ⟨εἰ⟩⁴ τὴν τῷ ὄντι ῥητορικὴν κακῶς εἴρηκεν
οὔτ᾿ εἰ τὴν δοκοῦσαν, ἔστι τοῦτο πρὸς λόγον, ὡς
ὀρθῶς ῥητορικήν γε εἰρήκει καλῶς, εἴπερ ἔσθ᾿⁵
ἕτερον τὴν δοκοῦσαν εἶναι ῥητορικὴν κακῶς εἰπεῖν.
μὴ γὰρ εἶναι τὸ τοιοῦτον ῥητορικήν, οὐκ αἰσχρὸν
εἶναι ῥητορικὴν χρῆν αὐτὸν λέγειν, ὥσπερ ἐκεῖνό πού
φησιν αὐτός, ὅτι εἰ μὲν θεῶν παῖδες, οὐ φιλο-
χρήματοι· εἰ δὲ φιλοχρήματοι, οὐ θεῶν παῖδες. ἀμ-
455 φότερα δὲ οὐκ ἔδει λέγειν. οὐκοῦν οὐδὲ ἐνταῦθα
456 ἀμφότερα ἐᾶν ὁ λόγος φαίνεται· ἐπεὶ καὶ αὐτὸ τοῦτο
153 D. ὑπὲρ αὐτοῦ Πλάτωνος ἡμεῖς νῦν ποιοῦμεν. εἰ γὰρ
ὅτι μάλιστα οὕτω διενοεῖτο, ὥσπερ ἔγωγε οὐκ
ἀντιλέγω, ἀλλ᾿ ὑπεξήρηται τὴν καθαρὰν καὶ τῷ ὄντι
ῥητορικήν, ἄξιον μὴ⁶ παρακρουσθῆναι μηδὲ ἀγνοη-

¹ om. VA.   ² om. codd. dett. Ddf.

been made between wisdom and roguery, moderation and stupidity, justice and simplicity, courage and audacity. And it is neither fair nor proper for a man to gloss over vices with the name of virtue nor to belittle the virtues by setting beside each virtue its counterpart in vice. So it is reasonable, in accordance 453 with the very logic of the matter, to examine oratory in terms of those who correctly practise it and in truth achieve it, even if no one ever has, but not in terms of those who have made it a cover for their greed and badness, and to distinguish slander and fawning from oratory, as we do trickery and conjuring from all philosophy.

So in these arguments Plato has accused flattery 454 and slander, not oratory. Whether he has slandered true oratory or that apparent oratory, makes no difference since he has also correctly praised oratory, while slandering that apparent oratory is another matter. Far from such a thing being oratory, it was improper for him to say that oratory was shameful, just as he argues somewhere [a] that if they are the sons of the Gods, they are not covetous, and if they are covetous, they are not the sons of the Gods. But both things cannot be said of them. So even 455 here the argument does not appear to allow both things to be said of oratory. Indeed, we act now on 456 Plato's behalf. For if this was really his intention, as I do not dispute, and he exempted the pure and real oratory, the masses ought not to be misled and

---

[a] *Republic* 391 c ff.

---

[3] codd. dett. : δὲ TQVA. [4] add. codd. dett.
[5] codd. dett. : ἐς VA, εἰς TQ.
[6] codd. dett. : μὲν TQVA Phot.

(153 D.)

σαι τοῦτο αὐτὸ τοὺς πολλούς, μηδὲ ὡς ψήφῳ κα-
θαρᾷ προσέχοντας θᾶττον ἢ συμφέρει βουλεύσα-
457 σθαι περὶ τῶν τηλικούτων. περὶ τοίνυν αὐτοῦ πάλιν
τοῦ μέρους[1] αὐτὸς ὡδὶ μαρτυρεῖ " Οὐκ οἶσθα ὅτι
ἐπὶ παντὶ ἐπιτηδεύματι οἱ μὲν πολλοὶ φαῦλοι καὶ
οὐδενὸς ἄξιοι, οἱ δὲ σπουδαῖοι ὀλίγοι καὶ παντὸς
ἄξιοι;[2] ἐπεὶ[3] γυμναστικὴ οὐ καλόν σοι δοκεῖ εἶναι καὶ χρηματιστικὴ καὶ ῥητορικὴ καὶ στρατηγία; Ἔμοιγε πάντως δήπου. Τί οὖν; ἐν ἑκάστῳ
τούτων τοὺς πολλοὺς πρὸς ἕκαστον τὸ ἔργον οὐ
καταγελάστους ὁρᾷς; Νὴ τὸν Δία καὶ μάλα ἀληθῆ
λέγεις. Τί οὖν; τούτου ἕνεκα αὐτός τε φεύξῃ πάντα τὰ ἐπιτηδεύματα καὶ τῷ υἱεῖ οὐκ ἐπιτρέψεις;"
458 οὐκοῦν χρή, ὦ Πλάτων, οὐδὲ τὴν ῥητορικὴν ἀπὸ
τῶν φαύλως μεταχειριζομένων κρίνειν, ἀλλὰ ἀπὸ
τῶν ὡς ἄριστα προϊσταμένων, ἢ γελοῖόν γε ἂν εἴη,
μᾶλλον δὲ ὑπερφυές, εἰ δι' ὧν παραδειγμάτων οὐκ
ἀξιοῖς φιλοσοφίαν φαῦλον[4] ἡγεῖσθαι, ταῦτα οὐκ
ἀρκέσει ῥητορικῇ, καὶ ταῦτα ἐν αὐτοῖς οὔσῃ τοῖς
παραδείγμασιν, ἃ μηδὲ κρίνειν πονηρὰ ὁμολογεῖς.
459 Εἶεν. τίνες οἱ τυγχάνοντες αὐτῆς ὀρθῶς, καὶ
τοῦτο ἐκ τῶν Πλάτωνος δείξομεν. "Τὸ μὲν δύνα-
154 D. σθαι, ὦ Φαῖδρε, ὥστε ἀγωνιστὴν τέλεον γενέσθαι
εἰκός, ἴσως δὲ καὶ ἀναγκαῖον, ἔχειν ὥσπερ τὰ ἄλλα·
εἰ μέν σοι ὑπάρχει φύσει ῥητορικῷ εἶναι, ἔσῃ
ῥήτωρ ἐλλόγιμος, προσλαβὼν ἐπιστήμην καὶ μελέ-
την· ὅτου δ' ἂν ἐλλείπῃς τούτων, ταύτῃ ἀτελὴς
ἔσῃ· ὅσον δὲ αὐτοῦ τέχνη "—ἀλλ' ἐῶ τό γε ἐφεξῆς.
460 εἰ τοίνυν δεῖ τὸν μέλλοντα ἔσεσθαι ῥητορικὸν φύσιν

───────

[1] αὖ τούτου πάλιν [τοῦ μέρους] Keil.
[2] οἱ δὲ—ἄξιοι om. VA.
[3] Ddf. ex Plat. : ἔτι TQVA.   [4] om. VA.

be unaware of this fact, nor satisfied, as it were, with a clear verdict, to deliberate more swiftly than is expedient about such important matters. On this 457 particular subject he again bears witness as follows [a] : " Do you not know that in every profession the masses are bad and worthless, but the serious few and most valuable ? Do not gymnastics and money-making and oratory and generalship seem to be a fair thing to you ? Yes, indeed. Well then ? Do you not see that in each of these the masses are ridiculous in their particular work ? Yes, by Zeus, you certainly speak the truth. Well, on this account will you avoid all professions and not permit your son to undertake one ? " So it is also fitting, Plato, not to 458 judge oratory from those who practise it badly, but from those who champion it as well as possible. Or it would be foolish, or rather, very strange if the examples through which you demand us not to believe that philosophy is bad, will not suffice for oratory, and at that while it is even used among examples which you admit that you do not judge as bad practices.

Well ! Who are they who properly succeed in 459 oratory ? We shall also show this from Plato's words [b] : " It is likely, Phaedrus, perhaps also necessary that the ability of becoming a perfect contestant is in the same state as other things. If you have the natural endowments for being an orator, you will be a distinguished orator, when you have added knowledge and practice. But in whatever of these you are deficient, in this respect you will be imperfect. But as far as it has art . . . " But I omit what follows. Then if someone who is 460 going to be an orator must possess at the same

Euthydemus 307 A-B.　　　　[b] *Phaedrus* 269 D.

καὶ τέχνην καὶ μελέτην ὁμοῦ κτήσασθαι, δῆλον ὅτι
ὁ¹ ἐκπεπτωκὼς τῆς τέχνης καὶ τῆς φύσεως τῆς
461 βελτίστης ἀτελής ἐστι ταύτῃ. πῶς οὖν τοῦτο δεῖ
ῥητορικῇ προστιθέναι; εἴπερ ὁ μὲν μὴ πάντα παρα-
σχόμενος παρὰ τὴν ἔνδειαν ἀτελής ἐστιν, τὰ δὲ
ἐπιτηδεύματα ἐκ τῶν κατορθούντων, οὐκ ἐκ τῶν
ἀποτυχόντων κρίνεται. ὃ δὲ δὴ μὴ μόνον τέχνης,
ἀλλὰ καὶ φύσεως καὶ μελέτης δεῖται, πῶς τοῦτο
ἔνεστιν μηδεμίαν εἶναι τέχνην φάσκειν, ἢ πῶς τὸν ἐλ-
λείποντα ὅτου δὴ μέρους ἀτελῆ κατὰ τοῦτο δίκαιον
λέγειν, τούτου ὅστις ἂν² διὰ πάντων τύχῃ, κολακείαν ἔνι φῆσαι μετέρχεσθαι;

462   Πανταχῇ δὲ καὶ διὰ πάντων ἡμῖν ἐκπίπτουσιν αἱ
ψῆφοι. πρῶτος δὲ Πλάτων αὐτὸς ψηφίζεται καὶ
μέσος φασὶν καὶ τελευταῖος· καὶ κινδυνεύω δοκῶν
ἀντιλέγειν Πλάτωνι παντὸς μᾶλλον συναγορεύειν.
463 εἰ δὲ δεῖ τι καὶ παῖξαι, δοκῶ μοι κατὰ τοὺς κωμῳ-
464 διοποιοὺς ὥσπερ ἀποδιδράσκοντα αὐτὸν ἕλξειν εἰς
155 D. τοὺς ῥήτορας. τί³ μαθὼν καλλωπίζεται; εἰ δέ
τινες καὶ ἄλλοι παραβῶντες ῥητορικὴν ψέγουσι,
μᾶλλον δὲ τονθορύζοντες ἐκ τοῦ ζόφου⁴ τοξεύοντες
κατὰ Ἀλκαῖον, ὧν οὐδὲ τὰ ὀνόματα ἀγαγεῖν ῥᾴδιον
εἰς λόγον, οὐχ οἷς καλοῦνταί φημι, πλὴν εἴ τις καὶ
τοῦτο προστίθησιν, ἀλλ᾿ οἷς γε χρώμενοι ταῦτα
σοφίζονται, τοσοῦτόν μοι πρὸς τούτους ἀποκεκρί-
σθω, ὅτι ῥητορικῇ παρὰ πόδας διδόασι τὴν δίκην.
465 πρὸς δὲ Πλάτωνα τὸν τῶν ῥητόρων πατέρα καὶ

---

¹ Iunt.: ὅτι τε VA : ὅτι TQ.
² codd. dett. Ddf. : ἐὰν TQVA.
³ Behr, qui etiam distinxit : ὅτι TQVA ; post ῥήτορας
lacunam indic. Reiske.
⁴ codd. dett. Jacobs, cf. p. 295. 8 ed. Keil : ψόφου TQVA,
cf. § 167 ; ψέφους Lobeck.

time natural ability, art, and practice, it is clear that whoever has failed in art, and lacks the best suited nature, is imperfect in this respect. How ought this 461 to be attributed to oratory, if he who has not provided everything is imperfect from his deficiency, and professions are judged from the successful, not the deficient? But what not only requires art, but also natural ability and practice, can this be denied to be an art? Or can it be said that he has pursued flattery, who has achieved the art of oratory in every way, when it is just to say that he who is deficient in some part of it is imperfect in that respect?

Everywhere and in every way the verdict is 462 given to our side. First, middle, and last, as they say, Plato votes for us. And while seeming to dispute with Plato, more than anything I may be in agreement with him. If a joke is appropriate, I think, 463 in the manner of the comic poets [a] that I shall drag him back to the orators, as a runaway slave. What possesses him to be so coy? But if others bawl 464 out and find fault with oratory,[b] or rather " mutter, shooting in the dark," to quote Alcaeus, [c]people whose words are not even easily understood, I do not mean their names, unless someone adds this too, but the words which they employ when they use these sophisms, against these let my answer only be that oratory punishes them on the spot.[d] But 465 against Plato, the father and teacher of orators, it

[a] CAF III, frg. 795 Kock.
[b] Apparently the Cynics are meant; they are more particularly attacked in or. iii, *cf.* Behr, *op. cit.*, p. 94, n. 2.
[c] Frg. 112 Bergk.
[d] *i.e.* they make fools of themselves by their incompetence in speaking. Their names are not easily understood because they are not pure Greek, but of barbaric origins.

(155 D.)

διδάσκαλον ἀναγκαῖον ἦν ὥσπερ φιλοτησίαν προ-
λαβόντα ἀντιπληρώσασθαι. δέχοιτο δὲ γενναίως,
ὅτι καὶ προῦπιεν· ἐπεὶ καὶ τὸν βαλόντα μὴ δεῖ[1]
466 ἐκφυγεῖν. παρὰ ⟨δὲ⟩[2] τῶν ἄλλων ἡμῖν συγγνώμη
δικαίως ἂν εἴη, τοὺς λογίους θεοὺς εἰ Πλάτωνος
τοῦ καλοῦ περὶ πλείονος ποιούμεθα. ἐξαιρεῖται δὲ
ἡμᾶς αἰτίας καὶ ὁ πάντα ἄριστος Ἀσκληπιός, ψῆφον οὐκ ἄτιμον αὐτὸς διδούς, οὐδὲ ⟨παυσόμεθα χάριν
ἔχοντες,⟩[3] τὰ μὲν ἐν μέτροις, τὰ δὲ οὑτωσὶ πεζῇ.

[1] Reiske : δεῖν TQVA.   [2] add. codd. dett.
[3] οὐδὲ αὐτὸς διδούς TQVA : οὐδὲ transposuit et senten-
tiam supplevit Behr.

[a] Cf. Behr, op. cit., p. 33, n. 52 : unemended the Greek
text implies that Asclepius expressed his approbation of
Aristides in prose and verse oracles, which seems an odd
remark. The good scholium on this passage (not yet pub-

was necessary for me, as if I had received a toast from his hands, to fill the cup in return. May he receive it with noble grace, because he pledged it too ; for it is not fitting for the man who strikes the first blow to run away. Others would justly pardon 466 us if we value the Gods of oratory above the good Plato. And Asclepius, best in everything, exempts us from Plato's accusation, when he too honours us with his approval, and we shall not cease to be grateful, in our verse as well as in our prose in the manner you see here.[a]

lished) rightly refers Asclepius' communications to dreams, but is not specific on how the " verse and prose " are to be understood. The scholium published in Dindorf, indeed, refers the " verse and prose " to Aristides, but this scholium is attested only in inferior MSS. and seems to have little authority. Its otherwise silly remarks have been aptly explained by Lenz, *The Aristeides Prolegomena*, pp. 57-58.

INDEX

TO ORATIONS I AND II

(References are to oration and section, Words are listed as they occur in the Greek text, but, with the exception of *some* literary citations, no note is taken of whether the word appears more than once in the given section. Brackets indicate that the word is not actually used, but only alluded to.)

ABYDUS i. 292
Acarnania i. 297
Achaeans i. 378, 381 ; ii. 88, 414, 415
Achaia i. 225, 278
Achilles ii. 387
Acrocorinth i. 270
Acropolis of Athens i. 16, 20, 41, 88, 191, 233, 352, 403 ; of heaven i. 19
Aegae i. 334
Aegean Sea i. (10, 11, 12, 14, 16, 17, 20, 23), 63, 102, (109, 117)
Aegina i. 215, 216 ; ii. 144, 370. Aeginetans i. 212
(Aegospotami) i. 252, 277
Aeschines son of Lysanias ii. 61, (62), 63, (64), 66, 76, 78, 83, 217 ; *Alcibiades* ii. 61, 62, 74, (77), 217
Aeschylus ii. 55 ; *Myrmidons* ii. 55 ; *Persians* i. 203
Africa (see also *s.v.* Libyans) i. 324 ; ii. 297. African strait ii. 145
Agamemnon ii. 414
Agesilaus i. 296
Ajax i. 286, (381). Ajaxes ii. 414
Alcaeus ii. 464
Alcibiades ii. 61, 74, (299), 335
Alcinous ii. 86, 87, 88

(Alcman) (ii. 129)
Alexander (= Paris) i. 128
Alexander I of Macedon i. 175
Alexander the Great i. 331 (334, 398)
Amazons i. 83, 84
Ambracia i. 229
Ammon ii. 44
Amphion ii. 394
Anaxagoras ii. 78, 258
anonymous i. 1, 3, 4, 5, 11, 49, 86, 90, 101, 114, 127, 136, 152, 188, 236, 238, 284, 297, 302, 303, 305, 306, 308, 309, 311, 312, 322, 388, 392 ; ii. 47, 48, 57, 66, 77, 79, 84, 85, 109, 113, 166, 168, 277, 335, 342, 378, 394, 412, 423, 463
Apollo i. 13, 62, 67, (87, 167, 382, 399) ; ii. (39, 40, 41, 46), 49, (52), 56, (57, 78, 80-83), 86, 88, 150 ; Apollo Musegetes ii. 19 ; Apollo Pythius ii. 34, 42
Araxes ii. 240
Arcadia i. 290 ; ii. 7. Arcadians i. 358
Archelaus ii. 237, 238, 242
Archilochus ii. (166), 406
Areopagus i. 46, 47, 48, (338), 367, 385
Ares i. 46 ; ii. 207

INDEX

Arginusae i. 241

Argives i. 80, 261, 357, 371 ; ii. 7, 413

Arion ii. 336, 376

(Aristides, Aelius) i. 329, 404 ; ii. 14, 16, 18, 66-74, 351, 429-438, 466

Aristides son of Lysimachus i. (165, 282, 391) ; ii. 346, (348, 351), 352, 353, 357, (358), 359, 360, 361

Ariston ii. 304, 445

Aristophanes *Acharnians* ii. 59, 380 ; *Clouds* ii. 380

(Artaxerxes I) i. 202, 204, 208, 209, 213, 274

(Artaxerxes II) i. 271, 275, 280, 293, 313 ; ii. 301

Artemis i. 13

Artemisium i. 128, (149), 159, (160), 167, (168)

Arthmius of Zelea i. 369

Asclepius ii. (67), 68, (69, 70), 75, (153), (430, 434), 466

Asia i. 13, (15), 64, 83, 93, 123, (124), 200, 201, 208, 237, 271, 275, 364 ; ii. 297

Assyrian Empire i. 335

Athena i. 12, 19, 41, 42, 43, 48, 154, 167, 339, 362, (379, 404) ; ii. (93) ; Athena Pronoïa i. 13 ; Athena Poliouchos i. 154 ; ii. 339 ; Athena's *peplos* i. 404

Athenians (see also *s.v.* Athens) i. 1, 6, 56, 57, 58, 81, 95, 97, 98, 100, 103, 111, 133, 148, 149, 150, 159, 165, 167, 172, 173, 175, 178, 180, 182, 183, 215, 220, 248, 250, 268, 277, 280, 308, 309, 313, 320, 327, 329, 330, 331, 334, 351, 357, 358, 359, 360, 363, 369, 377, 397, 402, 403 ; ii. 281, 321, 322, 331, 333, 335, 336, 342, 359, 360 ; autochthones i. 8, 25-34, 49, 73, 263, 358

Athens (see also *s.v.* Athenians) i. *passim* ; ii. 7, 13, 293, 351 ; annual sacrifices i. 341 ; arbitrator for others i. 361, 371 ; arts i. 32, 191, 354, 364 : buildings i. 354, 364 ; care of children of war-dead i. 53, 368 ; chariots i. 43, 350 ; climate i. 18, 19, 352, 353 ;

colonies i. 5, 15, 19, 55, 62, 64, 65, 66, 69-74, 76, 88, 99, 113, 328, 334, 336, *cf.* ii. 40 ; constitution i. 4, 43, 236, 237, 252-257, 259, 382-393 ; crops i. 18, 23, 24, 25, 31, 32, 34, 37, 49, 113, 336, 339, 342, 354, 358, 386 : olive i. 339, 362 : wine i. 339, 360 : wheat i. 38, 45, 50, 74, 339 ; demes and cities i. 53, 351 ; dialect i. 15, 322-330 ; embassies i. 370, 371 ; empire i. 212, 224, 227, 235, 281, 282, 283 (lasted seventy years), 293, 302-312, 327 (its dialect), 332, 391 ; exiles, reception of i. 50, 52-61, 67-73, 77, 81, 93, 113, 294, 315, 330, 336 ; first fruits, receives i. 37, 358 ; first men i. 8, 25-31, 33, 34, 49, 73, 113, 263, 336, 357, 358 ; foster-father i. 1, (54), 332 : nurse i. 25, 110 : father i. 140 : mother i. 315 ; funeral orations i. 4, 86, 368 ; ii. 342 ; games i. 38 ; generosity i. 5, 8, 10, 34-38, 49, 50, 56, 60, 62, 67, 70, 71, 72, 75, 77, 78, 81, 82, 137, 142, 144, 154, 155, 179, 205, 213, 222 (aid to Lacedaemonians in earthquake), 227, 228, 279, 294, 308, 336, 339, 342, 345, 358, 370, 386 ; giver of freedom i. 110 ; gods, relations with i. 4, 21, 32, 33, 34, 38, 40, 41, 42, 44, 45, 46, 49, 50, 52, 154, 192, 193, 217, 333, 335, 338, 341, 360, 363, 372, 374, 399 ; harbours i. 23, 352 ; laws i. 336, 343 ; libraries i. 354 ; marble-quarries i. 21, 364 ; mines i. 23 ; national assemblies i. 336, 373, 395 ; naval power i. 42, 133, 136, 137, 138, 140, 141, 168, 205, 212, 215, 232, 241, 327 ; oldest city i. 7, 61, 73, 304, (335), 357 ; oratory i. 2, 6, 43, 322, 329, (336), 343, 347, 354, 394, 397 ; philosophy i. 343, 397 ; poetry, comedy & tragedy i. 328, 343 ; reverence shown to i. 330-335, 398, 400, 402, 403 ; statues i. 354 (fallen from heaven), 364 ; temples i. 21, 104, 105, 117, 341, 354,

INDEX

364 ; topography i. 8-23, 336,
351 ; walls i. 191, 252, 267, 278,
351 ; warfare, general i. 4, 75,
318, 319, 336, 344-350, 354,
359, 394 ; war with Aeginetans
i. 212, 214, 215, 216 ; war with
Amazons i. 83, 84 ; war with
Boeotians 506 B.C. i. 91, 457
B.C. i. 212, 221 ; war with
Corinthians 459 B.C. i. 212, 214-
217 ; on behalf of the Corinthians 394 B.C. i. 269, 270, 312,
319 ; war with Dionysius I i.
313 ; war with Dorians 1100
B.C. i. 87, 506 B.C. i. 91 ; war
with Euboeans 506 B.C. i. 91,
447 B.C. i. 224, 278 ; war with
Eumolpus and Thracians i. 85,
87 ; war with Eurystheus i. 78,
79 ; war with Lacedaemonians
(Byzantium) i. 292, (Coronea)
i. 294, 295, 312, (Haliartus) i.
266-268, 294, (Lechaeum) i.
290, (Leucas) i. 313, (Mantinea)
i. 291, (Naxus) i. 297, (Phlius) i.
291, (Tanagra) i. 219, 220, 322,
(Thebes) i. 296, 395 B.C. i. 243,
266-271, 280, 293, 294, 319,
378 B.C. i. 294, 295, 312 ; war
with Peloponnesians 455 B.C.
i. 218, 433 B.C. i. 218-243, 252,
268, 277, 278, (Aegospotami) i.
252, 277, 279, (Ambracia) i.
229, (Arginusae) i. 241, 242,
(Corcyra) i. 229, (Corinthians)
i. 229, (Cythera) i. 229, (Decelea) i. 233, 235, 242, (Hellespont) i. 236, (Melos and
Scione) i. 302, 303, 309, 312,
(Mytilene) i. 310, (Naupactus)
i. 229, (Pharnabazus) i. 237,
(Pylus) i. 228, 229, 240, 277,
279, (Sicily) i. 232-234, 240 ; ii.
281, (Thrace) i. 229 ; war with
Persians, general i. 93, 335 ;
490 B.C. i. 13, 95-114, 141, 160,
167, (272), 273, 322, 347 ; ii.
341 ; 480 B.C. i. 23, 115-184,
249, 252, 273, 320, 321, 347,
369 ; ii. 240, 341 ; war with
Persians 479-448 B.C. i. 189,
193-209, 215, 216, 273 ; war
with Philip i. 314, 315, 316,
319 ; war with pirates i. 63 ;
war with Samus i. 224 ; Sardis,

sack of i. 94 ; war with Thebans (Seven against Thebes) i.
80, (after Leuctra) i. 301,
(Mantinea) i. 312, 319, 347,
360 ; war with the Thirty i.
253-258
Athos i. 121, 127, (203)
Atlantic i. 118, 119
Atreus, sons of i. 378
Attica i. 10-14, 16, 20, 23, 79, 83,
117, 157, 209, 233, 353, 360

BABYLON i. 94 ; ii. 301
Bacchants ii. 74, 75
Bacis ii. 46
barbarians (see also s.v. Persians
and s.v. Medes) i. 1, 4, 14, 15,
63, 64, 92, 93, 96, 99, 106, 107,
108, 112, 114, 125, 126, 129,
138, 139, 141, 143, 144, 145,
150, 157, 160, 163, 164, 167,
172, 178, 182, 183, 184, 190,
194, 195, 197, 206, 210, 211,
213, 221, 225, 226, 227, 231,
235, 237, 256, 272, 273, 281,
300, 301, 308, 313, 320, 322,
327, 333, 389 ; ii. 68, 321, 322,
324, 325, 326, 327, 331, 341 ;
cf. ii. 380 "speak somewhat
barbarously"
Boeotia i. 54, 57, 80, 182, 183,
219, 220, 267 ; ii. 109. Boeotians i. 91, 212, 220, 233, 322
Bosporus i. 324 ; ii. 240
bridge of Xerxes i. 127, 166, 203 ;
ii. 240
Byzantium i. 59, 198, 292, 294.
Byzantines i. 319

CADMEA i. 80, 293
Callaethyia ii. 7
Callicles ii. (226), 344, 346, 355
Callicratidas i. 242
Calliope ii. 391
Calypso ii. 145
Caria i. 83
Carians i. 241
Carthage ii. 297. Carthaginians
i. 232
Carystians i. 212
Cecrops i. 354 ; ii. 7
Cecryphalea i. 214
(Chabrias) i. 296

INDEX

Chaerephon ii. 331
Chaeronea i. 331
Chalcidians i. 319
chariot, invention of i. 350
Charybdis ii. 280
Chelidonean Islands i. 209, 274
Chersonesans i. 319
(Chrysippus) ii. 177
Cilicia i. 324. Cilicians i. 202
Cimon (*cf.* i. 203, 273) ; ii. 319, (321-325), (327-333), 334, (335), (340-343), (359)
Clarus ii. 44
Cleopatra ii. 237
cleruchies i. 118
Codrus i. 87, 88 ; ii. 8 ; sons (Medon and Neleus) i. 88
colours, mixture of ii. 161, 162
Conon i. 241, (243, 252, 280)
contests i. 105, 187, 188, 217, 240, 283, 336, 362, 375, 393 ; ii. 2, 3, 4
Corcyra i. 229, 297
Corinth i. 59, 270, 290, 294. Corinthians i. 212, 214, 216, 229, 269, 312, 319, 322, 361, 372
Cratinus ii. 72
Cretans i. 371
Criasus ii. 7
Crisean Gulf i. 218
Critias ii. 335
Crotopus ii. 7
Cyanean Islands i. 209, 274
Cyclades i. 11
(Cynics) i. 390 ; ii. 464
Cyprians i. 202. Cyprus i. 273
Cyrene ii. 40
(Cyrsilus) i. 158
Cyrus ii. 240
Cyrus, the Younger ii. 301
Cythera i. 229
Cyzicus i. 237

DAEDALUS ii. 118
daemon (=evil spirit) i. 231 ; *daemones* ii. 424
Darius I i. 95, 96, 97, 99-102, 114, 116, 125 ; ii. 240, 407
(Darius II) i. 235, 237
Datis i. (97, 100), 119
Decelea i. 233
Delium ii. 299
Delos i. 13, 363
Delphi i. 173, 190, 209, 363 ; ii. 35, 38, 42, 52, 83, 150

Demeter i. 36, 339
Demodocus ii. 87, 88, (89), 90
(Demosthenes, general) i. 233
Demosthenes, orator ii. 9, 72, 120, 186, 255, 280 ; *or. i* ii. 72, *or. iii* ii. 186, *or. x* ii. 280, *or. xxiv* ii. 255
Deucalion ii. 7
Diagoras ii. 258
Dion ii. 281, 285-288, 290, 292, 296, 297, 298, 321, 324, 326, 362
Dionysius I i. 293, 313 ; ii. 326
Dionysius II ii. 281, 282, 285, 296, 297, 311, 326, (327)
Dionysus i. 73, 339, (360) ; ii. 75
Dioscuri i. 374 ; ii. 148
Dodona ii. 42, 52
Dorians i. 54, 67, 87, 91
dreams i. 12, 137, 268 ; ii. 70, 71, 72, 75, 168, 400, (466) ; interpretation of ii. 168, 169
Dryopians i. 55

EARTHQUAKE in Laconia i. 222
Egestaeans i. 232
Egypt i. 216 ; ii. 144, 370 ; the Marsh i. 204. Egyptians i. 204, 215 ; ii. 68, 169, 426. Egyptian Sea i. 202. Egyptian ship ii. 371
Eleusinian Games i. 362. Eleusinian Mysteries i. 330, (341, 342), 363, 373. Eleusinium i. 373. Eleusis i.168 (apparitions from), 372
empire, theory and justification of i. 306-312
enoplius (war dance) i. 200
Epidaurians i. 212 ; ii. 153
Erechtheids i. 384
Erechtheus i. 87, 88, 379 ; daughter (Agraulos?) i. 87, wife (Praxithea) i. 87
Eretria i. 119. Eretrians i. 95, 102, 104
Erichthonius i. (43), 354
(Erinyes) i. 48
Euboea i. 91, 160, 278. Euboeans i. 91, 224, 319
Eumolpus i. 85, 87
Euripides ii. 55, 132, 394 ; *Antiope* ii. 394, *Hippolytus* ii. 55, *Melanippe the Wise* ii. 132 ; frg. inc. ii. 166, 168

INDEX

Europe i. 83, (110), 123, (124), 198, 207; ii. 297
Euryalus ii. 96
(Eurybiadas) i. 140, 148
(Eurymedon, general) i. 233
Eurymedon river i. 203, (273)
Eurystheus i. 52, 78, 79

FESTIVALS celebrated after Persian War i. 189, (192)
foster-fathers i. 1, 332; ii. 47; foster-children i. 36, 38; nurse i. 25, 110; father i. 140; mother i. 313
Four Hundred, the i. 236, 237, 253
(Furies) i. 48

GADIRA i. 66; ii. 273
Gargarus ii. 148
Gerania i. 219
Geryon ii. 229
Gods (in general or unnamed individual gods) i. 3, 4, 9, 20, 21, 32, 33, 34, 35, 37, 38, 40, 44, 45, 46, 47, 48, 49, 50, 51, 88, 93, 103, 104, 107, 108, 114, 115, 117, 126, 133, 138, 155, 167, 168, 189, 191, 192, 193, 217, 265, 298, 302, 307, 311, 329, 330, 338, 340, 341, 344, 360, 363, 366, 374, 382, 399, 401, 404; ii. 34, 39, 40, 41, 42, 43, 45, 46, 48, 52, 53, 54, 56, 57, 58, 59, 63, 67, 68, 69, 70, 71, 75, 78, 80, 81, 82, 83, 86, 87, 88, 89, 91, 92, 93, 95, 96, 102, 103, 109, 110, 113, 120, 126, 127, 128, 130, 142, 153, 166, 176, 207, 217, 230, 258, 288, 294, 321, 326, 336, 337, 338, 339, 379, 398, 411, 418, 420, 423, 424, 430, 434, 437, 440, 454, 466; of Oratory ii. 19, 57, 466
Gorgias ii. 13, 22, 28
Gorgon i. 128
Gorgon-like ii. 157, 372
Greece i. 9, 14, 15, 16, 50, 63, 64, 65, 69, 81, 93, 97, 98, 101, 103, 110, 113, 114, 124, 126, 131, 132, 143, 154, 174, 184, 189, 197, 201, 206, 207, 208, 209, 212, 221, 231, 232, 274, 297, 313, 315, 318, 319, 321, 331, 336, 344, 362, 389, 401, 403;
ii. 52, 240, 321, 322, 327, 404.
Greek(s) i. 4, 6, 8, 11, 14, 37, 40, 49, 54, 55, 56, 57, 62, 64, 65, 67, 71, 73, 77, 85, 86, 91, 92, 93, 94, 95, 97, 98, 99, 104, 107, 110, 111, 113, 115, 125, 126, 129, 131, 132, 133, 134, 137, 138, 143, 144, 145, 146, 149, 150, 157, 158, 159, 160, 161, 164, 165, 167, 168, 171, 172, 173, 178, 179, 180, 182, 183, 184, 190, 191, 192, 194, 195, 197, 201, 205, 206, 208, 209, 210, 211, 212, 213, 225, 226, 227, 228, 229, 231, 232, 235, 248, 262, 266, 268, 269, 271, 272, 274, 275, 277, 280, 282, 286, 293, 294, 301, 305, 308, 312, 313, 314, 315, 316, 319, 322, 326, 327, 329, 330, 333, 334, 335, 348, 350, 357, 358, 360, 367, 371, 373, 377, 391, 399, 402; ii. 19, 39, 47, 60, 68, 88, 323, 324, 325, 327, 331, 335, 346, 348
Gyges ii. 239
gymnastics ii. 22, 36, 149, 150, 151, 236, 249, 374, 375, 457

HADES i. 133
Haliartus i. 267, (294)
(Halirrhothius, son of Poseidon) i. 46
Halitherses ii. 93
Harmosts (Lacedaemonian governors) i. 292, 295
health ii. 5
Helen i. 128; ii. 234
Helicon ii. 103, 109
Hellespont i. 236, 252, 277, 327; ii. 240
Heniochi i. 325
Heracles i. 35, 50, (51), 52, (53), 67, 78, 324, (360), 374; ii. 63, 226, 227, 229, 307, 412
Heraclidae i (35, 52, 53, 54, 57, 67), 68, 71, 78, (79)
heralds (Persian) i. 97, 99, 101, 125, 174, 175; interpreter i. 99; demand for earth and water i. 117, 157, 174; heralds (Theban) i. 299, 300
Hercules see s.v. Heracles
Hermes ii. 19, 48, 56, (57), 207, 396, 397, 423; god of oratory,

INDEX

ii. 19, (57); various epithets ii. 423
(Herodotus) ii. 7, 239, 240
Hesiod ii. 9, 97, (99), 100, (103), 129, 391, 438; *Theogony* ii. 100, 391 (*bis*); *Works and Days* ii. 97, 98, 99, 103, 129
(Hipparinus, father of Dion) ii. 326
(Hipparinus, son of Dion) ii. 326
(Hipparinus, son of Dionysius I) ii. 326
Hippocentaurs ii. 196
Hippocrates ii. 120
Homer i. 328, (380); ii. 9, 12, (86), 90, (92, 93), 96, 97, 177, 193, 351, 357, 380, 387, (388), 389, 391, 395, 406, 413, (414), 417, (418, 419), 426, 428; *Iliad* (title) ii. 94; *Iliad* i. 12, 286, 377 ("catalogue of ships and cities"), 378 (*ter*), 379 (*bis*), 381; ii. 47, 86, 135, 177, 351, 380, 387 (*bis*), 395, 406, 413 (*ter*), 414 (*ter*), 417, 426; *Odyssey* (title) ii. 94; *Odyssey* ii. 86, 87 (*ter*), 88, 89, 90, 91, 92, 93 (*bis*), 94, 95 (*bis*), 96, 145, 193, 357, 389, 418, 426
Homeric ii. 135
Hyrcanian Gulf i. 119

Iasus ii. 7
Ida ii. 148
Idomeneus ii. 135
Iliad ii. 94. See also *s.v.* Homer
Ilium i. 378
India i. 25. Indian i. 94; ii. 426
Ionia i. 19, 55, 93, 327; ii. 40. Ionians i. 160
(Iphicrates) i. 313
islands (in the Aegean or Myrtoan sea) i. 10, 11, 13, 60, 63, 64, 102, 208, 235, 242, 280
Isthmus i. 217
Italy i. 313
Ithacesians i. 376

King (of Persia) i. 97, 99, 102, 115, 121, 122, 129, 160, 162, 164, 168, 170, 172, 174, 177, 178, 180, 189, 201, 202, 204, 206, 213, 235, 237, 271, 273, 274, 275, 280, 293, 313, 369; ii. 322

Lacedaemonians i. 147, 148, 160, 178, 180 (at Thermopylae, *cf.* i. 131), 182, 200, 212, 218, 219, 220, 221, 222, 229, 233, 237, 238, 240, 242, 243, 249, 250, 252, 254, 255, 256, 258, 259, 260, 266, 267, 271, 277, 280, 286, 288, 290, 293, 296, 298, 300, 301, 312, 313, 319, 320, 322, 326, 359, 366, 382; ii. 39, 129; compared to Athenians i. 238-240, 245-251, 256, 258, 260, 263, 271-289, 305, 308, 359, 382; constitution i. 382; earthquake i. 222; émigrés i. 263; empire i. 243, 250, 252, 254, 256, 266, 280-283, 301, 305: 11 years duration 283
Laconia i. 58, 222, 291
laws: illegal proposals ii. 21; purpose of laws ii. 212-233, 244, 245, 271; repeal of ii. 5, 254-256; taught at Athens i. 336, 343
Lechaeum i. 290
Leontini i. 232
Leos i. 87
Lesbos ii. 336
Leto i. 13
Leucas i. 313
Leuctra i. 250, 298
Libyans (see also *s.v.* Africa) i. 204
lieutenants of Persian king i. 97, 100, 189 (*cf.* i. 119)
Locrians i. 221
Lycaon ii. 7
Lycia i. 83
Lycurgus i. (365), 366; ii. 38, (39)
Lydian ii. 239
lyre players ii. 2
Lysander i. 267, 268
Lysanias ii. 66
Lysias ii. 52
Lysimachus ii. 346

Macedonia ii. 238. (Macedonians) i. 333; (empire) i. 335
(Maeotis) i. 66
man compared to animals i. 330; ii. 379, 395, 396, 403
Mantinea i. 312, 347. Mantineans i. 291
Marathon i. 13, 110, 114, 117, 126, 131, 160, 167, 256, (272), 322, 347; ii. 341

INDEX

Mardonius i. 170, 172, (173), 180, 182
Massagetae ii. 240
Massalia i. 66
Medes i. 139, 164, 212, 236, 252 ; ii. 240 ; " those who side with the Medes " i. 320, 321. (Median empire) i. 335
medicine ii. 22, 35, 62, 65, 67, 70, 75, 122, 149, 152-156, 185, 236, 247, 249, 250, 251, 258, 334, 374, 375, 411, 412, 433
Megara i. 215, 216, 219, 225, 278 ; ii. 285, 292, 293. Megarians i. 212, 214
Melians i. 302
(Menander) ii. 168
Menelaus ii. 95
Menestheus i. (377), 379
Mentor ii. 93
Messenians i. 57
Methymne i. 292. Methymnean ii. 376
Milesians i. 224
Miltiades (i. 107) ; ii. 319, (321-325, 327-333), 334, (335, 340, 341), 342, (343), 357, (359), 360, 361
Mithaecus ii. 343, 426
Muses ii. 19, 47, 49, 52, 54, 56, (57), 87 (sing.), 88 (sing.), 90 (sing. and plural), 91, 109 (sing.), 391
Mycale i. 198
(Myrtoan Sea) i. 20
Mysteries i. 12, 50, 111, 330, (341, 342), 363, 373, 374 ; (ii. 52, 54, 67, 73)
Mytilene i. 241
Mytilenaeans i. 310

NAUPACTUS i. 229
Naxians i. 212. Naxus i. 297
Nemea (Nemean lion) ii. 307
Nereids ii. 148
Nestor i. 378 ; ii. 93, 94, 95, 414, (415)
Nile ii. 351
Ninus i. 240
Nisaea i. 278
Nymphs ii. 75

ODYSSEUS ii. (88, 89), 90, (93, 96), 145, (193), 280, (415), 417

Odyssey ii. 94. See also *s.v.* Homer
Oenophyta i. 221
Olympia (games) i. 283 ; (site) ii. 156
Olympiads i. 283
oracles and seers i. 30, 37, 46, 87, 167, 173, 399 (*quater*), 401 ; ii. 34, 37-44, 47, 48, 49, 56, 78, 81, 82, 163-171 ; source of medical cures ii. 35, 36, 52, 62, 65, 66, 67, 70, 72, 73, 75
orator called demagogue ii. 189 ; ruler, patron, teacher ii. 190. See also *s.v.* oratory
oratory, general i. 2, 3, 5, 6, 43, 152, 322, 328, 329, 330, 343, 347, 394, 397 ; bond of life ii. 210, 424, *cf.* 401 ; cure for everything *cf.* i. 330 ; ii. 184, 209, 412 ; first fruits of ii. 398 ; four parts of virtue ii. 235, 236, 382 ; funeral orations i. 4, 86, 368 ; ii. 342 ; ideal oratory ii. 148, 425, 426, 429-437, 446-461 ; immutable ii. 5 ; purpose ii. 205-233, 244-246, 257, 268, 318 ; slandered by masses ii. 18 ; philosophy compared to, see philosophy. See also *s.v.* orator
(Orestes) i. 48, 338

PAEAN i. 108
Pamphylia i. 83, 273
Pan i. 108
Panathenaea i. 186, 230, 362, 404 ; ii. 156
Pandarus ii. 86
(Paris)=Alexander i. 128
Pausanias, king of Sparta i. 267
Peace of Callias i. 208, 209, 210, 225, 226, 274, 275, 276
Peace, King's i. 271, 272, 274, 275, 276, 293
Peace, Thirty Year i. 225, 226, 228, 278
peace, offers of (after Arginusae) i. 243 ; (after Cyzicus) i. 237, 240 ; (after Pylus) i. 240, 277
Pegae i. 225, 278
Pelasgians i. 55
Peleus ii. 387
Pella i. 334

Pelopidae i. 48
Peloponnesians i. 78, 87, 214, 216, 242, 250, 278, 293, 300. Peloponnesus i. 52, 54, 57, 64, 67, 68, 79, 218, 222, 233, 237, 299, 301, 369
Peneus i. 208
(Pentelicus) *cf.* i. 106
penteterid i. 230, 373
peplos i. 404
Pericles ii. 319, (321-325, 327-333), 334, (335), 336, 339, (340-343, 359), 360
Perinthians i. 319
Perioeci i. 222, 301
Persians (see also *s.v.* barbarians and *s.v.* Medes) i. 96, 98, 101, 165, 182, 183, 202, 203, 271, 313. (Persian empire) i. 335. Persian Gulf i. 119
Phaeacians ii. 86, 88, 96
Phaedrus ii. 52, 459
Pharnabazus i. 237
Pharus i. 204 ; ii. 145
Phasis i. 119
Phemius ii. 92
Phidias ii. 118, 120 ; (his statue of Athena) i. 364
Philip II i. 314, 316, 319, 331, (398)
philosophy compared to oratory ii. 25, 29, 30, 176, (*cf.* 258, 259), 305, 315, 316, 317, 380, 385, 451, 458
Phlius i. 291
Phocians i. 212, 219, 221
Phoenicians i. (160, 168), 202
Phoenix, tutor of Achilles ii. 387
(phoenix bird) ii. 426
Phoroneus ii. 7
Phrygians ii. 7
Phthiotians i. 376
Phyle i. 256
Pillars of Heracles i. 324
Pindar ii. (109), 148, 226, 229, 230, 231, 420 ; *Olympians* ii. 109, 110 (*bis*) ; *Pythians* ii. 148, 230 ; fragments i. 401 ; ii. 112, 226, 227, 229, 232, 420
Piraeus i. 255
Plataea i. (172), 180, 182, (183, 190). Plataeans i. 57, 59
Plato ii. title, 9, 11, 12, (13), 14, 15, 16, (19, 20, 23, 24, 28), 34, 41, 50, (51, 52), 54, (55, 58), 60,

61, 62, 63, (64), 66, (72), 73, 78, 83, 93, 96, 100, (105), 109, 113, 114, 132, (133), 137, (138, 141), 142, (144, 148, 149, 153), 154, (156, 157, 161, 162), 164, (165, 166), 171, (172, 173), 175, (176, 177, 178), 179, 184, (186), 187, (189, 194, 195, 196), 199, 201, 203, (226, 231, 234, 237), 239, (243), 251, 253, 257, (261), 262, (266, 267), 271, 272, (273, 275), 277, (278, 279), 280, (281), 284, 285, (286), 287, (288-294), 295, (296, 297, 298), 299, 301, 304, (305), 306, (307-310), 311, 313, 315, 319, (320), 321, (322, 323), 324, 327, (329, 330), 331, (332, 334), 339, 340, (341, 342), 343, (344, 346-349), 352, (354), 355, (356-359, 361-363, 370-372, 374-376, 378), 380, (381, 394), 424, 428, 430, (431-434, 436), 438, 440, 441, 442, (443), 445, 446, (447, 448), 454, 456, (457), 458, 459, 462, (463), 465, 466 ; decorated Painted Porch ii. 105 ; *Apology* ii. 299, 439, 441 ; *Epistle VII* ii. 285, 286, 287, 289, 290, 292, 294, 296, 298, 362 ; *Epistle VIII* ii. 321, 324, 326, 327 ; *Euthydemus* ii. 457 ; *Gorgias* ii. 13, 14, 20, 22, 23, 28, 33, 61, 132, 138, 145, 148, 149, 154, 157, 172, 178, 179, 194, 198, 199, 202, 226, 234, 236, 237, 242, 261, 262, 263, 266, 267, 271, 273, 279, 282, 288, 294, 297, 306, 307, 309, 310, 314, 316, 319, 321, 322, 323, 327, 328, 329, 330, 334, 336, 338, 342-363, 368-372, 374, 375, 376, 380, 381, 389, 394, 426, 431, 432, 434, 435, 440, 441, 442, 443, 444, 446, 447, 448, 454, 455, 456, 458, 461 ; *Laws* ii. 39, 50, 275, 304 ; *Menexenus* ii. 341, 342, 343 ; *Phaedo* ii. 11, 176 ; *Phaedrus* ii. 52, (*bis*), 58, 137, 156, 164, 459, 460 ; *Politicus* ii. 171, 438 ; *Protagoras* i. 401 ; ii. 394 ; *Republic* ii. 41, 251, 273, 304, 454 ; *Symposium* ii. 132, 299, 372, 424, 447 ; *Timaeus* ii. 445
Platonists and defenders of Plato

INDEX

ii. **12**, **60**, 132, **133**, 272, 321, 335, 440
Polus ii. 22, 262
Pontus ii. 40, 144, 370
Poseidon i. 41, 42, 46, *cf.* 338 ; ii. 148, 426 ; see also *s.v.* Halirrhothius
Potidaea ii. 299
Priam ii. 414
Priestesses at Delphi ii. 34, 35, 37-41, 52, 78 ; at Dodona ii. 42, 43
Prometheus ii. 396, 397
proverbs i. 37, 60, 81, 103, 166, 208, 216, 241, 322 ; ii. 237, 314, 337, 392, 406, 465
Prytaneum i. 30, 319, 401
Psyttalea i. (164, 165), 168
Pygmies ii. 395
Pylians i. 376
Pylus i. 229 ; ii. 93, 95
Pythian i. 62 ; ii. 34, 38, 39, 41, 42, 50, 78. Pythian Mission i. 363
Pytho ii. 34

RED SEA i. 119
Reverend Goddesses (Erinyes) i. 48
(Rome) i. 332, 333, 335, 398 ; ii. 430

SACRED MONTH i. 187
Salamis i. 128, (135, 136, 137 138), 145, (149), 157, (158)' 160, (161), 164, 165, (166, 168), 176, 180, 236, 347 ; ii. 341. Salaminian i. 381
Samos i. 224, 236
Samothracians i. 363
(Sarapis) ii. 68
Sardanapallus ii. 240
Sardis i. 94
Scamander ii. 351
Scionians i. 302, 312
Scylla ii. 377
Scythians ii. 240
Sestus i. 198
Seuthes i. 293
Seven Wise Men i. 365 ; ii. 34
Sibyl ii. 46, 52
Sicily i. 232, 233, 234, 235, 237, 240, 313, 350, ; ii. 144, 280, 293, 297, 324, 325, 362

Sicyonians i. 212, 291
(Smyrna) i. 328
Socrates i. 366 ; ii. 13, 22, (61, 62, 74), 76, 77, 78, 79, 81, 82, 217, 218, 242, 262, (263), 299, 331, 335, 344, 439 ; his *daimonion* ii. 80
Soli, of ii. 177
(Solon) i. 365
sophism i. 216 ; ii. 178, 464. sophist i. 306 ; ii. 93, 177. sophistry ii. 22, 28
Sophocles ii. 408, 428 ; *Oedipus Tyrannus* ii. 408 ; frg. i. 60
Sparta i. 299 ; Spartans see *s.v.* Lacedaemonians and *s.v.* Laconia
Spartoi (Sown-men) ii. 207
Speusippus ii. 331
Sporades i. 11
Stentor ii. 351. Stentorian ii. 109
Stesichorus ii. 234 ; *cf.* i. 128, 166
Stoa Poikile (Painted Porch) ii. 105
Strymon i. 198
Syracusan(s) ii. 281, 321. Syracuse ii. 281, 285, 326
Syria i. 324

TANAGRA i. 220, 322. Tanagraeans i. 54
Tanais i. 66
Telemachus ii. 93, 94, 95, 96
Telephus ii. 59
Terpander ii. 336
Teucer i. 286, (378)
Thasians i. 212. Thasus i. 59, 294
Thearion ii. 343, 426
Thebans i. 51, 58, 59, 250, 266, 269, 294, 296, 298, 299, 301, 312, 319, 331, 360. Thebes i. 54, 294, (296), 360
Themistocles (*cf.* i. 23), (139, 140, 148, 149, 160, 168, 169) ; ii. 319, (321-325, 327-333, 335), 336, 339, (340, 341), 342, (343), 357, (359), 361
theoria (sacred mission or festival) i. 31, 87, 363, 372. theoric fund ii. 397
Thermodon i. 83
Thermopylae i. 131, 154, 167
Theseus i. 35, 52, 360
Thespians i. 59

567

INDEX

Thessalians i. 54
Thirty Tyrants, the i. 252-257, 259. 261 ; ii. 335
Thracians i. 85, 292 ; kings i. 292. Thrace i. 59 (32 cities), 229, 292, 297, 327
(Thrasybulus) i. 253-257
Thucydides ii. 434
(Timotheus) i. 313
tragic poets ii. 2
Triptolemus i. (36), 199
Troezen i. 154 (Athenian decree), (156), 225, 278
Trojans ii. 234. Trojan times i. 375
Troy ii. 414. (Cf. i. 375 ; ii. 234)

UNIVERSE arose from four elements i. 388

VIRTUE, four parts of ii. 235, 236, 382, (451, 452)

WAR, nature of i. 194, 195. Wars (other than Athenian ; for these, see s.v. Athens) Cadmea seized i. 266, 293, 294 ; Carthaginian invasion of Sicily i. 232 ; Chaeronea i. 331 ; Corinthian war i. 269 ; Cyrus conquers Ionia i. 93 ; Cyrus against Massagetae ii. 240 ; Cyrus the Younger against Artaxerxes II ii. 301 ; Darius against Scythians ii. 240 ; Egyptian revolt from Persia i. 204, 215, 216 ; Leuctra i. 250, 298-301, 360 ; Medes against Ninus ii. 240 ; Persians, previous conquests of Egypt i. 204 ; Spartan invasion of Asia (400 B.C.) i. 93
wryneck i. 330

XENOPHON ii. 301 ; Anabasis ii. 301
Xerxes i. 115, 116, 117, (118, 119), 120, (121-123), 124, 127, 128, (129), 133, (157, 158, 160, 162), 166, (168, 170, 172-174, 177, 178, 180, 189, 201, 207, 208, 209), 249, 273, 369 ; ii. 240

ZELEA, of i. 369 ; ii. 86
Zethus ii. 394
Zeus i. 19, 120, 187, 322 ; ii. (42), 43, 48, 53, 55, 56, 88, 109, 121, 132, 148, 149, 166, 177, 196, 229, 247, 259, 273, 282, 297, 321, 345, 352, 365, 380, 391, 396, 411, 420, 457 ; Zeus Eleutherius i. 110, 190 ; Zeus Terastius ii. 275
Zeuxis ii. 120
Zoster i. 13

Printed in Great Britain by R. & R. CLARK, LIMITED, *Edinburgh*

THE LOEB CLASSICAL LIBRARY

VOLUMES ALREADY PUBLISHED

LATIN AUTHORS

AMMIANUS MARCELLINUS. J. C. Rolfe. 3 Vols.

APULEIUS: THE GOLDEN ASS (METAMORPHOSES). W. Adlington (1566). Revised by S. Gaselee.

ST. AUGUSTINE: CITY OF GOD. 7 Vols. Vol. I. G. E. McCracken. Vol. II. W. M. Green. Vol. III. D. Wiesen. Vol. IV. P. Levine. Vol. V. E. M. Sanford and W. M. Green. Vol. VI. W. C. Greene. Vol. VII. W. M. Green.

ST. AUGUSTINE, CONFESSIONS OF. W. Watts (1631). 2 Vols.

ST. AUGUSTINE: SELECT LETTERS. J. H. Baxter.

AUSONIUS. H. G. Evelyn White. 2 Vols.

BEDE. J. E. King. 2 Vols.

BOETHIUS; TRACTS AND DE CONSOLATIONE PHILOSOPHIAE. Rev. H. F. Stewart and E. K. Rand. Revised by S. J. Tester.

CAESAR: ALEXANDRIAN, AFRICAN AND SPANISH WARS. A. G. Way.

CAESAR: CIVIL WARS. A. G. Peskett.

CAESAR: GALLIC WAR. H. J. Edwards.

CATO AND VARRO: DE RE RUSTICA. H. B. Ash and W. D. Hooper.

CATULLUS. F. W. Cornish; TIBULLUS. J. B. Postgate; and PERVIGILIUM VENERIS. J. W. Mackail.

CELSUS: DE MEDICINA. W. G. Spencer. 3 Vols.

CICERO: BRUTUS AND ORATOR. G. L. Hendrickson and H. M. Hubbell.

CICERO: DE FINIBUS. H. Rackham.

CICERO: DE INVENTIONE, etc. H. M. Hubbell.

CICERO: DE NATURA DEORUM AND ACADEMICA. H. Rackham.

CICERO: DE OFFICIIS. Walter Miller.

CICERO: DE ORATORE, etc. 2 Vols. Vol. I: DE ORATORE, Books I and II. E. W. Sutton and H. Rackham. Vol. II: DE ORATORE, Book III; DE FATO; PARADOXA STOICORUM; DE PARTITIONE ORATORIA. H. Rackham.

CICERO: DE REPUBLICA, DE LEGIBUS, SOMNIUM SCIPIONIS. Clinton W. Keyes.

1

THE LOEB CLASSICAL LIBRARY

CICERO: DE SENECTUTE, DE AMICITIA, DE DIVINATIONE
W. A. Falconer.
CICERO: IN CATILINAM, PRO MURENA, PRO SULLA, PRO
FLACCO. Louis E. Lord.
CICERO: LETTERS TO ATTICUS. E. O. Winstedt. 3 Vols.
CICERO: LETTERS TO HIS FRIENDS. W. Glynn Williams,
M. Cary, M. Henderson. 4 Vols.
CICERO: PHILIPPICS. W. C. A. Ker.
CICERO: PRO ARCHIA, POST REDITUM, DE DOMO, DE HA-
RUSPICUM RESPONSIS, PRO PLANCIO. N. H. Watts.
CICERO: PRO CAECINA, PRO LEGE MANILIA, PRO CLUENTIO,
PRO RABIRIO. H. Grose Hodge.
CICERO: PRO CAELIO, DE PROVINCIIS CONSULARIBUS, PRO
BALBO. R. Gardner.
CICERO: PRO MILONE, IN PISONEM, PRO SCAURO, PRO
FONTEIO, PRO RABIRIO POSTUMO, PRO MARCELLO, PRO
LIGARIO, PRO REGE DEIOTARO. N. H. Watts.
CICERO: PRO QUINCTIO, PRO ROSCIO AMERINO, PRO ROSCIO
COMOEDO, CONTRA RULLUM. J. H. Freese.
CICERO: PRO SESTIO, IN VATINIUM. R. Gardner.
[CICERO]: RHETORICA AD HERENNIUM. H. Caplan.
CICERO: TUSCULAN DISPUTATIONS. J. E. King.
CICERO: VERRINE ORATIONS. L. H. G. Greenwood. 2 Vols.
CLAUDIAN. M. Platnauer. 2 Vols.
COLUMELLA: DE RE RUSTICA, DE ARBORIBUS. H. B. Ash,
E. S. Forster, E. Heffner. 3 Vols.
CURTIUS, Q.: HISTORY OF ALEXANDER. J. C. Rolfe. 2 Vols.
FLORUS. E. S. Forster; and CORNELIUS NEPOS. J. C. Rolfe.
FRONTINUS: STRATAGEMS AND AQUEDUCTS. C. E. Bennett
and M. B. McElwain.
FRONTO: CORRESPONDENCE. C. R. Haines. 2 Vols.
GELLIUS. J. C. Rolfe. 3 Vols.
HORACE: ODES AND EPODES. C. E. Bennett.
HORACE: SATIRES, EPISTLES, ARS POETICA. H. R. Fairclough.
JEROME: SELECT LETTERS. F. A. Wright.
JUVENAL AND PERSIUS. G. G. Ramsay.
LIVY. B. O. Foster, F. G. Moore, Evan T. Sage, A. C.
Schlesinger and R. M. Geer (General Index). 14 Vols.
LUCAN. J. D. Duff.
LUCRETIUS. W. H. D. Rouse.
MARTIAL. W. C. A. Ker. 2 Vols.
MINOR LATIN POETS: from PUBLILIUS SYRUS to RUTILIUS
NAMATIANUS, including GRATTIUS, CALPURNIUS SICULUS,
NEMESIANUS, AVIANUS, with " Aetna," " Phoenix " and
other poems. J. Wight Duff and Arnold M. Duff.

2

THE LOEB CLASSICAL LIBRARY

OVID : THE ART OF LOVE AND OTHER POEMS. J. H. Mozley.
OVID : FASTI. Sir James G. Frazer.
Ovid : HEROIDES AND AMORES. Grant Showerman.
OVID : METAMORPHOSES. F. J. Miller. 2 Vols.
OVID : TRISTIA AND EX PONTO. A. L. Wheeler.
PETRONIUS. M. Heseltine ; SENECA : APOCOLOCYNTOSIS.
  W. H. D. Rouse.
PHAEDRUS AND BABRIUS (Greek). B. E. Perry.
PLAUTUS. Paul Nixon. 5 Vols.
PLINY : LETTERS, PANEGYRICUS. B. Radice. 2 Vols.
PLINY : NATURAL HISTORY. 10 Vols. Vols. I-V. H. Rack-
  ham. Vols. VI-VIII. W. H. S. Jones. Vol. IX. H. Rack-
  ham. Vol. X. D. E. Eichholz.
PROPERTIUS. H. E. Butler.
PRUDENTIUS. H. J. Thomson. 2 Vols.
QUINTILIAN. H. E. Butler. 4 Vols.
REMAINS OF OLD LATIN. E. H. Warmington. 4 Vols.
  Vol. I (Ennius and Caecilius). Vol. II (Livius, Naevius,
  Pacuvius, Accius). Vol. III (Lucilius, Laws of the XII
  Tables). Vol. IV (Archaic Inscriptions).
SALLUST. J. C. Rolfe.
SCRIPTORES HISTORIAE AUGUSTAE. D. Magie. 3 Vols.
SENECA : APOCOLOCYNTOSIS. *Cf.* PETRONIUS.
SENECA : EPISTULAE MORALES. R. M. Gummere. 3 Vols.
SENECA : MORAL ESSAYS. J. W. Basore. 3 Vols.
SENECA : NATURALES QUAESTIONES. T. H. Corcoran. 2 Vols.
SENECA : TRAGEDIES. F. J. Miller. 2 Vols.
SIDONIUS : POEMS AND LETTERS. W. B. Anderson. 2 Vols
SILIUS ITALICUS. J. D. Duff. 2 Vols.
STATIUS. J. H. Mozley. 2 Vols.
SUETONIUS. J. C. Rolfe. 2 Vols.
TACITUS : AGRICOLA AND GERMANIA. M. Hutton : DIALOGUS.
  Sir Wm. Peterson. Revised by R. M. Ogilvie, E. H.
  Warmington, M. Winterbottom.
TACITUS : HISTORIES AND ANNALS. C. H. Moore and J.
  Jackson. 4 Vols.
TERENCE. John Sargeaunt. 2 Vols.
TERTULLIAN : APOLOGIA AND DE SPECTACULIS. T. R. Glover :
  MINUCIUS FELIX. G. H. Rendall.
VALERIUS FLACCUS. J. H. Mozley.
VARRO : DE LINGUA LATINA. R. G. Kent. 2 Vols.
VELLEIUS PATERCULUS AND RES GESTAE DIVI AUGUSTI.
  F. W. Shipley.
VIRGIL. H. R. Fairclough. 2 Vols.
VITRUVIUS : DE ARCHITECTURA. F. Granger. 2 Vols.

THE LOEB CLASSICAL LIBRARY

ACHILLES TATIUS. S. Gaselee.
AELIAN: ON THE NATURE OF ANIMALS. A. F. Scholfield
3 Vols.
AENEAS TACTICUS, ASCLEPIODOTUS AND ONASANDER. The
Illinois Greek Club.
AESCHINES. C. D. Adams.
AESCHYLUS. H. Weir Smyth. 2 Vols.
ALCIPHRON, AELIAN AND PHILOSTRATUS: LETTERS. A. R.
Benner and F. H. Fobes.
APOLLODORUS. Sir James G. Frazer. 2 Vols.
APOLLONIUS RHODIUS. R. C. Seaton.
THE APOSTOLIC FATHERS. Kirsopp Lake. 2 Vols.
APPIAN'S ROMAN HISTORY. Horace White. 4 Vols.
ARATUS. *Cf.* CALLIMACHUS.
ARISTIDES. C. A. Behr. 4 Vols. Vol. I.
ARISTOPHANES. Benjamin Bickley Rogers. 3 Vols. Verse
trans.
ARISTOTLE: ART OF RHETORIC. J. H. Freese.
ARISTOTLE: ATHENIAN CONSTITUTION, EUDEMIAN ETHICS.
VIRTUES AND VICES. H. Rackham.
ARISTOTLE: THE CATEGORIES. ON INTERPRETATION. H. P.
Cooke; PRIOR ANALYTICS. H. Tredennick.
ARISTOTLE: GENERATION OF ANIMALS. A. L. Peck.
ARISTOTLE: HISTORIA ANIMALIUM. A. L. Peck. 3 Vols
Vols. I and II.
ARISTOTLE: METAPHYSICS. H. Tredennick. 2 Vols.
ARISTOTLE: METEOROLOGICA. H. D. P. Lee.
ARISTOTLE: MINOR WORKS. W. S. Hett. "On Colours,"
"On Things Heard," "Physiognomics," "On Plants,"
"On Marvellous Things Heard," "Mechanical Prob-
lems," "On Invisible Lines," "Situations and Names of
Winds," "On Melissus, Xenophanes, and Gorgias."
ARISTOTLE: NICOMACHEAN ETHICS. H. Rackham.
ARISTOTLE: OECONOMICA AND MAGNA MORALIA. G. C.
Armstrong. (With METAPHYSICS, Vol II.)
ARISTOTLE: ON THE HEAVENS. W. K. C. Guthrie.
ARISTOTLE: ON THE SOUL, PARVA NATURALIA, ON BREATH.
W. S. Hett.
ARISTOTLE: PARTS OF ANIMALS. A. L. Peck: MOVEMENT
AND PROGRESSION OF ANIMALS. E. S. Forster.
ARISTOTLE: PHYSICS. Rev. P. Wicksteed and F. M. Corn-
ford. 2 Vols.

THE LOEB CLASSICAL LIBRARY

Aristotle: Poetics; Longinus on the Sublime. W. Hamilton Fyfe; Demetrius on Style. W. Rhys Roberts.

Aristotle: Politics. H. Rackham.

Aristotle: Posterior Analytics. H. Tredennick; Topics. F. S. Forster.

Aristotle: Problems. W. S. Hett. 2 Vols.

Aristotle: Rhetorica ad Alexandrum. H. Rackham (With Problems, Vol. II.)

Aristotle: Sophistical Refutations. Coming-to-be and Passing-away. E. S. Forster: On the Cosmos. D. J. Furley.

Arrian: History of Alexander and Indica. Rev. E. Iliffe Robson. 2 Vols.

Athenaeus: Deipnosophistae. C. B. Gulick. 7 Vols.

Babrius and Phaedrus (Latin). B. E. Perry.

St. Basil: Letters. R. J. Deferrari. 4 Vols.

Callimachus: Fragments. C. A. Trypanis.

Callimachus: Hymns and Epigrams, and Lycophron. A. W. Mair; Aratus. G. R. Mair.

Clement of Alexandria. Rev. G. W. Butterworth.

Colluthus. Cf. Oppian.

Daphnis and Chloe. Cf. Longus.

Demosthenes I: Olynthiacs, Philippics and Minor Orations: I-XVII and XX. J. H. Vince.

Demosthenes II: De Corona and De Falsa Legatione. C. A. Vince and J. H. Vince.

Demosthenes III: Meidias, Androtion, Aristocrates, Timocrates, Aristogeiton. J. H. Vince.

Demosthenes IV-VI: Private Orations and In Neaeram. A. T. Murray.

Demosthenes VII: Funeral Speech, Erotic Essay, Exordia and Letters. N. W. and N. J. DeWitt.

Dio Cassius: Roman History. E. Cary. 9 Vols.

Dio Chrysostom. 5 Vols. Vols. I and II. J. W. Cohoon. Vol. III. J. W. Cohoon and H. Lamar Crosby. Vols. IV and V. H. Lamar Crosby.

Diodorus Siculus. 12 Vols. Vols. I-VI. C. H. Oldfather. Vol. VII. C. L. Sherman. Vol. VIII. C. B. Welles. Vols. IX and X. Russel M. Geer. Vols. XI and XII. F. R. Walton. General Index. Russel M. Geer.

Diogenes Laertius. R. D. Hicks. 2 Vols. New Introduction by H. S. Long.

Dionysius of Halicarnassus: Roman Antiquities. Spelman's translation revised by E. Cary. 7 Vols.

Epictetus. W. A. Oldfather. 2 Vols.

THE LOEB CLASSICAL LIBRARY

EURIPIDES. A. S. Way. 4 Vols. Verse trans.
EUSEBIUS : ECCLESIASTICAL HISTORY. Kirsopp Lake and
J. E. L. Oulton. 2 Vols.
GALEN : ON THE NATURAL FACULTIES. A. J. Brock.
THE GREEK ANTHOLOGY. W. R. Paton. 5 Vols.
THE GREEK BUCOLIC POETS (THEOCRITUS, BION, MOSCHUS).
J. M. Edmonds.
GREEK ELEGY AND IAMBUS WITH THE ANACREONTEA. J. M.
Edmonds. 2 Vols.
GREEK MATHEMATICAL WORKS. Ivor Thomas. 2 Vols.
HERODES. *Cf.* THEOPHRASTUS : CHARACTERS.
HERODIAN : C. R. Whittaker. 2 Vols.
HERODOTUS. A. D. Godley. 4 Vols.
HESIOD AND THE HOMERIC HYMNS. H. G. Evelyn White.
HIPPOCRATES AND THE FRAGMENTS OF HERACLEITUS. W. H. S.
Jones and E. T. Withington. 4 Vols.
HOMER : ILIAD. A. T. Murray. 2 Vols.
HOMER : ODYSSEY. A. T. Murray. 2 Vols.
ISAEUS. E. S. Forster.
ISOCRATES. George Norlin and LaRue Van Hook. 3
Vols.
[ST. JOHN DAMASCENE] : BARLAAM AND IOASAPH. Rev. G. R.
Woodward, Harold Mattingly and D. M. Lang.
JOSEPHUS. 9 Vols. Vols. I-IV. H. St J. Thackeray. Vol.
V. H. St. J. Thackeray and Ralph Marcus. Vols. VI
and VII. Ralph Marcus. Vol. VIII. Ralph Marcus and
Allen Wikgren. Vol. IX. L. H. Feldman.
JULIAN. Wilmer Cave Wright. 3 Vols.
LIBANIUS : SELECTED WORKS. A. F. Norman. 3 Vols. Vol. I.
LONGUS : DAPHNIS AND CHLOE. Thornley's translation re-
vised by J. M. Edmonds ; and PARTHENIUS. S. Gaselee.
LUCIAN. 8 Vols. Vols I-V. A. M. Harmon. Vol. VI. K.
Kilburn. Vols. VII and VIII. M. D. Macleod.
LYCOPHRON. *Cf.* CALLIMACHUS.
LYRA GRAECA. J. M. Edmonds. 3 Vols.
LYSIAS. W. R. M. Lamb.
MANETHO. W. G. Waddell; PTOLEMY : TETRABIBLOS. F. E.
Robbins.
MARCUS AURELIUS. C. R. Haines.
MENANDER. F. G. Allinson.
MINOR ATTIC ORATORS. 2 Vols. K. J. Maidment and
J. O. Burtt.
NONNOS : DIONYSIACA. W. H. D. Rouse. 3 Vols.
OPPIAN, COLLUTHUS, TRYPHIODORUS. A. W. Mair.
PAPYRI. NON-LITERARY SELECTIONS. A. S. Hunt and C. C.

6

Edgar. 2 Vols. LITERARY SELECTIONS (Poetry). D. L. Page.

PARTHENIUS. *Cf.* LONGUS.

PAUSANIAS : DESCRIPTION OF GREECE. W. H. S. Jones. 4 Vols. and Companion Vol. arranged by R. E. Wycherley.

PHILO. 10 Vols. Vols. I-V. F. H. Colson and Rev. G. H. Whitaker. Vols. VI-X. F. H. Colson. General Index. Rev. J. W. Earp.
 Two Supplementary Vols. Translation only from an Armenian Text. Ralph Marcus.

PHILOSTRATUS : THE LIFE OF APOLLONIUS OF TYANA. F. C. Conybeare. 2 Vols.

PHILOSTRATUS : IMAGINES ; CALLISTRATUS : DESCRIPTIONS. A. Fairbanks.

PHILOSTRATUS AND EUNAPIUS : LIVES OF THE SOPHISTS. Wilmer Cave Wright.

PINDAR. Sir J. E. Sandys.

PLATO : CHARMIDES, ALCIBIADES, HIPPARCHUS, THE LOVERS, THEAGES, MINOS AND EPINOMIS. W. R. M. Lamb.

PLATO : CRATYLUS, PARMENIDES, GREATER HIPPIAS, LESSER HIPPIAS. H. N. Fowler.

PLATO : EUTHYPHRO, APOLOGY, CRITO, PHAEDO, PHAEDRUS. H. N. Fowler.

PLATO : LACHES, PROTAGORAS, MENO, EUTHYDEMUS. W. R. M. Lamb.

PLATO : LAWS. Rev. R. G. Bury. 2 Vols.

PLATO : LYSIS, SYMPOSIUM, GORGIAS. W. R. M. Lamb.

PLATO : REPUBLIC. Paul Shorey. 2 Vols.

PLATO : STATESMAN. PHILEBUS. H. N. Fowler ; ION. W. R. M. Lamb.

PLATO : THEAETETUS AND SOPHIST. H. N. Fowler.

PLATO : TIMAEUS, CRITIAS, CLITOPHO, MENEXENUS, EPISTULAE. Rev. R. G. Bury.

PLOTINUS. A. H. Armstrong. 6 Vols. Vols. I-III.

PLUTARCH : MORALIA. 16 Vols. Vols. I-V. F. C. Babbitt. Vol. VI. W. C. Helmbold. Vol. VII. P. H. De Lacy and B. Einarson. Vol. VIII. P. A. Clement, H. B. Hoffleit. Vol. IX. E. L. Minar, Jr., F. H. Sandbach, W. C. Helmbold. Vol. X. H. N. Fowler. Vol. XI. L. Pearson, F. H. Sandbach. Vol. XII. H. Cherniss, W. C. Helmbold. Vol. XIV. P. H. De Lacy and B. Einarson. Vol. XV. F. H. Sandbach.

PLUTARCH : THE PARALLEL LIVES. B. Perrin. 11 Vols.

POLYBIUS. W. R. Paton. 6 Vols.

PROCOPIUS : HISTORY OF THE WARS. H. B. Dewing. 7 Vols.

THE LOEB CLASSICAL LIBRARY

PTOLEMY : TETRABIBLOS. *Cf.* MANETHO.
QUINTUS SMYRNAEUS. A. S. Way. Verse trans.
SEXTUS EMPIRICUS. Rev. R. G. Bury. 4 Vols.
SOPHOCLES. F. Storr. 2 Vols. Verse trans.
STRABO : GEOGRAPHY. Horace L. Jones. 8 Vols.
THEOPHRASTUS : CHARACTERS. J. M. Edmonds ; HERODES, etc. A. D. Knox.
THEOPHRASTUS : ENQUIRY INTO PLANTS. Sir Arthur Hort. 2 Vols.
THUCYDIDES. C. F. Smith. 4 Vols.
TRYPHIODORUS. *Cf.* OPPIAN.
XENOPHON : ANABASIS. C. L. Brownson.
XENOPHON : CYROPAEDIA. Walter Miller. 2 Vols.
XENOPHON : HELLENICA. C. L. Brownson.
XENOPHON : MEMORABILIA AND OECONOMICUS. E. C. Marchant. SYMPOSIUM AND APOLOGY. O. J. Todd.
XENOPHON : SCRIPTA MINORA. E. C. Marchant and G. W. Bowersock.

VOLUMES IN PREPARATION

GREEK AUTHORS

MUSAEUS: HERO AND LEANDER. T. Gelzer and C. H. Whitman.
THEOPHRASTUS : DE CAUSIS PLANTARUM. G. K. K. Link and B. Einarson.

LATIN AUTHORS

ASCONIUS: COMMENTARIES ON CICERO'S ORATIONS. G. W. Bowersock.
BENEDICT : THE RULE. P. Meyvaert.
JUSTIN-TROGUS. R. Moss.
MANILIUS. G. P. Goold.

DESCRIPTIVE PROSPECTUS ON APPLICATION

CAMBRIDGE, MASS.   LONDON
HARVARD UNIV PRESS   WILLIAM HEINEMANN LTD

8